Praise for *The Regenerative Landscaper*

"Erik Ohlsen is one of the best permaculture designers, organizers, and educators, and this book draws on all those gifts. It's full of clear, practical advice on creating regenerative landscapes, useful for homeowners who want to plant a small garden, professionals who want to run an ecological design business, and activists who want to advocate for the best practices. He explains technical and scientific information clearly and in an engaging and easily understandable way. But most of all, he infuses all of the work with a deep love for the natural world and a spiritual connection to nature. I'll be using this book as a reference and a textbook for my students for years to come, recommending it to friends who want to learn about resilient land practices, and to anyone who needs some practical, grounded hope." —Starhawk, founder and executive, Earth Activist Training and author of *The Spiral Dance*

"As long as I've known Erik, he's had integrity and creativity in what he does. I'm overjoyed to see that he has finally taken the time to put his knowledge in book form. He's really shown us what can be done in this space, and this book is a perfect example of that. From sharing about regenerative practices to creating your own designs, this resource is a must in your household." —Ron Finley, Gangsta Gardener and founder of The Ron Finley Project

"Erik Ohlsen's *The Regenerative Landscaper: Design and Build Landscapes That Repair the Environment* combines the best of ecological science and the practice of regeneration. Regeneration, as Ohlsen makes clear, is cocreating with the living Earth—her intelligence, her laws, her patterns—and working in alignment with the water cycle and nutritional cycle to create circular living economies." —Vandana Shiva, author of *Agroecology and Regenerative Agriculture*

"I'm grateful Erik has put his decades of hands-on experience into an extensive book for all of us to learn from. The book is full of helpful photographs and illustrations. I especially like the detailed drawings of step-by-step, how-to information. Regenerative gardening, landscaping, and farming do a lot to stave off life's tendency toward entropy. This book adds a considerable amount of information to the literature." —Robert Kourik, author of *Sustainable Food Gardens*

"Erik's epic tome is a natural outcome of an amazing track record as one of the world's leading regenerative landscapers and educators. I really appreciate that this book is grounded in the practical experience that comes from years of work as a designer, consultant, project manager, and contractor—*The Regenerative Landscaper* will show others what is involved in running such an enterprise, be it a start-up or anyone looking to transition to more regenerative practices." —Darren J. Doherty, author of *The Regrarians Handbook*

"This is a well-written and incredibly thorough book on all things permaculture. Great reference book for those who want to dive deep!" —Diane Miessler, author of *Grow Your Soil*

"What an enjoyable and thoroughly erudite and engaging book! Erik's wisdom and experience shine out, and the breadth of his knowledge makes this a truly holistic approach to regenerative landscaping on any scale—from garden to farm and beyond." —Maddy Harland, editor and cofounder of *Permaculture* magazine

"*The Regenerative Landscaper* is an exceptional guide for anyone seeking a sustainable and self-sufficient lifestyle. The book provides clear and concise information on the principles of permaculture, including design, water management, soil improvement, and sustainable food production. It gives detailed step-by-step instructions to help you create a regenerative oasis. The book emphasizes the importance of taking action and includes information on planning, designing, implementing, adapting, and scaling your project. Erik's long years of experience guarantee this book will be a permaculture classic." —Sophie McKay, author of *The Practical Permaculture Project*

"With exemplary permacultural style, this book seamlessly spans the gamut of both designing and doing, from patterns to details, with purpose and pragmatism. Based on decades of experience, Erik Ohlsen has crafted a deeply informative and inspirational tome not only for 'landscapers in service of a thriving earth,' but in fact for everyone who feels the thrivalist calling to be in regenerative service to our living Earth and all its inhabitants." —Brock Dolman, Occidental Arts & Ecology Center cofounder and Permaculture Design Certification codirector

"Regenerative permaculture is a truly revolutionary approach to agriculture and land management that focuses on creating sustainable, self-sufficient ecosystems that benefit people and the planet. As Ohlsen engagingly presents them here, the principles and practices of regenerative permaculture can be applied to any scale, from a small backyard garden to a large food forest. Whether you are already a permie, or an interested farmer, a gardener, or simply someone striving toward sustainable living, this book will inspire and guide you on your journey toward regenerative permaculture." —Jessica Carew Kraft, author of *Why We Need to Be Wild*

"A viable human future will require deep transformation of the landscaper's craft. *The Regenerative Landscaper* melds Indigenous and scientific perspectives to produce this extraordinary practical handbook for the aspiring practitioner." —David Korten, author of *Change the Story, Change the Future* and *The Great Turning*

"I have been using regenerative principles on my ranch for nearly 30 years and I surely would have benefited from the knowledge that Erik shares in *The Regenerative Landscaper*. This book is a treasure trove of ecosystem healing principles, practices, and ideas. It is a must read for not only gardeners, farmers, ranchers, and land managers but anyone who wants to make a difference in healing our planet." —Gabe Brown, author of *Dirt to Soil*, rancher, and regenerative consultant

"Visionary and truly inspirational. Mind-bogglingly comprehensive. A holistic manual for doing our regenerative best as human participants in our human-imperiled, more-than-human world. My partner and I will be using this guidebook on our own riverside acres." —Bill Plotkin, PhD, author of *Soulcraft, Nature and the Human Soul,* and *The Journey of Soul Initiation*

THE REGENERATIVE LANDSCAPER

Design and Build Landscapes That Repair the Environment

Erik Ohlsen

Foreword by Penny Livingston

SYNERGETIC PRESS
SANTA FE • LONDON

Copyright © 2023 by Erik Ohlsen
All rights reserved.
Foreword copyright © 2023 by Penny Livingston
All rights reserved.

No part of this publication may be reproduced, stored in any retrieval system, or transmitted, in any form or by any means, electronic, mechanical, photocopying, recording, or otherwise without the prior permission of the publisher, except for the quotation of brief passages in reviews.

Published by Synergetic Press
1 Bluebird Court, Santa Fe, New Mexico 87508
& 24 Old Gloucester St. London, WCIN 3AL, England

Library of Congress Control Number: 2023937299

ISBN 9781957869087 (paperback)
ISBN 9781957869094 (ebook)

Cover design by Amanda Müller
Interior design by Howie Severson Design
Typesetting by Jonathan Hahn
Interior illustrations by Edward "Redbird" Willie
Managing Editor: Noelle Armstrong
Design and Production Manager: Amanda Müller
Production Editor: Allison Felus

Printed in the United States of America

For Toby

CONTENTS

Foreword by Penny Livingston   xviii
How to Use This Book   xxi
Introduction   xxii

Part I: The Wisdom of the Earth   1

Chapter 1: Earth's Design Intelligence   2
The Intelligence of Earth   2
   Interdependence   3
The Hydrologic Cycle: The Blue Planet   3
   Natural Water Storage   4
   Snowpack   4
   Vegetative/Animal Storage   4
   Rivers and Lakes   4
   Condensation   4
   Bacterial Rainmakers   5
   Fungal Rainmakers   5
   Water Runoff   5
The Carbon Cycle: Life's Origin   6
   Liquid Carbon Pathway   6
   Grassland and Forest Carbon   7
Photosynthesis: The Miracle of Life   7
   Forest Ecology   8
   Wetland Ecology   9
   Grasslands Ecology   10
Keystone Species   10
   Rivers of Salmon   10
   The Power of Bees   11
   Red Mangrove Coastlines   11
   Bioregional Keystone Species   11
Regenerative Disturbances   12
   Mimic Herd Migration   12
   Become Fire   13

Chapter 2: The Regenerative Mindset   14
Embrace Earth Wisdom   14
Landscapes Are Ecosystems   14
Animism and Science   15
Regenerative Landscaping Principles   16
   Reciprocity   17
   Give More than You Take   17
   Make the Least Harm   17
   Ecological Yield   17
   Contextual Design   18
   Problems Are Indicators   18
   Manage Cyclical Energy   18
   Closing Loops in the Landscape   19
   Relative Location   19
   Redundant Planning   19
   Timescale Management   19
   Design with Successions   19

Chapter 3: Land-Use Directive   20
A Toxic Legacy   20
   Regenerate the Degraded   21
   Weaving the Threads Together   21
Lawn Transformation Step by Step   22

Part II: Compose *with* the Land   27

Chapter 4: Contextual Design   28
When Is the Land?   29
   The Story of Place   29
Initial Questions to Ask   30
   The Curious Listener   30
Pattern Recognition   30
   Cycles (Evolution, Change, Management)   31
The Eagle and Flood Plain   32

Chapter 5: Awareness Practices 34
Walk the Land in Silence 34
   Reflective Sitting 35
   Community Land Walks 36
   The Sit Spot 36
   Tracking Journal 37

Chapter 6: Reading the Land 38
Water Patterns 38
   Springs and Seeps 39
   Low Lying Areas, Bog, Wetlands 39
   Look for Water in the Driest Time of Year 39
Vegetation 39
Animal Indicators 40
Natural History 40
Know Your Geology 40
Site Constraints 41
On-site Resources 41
In Field Soil Tests 42
Soil Textures Come in Many Combinations 43
   Observing the Soil Profile 43
Landforms 45
Microclimate 46
   Wind Patterns 47
   Sun Orientation 48
   Thermal Mass 49
   Fog 49
Infiltration Rate Test 49

Chapter 7: Create a Base Map 50
   Hand-Drawn Map 50
   Satellite Image 50
   Surveyed Map 50
   Satellite/Topo Overlay 51
Key Elements to Include in the Base Map 51
   Topography 51
   Structures 51
   Utilities 52
   Scale 52
Triangulation Mapping Simplified 52
Case Study: Site Assessment with Kendall Dunnigan 55

Chapter 8: Social Context 61
Social History 61
Know Your Neighbors 62
Project Stakeholders 62
Community Context 62

Chapter 9: Develop Your Vision 63
Attitudes and Behaviors 64
   Core Values Development 65
   Articulating Goals 65

Part III: Conceptual Landscape Design 69

Chapter 10: Conceptual Design Process 70
Creativity and Imagination 70
   Generating Ideas 71
   Unlimited Possibilities 72
Concept Planning 73
   Real Regeneration Versus Greenwashing 74
   Embodied Energy 75
   Land Access 75
   Question Your Motives 78
   Long-Term Design 79
   Design Timeline 79
Aesthetics 80
Case Study: The Permaculture Neighborhood Center 81

Chapter 11: Permaculture Design Wisdom 85
Permaculture Principles 86
   Stacking Functions 86
   Vertical Stacking 86
   Planned Redundancy 86
   Optimize Edge and Ecotones 87
   Design for Catastrophe 87
   Use On-site/Biological Resources 87
   Catch and Store Energy 87
Permaculture Zoning Strategy 88
Permaculture as a Way of Life 88

Chapter 12: Drafting Design Plans 89
   Communicating to Project Stakeholders 89
Drafting the Plan 89
   Hand Drafting 89

Digital Drafting 94
Using Elevations 94
Detail Drawings 95
Construction Drawings 96
Color Versus Black-and-White Renderings 96
Professional Design Tips with Emily Mallard 97
Taking Feedback 100
Finalizing Your Master Plan 100

Chapter 13: Design Plan Sets 101
Conceptual Master Plan 101
Planting Plan 102
Utilities Plan 102
Irrigation Plan 102
Hardscape Plan 103
Demolition Plan 103
Staging 103
Grading and Drainage Plan 103

Chapter 14: Phased Project Plan 105
Schedule Changes 105
Phase Abandonment 105
Sequencing 105
Creating a Project Schedule 106
Estimated Duration 106
Time of Year 106
Budgeted Labor/Materials 106
Sequencing (Critical Path) 107
Using a Gantt Chart 107
Project Choreographer 108

Chapter 15: Professional Design Relationships 109
Developing a Design Budget and Identifying Deliverables 109
Meetings 110
Project Parameters 111
Communication Is the Fuel 112
Unrealistic Schedules 112
Case Study: Sebastopol City Hall/Library Landscape 113

Part IV: The World of Soil 119

Chapter 16: Living Soil: The Foundation of Regenerative Landscapes 120
Five Principles of Soil Health 120
Create Living Soil 121
The Soil Community 121
Rhizosphere 121
Plant Exudates 121
Bacteria 122
Fungi 122
Protozoa 122
Nematodes 123
Arthropoda 123
Earthworms 123
Birds/Mammals 123
Feed Soil Life 123
Compacted and Hydrophobic Soils 124
Soil Decompaction Techniques and Tools 125
Broad Fork 125
Bucket Decompaction 126
Plants as Subsoilers 126
Case Study: Singing Frogs Farm 127
Soil Testing 130
Reading a Soils Report 131
Phospholipid Fatty Acid (PLFA) Test 132
The Haney Test 133
Slake Test 135
Develop a Soil Regeneration Plan 135

Chapter 17: No-Till Landscaping 137
Mulching 137
Cardboard/Newspaper 138
Wood Chips 140
Straw 140
Manure 141
Compost 142
Leaves 142
Chopped Plants 143
Materials Calculation Equation 143

Chapter 18: Vermiculture 145
The Power of a Worm Bin 145
Build a Worm Bin 146
Worm Bin Design 146
Drainage 148
Airflow 148
Lids 149
Placement 149
Prepping and Adding Worms 149
Feeding Your Worms 150

Caring for Worms   151
Harvesting Castings   151

Chapter 19: Composting   153
Compost Foundations   153
   Brown Material   153
   Green Material   154
   Manures   154
   Location   154
   Pests   154
Warm Composting   154
   Warm Composting Method   155
Hot Composting   156
   A Simple Hot Composting Method   156
Double Bin Compost System   156
Buying Compost   157

Chapter 20: Compost Tea and Plant Ferments   158
   Aerated Compost Tea   158
Compost Tea Recipe   158
   Commercial Brewers   159
   Liquid Comfrey Fertilizer   160
   Comfrey Fertilizer Recipe   160
Manure Tea   161

Chapter 21: Cover Cropping   162
   Timing   162
   Disturbances   163
Specific Seed for Specific Yields   163
   Nitrogen Fixers   163
   Taproot Plants   163
   Vegetables/Herbs   164
   Grain   164
   Insectary Plant Species   164
How to Broadcast Seed   164

Chapter 22: Hügelkultur   166
How to Build Hügelkultur   166
   Location   167
   Gather the Right Tools   167
   Dig the Trench   168
   Build in Layers   168
   Place the Final Layers   168
   Plant the Berm   169
The Benefits of Hügelkultur   169
   Microclimate Moderation   169
   Raised Planting Bed   169
   Water Harvesting   170
   Fungal Substrate   170
Concerns   170

Chapter 23: The Fungal Landscape   171
   Edible Mushrooms   171
   Medicinal Fungi   172
Case Study: In the Dark at Somerset House by Darren Springer   172
   Mushroom Cultivation Recipes   174
   Erosion Control   176
   Toxic Remediation with Fungi   176
   Landscapes of Fungi   176

Part V: Water in the Landscape   177

Chapter 24: Design Water Resilience   178
Water Conservation   178
   Regenerative Versus Degenerative Water Management   179
   Water Harvesting   180
   Droughts and Floods   181
   Landscapes of Water, Landscape of Life   181

Chapter 25: Identifying Water Sources   182
   Precipitation   182
   Rivers and Lakes   183
   Wells   183
   Freshwater Springs   183
   Municipal Water   184
   Responsible Water Management   184
Case Study: Laundry-to-Landscape Reuse by Connor Devane   184
Case Study: Why Small Solutions Matter by Trathen Heckman   188

Chapter 26: Managing and Harvesting Surface Water   193
Topography   193
Soils   193
Sources and Flows   193
   Tracking Water Outflows   194
Landscape Grading   194

   Contour 194
   Earthworks 195
   Avoid Damaging the Sacred 196
   Equipment for Installation 196
   Time of Year 197
   Sequencing Within the Whole Project 197
Water Infiltration Systems 197
   Size Appropriately 197
   Rain Gardens 198
   Building a Contour Water-Harvesting Swale 199
   Completing the Project 203
Spillways/Overflow 203
Combine Water Management Techniques 205

Chapter 27: Landscape Drainage Systems 206
Landscape Drainage Systems 206
   Grading 207
   Water Diversion Channels 207
   French Drains 207
   Drain Inlets/Pipe Conveyance 207
   Drainage and Erosion 208
   Drainage and Pollution 208

Chapter 28: Water Distribution 209
Gravity 209
Pumping Water 209
   Solar High Lift 210
   Well Pump 210
   Pressure Tank (Bladder Tank) 210
   Booster Pump 210
   Hand Pump 210
   Surface Flow 211
   Piping 211
   Natural Water Flows 211
Veins of the Land 211

Chapter 29: Roof Water Harvesting 212
Calculating Roof Water Catchment 212
Capture and Distribution 213
   Dry Line Conveyance 213
   Wet Line Conveyance 213
Tank Storage 215
   Siting Tanks 215
   Transfer Tanks 216
   Tank Foundations 216
   Gutter Retrofitting 216

   Using Rainwater 217
Harvesting Abundance 217

Chapter 30: Landscape Ponds 219
Design Functions 219
   Siting the Pond 220
   Engineering and Permits 221
   Excavation and Shaping 222
   Spillway and Leveling 222
   Installing the Underlayment 222
   Installing the Liner 223
   Rock Work 224
   Installing Pond Infrastructure 224
Case Study: WaterUP/Water School: Johads and Reviving Rivers in Rajasthan, India by Minni Jain and Louise Bingham 225
   Earthen Ponds 232
Locating a Pond 233
   Impoundment Ponds 233
Aquatic Plants for Pond Systems 236

Chapter 31: Irrigation Systems 238
Designing an Irrigation System 238
   Water Demand 238
   Sizing the System 238
Flood Irrigation 239
Overhead Sprinklers 239
Drip Irrigation 240
   Planning Your System 240
   Drip System Installation 242
Pipe-Laying Tricks 245
If You Suspect There Is a Leak in the Irrigation System 247
   Irrigation Maintenance 248

Chapter 32: Erosion Control 249
Elements of Erosion 249
   Velocity 250
   Roads: Problem and Solution 250
   Head Cuts 250
   Toe of the Slope 250
Biological Erosion Control 251
   Straw 251
   Broadcast Seeding 251
   Planted Overflows 252

    Contour Logs   252
    Erosion Gullies   252
How to Build a Brush Check Dam   253
Nonbiological Erosion Control   254
    Rock Armor   254
    Rock Check Dams   254
    Rock Walls   255
    Boulder Placement   256
    Zuni Bowls   256
    Water Crossings   257
Temporary Project-Based Erosion Control   258
You Are the Solution   259

Part VI: The Built Environment   161

Chapter 33: The Built Environment   262
Living in the Landscape   262
    Hardscape Versus Softscape   262
    Build to the Use   263
    Relative Location   263
    Natural Building   263
    Use of Concrete   264
    Materials Sourcing   264

Chapter 34: Architectural Elements   265
    Decks   265
    Benches   266
    Shou Sugi Ban   266
    Trellises/Arbors   267
    Raised Beds   267
    How to Build Wooden Raised Beds   267
Building a Cob Oven by Sasha Rabin   269
What Is Cob?   270
    Materials   270
    Cob Ovens   271
    Building the Foundation   272
    Setting the Hearth Bricks   272
    Creating the Door Opening   274
    Creating the Sand Form (the Void of the Oven)   275
    Layers of the Oven   275
    Earthen Plaster Recipe   277
    Oven Roof   277
    Oven Door   277
Cooking in Your Cob Oven   277
Materials and Tools for a Cob Oven   278
Recipes   279
    Clay Slip   279
    Chopped Straw   279
    Cob   280
    Basic Cob Recipe   280
    How to Mix Cob   280
    Ratios for Cob Mixes   281
    Make These Samples   281
Thermal Mass Versus Insulation   281

Chapter 35: Landscape Patios   282
Sizing   282
Surface Materials   282
Patio Foundations   282
Flagstone Patio   284
Pavers/Brick   284
Decomposed Granite   285

Chapter 36: Landscape Pathways   286
Water Runoff/Drainage   287
Shape and Flow   287
Materials for Pathways   287
    Gravel   287
    Flagstone   288
    Stepping Stones   289
    Wood Chips   290
    Vegetated Pathways   291
    Decomposed Granite   292
    Pathway Chases   292
    Water-Harvesting Pathway   293
    Landscape Steps   293

Chapter 37: Terrace and Rock Wall Systems   296
Walls or No Walls   296
To Consider When Excavating Terraces   297
    Staging Terrace Projects   297
    Combining Terraces, Swales, and Rain Gardens   298
Rock Walls and Alternatives   298
    Benefits of Rock Walls   298
    Disadvantages of Rock Walls   299
Urbanite Walls   299

Boulder Walls 299
Placing Boulders 300

Part VII: Planting Earth 301

Chapter 38: Revegetate the Planet 302
Repairing the World with Plants 302
An Ecological Planting Strategy 302
Plant Medicine 303
Plants for Controlling Erosion 303
Soil Building 303
Water Filtration 303
Food Production 303
Nutrient-Dense Food 304
Edible Landscaping 304

Plant Hardiness Zones 305

Chapter 39: Landscape Planting Plans 306
Assess Existing Vegetation 306
Plant Lists 306
Mapping Your Planting Plan 308
Useful Plants 308
The Right Plants for the Space 308
Extending Flowering Times 309
Evergreen Versus Deciduous 309
Permaculture Zoning in Planting Plans 311
Plan for Maturity 311
Choosing Plant Sizes 311

Chapter 40: Plant Communities 313
Structural Plant Combinations 313
Structural Growth Patterns of Trees and Plants 313
Zone by Zone 315

Plants by Function 315
Soil-Building Plants 315
Native Gardens 315
Drought-Tolerant Gardens 316
Cut Flowers 316
Medicinal and Culinary Herbs 316
Grains 316
Plant Fibers 317
Crafting Wood 317
Wetlands 317
Insectary Plants 317
Animal Forage 318

Native Plants Versus Exotic Plants 318

Case Study: EarthSeed Farm 320

Chapter 41: Regenerative Agroforestry 323
Food Forest Agroforestry 323
Orchards 324
Managing Biomass 324
Soil Seed Bank 326
Pollination 326
Prepping Planting Areas 327
Growth Pattern and Longevity 327
Extending Harvests 327

Planting Trees 328
Soil Structure 328
Orientation 329
Water Table 329
Tree Guards 330

Planting Trees by Seed 330
Seeds into the Ground 331
Seeding into Pots 331
Stratification 331
Wet Versus Dry Seed 331

Planting a Bare Root Tree 332

Choosing Fruit and Nut Cultivars 333
Chill Hour Requirements 333
Varieties You Like to Eat 334
Storing and Longevity 334
Cultivars for Fermentation 334

Hedgerows 335
Tips for Growing Regenerative Hedgerows 335

Chapter 42: Managing Trees Systems with Pruning 337
Dead 337
Diseased 338
Directional 338
Pruning for Size 338
Pruning for Shape 339
Pruning Times of the Year 339
Pruning Fruit Wood 339
Pruning Angles 340

Three Ways to Train Scaffold Branches 340
The Power of Your Cuts 341
Thinning Fruit 342
Coppicing 342
Pollarding 343

Chapter 43: Growing Vegetables   345
    Nutrient Density   345
    Saving Money   345
    Food Sovereignty   346
    Healthy Soil Equals Healthy Food   346
Four Seasons of Harvest   347
    Growing in the Right Season   347
    Frost Protection   347
    Greenhouse/Hoop House   348
Choosing Vegetable Varieties   348
    Grow What You Eat   349
    Growing in Season   349
    Perennial Vegetables   350
    Notable Perennial Vegetables   350
Planting in Cycles   351
Renewing Soil Health   351
Companion Planting   352
Harvesting   352
    Preserving the Harvest   353
    Harvest/Preservation Tips by Vegetable (A Short List)   354
Pests and Disease   357

Chapter 44: Plant Propagation   359
Propagate by Seed   359
    Sowing Seeds   359
    Depth of Seed Planted   360
    Covering Seeds   360
    Seeding in Ground Versus Pots   360
Grow Your Own Plants   361
    Cuttings   361
    Dig and Divide Roots   363
    Grafting   363

Chapter 45: Landscape Maintenance   364
Changing Cultural Aesthetics   364
Vegetation Management   364
    Mowing   365
    Nontoxic Herbicides   367
    Occultation   367
    The Art of Weeding   367

Chapter 46: Saving Seed   368
Pollination   368
    Self-Pollinated   368
    Insect-Pollinated   369
    Wind-Pollinated   369
    Hand-Pollination   369
When to Harvest Seed   369
    Harvesting Wet Seeds   369
Seed Processing   370
    Threshing   370
    Screening   370
    Winnowing   370
Seed Storage   371
    Labeling   371
    Share the Abundance   371
The Hidden Seeds   371
The Cultural Conservancy and Heron Shadow by Maya Harjo   372

Part VIII: Creatures of the Landscape   375

Chapter 47: Of Wing, Hoof, Claw, and Scale   376
Predator–Prey Relationships   376
Nature Awareness   377
    Bird Language   378
    Animal Ancestral Compulsion   378
Observing Animal Habitat   379
Animal Behaviors   380
    Leave Landscape Habitat Intact   380
    Insectary Superstars   381
    Integrated Pest Management (An Ecological Approach)   381

Chapter 48: Integrated Pest Management   382
Seasonality   382
Stressed Plants   383
Beneficial Predatory Insects   383
    Dragonfly   383
    Parasitoid Wasps   383
    Ladybugs   384
    Lacewings   384
    Tachinid Flies   384
    Hoverfly   384

Mammals   385
Attracting Birds to the Landscape   385
   Nesting   386
   Cover/Shelter   386
   Forage   387
   Bird Boxes   387
Mason Bee Habitat   388
   Making Mason Bee Hotels   388
Insectary Plants   389
   Flower Shapes   389
   Trap Crops   390
Burrowing Mammals   390
Reptiles   390
Amphibians   390
Lizard Habitat   391
Edge Effect   391
Avoid Insecticides (Conventional and Organic)   391
Habitat Ponds   392

Chapter 49: Fencing   393
Single Tall Fence   393
   Siting the Fence   393
   Choosing Fencing Materials   394
Double Low Fences   396
Electric Fencing   396

Chapter 50: Choosing the Right Animals   398
Beneficial Relationships   398
   Stocking   399
   Vegetation   399
   Terrain   400
   Frequency   400
   Human Resources   400
   Input/Output Analysis   401
Keeping Bees   402
   Beehives   403
   Log Hives   403
Sheep   404
Goats   406
Cows   407
Safety Considerations for Domesticated Animals   409

Chapter 51: Chicken Systems   410
   Varieties   410
Integrating Chickens into the Regenerative Landscape   411
   Determine If Chickens Are Appropriate for Your Project   411
   Locating the Chicken Coop   411
Protecting Your Chickens   412
   Permanent Runs   412
   Movable Systems   413
Harvesting   413
Basic Chicken Coop Design   414
Protection from Predators   415
Water Source   415
Food   416
Deep Bedding   416

Part IX: Restore the Wild   417

Chapter 52: Stewards of the Earth   418
Biodiversity   418
   Invasive Grasses   419
   Site Specific   419
   Emergency Resilience   419
   Reforestation   420
   Bring Back the Prairie   420
   Perennial Grasses and Herbs   421
Case Study: Mycoremediation with Dr. Mia Maltz   421
Seed Drilling   432
Build Relationships with Wild Plants   433
   Ethical Wild Harvesting Techniques   433
   Tending Wild Plants   434
   Stimulate Growth and Propagate   434
   Seasonality   434

Chapter 53: Lands of Fire   435
Catastrophic (High Intensity) Versus Good Fire (Low Intensity)   435
Fire Frequency   436
Lessons from the Fire   437
Animals and Fire Management   438
   Fuel Ladders   438

 Prescribed Burning   **439**
 Shaded Fuel Break   **439**
The Fires Will Return   **440**
Fireproofing the Landscape   **443**

Chapter 54: Regenerative Forest Management   **445**
Ecological Forest Management   **445**
 Selective Thinning   **446**
 Death and Decay   **446**
 Disease Vectors   **446**
 Selecting Trees to Cut   **446**
 Lop and Scatter   **447**
 Protect Existing Saplings   **448**
 Contour Brush Piles   **449**
 Biochar   **449**
Follow Indigenous Wisdom   **449**

Acknowledgments   **451**
References   **452**
Index   **465**

FOREWORD
by Penny Livingston

When I first met Erik in 1999, he was only 19 years old—one of my students at the Occidental Arts and Ecology Center, sitting among an exuberant bunch of enthusiastic young people ready to redesign the world, starting with the community of Sebastopol. He arrived as a part of Planting Earth Activation (PEA), a group that had been installing free gardens for interested community members.

Four years earlier, I had started a permaculture design and building company focused on designing landscapes and human settlements that have the stability and resiliency of a natural ecosystem. I was looking for people to work for me who loved working the land, enjoyed place-making, installing gardens, and building soil.

I was so impressed by the energy of this small but mighty group, eager to create positive change in their community. Of the group, Erik caught my eye for his vibrancy and his moving stories about how such generous offerings had affected the recipients of these gardens. Seeing in him a capacity to bring people together and get things done, I asked him if he was interested in getting paid to do this work and if he could organize his friends to work for me. I chose Erik because I saw in him a young man who embodied leadership with the Seven Sacred Attributes of the Lakota tradition, as told to me by my elder friend, Gilbert Walking Bull. These are qualities the clan mothers in his community would look for in young boys and men to decide who would make a good chief. I have been given permission by Gilbert Walking Bull to share these sacred attributes with others to help us learn and grow our leaders:

1. *Wowah'waka:* Inner quietness, sacred silence.
2. *Wocanto'knake:* Heartfelt love and compassion for all two-leggeds, being a caretaker of people.
3. *Wowaunsila:* Heartfelt love and compassion for all of creation, being a caretaker of the creation.
4. *Wowawokiye:* To be truly helpful; to discover our gifts, purpose, vision, and to follow through on it. Translating love and compassion into action.
5. *Wobliheca:* The experience of being fully alive and elated, enjoyment of each moment of life.
6. *Wowiyuski:* Positive powers; overwhelming, heartfelt joy; the childlike state of wonder and delight.
7. *Wozani:* The sacred state of health—soundness of mind, body, and spirit—the quickness of a coyote.

When Erik became my apprentice, I put him to the test. I wanted to see what this dynamic young man was made of. He showed up, worked hard, and was passionate about working the land and creating abundant landscapes. He passed every test I subjected him to.

When he was assisting a permaculture design course I was teaching in a very remote rural community in Northern California, I told him, "We need a pile of rocks for a hands-on project by tomorrow afternoon." Without batting an eye, he told me he had noticed a big pile by the side of the road a mile away. I knew that pile was there and simply wanted to see if he had noticed, and indeed he had! Part of our skill building is to learn to be resourceful by gleaning resources from nearby. In every task I put forward for Erik, he showed up with integrity, enthusiasm, and competency.

Over the years, I witnessed Erik growing into a dynamic, visionary leader, developing the skills and capacity to manifest his dreams and visions. He approaches land management from a spiritually connected intention, working in harmony with the earth, designing and implementing landscapes that the land is calling for. He has developed a gift and a skill for this art, along with a storytelling ability that leaves people with a sense of possibility and inspiration—he frames a story so that people can see themselves in it.

In 2001, I cofounded the Regenerative Design Institute (RDI) at the Commonweal Garden in Bolinas, California, to offer permaculture education to those who have an interest in this approach to design, land management, nontoxic building, and community organizing. We look to the natural world to discover nature's operating principles and learn from the deep and ancient wisdom it has to offer. At the garden, Erik taught hands-on practical skills with me, like how to properly plant a tree, how to lay out level water-harvesting ditches on the land, how to install irrigation systems, how to make good compost, and more. In 2005, Erik started a successful ecological landscaping business called Permaculture Artisans. As a designer, I felt complete confidence in recommending him to any client because I knew he would deliver quality service with integrity.

By 2012, he had developed a center for permaculture education and demonstration in Sebastopol, California, called Permaculture Skills Center. This center has inspired and trained hundreds of people in permaculture farming, landscaping, and earth-repair techniques. In 2015, Erik started the Ecological Landscape Immersion Program to teach others how to regenerate healthy ecosystems in the landscape design and implementation process. He not only fleshed out a number of step-by-step methods, techniques, and strategies, he also taught how to listen to both the land and the client, connecting the two in a cohesive project that resonated with the land steward and was beneficial to the overall landscape. He demonstrated how to increase landscape function by integrating soil, water, and vegetation with slope, sun, wildlife, and human connection. His decades of dedication, integrity, community connection, listening to the land, and openness to learning new things are all present in this extraordinary book.

If you think about it, there is a huge amount of land that is stewarded by both homeowners and renters as part of home residences. Imagine if everyone considered themselves a steward of an ecosystem in their yard rather than seeing it as just a landscape or garden. If whole communities adopted the ethics and principles of regenerative landscaping, we could do so much to reverse climate change by sequestering atmospheric carbon back into the earth as healthy soil and plants. It would eliminate the need for chemical fertilizers and biocides and would increase ecological health in urban and suburban communities.

The book you are holding in your hands is a complete work on permaculture and regenerative landscaping, but it also includes many other topics one might not consider related to ecological or regenerative landscaping. This is because Erik is a whole-systems thinker. A whole systems thinker can't separate nontoxic natural building from watershed health, land use, habitat development, and economy. They are all interconnected and related to each other. Reading this guide will bring to light in detail why and how these are related. An example of this interconnection is the relationship between water runoff and salmon spawning. If everyone could manage the water runoff on the land they are stewarding in a way that eliminates erosion, salmon would be able to complete their spawning process and the eggs would be allowed to hatch, thus bringing salmon back to abundant populations after being designated as nearly endangered.

So this is more than just a manual on regenerative landscaping. It offers a unique and comprehensive understanding of the design intelligence that the natural world has to offer us, with the capacity to change the world of landscaping, gardening, and earth stewardship. It helps us to become better human beings and aids us in remembering our original operating instructions for stewarding and tending the land in a good way, one yard at a time.

As we embark on an era of species extinction, climate change (global weirding!), and ecological collapse, this book is more important than ever. Grim statistics are coming more and more into our view. I have hope that we can still shift the pattern of destructive, extractive practices to a pattern and relationship of renewal and ecological health, providing abundance for humans as well as wildlife.

If you want to make an impact in the world, it isn't up to just you or even a few of us. It really depends on millions of people making positive change. *The Regenerative Landscaper* is a comprehensive how-to guide for ecological landscaping and a basis for ecological literacy, infused with Erik's profound knowledge and experience of permaculture and landscape design.

Upon gaining the knowledge offered here, you—the reader—will learn how to steward land and create ecologically rich, abundant gardens and landscapes. The more people who have access to the information offered here, the more ecosystems on this earth can be restored. When people understand that they are a keystone species, they can learn to behave like a probiotic on the earth, restoring ecosystem health one garden at a time. The world will change when people remember the sublime design intelligence of the natural world, with humanity as stewards of this beautiful garden planet.

NOVEMBER 2022

HOW TO USE THIS BOOK

The Regenerative Landscaper is organized to assist you, the reader, through your landscape projects from beginning to end. There are many reasons to create a regenerative landscape—beauty and function, resilience, sovereignty. Whatever your goal, this book guides your way.

Here I share with you the same project-sequencing approach I have used in professional landscaping for decades, bearing in mind that each designer dwells in a particular context that has its own emerging timeline.

You will be guided as you observe your project's context, conduct site analysis, create and install your design, and finally move into stewardship—or maintenance—of the land. Written like this, the process looks linear, but in truth it is dynamic and cyclical. Each project will veer onto its own path and follow its own natural trajectory, but the sequencing shared here is always indispensable.

If you are new to regenerative design, follow the progression of the book as laid out. If you are already highly experienced, you may skip around to relevant sections, step-by-step processes, and case studies as needed for your project. The index at the back of the book will help you find your desired topics.

The information in this book is comprehensive and time-tested. If you find yourself returning to *The Regenerative Landscaper* as a reference guide, then it has achieved its purpose.

INTRODUCTION

Imagine you step out your back door and are immediately greeted by birdsong. Trees sway in the breeze as you hook your basket onto your arm and set out to harvest fresh herbs for your breakfast. You enter your garden where an abundance of food and flowers await. Butterflies and insects buzz by, drinking from the sweet nectar your garden provides. Within ten minutes, you've filled your basket with just-ripe veggies, fruits, eggs, and herbs for your day. A bundle of cut flowers rests on top—an offering to beautify your home. This is a landscape of real abundance.

I remember the moment when I realized what true abundance and wealth was—abundance for my family but also for all the life in my garden. I was grazing on blueberries, cherries, and mulberries, watching plums ripen, the symphony of birdsong deafening. It was late spring, and I noticed that the diversity of birds and wildlife visiting the homestead had more than quadrupled in the five years since we built this landscape.

Bewick's wrens had nested in a bird box we had hung from an old maple. Brown creepers (a rare sight) had found a crack in the bark of a redwood tree and built a home there. House finches nested against the house on top of a forgotten broom. Numerous other species—quail, titmouse, bushtits, towhees, foxes, opossum, pygmy owls, red-shouldered hawks, barn owls, bats—all made their home on this one-acre homestead.

My belly was full of fruit and my mind calm as I watched two western pond turtles sun themselves among a half-dozen species of emerging dragonfly in the pond. This is what abundance looks like to me. I spent six months building that pond and now it is a temple of life and a place to soothe the soul.

This same lush landscape solves multiple environmental crises. It catches and stores water, which is becoming ever more critical for combating drought and fire. The biologically rich topsoil sequesters carbon and feeds a thriving plant community that, in turn, feeds the living web of soil. The garden serves as a true safe harbor for threatened and endangered birds and insects.

If this inspires you to act—if the voice in your head is saying *Yes!*—you're in the right place. In these pages, you will find step-by-step instructions for designing and turning your yard into a **regenerative landscape**. This book not only provides a plethora of ideas but acts as a practical (day-to-day, month-by-month) manual, documenting the entire process and mind-set you need to create ecological paradise.

I know this kind of landscape is possible because I've been doing this work for more than 20 years. I've had the privilege of building hundreds of regeneration projects—with private landowners, nonprofits, schools, and cities—mostly in the United States but also throughout the world. This work has given me hope that even during the darkest times, regenerative solutions bring about a more peaceful and abundant world. I hope this book infuses that same hope in you. You can use this book to create a healthier and more beautiful world for yourself, your family, and your community. When you become a steward of the land, your yard not only sustains but actively regenerates natural life-support systems of the environment. Once you understand the systems of your specific project, you can begin to enhance how they function. Achieve this and your landscape will respond in kind with beauty, food security, and climate stability.

We can do this one yard at a time: land at every scale—every barren, sacred piece of ground—plays a part. Your own front yard can repair the earth. As a result of your regenerative landscape, you play a part in managing a healthy water cycle, turning soil into carbon-harvesting reservoirs, and cultivating personal sustainability by growing medicinal herbs, fruits, and vegetables. Growing food and medicine can literally save you thousands of dollars a year in groceries while helping safeguard your and your family's health as you enjoy more nutrient-dense food. There has never been a better time to move in this direction.

At the root of all regenerative practices is the living wisdom of Indigenous people. Honoring the native people and practices of your area is an inextricable part of understanding the landscape. There is a common bond we all share that traces each of us back to our early ancestors. This bond represents the relationship between people and land; it is a gift but it comes with a great responsibility.

For thousands of years humans across the globe maintained a balanced partnership with their habitats. Much of that knowledge has been lost to colonization, but enough of the old ways remain to seed a new reciprocal relationship with landscapes. Humans are intelligent. But the process of colonization might cost us everything if we don't urgently change our cultural land-use practices. The ingenuity of our near ancestors and their relationship to their environment has, for better or worse, spawned human civilization as we know it. Selective plant breeding, domestication of animals, changing the physical shapes of landscapes—these abilities, now inherent in all human societies—have enabled people to transform land into food-growing systems (agriculture). The same knowledge that founded civilization has been used to disrupt and destroy living systems through industrial agriculture on a planetwide scale.

We are now at a crossroads. How we treat our landscapes and each other defines the fate of all future generations. We still have a choice. We can use this power either to destroy or to renew. Do we continue to take the destructive path, accelerating mass species extinction, poverty, and climate disasters? Or do we take the path of regeneration, where we dust off the ancestral ways and do the real work of repairing our ecosystems?

No matter our political ideology, culture, or religion, we are all united by a few basic elements, the forces that shape our planet. The forces of the sun, life-giving water, and the magic of the chlorophyll molecule—these systems undeniably connect every human and every living thing in the web of life. By picking up this book, *you are choosing renewal*. Inside, you will find comprehensive, easy-to-follow methods for transforming a patch of earth into a life-sustaining regenerative landscape. You'll discover answers to your questions, but you'll also discover how to *ask* the right questions—how to listen to the earth in all its complexity and splendor.

The regenerative path unfolds in front of you. The tools you need are here in your hands. Join me on this journey as we repair the land together.

PART I

The Wisdom of the Earth

1
Earth's Design Intelligence

Regenerative landscaping focuses on increasing the health and productivity of ecosystems: managing landscapes, farms, and gardens to enhance the life-giving processes occurring in these ecologies. This approach builds soil carbon, increasing soil's capacity to hold water and distribute nutrients to plant life. In a regenerative landscape, we manage a healthy and functioning hydrologic cycle, catching, storing, and infiltrating storm waters, reducing floods, erosion, and drought.

We are living through the sixth mass extinction,[1] an event marked by the disappearance of plant and animal species every day. Truly ecological landscapes focus on preserving biodiversity and building habitat for wildlife, turning landscapes into refuges for all manner of animal and plant life to thrive. Butterflies, bees, hummingbirds, snakes, lizards, frogs, mammals—think of all the diversity on this earth to celebrate and steward. But first, you need to recognize the habitat that already exists on a site and be careful not to destroy it in your landscaping work.

Many well-intentioned landscapers damage intact ecologies, blinded by their enthusiasm for making beautiful gardens. That is not the way of regeneration. Our choice to leave landscape systems alone is as important as our desire to change them. Learn the way of the site first so that your design will truly fit the context of the land. I will teach you how.

My goal is to help you design, develop, and manage regenerative landscapes. The landscape around your house, the local park, an agricultural operation—all scales are relevant—every single space can be an ecological model in your community.

This book provides the day-to-day practical methods of building regenerative landscapes, from understanding project context and reading natural patterns to drafting and presenting designs, from the installation of landscape systems to monitoring, maintenance, and long-term stewardship. Each part features case studies of real projects that showcase brilliant landscapes, regenerative designers, and farmers.

My dream is that you honor this book with dirty finger smudges, use leaves as bookmarks, and refer to it time and again for your design and installation projects. It's here for you when you forget what the next step is, when you need an extra bit of inspiration, and when you want to remember the creative ways people have already solved the problem you're up against.

THE INTELLIGENCE OF EARTH

For billions of years the earth developed and refined innovative systems for supporting life—the water cycle, the chlorophyll molecule, the shield against the sun (atmosphere), a dynamic surface composed of forests, wetlands, grasslands, mountains, deserts, oceans, and you and me. All these elements are woven into an interdependent whole—earth.

Understanding how ecosystems function to support communities of living organisms is the *first* layer of knowledge required to design regenerative landscapes. This host of relationships and cyclical processes that make up the design wisdom of the earth is our primary inspiration for regenerative design.

Ecosystems are composed of specific patterns and processes that work together to grow life. As regenerative landscapers, our task is to assist, enhance, and repair these life-support systems. When we do it correctly, we (by default) enrich humanity with resources—nutrient-dense food, clean water, herbal medicines, and immense beauty.

Interdependence

When living and nonliving things, including humans, are working together through mutually beneficial relationships, they are modeling interdependence. A tree provides a home for a squirrel; the squirrel plants the tree's seeds. A bison grazes on grass, and the grass utilizes the bison's manure to grow big and strong. There are infinite examples of these cooperative relationships, which leads us to the awareness that everything is dependent on everything else. When we break these connections, ecologies degenerate and collapse becomes imminent.

Ecological crisis has been culminating for hundreds of years through deforestation, desertification, biodiversity loss, dying oceans, and catastrophic climate events. Many life-support systems of the earth have been broken, and we are the ones who can mend them. Before we engage in this restoration, we need ecological literacy—the understanding of how rain is formed, how forests evolve, how the carbon cycle works, and much more.

THE HYDROLOGIC CYCLE: THE BLUE PLANET

Our wonderful blue Earth is the only known planet with water molecules in all of their three forms: solid (ice, snow), liquid (water), and gas (water vapor). The movement and distribution of these waters is called the hydrologic cycle. Three percent of the planet's water is freshwater and two-thirds of that is locked up in ice caps, glaciers, and inland seas. That leaves 1 percent of all the water on earth to provide for the terrestrial biosphere (plants, animals, humans).[2] Powered by our closest star, the sun, the water cycle constantly recycles freshwater through the processes of evaporation, condensation, and precipitation (rain, snow), with evaporation and its sibling, transpiration, being the main drivers of precipitation.

Evaporation: Movement from the sun and wind creates heat that evaporates water, turning it from liquid to gas. The water vapor rises into the atmosphere until it hits cold air, causing water molecules to condense into clouds. Eventually this water will return to the earth in the form of rain or snow. Evaporation constitutes nearly 90 percent of all atmospheric moisture.[3]

Transpiration: Trees and plants uptake water from their roots and transpire water vapor through their leaves, which enters the atmosphere. Much of the rain that falls on inland areas comes from rain clouds formed through forest transpiration.[4] This is one reason why humanity needs to be planting more trees a year than we remove. When we remove trees, we remove the rain. When we plant trees, we plant the rain.

Natural Water Storage

Once rain or snow falls to the ground, what happens next is of utmost importance. Every ecosystem has its own form of water storage, and caretaking these storage systems is part of our work as regenerative designers. Groundwater is one of the most significant water-storage systems, providing for most of the biological needs of life on land. Humans can make the largest restorative impact on groundwater by aiding stormwater infiltration and reducing our dependence on groundwater for agricultural and domestic uses.

Snowpack

In mountain regions, snowpack provides a remarkable form of freshwater storage, capturing winter snowstorms and then slowly feeding rivers and lakes through snow melt the rest of the year.

Vegetative/Animal Storage

In desert ecosystems, water is mainly stored in cacti and succulents, ingenious storage systems in regions with extreme arid conditions. All plants store some moisture. Animals (including humans) do as well. We are all just sacks of water, imbibing and excreting moisture all day, every day of our lives.

Rivers and Lakes

Bodies of freshwater, like lakes and rivers, make up nearly half of available freshwater sources. Rivers also distribute water and nutrients throughout the environment. The volume held in these bodies of water is dependent on factors such as the state of the groundwater table, snowpack, and regional precipitation events.

Condensation

When water vapor transforms from gas to liquid, it's called condensation. This happens when warmer air cools to its *dew point*—the temperature needed for airborne moisture to condense.

In addition to dew point, water molecules need surfaces to form into liquid. Condensation in the atmosphere is dependent upon *aerosols*—tiny particles that provide a surface for liquid water and, when combined, form clouds, storms, rain, and snow.

The same can be said for morning dew on grass or moisture on the outside of a glass filled with cold water. In these instances, the air has cooled to the dew point, condensing upon the grass and glass surfaces. (Have you ever drunk morning dew from the leaf of a plant? It's a highly recommended experience—just make sure the plant isn't poisonous!)

Aerosols in the atmosphere come in many forms: minerals, dust, pollen, and other fine particles that form cloud condensation nuclei (CCN).[5] These particles rise from the earth and catch air currents that draw them high into the atmosphere where they help form clouds.

A seldom studied yet vital component of our water cycle is dependent upon a special type of atmospheric aerosol: the biological kind. These primary biological aerosol particles (PBAP) seed the sky, providing cloud condensation nuclei to make rain.

Bacterial Rainmakers

The most effective bacteria for providing cloud condensation is called *Pseudomonas syringae*. This innovative organism is not only responsible for helping seed rain in the atmosphere, but it also causes ice nucleation. Ice nucleation happens when water vapor condenses directly into ice in cold temperatures. In this way, *P. syringae* help make snow, sleet, and ice. This bacteria, and others of its kind, are commonly parasitic to plants and trees, which is where they develop and release their rainmaking spores.[6]

Fungal Rainmakers

Fungal spores also provide biological aerosols for making rain. A large group of fungi called *Basidiospores* eject 50 million tons of airborne spores every year. These tiny particles float around the atmosphere, seeding clouds and falling back to earth to spread their kind.

Many of these mushrooms use a "surface tension catapult" process that turns the spore into a ballistospore with 25,000 G of force (10,000 times more than a rocket ship) to explode into the air. When a droplet of water forms and falls from the spore's surface, it releases the surface tension catapult, firing the spores into the air.[7]

With fungi and bacteria acting as biological aerosols, it's easy to conclude that forests and grassland ecosystems are vital components for not only the transpiration of moisture, but the seeding of clouds.

Water Runoff

Clean, accessible freshwater is being lost at an alarming rate with dangerous consequences for environments, watersheds, and human communities. Runoff is one of the biggest contributors to polluting water, eroding soils, and depleting freshwater sources. Agricultural soils, roads, pavement, houses—all these impervious systems have broken the natural capture and filtration of rainwater. This, along with overconsumption and chemical intensive agriculture, contribute the greatest impacts to the global freshwater supply.

Regenerative design offers many solutions for managing water runoff, with stewardship of freshwater providing the basis for all foundational design features. Landscape designers (hey, that's you!) have many opportunities to manage water cycles that clean, store, and increase availability of freshwater. That's good news because the process of aridification has increased dramatically around the planet with cracked, dry soils and shimmering waves of heat sprawling in its wake.

An arid landscape is an environment where evaporation exceeds precipitation. (Humid climates are the opposite! Precipitation exceeds evaporation.) Aridification—when the land becomes drier and drier over a long period of time—threatens an ecosystem's ability to hold water and therefore support biological communities. Often, this is due to a reduction of precipitation (rain, fog, sleet, snow), groundwater loss, increased evaporation, and lack of ground cover. As vegetation dries out, the aridification process intensifies and the surface of the soil heats up, which can lead to desertification.[8] That's why understanding the water cycle is foundational to restoring ecosystems.

THE CARBON CYCLE: LIFE'S ORIGIN

Like the water cycle, the carbon cycle provides the basis for life on earth. Eighteen percent of the human body is made of carbon. The stem and leaf mass of herbaceous plants is composed of nearly 45 percent carbon while nearly 50 percent of woody plants (trees) are made of carbon. We are all connected: people and trees and animals.

There are five main carbon sinks (systems that absorb carbon) on earth: the ocean, the atmosphere, stone/sediment (including fossil fuels), the interior mantle of the earth, and the terrestrial biosphere (plants, trees, soil). We as regenerative designers can directly influence only the terrestrial biosphere, thereby affecting the atmospheric carbon sink at the same time.[9]

The excessive amounts of carbon dioxide (CO_2) and other greenhouse gases entering the atmosphere have resulted in the trapping of heat, warming the earth and generating extreme climate events worldwide. Carbon dioxide operates under natural laws that we humans manipulate through activities like plowing the soil and burning fossil fuels, which can lead to disaster. However, we can do things differently. Planting trees, along with ecological grassland and ocean management, aids in the removal of excess carbon from the atmosphere through the power of photosynthesis. We either build landscapes and farms that release carbon dioxide (tilling, paving, draining), adding to catastrophe, *or* we build landscapes that sequester (draw down) CO_2 into trees, soils, and prairies.

Liquid Carbon Pathway

In the liquid carbon pathway, plants take in carbon dioxide through the process of photosynthesis, transform this CO_2 into a source of food, then offer it to a wide range of organisms. Up to 30 percent of the carbon a plant absorbs from the air is released as plant exudates from its roots into the soil. Fungi and bacteria feed on this carbon, making it available to other organisms, while feeding the plant minerals and nutrients in exchange for this carbon gift.[10] This model is a stunning display of reciprocity between a diversity of species—a web of relationships that keeps the living world alive.

By aiding terrestrial carbon sinks (the biosphere), we beneficially affect both carbon and water cycles. When we sequester carbon in plants and soil, we not only reduce the atmospheric load of carbon, but with every 1 percent increase of carbon per acre of soil, we increase its water-holding capacity by approximately 25,000 gallons! The soil is a literal reservoir for carbon and water, and a regenerative landscape will have ample amounts of both.

Grassland and Forest Carbon

Part of stewarding the carbon cycle includes protecting grasslands and forests from destruction. There are 10 to 12 billion acres of grazing grasslands on earth, constituting a massive carbon sink. Many perennial grasses develop 10 times the underground root growth compared to their above-ground leaf growth, providing a large liquid carbon pathway to feed carbon-storing soil life.[11]

In Northern California where I live (on unceded Pomo and Miwok land), we are home to the tallest trees in the world, the coastal redwood (*Sequoia sempervirens*). These ancient groves, with some trees over 3,000 years old, are the greatest carbon-storing forests in the world. It takes approximately the same amount of time for a fallen redwood tree to decompose as it did to grow. That means that a 1,000-year-old tree would release stored carbon over 1,000 years.

All old-growth forests represent major carbon storage systems. They can hold 30 to 70 percent more carbon than second- or third-generation forests. These ecosystems desperately need protection to keep the planet's climate in balance. So far, half of earth's forests have been lost and only a fifth of what remains is in pristine condition. In some areas we can reverse this trend through afforestation (planting trees), but protecting what's left is also necessary.

PHOTOSYNTHESIS: THE MIRACLE OF LIFE

The earth is innately regenerative, but the usable energy for growing living systems is reliant upon a green, vegetated landscape. Photosynthesis and its ability to turn sunlight into usable energy is one of the most fundamental gifts to life on the planet. This process is made possible by the tiny chlorophyll molecule. Here is how it all began.

Millions of years ago, microscopic ocean bacteria learned to convert sunlight into proteins and carbohydrates. These cyanobacteria were the first organisms to develop photosynthesis. Over time, these bacteria combined with other more complex organisms, leading to the birth of the plant kingdom.[12]

Chlorophyll is a green pigment molecule that makes its own food by using the energy of the sun and transforming it into sugars and proteins. Inside the cells of plants are tiny structures called chloroplasts. These chloroplasts are the homes where chlorophyll molecules are located inside plants. In the process of converting sunlight, carbon dioxide is absorbed from the air and oxygen is then released. This process comes with a small cost. For photosynthesis to take place, the chlorophyll molecule must consume minerals and nutrients to fuel the process. Every food web on earth, from marine environments to terrestrial landscapes, begins with photosynthesis, making the chlorophyll molecule the very basis for life on earth.

Planting gardens, reforesting degraded landscapes, growing food—at the center of each of these acts is the carbon-harvesting, sunlight-absorbing, oxygen-exhaling, matter-producing miracle of photosynthesis. Plants are the greatest allies in the work of regenerating the earth.

Forest Ecology

The world's forests are massive carbon sinks, making up nearly 45 percent of land-based carbon. Some forests convert up to 5,000 pounds of carbon dioxide per year per acre! Forests are living systems that provide key ecological functions to build soil, home animals, and manage micro and macro climate patterns.[13]

Currently forest covers approximately 30 percent of earth's terrestrial surface, making up more than 3 trillion trees. It sounds like a lot, but it is half as many trees as the earth sustained at the dawn of human civilization. Still, we are losing 15 billion trees a year to toilet paper production, timber, farmland expansion, and other human industry.

Forests modify weather in a variety of ways including surface albedo (reflection/absorption of light), transpiration (from vegetation), and wind absorption (aerodynamic roughness).

Tropical forests, for example, transpire enough moisture to generate large rain systems. This has several effects. The process of transpiration produces "evaporative cooling," which cools the forest floor during transpiration. At the same time, as new clouds are formed, their high albedo reflects sunlight away from the region and cools the land even further. They're like huge, natural air-conditioners.

Throughout the globe, clouds generated from the transpiration of forests are often the *only* precipitation source for inland environments, exemplifying how important a role forests play in managing a stable water cycle. After you drink a big glass of water, you might want to go hug a tree and say thanks.

Unlike surfaces like snow and ice, which reflect significant solar energy back into the atmosphere, forests absorb heat from the sun, warming the air in cold environments due to their low albedo but cooling the air in warm environments by keeping solid radiation from warming the soil surface (shade).

The water that a single tree transpires daily has a cooling effect equivalent to two domestic air conditioners.[14] The shade produced by forest canopy can cool the surface of the earth up to 20°F–45°F! This drastically reduces the heat island effect in our urban centers and can determine whether land is farmable in our agricultural landscapes.

The texture of the forest provides yet another climate moderation service. As wind moves across the surface of the earth, forests catch the moving air, slowing it down and absorbing the energy. The air releases energy, causing the forest to transpire faster, leading to the development of more clouds.

Some forests harvest fog, a unique way to cycle moisture. These systems, like the redwoods of Northern California, broom (capture) the fog, literally taking moisture in through canopy leaves to feed the trees. Fog is also caught along the needled leaves and drips down along the branches, grabbing nutrients on its way and finally reaching and nourishing the forest floor.

Most forests are fungal-dominated fire ecologies, producing a large amount of the earth's oxygen. One tree produces 260 pounds of oxygen per year; all together, all the trees on the planet exhale approximately 30 percent of earth's oxygen every day.[15]

When rain, snow, or hail fall, a forest creates its own nutrient-rich fertilizer. This is called "throughfall"—when precipitation moves through leaves, branches, and trunks of trees taking with it bird manure, dust, bacteria, and fungi that wash down to feed the forest floor.

Forests are a wonder of this green earth. That is why, as regenerative designers, we imitate the patterns and relationships that comprise forest ecologies in our design plans. Even the way we grow our food and fiber comes from emulated forest systems called agroforestry.

Replicating forests through agroforestry brings many benefits to the landscape: the production of leaf mulch and woody debris builds fertility, along with an increase in water-holding capacity, biological diversity, and carbon sequestration. Forest ecosystems are perennial and multigenerational. A landscape built like a forest becomes a long-term, low-maintenance, high-productivity system that creates multigenerational resilience for all of life.

Wetland Ecology

Wetlands are the most biologically productive ecosystems found on the planet. They are formed through webs of interdependent relationships between terrestrial and aquatic ecosystems (land and water). Wetland trees build fertile soil and protect waterways by holding the land together with their root masses.

Like forests, wetlands are an integral part of the carbon cycle. Covering 6 percent of Earth's land surface, wetlands (including marshes, bogs, swamps, river deltas, mangroves, tundra, lagoons, and river flood plains) store 10 to 20 percent of terrestrial carbon.[16] Wetlands also protect the land from storm surges. The bottomland riparian wetland forests along the Mississippi River once stored more than 60 days' worth of flood water. Now, due to these ecosystems being filled and drained, only 12 days of flood water can be stored.[17]

These are carbon-farming systems like no other on earth; the plant ecologies that thrive in many wetland systems are carbon-sequestering superstars. Wetlands are threatened with development, disappearing three times faster than forests. If all the wetlands on earth were removed, it would release an additional 771 million tons of greenhouse gas (representing one-fifth of all the carbon on earth) into the atmosphere.[18]

When land and water join, life blossoms; complex and interconnected food systems emerge, creating a thriving environment for many aquatic and terrestrial lifeforms. Self-replicating cycles are set in motion. Seed, fruit, and nuts fall into the water, feeding fish and aquatic life. Mammals, sea turtles, and thousands of other species of invertebrates, insects, amphibians, and reptiles all interact in a web of relationships. It's a dynamic cycle of growth, life, and death. These are systems that inspire some of the most effective water design strategies of a regenerative landscaper, utilizing the patterns of wetland ecosystems and many of their variations.

Ponds, blackwater systems, constructed wetlands, water harvesting gardens—any system where water is collected, infiltrated, and filtered can function as a wetland.

Grasslands Ecology

Lawns, the most widely spread human-built landscape in the world, attempt and fail to mimic grassland ecology. Lawns are grass-based systems devoid of the life grassland ecosystems support; they are monocultures designed only for the human-centered functions of recreation and status.

Grassland ecologies, however, are havens of life. These wild places are filled with perennial grass species—many with deep root systems—feeding the soil with nutrients, holding it against erosion, and drawing carbon deep into subterranean soils. Some grass roots penetrate dozens of feet into the ground, pulling organic matter and carbon into places where it can be stored for many years. A healthy grassland is composed of a high diversity of closely spaced grasses and herbaceous plants. Hundreds of species, from bison to butterfly, depend on these prairie biomes.

In landscape design, we can create and manage ecological grassland ecosystems by incorporating regionally native grasses, forbs, and shrubs into the design to simulate the best functions of native prairies, generating many yields along the way. We can even grow edible greens, medicinal roots, berries, and other food and medicine from within managed grassland ecologies.

KEYSTONE SPECIES

Every ecosystem on earth is composed of a unique set of relationships: patterns formed by species, climate, and soils, by water, rock, and sea. But some universal patterns are present throughout the planet's biosphere. One core pattern we observe is the presence of *keystone species*. These are species of plants, animals, or microorganisms that provide benefits on which the ecology is completely dependent. Remove the keystone species and the system begins to collapse. Every place we live—every home, park, and landscape project—is influenced by its relationship to the keystone species of that region.

Rivers of Salmon

I live in Northern California where creeks and rivers once ran thick with salmon. The Indigenous people of these lands have always revered salmon as sacred creatures of these waterways. As a keystone species, whole watersheds depend on salmon for bioregional survival and longevity. Some salmon species like the coho (*Oncorhynchus kisutch*) are endangered due to overfishing, watershed pollution, gravel mining, soil erosion, and other industrial practices that have destroyed salmon spawning grounds.

Born in the headwaters, young salmon are reared in the creeks and rivers of their birth for one to two years before venturing into the wilds of the ocean. There they travel far out to sea, eating fish and plankton. When mature salmon are ready to spawn (2–8 years old), they return to their natal rivers and creeks.[19]

Their journey in the ocean, where they grow large from marine food they eat, can span *thousands* of miles, yet they know the precise river mouth where they will return, back to the watershed of their birth. Once returned to home waters, more miracles occur. They swim against fast currents and jump waterfalls until they reach the headwaters. When they reach their spawning grounds, they use the last of their energy to seed the next generation of salmon. Then, they sacrifice their bodies and . . . die.

Upon death, the rich, fatty bodies of salmon return minerals and nutrients to the upper reaches of the watershed. Bears, eagles, and other scavengers take advantage of the martyred salmon and consume and distribute those nutrients across the environment. Salmon become not only food for wild animals but minerals and nutrients that trees, plants, and soil life also depend on. As we have seen throughout the Pacific coast and elsewhere in the world, when salmon disappear, the landscapes of their origin become susceptible to disease and famine.

The Power of Bees

Global food production as we know it is dependent on the small, humble bees (*Apis*) of our world. The common honeybee, along with native bees of each bioregion, are so widespread and integral to the human food system that 71 percent of food-producing plants we grow are pollinated by them. They are a keystone species for the survival of humanity. Not only do bees ensure fruits and vegetables are pollinated, but they are also responsible for mixing the pollen of insect-pollinated trees and flowering plants, helping the botanical world adapt to changing conditions, fend off disease, and reproduce each year. If bees continue to disappear (as they have recently due to industrial agriculture practices), thousands of species of plants and animals will disappear with them.[20]

Red Mangrove Coastlines

Keystone species come in many forms: animals, yes, but also trees, plants, even bacteria provide ecological services worthy of any keystone species. The red mangrove (*Rhizophora mangle*), a riparian tree that grows along subtropical coastal waters, is a keystone species that builds complex ecologies in its wake. Thousands of species of sea life—sea turtles, fish, manatees, dolphins, sharks, and many more—all thrive amongst the tangled root systems mangroves cast into the water's edge. Without these mangrove ecosystems, much of the life that depends on them would have to travel long distances to find safe havens and many would die along the way.

Bioregional Keystone Species

At every landscape scale—city urban backyard, thousand-acre snowy ranch, suburban homestead—keystone species are present and must be taken into consideration when designing new landscapes.

Identify the keystone species in your region. What is their habitat and how can you enrich these systems? What can you do to manage the land and implement support mechanisms to aid these key organisms? Sometimes their influences are indirect. For instance, salmon don't spawn on my homestead, but the activities of my landscape directly impact watershed health. If I allow surface water to shed from the land, taking sediment with it, I'll be directly adding to the plight of the salmon as downstream creeks and rivers get polluted by my erosive landscape.

Everything is connected in the webs of life. How does your landscape affect keystone species in your environment?

REGENERATIVE DISTURBANCES

Every ecosystem is held together by a network of patterns and processes that manage the organization and evolution of each environment. Many of these processes are initiated by some form of disturbance: a wildfire, a herd migration, a flood. These events may seem devastating, but in a balanced ecology they provide beneficial services. By understanding the roles disturbances play in the landscape, we can mimic and utilize those forces to regenerate ecosystems.

Some disturbances create conditions for new beneficial patterns to evolve in the landscape. We can call these "regenerative disturbances." Systems are always evolving and when one becomes stagnant, it can become diseased and dysfunctional. A disturbance breaks the stagnation and kickstarts new cycles.

Mimic Herd Migration

Many environments across the globe are managed (now or in the past) by the migration of ruminants. Ruminants are hooved animals that migrate through the seasons in large herds, eating grasses and broad-leafed plants along the way. The time a herd spends in one area and the path of its migration coincide with the movement of predators and access to food. This predator/prey relationship occurs throughout many environments and plays a significant role in sustained regenerative management of prairies and savannas. The roving herds reduce fuels for wildfires, keep opportunistic plants in check, and stomp organic matter into the soil.

Due to overhunting, industrialization, and private property ownership, along with other environmental and human causes, migrating herds across the world have mainly disappeared. To bring back these important migration patterns (especially where native animals disappeared) ranchers use domesticated animals (cows, sheep, goats) to mimic natural herd behavior. Many reading this book are not likely to manage a large herd of animals, but it is helpful to understand what benefits animals provide in managing the environment. In this way we can replicate their behavior in the landscape.

When animals move through a system regeneratively, they provide a series of benefits. They graze/browse vegetation, shearing off the tops and sometimes causing root die-off, which feeds the soil organic matter and (if not overgrazed) stimulates new growth in plants. They leave behind manure (fertilization), and in short durations stomp organic matter into the soil, creating ground contact with leaves and stems, allowing microorganisms to transform that organic matter into healthy topsoil. As animals graze on vegetation, they create conditions for a high diversity of plants to thrive. This ensures that no one species dominates by shading out the others.

We can simulate the benefits of animal disturbance in our own gardens and landscapes. On a small scale, we can do this by keeping chickens, ducks, goats, sheep, or maybe even a cow. But having animals in the system is not always appropriate or practical depending on the context. There are ways to mimic these kinds of disturbance patterns by being your own animal through mowing, scything, and pruning. (See chapter 50 for more about including animals in your regenerative landscape.)

Become Fire

Fire is a major disturbance, a natural pattern that has coevolved throughout many ecosystems called fire ecologies. In spite of human efforts to suppress new fires, these lands will inevitably burn. In fact, suppressing fire leads to an abundance of fuel that builds up over time, eventually leading to megafires.

Indigenous people have been introducing fire to the land for millennia, creating "good" fire through cultural burning as a vital tool for managing fire ecologies. Indigenous knowledge helps us decode fires past, but their wisdom is also paramount to how we live and manage our communities in fire zones today. We start with understanding the lessons fire teaches us and the various impacts flame, heat, and ash have on the land, both the regenerative and the catastrophic.

Fire is nature's way of removing disease, clearing forest understory, bringing in light to the forest floor, alkalinizing soil, and transforming minerals into bioavailable forms for plants and animals.

We use good fire to manage our environments, but we also simulate fire's effect on the land in other ways. Sustainable forestry, weeding, chopping, clearing, spreading ash—all these activities have similar effects to a low intensity fire. (See chapter 53 for more about fire in the regenerative landscape.)

2

The Regenerative Mindset

Regenerative design and stewardship are a set of practices, a mindset, that increase the health and productivity of ecosystems, resulting in the development of carbon- and water-holding rich soils, clean and abundant watersheds, and increased habitat for wildlife.

Everyone can approach landscaping through the lens of regenerative thinking. These tools and principles are not relegated to use by professionals and people with access to more resources.

Approaching a landscape project with a regenerative mindset requires a focus on designing relationships over elements. For example, if you are building a pond for water storage, you want to consider the many relationships and benefits a pond provides to your landscape. It is not only a water-storage system but also a microclimate moderator, a habitat attractor, a biomass generator, and so on. If you design relationally, you will place the pond and other elements strategically to synergize and capitalize on the resources provided by the pond. The same can be said about every layer and element in the design process. To design as nature, to generate landscapes that provide high yields, and to create energy-efficient regenerative systems, relationships must be the focus of the design process.

Even the most degraded landscapes—man-made deserts, clear-cut forests, asphalt parking lots—can be repaired. The application of regenerative design processes and principles can bring these systems back into ecological health. A patient mindset and trust in natural processes are key ingredients in ushering this level of ecological regeneration.

There is so much potential to repair the living world. We can all start right outside our backdoors, in our local parks or community gardens. Once you unlock the regenerative toolbox, you will see potential on every site. Advanced practitioners will notice that some landscapes are better left alone. Intervention is not always necessary, and sometimes our goals and well-intentioned activities can create more harm. For example, I've seen many practitioners cut down trees to build a "habitat" garden, essentially killing the habitat that was there. Learn to listen and observe landscape patterns, determining when it is more appropriate to do nothing.

EMBRACE EARTH WISDOM

At the heart of regenerative design is the practice of emulating and enhancing the design intelligence and patterns of ecosystems. As we have seen, earth has solutions to all the ecological crises we face today. We can design and build with the same wisdom, using the same focus on the patterns of relationships. When we partner with the life-sustaining processes of ecosystems, that's when we remember—we *are* earth's inherent wisdom, if we choose to be.

When we develop symbiotic relationships between humans and the ecosystems we inhabit, we reduce our use of energy, we stop creating waste, and we rebuild surplus resources of food, water, and habitat that once covered every landscape. We steward landscapes that enhance rather than destroy ecosystems. The more symbiotic relationships we develop with our environments, the faster we create resource-rich gardens and farms, landscapes, and cities, and develop resilience to catastrophe (wildfire, drought, flood, famine).

LANDSCAPES ARE ECOSYSTEMS

To design a landscape regeneratively is to design a fully functioning ecosystem where all elements (trees, water systems, animals, buildings, and so on) are woven together in interdependent relationships. This is the foundational approach to regenerative design: the understanding that no matter how much you impose your ideas onto a landscape, the inherent natural patterns will always intervene. That is why we compose with ecosystem forces—we utilize their intelligence and harmonize our designs to integrate fully with local environmental patterns. Even an asphalt parking lot is an ecosystem—though mostly a dead one—yet the forces of nature still apply, and eventually that asphalt will turn to soil, a process regenerative landscapers can speed up.

ANIMISM AND SCIENCE

Our cultural mindset has the greatest impact on our land-use patterns and, in the modern world, science sets the rules. Science asks the questions of what is and is not possible and pushes the boundaries of what we believe to be true or false. In the world of regenerative landscaping, science is a pillar, a backbone of understanding the environment and applying proven techniques to achieve regenerative goals. As you have already seen in this book, science helps us understand how water moves, how forests function, and how life thrives. Scientific breakthroughs have cured disease, given us warm, safe homes, and provided all the tools of convenience and enjoyment of the modern world.

But science has its own negative set of consequences. The more reductionist a scientific approach becomes, the easier it is to separate elements from other parts of the ecosystem. To break things down into their smallest components can break the webs and relationships that exist at the ecological level. This kind of science has doomed much of the living world with the production of harmful chemicals, fossil fuel technologies, and a take-first mindset.

A mere few thousand years in the past, all human inhabitants of earth—our ancestors—maintained animistic belief systems that not just aided survival in their raw environments but also helped these cultures live in ecological harmony with their habitats. These belief systems harnessed taboos, seasonal activities, and mythological stories that helped maintain a balance between civilization and ecology. Guiding practices developed from stories and beliefs that enhanced biological interactions in the environment.

Animism is the belief that nearly everything is alive: stones, waterfalls, tools, homes. An animistic worldview also considers the spirits of elements like trees and animals as intellectual entities, as nonhuman "persons." Often, trees or animals are considered relatives or even familial ancestors. When you believe that everything is alive, that plants and animals are relatives, when spiritual value is given to the land, destroying those entities becomes unethical and dangerous. These taboos translate into cultural activities that protect and celebrate landscape through seasonal observance, ritual, and ecological stewardship. Many Indigenous communities still practice these animistic ways to this very day.

As regenerative designers, we must bridge Indigenous knowledge with the application of earth sciences. I firmly believe that both Indigenous spiritual wisdom and cutting-edge ecological science must coexist—mutually beneficial to each other—to protect and regenerate what's left of the living biosphere in earth's current phase.

Yes, the earth will survive long after humans. Yes, the evolution of biology will spin forward, and new species and environments will emerge from the old. But I haven't given up on earth's current design plan. There are still ecosystems once broken that can be repaired. And still species we can keep from going extinct because of the modern human experiment.

Science can solve many problems with its focus on the intellectual process, asking questions, experimenting, and finding solutions to problems. But science doesn't work in the social ecosystem of the human heart. And the human heart is the greatest asset we possess for protecting the living world.

Indigenous spiritual wisdom and place-based understanding that has been cultivated over many, many generations provide a worldview that connects, acknowledging that humans are within the webs of life, not separate. Everything we do matters to everything else, invoking an understanding of the responsibility humans have for stewarding, rather than destroying, the health of other life forms.

The ethical standards of science are generally subjugated by the goals of funders, meaning it is virtually impossible for science to retain any sort of ethical code because the most powerful people on the planet control the most powerful scientific research and development of technology.

The spiritual ethos of animism, however, provides a blueprint for how cultures can form with standards that protect life. Let me be clear: I'm not asking you to adopt a new spiritual worldview. Alongside your existing belief system, I ask you to consider what kinds of values we need to care for the earth. The future of our world will be what we make of it. Will it reflect the love, reverence, and collective responsibility humans are capable of? Or will we continue to treat all life as a science experiment, a commodity to be exploited?

REGENERATIVE LANDSCAPING PRINCIPLES

Throughout the chapters of this book, I will provide examples of how to tangibly use the following principles as they pertain to design, water systems, soil health, planting strategies, and the built environment. These design principles are born from traditional ecological knowledge and the design practice known as permaculture design.

Reciprocity

All life forms in a cycle, a never-ending process of transformation, birth, life, death, and rebirth. When the cycles that make life break, systems will perish. In the landscape, we break some cycles, and we nurture others. Knowing which to break and which to nurture is a high level of regenerative design. Based on reciprocity, we always do the following.

Give More than You Take

Those seeking true regenerative design will take this principle to heart. It is the key mindset required for living in reciprocity with the land. You may find that applying reciprocity in modern-day landscaping is difficult and can seem insurmountable at times. You might be asking yourself, "Give more than I take? What constitutes the taking?"

When analyzing reciprocal relationships in the landscape, it is important to understand the concept of embodied energy. Every material you bring to your site, including compost, irrigation pipe, and heavy equipment, has an embodied energy cost. These tools and products, often required in landscape construction, represent part of the taking—mining, fossil fuel use, fabrication. These are extractive processes that harm the biosphere.

In this day and age, it is all too easy to take and consume. As regenerative designers, we must learn to give back. In our gardens and backyards, we have that chance. We get to give back by growing soil, planting forests, and cleaning water. We give back by making sure every landscape we touch is left better than we found it. In pristine landscapes, instead of changing them, we focus on protecting these sacred places and reducing harm.

Giving more than you take directs every decision you make. I've seen it many times: well-intentioned designers want to achieve a particular ideal (food forest or water harvesting, for example) and in doing so remove mature trees, scrape the soil off, or destroy important wildlife habitat. Sometimes these kinds of changes are necessary, always driven by context, but often enough they are unnecessary, only emerging as an idea of the designer and not based on the fundamental health of the ecosystem. And that is why reciprocity is essential to the everyday process of design and building of regenerative landscapes.

Make the Least Harm

All living organisms are sacred and thus all design, installation, and maintenance work considers the health of living beings and causes the least harm to the land while achieving the stated goals of the project.

Ecological Yield

The biggest difference between the regenerative landscape versus "green" or "sustainable" landscaping is that regeneration means leaving the ecosystem in *better* shape than you found it. Center to this approach is **obtaining ecological yields**. For small-scale farmers and edible landscapers, harvesting a yield that benefits humans is a primary goal. Food, herbal medicine, fiber, and fuel are all important yields that support people within the ecology. But if you only design for human needs, not considering the needs of the ecosystem, then your plan is not regenerative. Ecological yields, such as increased wildlife habitat, carbon sequestration, and increase in the water-holding capacity of soil are fundamental yields benefiting the landscape.

If our goal is to contribute to the benefit and welfare of our ecological communities, then ecosystem yields must be as important as a perceived human yield. In the end, every ecological yield is a human yield, as we are but one strand of many strands within the webs of life.

Contextual Design

Instead of fighting against natural forces, we embrace and integrate them into our plan. To fully understand our environments, we must **pay attention** to the patterns! We must observe, listen, and interact accordingly. As we recognize patterns across time and space, we can successfully integrate with the landscape in ecologically beneficial ways.

Take the time to be curious and ask lots of questions. Listen intently to the people and the patterns making up the landscape and let that inform your design process. Let that be the road map you use to generate a design that works on the site. This is the context you use to design the entire project.

Problems Are Indicators

Problems in the landscape are signs of disconnection—of misalignment—within the ecological webs. An indicator is usually not the root of the problem itself but a symptom. As designers, we need to ask the deeper questions and follow the signs (indicators) that lead to better understanding of how landscape systems are out of balance. Investigating an ecology is an act of listening, and this process will always yield solutions—gathered wisdom that fundamentally changes your design and implementation strategies. Problems are always indicators of elements in the system that need support and reconnection to the whole.

Manage Cyclical Energy

Managing the cycles of energy (sunlight, water, wind, photosynthesis, carbon, etc.) is always at hand in the ecosystems we inhabit. In our modern civilization, the consumptive mentality of taking resources from the earth has resulted in major imbalances. For example, if you cut all the trees of a forest, you also take away the rain.

Our job as regenerative designers is to create landscapes that catch and store energy in numerous ways—cycling carbon, oxygen, nitrogen, sunlight, cool air, and water. A regenerative system, like intact ecosystems, catches and stores more energy than it consumes. In doing this, these landscapes create conditions for higher complexities of life. **Capture energy**—water, sunlight, air, nutrients—and keep that energy in the system for as long as possible. The forces of nature are present on every site. The more we capture and store available energy, the less we rely on human technology like fossil fuels for landscape stewardship.

Closing Loops in the Landscape

In conventional landscapes, excessive waste is produced in the design, installation, and maintenance of these sites. In nature there is no waste. A regenerative design emulates nature's efficiency and thus, once established, will also create no waste.

One way this is achieved is by making sure our landscapes are closed-loop systems, meaning that all resources produced inside of the landscape stay in the landscape. The waste of one element is always the food of another.

Relative Location

Every element is placed in relation to other elements and functions, so the landscape gains incredible efficiency and harvests many forms of energy. This sort of design enables the system to manage itself. To design a system that self-regulates, you place components to support and feed from each other. The "waste" of one supports the needs of the other and vice versa. If you can't see how an element in your project (pathway, water feature, tree) connects to others, then it's likely not in the right location.

Redundant Planning

Every function within a landscape needs to have a backup plan. For instance, water must come from more than one source. So should food. If we base all water needs on a single source and that source dries up—the well pump breaks or the county is threatened by drought—that single water source won't sustain the life we've built around it. Each function in your design must be supported by multiple sources.

Timescale Management

In the regenerative landscape we manage timescales in multiple ways. It starts with your own vision for a project. How long will it take? When is a good time to start? How will it be maintained?

Managing the timescale also requires an understanding of the succession of the environment you're working in. Is it a grassland? A desert? A forest? What is or was this landscape like in its natural state? Was it ever an old-growth forest or an ancient oak savanna? These questions lead to important discoveries that deepen the understanding of a place. *When* are you in the evolution of the land? How does the region where you are working naturally evolve and where is the project site within that succession?

Design with Successions

In nature, successions are the foundation of evolving landscapes. If a catastrophic firestorm (like those in California in 2016 and later) rages through a valley at high intensity and burns all the forest to the ground, a new succession will take place—but it will take time to create conditions for a forest to thrive there again. Fast-growing pioneer plants will take over first, then shrubs will advance, followed by young trees. Each succession is creating the way for the next succession to evolve from the previous one. In regenerative design we speed up or slow down natural successions depending on the goals and ecological yields we are designing for.

3
Land-Use Directive

Conventional landscaping has created a host of issues, including the overuse of chemicals, water-chugging lawns, widespread soil compaction, and destruction of wildlife habitat. But it doesn't have to be that way. In this book, we get to change the landscape industry together and transform it into a healing force for restoring ecosystems. As a designer, a homesteader, or a renter, apply the principles of regenerative design to your landscape, unlock abundance, and savor the joy of taking responsibility for the lands you walk upon.

Opportunities to restore the land are around you right now. When you walk around your neighborhood, city, or countryside, notice the shapes and sounds of the world. Bring your awareness to the landscapes surrounding people's homes, the landscapes meandering through public parks, and the softened edges around parking lots. Take note of how much land there truly is within your community. In the modern world, much of what you'll observe in human settlements are nonfunctional planting systems and neglected parks. People's disdain for the land can be seen everywhere.

But deep down, every one of us enjoys the beauty of vibrant, healthy landscapes. We, as regenerative designers, are tasked with inspiring a new model for landscaping by bringing beauty, function, and ecology back into our towns and neighborhoods.

A TOXIC LEGACY

Use of chemicals—for fertilization, pest management, or vegetation management—runs counter to the regenerative goals of building healthy soil and protecting biodiversity. The work of restoring and stewarding landscapes can be performed without chemicals, but much of the Western world hasn't caught on to this truth yet. The modern practice of using chemicals at all phases of land work has infiltrated the minds of the Western world in profound and damaging ways.

The scale of degenerative landscapes is astronomical. In the United States alone, approximately 40 million acres are covered in lawns,[1] with an estimated 235,224 trillion gallons of water used every year.[2] Take a moment to let that settle in. Much of that water use is required to maintain lawns. Can anyone look at those numbers and not think that this is madness? We can change this! Here in this book, I will show you how.

To transform lawns into ecological landscapes is a noble act. This alone will cause a significant shift in overall land use on the planet. In the United States, the landscaping industry in the year 2020 was worth over $105 billion. In many parts of the world an awakening has been taking place; people are transforming their lawns into water-friendly landscapes. Thankfully, in drought-stricken areas like California and the southwest United States, a new landscaping trend has emerged, moving away from lawns to the water-conserving land practices discussed throughout this book.

Homeowners use up to ten times more chemical pesticides per year on their lawns than farmers use on crops. Nearly 80 million pounds of pesticides are used on US lawns annually. On top of this, every year 90 million pounds of chemical fertilizers are used on lawns and 26.7 million tons of air pollutants are introduced from mowing. Yale University has estimated that the United States uses more than 600 million gallons of gas to mow and trim lawns each year.[3]

Regenerative landscaping is an imperative land-use approach to stop practices that destroy soil, poison waters, and kill off the world's biodiversity. At the core of this shift is moving away from lawns and other resource-addicted landscape systems. Our job now, in the 21st century, is to focus all our efforts on renovating the landscape and agricultural industries by implementing an ecological value-based system.

The needs of natural systems must be at the root of landscape design. In doing this, we will instill a landscape approach that protects ecological services and generates surplus resources for all of life.

Many folks have small lawns, and these little grasslands may not seem like they have much impact. But when we add all the small lawns together, the impacts on watersheds, public health, and biodiversity are widespread and unsustainable. That said, small lawns do have a place if you use them regularly for relaxing, sports, and giving children a place to play, providing a function that fits your context. The reality is that most lawns are hardly used and represent only a great waste of resources, labor, and money for simple aesthetics.

We can do this differently! Converting lawns into regenerative landscapes is almost always relatively easy, fun, and makes for great community-building experiences or a useful way to invest resources.

Regenerate the Degraded

Cities, farmland, forests, landscapes—the reach of human development is vast, and so is the degradation of these lands. A few hundred years of turning forests into deserts, deserts into cities, and oceans into waste dumps have damaged the surface of the earth as we know it. As regenerative designers, our job is to put the pieces of unraveled landscapes back together, the hills and valleys, the forests and meadows, the lands that have been ravaged, abused, and used for their resources; we are here to rehabilitate those once wild places. This is the regenerative work of our times.

With regenerative design, we turn problems into solutions. We regrow the forests, we build topsoil, and we transform waste into ecosystems.

Weaving the Threads Together

Now you have the context of some of earth's wisdom, the state of the landscape industry, principles of regenerative design, and hopefully, the continued willingness to restore landscapes.

Where humans have been a problem, where our land-use practices have destroyed ecology—now we restore the land. As you strive forward in this book, take with you the design intelligence of the earth. In your design process, be the forest, be the watershed, be good fire, consider yourself a keystone species, and aid every landscape you walk along with your support.

A regenerative landscaper is a weaver of earth's living processes. Never forget that when you design, build, or maintain a landscape, you are making decisions that affect the whole ecosystem and the future of life in that place. Where you locate elements, what you choose to destroy and what you choose to leave unharmed, your interaction with water and sun—all of these are threads in the tapestry you are weaving onto the land. Focus on the connections (most importantly, your own) and, above all, never stop listening to what the land is telling you.

Up ahead, all the threads of the regenerative landscape will be revealed, and by the end of this book, you'll have everything you need to expertly design and build regenerative landscapes.

LAWN TRANSFORMATION STEP BY STEP

Step 1: Analysis and Design. Every lawn project, no matter the scale, requires an investment of observation, context analysis, and design before work can commence. In *very* small projects that time may only be an hour of planning, whereas larger projects can take much longer.

For lawn conversion, you need address these questions:

If an irrigation system is required, does the irrigation system need to be converted from sprinklers to drip?

What kind of soil are you working with? How much compost and other soil amendments will be needed for the lawn transformation?

What kind of planting systems are replacing the lawn? Are larger plants (five-gallon or larger) going to be planted?

Are earthworks or other terraforming needed to achieve a water-wise design?

Step 2: Excavate Edges (When Appropriate). The first step in lawn transformation work is preparing the site for sheet mulching. If the existing lawn is growing up to hard edges (concrete walkway, steel or rock edging, patio), it will be necessary to dig those edges out to ensure that sheet mulching materials (compost, cardboard, wood chips) don't slide onto hard surfaces.

Dig the sides out as if excavating a shallow trench. I suggest digging down four to six inches and a foot in width. In most cases the material you dig out is spread or "feathered" over the top of the lawn area adjacent to the edges. Excavate edges in this way to allow for compost, cardboard, and mulch placed such that the final grade of mulch rests at the same grade, or level, as the edging materials. In this way, mulch won't slide onto pathways and patios.

Step 3: Earthworks, Hardscaping (Optional). If the design calls for any kind of earthworks or hardscaping, this would be the time to do it. Most lawn transformations (at least those on a tight budget) will not call for drastic changes to the topography, but we *always* design to the context of a site and rain gardens, pathways, ponds, will be appropriate for some projects. If your project calls for elements that involve changing the topography or installation of architectural elements, the excavation, grading, and foundations for these systems are best implemented at this phase of the project.

Step 4: Renovate the Irrigation System. In drier climates, all lawns will have an irrigation system. Sprinklers are preferred by most lawn installers, and these systems will need to be renovated at this phase. There are simple conversions that allow you to easily cap sprinkler heads and convert the sprinkler system to a drip system for your new landscape. Conversion kits are fast and affordable and keep you from having to make new connections to water lines and irrigation manifolds (unless manifolds need attention!).

For some projects, a new irrigation system may need to be assembled. In that case, make sure any trenches, excavating, pipe/timer wire placement, and valve manifold development is complete at this phase of the project.

Step 5: Compost and Mulch Placement. This is where the process gets seriously fun. After transforming hundreds of thousands of square feet of lawns over the years, I can confirm that digging out and removing grass is *not* the most effective approach to lawn conversion. Remember, the main goal of regenerative landscaping is to increase the ecological health of environments through building living soil, water infiltration systems, and habitat enhancement. Always seek to do the least harm during project installation.

That is why we leave the grass in place whenever possible and use the sheet mulching method to turn the lawn into a soil building system, feeding soil microorganisms with organic matter by decomposing the leaves and roots of the lawn. If you are concerned about chemicals previously used on the grass, bioremediation (using mushrooms, bacteria, and plants to remove toxins) can be incorporated into the sheet mulching and planting plan to clean toxic soils. In some cases, the soil is contaminated with lead and *does* need to be removed if vegetables need to be planted there. Otherwise. . . .

Lawn Sheet Mulching. At this phase of the project, all the edges should be excavated and soil grades finalized, all trenches need to be filled, and any new hardscapes inside the area installed.

Place Compost. For the greatest carbon sequestering and biological activity in the soil, use enough compost to cover the whole lawn area in a minimum of two inches. This is the first layer of material to be placed and gets put *directly* on the grass (it sounds crazy but it works!). If the budget doesn't allow for this expense or planting will be delayed for an extended amount

(continued)

of time (more than six months after sheet mulching), then skip adding compost at this phase. Compost can also be added to the root zones of plants during the planting phase.

Place Cardboard. Acquire enough cardboard and/or newspaper to cover the lawn area entirely. If newspaper is what you have on hand, make sure to use it in layers at least eight pages thick. Cardboard and newspaper should be placed over the compost-covered lawn and overlapped at all edges by two or more inches. Most cardboard and newspaper can be resourced for free. Bicycle shops, solar installers, appliance stores are all great sources for recycled cardboard that would otherwise become waste. For large projects, at my company Permaculture Artisans, we purchase rolls of recycled cardboard from paper and packaging companies. For reclaimed cardboard, remove tape and make sure to *wet thoroughly* at the time of installation.

Place Mulch. Compost is down, cardboard is placed on top, and now it's time to cover the cardboard with mulch. Wood chips are the best choice if they are available in your bioregion. Straw, leaves, and plant debris (though this last option is not aesthetic if you are doing this for a client) are all good options if wood chips are not available or are too expensive.

Place mulch at a depth of at least four to six inches, making sure the mulch material doesn't rise above the grade at any hard edge (walkways, patios) of the worksite. Ensure that *all* cardboard/newspaper is *completely* covered with mulch. Any cardboard material not covered will dry out and could cause small problems later on.

Step 6: Planting Systems. Yay! If you have come this far in your project, you have made it to the planting phase. If you are planting trees or plants that come in 15-gallon pots or larger, you may want to plant those at the beginning of Step 5, after you have placed compost but *before* you put down cardboard. We plant large plants before mulching because it can be difficult to go back and dig large holes through the mulch. For 5-gallon pot size plantings or smaller, it is better to mulch before planting.

Use planting best practices when putting shrubs and trees into the ground. This may include adding mycorrhizal fungi inoculants, soaking with compost teas, adding soil amendments such as oyster shell and rock dust, or protection such as gopher wire baskets or tree guards.

Plant Placement. Before you put plants in the ground, first place them where you want them or how they are shown on a planting plan. When you place plants prior to planting (say that 10 times fast), dig a hole in the mulch and cut the cardboard beneath (an X cut works well), then place the plant there, still in its pot. We do this because plant installers sometimes get confused and plant next to the original placement rather than in the exact spot. Don't ask me why it happens, but it is common and should be avoided. Also, it is always a best practice to lay all plant materials on the ground to make sure placement is aesthetic and functional before final plant installation.

Step 7: Final Irrigation Install. The final step in your lawn transformation project is completing the irrigation system. In Step 1, you should have converted or renovated the irrigation infrastructure (hard lines, valves, timers, filters). In this final step of the process, you need to run drip hose out to your plants if you live in a climate that requires irrigation in dry months. If transforming your lawn into a native or drought-tolerant landscape, you can plant at the appropriate time of year and some of your plantings may not require any irrigation, but in most cases supplemental water is needed in the first couple years.

In chapter 31, you can find complete details for building an irrigation system. For now, know that this phase of your transformation will be running drip hoses to plants, installing emitters or using in-line drip (drip hose with built-in emitters), and burying drip hose in the mulch. Once you've run all your drip lines and buried them, you must check the irrigation system for leaks and pressure. Turn everything on (one valve at a time) and make sure the system is working correctly.

Step 8: Monitoring. For a few months to year after planting, monitor the landscape closely. Make sure your plants look healthy and that no cardboard has become exposed. If you find exposed cardboard, cover it immediately with more mulch. You may want to add compost tea applications in the first few months to keep the plant community happy during their transition into the newly transformed landscape.

PART II

Compose *with* the Land

4
Contextual Design

Regenerative landscape design is a practice of integrating layers upon layers of context, imagination, and physical material. It is the harmony of earth and water, of plants and sunlight, of animals and people. Much of the professional trades of the 21st century have lost this nuanced understanding of how natural systems function and the beneficial processes ecosystems provide human culture. The basics of cleaning water, filtering air, sequestering carbon, crop pollination, food production—these are daily services nature provides the inhabitants of earth, services we humans take for granted. This loss of context has led to disastrous developmental practices in everything from building construction to landscape installation. If we want to regenerate the land, we must design with context in mind again.

The ecosystems of earth, like human cultures, are incredibly diverse; the languages, tastes, shapes, and sounds are unique to each place, to each ridge and valley. Every landscape design must first and foremost emerge from the context, the on-the-ground existing patterns of land and people.

What is context? Context is the reality of the ecosystem. It's the reality of your inner and outer world. It's who you are, your ancestral history, your personal past, your family, your culture, your talents, and your passions. Context is also nature—the nature of the land, the shapes, the plants, animals, climates, waters, rocks, soils, everything that makes up the landscape ecosystem.

The more we understand all these layers of relationship that are affecting us, the better we design systems that work within the constraints of the land and our own life context.

When you step onto the site for the first time, don't be a designer. Take the time to listen, observe, and learn what the landscape in its current form is communicating to you. The voice of the land is the most important voice to listen to as a regenerative designer. It is our job to learn that language and translate it for everyone else. When you walk onto a site with the designer's mind, you will automatically want to change what is there and impose your vision on the land. First be only an observer, only compose *with* the land. Surrender your senses, still your thoughts, and immerse yourself completely into the patterns of the landscape. Learn to walk the land like this and you will be rewarded with pattern knowledge. If this concept is new to you, don't worry; this entire section is devoted to teaching you how to read landscapes in this way.

WHEN IS THE LAND?

Every place on earth is dominated by sets of cycles. Some of those cycles happen in short periods of time: the four seasons in a year, the bloom time of a plant, the harvest time of a tree. Cycles that govern environments happen in larger spans of time. They could take place over years, decades, and centuries. Many ecologies "reset" through large-scale disturbances. These disturbances, often regenerative to the land, come in the form of wildfire, the movements of large ruminant herds, floods, and storms. These extreme events occurring in the landscape provide sets of functions, both ending and beginning meta-cycles.

Since the invention of agriculture, approximately 10,000 years ago, humans have become major interventionists in the cycles of natural systems. Our ingenuity for better or for worse (often for worse) has changed the natural cycles and ecological succession of environments. When assessing the patterns and context of the site, it's important to ask the land: "When are you?" Which cycle is the land in currently? To answer this question, you must use historical reference to understand not only the natural history of the site and the growth and death of dominant vegetation types and watershed extremes, but also the social history—the ways the land has been manipulated or managed by human activities, within both Indigenous and settler contexts.

What are the cycles of death and birth the land endures until it reaches a dominant vegetation type like an old-growth forest or a prairie? This deeper understanding of the "when" helps you, as a designer, make decisions about soil health, goals for managing vegetation, and stewarding the land to meet both the goals of the project and the regenerative needs of the ecology in a symbiotic way.

The Story of Place

Every ridge and valley, wetland, and desert has a rich and layered story dating back millennia. Before you design a landscape, learn the story of that place. Start at the pattern level, the climate, known social and natural histories, and then dig into the details. Whatever the site is, from ridges to floodplains to forests, devote as much time as you can to learn the stories of the landscape. Go back as far as you can; even the geologic processes that happened millions of years ago are impacting that site today.

Over hundreds of thousands of years of evolution, the landscape becomes imprinted with its events, cycles, and communities. Specific patterns that are characteristic of only this place are highly likely. Indigenous communities may have settled there and left marks found in the shape of the land and the trees and plants still growing today. Fire, wind, and water all interact in specific ways depending on topography, temperature changes, solar orientation, and so on. The land may have once been an old forest harvested for timber, the road scars still directing water runoff today. Attend to small details and continue to ask nuanced questions every day.

> ## INITIAL QUESTIONS TO ASK
>
> **Geological:** What is the parent material of your soil? What geological formations exist on-site?
> **Biological:** What kinds of animals used to/still roam, nest, and scratch on that land? Which ones have gone extinct? What possible roles did they play in helping to manage the environment?
> **Social:** What kind of relationship does the land have with humans, either now or in the past?
> **Hydrological:** How does water interact with the landscape?
>
> Continue questioning like this each day for the rest of your relationship with the landscape. Stay curious and open to wonder because the natural world is always changing and evolving. Even a gravel lot in the middle of a city has a rich story, with natural forces trying to reclaim their place.

The Curious Listener

The recipe for long-term success, for your intended outcomes to manifest, is first be a humble listener, second a designer, and third a builder.

As you get better at listening to the cues of the land, you will discover that sometimes the best plan is to do nothing, sometimes the best plan is to wait, and sometimes the best plan is to drop everything you thought you were doing and immediately change direction. Knowing when a project falls into these different modes of action and nonaction only emerges through listening and observing.

Walk out onto the land and read the landscape, read what the vegetation is telling you. Listen to the birds and learn the kind of information they are sharing with their songs and behaviors. Feel the wind and the sun and ponder what they tell you about the environment. Your body is literally designed to take in ecological information when you choose to bring awareness to it.

PATTERN RECOGNITION

Recognizing patterns on the landscape is more than seeing individual components; it is about seeing relationships—the forest for the trees. It's recognizing how the whole has emerged from the set of elements, entities, interactions, and cycles playing out on the site. These forces make up the form and function of the entire landscape.

In the landscape, you can observe the following.

- **Elements (Structures).** *Elements* broadly describes physical structures in the landscape. Houses, ponds, garden beds, chicken coops—these are examples of elements that we integrate into our landscape design process, often existing in various states on a project before we begin. Prior to design, we need to take time to understand each element and how its function in the landscape plays a beneficial or detrimental role to the land and to the other elements.
- **Entities (Plants, Animals, Humans).** We inhabit a living planet, and that means that every landscape project is filled with living entities. Plants, insects, animals, and waterways are all living beings. Many Indigenous and animistic worldviews also include stones and landforms as living entities. We are responsible for all this life when we design and change landscapes.

    The greatest achievement of a regenerative landscape is to increase the ability for living entities to thrive in the environment *without* causing more harm. During the observational process, get to know all the living entities you can discover and what roles they play in the ecological circle of reciprocity.
- **Interactions (Relationships).** The invisible is as important as the visible. Thousands of relationships and interactions take place on the land every day, every minute. When learning about the intricate patterns of a project, look beyond individual elements and entities and discover the web of relationships taking place. Some of these relationships may be harmful to the whole, and some will be key aspects of resilience for that ecology.

A regenerative design not only considers the existing relationships and interactions on-site but also focuses on enhancing beneficial relationships and reworking nonbeneficial interactions. Most often, the interactions that have a detrimental effect on the system indicate a lack of important entities, elements, or connections. As a designer, your task is to weave elements and entities into beneficial and dynamic relationships. It could be as simple as removing an asphalt parking lot so the land can drink water, planting trees for shade, or packing brush into an erosive gully.

Cycles (Evolution, Change, Management)

Living systems, including human-engineered landscapes, are always evolving. Landscape designers will never stop the movement of time and change; therefore, they need to understand the current cycles and evolutionary succession taking place on-site before beginning. Are there young or old trees? Has the land freshly burned in a wildfire? These all indicate where the land is in its evolutionarily and cyclical process. Once you clearly understand the current cycle, you can speed up some evolutionary processes while slowing down others.

Humans have the power to intervene in the natural cycles of time and change on the land, which is part of why landscaping can be so destructive. Don't take this power lightly. We each have this ability *and* the *responsibility* that comes with it. Many adults, if they really wanted to, could cut down a 50-year-old tree in a single afternoon.

Humans have also created machines that can speed up the evolutionary process. Bulldozers, if used appropriately and in the right context, can be a major benefit to regenerative landscapes, but most often they are used for the complete destruction and obliteration of whole ecosystems. They can knock down trees in a single pass, scrape millions of years of developed topsoil in a day, and level mountains and valleys in a few months or years.

If you're going to manipulate the evolutionary timeline of the environment, do it for the sake of living systems or you will kill the life of the land.

When we incorporate an understanding of cyclical change into our regenerative design, we become the keystone species in the repair of landscapes. We can speed up cycles of regeneration through the building of topsoil, the planting of a forest, and the hydration of a watershed.

THE EAGLE AND THE FLOOD PLAIN

Sometimes your observations will take you by surprise, like the time a bald eagle taught me about a wetland. This happened at the Laguna de Santa Rosa, an ancient wetland and the closest immediate waterway in the town where I live. It was a late winter day, and I was driving from my home to my favorite local hiking trail at the Laguna. The previous night, an impressive storm had dumped a few inches of blessed rain. The Laguna had spilled its banks and flooded nearby pastures like it has done for thousands of years. As I crossed the bridge that takes me over the main stem of the wetland, I looked to the north and there, banking around for another dive, was a bald eagle. Where I live, seeing a bald eagle is like a spiritual experience. They mostly died off in the twentieth century from the agricultural use of the pesticide dichlorodiphenyltrichloroethane (DDT).[1] The eagles only began to make a comeback at the end of the last millennia.

I was mesmerized and pulled over to the side of the road to watch the great bird. As I stopped my car, I saw it swoop into a flooded pasture where water was only a few inches deep. The eagle dropped down and, as I watched, broke the surface of the water for an instant before rising skyward, a large fish trapped in its piercing talons. It flew back around and landed in one of the old oaks that keep watch on these lands. I stood for a moment, watching it pick apart its meal, and thought about what I just witnessed. Then it hit me, understanding dawning on me as a series of implications came into focus.

Floodplain connectivity is the phenomenon that occurs in healthy watersheds when a waterway floods its normal banks into the "floodplain"—an area usually shaped like a large, flat terraced zone, worked by water over time. In the case of the Laguna, the main stem of the wetland had flooded the surrounding pastures overnight. Those flooded waters were soaking into soil that is usually not covered in water. Millions of grubs and insects that live in the soil surge out from under the ground when it's saturated with water. This creates a banquet for fish and other aquatic creatures who can now break free from the main water channel and feast on the floodplain grub buffet. Those fish, in turn, have left deeper waters, where they can better hide from aerial predators—in this case, becoming an easy meal for the great eagle.

Look at how many connections, how many recognitions of pattern can be observed through this one small action that took no more than 30 seconds—an eagle catching a fish. When recognizing patterns in nature, profound realizations often occur when you least expect it, when your mind is in a state of wonder or curiosity. If I was doing a project in the vicinity of this Laguna floodplain, I would consider this dynamic relationship and whether my design goals protected and enhanced floodplain connectivity and wildlife diversity.

5
Awareness Practices

Developing an awareness of natural systems requires rigorous practice. The more you train all five senses to the rhythms, sounds, smells, and patterns of ecosystems, the easier and more intuitive it will become. The biggest challenge in keeping your awareness keen and your eyes sharp is to stop focusing on your thoughts. Stop designing entirely and allow your awareness to catch an ocean breeze, the waft of blooming wildflowers, the change of elevation as you walk, or the movements—no matter how small—of animals.

The land speaks in so many ways. At different times of day, at different times of year, it tells you stories it wants you to hear. The land always gives you information (data) about your surroundings, about what is possible in the landscape, about what's necessary for systemic vitality, and how the ecology generates abundance. Most of us are so consumed by our thoughts that 99 percent of the time we don't hear the messages the land is offering us.

For tens of thousands of years, Indigenous cultures throughout the world developed nuanced and advanced ways of listening and interacting with the land. While many of the old ways have been lost, erased by colonial and religious purging, the ancient knowledge still exists among wisdom keepers throughout the world. This place-based knowledge is the root of many of our regenerative design strategies, including the fundamental practice of reading the land.

WALK THE LAND IN SILENCE

Time to be quiet and alone on a landscape is crucial to the regenerative design process, allowing the designer to completely focus on natural patterns without distractions. One of my favorite practices is silent focused walking. Here's the process I use to make these adventures meaningful to the design process.

Make sure you've given yourself enough time to walk the site without feeling rushed. This type of observational exercise requires a calm state of mind, and it will take you at least the first 20 to 30 minutes to get your mental focus tuned to the present moment. During the walk, make sure to both wander and sit. Take in all the shapes, patterns, and sensations you can find. In general, an awareness walk should take a minimum of two hours but if the site is quite large, it could easily take three to four hours or longer. Take a tracking journal with you to record any notable observations. Place leaves, feathers, flowers into your journal as part of your record of the site. These notes will be invaluable when you move into the design phase.

Be prepared for inclement weather. Sun hat in the summer, jacket in the winter, food, and water—take what's necessary so you can be comfortable for an extended period of time and not distracted by thirst or hunger. If you do find the sun too hot or a cold wind biting at your neck, take a special note of this! Where did the cold bite hardest? Where did the sun make you wilt? These are clues to microclimates.

Observational tools such as binoculars, mobile GPS units, soil test kits, animal field guides, and other similar resources make great additions to your walk. I recognize that it is the twenty-first century and most folks have smartphones. There are many valuable applications for your pocket computer: apps for reading the sun and moon locations, plant identification, soil type, and so much more. Your phone can make a powerful ally for land analysis, but I would not rely on it too heavily just yet. The kind of awareness walk we're talking about here is about dropping into a deeper perception of natural patterns, which no tool will tell you better than your body's own sensors. Looking at your phone and getting distracted by various applications and incoming communications will pull you out of the ideal mindset. You can always come back again for a more reductionist analysis later and use all the technology you want.

Having a printed site map or satellite image of the landscape will aid your understanding of topography, solar orientation, and other landscape features while you traverse the project. I like to put a satellite image in my tracking journal and place numbers or symbols on the map that correspond to notes I take about significant birds, trees, and other wonders.

Reflective Sitting

I often stop and sit for long periods of time in special places I'm drawn to, asking questions of the land. As part of this practice, walk the same trail or area multiple times from different directions, creating loops and crisscrosses, observing from different angles, and approaching from diverse perspectives, finding new places to sit and reflect. This practice offers a rich understanding of how the landscape is formed, how it may have evolved, and why elements like vegetation types and water courses are located as they are.

Those of you who practice meditation understand what it's like to take time to clear your mind. The difference between this process and meditation is that, as you clear your mind, you will bring focus to the environment around you. In this way, you notice details like tiny sprouts growing at your feet or the difference between poppies, yarrow, ryegrass, and mushrooms, all growing together. If you allow your mind to wander without focusing attention on the environment, you may miss these nuanced yet important indicators about the land's interactions. It's humbling to discover that no matter how many times you bring your awareness to the land, you will never observe or understand everything happening there. Each time you focus attention on the features of a site, you unearth new knowledge.

A regenerative designer needs to tune their senses to the highest frequency possible. It can be a struggle to become fully aware of the existing landscape. It's all too easy to get caught up in design concepts instead, but your awareness will yield rewards. Like the time I noticed ants cultivating fungi on a south-facing drought-stricken hillside. Or the time I discovered a fig tree that had colonized two entire acres by itself—how its main root system sprouted from a freshwater spring and its successive branches grew tall, eventually falling over and touching the ground, where new roots formed new trees and slowly spread across the land. Or watching an army of goldfinches move through a garden, eating the aphids off every brassica, and how, upon closer inspection, those brassicas were coated with the greatest diversity of insects in the garden: parasitoid wasps, tachinid flies, spiders, ladybug larva, adult ladybugs, lacewings, and so on. These are the gifts you discover when you bring awareness to the land.

Community Land Walks

There are times when walking a project site with clients, partners, and other project stakeholders is necessary. These are important moments to vision, design, share observations, and generally connect with the land as a community.

The Sit Spot

The practice of sitting on the land has its origin in many cultures around the world. From meditation and yoga to divination and prayer, being with the land in stillness is a central activity valued by animist cultures.

For our purposes as land designers, we sit on the land to learn the language of landscape. The method described below has its origin in the Nature Awareness schools in the Americas developed by notable trackers such as Tom Brown, Jon Young, and others. Going further back, these practices were passed down from Native Americans and the Kalahari San people. Today we call this method the Sit Spot.

The Sit Spot is a place outside you visit repeatedly, as often as possible. In this way, you track the movements of animals, hear the messages of birds, see changes in plant growth, soil health, and climate in nuanced and profound ways. Here is how to develop your own sit spot practice. Anywhere outdoors can be used as a sit spot. Finding a place on the land away from distractions is ideal, but if you live in an urban environment, even your front or back stoop will do. Everywhere is nature. Wherever you choose, make sure it is convenient for you to visit again and again. This is imperative for developing an easy rhythm for your sit spot practice. If your landscape project is not your home then choose a spot at the site, and go as often as you're able.

Sitting on the land requires surrendering your time and focus. I suggest you bring the fewest number of items with you as possible—a blanket or a chair if it will make you more comfortable and water to drink. If possible, don't bring a phone or other computers with you. You need the least amount of distraction; see if you can leave conveniences behind. The best company is a notebook for writing down your observations and inspirations.

Studies have shown it takes an average of 25 minutes for wildlife to settle into their "baseline" rhythm—a state reflecting a calm demeanor like eating or exploring—once they've been disturbed. There's a good chance that walking to your sit spot will disturb the baseline state of wildlife, so a minimum of 25 minutes in your sit spot is recommended, though an hour is ideal.

Given enough time in your sit spot, the ecosystem community will settle down and go about their normal business.

Going out to sit on the land requires discipline. The chatter in your mind will insist you don't have time and after a few minutes you'll feel like you spent too much time already. Whatever the chatter in your mind, don't give up on the sit spot. Your mind will calm just like the surrounding wildlife. When it does, bring your full attention to where you are. Experience the landscape with more than your eyes; involve all your senses. Which sounds are present? What's the farthest sound you can hear? Are there odors you smell or sensations like warmth or cold you can feel? What shapes have formed around you? Notice the slope of the ground, a tree stretching tall, a dancing blade of grass, the crisp lines of an electrical grid. Who inhabits this space?

Open yourself to every wonderful possibility. Take it all in and let the transmission from the land into your senses. The reciprocity you offer is the attention you give. After a while, make notes of what you discover. As you return each day or week, track any changes that occur. Is the same bird sitting on that pole again? Are squirrels chattering in the same tree? Have the plants begun to flower or are trees about to lose their leaves?

Add the sit spot practice to your site analysis routine and document your findings. You will be amazed at the discoveries you make and the new direction your project will take because of the deep relationship you have developed.

Tracking Journal

Using a journal to track observations on the land is a great way to record data during the site assessment phase. As you walk and sit and listen to landscape patterns, jot down what you see and hear in a notebook. If using a smartphone or tablet is more your style, that is fine too, but this will pose a few limitations. With a physical journal, you can write, draw, and tape items into the book. You may save an unrecognizable feather or a leaf with associated notes logging where and when it was found. For example, if I see an unknown hawk hunting in a particular area every morning during a sit spot practice, this observation gets noted in my journal and on my base map as "hawk hunting zone." Then, I research the species and add that new information to my journal.

The names and habits of plants, animal behaviors, fungal observations, special features, climatic patterns—all of it goes in the tracking journal. Print out a satellite image or a map of the site and include that in the journal too. As observations are made, label them with a symbol or note on the map or image. All this data deepens your understanding and relationship to the landscape.

6

Reading the Land

At some point in the process, you move beyond passive observation and curious listening to a dedicated data-gathering phase. I like to call this "gathering evidence." This is when you document all the features of the site in earnest. Vegetation types, microclimate, animal species, topography, legal constraints, water sources, natural history, social history, threats of natural disaster, and so on. The following sections will touch on all these layers of the existing landscape, what you should be looking for, and how to research, monitor, and document them.

WATER PATTERNS

Reading water in all its forms is crucial to the site analysis phase. How does water move on the site throughout the year and during storm events? Are there perennial waterways (water that flows all year long)? Are there springs? Sleuth out everything you can about water on the site. If you're observing during the dry time of year or in an arid environment, the effects of water are still present. The patterns of water can be seen everywhere if you know how to see them. Water has sculpted the land, possibly causing erosion, gathering in and greening low areas, and rushing off steep grades. Here's a hint: topography plays a major role as do climate and impervious surfaces like roads and buildings. Learn about all water sources in the landscape—city water, wells, rainwater, springs, greywater—all are central to creating a regenerative design.

When observing water sources there are several factors to consider. First and foremost is quantity. How much water do you have to use for your landscape? It's possible there are no water sources, and the landscape will be dependent upon rain. Wells and springs are generally rated by gallons per minute (GPM) or gallons per hour (GPH). This gives a clear sense how much water the well or spring is producing. From this we can develop a water budget for the landscape based on the appropriate use and management of the sources. Doing this in a regenerative and a reciprocal way means not taking too much from your water source and designing for the least amount of water usage modeling a high form of ecological regeneration.

For instance, at my one-acre homestead we have a well that pumps 25 gallons per minute. That is an immense volume of water, and I would never design a system that needs to use a quantity like that. We did, however, establish a one-acre food forest garden and used our well sparingly to establish trees and perennial plants on drip irrigation. That water use helped the development of the forest garden, which in turn cools the ground with shade, reducing evaporation in a landscape shaped to catch and store all rainwater, recharging the aquifer. It's a reciprocal relationship generating abundance for all living beings on the land.

If your water source is municipal (a city or county water system), then quantity and financial cost are interlinked. If you are charged for every gallon of water you use, then you need to be strategic about not only your water budget but also the phasing of plantings (cheaper during the rainy season, for example). Your entire water conservation approach can also conserve money. At the time of writing this book, the region where I live is in severe drought. Some farms and vineyards have had to cut water to hundreds of acres of planted crops. With municipal systems, the entire community has a collective responsibility to the water source of the region. In this case, the Eel and Russian Rivers (and associated reservoirs) are threatened, and everyone who depends on these watersheds needs to come together to reduce their water budgets, both in the house and on the land.

For many communities around the world, caught and stored rainwater is the main, if not the only, source of water. When rainwater is your source, storage becomes the key design element. If you live in a climate that rains infrequently, it is necessary to store as much rainwater as you can between storms. Some water sources are seasonal: they dry up at certain times of the year and flow abundantly at other times. All of this gets worked into your future design strategy.

Springs and Seeps

Wetlands, freshwater springs, seasonal seeps, and erosion gullies are some of the ways water reveals itself in the landscape. Wherever you are in the world, indicators like plants, animal behavior, and other landscape features will direct you to the patterns of water on the land.

Low Lying Areas, Bog, Wetlands

Wetland areas pose significant challenges but also provide an abundance of resources for ecosystem productivity. At my land-based education center, we developed an ecological paradise called the Permaculture Skills Center in the floodplain of a wetland, the Laguna de Santa Rosa. Water-loving plants like pennyroyal, yellow dock, and juncus grass grow in abundance on this land, indicating a bog. We had to adjust our planting strategy, taking the saturated winter soils into account. We can't plant trees (unless they're well-suited natives) at grade. Instead, nonnative trees are placed out of the high water table by planting them on mounds or berms to avoid root rot.

Look for Water in the Driest Time of Year

When looking for springs, seeps, and seasonal water flows, the driest time of year may be the best time to discover expressions of water. When I'm on a consultation and find green grasses in the middle of a pasture, it means a spring, seep, broken waterline, or leach field is present.

VEGETATION

Vegetation includes all plants, trees, lichens, and algaes existing in the landscape. These are your photosynthesizers, the aspects of the landscape that draw down carbon; grow food, medicine, fiber, and fuel; provide habitat; and aid in the creation of rain. The green entities growing on a site give you key information about everything from soil type to climate to the wildlife community.

The dominant vegetation (e.g., forest canopy, grassland, wetland plants) can reflect either a native ecology or a landscape dominated by opportunistic (invasive) species that need to be managed if establishing a diversity of species there.

The deeper into the realm of plants you go, the more meaning you get each time you see a particular species. Some species indicate year-round water, others acidic soil, and yet others only grow on forms of rock. Plants are translators of ecosystems, and learning their language is learning the language of the earth.

You can also analyze seasonal changes in vegetation. Some trees are evergreen, keeping their leaves all year long, while others are deciduous, dropping the leaves to the ground every year. These characteristics change everything about the environment, affecting soil health, temperature gradients, and plant biodiversity.

The plant kingdom gives us much to contemplate and guides the entire process of landscape. Open yourself to all the wonders of the green world, from the tiny mosses that sprawl across compacted soils to the mighty evergreens that harvest fog from the sky and everything in between.

ANIMAL INDICATORS

We share the earth with wild creatures that teach us vast knowledge about each ecosystem. From the species of animals, to what they eat, to their daily behaviors, these creatures are indicators of many characteristics of an environment—a dung beetle indicates fertile ground, a rattlesnake indicates rocky soil, and the presence of dragonflies indicate a wetland.

Learn everything you can about the animals that live in the landscape, their behaviors, and what they may indicate about the land. It takes time to understand the animal community so be patient with the results. Some creatures may come to visit during migratory periods. Other seasonal changes may affect species one year differently than another. Every creature, big and small, has something to teach you about the land. Listen to them, honor them, grow with them.

NATURAL HISTORY

Research the natural history and succession of evolution of the site. What was it like prior to the Industrial Age? Was it an old-growth forest, grassland, or high desert? What was it before it was turned into a subdivision or transformed into an agricultural area? What were the natural ecosystem patterns like 1,000 years ago, 5,000 years ago, 10,000 years ago?

The purpose isn't necessarily to bring the land back to how it was 1,000 years ago. Your context and goals will guide how natural history is incorporated into the design process. If you're reading the landscape of a pristine, undeveloped place, your approach might shift to managing and protecting the ecology as it is.

KNOW YOUR GEOLOGY

Part of due diligence is asking the right questions. Explore the patterns governing a project from every angle, timescale, and influence, including the geology—a major factor in the development of both topographical landforms and soil structure. Taking it one step further, topography and soil structure influence the movement and flow of water and the types of vegetation that can grow on the site. *Parent material* refers to the mineral material that makes up the basis for, or is the "parent" of, the soils you have on a site. Water, soil, vegetation, and even climate are all influenced by the geologic forces governing the landscape.

Geologic features can create major constraints to landscape design. Some landscapes have a shallow soil profile, sitting on impervious bedrock. This type of environment limits what can grow, how water is captured and stored, and what kinds of infrastructure can be built. Whatever region you work in, it's a good practice to get to know the various types of geology in your region. As you understand more about how water, soil, and plants interact with different geological formations and geological landscapes, you will learn what to look for, what's possible in each area, and what activities to avoid.

SITE CONSTRAINTS

Each landscape has a range of constraints that will guide the design process—some fixed and some changeable—including erosion, pollution, topography, and whether it is forested.

Don't ignore constraints when developing design concepts, as they sometimes make the process easier and lead to unique and unexpected solutions. For example, we might discover only one appropriate location to place a house due to limitations of slope, drainage, or other issues. Embrace the process; these are moments where the design is taking shape on its own.

Some projects don't turn out how we hope. Through the assessment phase one can discover project nonstarters like pollution, lack of water, and so on. Ecological constraints like these must be identified before delving too deeply into the landscape project. Don't move forward designing a project you know will fail. It is surprising how many times people ignore the constraints of the site because it's inconvenient. In rare instances, the site assessment process leads the designer to a conclusion that the project goals are completely unattainable. A short list of constraints impacting landscape projects includes shallow topsoil on bedrock, excessive flooding in the winter, lack of any source of water, toxic pollution, noise from major highways, toxic agricultural neighbors, contaminated water sources, extreme fire danger, saline soil, floodplain, active earthquake faults, proximity to industrial factories, insufficient sun orientation, and constant or damaging winds.

As you can see, some of these examples would be obvious to project stakeholders immediately (proximity to a freeway, for instance), while other constraints will require more research and identification to reveal problems specific to the landscape (water quality, soil health).

ON-SITE RESOURCES

The conventional landscape approach often makes use of tremendous energy and resources originating from off the site. These materials represent high embodied energy costs and a large carbon footprint. A regenerative landscape is developed the opposite way, using on-site resources as the first choice in the build and management process. Using on-site resources heavily influences the design build approach as decisions are made based on readily available materials and energy flows from the project site.

When I moved to my homestead, a eucalyptus forest had taken over much of the land. Most people see eucalyptus trees as a major constraint, but I saw them as a valuable resource. Because many of these trees were dropping large branches, they were labeled by arborists as hazards and destined to be removed. All of the biomass from every tree was utilized on-site to build retaining walls, grow mushrooms, and chopped up for firewood and timber. The 250 yards of wood chip mulch ground from eucalyptus branches became one of the key resources in jumpstarting our orchards and gardens.

(Note: You may find sources that tell you not to use eucalyptus chips to jumpstart a garden. While it is true that living eucalyptus trees are allelopathic, meaning not much can grow underneath them, once eucalyptus trees have been cut and chipped, the allelopathic ingredients become inert and the biomass becomes readily available to fungi and bacteria for decomposition. Our thriving homestead is a testament to this fact.)

IN FIELD SOIL TESTS

Shake Test

The soil shake test is a tried-and-true method for analyzing soil structure. This will give you a glimpse into the percentages of clay, silt, and sand present in the soil. Take a mason jar and fill it halfway full of well-crumbled soil from the site. Then fill the jar with water to cover the soil, leaving an inch gap between the lid and the water line. Next, tighten the lid and shake vigorously. Shake, shake, shake. Keep shaking for 20 minutes to ensure all the soil particles are suspended in the water.

Set the jar down in a place where it can be undisturbed for 24–72 hours, or until all suspended soil particles have settled in the jar. Once the sample has settled, it will show you a reading of the composition of the soil. Sand settles first as it's the heaviest material, followed by silt, and then the smallest clay particles settle last. Any organic matter will float on top.

Ribbon Test

The ribbon test is another great technique for analyzing soil in the field. It is a quick and efficient way of getting a snapshot of the composition (percentages of sand, clay, silt) of the soil.

Step 1: Grab a small handful of soil and add enough water to roll it into a ball. If you can't make a ball, the soil is very sandy.
Step 2: Feel the texture of the ball by pressing it with your fingers. Is it gritty with sand, silky with silt, or sticky with clay?

Step 3: Roll the ball again and, with your thumb, gently press it out over your finger to make a hanging ribbon.

Step 4: How long of a ribbon can you make? A short ribbon means your soil is loamy (combination of sand and clay) and a longer ribbon means there is more clay in the soil. Incredibly the length of the ribbon can tell you exactly what kind of soil texture you have.

SOIL TEXTURES COME IN MANY COMBINATIONS

Sand: Cannot be made into a ball.

Loamy sand: Will form a ¼-inch ribbon.

Clay sand: Will form a ¼- to ½-inch ribbon. Sticky when wet.

Silty loam: Will form a ½- to ¾-inch ribbon. Very sandy to the touch.

Light sandy clay loam: Will form a ¾- to 1-inch ribbon. Sandy to the touch.

Loam: Will form about a 1-inch ribbon. Feels smooth with organic matter present.

Sandy loam: Will form a 1-inch to 1½-inch ribbon. Sandy to the touch.

Clay loam: Will form a 1½- to 2-inch ribbon. Smooth to the touch.

Sandy clay and light clay: Will form a 2-inch to 3-inch ribbon. If sandy, you can feel and hear sand grains. If light clay, it will be smooth to the touch. When pressing with fingers, a slight resistance.

Light medium clay: Will form a 3- to 3¼-inch ribbon. Smooth to the touch and moderate resistance when pressing.

Medium clay: Will form a 3¼ inch to 4-inch ribbon. Can be rolled into long ribbons with strong resistance to pressing with fingers.

Heavy clay: Has no problem forming a ribbon over 4 inches. Can be rolled into long ribbons without fracturing and is quite resistant to pressing.

Observing the Soil Profile

The composition of soil determines many factors about the landscape including the capacity for holding water, plant productivity, erosion, and stability—all major factors we consider in the design and development of landscape. Whether the soil is high in clay, more sandy, or full of silt will affect our entire landscape approach and guide our decision-making process.

There are two solid ways to investigate the soil profile on a landscape project. The first method is to find an area where the soil profile is already visible; look for areas with significant erosion, like a gully, a head cut, or a creek bank where you can see four to six feet of exposed soil.

If an erosive feature does not exist, the second way to look at the soil profile is to dig a test pit. Test pits are generally six feet deep, dug using an excavator or backhoe.

The goal is to look at the stratified layers of soil and parent material that make up the soil profile. These stratified layers are generally formed in horizontal bands and will show the designer the depth of topsoil, veins of clay, hard pan, and gravel deposits.

I live in a soil type called Gold Ridge loam. Commonly, we find approximately 12 to 18 inches of a sandy loam topsoil, sitting on approximately three to four feet of golden clay-loam. Beneath that we will sometimes find veins of heavy clay that can be anywhere from six inches to two feet. Often enough, the heavy clay sits atop a gravel deposit. This is how we read soil profiles, identifying the different types of soils and aggregates that make up each layer. When checking the soil profile or digging a test pit, you can also identify if there's a hardpan (a compacted or impervious soil horizon below the surface) or if compaction is present.

Don't worry about digging a test pit if the project doesn't have cause for it. This is information that is nice to have but not always necessary for a landscape project. If, however, you plan to build ponds, foundations for buildings, or other significant earthworks like large terraces, then knowing the soil profile will be quite useful. In building large ponds, for instance, identifying the different soil horizons and their composition is a key initial assessment that determines the kind of pond you can build and what materials will be required to build it. Heavy clay soils make for good ponds while sandy loam soils do not.

The soil profile can also give you a glimpse of the natural history of that region. Fossils, shells, petrified wood, and other natural artifacts can all be discovered at varying depth of the soil profile, telling you of ages gone by when the land was covered in sea or old forests.

Drainage. A "pit test" can be used to determine the soil's ability to hold or drain water. Dig a hole into the soil profile a minimum of a foot and a half to two feet deep. Fill it with water and time how long it takes the water to infiltrate. It's going to be different if it's the middle of the wet season or the dry season.

Soil Moisture. As landscapers, we often anticipate when the soil will dry out enough to dig without damaging soil structure. We never disturb soil when it's too wet as it will cause compaction and destroy its structure. One of the ways to test soil moisture in temperate climates is in the springtime. This is where the "squeeze" method comes into play. To test soil moisture, grab a handful of soil you want to test and squeeze it into a clump in your hand. If water immediately drips out like it would a wet sponge, then the soil is still too wet to be disturbed. That means no tilling, no driving on the surface, and limited digging of any kind. When the soil is this wet, all activities that disturb soil will increase soil compaction and cause a variety of potential issues in the landscape.

If no water squeezes out, but it compacts into a tight ball, then further test by poking it with your forefinger. If this ball doesn't break apart easily into small aggregates but instead breaks in half, remaining in large clumps, then the soil is still too wet to disturb. If you're able to break the ball up into lots of little clumps or it becomes a crumbly texture (good tilth), that indicates it's dry enough to work.

Organic Matter. Typically, if soil has a dark color, it has a higher level of organic matter content. When lacking dark colors, it may indicate the soil is stripped of organic matter and devoid of a robust soil ecology. In addition, look for life in the soil like worms or insects. To go deeper, microscopy (use of a microscope) can help identify bacteria, protozoa, and fungi.[1]

Plant Indicators. Plants divulge much about soil. Stunted plants commonly indicate a hardpan, while wetland plant communities indicate saturated and/or poorly drained soil. The more you dive into plants and their indicators, the more you will learn about water, minerals, climate, soils, and wildlife.

Once while out on consultation with a client, I brought in a soil scientist to consult with us. We were standing at the edge of a 10-acre fenced pasture and the soil scientist, without ever setting a foot in the field, turned to me and said, "This field is deficient in magnesium."

I thought, *What? You haven't even walked in the field. How could you possibly know just by looking at it from the fence line?* It turns out, he could see very few if any legumes. This one plant indicator revealed to him a mineral deficiency. When we sent a soil sample to the lab, guess what they discovered? There was a magnesium deficiency in that field.

Climate. What do plants indicate about climate? I live in Northern California, where the fog belt allows the tallest trees on the planet—the coast redwoods—to grow. In my temperate climate there are many frost areas in the winter, limiting the growth of subtropical species such as citrus and avocado, along with some frost-free zones we call "banana belts." If I walk in a landscape and see healthy mature citrus trees like lemon or orange trees, then I know that I'm in a banana belt and consequently a frost-free area. In this way, trees and plants convey much about the climate. Even without a full landscape analysis, by virtue of a single tree species, I can learn much about the microclimate surrounding me.

LANDFORMS

To understand the patterns of water and climate, you must understand the topographical shape of the land and its various landforms. This shape and orientation of the landscape dictates the pattern of the ecology, informing everything from water flow and microclimate to natural disasters. Comprehension of different landforms and the way water responds to them is key knowledge for ecological designers.

Main Ridges. Watersheds are basins separated by main ridges. When it rains, these ridges act as water divide lines—water landing on one side of the ridge enters one watershed and the water landing on the other side of the ridge enters a completely different watershed. Main ridges are often but not always the highest elevation points of a region.

Secondary Ridges. If main ridges are the tallest ridges of a watershed, secondary ridges are like fingers that branch off the main ridge. These finger ridges create their own sets of valleys and drainages, all flowing into the same creek or river of their watershed.

These smaller ridges affect microclimate in numerous ways. As cold air sinks, hot air rises, creating a host of different convection cycles and microclimate variables.[2] When analyzing landforms, please pay close attention to the variety of distinct climate features that are dictated by the various kinds of ridges you encounter.

Saddles. The basin-shaped area between two peaks or knolls is called a saddle. This unique landform sits high in the watershed as a natural collection point for water. A saddle can be used as a strategic location for a pond or other infrastructure due to this vantage point.

Primary Valley. The primary valley is the main valley characterized by the largest waterway. A watershed flows from main ridges and secondary ridges, finding its way to a river that carves the main valley. This is often the lowest point of the valley, descending to lower and lower elevations as the main river or creek winds its way towards the sea.

Secondary Valleys. Secondary valleys are the smaller valleys defined by two secondary ridges. These valleys often have steep grades to them and reside higher in the watershed than the main valley.

Because secondary valleys are located higher in the watershed, they often provide incredible vantage points for collecting and moving water. In these strategic locations landscape designers can utilize gravity for dispersing collected and stored water.

Natural Drainages. Natural drainages come in many forms: streams, creeks, rivers, washes, gullies, arroyos, and seeps. These drainage structures can be either year-round waterways or seasonal systems. Use plant and animal indicators, observational changes throughout the year, and local knowledge to determine the seasonality of natural drainages. Check with local ordinance to identify any legal protections or conflicts with working in or near natural waterways.

Roads and Erosion. Roads have the power to affect topography, water flow, erosion, and microclimates. While they can be built to enhance ecological function, many of the roads we inherit in today's landscapes have a degenerative effect on the land.

Pay close attention to the way the road influences water and erosion. As decades go by, badly designed roads can lead to the destruction of streams and creeks and the habitats they provide for wildlife.

As water gets channeled down the road, increasing in volume and velocity, it can act like a larger-than-life drill that cuts into the soil, washing it downstream and creating crevices or gullies throughout the landscape. This in turn decreases the water table of the entire region as the channels cut deeper and deeper into the land, draining precious subsurface waters quickly and dangerously into downstream waterways.

During your site assessment process, focus some energy on the drainage and erosion patterns caused by driveways, roads, and their associated drains, culverts, and ditches.

Badly designed culverts are the enemy of watersheds, but it all starts with the roads themselves. Wrongly placed roads cut through the land, diverting the natural flow of water and sometimes collecting that water in damaging ways. Culverts then become the release valves for roads: once a large amount of water has been collected, it gets directed to a culvert where it fires out the pipe like a shotgun.

MICROCLIMATE

All landscapes have small-scale differences in the way heat and cold, sun and shade, wind and shelter, act across the terrain. Observant designers will detect drastic changes from the sunny

Erosion gully formed from excessive water runoff coming from upslope road culvert. Photo credit: Erik Ohlsen

south side of the building to a tree-shaded north side, from the bottom of the hill to the top of the ridge.

Analyzing microclimates yields important information about frost zones, banana belts, protected areas, and more, driving the design process, plant choices, and the location of infrastructure like decks, animal pens, and vegetable gardens.

Wind Patterns

Wind is a powerful sun-driven force across the land. It has the ability to completely change the landscape and the climate. You will want to map the direction of prevailing winds and storm winds, along with other effects wind may have on the land. Anyone who ventures along the coast or climbs to the top of mountains will see how trees are shaped by wind. Many trees in these high wind zones are twisted and bent from the force of prevailing winds. One easy observation to make is to identify if the tips of tall trees are bent in a specific direction. If you notice this pattern, it is likely a result of prevailing wind and it is something we call wind flagging.

While prevailing winds are most likely to affect the landscape, storm winds can cause a different set of issues. Because large trees often grow more roots on the side of the trunk where the prevailing wind blows, they are more susceptible to damage from storm winds coming from a different direction. That is one reason why tree falls are common during storm events.

Many ecologies around the world also have fire winds. In coastal communities, these are called offshore winds as they originate inland, blowing hot air toward the coast. This blast of inland heat carried by fire winds dries out vegetation and can cause an ignition to expand into a fast-moving fire.[3]

On my own homestead, we have at least four different kinds of wind. Our storm wind usually hails from the south, while our prevailing wind pushes off the coast and hits us from the northwest. We are located miles from the coastline and always enjoy what we call "coastal air-conditioning" from our prevailing northwest winds. As we've learned multiple times since the year 2017, the fire winds—which feel more like a blow dryer—can come suddenly with incredible strength from the east, carrying numerous fires into our region.

We also have a fourth type of wind. To the west of our homestead, the land rises to a knoll. From the top of the ridge comes the strongest prevailing wind. Half of our property is surrounded by oak, pine, and redwood trees. This part of the land is very sheltered, and the wind is always gentle. On the other half of the property, we are exposed to the neighboring pastures that sit between us and the ridge to the west. As the wind whips out of the west and through these pastures, it hits this section of our homestead with a surprising force. It often brings cool air with it, dropping the temperature as much as 15°F cooler than anywhere else on the homestead. As part of our design process, we considered this area as a possible site for a wind generator.

Topography, macroclimate, cityscapes, forests, and deserts—all have their own unique relationship with wind. Your job as a landscaper is to use this context throughout the design and build process.

Sun Orientation

Let's face it, every landscape is completely driven by the sun. From hydrology and photosynthesis to carbon cycling, macro and microclimate, every natural cycle in the landscape is derived from, or affected by, solar energy.

When mapping the sun in our site assessment process, we look toward the "orientation" of the sun to describe which way the land or elements such as houses, greenhouses, and vegetable gardens are facing. Topography, vegetation, geological formations, and geographic location can all affect orientation to the sun. If the project is on the north side of a steep slope in the Northern Hemisphere, it will get very little sun, whereas a project in the middle of a flat prairie may have sun all day.

An evergreen tree on the sun side of the house will cast shade even in the sunniest climates. Track the patterns of sun and shade carefully, utilizing elements like sun azimuth finders and making your own sundial to help you identify how the sun will move and change on the land throughout the entire year. This last point is key as the land will look very different at summer solstice than it will at winter solstice. These two extremes—the winter solstice giving you the lowest point the sun will reach on the horizon and the summer solstice the highest point the sun will reach in the sky—gives you the full spectrum of the sun's movement in a year.

Ancient cultures have tracked the sun in this way for millennia. Many megalithic structures around the world were built to track solstices and equinoxes and act as solar calendars. You certainly could design your own landscape to function in this way, but in the twenty-first century many new technologies exist that make tracking the sun easy at any time of the year.

Special tools to see the azimuth of the sun throughout the year have existed for decades and azimuth finders now exist on smartphones. With many of these applications, one can even take photos and use them later in the design process or for presenting to project stakeholders. Using an app called Sunseeker, I can see the path of the sun through my phone at all times of the year. We use this in detailed ways: If there is a tall tree to the west, we may look at when the sun goes behind that tree during winter solstice versus summer solstice. The entire design will reflect this discovery through decisions like the placement of new trees or the location of patios and ponds.

All design is driven by context—a project site that remains shady throughout the year or a hot, exposed plain will require different approaches.

Thermal Mass

Thermal mass is material that absorbs heat during the day and releases it at night. Stone, brick, concrete, soil, and water all have the properties of thermal mass. With so many materials with this magical property, it is easy to see how microclimates can be influenced by thermal exchanges. If the landscape boasts rocky soils or outcroppings, thermal mass will play a role in microclimates.[4]

Fog

Some parts of the world (like where I live) are extreme fog areas. Fog provides moisture that can be much needed during droughts, but can also carry plant diseases, both factors to consider during site assessment. Specific trees and plants evolved with fog cycles have developed methods to "comb" fog with their leaves, dripping residual moisture to the ground. In dense fog zones, fog catchment systems can be built to catch water and can harvest many gallons per day.

INFILTRATION RATE TEST

This is an exceptional process for testing the infiltration rate of landscape soils. It will give a reading of how fast 1 inch of rain will infiltrate into the ground.

Materials

3-inch-diameter (wide) plastic/metal pipe by 5 inches long
Plastic wrap
Piece of wood (approximately 2 by 4 by 6 inches)
Small sledge
Stopwatch
Small container with a measurement of 107 mm or 1 inch for an exact measure of water. (This amount only works with a 3-inch pipe. If the pipe width is different, research the calculation to make sure you are only placing 1 inch of water into the test tube at a time.)

Directions

1. Mark 3 inches on the outside of the plastic/metal pipe.
2. Pound the pipe into ground until it is 3 inches deep (use a piece of wood and a sledge to pound it in without breaking it).
3. Place the plastic wrap inside the pipe (to hold an inch of water).
4. Use distilled or rainwater if you can and pour into the tube (pipe) on top of the plastic wrap. Carefully pull the plastic out, letting the water enter the tube all at once. Start stopwatch.
5. Take a reading twice so that you have put 2 inches of water into the test hole unless the ground has been irrigated or saturated with rain recently.

7
Create a Base Map

The first type of map a designer must develop is a base map—a map of existing conditions. The base map is the tool you use to document site observations prior to the conceptual design process. There are several ways to develop the base map, from a simple downloaded satellite image to a complex, professionally surveyed plan. Find the solution that best fits your skill set, project context, and budget.

Hand-Drawn Map

Hand drawing a landscape base map is an old-school yet completely effective method for developing this vital design tool. Check out the section below on triangulation to get the step-by-step process for developing a hand-drawn base map.

Satellite Image

Using a satellite image from Google Earth or other accessible providers is the quickest way to get a simple base map developed. This method has a few upsides but also some drawbacks.

Scaling your base map can be difficult on a satellite image if you don't have access to more advanced tools. One way to get around that is to use a fixed structure (house, barn, road) as a reference to figure out the scale that associates with your satellite image. For example, if you print out a satellite image of your project and want to know the distance between elements and entities, begin by measuring the fixed structure on the map. Let's say you're measuring one side of a house. When measuring with the ruler on your satellite image, you might conclude that the length of the house is 1 inch on your printed image. Now, measure the actual length of the house in the field. Let's say it is 50 feet. That means that 1 inch on your satellite image equals 50 feet. Now you can scale the satellite image to develop the rest of your base map and eventually the design.

(Note: This method for discovering the scale of your image is only true for the size of the image you printed. If you print that same image larger or smaller or zoom in to the digital satellite image and print a smaller area of the site, the scale will change. In that case, it makes sense to put a scale bar on the original base map (more on this below). In this way, the scale bar will enlarge or reduce along with the image if you zoom in or change the size.)

Surveyed Map

Some projects will require a professional mapping or surveying plan to achieve approval for permitting, property assessment, and engineered designs. This is by far the most accurate and high-quality map you can get for the project, but it is also the most expensive version of a base map.

Surveyors (usually civil engineers) can develop a map that certifies the exact property boundaries and property lines. For large-scale projects that require extensive permitting or for real estate endeavors, a licensed surveyor will be required to develop the map and certify property boundaries.

On the other hand, if exact property lines are not necessary for your design process but a high-quality digital base map is still desired or needed, then a digital mapping company of any kind (not necessarily a licensed surveyor) will suffice. All these mapping professionals utilize the latest technology: total stations, drone mapping, satellite uploads, and LIDAR (light detection and ranging) data to create the digital map.

In the end, you must decide what kind of map is right for you. Your context-driven approach to this process will yield the correct answer. The project budget, permit requirements if any, and project stakeholders all need to be considered when deciding on the appropriate base map.

Satellite/Topo Overlay

A satellite image with a topographical overlay offers layers such as contours, vegetation, existing structures, and so on all in one place, making it especially useful during landscape assessment. In the landscape industry these maps are called ortho-topo maps.

KEY ELEMENTS TO INCLUDE IN THE BASE MAP

Topography

A topographical map represents the elevational characteristics of the land. Using contour lines, the map renders an image of not only elevational points but also the steepness of grade between contour lines. A contour line on a map represents one elevational plane across the map. That means that every point along the same contour line is at the same elevation. The closer the lines are together, the steeper the grade. The most common elevational changes between contour lines vary from 1 foot, 2 feet, 5 feet, 10 feet, 20 feet, and 40 feet. For landscape base maps, it is best to develop topo maps with contour lines every 1–2 feet for smaller projects and every 5 feet for larger projects.

Developing your own topographical map by hand can be challenging and requires a set of specific tools to develop accuracy. A-frame levels, water levels, laser levels, total stations, drones, and airplanes can all be used to find contours and develop topographical maps. In some areas of the world LIDAR sensors have been used to develop publicly accessible topographical maps down to 1-foot contour lines.

Structures

Every fixed structure needs to be represented on the base map. Fixed structures include houses, barns, greenhouses, tool sheds, roads, walls, fences, swimming pools, ponds, etc.

Utilities

Overhead and underground utilities both appear on the base map, with buried utilities taking priority because they can pose major constraints during landscape installation. Utilities include electrical lines, gas lines, communication lines, water lines, septic systems, and so on. In the United States, dial 811 and public utility companies will come to your site for free to mark any publicly buried lines existing on the project site. It may be difficult to trace the path of utilities that have been installed independently, however. Do extensive research including visiting planning departments, looking over old maps, and following existing utility boxes, stub outs, and standpipes to determine where these systems may hide on-site. It's like a grand scavenger hunt, and the reward is that you won't destroy the septic system or cut an electrical line next time you dig!

Scale

Whatever scale the map is created in, make sure you write that down on the map along with a scale bar. This will make the map usable and readable during design and installation. The scale is usually written in the title block of the map within a border around the map.

From a project management perspective, working with a map's scale helps in the installation and planning process. When it comes time to estimate materials and labor to install a project, generate "take offs" from the scaled design to approximate everything required to build the landscape.

Depending on the size of the property, the scale of the base map will need to be adjusted. If working on a small urban lot, a smaller scale like 1 inch =10 feet can be used, but for larger projects like a 500-acre ranch, a scale of 1 inch = 100 feet might be more appropriate.

TRIANGULATION MAPPING SIMPLIFIED

Triangulation is a surveying method using triangles to find points in the landscape. Through a series of chaining together these triangles, one can lay out the existing features of the landscape onto a base map. Triangulation is used for very complex mapping projects, but for our purposes here, we are going to use a simple version of this technique that anyone can learn quickly to create scaled maps for landscape.

First, gather the necessary tools to map the project.

Tape measure. 100-foot and 300-foot tape measures are excellent tools for measuring from one point to another to create the triangles. A measuring wheel will also work. Smaller tape measures can work but are less efficient as many of the areas we measure will be longer than 25 feet.

Mobile drafting board. When out in the field triangulating points, you will be frequently marking a large sheet of paper; a large mobile drafting board is indispensable for this task. Later you can trace over the penciled map and scan for digital use.

Pencil compass. A large, high-quality pencil compass is a required tool for identifying the triangulated points on your developing map in the field.

Scaled ruler. An architect or engineering scale, which looks like a prism-shaped ruler, is vital for creating a landscape map. An engineer scale has values such as 1 inch = 10 feet or 1 inch = 40 feet and so on. An architect scale uses fractions showing values like ¼ inch = 10 feet or 1/8 inch = 1 foot. For landscape design, an engineer scale is usually the best option, though either can work.

Pencils and eraser. During triangulation, the map should be initially drafted using multiple pencils with different sized tips to make various line weights distinguishing features like roads, fences, and buildings from one another.

You will need a good eraser not only to fix and redraw mistakes but also to erase the arcs made by the pencil compass when finding new points.

Vellum paper. Vellum is an excellent paper to use for drafting a base map. It takes well to pencil, erases easily, and is light enough to be used for tracing. It comes in rolls and sheets.

Directions

1. Choose a scale to use in drawing the map. Using the scale ruler (engineer or architectural), decide whether your map will be scaled at 1 inch = 10 feet or something else. Choose a scale that is best for the project and your skill set.

2. Place a piece of vellum paper onto your mobile drafting board. A C-size 18 by 24 inches is common but you can also use a B-size sheet 11 by 17 or a D size sheet 24 by 36.

3. Start by locating fixed reference points like the corner of buildings and fences, fence posts, or trees as starting places to map the entire project site. For instance, measure the distance between two corners of a building. Place those two points (let's call them point A and point B) on the map and draw a line between them. Place this line roughly in an area that makes sense on your sheet of paper using a scale that allows you to fit the entire project area on the sheet. For example, let's say your map scale is 1 inch = 100 feet and the actual distance from one building corner to the other is 50 feet. When you place the two building corners on the map, they would be placed ½ inch from each other since ½ inch equals 50 feet.

(continued)

4. Once point A and point B are placed at scale on the map, you locate a third point (point C) to make a triangle. First measure the distance from point A to point C. Let's make point C an oak tree. Let's say the actual distance from point A to point C in the landscape is 75 feet. Take a note of this and then measure the distance between point B and point C. Let's say this distance is 25 feet in the landscape. Take a note of this.

5. Here's where the magic unfolds. You would now find point C on the map to place it at scale. Take your pencil compass and open its width to the equivalent of 75 feet. In this case, with a scale of 1 inch equals 100 feet, 75 feet is equal to ¾ inch. Spread the legs of your pencil compass to 3/4 inch.

    Now place the spike down onto Point A, the pencil point touching down 3/4 inches away. Draw a small pencil arc in the general vicinity of where you think point C (the oak tree) would be.

    Now do the same thing between point B and point C. At 25 feet and with a scale of 1 inch = 100 feet, 1/4 inch would be the width between the legs of your pencil compass. Stick the spike at point B and scratch a small pencil arc 1/4 inch away. When you make the second arc, ensure that it crosses the first arc you made between point A and point C. The point where the two pencil arcs cross is the location of your oak tree. Now place your oak tree on the map by measuring the circumference of the trunk and place that on the map at point C.

6. Moving forward, you can continually make triangles like this using the oak tree, a fence post, a building corner, and so on. Once you find three points you can "daisy chain" from there and find all the other points you need to create the entire base map to scale.

    Erase the pencil arcs made by the compass as you go. You will continually measure points in the field, use the pencil compass to find them on the map, and mark them down. As your triangulated base map develops, you may begin to use different pencil weights to thicken lines like fences or use symbols to represent specific trees or water features.

7. This initial base map can later be traced by placing another piece of vellum on top of it, holding it in place with drafting tape, and tracing a clean version of the map. This second version will be much clearer, without eraser marks and smudges and other imperfections that get picked up in the field during triangulation. You can even trace the second version in ink to create a professional-looking map.

8. Depending on the method you use in drafting the conceptual design, you can draw directly onto the rendered base map or scan and upload it digitally to a computer software for digital drafting. Design drafting will be discussed in chapter 13.

CASE STUDY: SITE ASSESSMENT WITH KENDALL DUNNIGAN

Kendall Dunnigan is the Permaculture Program Director at the Occidental Arts & Ecology Center in Sonoma County, California. She has decades of experience working with communities and landscapes throughout the planet developing regenerative farms, landscapes, and organizations. She has taught dozens of permaculture design courses and helped thousands of students learn the skills of repairing the earth's living systems.

Kendall is unique in her ability to work in many climates and cultures around the world, and she has developed a *site assessment protocol* that is highly efficient and detailed in scope.

For this case study, rather than focusing on a specific project, we focus on Kendall's site assessment process, which she has honed over decades as a teacher and consultant.

Virtual Site Assessment

Kendall takes the site assessment process and her clients' and students' time seriously. To achieve this, she developed a "virtual" site assessment process that generates a mind-blowing amount of usable data she uses to understand landscapes before stepping onto project sites.

Kendall recognizes that the more she knows about the landscape, the region, the topography, the culture, and the microclimate before she visits the site, the more quickly and easily on-site assessment can go, thus more effectively serving her clients and the ecosystem's need for regeneration.

Here are the elements Kendall uses in her virtual site assessment.

For each project, she uses Google Slides to organize project data, base maps, and design concepts. This tool allows her not only to access projects from anywhere in the world but also to develop collaborative systems with her project's stakeholders. These Google Slides projects are living documents that constantly evolve as new information is gathered and designs are developed.

Copy her template here: https://tinyurl.com/ycyxhksb.

To further organize her projects, Kendall uses an adapted Keyline Scale of Permanence, first developed in the 1930s by P. A. Yeomans:[1]

1. Climate (including Sector Analysis)
2. Landform (Geography & Geology)
3. Water
4. Roads/Access (Physical, Cultural and Legal Access)
5. Vegetation/Wildlands (Flora & Fauna)
6. Structures/Infrastructure (Energy, Fences, etc.)
7. Patterns of Use (Zones)
8. Soil/Waste Systems

(continued)

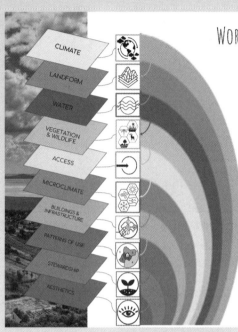

Modified keyline scale of permanence by Kendall Dunnigan.

The scale of permanence divides the landscape process into eight categories. These criteria are numbered by their permanence or the ability to be changed by human intervention, meaning that the element that we as designers can affect the least is number 1 and the element we can affect the most is number 8. By arranging the project in this way, Kendall places data in these various categories into her Google Slides systems, enabling easy reference and organization as well as generating a prioritization strategy for projects.

The next step is to identify the location of the project geographically and culturally. She works using satellite images (Google Earth and other sources) and maps to pinpoint the project location relative to both its regional influences (cities, communities) and its localized topography (mountains, rivers, etc.). These are zoomed out 3D images of the site showing the shape of the land and pictures of the project site outlined inside the surrounding region. Additional maps added at this point are parcel maps, watershed maps, LIDAR, indigenous territories, historical maps, and any other maps that inform you about the site.

One of the major tasks in assessing a landscape project is developing the base map. Various methods for developing base maps are detailed in this chapter, but Kendall shares with us an affordable and powerful way to develop a topographical base map on your own. By combining the power of digital earth terrain data with a design software called Sketch Up or an inexpensive 2D app called SmartDraw, Kendall produces usable topography satellite overlays (ortho/topo maps) from her computer.

Here's an overview of her process:

In Sketch Up, geolocate the project location and upload the terrain data. Grab an area that is slightly larger than the project site to see how surrounding topography influences the landscape.

Once the geolocated project terrain data is uploaded in Sketch Up, command the software to mark lines along elevation points you choose (you can find several excellent YouTube videos to teach you how to do this). For instance, you can choose 5-foot elevations and the software will place contour lines for every 5 feet. It's an incredible trick for creating a cheap topography map.

Detailing the whole workflow in Sketch Up is beyond the scope of this book but online tutorials exist to show you exactly how to do this for yourself. Thanks for the tip, Kendall!

One of Kendall's practices for researching the natural and social history of a land is finding historical images of the project site if possible.[2] Within Google Earth, one can view satellite images from the past (going back a few decades) but those images are often grainy or nonexistent. Better resources can be found on the internet with some extensive research, and many of these old images will surprise you. They may show buildings that existed but are now long gone and forgotten, agricultural endeavors, and/or raw land prior to industry and development.

Part of Kendall's historical research always includes identifying the Indigenous territory she is working in. Online resources like the Decolonial Atlas (https://decolonialatlas.wordpress.com/) and the native land map (https://native-land.ca/) are excellent resources to ascertain who are the first peoples of the land.

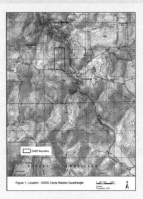
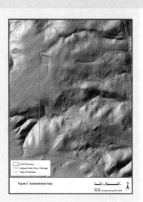

Topographical maps.

(continued)

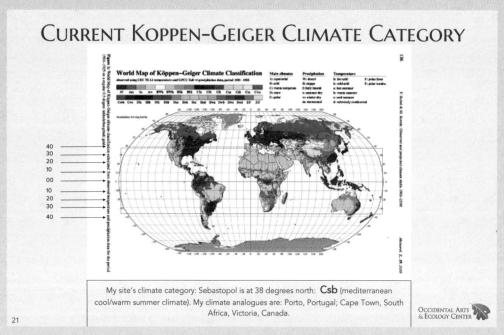

Climate analogues.

Regenerative landscapers design within multigenerational timelines to ensure a thriving future for earth's descendants and need to address climate change head on. Kendall has developed a workflow for identifying the climate projections of a landscape, using that information to advise the design process.

This step in the virtual site assessment allows designers to understand where and when a site is on the earth and in time. Kendall conducts a detailed climate analysis for the current time and projects for 2080 typically (because there are excellent projections for 2080 and it is within an understandable timeframe). She looks for climate analogues for a site (a climate analogue is a place on earth that has a similar climate to your landscape project). This information expands the variety of data and understanding used in developing a conceptual landscape design. Kendall takes this even further by addressing the future climate *projection* for her projects. The University of Maryland has a visual future climate analogue map online[3] that shows your current locations and the location your site will be most like in 2080. For example, Santa Rosa, California, will have a climate more similar to Tijuana, Mexico, in 2080, which is critical for choosing plant varieties and water regimes that will result in multidecade design success.

Once the climate projection is identified for a site, Kendall searches for climate analogues that fit the projected climate of the project site. Once a climate analogue has been identified, she researches the current and historical regenerative practices (often informed by Indigenous traditional ecological knowledge of the regions). Following this trail of clues, Kendall can begin to identify practices, plant species, ecological threats, and other essential knowledge for designing a landscape project's resilience to future climate change.

Precipitation is included in the climate assessment along with other virtual sector information that can be collected such as wind direction and speeds, flooding, etc. Documented precipitation (rain, snow) data is plentiful and easily accessible online. Kendall researches average rainfall for every site, tracking shifting trends and changes in averages over the decades. These data point developments reveal patterns vital to the regenerative design process as we designers ponder the implications of floods, droughts, and water security.

Online soil information is widespread. The US Geological Survey (USGS) has catalogued soils across the United States, providing details about subsoil and topsoil in every region of the country. As an initial soil assessment process, this data is highly valuable. Similar resources exist in countries across the world. In addition, Kendall gets chemical and biological soil tests to understand not only the broad soil type as identified with the USGS data but also the specific chemistry and ecological soil health of the site.

Once Kendall has created a topo/satellite map and collected the above information, she develops a set of maps that are populated with a wide range of data about the site. A *sector map* is one of the first layers created. This marks the direction of incoming forces of energy

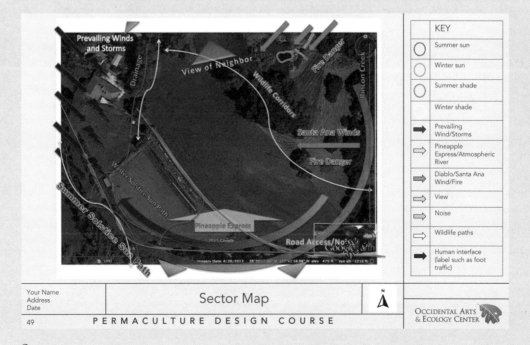

Sector map.

(continued)

to the site. Fire danger, prevailing winds, sun orientation, wildlife pathways, noise/pollution, and any other force of energy that impacts the project will be placed with incoming arrows and text onto the topographical map. The sector maps begin virtually and then are completed during the on-site assessment.

Important Reminder

Kendall reminds us that no matter how developed our base maps, ***the map is not the territory.*** In the end, no amount of virtual research, surveyed landscapes, or conceptual designs render all the truths of the land. The only way to truly understand a landscape is to walk, run, sit, sleep, breathe, and taste the ecology. Even then, our visits to the site are only snapshots in endlessly changing ecosystems.

8
Social Context

Human needs, along with social and cultural patterns, play a major role in land use and a community's relationship to landscape. The context of social patterns leads you, as a designer, to a richer level of concept planning. Your stated goals and vision will be informed and adjusted through this lens of social assessment.

Within the social sphere of our communities, we find contextual factors that affect the land, the community, and potentially the landscape project. Factors such as poverty, racism, classism, differing cultural identities, languages, and age groups are all aspects that make up the social fabric within a community. These underlying social patterns form layers of cultural context that should not be taken lightly in the design and implementation of a landscape project. If you live in the United States, the land you are stewarding was colonized and stolen from Indigenous peoples by colonialists. Acknowledging you're on stolen land, working to support local tribes, identifying sacred sites, and taking seriously the history of slavery and genocide on the land will help guide the designer to make decisions that care for the whole—the whole landscape and the whole community.

Other social conditions need to be assessed. If the project is near a school, consider the traffic, access to kids and parents, and other audio and visual elements that affect the landscape. In this way, the design gets guided by these challenges, hoping to solve potential issues through the design process. Is the project in an urban food desert? Maybe the landscape can feature food-producing trees and plants along public access ways to provide fresh food to the neighborhood. Local food gleaners and soup kitchens could utilize the nutrient-dense resources found in this landscape.

Another issue could be that the neighbors next door enjoy large parties and loud music while the people living in the landscape you're designing need quiet and solitude. A case like this might lead the designer to develop sound walls, privacy, and moving water elements that can drown out the loud neighbors and provide a tranquil experience.

SOCIAL HISTORY

What is the history of the Indigenous people of the land? Are there still Indigenous people on the land? What kinds of food sources did/do they use? What kinds of structures did they live in? How did they/do they relate to the land? Many Indigenous communities foster balanced and sustained ways of ecologically living with the environment. Learning from their wisdom can inspire a landscape design that models an Indigenous approach to land management (always acknowledge/support Indigenous communities and credit them in your work). The better we understand the native approach to managing landscapes, the more we can emulate the success of thousands of years of innovative management techniques.

What are other historical traces of human activity? Take special note of existing infrastructure. Is there an old mine or a garbage dump on-site? For instance, at the Permaculture Skills Center, our neighbors on the east side of the property mentioned to us that the remains of an old rodeo rink were found on their property. This one discovery enabled us to see the whole landscape in a different way. We saw beyond the five acres we steward and began to look at it from the point of view of the 100-acre ranch, our project a small piece in the middle.

KNOW YOUR NEIGHBORS

It helps to know your neighbors for many reasons. Hopefully the neighbors are friendly and a good relationship can develop, but that's not guaranteed. Whether friends or not, pay attention to the neighbor's land-use activities. Are they spraying chemicals, do they have loud animals, or are they directing stormwater onto your project site? Or do they share their resources—grow food for the neighborhood, love to fix things, and be of service to the community? Consider all the ways neighbors' activities impact the landscape, good and bad, as you start the design phase. Most people want to make good neighbors, but sometimes it's necessary to block out neighbors with privacy plantings and fences. Knowing your neighbors will help you decide how to treat the edges of the property. Are you building a higher fence or installing a gate?

PROJECT STAKEHOLDERS

For the sake of this book, the term *project stakeholder* refers to any person, entity, or organization with a direct relationship with the project. This could be a client, a family member, a neighbor, a colleague, a coworker, a community member, a municipality, a contractor, a business, and so on. This also means the ecological stakeholders or entities—the waterways, animals, trees, insects, and soil biology.

Each project will have its own specific blend of project stakeholders. Throughout the book, this term will be used within the context of decision making, landscape design, installation, and any other communication between entities required during the project.

COMMUNITY CONTEXT

Whatever community you're working in, whether it's the place where you live, a community that you identify with, or another community you're working within, you need to understand how culture affects that community. A community can represent many different types of groups, including cities, neighborhoods, schools, sports teams, or business staff. If your project involves working directly with a specific community like a school, then taking time to understand the culture of that school, the desires, problems, expressions, and motivations of that culture will be vital knowledge during the design process.

9
Develop Your Vision

Before starting any landscape project, clarify your vision for the entire process—the design, implementation, and overall stewardship. To instigate the visioning process, it helps to look at your dreams for the future. This is a fun process so give it the time it deserves. Enjoy! Walk yourself and other project stakeholders through the following scenarios: Seven years from now, you step out your home into the landscape. What is your experience as you wander through the land? How do you feel walking there? What sights do you see? What sounds do you hear? What yields do you harvest?

The seven-year vision is a great place to start, especially when making a sensory experience out of the visioning process. Take extensive, unedited notes during this process. Later these can be developed into a usable document to help form a landscape design concept. If your project is more temporary than a seven-year cycle, change the time frame to meet the project's needs.

Follow the same visioning process again but this time, cast forward 50 years. This version requires the expansion of the scope of your project's impact. Obstacles will begin to surface. You may be renting the space, or you may be an elder who won't be around in 50 years. However, none of that matters; this is a vision of the land that grows beyond you.

When you cast forward 50 years, consider what the next generation will inherit in this landscape. Consider birds, trees, and watersheds. Expand your scope as wide as possible to see how this project fits into the evolutionarily (successional) timeframe of the entire living ecology.

Casting your vision into the future like this requires a broad and open mind. Try not to get fixated on details just yet (those will come) but keep the vision expansive. As a clear vision within these timescales gets generated, make sure to write everything down in detail. You will come back to this later.

Now that you have visioned the physical experience, let's take a comprehensive look at the social patterns and processes you envision for the project. Remember, every landscape project has a social layer. Even when working by yourself in the woods, there's a nonhuman community requiring your attention.

Money, time, equipment, and communication are all topics that need to be discussed thoroughly and can and will bring up uncomfortable emotions. Sometimes, it's even necessary for people to step away from the project, for contractors to be hired or fired, and in extreme cases projects like these even send people into therapy!

Much of my career as a professional landscape designer has been spent having hard conversations with my clients, staff, colleagues, and other project stakeholders. Therefore, the necessity of developing a vision for social processes on your project cannot be overstated.

To plan out the social vision for the project. Here is a set of questions to ponder:

What kind of people do you want to work with?

How attached are you or others to specific timelines?

How necessary is it to stay at or under budget?

When the situation gets tense, what kinds of conflict resolution processes are being used?

What are the best forms of communication? Is an email or text efficient enough or is a phone call or in-person meeting necessary?

ATTITUDES AND BEHAVIORS

Each of us has a unique approach to stress and communication. Some are highly organized, others more flexible, and some folks just want to have fun all the time. There is no judgment about the unique person you are, but it is good to know your preferences when starting a landscape project. When developing a vision, it's good practice to evaluate your own tendencies during stressful situations, and the kind of working atmosphere you thrive in. Designing and building landscapes is fun but can also be quite stressful.

Write down a vision for the sort of work environment that best suits you. Maybe you're more introverted and need opportunities to work alone with plenty of preparation time for any meetings with other project stakeholders. Maybe you thrive in social spaces, have a flexible schedule, and are happy to have project partners contact you day and night. For me, I need time alone to understand a project, and I generally can't make big decisions without sufficient time to digest the situation.

Ask yourself, *What kinds of attitudes and behaviors do you expect from other project stakeholders?* This key question helps you determine the right people to bring into the project as well as providing the basis for a clear set of agreements to make with those working with you.

Some readers might be wondering at this point how much of this truly pertains to their landscape endeavor. For many years I felt the same, separating the physical work of designing gardens and farms from the social processes that took place during these projects.

At this point, I've been on enough projects to know that the social layer is usually the one that dooms a project. The social patterns discussed here are of utmost importance to the success of your project. I've seen couples split up, projects abandoned halfway through, hundreds of thousands of dollars wasted, and worse. It seems to be the nature of humans to rush into projects without creating social structures that ensure success.

I don't want you to make those same mistakes so please don't take this part of the book lightly. For some of you, the next section will save you tremendous amounts of time, stress, and money.

Core Values Development

Compress your vision into a set of core values or principles that represent the definitive conduct, needs, behaviors, and overarching ethics needed to meet the vision of your project.

Be patient in developing your values. They may bend and transform over time and that is OK. Keep your principles to a minimum; I suggest developing no more than five. If you create too many, you start to develop contradictions and confusion among your value systems.

Here are a few examples of core values. Notice how each value takes on a different sphere of the project.

Cause the Least Harm. All project decisions are made with the "least harm" principle. All living organisms are sacred and thus all installation and maintenance work considers the health of living beings and causes the least harm to the land while achieving the stated goals of the project.

The Land Has a Voice. No decision is made or action taken before consulting the land itself. Spend quiet time with trees, listen to the birds, and observe through the seasons. Observations and revelations discovered during this process are always shared as an equal project stakeholder when making decisions.

Fiscal Sustainability. Monetary resources are finite and therefore all project decisions must adhere to a rigorous and clear budget.

Attitude of Kindness. All people deserve to be treated with kindness and respect. Do not tolerate put-downs, gossip, or lying on your projects. The right team is as important as the finished result; therefore, choose project workers and contractors by the demeanor and energy they bring to your project.

Vision Statement. If you've followed the vision development process so far, you're nearly ready to find the essence of the project. The vision statement is the seed, the pearl, the heart of the entire project. Again, it requires patience to get this right, so don't rush it. You've developed visions, thought about the social layer as well as the physical layer, and created a set of values.

Now you need to condense all of that into a single paragraph. In this way, you capture the essence of your vision, your hopes, your needs, and your constraints. Write a few different versions of what a single paragraph might look like that encompasses your entire vision.

Once you've written down a few versions, some sentences will resonate strongly with you. Begin combining the most potent language that speaks the truth of your vision and who you are.

Now that you have your core vision statement, you can print it out and stick it to your computer, hang it up in your office, and share with other project stakeholders.

Every now and again, you'll want to edit your vision statement. Maybe something has changed in your life or the life of the project. It's OK to change and edit your vision statement as many times as you need. Let it be a living document that evolves with you and the landscape.

Articulating Goals

In addition to understanding the context of a site, you also need to know where you are trying to go with the project and how to get there. Now it's time to expand on your vision. Here you move from a broad level of thinking into a detailed planning process. For those that love to make lists, your moment has come.

Here are some questions to ask as you refine your vision. For each set of questions, list out as much detail as you can about timelines, species, and other hopes and dreams.

What is the budget for this project? Is it best to build the project all in one phase or spread the budget out over several years? If the latter, what does the yearly budget look like? What is the ideal project timeline?

Does this project call for food production? If so, will it be perennial food production such as fruit and nut trees? Annual food production such as vegetables? Animal products such as eggs and meat?

What are the ecological goals (yields) of the project? Creating habitat for a specific endangered animal? Sequestering carbon? List all your ecological goals here.

What kinds of water systems will be required for your vision to work? What is the entire relationship of landscape and water? Get specific and list your water ideas.

Are there family and community functions happening in your vision? What kinds of spaces need to be built to provide for celebration, recreation, and relaxation?

What changes to existing infrastructure are required to make your vision work? Are there buildings, fences, or hardscapes that must be removed? Do new structures need to be built or remodeled? Create a list of outdoor spaces people might utilize like decks, pathways, patios, a greenhouse, a tool shed, social gathering spaces, a pool, camping zones, etc.

What details are missing? Add to this list any other factors you can think of.

Look back at your seven-year and 50-year visions. In this next step, you will reverse engineer your vision back from the future to the present day. What are the cycles, processes, materials, and changes that need to be made to achieve your future visions?

As you work back through the process, begin to identify a series of milestones. These are major achievements in the process of developing the landscape. As you develop these milestones, you are inadvertently creating a set of goals and a timeline.

For instance, maybe you envision walking into a lush and shady landscape where food is harvestable throughout the year. To reverse engineer this, you must consider some factors. This landscape is going to require trees and (depending on species) additional water. Are there trees existing on the landscape now or is it barren? If barren, what kinds of species can be planted and what water infrastructure is required to bring this vision to reality? Trees take time to establish, so you will need to plant them soon if you hope to have shade in the near future. But water takes precedence over planting. Are you planting species that grow native to your region and require less water or do you want to establish nonnative edible or soil-building trees that need more water in the first few years? This sort of reverse engineering helps define all the steps that are required to achieve that vision. Unless you are planting native during the rainy season, identifying a water source will likely come before planting trees.

Maybe part of your vision includes having a place for guests to sleep in the garden. That could look as simple as a camping site or as luxurious as a guest house. If the latter, then what you envision will probably take a fair amount of time to build. Does the site currently offer a location for such a structure? What kinds of activities are required to lay the groundwork to build the guest house? Do you imagine running water and electricity to this structure? As you can see, every one of these reversed engineered design concepts brings up more and more questions, and these explorations help you refine your vision and manage the project realistically.

Not only does reverse engineering help develop a set of milestones but this process also generates a rough timeline of activities and the sequence that is best taken to make your vision a reality. Your priorities will emerge as part of this process, providing a foundation for managing the project, creating the budget, and ensuring you are making decisions that lead you in the right direction. At all phases of this process, ensure that you are going back to your core values and vision statement to determine if your developing goals fit with your guiding principles.

As you begin to develop a phased timeline for your project with various goals, you can begin to assign budgets, professionals you'll need to contact, and other planning levels that you need to achieve each milestone. All of this becomes the springboard for the design process, detailed in part III.

A distinction needs to be made between desired goals and functional goals. For example, maybe a swimming pond is part of your dream project but what you really need is water and a way to stay cool in the summer. You may run into obstacles achieving project-specific goals such as a swimming pond (budget, topography— any number of factors may make a specific goal unfeasible), but this doesn't mean the overarching goal of coolness in the summer and enjoying a water feature can't be achieved in ways more appropriate to the context of the project.

Everything comes back to context, which always changes through time. Your interests, abilities, and resources will all change—at times suddenly. Part of weathering change is adjusting your goals as your life context evolves. These are just the rolling waves of life, and you get to integrate them into the new you that is being born.

PART III
Conceptual Landscape Design

10
Conceptual Design Process

The conceptual design process is when we develop a full plan for the regenerative landscape. It's called "conceptual" because the process of landscape design will take many iterations, eventually evolving into a master plan. To achieve a design plan that is ready for installation, we must start with a set of conceptual ideas.

Here, I share the processes that I have worked and had success with over decades. If you have alternative methods of analyzing and conceptualizing design elements, I encourage you to bring your skill sets to the table and I hope what I offer here adds to your design toolkit. I only ask that, in every design you develop, you implement regenerative design principles throughout the process to facilitate the constant increase of ecological abundance on the site.

If you do your job correctly, your design plan will reflect the resources and constraints of the site and the project's entire context, including the social, cultural, and ecological impacts. This context combined with the stated visions, goals, and values will provide you with the foundation you'll need to generate a regenerative landscape design plan.

As you journey through different design drafting models, remember, these are just tools. When you put this work into practice, you will immediately see the benefits of drafting plans and their potential for communicating regenerative landscape design. A well-made design plan is a powerful tool for presenting concepts, guiding installation, and communicating about the various aspects of the project with project stakeholders.

CREATIVITY AND IMAGINATION

The best designers in the world, in every trade, are constantly breaking conventions and dreaming up new artistic expressions that expand our belief about what's possible. As you step into the design process and mesh the tools given to you in this book with your own life experience, get playful and imaginative within the context of your project. Look for design ideas that strike you as functional, gorgeous, and unexpected. Often the "aha" creative moments happen when the designer's mind widens beyond thinking and instead rests in the state of listening discussed in part II. In these moments we discover the most simple and powerful solutions to landscape challenges.

To maximize your creative force, consider what processes that work best for you. Some people work better in a team, bouncing ideas off others in creative ways, while others require solitude for their creativity to spark. For me, solitude on the project is paramount. It's easy to achieve this on my own homestead but it becomes trickier when working for clients. Clients often wander the land by my side asking questions and learning through my assessment process. This service, which I have provided for decades, is usually worthless (for me) in terms of generating creative ideas. If you are working for or with others, you may need time alone on the project to activate another level of creativity. You may love to share your ideas with others but can end up justifying someone else's design concept rather than letting your artistic juices flow unhindered.

For me, solo walks and hikes on a project are the most valuable. In these creativity sessions, I am in the deep awareness phase where I pay attention to everything happening on the site holistically. The patterns, the vegetation, the way the wind blows across the leaves, the length and shapes of shadows, the traces of water in all its forms—the land speaks volumes, and my imagination gets to run wild. I try not to have destinations in mind during these walks and let myself get pulled through the space like a spider's web weaving back and forth, connecting all the elements into a grand matrix. Then, in unexpected moments, design concepts flood into my mind, forming the basis for the landscape design plan.

Generating Ideas

Landscape design is more than function—it's flow, it's beauty, and it's art. As an art, there are thousands of ways to achieve the same necessary functions while drastically changing the experience and the aesthetics. Your landscape plan should reflect your own eye for beauty, your own sense of what it means to experience the landscape. Combine this with project stakeholders' visions and ideas, and a design concept begins to form.

Not everyone has the capacity to generate a detailed vision right away, which is completely normal. For some of us, it takes a bit longer to know not only what we want in a landscape design but also what the land is asking for. Confidence in aesthetic preferences doesn't always come easily, and you may find yourself looking for inspiration.

One of the best ways to gain inspiration is to tour established landscapes, visit botanical gardens, and explore pristine natural environments. All these places provide their own models of regeneration, their own aesthetic character. As you venture through these lands, take note of what you love and what you don't love.

When you're not exploring landscapes in real life, explore them virtually. Find pictures online, look at magazines, and research as many possibilities as you can. Save the aesthetics and patterns that jump out immediately in your project files.

When you integrate the context of a site with your goals and your visions, then sprinkle your own artistic pollen into the mix, the conceptual design phase will be a rich and enjoyable process, but it can also be paralyzing. In many regenerative design circles, we call this paralysis by analysis. This happens when the designer gets overwhelmed by all the possibilities and data and gets overly concerned about making design mistakes and therefore unable to move forward with the project. I have friends who have been stuck in paralysis for over a decade, always trying to initiate their projects but in the end never taking real action, their landscape projects never coming to fruition.

If you find yourself in a similar place in your project, here are two suggestions for breaking through the paralysis in your landscape design process. First, realize that often design paralysis comes from specific issues and not the project as a whole. It's true that even specific issues can affect the entire project but, 99 percent of the time, there *are* aspects you can move forward, independent of problems you haven't figured out solutions to yet. My suggestion is to keep forward momentum rather than letting the project stagnate. Momentum is a powerful phenomenon for artists and designers, and when you stop feeding the ever-evolving pattern that comes with it, the stagnation that follows could lead you to paralysis and even abandonment of the project. I've seen it happen too many times!

When hitting an obstacle, be like water. Integrate the obstacle into your plan and keep moving around and through it until it has been fully digested and transforms into a solution rather than a problem.

Second, if aesthetics, rather than general site constraints, are the issue leading to paralysis—if as an artistic designer you are unable to make decisions about color, texture, placement—then laying the plan out on the physical landscape is my best advice. Designers often sequester themselves behind their desks, thinking the design plan will emerge out of their brains. In some way it does, but when that's not working, the landscape itself must be consulted to help you make decisions.

Using survey flags, stakes, ground paint, rope, or any other appropriate medium, begin placing all the features of your landscape concept on the site—pathways, water features, planting areas, and so on. You will be amazed how quickly the landscape communicates its truths to you. As you walk through your mockup of the landscape, I guarantee new ideas will come, solutions to problems will be revealed, and your momentum will be renewed.

Unlimited Possibilities

Don't limit yourself to what's possible. Work within the context, but from there think big, bold, and extraordinary. Step outside the mental box your culture has trapped you in. Allow your imagination to run wild and free like an antelope across the plains. Don't worry, it doesn't matter how bold and crazy your ideas are—you haven't built anything yet, and there's no danger in being a little crazy with your imagination at this phase. We all do it, even if we don't speak it out loud! When it comes to design, you are your greatest limitation. Allowing yourself full freedom to generate ideas outside the norm will always yield something usable and unexpected. Even if 90 percent of your wild idea doesn't make sense, the 10 percent that does may just bring the entire landscape design to life. At the very least, give yourself this process because it's fun and can help you shake up any stagnation you may feel in the design process.

My only caution is if you're working with project stakeholders who won't appreciate bold innovation. This process may not be best undertaken in a group setting, depending on who's

CONCEPTUAL DESIGN PROCESS 73

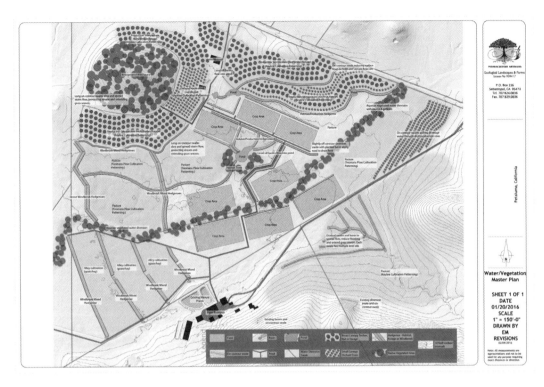

Full design rendering of 100-acre regenerative agriculture system. Designed by Erik Ohlsen and Emily Mallard.

there. Know the community you're working with and whether generating outside the box would be a good fit for them.

CONCEPT PLANNING

The landscape concept plan is where we bring all the threads of design together. We combine the site assessment discoveries (context) with the vision and foster ideas to accomplish our goals. By weaving context, visions, and goals, we begin to generate innovative ideas while applying the regenerative design principles.

In this phase, you begin to cultivate solutions to problems discovered during project assessment while placing landscape elements into a relational design pattern. Concept planning is a fun and creative part of the process where the bulk of the regenerative landscape plan is formed. As you generate ideas, keep workshopping with different ways of setting up the plan— play around with diverse combinations of connections and flows between landscape elements.

The conceptual design is the heart of the design process, so invest the time required to make it worthwhile. Later in the process you will refine your ideas until a "master" plan is revealed. For now, generate ideas and keep the plan in a draft process. Stay open to making revisions, getting feedback, and reworking the design until a design plan emerges that is worth implementing.

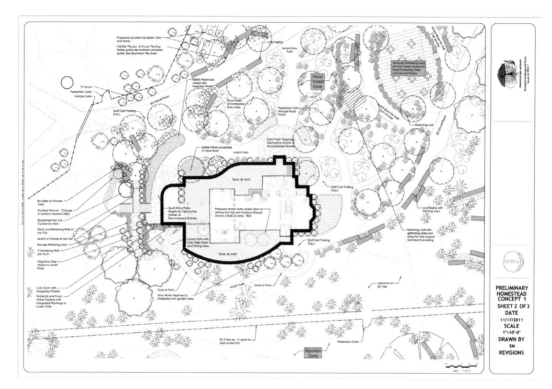

Homestead landscape design concept. Designed by Erik Ohlsen and Emily Mallard.

Real Regeneration Versus Greenwashing

Before moving ahead, it's important we take a moment to recalibrate your motivations for the project. Since you are reading this book, my assumption is that your goal is to create a truly regenerative landscape system. I applaud this goal but also need to warn you. As you navigate the design process, you will be making many decisions that impact the ecosystem and community. Even more decisions will be made during implementation and, in this modern era, it is all too easy to cut corners and choose industrial methods to save money and time. The term *regenerative design*, like *permaculture*, or *sustainability*, is often used to cast projects in a "green" or ecological light that may not be truly regenerative. We call this greenwashing. Many projects incorporate aspects of a regenerative approach but then fall short of having a true regenerative impact on the ecosystem. Only you and your project stakeholders can decide what level of regeneration you incorporate into the project. My hope is that a deep respect for ecosystems and ecological communities guides your every move.

As modern-day humans, we still have a lot to learn about what it means to live in true balance with our environments. We are relearning the ecological ways of our ancestors, remembering what it means to be human, and transitioning away from the industrial, consumer based, profit-driven economic models of the twentieth and twenty-first century. This book attempts to balance both the transition from an industrial economy to a regenerative one *and* the true, deeper expression of regeneration.

Embodied Energy

Embodied energy consumption provides a strong basis for measuring the regeneration of a landscape process by tracking how much energy, materials, and labor goes into every product and service utilized on your project. What is the overall carbon footprint of the project? How much fossil fuel consumption is required to make the project happen? These are difficult and fundamental questions we must ask when we decide whether a project is truly regenerative or on the transitional edge from industrial to regenerative. I'm not trying to make a judgment here, only to point out the importance of this type of assessment and questioning.

It really comes back to your motive. It's about your priorities, what you're willing to give up, and how long you're willing to wait to achieve your goals. In general, a slower approach that utilizes fewer energy inputs and fewer off-site materials, and works within the natural successions of the landscape, will be more regenerative.

It might be clear for you that you need that flagstone patio, you won't be satisfied without the swimming pool, or your project site is so degraded and covered in cement that large-scale use of equipment and fossil fuels are necessary to transition to regeneration. This may absolutely be the case and your goals will be to offset your embodied energy consumption by catching stormwater in the landscape and planting intensively to build soil, grow food, and other techniques to sequester carbon and reduce your consumption moving forward.

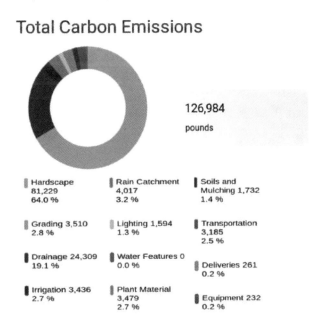

Using a carbon calculator like this one provided by BOND Landscape Calculator www.bondc6.com, landscapers can estimate the total carbon emissions of a proposed landscape installation.

Land Access

Regenerative landscaping will always require at least one major resource: access to land. To ignore the complex issues of land accessibility, private property ownership, and the dark history of land grabs would be a disservice to a conversation about regeneration. If regenerative landscaping was only possible through property ownership, then we'd be talking about regeneration only for the few and privileged. That is not the intention of this book. I firmly believe that all people have a right to live in direct relationship with the land, to grow their own food and medicine, and to live with dignity and safety upon the lands they inhabit. In the current capitalist economy, this ideal is far from the reality. The concept of private land ownership is one of the biggest travesties of humankind. When settlers came to the Americas, most, if not all, native communities managed land in "territories" but never in ownership. How could one own the land? The land is a living being composed of other living beings like plants, animals, fungi, and watersheds. A North American Indigenous worldview sees humans as a part of the ecosystem; therefore it is not possible to "own" the landscape.

Once American settlers began claiming land ownership, they limited the native people's access to the land and began to convert pristine natural systems into Eurocentric homesteads. Over the centuries, greater and greater areas of land became "owned" by those with power and privilege, leading to the situation we have today where nearly all land is privately owned or inaccessible to the populace.[1]

The Land Back movement, led by Indigenous people, has risen as a response to the centuries of land theft. Land Back recognizes that disconnecting Indigenous people from their land has resulted in decimated watersheds, destroyed topsoil, and the extinction of thousands of animal and plant species. On the other hand, in the twenty-first century, 80 percent of the world's remaining biodiversity is managed in what is left of sovereign native territories.[2] Giving land back to Indigenous people is one of the best ways to regenerate Earth's biological systems. With so much devastation, death, and grief caused by settler colonialism, giving land back is also a first step in reconciling the tragic past and bringing healing to our communities.

It's not just native communities that suffer from a system based on private property ownership. Black Americans have also suffered centuries of inequality, abuse, and a lack of access to land. When President Franklin D. Roosevelt signed the New Deal into law in 1933 to pull Americans out of Depression era poverty, creating the Federal Housing Administration to provide federal-backed loans to help people buy homes and stimulate the economy, Black Americans were excluded from this wealth building.[3]

As part of the federal housing program, Black neighborhoods were "redlined" on development maps, delineated as less valuable and dangerous. Black Americans were rejected from the loan program and thus were less able to buy their own homes. Furthermore, mortgage insurance companies would not insure Black-owned homes or neighborhoods in close proximity to Black neighborhoods. Housing developers resorted to full segregation tactics, using walls and freeways to separate Black and White neighborhoods in order to receive mortgage insurance.

This redlining, and the racist and segregationist tactics that came with it, created a *massive* wealth gap between White and Black Americans that still exists today. Many White Americans who received loans and bought homes were capable of generating enough value from their investments to pass this wealth to their heirs and next of kin. This grew a large, White middle class in the United States while suppressing the wealth of Black communities at the same time.

This is just one of many ways that racism has been institutionalized in the United States and why Black farmers and Black communities in general have lacked the wealth and access to own land. All of this makes the call for reparations even stronger and even more legitimate for Black Americans who have suffered centuries of institutionalized racism.

The current global economy has severed access to the land from most of humanity. This means most people couldn't grow their own long-term, food-producing, regenerative landscape even if they wanted to. This is at odds with the reciprocal nature of regeneration and has led to an economy based on global food imports and exports rather than hyper-local food production. We can and will change this problem—many creative options exist right now. If you're reading this book and don't have access to land, don't give up. Below you will find creative ways of engaging directly with landscapes even when they are not your own.

In 1999, I cofounded an organization called Planting Earth Activation (PEA). Our goal was to give away seeds and food-producing gardens to the community for free. We planted over 200 gardens in two years, producing food, seeds, and ecological yields. Hundreds of landscapes we helped create, but not even one did I own. Most of them, I never even returned to. A few of these landscapes became gardens where I was invited to visit, harvest, and enjoy whenever I wanted. After that experience, I realized how many people want ecological gardens and landscapes but don't know where to start. For most of these people, the work, cost, and lack of know-how made creating a regenerative landscape out of reach. When an inspired group of young people came by offering to give them gardens, to take care of them, and to share the harvest, it was an offer many couldn't refuse. Throughout those years working with PEA, we planted gardens at people's homes, in community gardens, and directly onto public land. We also worked with schools, businesses, and nonprofit organizations developing regenerative landscapes everywhere we went. These projects represented a new way of accessing land for ecological restoration and community resilience.

When I speak about the free gardens we built for people, some folks express concern about designing and building landscapes on "other peoples'" land. Comments like, "Why would I spend my time and energy on someone else's property?" are common. I understand the sentiments profoundly. I built many gardens that were subsequently bulldozed or damaged when new people moved to the site. Those experiences were disheartening and enraging. But many of the landscapes we gave away are still flourishing decades later. In my own town, I could visit at least thirty publicly accessible fruit trees I helped plant that are still lining sidewalks, city lots, and parks.

With reciprocity at the core of regeneration, I encourage you to move beyond mental obstacles like "I don't own the property" and toward common ecological goals of building soil, creating habitat, producing food, and managing water. I developed extensive gardens in every rental house I ever lived in, and during the years I occupied those spaces, I enjoyed those gardens immensely. I saved money by growing my own food and my homes always represented the world I dreamed of creating. When I left those rentals, I left gardens in my wake, and many are still going strong today.

Don't be afraid to regenerate whatever land that you are able to access. Ownership is only a concept, but the land is 100 percent real. If you have access to it, give it your love and attention for the sake of the ecosystem and generate *ecological yields*. You will be rewarded for your work, I guarantee you. Don't feel bad about leaving regenerative landscapes in the trail of your life. When you leave you can still take your gardens with you. When I leave a garden, I propagate my favorite plants through cuttings, seed saving, scion wood, and root division and plant these in my next garden. Because of this practice, some of the plants on my current homestead are genetic clones from the very first gardens I planted decades ago.

If you live in an apartment, are currently houseless or nomadic, access someone else's landscapes if you can. Many people relish the idea of having support in building out a regenerative landscape. You can be the force that makes it happen by creating simple land access agreements with friends, neighbors, and family members. Developing relationships like these allow you to nurture landscapes, obtain a harvest, and help others steward their landscapes with care and integrity. Shared harvests (and harvest parties) are almost always a win-win situation—and fun too.

To be real, sometimes these agreements don't work out very well and you will feel burned. It happened to me many times, but I still cherish each learning opportunity. These relationships are risky, but one project lost is not the end of your journey restoring the land. Remember, you are a service more to the land than to the person. If you don't give up, you *will* find relationships that are mutually beneficial and nourishing to you and the community.

Designated community gardens are a great place to access land and develop regenerative systems. Most community gardens are understaffed and underfunded, and if you bring your passion and energy to a public garden, it will likely be received enthusiastically. You might talk them into planting an orchard or expanding the garden into the neighboring lot.

Don't be turned off by these land-based prospects. If regenerative landscaping is a passion of yours, get creative, build relationships with people, and find access to diverse landscapes throughout your community.

Question Your Motives

Get in touch with your true motivations and needs. Be honest with yourself—this way you can ensure you meet those goals and be happy that you did. If your motivation is regeneration at the highest scale, if your main priority is to restore ecosystem function, to do less harm in the process of implementation, and to work with natural and native ecologies and their repair mechanisms, then you will be operating at a different level. You will ask different questions; you will sacrifice speed for long-term regeneration and reduced ecological harm. This is an ideal scenario but a rare goal for most people.

We must consider how the work we do affects our lives and daily consumption. We may plant edibles over ornamentals to grow our own healthy, nutritious food and reduce our carbon footprint that way. Or, taking that concept to a new level, you might build an enormous regenerative agriculture farm, with thousands of acres dedicated to sequestering carbon, building soil, catching water, creating habitat, and feeding the populace. Everyone will approach the scale of regeneration differently, so know where it is that you're reaching toward. Be clear with yourself and honest about the materials you use and the energy consumption embodied in the project. Take the time to map out the potential gains over the years. A project may take a significant amount of energy to implement, but 10 years later, because of good design, its restorative qualities to the environment gain traction every year until the net positive gain of soil, water, and habitat far outweigh the initial consumptive energy costs.

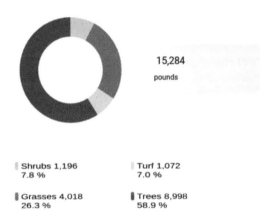

To offset the carbon emissions of a project, we sequester carbon through our planting systems. This Annual Carbon Sequestration Example was provided by BOND Landscape Calculator www.bondc6.com.

Long-Term Design

Designing for the long term is designing for regeneration. Developing a vision for the landscape that extends not months but years and—to a greater level—not years but decades or generations gets us closer to the primary goal of restoring and regenerating ecosystems. We live in a culture obsessed with short-term thinking and instant gratification, and it's important to recognize that part of your thinking is influenced by the dominant cultural paradigm.

Even in the high-paced version of regenerative landscaping found in the professional landscape and farm industry, there's still room for long-term thinking and long-term effects. Throughout your design process, see if you can keep the scale of the design, its impact on the environment, and the process of designing and installing the project in the most long-term scale imaginable. The more dedicated you are to this approach, the less harm you will inflict on the ecosystem.

Design Timeline

The scale and context of each project will always differ, but the deliverables you create can take the same amount of time regardless of the size or scale of the project. The keyword here is deliverables, trade speak for the curated or physical items a designer provides to a client.

You may be designing a landscape just for yourself or your community, but it is still helpful to think in these tangible terms. What exactly do you want to create with your design? Which kind of maps, graphics, layout schemes do you plan to produce? Getting clear on deliverables will help determine how long the design takes.

The tools and processes used in your landscape design also affect how long it takes to complete aspects of the design. Different types of deliverables will change the timeline and budget, which is why a well-planned design process is crucial. Skilled time management also aids in the estimation of project duration and budget for each phase of the project.

It's a mistake to rush a design project. There *are* situations when rushing a design is required, but that is far from ideal. It is equally problematic to have no timeline for your design process which signals to project stakeholders (and your subconscious) that the design is not a priority. With all that in mind, make sure to create a time frame and hold yourself accountable, while maintaining flexibility as a natural timeline materializes based on project context, constraints, and stakeholder actions.

AESTHETICS

In a strange paradox, building development has moved further from artistic expression, toward cheap efficiency, whereas landscape development focuses on aesthetics while sacrificing function. I understand why people want their landscapes to be beautiful. That's what I want too! But fostering natural beauty is easy. As a regenerative designer, we can integrate that beauty with ecological function.

The conventional focus on landscape aesthetics mirrors society's obsession with physical human beauty, always looking at the surface and never prioritizing what is within or the whole being. While aesthetics is a key part of design, in a regenerative landscape beauty comes through—and not at the expense of—function. We trust in the process of nature's inherent beauty to emerge with grandeur in the process of regeneration. The imagination of the designer is unlimited, but landscapes have constraints. We can always ensure that function and beauty are stacked together throughout every phase of the project. Trust that, focus on ecological yields, and let your creativity run wild within that context. Nothing will be more beautiful.

Another aesthetic issue is the conventional landscaping approach of overly clean maintenance. A tidy and well-kept garden isn't necessarily a problem, but this can become an ecological disaster. For example, in the fall when deciduous trees drop their leaves, landscape maintainers have an almost obsessive need to rake and blow all the leaves into tidy piles that are bagged and taken to waste disposal stations. This is a travesty as many insects, birds, and mammals use the downed leaves for overwintering. Fallen leaves also create a natural mulch, feeding fungi and soil microorganisms.[4]

Most often, subtle technique yields the greatest beauty. What is beauty if not the expression of emotions that rise to the surface when we experience what we find beautiful? You carry that sort of measuring tool inside your own heart. Chances are, if you design and build a landscape that feels beautiful to you, it will feel beautiful to others. That said, we all have different parameters for beauty, and we can't expect everyone to have the same experience. Be true to you, true to what the landscape tells you, and you won't go wrong.

CASE STUDY: THE PERMACULTURE NEIGHBORHOOD CENTER

The Permaculture Neighborhood Center is a 1/3-acre lot in a suburban neighborhood. It began as a parking lot and was transformed into a cohousing community, educational center, and food forest.

When my wife and I became stewards of this site, it had a huge asphalt area that covered much of the space along with a large compacted gravel zone. When it rained, water flowed down the asphalt and up against the house, damaging the foundation. As a seasoned ecological designer, I was able to look past the hardened surfaces to see great possibilities that awaited.

The more you attune to what's possible, the more you start looking at parking lots and other damaged lands not for what they are, but for what they can become. As you exercise this creative muscle and learn to see *beyond* the damage, you will instead see the full potential of restoration.

Responsibility, reciprocity, possibility . . . these were my mantras as I considered how to approach this project. Because the land was damaged and constricted, my first offering would be letting the soil breathe by removing the asphalt and concrete. If I could help this land heal, maybe it would gift us in the form of food and beauty. Below is how we did it one step at a time.

Step 1: Demolition

When the starting canvas is concrete, asphalt, or other hardscaping (all three on this project), the first action to take is often demolition and the removal of these hard, water-shedding surfaces. Removing materials in large quantities requires the use of equipment for lifting and breaking and trucks for hauling if the broken pieces can't be reused on-site.

In a small space like this, there wasn't much room to reuse all these materials. Taking much of it off-site was a decision driven by our context. We delivered these materials to a local landscape materials company to be ground up and reused as road base. Some concrete we kept on-site to be used for walls and stepping stones. Many quarries and landscape materials companies will take concrete, asphalt, and rock debris at no cost. Big energy may be required at the beginning of a project like this. Taking time to weigh all your options is crucial.

On this site, the impervious surfaces suffocated the soil, shedding water when it rained. When water can't infiltrate the soil, it can lead to a depletion of groundwater aquifers and intensified runoff patterns, producing flooding downslope. This kind of water runoff erodes soil and carries sediment and toxins from roads and agricultural lands into local waterways. The effect of runoff in our landscapes is devastating—it induces flooding in low-lying areas, fills waterways with sediment, and poisons whole watersheds.

(continued)

In this case, we removed the main runoff culprit—impervious asphalt and concrete. Now the land can breathe again, and the soil can absorb stormwater, recharging groundwater aquifers. After demolition, a very intense phase, we began the regeneration process.

Step 2: Managing Stormwater

Imagine if every unused asphalt lot you see, or every lonely lawn, could be transformed into an ecological oasis; this would change the world. Our vision for this site was to build an ecological food-producing forest. That starts with water.

Once the soil was free from its concrete prison, we got to work on water management. The lot had a slight slope to it heading to the main house located at the bottom. The long narrow lot was surrounded by nine neighboring houses, making for an immense amount of water runoff potential. Soil type always determines water infiltration capacity. With our sandy soils, we were able to catch and infiltrate over 400,000 gallons of water a year.

After a visit to the planning department, we discovered that, upslope from our project, there were two houses with a combined drainage system flowing into one large pipe that was trenched through our site and out into the storm drain. During our landscape installation, we cut into that pipe, placed a 6-inch valve, and opened all that water to the site for infiltration. That equated to nearly 200,000 gallons of water a year we let onto the property at the top of the slope. In large rain events or other emergencies, we could close the valve, sending the water to the storm drain and giving us great flexibility in times of need.

To achieve our goal of catching and infiltrating as much water as possible, the land needed shaping. Three large terraces, seven contoured ditches (swales), and three rain gardens (shallow basins) were installed. These earthworks provided ample areas to direct infiltrating water, while also supplying diverse zones with moist soils for planting.

We directed drainage from many neighbors' buildings, daylighting (releasing) the water into the infiltration structures of the landscape. By keeping the water on the land, we mitigated flooding, providing an important service for the whole neighborhood.

To add to our water security, we installed 4,500 gallons of water storage tanks to collect rain from the roof of the house.

Step 3: Designing Pathways

Once demolition and earthworks were complete, it was time to lay out pathways. The main pathway connected the series of terraces and multiple gathering areas (a covered patio and an outdoor eating area). Smaller pathways provided access to the orchards, greenhouse, perennial garden beds, veggie gardens, and children's play areas. To keep the project low budget and the carbon footprint small, all pathways on-site were covered in locally sourced wood chips.

Step 4: Building Soil Fertility

On this urban homestead, we tested the soil after demolition and discovered it needed a calcium and PH boost. We purchased oyster shell lime and rock dust and spread it across the landscape. We sowed cover crops over the site before the first winter to build organic matter and fix nitrogen into the soil using a mix of green manure plants like vetch, bell beans, favas, clovers, oats, and native wildflowers. After broadcasting the seed, we spread a light layer of straw on top to protect the seeds from birds.

Once the cover crop hit peak bloom the next spring, we slashed and left it in place. We then placed compost, cardboard, and wood chips (in that order) over all the planting and cover crop areas. This sheet mulch added nutrients and organic matter to the soil, creating an organic carbon sponge for planting.

Step 5: Outdoor Living

Outdoor living was a priority for us. We built a covered patio just off the back of the house for year-round enjoyment. The patio solved the drainage issue against the house at the same time. We sloped the patio at a 1 percent slope (1/8 inch per foot) away from the house's foundation, protecting it from further water damage. Surfaced with flagstone and complete with a wood-fired cob oven, bench, sink, counter, and cupboards, this all-weather space made for an incredible year-round place to gather with family, friends, and extended community. The cob oven became a central cultural hearth where neighbors, students, business staff, and community cookouts could assemble.

A large habitat pond was built the first summer as a haven for birds, damselflies, and pollinators. With our small lot and sandy soils, this pond had to be built using a 40-milliliter EPDM liner. Four feet deep in the center, with a waterfall and planted wetland, this water feature became a favorite place to relax and observe the seasons. Every year, a spectacle of hundreds of damselflies birthed from the pond over a short period of time. Once able to cruise the neighborhood, those damselflies spent their days eating insects, providing an important pest management service.

Step 6: Planting the Edible Forest

In one year, from asphalt demolition to project-wide planting, the site was transformed. We grew hundreds of pounds of food for our family and built habitats of all kinds for a diversity of wild organisms.

Over 80 fruit trees were planted along with fast-growing nitrogen-fixing trees. Among the growing edible forest, we planted herbs, flowers, and berries. On the north side of the house,

(continued)

we inoculated oak logs with shiitake mushroom spawn. Our food production systems were completed with a chicken coop and perimeter chicken run, which ran partly around the garden, giving our dozen chickens ample space to forage and roam.

Once a paved lot, now an edible paradise. The trees grew up, the fences were colonized by edibles, the pond grew lush, and the whole site became abundant with life and birdsong. This sanctuary became a destination where thousands of folks came for garden tours, educational classes, and parties, where the wonders of nature were celebrated and where families and communities grew and thrived together.

11
Permaculture Design Wisdom

As you move into the conceptual design process, the principle of designing relationships as opposed to elements needs to be kept at the front of your mind. At this phase, relationship design should be in full effect, locating elements relative to each other, as well as entities and energy flows such as sun, wind, and water to provide the container in which a design concept is developed. You are designing an ecosystem more than a landscape, an integrated part of the surrounding environment, developing interactions with the bioregion and the world. This holistic approach to design is one of the great benefits of a permaculture design approach.

If you are familiar with permaculture design, you will notice its influence throughout the pages of this book. Permaculture design heavily impacts my work in regenerative landscaping and my slant on life in general. As a design system, permaculture is primarily a principle-based approach to ecologically reintegrate human civilization within natural earth cycles. The permaculture design system was developed by Bill Mollison and David Holmgren, born from the following foundations.

- **A mutual benefit between humans and ecology.** This principle is foremost in permaculture, which recognizes that the true needs of humans and the needs of the earth are the same and are attained through mutually beneficial relationships. Human culture can be a force for regenerative stewardship of the environment when working within ecological constraints. Permaculture was developed with three core ethics to help guide our endeavors toward this goal. The three ethics are: care for earth, care for people, and reinvest surplus back into earth and people. This book shares dozens of ways to accomplish these ethics through the entire regenerative landscaping approach.

- **Techniques inspired by ancient and traditional knowledge.** Indigenous communities throughout the world are the primary inspiration for many permaculture practices being implemented today. While many of these techniques have taken on new names in modern society, the origins are rooted in the thousands of years of regenerative stewardship practiced by native cultures. Permaculture has sometimes come under criticism because many new permaculture teachers and practitioners don't acknowledge the Indigenous origins of their strategy and therefore present the work as if it's new. This results in an erasure of traditional knowledge and the native cultures still practicing them today.

- **The patterns and processes of the earth's wisdom.** As explored in part I of this book, earth's natural wisdom and its ability to create abundant living systems through catching and conserving energy are always primary models for the permaculture approach. Go for a hike, sit by a river, explore a desert canyon, and you will find inspiration for ecological landscape systems. Pattern recognition is a core practice of permaculture design and one that often gets overlooked by modern practitioners.

PERMACULTURE PRINCIPLES

Throughout this book, I have seeded principles of permaculture where they can best be integrated into aspects of your regenerative landscape. On the whole, there are anywhere from 12 to 30 principles, depending on who you ask and which permaculture lineage you are learning from. We are not exploring every one in depth here as they are embedded in the regenerative design principles found throughout the book. Several powerful design principles that enable you to develop energy efficient landscape designs are highlighted below.

Stacking Functions

When it comes to design efficiency and energy conservation, this brilliant approach inspires us to design relationships. When every element (pond, fence, patio) supports *multiple* functions, the landscape better functions as an ecosystem. In pristine natural environments you will always find each element or entity providing many functions to the whole. Our regenerative landscapes must work the same way.

This principle asks us to think outside the box about what's possible. For example, the pond on my homestead is more than a beautification project. Rainwater from our house flows into the pond, making it a water storage and catchment system. The pond is also a natural swimming pool for recreation and a habitat for a diversity of birds, amphibians, mammals, and insects. That's more than four functions "stacked" into the pond, linking it to the whole ecosystem through interactive relationship design.

Vertical Stacking

Landscapes are designed not only in the horizontal plane but also on the vertical plane. This is an often-overlooked aspect of landscape design. Look beyond just the ground or your sight line—look up. How can you use the vertical space to generate ecological and human yields or special features to give texture to the landscape? Beyond trees—an obvious choice for vertical design—consider architectural elements like trellises, fences, and buildings.

Planned Redundancy

When we are stacking functions, we make sure that every element supports many functions and use planned redundancy to ensure that every function is supported by multiple elements. If you study how ecosystems work, one of the brilliant features of earth's wisdom is that every functional need of the environment is supported in multiple ways. This is resilience in action. Every season brings new and different challenges; if the landscape is dependent on one water source, or one nutrient source, or one food source, the whole system could unravel if disaster or a seasonal change strikes and damages that singular source.

Throughout each layer of the design, make sure these redundancies are integrated into the system and have as many backup systems as you can imagine for every functional need to make sure the landscape, including the human community, has resilience to unexpected changes.

Optimize Edge and Ecotones

In design, we leverage the phenomenon of *edges* in nature to create an "edge effect." When two or more systems come together, the edges mix and create a new system called an ecotone. A forest and a meadow, a river and its earthen bank—at these ecotones, diversity thrives and biological productivity compounds. The more we harness the power of edges, the higher yields and greater diversity the landscape can manage.

Design for Catastrophe

Consider the potential catastrophes that might befall the landscape project. The climate, solar orientation, social and cultural patterns, and geography ensure that every site will have different risks. Fire, hurricane, drought, flood, pollution, angry neighbors—what are possible threats to the landscape you're creating? Your job as the designer is to prepare for these emergencies. Size systems for extreme events, develop energy and water backup systems (planned redundancy), and store resources for times of need.

Use On-site/Biological Resources

The resources you use in your landscape will determine a lot about your regenerative values. As described elsewhere, materials with high embodied energy costs like mined stone and plastic products are inherently degenerative to the planet. If you're going for the greatest integrity within ecological regeneration, these types of products should be avoided. Any natural product sourced from off-site will have its own embodied energy costs in the transport alone.

The best place to source materials for your landscape project is from the project site itself. This approach can lead to much creativity. For instance, if you need to build a retaining wall but don't want to incur the embodied energy costs of transporting stone from off-site, you might use logs harvested from the project to build your retaining walls or employ biological means of erosion control (such as a root mat planting system) instead of a wall. Investigate the resources available on-site at this very moment and determine whether they can provide solutions to design/build challenges. Think creatively about making use of whatever is present rather than purchasing new materials and transporting them to the project.

Catch and Store Energy

The cycling of energy is the cycling of life. For our landscapes to thrive, energy catchment and storage is at the heart of success. Catch and store water, catch and store sunlight, catch and store nutrients— all these forms of energy make up the fuel that powers life in ecosystems.

PERMACULTURE ZONING STRATEGY

There are five zones in permaculture, each zone representing areas of the landscape relative to the time it takes to manage the elements in each zone. This approach is about designing a landscape that conserves energy and accounts for the time management resources of the landscape stewards/maintainers. This is achieved by placing elements within zones based on their management intensity. First you must decipher the management needs and accessibility of each element and then place them into the respective zones.

- **Zone 1**. Elements that require daily maintenance or accessibility should be placed closest to the house (e.g., lettuce, strawberries, summer squash, outdoor eating, culinary herbs, egg production).
- **Zone 2**. Elements that require weekly maintenance or accessibility should be placed relatively close to the house (fruit trees, worm bins, wood stove or outdoor fire pit, medicinal herbs, berry patch, animals, workshop, etc.).
- **Zone 3**. Elements that require monthly maintenance or accessibility can be placed farther away (nut trees, winter squash, grain crops, ponds, windbreaks, coppice groves, compost pile, curing wood, etc.).
- **Zone 4**. Wilder places require only periodic tending (e.g., erosion control, forest thinning, grazing, control burns, wildcrafting).
- **Zone 5**. Pristine environments need interaction only through observation (backpacking, boating, hiking, camping, etc.).

Many traditional landscape and architectural approaches tend to overcomplicate the design, placing elements far away and disconnected from each other, prioritizing aesthetic over function. As regenerative designers, we thrive at the edges of function and beauty, always placing elements in relative location to each other and to the stewards of the land.

Using the zone planning approach, ensure that pathways are part of the zone layout. Pathways are the distribution networks that connect one zone to another. Path layout must be carefully considered during the zone planning phase as they can be considered zone 1 or zone 2 when designed with easy access in mind. Place elements that require more attention along the same path. That way, every time you walk that path, the management of these elements can be monitored and cared for as needed. If needy elements are placed haphazardly around the landscape or along a variety of different pathways, it is likely that many landscape maintenance needs or harvests will be missed.

PERMACULTURE AS A WAY OF LIFE

The design principles of permaculture have an impact far beyond the landscape, garden, and farm. Carry these principles (and the regenerative design principles of part I) into your life and your work. Everything from economy, education, and governance can be designed intentionally with ecological systems thinking, social and cultural regeneration, and a changing climate in mind. Though the problems of the world seem large, I still believe humanity can be a force for good when we apply the principles of regeneration to all our ways of life.

12
Drafting Design Plans

Depending on your goals and who the design is for, creating a draft design plan may or may not be imperative, but it is always advised. At my landscape design company, Permaculture Artisans, we always provide either a hand-drawn or computer-drafted plan that communicates the design concepts.

Communicating to Project Stakeholders

Remember, a project stakeholder could be a neighbor, a parent, a client, a friend, a family member, or a partner. Depending on the needs of project stakeholders, having a drafted plan may be necessary or not required at all.

If you've been mulling over problems such as privacy from neighbors, drainage issues, siting the vegetable garden, or placing an outdoor patio, having solutions mapped out on a plan can be an effective way to share your ideas with project stakeholders and make collective decisions.

DRAFTING THE PLAN

There are many options for drafting plans and the rest of this chapter will be devoted to introducing you to them. You will find a special focus on drafting by hand as that is the most readily available and timeless workflow for most readers.

Several kinds of illustrations and design renderings may be required for a project. Below are the most common types of illustrations needed for landscape projects and when you would need them.

Hand Drafting

For most of you, a hand-drafted plan will be sufficient for your project. Some of you are gifted artists and drafting a plan will be easy and beautiful. For others this can be an intimidating process. If you're like me, you struggle with drawing and that is perfectly fine. Even those without inherent drawing skills can learn enough to make usable concept plans. All you need is the right set of tools, a bit of practice, and a lot of patience. It's worth it—take the leap!

Step 1: Paper Size and Scale. This is the most important beginning step. If you get the size and scale correct, everything should stay in scale as your design plan develops and you add new features. First you must decide what area your design will encompass. The larger the area, the bigger distances the graphic scale will need to account for. Next, choose a paper size to start with. I highly suggest using a large sheet of paper that is no smaller than 11 by 17 inches and no bigger than 24 by 36. Make sure to use common paper sizes like these to make copying easier later.

You want your plan to be at scale. This means the distances between elements on the design plan reflect the actual distances on the project site. That way, when you draw out a beautiful

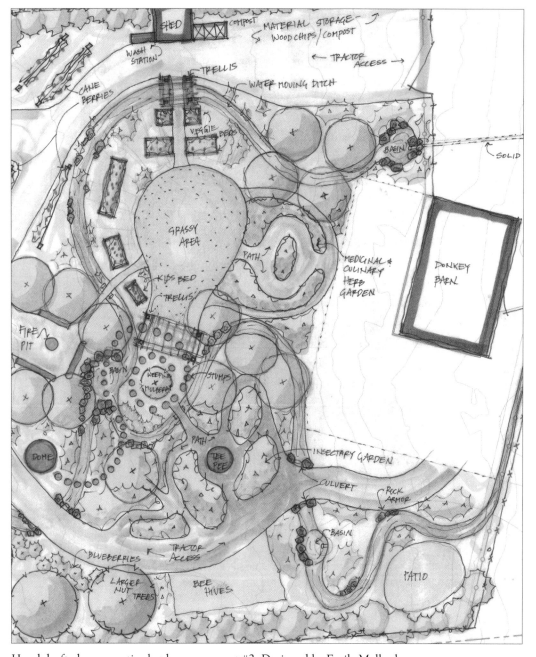

Hand-drafted regenerative landscape concept #2. Designed by Emily Mallard.

orchard on the plan, placing trees at 20-foot increments, the map will reflect the 20 feet of distance apart on the site. This goes for any design concept. A simple scale to use is 1 inch equals 10 feet. Every inch on the drafted plan, represents 10 feet of space on the real landscape. As you develop your design, use the scale for every element you place onto the map. If done correctly, when you or others install the landscape in the real world, the sizes and distances of landscape features will match up with the plan. (That's the goal though it doesn't always work perfectly as the map is not the territory, but taking the time to get it right is always valuable.)

Here are some common scales used in landscape architecture. 1:5, 1:10, 1:20, 1:50, 1:100, 1:200. The larger scales work better for bigger landscapes and farms and the reduced scales work better for smaller designs. For your purpose, the most important factor is whether the scale you're using allows you to fit the full landscape area onto the sheet of paper you have chosen. For instance, if you are designing a very large site, let's say 20 acres, then a scale that reads 1 inch equals 10 feet (1:10) would hardly fit even 1 acre on the page. For 10 acres, a 1:200 or even bigger would be a better choice. When you produce the drafted plan, *always* write the scale you used on the plan.

Once you have chosen a size sheet of paper, determined the project size, and selected a graphic scale you can move to the next step.

Step 2: Graphic Scale. A graphic scale is a physical scale placed on the original design that represents distance in feet (or meters). This way, whether you make the map bigger or smaller or print out a zoomed in section of the plan, folks reading the map can use the scale bar to orient themselves to the dimensions and distances represented on the map.

Step 3: Creating the Title Block. Every drafted plan must have a title block. This is a border around the design plan where important information is written.

At a minimum your title block needs to include:

- The job name/project title. Usually, the title of the project includes the last name of the project's owner. A plan for my home would be called "Ohlsen Homestead" unless I had another name for the homestead. If this is a farming project, a community garden, or a school garden, title the project appropriately by putting the name of the farm or organization in the title block. A subtitle can be added below the main title, such as "vegetable garden," "playground," or whatever the subject of the design might be.
- Always place a North arrow on the design. While some designers may put the North arrow on the map itself, it is more common and a better practice to place the North arrow in the title block. Designs are usually oriented to North, so the North arrow should be pointing up when reading the map.
- Include the scale that you're using in the title block as well as the scale bar.
- Place the initials or name of the designer/designers in the title block. At my design company, we also label each revision with the date the plan was revised and who did the revision.

- The title block is a good place to put any organizational logo(s) or contact information like website, phone number, and address of any businesses, municipalities, or organizations involved in the design.
- Other pertinent information like professional licensing, permit stamps, etc. can be added to the title block.

Step 4: Shapes and Lines. Readability and clarity should always be at the forefront of your goals for rendering a plan. How you use shapes, patterns, and line weights will aid or hinder your success in drafting a well-structured and understandable design plan.

- **Line Weights.** Line weights are the relative darkness or lightness of a line in the design plan. Use darker and lighter lines to engage the reader and create depth in the design plan. Line weight also helps with distinguishing landscape elements from each other (you can use different line weights to distinguish a fence line, a barn, and an existing tree). A common practice among design professionals is to use darker lines for elements closer in view and lighter lines for those farther away. In a plan view, a tall tree would have a darker line and a small shrub a lighter line. An elevational or detail drawing would use thicker lines for images in the foreground and lighter lines (weights) for elements in the background. You can also assign a thickness to specific elements like giving darker lines to buildings and roads and lighter lines for plant systems. Whatever line weight system you decide to use, make sure to *stay consistent* throughout the plan.

  During the drafting process have a variety of colored and gray pencils of different thicknesses on hand.

  You can also distinguish features by the type of line you use (solid, dashed, wavy, double, or single lines combined with hatch marks, and so forth). This is a quick and easy method for distinguishing the difference between a water line, a fence, an electrical line, and a pathway—any elements that extend across the landscape.

- **Hatching Marks.** Differentiating between a gravel pathway and a wood chipped pathway is a great example of where hatch marks shine in the drafting process. While both are pathways, they are designed with different materials and thus must be shown differently on your concept plan. Hatch marks can be used to represent many types of elements— buildings, grassy areas, waterways, berry patches, farming zones, and so on. If the concept plan does not require a detailed planting plan, hatch marks are a valuable tool for differentiating a diversity of plant species (color shading also serves this purpose).

  Hatch marks come in many different forms: spread out lines, crisscrossing lines, nets, dots, nearly any pattern will work. The best use of hatch marks is when they improve the readability of the map and accentuate notable elements. Utilize this technique sparingly, avoiding too many complicated patterns that make the map look busy and confusing, and you will get great results.

- **Symbols.** In the design world we use symbols for common elements like electrical boxes, irrigation valves, doors, specific kinds of trees—symbols for everything.

    One of the most important symbols to use as landscape designers are tree and plant symbols. Many regenerative landscape designs require a planting plan, and these elaborate plans get confusing.

    In a true planting plan, the designer needs to place *every* plant on the design map. This could include hundreds or thousands of plants representing the different sizes and shapes of species. Evergreen and deciduous trees are a great example. Placing these trees in a design plan needs to be well thought out as these trees have very distinctive growth habits. Contrasting symbols for each type of tree will help create a clear design plan.

    Luckily, there are stencils for many common symbols, including stencils for tree symbols with varying sizes and shapes to help you match the correct scale with the symbol when drawing the tree onto the plan. Stencils makes the task of drafting more expedient while the use of symbols in general provides better consistency throughout the design plan.

Step 5: Tracing the Design Concept. Now you're ready to create the actual design map. Everything described above should help you feel prepared for the task of drafting concepts. Once you have your space set and the drafting tools at the ready, tape the base map (discussed in part II) to your drafting desk. Over the base map, affix a large piece of vellum tracing paper with drafting tape.

Now trace the base map onto the tracing paper, including all the existing structures that will be kept in the design moving forward. Elements that will be removed can be left out of tracing at this time (for instance, if a fence is going to be removed and not replaced, don't trace it onto the new design).

From here you begin to draft your conceptual design plans in as much detail as appropriate. When creating the design, remember to draw on the tracing paper and retrace on new paper when needed.

Don't rush this part of the process. Let your creativity soar and have fun while drafting the landscape design concept. This part of the process can unveil new ideas as you integrate the context, goals, regenerative principles, imagination, and concepts into a whole systems design plan.

Step 6: Revisions and Drafts. In most cases, your first conceptual design will only be a rough draft. Get feedback on your plan once you have the first draft complete. Share the plan with other project stakeholders for their thoughts and/or go into the field and walk the land with the drafted plan in hand. Imagine how your current design concepts fit the land and mark up a *copy* of the map. Don't be afraid to completely change your design around if it's called for.

It's a lot of work to keep redrawing the plan, but it will always be better to revise until you have a concept that truly fits the context of the site, people, and goals you're trying to achieve. It's going to take multiple revisions to get there. If you accept this fact at the beginning, it will make the process much easier.

Your next version will be much better than the first and now you've had a chance to exhaust different ideas and gain feedback so you will be much closer to the mark now.

Once you get a second design drafted, repeat the whole feedback process again. This time, if you were listening clearly to the feedback the land and project stakeholders gave you, there will likely be less changes to make on the third go around. Because you are tracing each new layer using the hand drafted method, it will become easier and easier each time you retrace aspects of the design that are unchanging.

Step 7: From Analog to Digital. Presenting plans and printing out the final design require digitizing the plan. This is easily done through a scanner and a small bit of layout in an appropriate computer software. The minimum goal is to put the design into a format where it can be emailed and copies can be easily printed.

A more advanced process would include importing the scaled drawing into a program like Adobe Photoshop or Illustrator and adding design elements like color rendering, title blocks, and construction notes. A digitized design plan provides many options for sharing, working collaboratively online, and adding new layers going forward. Most landscape designers who use hand drafting to develop the original plan move to a digital format once the initial plan has been completed.

Digital Drafting

Computer-automated design is a game changer when it comes to drafting plans. At Permaculture Artisans we use the industry standard AutoCAD (a computer-automated design drafting software), enabling us to work seamlessly with engineers, architects, county governments, and other professionals. Software programs like AutoCAD are powerful and, for an ecological design company like ours, necessary. But this level is not necessary for most regenerative designers.

If you want to design on the computer but avoid the high price and learning curve of big programs like AutoCAD, there are several great alternatives, some free and many affordable. Do your own research and find one that fits your needs. Adobe Illustrator is a common favorite in landscape design for its many functions and great user friendliness.

With the onset of tablet computers and intelligent styluses, the design possibilities have evolved yet again. Drawing applications for tablet computers have gotten so good that some designers exclusively use these tools for design. The Procreate app on an Apple iPad using an Ipencil is a popular combination for high quality design drafting.

These digital tools, whether a tablet computer, AutoCAD on a desktop, or Illustrator on a laptop, all provide traditional design features such as line weights, hatch marks, line breaks, symbols, and annotation abilities—the same strategies are applied to both digital and hand-drawn methods.

Using Elevations

Labeling contour lines with elevation markers is an excellent practice for incorporating topographical data into concept plans. More important, adding elevation references to plans and construction details will aid the installation crews referring to your plans. Elevations tell designers and installers where a location is relative to sea level and other elements in the landscape.

Topographical maps label every 5 to 10 contour lines with an elevational number. Engineers and architects label the elevations of many, many points to ensure that installation is done correctly. The locations of building corners, grade changes from the top of a swale to bottom, pitch of a road, and all manner of detail are included in plans of this level. Most landscape design plans won't require that degree of detail, though it does make the building process more fluid. At a bare minimum, label two contour lines (or points) on your map with their elevational value to give designers and builders a reference to locate the elevations of everything else in the design.

With elevational data in hand, landscape builders will locate a point that corresponds to the map and mark it at the correct elevation. From there, laying out the landscape on-site and marking the placement of ponds, pathways, terraces, trees and so forth can commence. This leads to better precision as the design is translated from the map to the physical project site.

Detail Drawings

Detail drawings are advanced renderings of specific parts of a project, most useful for construction purposes. It could be a graywater system, the side view of a landscape when it's mature, or the detail of an irrigation box. This refined imagery aids not only in construction but also in communicating designs to project stakeholders, getting permits approved, and gaining funding for a project.

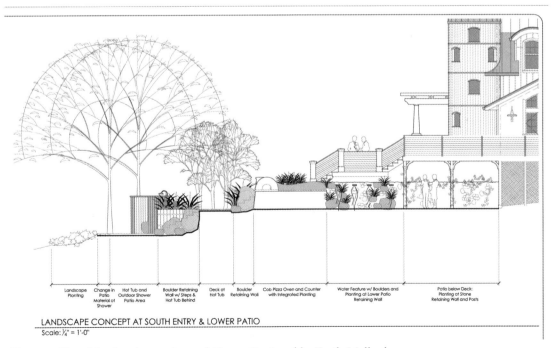

Elevation Detail for Landscape Around Home. Designed by Emily Mallard.

As you can see, detail drawings require another level of illustration skills beyond simple concept designs. If you possess skills like these or have a will to learn, knowing how to make these drawings could open many doors in the design world and greatly enhance your entire design process. Just remember, if you're being hired to develop detailed graphics for clients, these illustrations take time and will add to the overall design budget.

If making details like this is daunting for you (as it is for me) but still required for the project, then hire this phase out to a skilled illustrator. Only invest in detail drawings if it's necessary or helps you achieve a superior installation. Many landscape projects go over budget, so simplifying your overall process is generally productive and extra details may not be worth the investment of time and money.

Construction Drawings

Construction drawings are detailed drawings that include specific information to help installation crews build to the design specifications. This data often shows up in the form of measurements—the length and width of architectural elements, the quantity and type of plants, the volume of compost to be applied, the volume of soil to be excavated, aesthetics, and more. Orientation of elements and details about the transitional zones are all aspects of a design that may require specific information for construction.

Moving from design concepts into the installation phase is exciting and sometimes scary. This is when you face the biggest risk of something going wrong. Construction drawings and their accompanying set of notes are here to help ensure that design concepts keep their integrity during installation. Construction notes provide a detailed narrative for how the work is to be completed and are sometimes written on a separate sheet of paper with labels that correspond to drawings and other notes included on the construction drawing.

(Note: Even when it comes to construction details, the map is not the territory. It is common that small to large adjustments must be made in the field to adapt to new information or problems discovered during the building process. Don't be alarmed if this happens. Do the best you can by providing as much detail as possible to guide the process, while assuming some changes will occur in the field.)

Color Versus Black-and-White Renderings

Because adding color to designs is expensive to render in print, the majority of landscape design and construction graphics are developed in black and white. Black and white is sufficient for construction drawings and general design concepts but there is a case to be made for colored designs.

Because a color rendering of a landscape design is beautiful, it can be a powerful tool for inspiring project stakeholders. If you are a professional landscaper looking to win a big contract, a color rendering will almost always be more impressive to the client. Color helps communicate function, texture, and flow better than black and white.

When working with schools and municipalities, I always default to colored designs. Generally, we need to win the approval of administrative staff, city council members, and other decision-making stakeholders. The more information that can be provided by the design, the more beautiful the design's aesthetic, the more likely the project will gain approval.

If you choose to go with color, make sure you create a black-and-white design first. Save and copy that version in case you need to go back later to make changes (it's easier to make changes in black and white) or a black-and-white image is required for some reason.

PROFESSIONAL DESIGN TIPS WITH EMILY MALLARD

For several years, I had the pleasure of working with an incredible landscape designer named Emily Mallard. As a designer and trained landscape architect, she brought a high level of artistic talent, professionalism, and well-developed design skills that helped put my landscape company, Permaculture Artisans, on the map.

Over the years, Emily and I developed a joyful and effective process of working together on designs. Emily had several skills that I was never able to master, making our collaborations all the richer. One of Emily's specialties is making designs come to life during the conceptual drafting and planning phase.

I asked if she could provide some tips and best practices. Here is some advice from Emily Mallard for developing your own conceptual design plan.

Understand Project Stakeholders. Emily's project stakeholders are normally clients. She puts great emphasis on understanding not only their goals and visions but also who they are and their relationships with each other. Her designs of pathways, planting areas, and various outdoor spaces reflect the human needs and patterns of her clients both as individuals and as family units. I find this lens inspiring as it looks at the whole context of the project including the human element.

Starting a New Landscape Concept. As discussed elsewhere in the book, knowing where to begin designing can be intimidating. Of course you start with context, reading the land, and observation. But from there, developing a conceptual plan can lead to paralysis by analysis.

For Emily, the initial drafted sketch is the part of the site analysis that kicks off the whole design process. She has a simple and powerful way to begin her design concepts: She always starts with laying out pathways and waterways, these being the core circulation and flow systems of the landscape. Pathways facilitate how humans move through the space, which promotes ongoing management and relationships. These generally have starting and ending points that make practical sense and, in some cases, are already decided as part of existing infrastructure.

Water is a force that requires humility and respect. As such, how water is moved in the landscape is required at the beginning of any design phase to create the bones (structure)

(continued)

of the landscape. Once pathways and waterways are clearly positioned, Emily then begins to place new elements like orchards, ponds, vegetable gardens, rock walls, and so on in the remaining spaces. She says this method often primes the design to *self-create* once path and water flows have been determined.

A clear idea of the desired landscape aesthetic clients are hoping for is encompassed in this first phase of the design process. Emily initially lumps aesthetics into two categories, contemporary (clean lines), or natural (organic wavy lines). With these broad aesthetic parameters clarified, she begins the design.

Hand-Drafted Revisions. When it comes to hand-drafting design concepts Emily has some important advice for you. First off, tracing paper is your friend. When you develop your concept, you start with your base map, then place a piece of tracing paper over the top using drafting tape. Then sketch out (in dark ink, Sharpie) the existing elements that are staying. This could be a house, a driveway, a road, a wall, a water tank, any existing element that will not be removed as part of the design and installation process gets traced in dark ink.

Once this layer is down, she will begin adding design concepts. When adding new elements, she uses colored erasable pencils. Color helps to differentiate aspects of the design like water systems, pathways, planting areas, and gathering zones. As she works through her process, she usually doesn't erase ideas that require change. Instead she retraces the entire plan multiple times before a presentable draft is complete. For Emily, this part of the process is crucial for the design plan to unfold. I asked her why her practice involved always adding new sheets of trace rather than erasing previous layers and starting over on the same sheet. Her response was brilliant. You never know when an idea has merit. By erasing her first concepts, she might be throwing away a usable idea that will make sense later.

As her process evolves, she may go back to older versions and incorporate aspects of those into the final plan. Once she has drawn a few rough concepts, she begins to make solid decisions about landscape elements and placement. Her final phase of developing the initial concept plan is to retrace the whole plan with all the best elements and concepts woven together. At this point she will scan the design plan and import into Photoshop (any similar application will do) to add a title block, a North arrow and scale bar—all critical information that needs to be on every finished design plan. One important note: Though every project is different, Emily suggests a scale of 1inch = 10 feet for most suburban and urban projects.

But this is still only the beginning. Presenting the plan to clients and gaining feedback is next. She always brings two hard copies of the plan to the design presentation so new ideas and constructive feedback can be drawn directly on one of the maps with red ink in front of clients. Emily says this helps clients see that she is capturing their design feedback. She purposely presents a slightly rough version of the design concept during the first presentation to make clients feel more comfortable making changes. She says that a fully polished first draft design can be intimidating to project stakeholders and could lead to a shutdown of authentic feedback from these clients. Also, keeping the first draft rough keeps her from spending too much time perfecting a plan that will ultimately change—possibly drastically.

The unmarked copy of the plan is given to the clients to keep and mull over after the meeting has ended. Emily waits a week or two before incorporating revisions as her hard-won experience has shown her that clients will often have new ideas or change previous feedback once they have had a couple weeks to think about the design. This is the sort of advice you can only get from those with vast experience! After checking in with clients a final time to make sure no further changes are to be made, *then* Emily will revise the design incorporating all client feedback.

The hard copy of the design plan with redlined feedback becomes the basis for this next revision phase. In this step she takes another fresh sheet of trace and redraws the plan *again*, incorporating all the feedback.

She then repeats the process of printing out hard copies of the plan, presenting to clients, and receiving feedback. As you can imagine, there's a lot of work involved in redoing the design and retracing the steps, but the benefits are enormous. The "final" plan will reflect all the hard work, stakeholder feedback, and design solutions developed throughout the process.

The Benefits of Computer Drafting. For most of her projects, Emily uses AutoCAD computer software for landscape design. This software can take six months to a year or more to learn, but Emily stands by its effectiveness. She explains that making revisions on a digital plan is quick and easy compared to a hand-drafted plan where retracing the entire design is required. With computer design software, deleting and reworking sections of a plan is done specifically to features that require a change without having to redo the entire plan.

In addition, digital software like AutoCAD embeds distance and length into the design plan. When it comes to estimating or building a project, takeoffs (measurements/volumes derived from the design plan) from digital design software can save dozens of hours of time calculating the exact sizes and volumes of landscape elements. Finally, the ability to click layers on and off is a huge advantage when presenting specific aspects of design to clients.

Emily had this to say about the more popular design programs: AutoCAD is the most precise, making it the best fit for professionals. Adobe Illustrator is the most user-friendly, making it a good starting point for hobby designers, do-it-yourselfers, and novices. Sketchup is useful for taking a digital file in and rendering it in 3D. Many digital design programs exist and will work well for your landscape design projects. Talk to local professionals to see what they use, and make sure that whatever program you are using "talks" to programs used by colleagues, local professionals, and project stakeholders.

(continued)

> **The Impermanence of Design.** To be a landscaper designer is to maintain flexibility in how a design is eventually constructed. By the time a landscape design is implemented, Emily may no longer be on the project or she may be kept on as a consultant during the installation, as is typical in the landscape industry. She has learned to accept this part of the process. As you know from elsewhere in this book, the design is not the territory, and concepts and ideas are always in a state of change. This means that decisions will be made in the field that will change the design once building begins. This is to be expected and requires a level of humility in designers who aren't also building the landscape. To work with landscapes is to accept that everything is continuously changing in unending succession forever—a practical rule for all aspects of life.

Taking Feedback

People will critique your designs as they do any form of art. Some comments will have merit and some will make no sense at all. In all cases, stay open to receiving feedback. During this part of the process, your mistakes and strengths will be revealed, giving you a chance to fix issues before additional time and money is spent on the project—this is always a good thing. If you are a professional delivering designs to clients, this will be especially valuable to you. If you are not a professional, the issues raised from receiving feedback are still important. Don't let your ego get in the way of improving your final design.

Finalizing Your Master Plan

After presenting a revised design plan and incorporating feedback from project stakeholders, you now move toward finalizing the master plan—the final agreed-upon plan that will be used during installation. It's important to note that the design is *never* complete. We may develop a finalized master plan and use this for installation, but as we know, changes will always be made in the field. New information and situations will arise, needs and goals will change, and the ecology will continue to cycle and evolve in unexpected ways.

Keep this in mind throughout the entire process of design, building, and management. Still, arriving at a "final" master plan is a moment to be celebrated. This occurs *after* the final presentation of the revised concepts, incorporates all previous feedback and new information, and should be close to a complete plan.

13
Design Plan Sets

Big projects may require an extensive variety of design deliverables. Put together, these are often called plan sets, and they include many layers, details, and notes about the project. A plan set is different from a general concept plan because it contains different design layers meant to guide installation. Every layer represents a different aspect of the project—the planting plan, the hardscaping plan, a utilities plan—each represented by its own design sketch with construction details.

Conceptual Master Plan

Much of this book is devoted to teaching you how to create a conceptual master plan. This is a general design of the entire scope of the landscape that includes everything possible (earthworks, water features, pathways, planting areas, built structures, etc.) integrated into a single design graphic. This is the best possible tool to use in landscape design; however, many of the details for each layer are left out of conceptual master plans as they would become confusing and cumbersome.

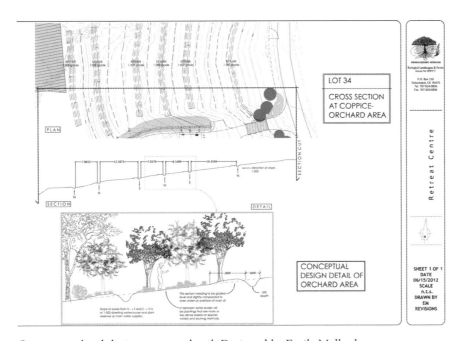

Contour orchard design concept detail. Designed by Emily Mallard.

Planting Plan

A true planting plan represents a design graphic with every plant placed in its location and quantity on the map. Existing trees and plants may be included, but the most important aspect of a planting plan is that it guides the people installing plants through the full layout of the entire planting system. A conceptual master plan generally doesn't go into this level of detail. A concept plan will often have areas of use labeled such as "food forest" or "vegetable garden" but without labeling each individual plant. There is a middle ground, and some plant labeling can be incorporated into a master plan strategically, especially larger shrubs and tree species.

A planting plan delivers a high level of detail and assists landscape builders in creating a budget for acquiring the needed plants.

Utilities Plan

Utilities include electrical, water, septic/sewer, telephone, internet, and so on. With few exceptions, utilities are buried in the ground. If additional utilities need to be installed for the landscape project, you will need a utilities plan to show where trenches must be excavated and where manifolds and terminal boxes should be placed.

Utility plans show all existing utilities (discovered during your site assessment process) and any new suggested utilities. Construction notes are added to the plan when appropriate, including notes about where protective fencing is needed to ensure special trees and other landscape features are not disturbed during the digging and backfilling of utility trenches. Landscapes need to be protected when contractors bring out equipment. Too many ecosystems have suffered from an equipment operator unknowingly digging through the roots of an old tree, compacting a freshwater spring, or scraping off rare native grasses.

Digging trenches for utilities is especially dangerous because there is potential for severing existing utilities, leading to expensive repair costs, safety hazards (cutting a gas line), and even death (cutting an electric main).

A utility plan should consider both safety measures and installation efficiency. When laying out the placement of a trench, consider the disturbance of soil and plant communities and what the use of that zone will be after trenching is complete. Even before the first bucket of soil is excavated, you can see how many reasons there are to have a well-thought-out utility plan.

Irrigation Plan

Irrigation plans are commonly added to utility plans but can also be treated as a standalone layer in plan sets, separating the landscape into irrigation zones—planting areas watered by the same irrigation valve or designated by plant functions (vegetable garden, windbreak, native planting). It is common to place plants that require similar irrigation needs in the same zone.

In addition to irrigation zones, an irrigation plan will call out where standpipes (hose bibs), irrigation manifolds, filters, and surface-installed drip lines will be placed. If the water system is gravity fed, air vents and water tanks will also be added to the plan. Since irrigation systems are so expensive to install, taking the time to lay out a detailed plan will help you make budget, design, and installation decisions.

Hardscape Plan

Hardscaping is a general term used for permanent infrastructure like hardened walkways, decks, patios, walls, pools, and foundations and architectural elements like trellises, gazebos, and outbuildings.

A dedicated hardscape plan will be used as a tool for installation and, because hardscapes are usually the most expensive aspect of a project, detailed plans are necessary. When building a rock wall, flagstone patio, or a deck off the back of the house, many costly factors come into play. The materials for these built elements are generally large, heavy, and expensive. Truck deliveries, equipment rentals, and equipment access all become necessary additions to the project budget.

A hardscape plan represents the size of hardscapes, the volume of material required, and sometimes construction notes.

Demolition Plan

The first phase on most projects is demolition, where elements of existing landscapes need to be changed, deconstructed, or removed. Once the demolition phase is over, the new landscape is constructed.

A demolition plan details which parts of the existing landscape need to be removed or changed. On the plan itself, details can be included such as how the demolition is to be executed, equipment access, routes for taking material on and off the landscape, and interim staging of materials. It is also helpful to include protected areas demolition technicians need to avoid during the process like trees, sensitive neighbors, and other areas of concern.

Staging

Identify staging areas for tools, equipment, and materials placed prior to or during installation. Consider how to keep access flows open and support the coming and going of deliveries.

This part of the process is not generally its own layer on a plan set. I have singled it out here because of its importance. Strategic project staging is a layer that can be added to many of the other plan sets. Demolition (especially), hardscaping, and grading—all these layers require the movement of significant amounts of materials and possibly equipment. Providing notes about access, staging, and deliveries is crucial information that benefits many layers of a landscape plan set.

Grading and Drainage Plan

Grading and drainage is one of the more important layers in a plan set. This part of the process is frequently the first activity to take place when building a landscape, so the demolition phase is typically added to the grading plan.

Making mistakes during grading and earthworks could lead to catastrophic consequences in the landscape. Water and erosion are powerful forces that renew and destroy ecosystems and, as regenerative landscapers, we have a specific approach to managing water ecologically. These regenerative water solutions are presented in the grading and drainage plan. If the project requires earthworks—moving and grading the earth for pathways, ponds, terraces, roads, and structures—all that earth moving is revealed on this layer of the plan.

In addition, any drainage systems—drain inlets, french drains, culverts, downspouts—are included on this layer. Civil engineers essentially create grading and drainage plans as a main deliverable provided to clients. In this book, you won't become a civil engineer, but if you read carefully and implement the practices provided, you can become a confident water designer over time. In fact, while there are a lot of civil engineers I love, I've met just as many who are stuck in an old paradigm of water management that dehydrates and destroys ecosystems. That is why you, as an aspiring or experienced regenerative designer, are so needed in this world.

14
Phased Project Plan

A serious landscape designer will develop a phasing plan for the development of the project. Practically speaking, the phasing plan is a perfect time to estimate labor, materials, and financial budgets. But this approach also acknowledges that a reciprocal and regenerative relationship with the landscape—a living organism—must be done over the cycles and seasons. Combine reciprocal relationships with practical planning and you have a powerful tool for regeneration.

A phasing plan that begins during the conceptual design phase will set the project up for success when implementation on the ground begins. Developing the phase plan is a visioning and exploration exercise filled with ideas, hopes, and dreams. Create a plan that includes a long enough scope—one year, three years, five years, or longer is ideal.

Following are some patterns to look for while you are creating the phased project plan.

Schedule Changes

As you produce the forecasted landscape design and implementation schedule, accept that any schedule you make will have to be flexible. As the project moves forward, *changes will occur*. A project schedule is not set in stone but rather a guide that fuels project momentum and gives project stakeholders the ability to plan for the future.

Phase Abandonment

Phased landscape plans will look quite different halfway through the process than at the beginning, and the final plan will have evolved even more by the end. Design and building milestones will be placed on the schedule at the beginning, but as the work gets underway, expect that some parts of the plan will be abandoned altogether. Budget constraints and other issues will emerge, and when they do, resources will be redirected to higher priority aspects of the project. Sometimes we have to cut our losses, like cutting the end of a tree branch that is too heavy and threatens to drag the entire tree over.

Sequencing

Sequencing—the way you will move from one phase or project to another—is one of the most important features of a phasing plan. For example, we almost always perform the grading and earthworks in the landscape before the planting phase. This ensures that the final soil levels are graded prior to placing roots in the ground so that plants aren't disturbed.

Sequencing a project (as shown in the Gantt chart below) happens from the macro-level patterns to micro-level details. Deciding that earthworks come before planting is a macro-level pattern, and all the smaller steps during the implementation of the earthworks are examples of micro-level sequencing.

For instance, sequencing earthworks might include waiting for the correct season, accessing equipment, identifying areas that need protection from machines, and deciding where to begin to cause the least amount of damage during the process. Because this is a regenerative landscape, with the goal of decreasing harm to ecosystems and increasing ecological yields, there will be many factors to contemplate.

Appropriate sequencing of the project empowers you to identify needs for immediate landscape management while you plan for more extensive later phases. While it takes time to design and implement earthworks, build a greenhouse, or decide the placement of a pond, in the meantime you can put up birdhouses, create native bee habitats, sow appropriate cover crops, or bring in chickens, bringing in ecological yields without getting in the way of bigger picture design and landscape development. There is no reason to wait to take positive actions for the restoration of the land as long as you understand the context. Activities that build ecological resilience without causing harm or wasting resources should be implemented and celebrated.

CREATING A PROJECT SCHEDULE

Creating a project schedule will aid you in seeing the distinctive parts of the project starting now and casting forward into the future. Think of it as a puzzle you create and then solve.

The best tool for creating a project schedule is a Gantt chart (see the example below). This brilliant scheduling tool provides a template for complete project planning.

The Gantt chart is a type of calendar or spreadsheet where you sequence project phases—design, water/soil testing, earthworks, water system implementation, agricultural activities, and every other phase that fits the project timeline. Break up phases into categories using common sense and driven by the project's context.

Estimated Duration

Estimate how long each phase will take. At the beginning, your estimate will be off, but as phases of the project are completed and you begin to prioritize future phases, you can adjust the duration of each phase to fit the most accurate estimate.

Time of Year

When developing the project schedule, placing phases into the appropriate season—a foundational principle of regenerative landscaping—is an easy first step.

Budgeted Labor/Materials

Phase planning is also a budgeting activity. Begin to assign labor and material costs for each phase in the plan. Estimated duration ties in directly with projected labor costs. If an overall budget already exists for the project, assigning costs to scheduled phases is crucial. You'll quickly get a sense of how far the budget will go and can begin cutting less realistic activities from the Gantt chart.

Sequencing (Critical Path)

The *critical path*, in trade jargon, is the fastest path to reach a project's completion. Placing each activity in the correct order on the Gantt chart will give you a vision of the whole project. This shows you how to prioritize which phases need immediate attention and which elements can wait.

USING A GANTT CHART

Gantt charts offer even more detailed options to aid overall planning and project estimating. For making the actual Gantt chart, many templates and software programs exist online. Feel free to use the examples in this chapter as a starting point to create your own Gantt chart using

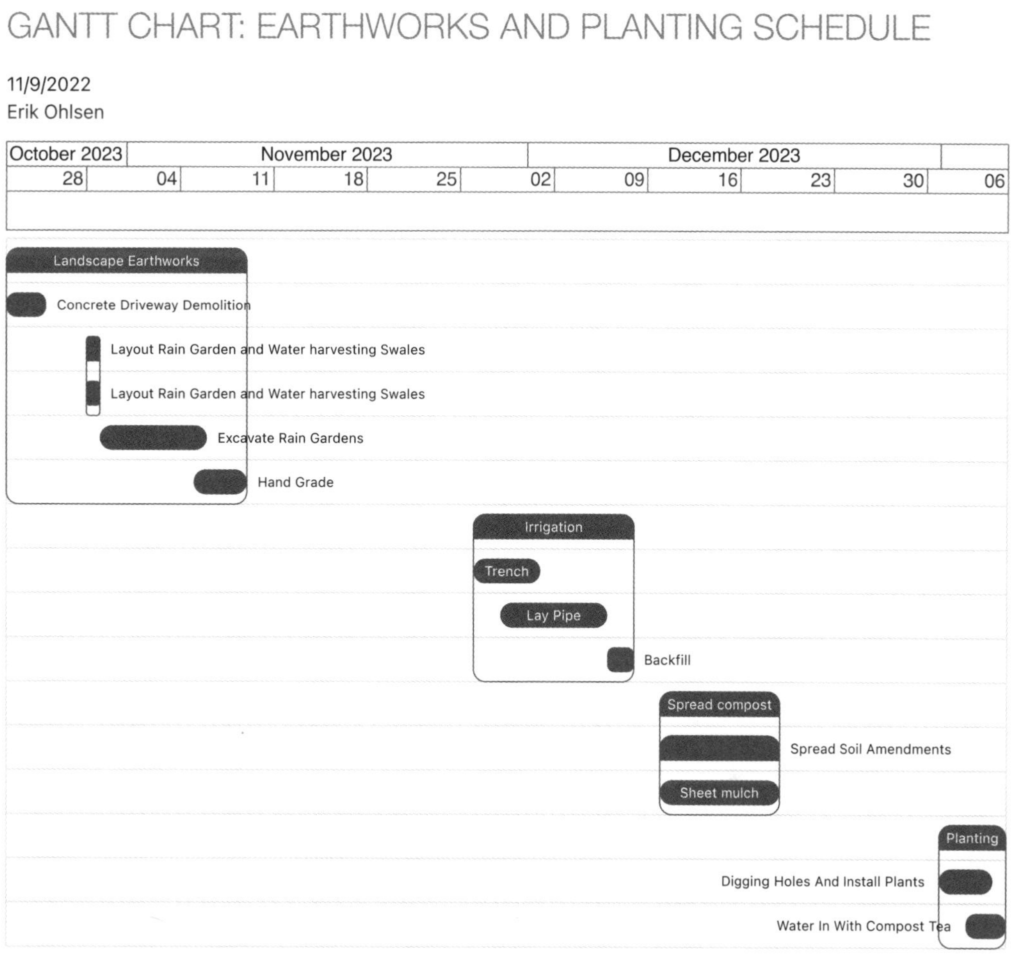

GANTT CHART: EARTHWORKS AND PLANTING SCHEDULE

11/9/2022
Erik Ohlsen

October 2023			November 2023				December 2023				
28	04		11	18		25	02	09	16	23	30	06

Landscape Earthworks
- Concrete Driveway Demolition
- Layout Rain Garden and Water harvesting Swales
- Layout Rain Garden and Water harvesting Swales
- Excavate Rain Gardens
- Hand Grade

Irrigation
- Trench
- Lay Pipe
- Backfill

- Spread compost
- Spread Soil Amendments
- Sheet mulch

Planting
- Digging Holes And Install Plants
- Water In With Compost Tea

A simple Gantt Chart Example. These can be as complicated or as simple as you make them.

a simple spreadsheet program. Some software programs integrate Gantt charts with budgeting software and other professional business tools. I use a stand-alone software program on a tablet computer.

With so many options, it's helpful to know what to look for. Following is a series of the common components included in a Gantt chart.

Using the basic **Calendar** function of the Gantt chart allows you to place project phases by dates and times. Use **Titles** to categorize action items and project phases. Most Gantt charts allow you to categorize and subcategorize as many times as needed. A Planting Plan category can be added and then broken into smaller steps of site preparation, planting, irrigating, mulching, and so on. Consider the **Duration** of each step. Does an action item take one day, one week, or one month? Whatever the projected duration is, give that value to the action item on the Gantt chart. Factor in **Cost** and a projected cost value to each action item. You can also **Assign Workers** in your Gantt chart, assigning people to action items and phases to keep everyone's responsibilities organized and in one place. Develop **Task Lists** for each action item or each day. The Gantt chart allows you to constantly break down phases, actions, and tasks. Remember your **Critical Path** when developing the appropriate sequence for the project. If you're a professional, Gantt charts also include **Projected Profits**, as well as **Progress Reports** on updated charts to communicate the current state of a project to stakeholders. Because large Gantt charts can be difficult to print when data is laid out in wide formats, many Gantt chart programs offer the ability to export Gantt Charts into PDFs, JPEGs, and other formats to enable easy sharing and presenting to project stakeholders.

Project Choreographer

A phased project-planning process puts you at the center of the flow of information, progress, and activity of a project. In this way, you become a choreographer of the process of regeneration. Here you pull the threads from each phase, each element, and each entity, weaving them into a harmonious chorus of interdependence through cycles and seasons. This level of planning during the design process is highly professional, practical, and keeps projects on the path towards creation. The sooner you engage a phased approach, the sooner you will focus on the best next step to take.

15
Professional Design Relationships

Readers of this book fall into many categories. Some of you are do-it-yourselfers, others are landscape professionals providing services, and still others are enthusiastic regenerative-minded folks looking for support in creating their own ecological paradise—in other words, potential landscape design clients.

I've been a professional landscape designer since the year 2000. From my vantage point, I understand the risks, rewards, and challenges of providing services to clients. On the other hand, I've also been a client, and I've coached others who are clients navigating a process with a professional landscape designer. The goal for this chapter is to provide clarity and support for all perspectives of this equation. The relationships between landscape professionals and their clients can be beautiful but can also turn ugly. Here we will go through key aspects of this professional relationship that can help all project stakeholders work together to meet budgets, goals, and core values.

DEVELOPING A DESIGN BUDGET AND IDENTIFYING DELIVERABLES

Relationships based on the exchange of money have inherent tension from the get-go. As a client, you only have so much to spend, so you want to get a professional service and not get ripped off. As a professional landscaper, you want to provide a beautiful service for your client, get paid for the time you spend on a project, and meet the financial obligations of running your business.

These are the two points of view that need to match for the professional relationship to be successful—not everybody is a good match for each other. Some relationships between a client and a professional will not end well. Go back to your core values (discussed in part II) to help guide your decision-making when it comes to entering professional design contracts. The more disciplined you are in implementing your core values, the less likely you will enter poor relationships.

Entering a design contract requires agreements. All parties must agree on the terms of the contract, the budget, and the time it will take to complete the work. This is tricky because nine out of ten times the cost of professional design services is shocking to clients. Experienced regenerative designers have spent years studying and apprenticing to gain their specialized skills and thus charge for their time accordingly. The professional landscape design process also takes an enormous amount of time, much of it invisible and unknown to most clients.

Talking about money—it's never easy, but it is the key conversation to have before agreeing to work together. As a designer, you need to develop a sense of what it takes you to create deliverables, the end products you provide your clients for services rendered. This could be conceptual design plans, consultation notes, project management, and so forth. Clients, on the other hand, need to have a strong sense of what they're after. As a client, you need to decide if a fancy color rendered design is necessary or if a well-designed black-and-white plan will do, understanding that higher quality maps, graphics, and design plan sets are going to cost more and—since many of these services are highly specialized—the costs won't be cheap.

Part of the designer's role in the relationship is to coach clients toward clarity about their project's context and what kinds of deliverables they need, and to help the client develop a plan that will meet their goals and budget. In business they say, "you get what you pay for," and that certainly rings true much of the time. But just as often people end up paying far more than they need to, making clear communication and a deep understanding of the end goal parts of the process that can't be skipped.

Once these conversations have been had and everyone is on the same page, agreements and contracts are made, including how payments and client deliverables will be processed. Frequently, a designer requires an upfront deposit to get going on the project with a payment schedule moving forward.

Beyond an upfront deposit, I caution designers against charging clients for time worked without providing design deliverables (even early drafted plans are enough). Clients truly appreciate being kept in the loop around the progress of a design plan when paying for the last round of work. If you're going to charge them, you should demonstrate corresponding progress.

The best (and most regenerative) landscape designs take time to create. There is an endless amount of context, data, and knowledge required to understand any landscape or community context. The more time that is allotted, the better the design will be. I also understand that clients need to see action and have specific goals with specific timelines. Finding that sweet spot, where the client accepts a longer process but the landscape designer adheres to tight deadlines, is the best possible scenario.

Color designs, black-and-white, hand-drafted or computer-generated detail drawings, construction notes, and plan sets—these are all significant deliverables that are best decided upon during the contract negotiation. Any moderate scale design requires a minimum of six weeks. For very large projects, years of design work could be required.

Meetings

I find meetings to be the number one gray area when it comes to managing design contracts. Every project is unique, and the frequency and duration of meetings varies wildly. Time spent walking the site, having phone conversations, and sitting down together can quickly add up. You may end up shocked to find that you spent half of the design budget on meetings, and this will cause problems. As the designer, it will be difficult to charge the client for all the time spent if you know the budget is tight and completing the design with the remaining budget is

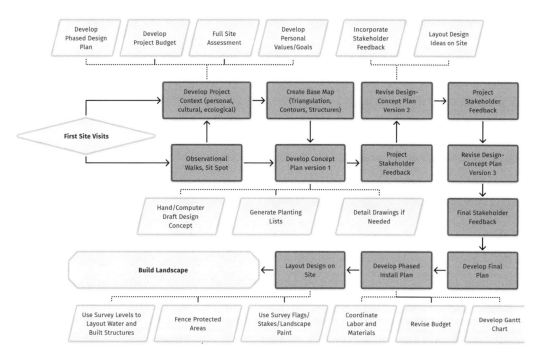

Professional Conceptual Design Process.

impossible. On the other hand, clients want to feel held in the process through meetings where they can ask questions and gain clarity.

There's no one solution for this problem of budgeting for meetings and communication. Building relationships with each other is important, and the best designers won't charge for every minute they spend with a client. The best designers also won't let a project get out of control when client communication needs begin to sink the design budget.

After experiencing this issue firsthand over many years, I developed a hybrid process where specific meetings are included in the budget (design presentations, site analysis, presentation of final design); I charge extra for the time and materials of any additional meetings beyond that. This means that we provide a budget for the minimum meetings necessary and are open to spending more time together if the client knows they will be charged for that time. That said, I always spend time with clients that I don't charge for because relationships are important to me, and I enjoy investing in my clients.

When you're the client, find that balance between making sure your needs for communication are met without taking advantage of the designer's time by sending endless emails and scheduling unnecessary multihour meetings. Expect to be charged for long meetings and return visits if you decide to change your goals around a project.

Project Parameters

The importance of deciding the parameters of a project, both in the size/area of the design and the scope of time, cannot be overstated. Whether client or designer, always use your personal context, your core values, and your goals to guide this process. What is the design really, truly asking for?

The *size and area* of the design. An overall project may take place on a five-acre site, but the project itself only happens around the house. Or does it? The area in question should be decided upon by looking through a few contextual layers. What are the immediate goals of a client, what is the design budget, and what other parameters impact the scope? Answers to these questions will help choose the correct scale of the project.

Next, clarify the *scope of time*. This one is a bit tricky. As regenerative designers we always design in multigenerational time frames. Our job is to bridge the landscape's past with its multigenerational future. For instance, we can build terrace walls and plant trees that live thousands of years but, in the modern-day economy, most projects won't fit that sort of time scale. As clients get clarity on their goals and budgets, you will decide how quickly the project will be built. Even tiny projects can be so highly detailed and designed that they take months or years to build. How fast is fast enough to get a project designed and built? Most clients don't want to wait years—life is short, children grow, and they want their regenerative landscapes as soon as possible to raise their families and enjoy life close to the land. The question is, how regenerative is the process if it is rushed?

How will this landscape get built? Is there a budget for building, or are clients building the project themselves? These conversations should be had prior to the landscape design phase.

I've seen it dozens of times. I'm hired to build a landscape for someone, stepping into their dream, listening to their hopes, and taking on the endeavor of manifesting it all. They love the design process, they love the design, but when it comes time to build, a huge discrepancy materializes. The incredible design that the client loves will cost tens of thousands of dollars more than the client can pay. Or money is not the issue, but it will take too long.

Notice a pattern with these problems? All of this comes down to differences in context, vision, and goals. All of it requires upfront and ongoing communication.

Communication Is the Fuel

A common mistake people make in a professional relationship is not following through with timely communication. Communication, however, is the fuel of a successful project. It is what feeds the process, keeps it smooth, keeps it effective, and keeps people happy. Effective communication of project parameters, design ideas, installation time frames, and schedules are all key ingredients to get across in the presentation of your designs. Whether you're communicating positive updates on the project or taking on challenging topics like extra costs incurred, you must keep communication fluid and honest.

Unrealistic Schedules

Build enough time into your estimation for the whole project. If you miscalculate the duration of a project in a big way, it will seriously cost you. You need to be realistic (almost overly so) about what it takes to perform design and installation tasks. Don't just estimate from your gut or what you think a task will cost. Take the time to measure the site and develop accurate material and labor costs.

Know this going into the design process: nearly every project will take longer than you think. Once you accept this truth, you can incorporate cushions into your cost and time estimates so there will be room for going over the original approximation. Incorporate an ongoing communication plan with project stakeholders to analyze progress before going over allotted time and financial projections.

Both your projections and *how* you accomplish the work will impact the schedule. How can you set the project up for incredible efficiency? Plan the installation in such a way that materials are moved only once, staged equipment/materials are placed out of the way of work being done, and work is done at the right time of year to avoid seasonal problems. Avoid wasting money on equipment rentals or labor by hiring the most efficient crew. There are many ways to sabotage project schedules and estimates if thoughtful planning is not implemented.

CASE STUDY: SEBASTOPOL CITY HALL/LIBRARY LANDSCAPE

I live in a town called Sebastopol in Northern California about an hour north of San Francisco. In 2013 I was approached by the city and community members to join a team that would design the landscape around conjoined properties: Sebastopol City Hall and Library. The City Hall/Library are located on the main highway going through town, so this project had a high profile from both a community and a geographical point of view.

I joined the design team as a volunteer, collaborating with master gardeners, artists, city council members, and city staff who made up the landscape design committee. The committee spent two years, meeting once a month, to develop principles, guidelines, and finally a design plan for the landscape project. It was a great experience and the result was incredibly satisfying.

As a collective, we generated many innovative ideas for the project, combining the group's ideas to create a unique and impressive final design that incorporated art, food, education, and beauty. The roads, parking lots, various buildings, and alleyways of this project created *many* microclimates, giving us a template for ecological diversity. We wanted this landscape to tell the story of our bioregion and the communities of people that have affected it over millennia. Folks who visit the landscape get to walk through a living cultural history museum where the plants themselves convey the lessons.

California Native Landscape

The first area of the City Hall/Library landscape pays homage to the original (and continued) inhabitants of these lands, the Southern Pomo and Coast Miwok. Here, plants that Indigenous

(continued)

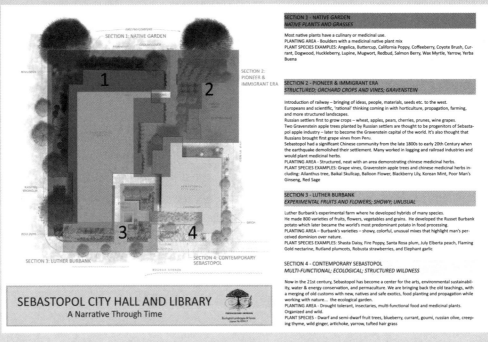

Sebastopol city hall and library conceptual design plan. Designed by Erik Ohlsen, Emily Mallard, and community committee.

people have used for thousands of years were installed. This community of plants was also chosen for the specific microclimate and soils of the project area. Much of these florae are edible, medical, or fiber-generating and have multiple uses throughout local native communities.

Native Plant Species

Angelica (*Angelica hendersonii*)
Coffeeberry (*Rhamnus californica*)
Coyote Brush (*Baccharis pilularis*)
Yarrow (*Achillea millefolium*)
Yerba Buena (*Clinopodium douglasii*)
Dogwood (*Cornus sericea ssp. occidentalis*)
Huckleberry (*Vaccinium ovatum*)
Mugwort (*Artemisia douglasiana*)
Willow (*Salix hookeriana*)
Toyon (*Heteromeles arbutifolia*)
Wax Myrtle (*Myrica californica*)
Salmonberry (*Rubes spectabilis*)

Pioneer Immigrant Era

The second area represents the agrarian settler roots of the community. This bioregion is still dotted with 100-year-old apple and pear groves and 100-year-old head-trained vineyards. Once the land was taken from native people, it was transformed into a heavily agrarian community, once called the apple center of the world. A section of the city hall landscape was dedicated to food-producing plants and trees representing the old-time settler homesteads.

A large population of Chinese immigrants once inhabited these lands during the settler era; a special community of plants was dedicated to their presence as part of the Pioneer Area of the landscape design.

Settler Era Species

Table/Wine Grapes (*Vitis vinifera*)
Apple (*Malus domestica*)
Fig (*Ficus carica*)
Almond (*Prunus amygdalus* 'All in one')
European Plum (*Prunus cocomilia*)
Pomegranate (*Punica granatum*)

Chinese Medicinal Herbs

Baikal Skullcap (*Scutellaria baicalensis*)
Balloon Flower (*Platycodon grandiflorus*)
Blackberry Lily (*Iris domestica*)
Korean Mint (*Agastache rugosa*)
Poor Man's Ginseng/Dang Shen (*Codonopsis pilosula*)
Red Sage (*Salvia miltiorrhiza*)

Luther Burbank Garden

Many know the work of Luther Burbank, renowned botanist and plant breeder. He hybridized many fruits and vegetables that people still consume around the world today. The russet potato is probably the most widespread of such creations. Luther Burbank lived in the town of Sebastopol, where he managed his experimental farm, the remnants of which still exist less than a mile from the Sebastopol City Hall and Library. We dedicated the third area of the landscape specifically to plant species he developed in this community.

(continued)

Luther Burbank Species

Shasta Daisy (*Leucanthemum superbum*)
Fire Poppy (*Papaver californicum*)
Santa Rosa Plum (*Prunus salicina*)
July Elberta Peach (*Prunus persica* 'Burbank Elberta')
Flaming Gold Peach (*Prunus persica* 'Flaming Gold')
Rutland Plumcots (*Prunus armeniaca* 'Rutland')
Robusta Strawberries (*Fragaria ananassa* 'Robusta')

Modern Ecological Garden

The final zone was developed as a model for the modern-day regenerative landscape. It is a multifunctional, multi-strata food forest incorporating edible, pollinator-attracting, and nitrogen-fixing plant communities. A rainwater catchment system was also included in this area.

Ecological Garden Species

Japanese Persimmon (*Diospyros kaki*)
Provence Lavender (*Lavandula intermedia* 'Provence')
Goumi (*Elaeagnus multiflora*)
Silver Lupine (*Lupinus albifrons*)
Meyer Lemon (*Citrus meyeri*)
Valencia Orange (*Citrus sinensis* 'Valencia')
Pineapple Guava/Feijoa (*Acca sellowiana*)
Oregano (*Origanum vulgare*)
Wolfberry (*Lycium barbarum*)

Community Landscape Installation

When it came time to install the landscape, we teamed up with local heroes at the Daily Acts Organization (DAO). They organize public garden installations, weaving education, celebration, and action into every event. Over the course of two years, DAO organized installation days where the community volunteered to build aspects of the design.

Hundreds of hands and hearts poured their energy into the creation of this public living history food forest. I facilitated some installation days myself, giving educational workshops and tours throughout the process.

The trees are now mature and bearing fruit and the habitat has grown in. Every month, thousands of people visit these gardens, immersed in the rich ecological history of the bioregion.

PROFESSIONAL DESIGN RELATIONSHIPS

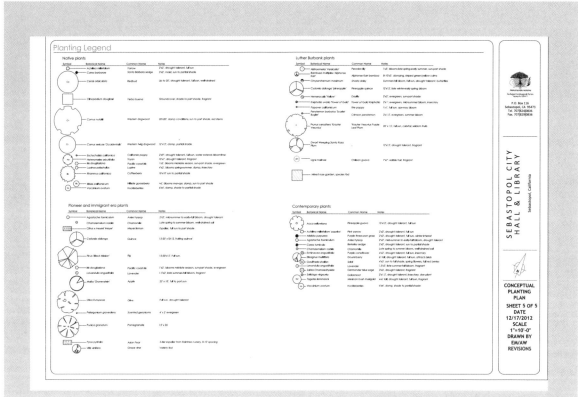

Sebastopol city hall and library planting plan legend. Designed by Erik Ohlsen and Emily Mallard.

PART IV
The World of Soil

16
Living Soil: The Foundation of Regenerative Landscapes

Regenerating soil is one of the greatest actions we take to repair ecosystems, subvert social collapse, and regenerate healthy ecologies. The soil represents a confluence of many aspects of life on earth. The state of the soil dictates water quality, air quality, and food nutrient density—which in turn dictate economy, culture, and climate.

Consider the massive role farming plays in sustaining modern society. Then think about the widespread destructive practices of industrial agriculture, including soil tillage, overgrazing, the application of chemicals, and the planting of genetically modified species. It's not hard to grasp why 24 billion tons of soil[1] are lost to erosion each year when 50 percent of habitable land on earth is being used for agriculture.[2] As landscapers, we make many decisions that affect soil. The industrial landscape model is a destructive force that uses chemicals, monoculture, and plowing—literally killing the life of soil. Landscape implementation devastates soil through the processes of clearing land, building hardscapes, and excavating earthworks. As a regenerative landscaper, it's your job not only to have a soil fertility plan but also to do *the least harm* at every phase of the project; to protect the soil at all times. Soil truly is the backbone of civilization. Every square inch matters. Urban gardens, small homesteads, ranches, parks, school grounds—it's our responsibility, yours and mine, to care for the world of soil.

Five principles of soil health were developed by the National Resources Conservation Service (NRCS) of the USDA. These principles are based on years of science and observation. They make up the backbone of no-till and regenerative agriculture methodologies worldwide and lead to the management and development of a deep soil carbon sponge.

Looking through the lens of pattern recognition, it's easy to see how these principles mimic the wisdom found in pristine forests and grasslands where ecosystems evolved with Indigenous management for tens of thousands of years. These principles are unpacked throughout the following chapters—the implementation of these concepts weaves through everything in the landscape, from soil building, food production, and water harvesting to erosion control, land stewardship, and every interaction we have with the ecosystem.

FIVE PRINCIPLES OF SOIL HEALTH *(Adapted from the Natural Resources Conservation Service)*[3]

1. Disturb the soil as little as possible.
2. Keep living roots in the ground at all times.

3. Plant diversity.
4. Keep soil covered.
5. Integrate animals.

CREATE LIVING SOIL

Nearly all terrestrial life is dependent upon the few inches of topsoil that make up the skin of planet earth. This topsoil is the bank where nutrients, water, and life are stored—where plant and animal kingdoms are sustained in life and where they return in death. As threads inside the great webs of life, we humans are equally dependent upon the soil and will return to it someday.

Living soil, flourishing with microbiology, is the earth's carbon sponge and ultimately the foundation for all regenerative landscapes. It is this microbiology, the living organisms that make up the soil community, where all the vital interactions occur for sustaining terrestrial life. The processes of decomposition, nutrient distribution, water absorption, carbon sequestration, and mineral bioavailability all happen through the behaviors of the soil's biological community. This is soil that is wholly alive.

The goal of every regenerative landscape is to nourish living soil, feeding the biological interactions therein. Below we will explore the community of soil organisms, how to feed them, repair degraded soil, build carbon batteries, and reverse the ecological devastation of human development—solutions await in the following chapters.

The Soil Community

A diverse community of microorganisms make up a healthy soil ecosystem. Working together, bacteria, protozoa, nematodes, fungi, plants, and arthropods work the miracles of carbon sequestration, nutrient distribution, and decomposition within the rhizosphere and beyond. The structure of healthy soil is of the utmost importance, and a vibrant soil biology results in healthy soil structure. Every element plays a crucial role. For example, fungi and bacteria create biological glues such as glomalin, which bind soil particles together, attach water and nutrients, and mitigate erosion and drought.[4]

Rhizosphere

The rhizosphere is the key layer of earth's carbon sponge. In this zone, which exists between 1 and 10 inches from the surface, the majority of interactions between plant roots, mycorrhizal fungi, bacteria, nematodes, and other organisms take place. Life is born from the rhizosphere that all soil-based life depends upon. The rhizosphere is where plants absorb most of their nutrients and release plant exudates, while the soil community breaks down minerals, nutrients, and water, making them more accessible.[5]

Plant Exudates

One of the great processes of reciprocity is the exchange between plants and soil microorganisms—an entire economy of trade and commerce happening below the surface. Plants excrete exudates (amino acids, sugars, and other nutrients) that attract bacteria and fungi. The bacteria and fungi feed on the exudates. In trade for these gifts, they provide a number of benefits to plants. They break rocks into absorbable minerals, decompose organic matter into nutrients, and so much more. They even protect plant roots from pests and disease to ensure this great subterranean economy continues to thrive.[6]

A diversity of plants increases these interactions as different plant species provide a variety of plant exudates to the soil, therefore cultivating a wide mixture of microorganisms. The more variety of plant roots, the more diverse the soil community. This is true resilience—by utilizing these ecological processes, fertility in the landscape is achieved with simple and effective means.

Bacteria

Thousands of species of bacteria live in soil, on plant roots, and on plant tissues. One example is *Rhizobia*, a large family of bacteria that thrive in the rhizosphere. There are many functions, interactions, and species of bacteria, but at this point in our understanding of soil science, we know very little about most of them. What we do know is that the activities of bacteria in the root zone offer a plethora of benefits to plant communities. They are attracted to and feed on plant exudates and they provide food to other beneficial organisms. They protect plant roots from pests and disease, fix nitrogen (building soil fertility), decompose organic matter, and enrich the rhizosphere with numerous other reciprocal interactions. Bacteria reproduce quickly and in great numbers, functioning as massive storehouses of carbon and other nutrients. Other organisms feed upon these bacterial blooms, further transforming the bacterial nutrient storages into accessible plant nutrients.[7]

Fungi

The science of fungi is still very young with new revelations published each year. As young a science as it is, the breakthroughs in understanding fungal interactions in the soil have been nothing short of breathtaking.

Fungi make up 55 percent of the organic matter found in soil, providing a host of functions from decomposition of biomass to remediation of toxic substances. Fungi use their external secretions to consume root exudates, bacteria, and other organisms, transforming their nutrient loads in the mycelial body. This mycelium (underground parts of fungi) creates spongy webs of biomass that absorb and retain water while binding soil particles. Fungi also protect plants from root-eating nematodes and other pests to ensure optimal plant health.[8]

Mycorrhizal fungi are a special family of fungi that attach to the root hairs of plants (90 percent of the plant world depends on mycorrhizae) and distribute sugars and nutrients from the soil into plant roots and also from plant to plant. Young trees thrive in the shade through mycorrhizal interactions when their tall mothers, who draw nutrients down through photosynthesis into their roots, send nutrients to saplings through fungal networks.

Protozoa

These soil organisms graze on bacteria in the rhizosphere. Think of them as the grazing herds of the soil realm. They eat bacteria, fungi, other protozoa, and organic matter, all while secreting biowastes that provide bioavailable nutrients to plants. They are the great transformers of the soil world that feed on and are fed upon by other organisms. Without protozoa, the nutrient cycling process would be broken and diminished.

Nematodes

Nematodes come in great variety, both beneficial and pathogenic to plants. They provide a number of services that add to the continuous cycles of life, death, and nutrient transformation in the soil. They feed on protozoa, bacteria, fungi, pests, and each other, keeping populations balanced. These behaviors add to nutrient availability in plants and storage of carbon, water, and minerals in the soil. Some nematodes are pathogenic and will bore into the roots of plants, but a healthy soil ecosystem will keep these actions in check as fungi and other organisms will protect plant roots against their attacks.

Arthropoda

Arthropods and microarthropods continue this feeding frenzy found in the rhizosphere. These organisms burrow into the soil benefiting gas exchanges farther into the soil's depths. They feed on nematodes, fungi, and bacteria and add to the development of soil structure and nutrient bioavailability. They feed on each other in a constant trophic cycle of death, decay, and rebirth.

Earthworms

These precious organisms feed on soil life, organic matter, and minerals, passing food through their gizzards and inoculating it with a host of bacteria and humic acids that continue the process of soil regeneration. Earthworms make tiny furrows through the soil, creating homes for soil organisms, aerating the soil, and increasing water infiltration.

Birds/Mammals

Standing at the top of this food web are birds and mammals. Birds eat arthropods, feed on seeds, drop their guano to the soil, and move fungal spores and bacteria from place to place, offering many acts of reciprocity—feeding soil life, planting seeds, and managing ecosystems. This is just one facet of integrating animals to build soil.

Burrowing mammals aerate the soil, providing habitat for an array of other soil organisms. They shred organic matter in preparation for decomposition. Burrowing mammals are considered pests as some feed on plant roots, damaging planting systems, but when in balance they contribute to the living soil community that make up the rhizosphere.

FEED SOIL LIFE

Regenerative landscapes, as intact ecosystems, have a diverse and robust community of soil life born of the gift economy generated by the trade of sugars and carbon harvested from photosynthesis for the minerals and nutrients given by soil life. These are webs of relationships, of reciprocity, of life, and your role is to feed them. This is your part in the dance of reciprocity, your role as a contributor within the ecological gift economy. Feed soil life, and feed them more. Feed them by planting, feed them by protecting the surface of the soil, by adding organic matter, and keeping living roots alive and growing at all times.

These are the foundations of regenerative landscapes, the foundations of thriving ecologies, the foundations of humanity.

COMPACTED AND HYDROPHOBIC SOILS

Human development, including modern landscaping, has an enormous negative impact on the world's soils. These influences lead to numerous catastrophes for ecosystems and human civilization.

Billions of tons of topsoil wash away from our forests, grasslands, cities, farms, and landscapes every year. Eventually, all that soil makes it into creeks, streams, rivers, and oceans. The sediment spilling into waterways causes a breakdown of the aquatic food web resulting in water pollution, species extinction, and warming of waterways, which increases evaporation and drought conditions. On landscape projects, you will often find degraded, damaged, and compacted soils. As regenerative landscapers, one of our primary goals is to regenerate the soil, which fortunately is almost always doable.

Before you can make it better, it's important to understand what the issues are. We discuss soil tests throughout this section of the book and elsewhere. Soil assessment will yield much guidance starting with the look and feel of the soil upon your first observation.

Highly compacted soil has less biological life, is unable to absorb water, and hosts an unlivable home for most plant communities, though several tough species still flourish. Sadly, much of human development leads to compacted soils; in fact, most building development requires a 90 percent compaction rate of the soils underneath and around buildings. This makes sense when you want solid foundations and no water to penetrate, but when it comes to gardening, farming, landscaping, and restoration, we want our soils to be loose, with a thriving biological soil community and the ability to absorb and infiltrate water.

The world is a diverse place and some soils have naturally evolved to be more compacted and less absorptive. If these are features of natural succession, then specific soil communities will have evolved to generate intact ecosystems despite the compaction. Systems like these need to be honored for their own intelligence and protected/managed accordingly. But this is the exception to the rule. In most cases, compacted landscape soil is due to human activities, whether it be conventional agriculture, deforestation, road cuts, house building, or the poor timing of a tractor driven across wet soil.

When soil is compacted, devegetated, sun exposed, with a hot surface temperature, it becomes hydrophobic. This means that when rain falls, rather than absorbing and infiltrating into the ground, water runs across the soil surface, moving sediment and causing erosion.

Keeping the soil covered at all times with mulch or vegetation is one simple way to reduce a hydrophobic condition. If the soil is heavily compacted, however, other means will be necessary to invite water back into the soil.

Soil Decompaction Techniques and Tools

Soils that have extreme compaction due to agriculture, overgrazing, misuse of machines, and other forms of development sometimes need a more surgical approach to regeneration. In these cases, no-till mulching and planting systems will not be sufficient for any near-term benefits. To speed up the process of rehabilitating the soil, a subsoiling tool is beneficial. There are many kinds of subsoiling tools: the Keyline plow, ripper bars, and everything in between. While much of the industry uses simple ripping bars (usually pulled by bulldozers) stuck into the ground to depths of one to three feet to break up hardpan and loosen soil, more sensitive subsoiling tools like a keyline plow are a better match for a regenerative approach.

The more common ripping procedure decompacts the soil but has major drawbacks. It is a very invasive tool that tears up the ground. When a ripping bar is dragged through the soil it pulls subsoil out of the ground, flinging it on the surface. This inversion is detrimental to soil health as the soil horizons and their biological counterparts are displaced during the ripping process. This is why regenerative landscapers prefer the keyline plow (and similar tools), which is designed not only to cut and open soil at depth (4 to 24 inches), but to do so with the least amount of negative impact. These are subsoiling tools that have a cutting blade on them (rather than a flat bar), allowing them to slice through the soil like a knife slices through warm butter. At the base or "foot" of the plow is a wider protruding section that creates tiny furrows in the land, keeping soil horizons intact (noninversion). This noninversion plow loosens soil, aiding water infiltration, oxygenation, and nutrient distribution, all helpful to the root growth of plants. To keep the soil surface undisturbed, keyline plows use coulter blades (cutting disks) that open the surface of the soil just before the plow is dragged through. This allows the subsoil shank to cut through fully vegetated pastures leaving grasses and herbs intact.

Tools like these are powerful but not always appropriate. Working with the principle of *do the least harm*, much observation and discernment is necessary before choosing such a surgical approach.

Subsoiling sessions are frequently performed when the ground is moist but not wet. During or immediately after subsoiling, the land is prepared for sowing seeds, spreading compost, spraying compost teas, and direct planting.

Broad Fork

Broad forks are a subsoiling hand tool often used on no-till farms to prep planting beds without inverting the soil. They are large and heavy forks with many 8- to 12-inch metal tines. These are pushed into the ground and rocked back and forth by the two large handles. Broad forks are used to loosen compacted soil but also in bed preparation to draw more air into the soil, allowing for deeper plant rooting depths, and for incorporating soil amendments like oyster shell, rock dust, and compost. The broad fork is an important soil prep tool for every regenerative landscaper.

Use the broad fork sparingly. Overzealous practitioners use the broad fork as a tilling machine, lifting up and flipping (inverting) the soil. This has adverse effects on soil biology and is not advised. The best use of the fork is to insert it in the ground, push the tines all the way in (or as far as you can), and pull back on the handles enough to loosen the soil without lifting it up and out of the ground.

Once you've loosened the soil, pull the forks out of the ground and place them back down 12 to 18 inches past your last forking and follow the same process. Repeat this process throughout the entire planting area for best results. Broad forking is frequently followed by composting, mulching, seeding and/or planting.

Bucket Decompaction

Bucket soil decompaction refers to using an excavator or backhoe bucket to loosen the soil. This is a highly disruptive method but well suited to specific situations where mechanical help is needed. The critical approach to this method is making sure not to invert the soil during the process. This is difficult for equipment operators who have little experience but an experienced operator (or a novice who operates slowly and carefully) can take an excavator bucket and push its teeth into the ground without flipping the soil. Like using a spader or a broad fork, this process is repeated across the entire area as a way to loosen and chop up the surface of the soil without flipping it over. It is not a process of excavation—instead, push the teeth of the bucket into the ground and then remove them to break up compacted soil.

Plants as Subsoilers

Ecosystems have their own powerful subsoilers, many in the form of plants. A lot has been written about the roots of plants driving deep into the soil and breaking up hardpan, but often this is hyperbole. This is one of those myths that carry truth but isn't always what it seems. Taprooting plants, many trees, and especially perennial grasses do drive their roots deep into the soil, and over time they can break down compacted layers. These processes take time, though, and one season of daikon radish won't do. The trick with using plants as subsoilers is more about their association with the soil microbial community than the plants by themselves. As roots drive into compacted soil, they create food and habitat for microorganisms, which transform the soil into a less hydrophobic and less compacted state. Using daikon radish as an example, you can let the roots do what they can as they grow, but allowing them to compost into the ground after the growing season is the real benefit. Slashing them at the base or smothering them to activate decomposition will pump organic matter and biological foods into the ground.

With patience, the appropriate tree and plant species will slowly puncture compacted soil and, given generations of time, will even turn stone into soil. When mixing cover crop seed for dispersal, if the soil is devoid of organic matter, hydrophobic, or has a hardpan, always add deep-rooting crops like mustard, daikon, mangels, and appropriate grasses (when these species fit the context, and never in wildland scenarios unless using native species).

CASE STUDY: SINGING FROGS FARM

Nestled in California's coastal range is a farm that puts nature first. Paul and Elizabeth Kaiser of Singing Frogs Farms have developed an innovative system, one founded on the proliferation of and reverence for soil life, a farm created for winged ones, four-legged beings, and humans in equal measure.

The Kaisers' mission was to steward land for wildlife when they bought their farm in 2007. They believed organic farming would be a proficient method to care for the land, create habitat for life, and pay their expenses. Their story exemplifies what happens when, instead of imposing your will upon the land, you listen to the feedback given by the ecology in response to your land-use practices. If paying humble attention to landscape patterns, you may find yourself, like the Kaisers, completely changing your landscape approach midstride. There is a big difference between regenerative and conventional land stewardship. The regenerative approach reflects the worldview of being a part of the land, of working within the constraints and resources of the ecology and recognizing that the health of the landscape reflects the health of the whole community. True regeneration means striving to cause the least harm while developing the greatest ecological yields. This is what the Kaisers' story and practices represent.

In the first couple of years on their organic farm, a few notable experiences changed the course of their trajectory. They had inherited and implemented their predecessors' farming methods. These organic practices included tractor tillage to prep beds, cover cropping, winter rest, and single crops per bed. Sounds pretty good, right? These are common organic farming methods but, as it turns out, not ideal for the health of soil. The Kaisers struggled under these practices. The wet winter on floodplain soils meant no sales for months and required them to lay off trained farm workers. They couldn't till beds on wet ground, sometimes waiting until April or May before putting a crop in the ground. It wasn't working out financially; change had to come. But change came from an unexpected source. . . .

For the Kaisers, building a haven for wildlife was central to their goals. The organic tillage system seemed to be working counter to their context of reciprocity, but they didn't know yet what the solution would be. Then something extraordinary happened. Paul's recollection of this moment was emotional to listen to. He was on his tractor plowing yet another green covered bed. The typical carnage of dead reptiles and dust clouds followed in the wake of the tiller blades. The descending ravens (*Corvis corax*) and crows (*Corvus brachyrhynchos*) picked at the dead and dying animals.

On one particular pass, a brave mother killdeer (*Charadrius vociferus*) got Paul's attention. As the tractor plowed forward, the killdeer took a stand, unwilling to move, screaming and pleading for the tractor to stop . . . and it did. Paul heard the crying mother and turned the

(continued)

tractor off. In Paul's words, "She literally risked her life to protect her full nest of eggs." A full clutch of killdeer eggs was mere feet from being plowed under.

That was the last year the Kaisers used tillage on their farm. That year they honored the killdeer by designing their farm beds around the nest, but the whole experience did not sit well for them. The organic tillage farming model was counter to their values and goals and they would never go back.

Over the next few years, as they developed an incredible regenerative agriculture model putting ecological life first, the land and farm flourished around them. The health of wildlife and soil became the most important indicators of their success. They adopted the five no-till principles described at the beginning of this chapter.

Here are a number of solutions they implemented to develop their now world-class agroecological farm, Singing Frogs Farm.

Leave the Soil Intact

This was the first of many changes the Kaisers made to build the best farming soil in the world. Tillage releases enormous amounts of carbon to the atmosphere, shreds fungal hyphae, destroys beneficial bacterial communities, and kills wildlife.

Leave Roots in the Ground

Part of an exemplary no-till practice is to *not* pull plants up by their roots but instead to cut them at the base and leave the roots in the ground to decompose, feeding the soil biology. On Singing Frogs Farm, when a crop like broccoli is harvested for their CSA, they leave the roots in the ground, planting their next crop around the decomposing broccoli root balls once the stem has been cut below the ground.

Maximize Photosynthesis

Keeping the soil covered with living plants requires an intensive planting system. At Singing Frogs Farm, they don't plant just one crop in a bed at a time but intercrop up to two crops per bed at the height of the growing season. Often, these interplanted crops are planted at different times; for instance, a crop of tomatoes are planted in April with two successions of lettuce interplanted in the same bed. Before the tomatoes stop producing in the fall, a crop of cauliflowers are interplanted in the same bed, making use of the shade the old tomatoes provide. Eventually the tomatoes come out as the weather turns cold and there is less sun. Then cauliflowers take over the bed. This level of intensity allows the farm to harvest more crops from each bed than a traditional organic farm would. With short duration crops, the Kaisers can grow nine successions of crops in a single farm bed in a 12-month cycle! This benefits the soil by maximizing photosynthesis and maintaining a diversity of root systems in each bed, which provides a wider range of plant exudates to feed soil biology and results in a more diverse and resilient soil community.

This intensive planting approach also reduced their irrigation needs by 15 to 20 percent.

Surface Applied Compost

At Singing Frogs Farm, they build incredible compost that gets reapplied to the farm beds throughout the year. Rather than till their compost applications into farming beds, ⅛ to ¼ inch of compost is applied on the surface. They are always looking at diversifying the microbiology and often add a mix of different composts from their local bioregion to their own homemade sources when adding to the surface of a bed.

The surface-applied compost gets integrated into deeper soil layers by earthworms, fungi, and the rest of the living soil community.

Year-Round Production

With their no-till farming approach, the Kaisers benefit from year-round production on the farm, differentiating themselves from most organic farmers in the region. A farm that uses a tilling culture can't prep beds during the wet season and therefore can't produce a crop during those months. But the Kaisers' no-till solution allows them to plant and harvest at all times of the year in their temperate climate.

The new year-round farming method enables them to employ farmworkers in all seasons, which ensures that well-trained staff can stay on the farm for years instead of months.

Pollinator Hedges

Implementing the agroecology principles of their farming approach, the Kaisers developed perennial hedgerows between blocks of farming beds to feed and house pollinators, birds, snakes, beneficial predatory insects, and other wildlife. In 2013, Singing Frogs Farm won a national pollinators award for the noticeable effect their hedgerows had for creating safe havens for pollinators.

The beneficial insects and birds benefit the farm by managing pests and increasing crop pollination. The hedgerows protect the soil from sun and evaporation, keeping moisture in the ground to feed soil microbial and plant communities alike.

Occultation

As any vegetable gardener or farmer knows, prepping a bed for planting is the most intensive act of labor needed for growing crops. Tractor tilling and double digging are two of the most

(continued)

common practices gardeners and farmers use for prepping vegetable beds. Broad forking, as discussed elsewhere, has a place in bed prep and has been used at Singing Frogs Farm in their early no-till days. Another process for prepping a bed is called occultation. At the Kaisers' scale, transitioning heavily vegetated beds and winter cover crops requires a no-till system that is low labor, the least impactful to the soil, and inexpensive. Occultation meets those needs and then some.

Occultation is the process of placing black tarps over the ground to smother out existing vegetation. The black tarps absorb heat from the sun, gently heating the soil surface and increasing decomposition. In this way, practitioners transform an area of the landscape with minimal labor, never disturbing the soil. After two to three weeks of occultation (depending on the time of year), the vegetation underneath will have died off and begun to decompose. At that point, the black tarp is removed to be used elsewhere or folded up for another time so the area can be prepped further with soil amendments, compost, and mulch followed by planting.

It's important to note that the Kaisers' use of occultation does not leave tarps covering areas for long periods of time. Keeping to the principle of having living roots covering the ground at all times, their goal is to quickly decompose one vegetation type and plant the next one as soon as possible.

In hot summer months, leaving a black tarp on the ground can be detrimental if it heats the soil surface for too long. Eventually, the biology in the soil will begin to die off. It's a powerful tool to be used sparingly and strategically.

Proof of Concept

The proof of the Kaisers' no-till methods is found in the quality of the food they grow, the vibrant and fecund life that exists on their farm, and the data found in their soil tests, pollinator monitoring, and water testing.[9]

In the soil testing section below, the Kaisers share the results of their soil tests and how to read them. As you will see, the soil they are growing is extraordinary, just like them and the lands they steward. You can do this too!

SOIL TESTING

It is crucial to assess and test landscape soils. Soil assessment strategies include tests for structure, composition, drainage, and profile. In this section, the focus is on testing soil for nutrients, organic matter content, biology, and minerals. The best way to acquire this type of soil data is through a laboratory-based soil test. These tests are generally straightforward and relatively inexpensive.

The first step is to take a soil sample(s) to send off to a soil-testing lab. To take the soil sample you must dig six to eight inches into the ground. Once the hole is dug, dig out one to two cups of soil and place in a Ziploc bag. Follow the same procedure in three or four other places in the vicinity of the first sample. Samples taken 40 or so feet away from each other are plenty. Now mix all the samples together in one Ziploc bag. You can now ship the samples to a laboratory of your choosing. (Lab recommendations are made below.)

On large sites, multiple samples (from three or four holes) will be necessary. Take samples in areas similar to each other—for instance, one set of samples from a floodplain and another set of samples from the ridge top. Do this rather than mix floodplain and ridge soil. Follow common sense in this way on your own projects. Follow the same procedures for every sample and send them all to the same lab.

Reading a Soils Report

Elizabeth and Paul Kaiser of Singing Frogs Farm graciously share a variety of soil tests from their carbon sequestering, no-till regenerative farm below as examples for how to assess and use these soil-testing methodologies in a regenerative landscape.

Traditional laboratory soil tests look at the mineral and chemical composition of the soil, providing data on the big three macronutrients—nitrogen, phosphorus, and potassium (NPK)—and micronutrients such as calcium, magnesium, and so on.

A test of this sort gives a snapshot of available nutrients in the soil but is limited in scope. This data is mostly useful for identifying major deficiencies, which will give you direction on remineralization needs in the landscape. These soil tests often come with a host of recommendations from the laboratory to add specific soil amendments to the landscape to get mineral and nutrient ratios into an optimal range.

Discussing soil testing with the Kaisers is always illuminating. While knowing about a calcium deficiency, for example, is beneficial, the focus on biology is paramount compared to the focus on the macro and micro nutrients of the soil. Soil biology is the factor that makes nutrients available to plants, and in association with the right plant communities, compost, and organic matter additions, it's the biology that makes the soil sing.

For this reason, the Kaisers suggest sending your soil to laboratories that test the biology. As you can see from the soil tests, there are a number of excellent data points presented by laboratories testing for soil biology. The Kaisers use Ward Laboratories and test their soil using both the phospholipid fatty acid (PLFA) and Haney tests. These tests show vital information for understanding organic matter, carbon, nutrient availability, and the presence of soil microorganisms.

As we know, a 1 percent increase of carbon over one acre increases the water-holding capacity by up to 25,000 gallons. Reading the organic matter content of landscape soil (via soil tests) is also reading the story of water—make the connections. These are powerful statistics. As Paul says, *the greatest use of a soil test isn't the first test you take but the subsequent tests taken in the same location at the same time of year.* By repeating soil tests in the same location at the same time of year, you document whether your soil-regeneration techniques are making a difference. These numbers, especially for farmers and professional landscapers, prove the regenerative strategies discussed in this book are effective and necessary.

For the sake of your regenerative landscape projects, focus more on the biological aspect of soil tests and less on the macro- and micronutrients. Focus on organic matter, carbon, and biology. That is the biggest takeaway of the tests presented below. Seasonality and changes in microclimate will affect soil tests. That is why it is advised to test at the same time of year in the same locations. A test taken in winter will differ drastically from a test taken in a dry summer. The tests presented in this book are just snapshots of a time on Singing Frogs Farm. Since the Kaisers began testing their soils, a dramatic increase in organic matter and biological activity has taken place, the trend continuing for more than a decade. Successional changes will always affect the land and the soil will continue to change with time in a living ecosystem. This is true for every one of your landscapes.

Phospholipid Fatty Acid (PLFA) Test

The PLFA measures the biological activity in the soil. The data generates a glimpse of fungal, bacterial, and protozoa populations. In this case, you can see data for Actinomycetes and Rhizobia bacteria, mycorrhizal and saprophytic fungi, protozoa, and undifferentiated (this category likely including nematodes and dozens of other species of soil life).

In addition, overall biological scores are given, delivering a benchmark for knowing the total microbial community at the time the sample was taken. As the Kaisers suggest, use these tests as comparisons year after year to prove the work you are doing to regenerate soil is working. If the test shows diminishing results from year to year, adjust your practices and/or research what the issue is.

On the PLFA test provided by Singing Frogs Farm you can see that their overall living microbial biomass numbers are 10,000. This is more than twice the number given as "excellent" on the test. This particular test was taken during the dry season, which provides a lower microbial number compared to the Singing Frogs Farm wetter season tests where they have had Total Living Microbial Biomass scores over 20,000! What a proof of concept for no-till regenerative soil building practices. The Kaisers are doing this on a farm where vegetables are being sold every week, meaning this is a farm harvesting crops and still yielding these numbers. Modeling your own regenerative landscape endeavors after the Singing Frogs Farm model will likely yield your own incredible results.

Note: Soil science is moving fast and testing soil biology in other ways such as using microscopy is also on the cutting edge of understanding soil health and how we can better care for the sacred soils of earth.

The Haney Test

The Haney test is the gold standard soil test for regenerative land stewards. This test provides you with information about organic matter percentage, active carbon, and nutrient extracts. What's so remarkable about nutrient extracts data is that the Haney tests for nitrogen, phosphorus, potassium, zinc, manganese, calcium, magnesium, sodium, copper, and aluminum using a process that mimics the biological extraction of nutrients for the soil. This means that the numbers you see on a Haney test resemble the actual absorbability of these nutrients for plants, not just total percentages present in the soil, so this is a much more accurate way of reading the nutrient availability of soil. Look at the Haney test example provided by Singing Frogs Farm to see how this data is presented. The Haney test even provides an overall grade for the health of your soil. The Singing Frogs Farm calculation came in at 25.10 on the presented Haney test. This is more than twice the best results of an excellent score for an organic farm, which usually comes in at 11.0–13.0.

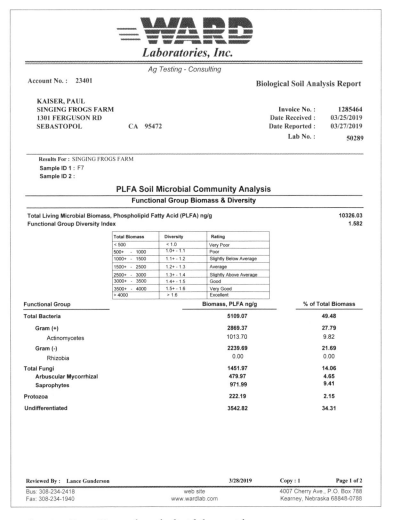

Singing Frogs Farm phospholipid fatty acid test.

Biological Soil Analysis Report

Account No.: 23401

KAISER, PAUL
SINGING FROGS FARM
1301 FERGUSON RD
SEBASTOPOL CA 95472

Invoice No.: 1285229
Date Received: 03/22/2019
Date Reported: 03/26/2019

Results For: SINGING FROGS FARM
Sample ID 1: F2B
Sample ID 2:
Lab No.: 1786
Sample ID 3:
Sample ID 4:
Soil Depth: 4 - 8 in

Haney - Soil Health Analysis

1:1 Soil pH	7.1	ICAP Sulfur, ppm S	12
1:1 Soluble Salts, mmho/cm	0.26	ICAP Calcium, ppm Ca	1293
Excess Lime Rating	NONE	ICAP Magnesium, ppm Mg	263
Organic Matter, %LOI	6.7	ICAP Sodium, ppm Na	23
		ICAP Aluminum, ppm Al	58.9
Soil Respiration CO_2-C, ppm C	195.8	**Calculations**	
Water Extract		Microbially Active Carbon (%MAC)	65.3
Total Nitrogen, ppm N	51.9	Organic C : Organic N	10.8
Organic Nitrogen, ppm N	27.9	Organic N : Inorganic N	1.1
Total Organic Carbon, ppm C	300	Organic Nitrogen Release, ppm N	27.9
H3A Extract		Organic Nitrogen Reserve, ppm N	0.0
Nitrate, ppm NO_3-N	22.6	Organic Phosphorus Release, ppm P	15.4
Ammonium, ppm NH_4-N	3.3	Organic Phosphorus Reserve, ppm P	< 0.1
Inorganic Nitrogen, ppm N	25.9	**Soil Health**	
Total (ICAP) Phosphorus, ppm P	193	Soil Health Calculation	25.10
Inorganic (FIA) Phosphorus, ppm P	177.4	Cover Crop Suggestion	10% Legume 90% Grass
Organic Phosphorus, ppm P	15.4		
ICAP Potassium, ppm K	287		
ICAP Zinc, ppm Zn	2.47		
ICAP Iron, ppm Fe	88.0		
ICAP Manganese, ppm Mn	3.1		
ICAP Copper, ppm Cu	0.14		

Reviewed By: Lance Gunderson   3/26/2019   Copy: 1   Page 1 of 2

Bus: 308-234-2418
Fax: 308-234-1940
web site
www.wardlab.com
4007 Cherry Ave., P.O. Box 788
Kearney, Nebraska 68848-0788

Singing Frogs Farm Haney test results.

Slake Test

The slake test is an easy home test that shows the presence or lack of soil microbiology. Here is how it works:

1. Fill two glass jars, 2 quarts or larger, with water.
2. Place an item inside each jar at the bottom to rest a clump of soil upon. A smaller upside-down jar, a shaped piece of metal mesh, or a small bit of brick can all work as a small "table" at the bottom of the jar.
3. In the landscape, dig a shovel-sized hole 6–8 inches into the soil. Excavate a clump of soil about the size of a lemon. Dig a similar clump of soil from the edge of the project site or a nearby location.
4. Place one clump of soil in each of the two jars. Rest it on your makeshift table at the bottom of the jar.
5. Here the soil magic is unveiled. If the clump of soil begins to disintegrate under contact with the water, easily falling apart and making the water cloudy, that means little to no biology is present in the soil. If, however, the soil holds together, doesn't disintegrate in the water, and the water itself stays clear, not cloudy, that displays the presence of a vigorous biological community in the soil. (A healthy biological community secretes many humic compounds such as glomalin.[10] These substances hold soil aggregates together, keeping them bound under the compression of water. That means, when it rains or the soil is under heavy water pressure, the nutrients in the soil do not leech away as they hold fast to pores of the soil.)

DEVELOP A SOIL REGENERATION PLAN

Once your soil is assessed through a multitude of tests and indicators, now it's time to create a soil regeneration plan for the landscape. As with everything in this book, this is completely driven by the context: your plan must reflect the characteristics of the site, soil test results, long-term landscape goals, budget, and so forth.

All these details will point to the specific strategies required for managing and developing soil health on a specific project. If your assessment process hasn't yielded many answers, or you haven't done any assessment, it is still OK to begin development of a soil regeneration plan as long as you update the plan when new information arises. Keep in mind that some soil building activities cause *no harm* to the landscape whatsoever, while others must be implemented using very nuanced and precise methods to avoid causing damage to the land.

For example, adding compost, applications of aerated compost tea, mycorrhizal fungi added during planting, and mulch applications will usually yield beneficial results. The small percentage of times where the effect is negative is due to rare and specific circumstances of the site.

A few techniques described in the following chapters need to be applied with discretion. Adding soil amendments like calcium, changing the pH, or running a subsoiling ripper through the site are beneficial in many landscapes but sometimes have detrimental effects, depending on the state of the soil.

Your soil regeneration plan must take a phased approach, implemented at specific times. For instance, I've had projects that get approved in the fall, but work cannot commence until spring. On the other hand, these areas that will be transformed into new landscapes or farms can be covered cropped immediately to take advantage of a wet season.

In my climate, cover cropping in the fall would be Phase One of a soil regeneration plan, followed by Phase Two, in springtime when the landscape is developed. Those cover crops will be worked into the soil, providing the basis for the new landscape. In Phase Three, once the landscape infrastructure has been installed, we usually add compost, soil amendments, mulch, and so on to jumpstart the biology and feed the soil organic matter.

In Phase Four or Five, I might be planting perennial soil-building species like groundcover clovers (*Trifolium*), black locust (*Robinia pseudoacacia*), mulch-producing trees like maples (*Acer*), oaks (*Quercas*), and other such species that will continually feed organic matter to the soil, fix nitrogen, and grow soil for generations.

If you're planning on growing food intensively—vegetables, herbs, berries, and short-lived fruits—schedule ongoing soil-building activities like applications of compost tea and yearly applications of mulch and compost to continually enhance the soil on a monthly and yearly basis going forward. Implementing diverse and strategically timed practices slowly usher the soil of a landscape toward a deeper and richer topsoil. A soil-regeneration plan will look very different for each landscape. Customize yours to consider not only the first year but subsequent years and decades.

The way people have treated the earth's soil over the last couple hundred years has generated an enormous deficit of arable soil. Referencing the keyline scale of permanence as discussed in part II, we find that soil is one of the elements where we can have the most impact and therefore create the most change.

By developing a multiyear and multigenerational soil-regeneration plan, you set the landscape up for not only short-term success but also a thriving future for our descendants.

17
No-Till Landscaping

Through tilling, agriculture and landscaping are major contributors to a majority of carbon dioxide emissions released into the atmosphere.[1] At the same time, these land use industries are one of the major solutions to sequestering carbon back into the land. The power of regenerative landscapes is the ability to produce ecological yields (carbon sequester) *and* human yields (food) at the same time. Through no-till practices, agriculture and landscape industries become solutions to so many crises facing humanity.

Limiting soil disturbance maintains healthy soil structure, microbiological diversity, and carbon storage. Every time we disturb or till the soil, we are releasing carbon into the atmosphere in great numbers, destroying the soil structure, and killing off billions of soil organisms.[2]

Soil disturbance happens in a number of ways (not solely tillage) and for many reasons. Landscape grading and earthworks are major soil disturbances. Digging the foundation for a house, barn, or greenhouse is a major disturbance. Building ponds, roads, swales, and terraces massively disrupts the soil. All of these infrastructure decisions lead to soil destruction. On many projects, these infrastructure installations are necessary, initially damaging yet still leading to vibrant regenerative landscapes. Knowing the effect project installation will have on soil helps you, as the designer, work toward the *least harm for the greatest effect.*

Prepping the landscape for planting, whether it be a farm, a kitchen garden, or a sprawling landscape, is a time where soil disturbance and tilling can be avoided (no matter what conventional practitioners tell you). Keeping the soil intact enables the soil biology to function optimally in the landscape. The context of some projects does call for a one-time till to handle soil compaction or other issues as described in the subsoiling section. That said, avoiding tilling and soil disturbance is the most ecological approach. If you have to disturb the soil, your goal should be to never do it again. Instead, regenerative landscaping mimics how forests grow soil through a process of adding layers upon layers of organic matter—compost, mulch, and soil amendments—and/or seeding directly into the existing soil surface.

MULCHING

Arguably, the richest soils in the world form beneath the canopies of forest ecosystems. Forests are good at building soil because every year they deposit leaves, bark, and decaying logs to the forest floor, keeping the soil covered at all times. This biomass becomes food for fungi and microorganisms that turn these carbon-filled materials into deep topsoil. Soils like these hold millions of gallons of water per acre[3] and store hundreds of gigatons of soil carbon.[4]

In most small to medium landscape projects, a similar approach of layering biomass onto the surface can be implemented to achieve forest rich soil with no tilling. Mulching and sheet mulching are the primary way to mimic forest soil in the landscape. For the sake of this book, mulch is any kind of material that can be placed on top of the ground to reduce weed growth, retain moisture, cool the soil surface, and feed soil organisms.

Plastic and rubber mulch exist but I do not advise using them in a regenerative landscape. Temporary use of plastic for an occultation has its place in a no-till system; otherwise, stay away from these products to reduce the use of plastic. For now, stick to biodegradable mulches.

Mulch covers the soil surface, protecting it from erosion, evaporation, and crustification. Using mulch strategically suppresses weeds, feeds fungi and bacteria in the soil, and holds water. It also reduces the need for irrigation by at least 30 percent and more in some cases.[5] Mulching sounds simple but can get complicated fast. You might find yourself in analysis paralysis trying to decide what types of materials you should or shouldn't use and how thickly to apply them. All that gets clarified below.

Cardboard/Newspaper

Cardboard and newspaper are used in sheet mulching. Cardboard and newspaper are laid on the ground, followed by compost or mulch. Cardboard and newspaper are biodegradable and attract worms, fungi, and other beneficial soil organisms. The cardboard absorbs and holds water while also suppressing vegetation underneath. Most undesired plants ("weeds") found in the landscape are adequately suppressed by applications of thick cardboard/newspaper covered in mulch on the landscape.

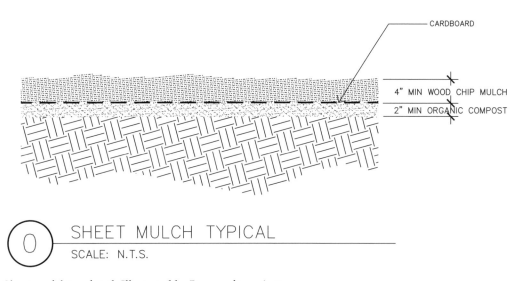

Sheet mulching detail. Illustrated by Permaculture Artisans.

The most vigorous weeds cannot be suppressed by sheet mulching; in fact, placing cardboard over them may aid their spread as their rhizomes surge beneath the cardboard to dominate new areas of the landscape.

(Note: For a simple sheet mulching recipe, go to the Lawn Transformation Step by Step case study found on page 22.)

If using cardboard, use a minimum of one layer with all the inner edges overlapped by a minimum of two inches to suppressing weeds. For blackberries, poison oak, and other woody, rhizomatous vegetation, apply two or more layers of thick cardboard to achieve plant suppression.

With newspaper, use a minimum of eight sheets thick in a sheet mulch. Just as with cardboard, overlap the newspaper a minimum of two inches to make sure no weeds slip between the cracks.

Cardboard and newspaper are recycled waste products and available for free in most communities. I find bike shops, appliance stores, and solar companies have the biggest and best recycled cardboard, although almost any cardboard will do. A lot of recycled cardboard comes covered with tape and staples. Remove the tape before putting cardboard down as mulch. Do *not* use wax-coated food boxes.

When you place cardboard as mulch in a sloping environment, always start at the top of the slope and overlap the layers as you work your way down the slope—the opposite as when installing shingles on a roof. Rather than speeding up the flow of water like roof tiles, our goal is to slow and capture as much water as possible, turning every seam into a mini water catchment device.

Much concern has been shared by some who warn about glues and inks on cardboard and newspaper. Most newspapers in the United States are printed with soy-based inks now and are fully biodegradable (but lead may be present in newspaper ink elsewhere in the world). Some cardboard will have more glue than others. If large seams of glue are present on bigger boxes, cut those sections out before using them. In my personal experience, I have never witnessed cardboard having a detrimental effect on soil.

Nearly all organic certification requirements allow for the use of cardboard and newspaper as a mulch. It is true that some glues and inks may be present, but fungi and bacteria will decompose and transform most if not all of these materials.

As a no-till method that keeps soil ecosystems intact, reduces the use of fossil fuels, redirects a waste stream, and builds carbon-sequestering soil—these materials boast extreme effectiveness.

Always wet the cardboard or newspaper before putting layers of mulch or compost on top. This aids fungal and microorganism production and helps integrate the surface layers with the cardboard. Watering also helps weigh down the cardboard on windy days to avoid having to chase dry sheets around the landscape.

Finally, cardboard and newspaper should be completely covered with mulch or compost and never left exposed to the sun and wind. The goal is for them to decompose safely into the soil; any exposure to sun and wind will dry the cardboard out, creating an unsightly mess.

A minimum of three inches of mulch should be placed on top of cardboard to keep it from showing, though six or more inches is common.

Wood Chips

Wood chips are one of the greatest mulches available for landscapes. In most cities, suburban communities, and rural landscapes, wood chips are easily found. Developing relationships with local arborists can yield a free source of chips, as does obtaining your own wood chipper if you're managing a forested landscape. At a minimum, most landscape and compost supply vendors will have a variety of affordable wood chips available to purchase.

Using wood chips as a final mulch layer is beautiful and widely used as a landscape aesthetic. Wood chips feed soil fungi and absorb and hold water as a sponge, eventually decomposing into rich topsoil. Because of the lignin in the wood chips, burying them underneath compost or soil is not advised. If they are buried, the biology in the soil may use existing nitrogen sources as energy to fuel the decomposition process of the lignin in the wood chips. Placing them on top of the soil, however, mitigates this issue completely while still providing an excellent food source for soil biology to consume as desired.

There are so many ecological uses for wood chips that entire books have been written on the subject—mulching, composting, mushroom cultivation, vermiculture, compost toilet additive, erosion control, beautification, potting soil, and so much more. With so many incredible uses, I can never understand why folks haul wood chips away from downed trees rather than returning them to the landscape.

In 2017 a gigantic wildfire consumed the hills around my hometown and part of the town as well. In the aftermath of the fire, thousands upon thousands of damaged trees were cut, chipped, then hauled out of the county. I was perplexed. With winter rains around the corner, the community scrambled to protect watersheds from potential erosion from the fire scars. Thousands of yards of wood chips were hauled out of the county when we needed them most for erosion control, water retention, and substrate for new fungal growth. This is the kind of shortsightedness a culture shows when it is completely disconnected from its ecology. It is the antithesis of regenerative design.

Some arborist companies use glyphosate and other herbicides during tree removal. Occasionally, these chemicals find their way into the wood chips. Painted wood chips have also been invented and sold worldwide as mulch. Stay away, stay far away from these chemical products.

Straw

Straw is another material that is readily available in many communities throughout the world and used for an array of functions on the regenerative homestead. Straw can be grown and harvested on the land or purchased from feed stores or neighboring ranches. Straw bales are cheap and easily transportable. I have many friends who even transport straw bales in cars without the need for a truck.

Straw is useful for mulching, erosion control, composting, vermiculture, mushroom cultivation, and in natural building projects for insulation, tensile strength within cob building materials (mixture of clay, sand, straw), and chopped up finely to add to earthen plasters.

When sourcing straw, keep in mind where it was grown and whether toxic chemicals were used. Sometimes straw comes laden with agricultural chemicals. Certified organic straw is available but less accessible in most communities. Interestingly, farms that grow organic crops can use any straw mulch on their farms.

Using straw as a mulch—as a forest-floor-mimicking-material—is effective and easy. Straw breaks down faster than wood chips and, if not placed thickly enough on the surface, it will disappear quickly as the season progresses. If you're putting straw directly on cardboard for sheet mulching, use a minimum of four inches of fluffed-up straw or a three-inch straw flake. Most of the time, straw is spread loosely on the surface, but sometimes flakes are called for. A straw flake is a section of straw bale that is peeled away from the compressed bale. It comes off the bail in a rectangular tile and can be used for erosion control, path mulch, and—in cases where sheet mulch is used—to suppress undesirable plants. Because it's compressed, the downside of using straw flake is that not many plants can grow through to the surface, so it should not be used where you're planting seed.

Manure

Sources for manure might include cows, horses, chickens, sheep, ducks, and so on. Each type of manure has a different effect. When it's decomposing, some types of manure get hotter than others, which can pose risks to plants. So using manure as a mulch and landscape additive should be done with caution and care.

The age of the manure makes a big difference in its usability. Raw manure of any kind is nearly always too hot to apply to planting systems (rabbit droppings are a notable exception) and can be spread in a sheet mulch or part of a bed prep and left to "rest" for at least three months before planting.

Composted manure—manure that has aged and gone through its thermophilic process—is a much safer and immediate resource to use in landscape soil preparation. Manure is high in nitrogen and therefore provides a strong base for landscape fertility, while also providing a robust addition of organic matter and microbial inoculant.

Cow and horse manure are the best (and often the most accessible) manures to use in the landscape because they don't burn as hot as other manures, and they compost quickly. In a sheet mulch, composted manure is best placed directly onto the existing soil or vegetation as the first layer, followed by cardboard or newspaper, and finally straw, wood chips, or similar materials spread thickly on top. As a top-dressing material, manure is not always the best if your goal is to smother out competing and undesirable vegetation types. Most seeds will sprout readily in well-aged manure and grow vigorously due to the accessible nutrients. If managing weeds is not an issue, then aged manures can be used as a top dressing for food forest, orchards, garden beds, landscape areas, and—on a larger scale—ranch and farm pastures. Layering manure on top of the ground is best done in shallow layers of one to two inches as opposed to the thicker layers for straw and wood chips. Spread composted manure on pastures and around existing planting systems to instigate vigorous growth. This works wonders.

Manures, whether raw or composted, make an excellent addition to building compost piles and will decompose with other materials into a biologically alive compost.

There are two big concerns when using manure in the landscape. Many manure sources come from large piles that have been sitting at ranches and farms for many years. Over time, seeds from the surrounding areas blow into the manure, lacing it with millions of potential weed seeds. If the manure was piled in a tall pile, it's likely that it heated up enough to kill most seeds, but this is not always the case. Bringing manure onto the land is likely to bring new seeds, which may or may not be desirable.

The second issue with using manure is the potential for toxic antibiotics and deworming agents to be present. Many if not most ranchers give deworming agents and antibiotics to their animals. These chemicals, once applied, may have adverse effects in sensitive soil ecosystems. Most notably, a connection has been made between the presence of dewormers and the absence of soil-building superstar dung beetles (*Scarabaeidae, Geotrupidae*), which collect, eat, and bury manure in ground feeding soil life.[6]

Compost

Compost is one of the greatest gifts you can give to a regenerative landscape. High quality compost has a balance of macro and micro nutrients, minerals, and is alive with beneficial fungi and bacteria. Adding compost to your regenerative landscape, farm, homestead, or ranch will nearly always yield positive results.

For use in no-till mulching systems, compost is normally added on top of a prepped landscape area. Many no-till farmers spread compost over their beds after a harvest has been made. In a sheet-mulching system, compost can be placed underneath cardboard to separate it from wood chips in the top layer or added in thicker volumes on top of the cardboard, planting directly into the compost after a short rest period.

Not all compost is the same; commercially generated composts are more sterile (less biology) and therefore less effective than homemade compost. Get to know the different compost sources, their benefits and drawbacks, before deciding what sort of application is best. A thin layer spread on top of the ground is always beneficial (except along waterways) whereas compost on top of cardboard in a sheet-mulching set up isn't always the best use, depending on the quality of the compost. Homemade compost can be used in this way as well as some aged commercial composts.

Weed seeds and disease can be spread through composts that didn't reach hot enough temperatures (130°F–160°F) to be considered thermophilic. Use of a compost thermometer to track temperature fluctuations is advised when making homemade compost. Commercial compost is sometimes too hot (above 160°F) and therefore sterile with few usable nutrients.

Leaves

Leaves are one of the great gifts of reciprocity when trees return them to the land in which they were born. Yet every year in the fall, the leaf blowers, the rakes, and the garbage trucks are alive in their efforts to clean and remove all the leaves from the ground.Leaf fall is an important ecological cycle that regenerative landscapers depend on and encourage in the landscape. When deciduous trees drop their leaves to the ground, a number of ecological yields are met. The soil is fed organic matter, thousands of species of insects and animals make their homes in the leaves, and the soil becomes insulated from wind, rain, and sun, while the leaves also absorb water in their spongy depths.

Our human environments are covered in impervious materials like driveways, parking lots, roads, rooftops, patios, gravel pathways, and more. In these contexts, leaving leaves on the ground makes less sense as the soil biology is not able to transfer the biomass into soil. Gathering and using these leaves to mulch gardens, layer into sheet mulch, feed worms, or build compost are excellent high value uses of this gift from the trees.

In 2008, my family and I moved to a new neighborhood. The new land we stewarded was devoid of organic matter and life. One of my first activities that fall was knocking on my neighbor's doors and asking if I could haul away the large bags of leaves they had left at the curb. I kept biomass from being trucked away from the neighborhood, while giving my new suburban homestead a major organic matter jumpstart. Maybe your neighborhood or town has a similar issue? Let other people's concept of "waste" be your treasure, the gift you give the soil.

Chopped Plants

My favorite production of mulch material comes when cutting back gardens. Annual plants, herbs, and other species need to be harvested and pruned to optimize the landscape. These actions produce locally sourced biomass—sometimes in great quality and quantity. Use this material to build compost or as mulch directly on the surface of the landscape or on top of cardboard as sheet mulch. Just imagine yourself as a soil-building bear in your garden ecosystem–breaking, rooting, and stomping biomass into the soil.

The trick with using chopped plant material as mulch is taking the time to cut it into medium to small pieces. You don't have to chop it as fine as confetti, but cutting it into pieces no bigger than four to six inches (or smaller) is ideal. With material like this, you are using the landscape as a mulch generator, keeping materials as local as possible, returning minerals and nutrients to their source, and feeding the microbiology in all the ways discussed in this book.

In agroforestry and permaculture circles this is called "chop and drop," a well-suited name for the process it describes. Taking it further, if your landscape management plan encompasses a chop-and-drop system, then you choose the species to plant in the landscape for their abilities to fix nitrogen, generate large amounts of biomass, and regrow from pruning and chopping. This is an intentional nutrient pump landscape, where soil-building species are harvested throughout the year to constantly build soil and sequester carbon.

MATERIALS CALCULATION EQUATION

Adding compost, wood chips, and manure to the landscape is a big task and can become quite expensive when purchasing large amounts. It is helpful to estimate volumes by cubic yards (in the United States and Canada) in order to not over- or underpurchase/source materials. If a sheet mulch is calling for three inches of compost and six inches of wood chips over a 1,000-foot (100 feet by 10 feet) area, how many cubic yards of compost and wood chips are needed for this project?

Use this equation to make materials estimates:

Length x Width x Height ÷ 27 = Cubic Yards

In our scenario above, the equation to estimate how many wood chips looks like this:

100 feet x 10 feet x .5 foot ÷ 27 = 18.5 cubic yards

For the compost required:

100 feet x 10 feet x .25 ÷ 27 = 9.25 cubic yards (purchase 9.5 or 10 yards as a quarter-yard isn't a sellable unit)

18
Vermiculture

I have been cultivating my own worms since 1999. Every place I've ever lived since then I have brought my worms with me and they have been consuming the waste from my kitchen all this time. All of the food waste that my family and I have produced across decades has been fed to these worms, and they have transformed our leftovers into biologically alive soil called worm castings. These castings are then given to trees, vegetables, and herbs to feed their rooted soils with life.

THE POWER OF A WORM BIN

Growing worms is an act of regeneration and abundance. One established worm bin can seed new bins—over the years, our worms have been used to inoculate hundreds of bins for clients, neighbors, schools, and friends.

In the United States alone, 30 percent of all food produced is thrown away.[1] That number is hard to swallow when you consider all the energy used in growing and producing that food—the deforestation of the land, the plowing of the soil, the planting of the seeds (sometimes laced with toxins), the application of chemicals, the water used to irrigate, the labor to plant, harvest, and process, the transportation to deliver to factories for processing and to stores for consumption. Then there is the time it takes to prepare and cook your food. And in the end 30 percent of that is tossed into the garbage. If each person or each family fed worms their food waste at home, we would all live in gardens of abundance.

The worm bin is a simple and effective solution with one common problem—people *mismanage* them, leading to moldy, fruit fly-ridden heaps. I have seen too many vermiculture systems that went defunct, abandoned to rats, mice, and mold. This need not be the case for you. All it requires are a few simple best practices to correctly maintain your worms. With simple best practices in play, you are guaranteed success.

The biggest issue you'll have to address will be taking the compost out of the kitchen before it starts rotting (I never succeed at this). When the material does leave the kitchen, fruit flies and rotting smells with it, it only takes five minutes to feed the worm bin. To guarantee happy worms and an eventual harvest of precious worm castings, follow the instructions below for a simple worm bin design and best practices for feeding, managing, and harvesting from your bin.

Build a Worm Bin

The relationship between vermiculture and my kitchen compost bin over the years has been intimate and profound, resulting in the harvest of dozens of cubic yards of the highest quality soil amendments on the planet.

When it comes to setting up a vermiculture system, I have experimented with just about every design and technique. I've had many failures and many successes and, in the end, I find the simplest worm bins are the best. The system I use is low maintenance, highly effective, and can be made with all reclaimed material.

The species of worm used for these bins is *Eisenia fetida*, also known as red wigglers, compost worms, red worms, and many other names. This worm species has a voracious appetite and under healthy conditions they eat half their body weight in a day. If you have 10 pounds of worms in your bin, they could eat five pounds of food in a single day. They transform that food into vermicompost and transform the vermicompost into worm castings. Truly remarkable.

Worm castings are a biologically alive, water-soluble, bioavailable spectrum of nutrients that give most plants much of what they need to grow healthy. There are nine species of beneficial bacteria in the gut of the worm that inoculate the castings, creating an incredible soil inoculant to bring life into soil.[2]

Worm Bin Design

Let's get the concept of "bins" out of the way first. When we say bins, we are describing a container of some kind that the worms live inside where you add your compost scraps for worms to feed on. In most cases, the vermicompost and subsequent castings get deposited in the same bin and eventually have to be harvested out.

Many commercial worm bins are available on the market. Every fancy system imaginable can be purchased as a kit or built yourself. There are stacked bins where worms move vertically up from one stacked bin to another, leaving castings behind for easy harvest. There are worm bins that operate under the same concept but the worms travel through a screen horizontally from one section of a bin to another. There are any number of different innovations that almost always focus on how to get the castings out of the worm bin. To emphasize, a fancy worm bin's main goal is to make it easier to harvest the castings. This is an understandable challenge and will be addressed below.

The biggest problem with the variety of fancy worm bins on the market is they are often more difficult to use and therefore get neglected and eventually abandoned. Somewhere out there, there are stacks upon stacks of these bins being sent to a landfill. I find it strange, because a worm bin is one of the most practical and easy systems to create out of reclaimed materials—no need to purchase anything.

Use any kind of reclaimed plastic bin, wood bin (in good condition), bathtub, or any receptacle that you're able to put drainage holes in with a lid on top— all these will work. One issue to consider is whether the bin has been used to store toxic chemicals. Worms are very sensitive and will die when exposed to toxic residue. Extra deep bins should also be avoided: Until you're a vermiculture pro, don't use bins deeper than 24 inches because anaerobic conditions will manifest at the bottom of the bin. Remember, these *Eisenia fetida* are worms that move *horizontally* through the soil, so wider, shallower bins provide a better home.

There are three general categories with customizations for choosing a suitable worm bin.

Plastic Bins. Choose a bin that is shallow and wide but no shallower than 12 inches and no deeper than 24 inches. Otherwise, the width and length of the bin are flexible.

Plastic bins will need to have holes drilled in both the bottom and the sides to enable drainage and airflow. There are thousands of reclaimable plastic bins but stay away from polyvinyl chloride (PVC). The off-gas from this type of plastic could pollute your worm castings and/or create an inhospitable environment for your worms. Use only food-grade plastics such as polyethylene or high-density polyethylene (HDPE).

Wooden Bins. Wood boxes also make excellent worm bins. A reclaimed wooden box or one you build yourself make great options. Make sure the wood is in salvageable condition to give your worm bin a good start.

Stay away from elaborate wooden worm box designs. I can't tell you how many times I've seen people take that route and either never finish building the bin, spend too much money, or the complex design fails altogether once complete. Simple is better. Keep repeating that to yourself when it has to do with vermiculture.

Depending on the type of wood and the fabrication, the wooden box will likely need drainage holes drilled into the bottom. Wood breathes, which makes airflow into the bin more abundant than with a plastic bin. Assess the material of the bin you're using—it's possible no side holes for ventilation will be required, especially if the bin is made out of wooden planks or slats. These may provide enough openings for air flow. If it's thick, old-growth single slabbed wood, you will need to drill air holes in the sides.

One advantage of wood is that it's natural; the disadvantage is that it will rot over time. With that in mind, some folks line the inside of the bin with a piece of geotextile fabric or drain cloth to protect the wood from water.

Do not stain the wood with a chemical finish! This will make it toxic and less habitable to the worms while polluting the finished worm castings. My traditional method is to use untreated wood with no liners for a fully natural experience. Eventually the bins break down and I make or reclaim another bin. It's as simple as that.

Bathtub. Reclaimed bathtubs make great worm bins! They are shallow and wide and long lasting, with good drainage already built in. To set up a bathtub worm bin, consider putting a filter around the drain. This will ensure that the worms and castings don't slide through the large drain hole. An upside-down planting flat covered in a small piece of geotextile fabric works great as a filter. You'll need to create a space around the drain where worms and castings can't get in. Other than that, follow the rest of the directions below and you will have an effective and long-lasting worm bin to enjoy for decades to come.

There are two major drawbacks to using a bathtub worm bin. Bathtubs tend to be large, awkward, and heavy. Transportation and placement may cause headaches and should be considered before deciding to use a bathtub in this way. Second, you will need to fasten a lid that completely covers the top of the worm bin to keep from animals getting in. A simple reclaimed exterior door can be used and is quite an elegant solution. The problem is that a door or lid of this size can be quite heavy and is dangerous for children (adults too) to use. Imagine a waterlogged door blowing shut on your or your kid's head while feeding the worms. Ouch! Two small lids are a good option. That way only half the bin gets opened at a time. Also, make sure the lid bends all the way back and rests open when the lid is up.

Drainage

Without good drainage your worms will be left in an anaerobic (without air) and waterlogged environment. Conditions like these cause worms to leave the bin (I've seen it many times) and upon your next visit you'll wonder what the stinky, soggy mess is about and where the worms have gone. Avoid this situation by ensuring good drainage for your worm bin. There are two ways to do this.

1. Make sure the bin itself has good drainage. If you've built your system correctly, there should be a lid that keeps rain and snow from getting into the bin. This is vital, but worms also need moisture. Starting a worm bin requires a fair amount of moisture (usually a full soaking of the "bedding" with a hose). When you start feeding the worms kitchen scraps, you will also be adding significant moisture to the bin. Once worms create vermicompost and castings, even more moisture will be held in the bin. Worm castings are full of humic acid and have an incredible ability to hold water. This makes a great soil additive but won't be great in a bin with bad drainage.

2. The worm bin needs to be placed off the ground. I generally place my bins on reclaimed cinder blocks, bricks, or old scraps of lumber. You determine what the best foundations are for your worm bin, ensuring it meets your various contextual needs, but you must have something to raise the bin off the ground. Since the bin needs to drain, liquid coming from the bin needs a place to go. If the bin is directly on the ground, moisture will have nowhere to go and this will create a soggy environment. In addition, keeping the bin off the ground reduces undesired pest pressure from rats, ants, and other animals.

Airflow

Worms need air to thrive, so the environment you provide for them will need adequate airflow. Sometimes it will be necessary to drill small holes in the sides of the bin (no bigger than 1/8 inch to 1/4 inch) to ensure proper airflow.

Bathtubs have a wide tapered top, allowing plenty of air to cycle in the bin, so they don't require air holes. Like everything with worms, there's no need to get fancy. Just make sure you're not putting worms into airtight containers and you're on the right track.

Lids

I've heard it many times: "I can't have a compost pile because of rats." Or "I can't have a worm bin because of rats." These are myths. Every worm bin must have a lid. I repeat, every worm bin must have a lid. There are large-scale vermiculture systems that are open air, but unless you're operating at a large scale, this will not be viable for most reading this book. Also, so much can go wrong in an open-air environment if you do not build or manage the worm farm correctly.

As long as the lid on your bin is secure and heavy enough that a raccoon can't lift it, no rats will get in either. If you live in bear country, your lid will have to be very secure and an indoor worm bin suddenly looks like a better choice.

The lids on my own bins are literally pieces of plywood cut to the right size. I've been using these pieces of plywood for many years without any issues at all. Many people will hinge the lid but I just rest them on top and lift them off when I feed or manage the bin. It is very easy and fits my context, but if you need something more beautiful then by all means make a nice lid that hinges to the bin. Just be warned, heavy lids that have trouble staying open can be dangerous. I've seen too many heads smashed by these lids. Get that part right!

Placement

For a successful vermiculture endeavor, the placement of the system is crucial. *Eisenia fetida* worms have a wide range of temperatures they can withstand but optimally they are kept in temperatures that are not too hot or too cold. Sunlight is dangerous for worms; therefore, placing a worm bin in direct sunlight will cause failure. You need to place your worm bin in a dark, cool location. In arid and drier temperate climates, a moist area would be optimal. In cold, northern climates, place your bin in a greenhouse, inside a barn or a garage, or in another warm area to keep worms active in winter.

In my semi-dry temperate region (in the Northern Hemisphere), I always place worm bins on the north side of the house as close to a kitchen entrance as possible.

Apply the principle of *relative location* and permaculture zoning by placing worm bins along zone one pathways or close to house entrances. A worm bin placed too far away, which could be deemed inconvenient for feeding kitchen compost, will be a worm bin that doesn't get used often enough. What size container do you have in your kitchen to put compost scraps in and how often do you take it outside? If your worm bin is too far away, your compost may end up sitting in your house longer than you'd like. Anyone who composts their kitchen scraps knows what I'm talking about. Place the worm bin in a convenient location to access readily and easily when the kitchen compost is taken out.

Prepping and Adding Worms

The worm bin is made, the site is chosen, and now it's time to activate the bin. The first action you need to take is to put "bedding" in the bin. Start with a single layer of cardboard on the bottom and wet it thoroughly. This provides a wet sponge at the bottom of the bin to help keep the new worm bin from drying out. The piece of cardboard also slows down the movement of moisture through the drainage holes, which you want at the start of a new vermiculture system.

Place the rest of the bedding material on top of the wet cardboard, filling the bin three-quarters full. Bedding material can include:

- shredded paper
- shredded cardboard
- leaves (my favorite)
- straw
- composted manure (use sparingly)

Your bedding should mostly be made up of paper, leaves, or straw, whatever you have available. Add one shovel full of native soil. This soil will provide grit for the worms to use when consuming your food waste; red worms have gizzards like birds and use grit to digest food. The other benefit of native soil is the addition of indigenous microorganisms to the worm system. These microorganisms have evolved on the same land as your worm bin and aid important microbial interactions when returned to the landscape as worm castings.

The bedding material should be thoroughly wet once you've placed it in the bin. Worms thrive in moist (but not overly moist) environments and dry materials need to be fully wet before the worms live there.

Once the wet bedding is installed you are ready to add the worms. There's no exact unit to volume ratio of how many worms to use to start a bin. My approximation would be a 1-gallon pot of worms for a 10-gallon-size container. Extrapolate from there if you must to estimate how many worms you need for your worm bin. Don't get discouraged if you can't get large volumes of worms. They reproduce extremely fast and need time to acclimate in the bin anyway. Even a small number of worms in a large bin will be plenty to initiate the process. It will take a little more time before you're able to feed large amounts of kitchen waste to them but within a few months the populations will soar and that will not be an issue. Be patient with your worms; add whatever amount you're able to acquire and it will be enough.

At the beginning stages, before you add any food but when the worms are placed in their bedding, there will be an acclimation period. It will take a couple weeks for the worms to adjust to their new home and they *can't be fed during this time*. They will feed on the bedding as needed until they are adjusted.

FEEDING YOUR WORMS

Feeding your worms kitchen food scraps is easy as long as you do it using the correct method. Taking your food waste out to the worm bin, dumping it on top, and leaving is not adequate. Dumping compostable material on top of the bin will lead to an increase in fruit flies, mold, and other unwanted pests. Here's the best method:

1. Dig a hole in the bedding/castings of the bin.
2. Dump your food scraps into the hole.
3. Cover up the food scraps with the bedding/casting material that you pushed aside for the hole.
4. Add new bedding by spreading a thin layer of leaves, paper, or straw on top. Then close the lid and you're done.

This foolproof method for feeding your worms keeps pets at bay, your worms happy with a scrumptious meal, reduces odor, and keeps the important balance between bedding, food scraps, and castings. Adding a layer of bedding each time you feed ensures that there's always bedding for the worms and creates a barrier from pests. Worms hardly ever emerge onto the surface of the bin. If you dump your food scraps there, it will be difficult for them to access because they prefer to stay underneath the top layer of bedding.

CARING FOR WORMS

Every time you feed your worms is an opportunity to check the health of the bin. I keep a small garden fork next to my bin that I use for feedings. During the feeding I sometimes loosen up the bottom of the bin (especially once it's full of castings) to aerate the worm bin. This periodic aerating reduces bad odor, keeps beneficial microorganisms happy, and increases the speed at which food scraps are transformed into worm castings.

Almost every problem you might run into with your worm bin—molds, anaerobic conditions, pests—can be solved by simply aerating the bin and adding more bedding. Aeration and bedding are the two optimal ingredients for keeping the worm bin healthy.

HARVESTING CASTINGS

Harvesting the castings is done simply in my system. Here are two ways to harvest the castings of a simple bin:

1. Make a worm castings tea. The nutrients and biology you want to harvest from a worm bin to help your landscape grow are all water soluble. Take a five-gallon bucket and put a fine meshed screen (no bigger than 1/4 inch) or colander over the top of the bucket.

    Dig out a shovelful or handfuls of the most composted worm castings from the bin. This material is normally found in one of the corners of the bin or along the sides. These castings should look like black soil with very little chunky material mixed in. Place the castings onto the mesh screen. Gently run water onto the castings and into the bucket. The water-soluble particles of the castings will wash into the bucket with the water. Chunkier material and undigested food scraps, along with any worms, will be left on top of the mesh.

    Once all the water-soluble castings have washed into the bucket, dump the worms and chunky material left on the screen back into the worm bin and cover with bedding.

Five gallons of worm casting tea can be further diluted into another 25 gallons of water. Stir it up in buckets to mix and aerate before applying it as a soil soak around your landscape plants in the garden.

2. Place a tarp in direct sunlight. Dig the castings out of the bin and place them onto the tarp. If it is not sunny out or all you have is shade, this will not work as well. When you dig the castings out of the worm bin, be careful not to excavate too much undigested food scraps with them. (Ideally, you've let this worm bin rest without feeding for two to three weeks before harvesting.)

The castings you pile on the tarp will have worms mixed throughout. Stack the pile into a tall tower. Worms don't like sunlight and will dive into the castings away from the sun. Scrape the castings off the top of the tall mound where no worms are present. The worms beneath will dive deeper into the pile. Repeat the process until you're left with a small pile of castings densely populated with worms. Return these to the worm bin and use the clean castings in the landscape or nursery.

If you're adding worm castings to your landscape, garden, or small homestead, there is little concern about accidentally releasing some red wiggler worms to the landscape. However, if you're working in a wildland environment, only use worm castings as a tea to avoid releasing worms into the wild. Northern forest ecosystems suffer from the introduction of worms (especially earthworms, less so red wigglers) because they consume forest duff too quickly, affecting fungal growth, water absorbability, and the organisms that depend on thick forest mulch.[3] Using *Eisenia fetida*, red worms, is of less concern than earthworms as they live in the top 12 inches of the soil, often getting eaten or dying out in dry conditions.

19
Composting

Composting is the act of speeding up the decomposition process of organic matter into a nutrient-rich, biologically alive additive for your landscape, homestead, and farm. The materials used in your compost are best sourced *on the landscape first*, as locally as possible second, and exporting from off-site a last resort (though quite common).

Methods for composting vary from practitioner to practitioner and debates on the best composting method could last an entire cycle of the moon. Some reading this book have a strong feeling about the best compost method and will never be shaken from their stance. I respect that. Below you will find three composting methods that are effective, proven, and easy to produce.

The first context question to ask is, what materials are you composting? For most readers, these will be the materials generated from your landscape— prunings from shrubs and trees, harvested vegetables, cut herbs, deadheaded flowers, fallen fruit, and kitchen scraps. For those stewarding animals, manure from chickens, ducks, sheep, and goats are added to the composting list. In addition, leaf fall, pine needles, shredded paper, and wood chips are all materials that might be generated in the landscape or neighborhood.

The second context question is, what are your goals? If the goal is simply to decompose excess organic matter with the hopes of harvesting black gold, then the warm composting system described below will be a perfect fit.

If, however, diseased plant material and weed seeds are a persistent issue for you, then the hot composting method is your best choice.

COMPOST FOUNDATIONS

Both the warm and hot methods have the same foundational approach. For best results, a ratio of 30 parts carbon to 1 part nitrogen is ideal. This is sometimes seen as 30:1 C/N. Like all good recipes, fluctuations will always vary and this is not a perfect science. A simple approach to achieve something close to these numbers is to use 1/3 brown material, 1/3 green material, and 1/3 manure.

Brown Material

Brown material consists of high-carbon sources that have already gone into an oxidized or dead phase. Straw, leaves, wood chips, dead and brown plant material, pine needles, and shredded papers all constitute your brown material.

Green Material

Sources for green material come from vegetative plant matter that hasn't decomposed yet. Grass clippings, material from cutting back herbaceous plants, vegetable plant bodies, and so forth. This material is a mix of carbon and nitrogen; because it's green, it will heat up the pile when it decomposes.

Manures

Depending on the source of the manure—chicken, goat, cow, and so forth, the carbon to nitrogen ratio of the manure will be different. Some are higher in nitrogen and heat up a great deal, others less so. The manure added to your compost pile presents the greatest biological inoculant for the compost. Manures are alive with billions of bacteria and function as the main nitrogen source for the compost pile.

Don't stress too much about getting the ratios exact. It's better to work with what you have, sourcing materials from the land or as locally as possible, as opposed to testing the carbon and nitrogen ratios of every material to get exact percentages. Trust me, every person reading this can make excellent compost with a little bit of effort.

Location

Hot composts are best made in a shady/semi-shady location where summer suns won't dry out and overheat the compost.

Pests

Rats, raccoons, and other pests are attracted to compost piles, mainly warm piles, and do pose a nuisance. In urban communities, using a compost structure like a plastic or wooden bin to keep critters from gaining access is best. A well-made hot compost pile, however, generally has fewer pest issues.

WARM COMPOSTING

Warm composting requires time and patience. These are compost piles that are built to rest in situ for three or more months.

I took my first composting class when I was 19 years old, having the privilege to learn composting from a biodynamic farmer at the Santa Rosa Junior College. His warm compost method was an inspiration. The compost built under his tutelage was fascinating, and months later the final result, extraordinary—compost filled with soil organisms, with a rich dark color, perfect soil structure, and the ability to hold water like a sponge.

The benefits of using the warm compost method are found in the rich biological life established in the final compost. Since these piles don't reach temperatures above 130°F, a larger diversity of fungi and bacteria proliferate in the pile. Hotter composting methods going above 140°F kill off much of the life, sterilizing the compost. The slower process of warm composting also yields more material in the end because less heat and gas-off means more material.

Decomposing undisturbed for months at a time is ideal for fungal growth, which experts say is the optimal compost to use in the landscape.[1]

Warm Composting Method

1. Fork and prep the ground beneath where the compost will sit. Prepping the earth below the compost pile helps air and biological exchanges occur between the pile and the earth below.
2. Place the primary layer—the larger and woodier material—onto the prepared ground. We would put fruit tree prunings, sunflower stalks, and so on in a layer roughly six inches thick to build the base for the compost pile. The reason for placing this bulky material at the bottom is to ensure that an ample amount of air enters the pile from below. Chop up this material into small pieces to aid in decomposition.
3. On top of the bulky woody layer, add the first layer of greens to a depth of three inches. Slashed cover crops, cut back herbs, and old vegetable plants all work. Chop and fork green material as you layer it. Ensure that the side of the pile is vertical as you build up.
4. Add a one-inch first layer of manure on top of the greens layer. Don't forget to aerate with a garden fork and rake to the edge of the layer below.
5. Build your warm compost pile by adding three-inch layers of green material followed by a one-inch layer of manure, followed by three inches of brown—for example, three inches of sliced vegetable plants, one inch of manure, three inches of straw. Then start the cycle again. For every layer you add, fork it into the next layer to ensure adequate air moves up and down through the pile. Additionally, misting/watering each layer as you build the pile is ideal. If the material is already heavily moist (kitchen scraps), less moisture is needed, but brown materials will require additional moisture. Essentially, you water and aerate the pile as you build it tall, layer after layer.

    Ideally, build your warm compost pile to a minimum of four feet tall. By building it to this height, it will ensure that the compost pile heats up to approximately 130°F. If your pile is too small, you can still make excellent compost, but it will take much, much longer to fully decompose.
6. Once the pile has been layered, aerated, chopped, and watered, it's time to cover the compost. My old teacher used a thick layer of straw to cover the pile. This protects the biological life growing, eating, and decomposing the compost pile from wind, rain, and sun. Most modern-day compost builders cover their piles with black tarps. A black tarp will also help keep the pile warmer and protect, to some degree, against pests such as raccoons and rats.
7. While the compost is in its decomposition phase for the next few months, periodically add plant ferments, compost teas, and microorganism inoculants (see chapter 20) to continue feeding the pile biological life and moisture. Use a compost thermometer to gauge the temperature and whether the compost would benefit from additives like manure or compost tea to stay activated.
8. The longer you wait to harvest the compost, the more time for fungi, worms, and bacteria to transform organic matter into rich, humic compost. Hotter climates will see a faster

transformation of warm compost and colder climates may need extra time to finish. In general, three months is an ideal window toward finished compost.

The results of composting in this way will be nothing short of astounding if done right.

HOT COMPOSTING

Thermophilic composting is the most common method used in municipal and commercial facilities. It's called thermophilic after bacteria of the same name that are active in hot compost between 140°F and 180°F. These heat-loving bacteria quickly decompose organic matter while the rest of the biology dies off, sacrificing their bodies to the compost pile. On the plus side, sterilizing compost this way kills off disease and weed seeds, leading to a clean final compost in as little as three weeks. The finished compost can be left to rest to allow greater numbers of fungi and bacteria to proliferate after the thermophilic process has been completed.

A Simple Hot Composting Method

1. A hot compost pile needs to be tall and turned regularly. The location requires adequate space to turn the pile.
2. Build a compost pile in layers as described for the warm composting. Make sure the pile is four feet tall or higher. This time, add two plastic pipes—2 inches wide by 4 1/2 feet tall—to the compost pile. Drill holes up and down the surface of these pipes. Hollowed-out bamboo can be used as a natural substitute.

    The pipe is placed in the compost pile with one end at the bottom sticking upright. Your layers of biomass are placed around the pipes. These pipes ensure optimal air exchange throughout the entire pile, keeping it well oxygenated and highly active. Cover the pile with a black tarp.
3. Turn the pile completely once a week. When turning, use the same method as before, aerating each layer with a garden fork and watering to ensure plenty of air and moisture is in the pile. Reuse the pipes in the freshly turned compost pile.
4. After three weeks, let the pile rest for a minimum of one week. This will allow the soil biology to colonize the cooling pile. Now your compost is ready to be fed back to the landscape. Bon appétit!

DOUBLE BIN COMPOST SYSTEM

Building compost needs to be practical. If your compost pile needs to be designed for daily or weekly additions of kitchen scraps and cut plant materials, then a double bin system is advised.

A double bin system consists of two compost piles right next to each other. Usually these are separated by pallets, wood slats, or wire mesh, and often they are enclosed within built structures to keep pests out. One pile is dedicated to daily or weekly feeding of kitchen scraps and landscape plant material while the second pile rests as a "warm" compost left undisturbed to age into finished compost. An alternative is to turn the resting pile into a "hot" compost as described above.

Once the pile being fed regularly gets large enough, it is left to rest and the second bin is harvested as compost for the landscape. Now the empty second bin is ready to become the feeding pile and the whole cycle repeats.

Managing a compost pile that you feed frequently is similar to managing a worm bin. When you feed kitchen scraps to the pile, don't dump them on the top and walk away. Dig a hole in the pile, dump the kitchen scraps in, and cover them. Then cover the pile with a thin layer of brown material like straw, wood chips, or leaves. This will keep the pile well balanced and deter pests.

Compost piles that are fed regularly do pose a pest problem, which can be solved by creating the bin. This is similar to a worm bin except the bottom is in full ground contact with wood or wire mesh for walls. A sturdy lid on top is a must to keep rats and raccoons out of the compost.

BUYING COMPOST

Purchased compost is an excellent way to add biologically available nutrients, organic matter, and microbial life to the landscape. That said, there are many red flags to look out for when purchasing compost. Commercially produced compost is created through a mechanical thermophilic composting process. Commercial producers burn out weed seeds and disease to give their customers the cleanest possible product. The downside is that these composts sometimes arrive with little life in them.

In my own region, many years ago, compost from a privately owned commercial compost facility was laced with a chemical called clopyralid. This chemical wouldn't break down and was still present even after being composted at high temperatures. Landscapers and farmers were unknowingly putting this chemical-laden compost onto their projects, resulting in poor plant growth. Investigate before trusting a compost source. Organic compost can be found and hopefully yields great results but is often expensive. Do your research and know the source of your compost. Talk with farmers and landscapers familiar with a product before buying it. Trial and error is the next best test of compost quality if other research methods fail. A high quality compost will grow the garden quickly with large healthy plants. If you don't get these results, the compost may be the problem.

An advanced approach to purchasing compost is to get two or three kinds to mix together. Mixing multiple kinds of compost creates a highly diverse microbial inoculant that boosts life in landscape soil. A single type of compost might be dominated by bacteria and another type might be more fungal. When mixed together, these become powerhouse resources for the landscape.

Choosing what volume of compost to buy depends on your context. Once you have a reasonable landscape design plan, generate an estimate for the volumes of compost you need. Use the cubic yardage equation (found in chapter 18) to decide how much material is needed to cover the landscape.

20

Compost Tea and Plant Ferments

Many liquid fertilizers and biological inoculants are made from the landscape. You can make compost tea, worm casting tea, plant ferments, manure tea, and other microorganism inoculants to keep your planting systems hardy and the soil teeming with life.

AERATED COMPOST TEA

The use of aerated compost tea is gaining in popularity throughout the organic and regenerative worlds and for good reason. Dr. Elaine Ingram of the Soil Food Web training program has spent years brewing and studying these products and has developed many, many recipes for making compost tea that serve a variety of functions, including recipes that cater to fungal or bacterial inoculation. The science of compost tea is evolving quickly.

Compost teas need to be thought of as inoculant. They are not necessarily fertilizers but rather large doses of bacteria, fungi, and protozoa that activate all the beneficial functions found in a healthy soil biology.

Compost Tea Recipe

Here is a simple compost tea recipe that can be prepared, brewed, and applied to the soil within 24–36 hours. This recipe will produce a fantastic microbial inoculation for the soil. If, however, you need a highly fungal tea or a highly bacterial tea, do your own research to learn what kinds of additional fungal or bacterial additives will brew the kind of tea you require.

Materials Needed

5-gallon bucket
Strong aquarium bubbler with two or more air stones attached
Extension cord if plugging in an air bubbler away from an electrical outlet
1 stirring stick
1 gallon well-aged compost (not commercially purchased thermophilic compost) or
    1 gallon worm castings
1 cup kelp meal
1 cup rock dust (find at a nursery, farm store, landscape material vendor, or online)
1 ounce molasses

Directions

1. Combine all ingredients into the 5-gallon bucket and fill with non-chlorinated water, leaving 2 inches at the top of the bucket.
2. Stir vigorously. Spin vigorously clockwise, then counterclockwise, until bubbles and froth form on the surface.
3. Place the air stones attached to the aquarium bubbler into the bottom of the bucket and turn on. A vibrating, bubbling sound should emit from the bucket while air bubbles form on the surface.
4. Leave the air bubbler on and the bucket untouched for at least 24 hours.
5. After 24–36 hours, turn the air bubbler off and stir the contents vigorously once again. The aerated compost tea is now ready for application.
6. You can dilute the tea up to a ratio of 1:25—1 part compost tea to 25 parts nonchlorinated water. Compost tea is not a nitrogen-rich fertilizer and can be applied safely to the landscape without dilution, but diluting it makes it last longer while covering larger areas. Use immediately—do not allow the tea to rest for more than a few hours before application.

Freshly aerated compost tea can be used in several ways:

- When planting bare root trees and berries, soak them in the compost tea prior to planting.
- Add powdered mycorrhizal fungi inoculants to the fresh compost tea after brewing and just before application.
- Use compost tea as a soil soak around plants including young nursery plants, indoor plants, and everywhere in the landscape.
- Compost tea can be used as foliar spray (a mist sprayed on leaves of plants) but must be filtered before spraying through a backpack jet sprayer or spray bottle. An alternative brewing method for foliar application is to combine all organic materials into cheesecloth or a sock and steep them in a bucket of water (like a steeping teabag) with aeration (when the bubbler is on). This method provides a prefiltered compost tea that is appropriate for use in backpack sprayers and spray bottles. Warning: Unfiltered compost tea *will* clog spray systems which is utterly annoying!
- Using similar ratios and expanding the recipe for larger systems is acceptable. You can make 50-gallon systems or even larger. The larger the system, the more air needs to be pumped into the tea, which means small aquarium bubblers won't suffice.

COMMERCIAL BREWERS

Many compost tea brewers are available to purchase. Different sizes and technologies are produced all the time. If you're enthusiastic about compost teas and have the budget, a large commercial compost tea brewer can be a great investment, especially for production farms and orchards. I enjoy commercial tea brewing systems and have one myself, but this book is about what's practical. Most readers will be served by an affordable homemade compost tea brewer.

LIQUID COMFREY FERTILIZER

Comfrey is a vigorous herbaceous perennial that has a multitude of uses in the regenerative landscape. The leaves, stems, and flowers of comfrey are used to create a well-balanced liquid fertilizer. Comfrey grows vigorously and tolerates the leaves being cut multiple times a year, making comfrey a generous biomass producer in the landscape. Comfrey fertilizer can be made throughout the year and given to the landscape as a bioavailable liquid fertilizer.

While manures provide higher amounts of NPK per gallon, comfrey fertilizer is easily grown and accessible most of the year if planted in the landscape. Comfrey is filled with nutrients and, once fermented, provides a dose of available nitrogen and minerals. (Note: A similar plant ferment can be made from nettles.)

Comfrey Fertilizer Recipe

1. Get a 5-gallon or a 55-gallon bucket. If you have access to vast swaths of comfrey hedges, the 55-gallon bucket can be used to brew enough comfrey feed for a multiacre farm. A 5-gallon bucket will suffice for smaller sites.
2. Harvest the comfrey, cutting the stems and leaves away from the base. (Don't worry—it will sprout back.)
3. Chop the leaves and stems into small 3-inch pieces and fill the 5-gallon bucket two-thirds full. Add water to just cover the comfrey leaves.
4. Place a stone or a brick or something similar on top of the comfrey leaves to push them down into the water, using it to keep the leaves submerged.
5. Let this concoction sit for three to four weeks. During this time it will be fermenting into a dark green fertilizer. It will start to stink, so keep your comfrey fertilizer away from sensitive noses.
6. Once three to four weeks have passed, pull the weight out of the bucket, strain the liquid, and compost whatever fermented leaves and stems are left.

The comfrey liquid fertilizer is now ready to be used. It is extremely concentrated and should only be applied at a dilution rate of 1:25—1 gallon of comfrey fertilizer to 25 gallons of water. If you are using city water, dechlorinate it first by letting it sit out for twenty-four hours. Comfrey fertilizer can be applied once a month and stored for up to six months in cool, dark conditions. If you're implementing other regenerative soil management techniques, less frequent applications of comfrey fertilizer are appropriate. Liquid comfrey can also be added to composting piles to feed and activate the microbiology.

MANURE TEA

To make a strong liquid fertilizer with a high dose of nitrogen to feed landscape plants, look no further than manure tea. This age-old farming technique is as simple as it sounds.

1. In a bucket, dilute manure to a 1:10 ratio—1 gallon of manure (use *only* manure aged more than three months or composted) to 10 gallons of dechlorinated water.
2. Stir the concoction forcefully for 10 to 20 minutes. The longer you stir, the better, but your arm will get tired! Stir it one direction to create a vortex in the tea and then agitate it by stirring against the flow, going back and forth in this way. The goal is to break up as much manure as possible into water-soluble form.
3. Apply manure tea as a soil soak around desired plants. Warning: manure tea is very high in nitrogen and best used sparingly. Do not apply to young plants or seed starts. Avoid applying the manure tea onto the leaves of plants as the strong concentration of nitrogen will burn them. Horse and cow manure are best used for manure tea because manure from chickens and ducks will be too strong for many plants and pose other detrimental effects. The source of manure is significant as some manures are laced with antibiotics and deworming chemicals. **Never use fresh manure for your tea.**
4. Always use the entire batch of tea on the same day. You don't want to have manure fermenting around your landscape.

21
Cover Cropping

Plants are soil builders—they transform sunlight, sequester carbon, grind minerals, fix nitrogen, and feed soil microbiology. Through cover cropping, the many soil-building benefits of plants are harnessed.

By sowing thousands of seeds across the landscape at the right time of year, many regenerative yields are generated. Food is produced, along with herbal medicine, forage for birds, and pollinator habitats. By diversifying the seeds you sow—using mixes of 10 or more species—you optimize the soil microbial community with a wide palette of plant exudate food sources.[1]

Cover crops are usually short-lived annual systems that grow quickly to be returned to the soil the next season. You can also use perennial soil-building species to establish ongoing fertility. In the process of building a regenerative landscape, cover crops are used intensively in the first one to two years until perennial systems establish. On farms and ranches, cover crops may be utilized year after year between annual crops. Apply *contextual design* and plan accordingly for your specific project.

One advantage cover cropping has over other systems is the ability to cover large areas of land with beneficial species for little expense. Seeding an acre of land is much cheaper than planting an acre with plant starts. I've seeded five acres in a day by myself, by hand. Someday maybe you will do the same. I hope you do! This is a powerful approach with a lot of flexibility when getting the species, timing, and methodology correct.

Timing

Timing is key to success (timescale succession). The best time to sow is during or just before the first real rain of the season. In my region, this is generally the end of October or beginning of November. Sowing seeds at this time requires no additional irrigation as you are seeding with the rain. In this way you literally regenerate dozens if not hundreds of acres with no irrigation and no maintenance for months. In other regions, the time of seeding needs to fit your climate.

December through January (in the Northern Hemisphere) is usually too cold for many seed varieties to germinate, so seeding is best done before the cold sets in or in springtime after the thaw. In snowless temperate climates, winter grain and clover varieties still sprout during the cold months but they're limited.

Early to late spring is another opportunistic time to seed while the soil is still moist and warming up to the sun. Once the hotter seasons kick in, the window for broadcast seeding diminishes unless your climate is filled with summer rains and monsoons.

Disturbances

Success in your seeding endeavors requires a disturbance to the soil surface prior to seeding. It might mean seeding into freshly grazed pastures. If tilling of some kind has scarred the land, seeding into these prepped seedbeds work wonders. Seeding into subsoiler furrows, on top of backfilled trenches, into the tread marks of tractors, throughout a forest clear-cut, after a wildfire—these are excellent situations where disturbed soil is ripe for seeding. If the context calls for it, sheet mulch an area with compost above cardboard and seed directly into it.

Broadcasting seed following large earthwork projects is critical. Your regenerative landscape may call for new terraces, water-harvesting swales, ponds, garden beds, graded pathways, building foundations, and so on. When the grading work is complete, the soil will look damaged and barren. Have your seeding plan ready.

SPECIFIC SEED FOR SPECIFIC YIELDS

What exactly are your goals? This is the first question to ask before you purchase seed. Is this project a future farm, an ecological landscape, a native grass meadow? What are the existing soils like? Overcompacted? Well drained? Full of opportunistic weeds? Answers to these questions illuminate the context and assist your decision-making process. Choose specific species for specific outcomes.

Nitrogen Fixers

Nitrogen-fixing plants are soil-building species with symbiotic relationships with rhizobia bacteria. The plants offer their roots as host for the bacteria who are fixing or gathering nitrogen out of the atmosphere into nodules along the roots. The plant uptakes this nitrogen into its tissues, releasing it to the soil in bioavailable form upon decomposition.[2]

Nitrogen fixers come in many forms: annuals, perennials, ground covers, shrubs, vines, herbaceous, and so on. The entire family of legumes are nitrogen fixers, so most cover crop seed mixes include legumes as a central feature. Learning about the growth habits of various nitrogen-fixing plants like clover, vetch, bell bean, fava bean, and peas will help you determine the best way to accomplish your goals. In common practice, nitrogen-fixing plants are cut back in order to make the nitrogen available to landscape crops. Their flowering stage is the optimal time to cut legumes for nitrogen harvest. I always leave a small percentage uncut to go to seed for saving until the next season.

Taproot Plants

Broadleaf taprooting plants—daikon radish, mangel beets, and turnips—provide another host of functions for developing rich soil. These plants generally have taproots that drive into the soil, developing a large amount of subsurface biomass within their large root systems. When these crops are cut back or smothered in mulch, they dose the soil with large volumes of organic matter. If your landscape soil is barren and lacking organic matter, taproot species are here to help.

Vegetables/Herbs

Sow vegetables and herbs using a broadcast seeding method as well. Mustards, kales, beets, carrots, turnips, parsnips, lettuces, peas, fava beans, calendula, arugula, strovita, red clover, parsley, cilantro, dill, and fennel will readily germinate in a seeding system if sown at the right time of year. The best part is, if done right, these crops grow with no irrigation or maintenance, producing harvests in the springtime. This is a great way to grow food and medicine with low costs and high yields.

Grain

Most of the grains we eat are sown in either spring or fall, making them great candidates to seed with rains. Winter wheat, cereal rye, oats, and barley are some of the most vigorous cold season species, providing harvest for humans, animals (as forage), and the land.

Insectary Plant Species

Sowing wildflower seeds is an act of art and restoration. Many wildflowers and flowering herbs germinate easily and vigorously. This is one of the quickest ways to add color and beauty to the landscape while attracting pollinators—bees, birds, parasitoid wasps, butterflies, lacewings, ladybugs, and many more. These creatures manage pests throughout the landscape and pollinate crops. Many flowering seed varieties are either perennial or readily reseed themselves to return each year. But they only reseed if you let them go to seed, which means you need to plan ahead for how you will manage these species when they are mature.

HOW TO BROADCAST SEED

Soaking Seeds. Many seeds germinate better with a presoaking. Legumes especially germinate with improved vitality when soaked in water, compost tea, or bacterial inoculant for a good hour before dispersal.

Because legumes have a symbiotic relationship with rhizobia bacteria, soaking seeds in a rhizobium bacteria inoculant achieves greater nitrogen-fixing results. Bacterial inoculants are readily available for purchase and come as black powder that is mixed with the water for soaking the seeds.

Casting Seeds. Many methods work to broadcast seeds. One ancient and effective method is to mix them in a bucket and toss them with your hand. Different techniques exist for how to throw the seeds—throwing them high into the air and letting them fall where they may or flinging them out of your hand between thumb and forefinger are two common techniques.

Using broadcast seeding tools is an excellent way to achieve even cover, making your seeds go a long way. A walk-behind manual seeder tool works great, as will seed bags filled with your seed mix and slung over your shoulder. As you walk the landscape, you spin a seed plate at the bottom of the bag, which flings seeds in front of you in an even fan. This method is beautiful and primal and my favorite way to seed large landscapes.

There are many seeding attachments that fit to tractors. For larger projects, these could fit the context better than seeding by hand. Look into all the different styles and find a seeding attachment that best meets your needs.

Covering Seeds. Once seeds have been broadcast across the landscape, consider lightly raking them into the surface or covering them with a light layer of straw or wood chips. These actions protect the seed from hungry birds and from drying out in the sun.

22
Hügelkultur

When shrubs and trees are cut or removed during the landscape-building process, most people don't know what to do with the resulting biomass. Hügelkultur provides a way to incorporate woody debris into the landscape in a way that builds soil fertility as well as providing other ecological yields. Hügelkultur essentially means building a mound or raised bed of material that will enrich the soil. Rather than hauling wood debris off-site or burning it in a pile (common land management practices), building mounds keeps biomass on-site, putting carbon in the ground rather than sending it into the atmosphere. (Using burn piles does have an ecological function in large-scale regenerative landscapes and is discussed in part IX of this book.) The term *hügelkultur*, meaning "mound culture," comes from Germany and Austria. This technique has been in use for hundreds of years and became popular in the twenty-first century due to the inspiring work of Austrian permaculturist Sepp Holzer.

In this chapter, the uses and building techniques of hügelkultur will empower you to incorporate these systems into your landscapes. As always, context is the driver, and hügelkultur systems need only be developed when surplus or renewable sources of woody debris exist on the site. Trucking in material from off-site will waste fossil fuel resources when other techniques to build a regenerative landscape are available with on-site materials.

Moving biomass off-site, though a common practice, is literally mining the landscape. Woody material represents minerals, nutrients, and biological exchanges taking place on the land. Capturing and returning those nutrients to the soil continues the regenerative processes that trees provided before they were cut down.

HOW TO BUILD HÜGELKULTUR

Before deciding to build a hügelkultur, make sure you have access to woody debris such as tree trunks, logs, and branches. This material absorbs water in the wet season, retaining moisture into the dry season. To build a proper mound system, a moderate to large volume of material is required. Unless a friend or neighbor has significant woody debris or other sources that *need* a carbon sink, the regenerative method would avoid bringing material from off-site to build the project.

Some have advised avoiding certain types of wood like eucalyptus (always demonized for its allelopathic nature) for building hügelkultur or adding wood chips to landscape and gardens. The effect these trees have on the ecology during their growth is quite different from how their woody material acts once it decomposes. When fungi, bacteria, and other soil organisms

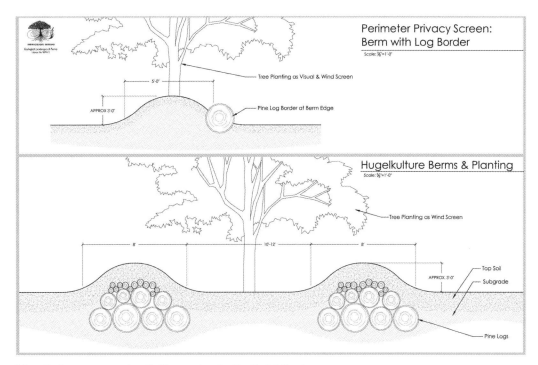

Hügelkultur concept detail. Illustration by Emily Mallard.

consume these materials, the logs and branches *will turn to living soil*. In the long term, the type of wood doesn't matter, but in the beginning, hardwood versus softwood or wood that rots quickly versus wood that doesn't *will* change how the system functions in the first few years.

Location

The concept of *relative location* must be applied when deciding the placement of hügelkultur. Because it is a raised bed, it provides many microclimate benefits while also creating a sound barrier and an area perfect for privacy plantings. As a windbreak, a hügelkultur system creates a protected area for trees and plants that need shielding from the wind. Plant *behind the wind side* of the raised mound on the natural soil grade to achieve this, *not* on top of the berm.

To harvest water, the hügelkultur must be placed in a beneficial relationship to the flow of water. Building on contour or placing the mound on the downslope side of a rain garden are two proven methods for incorporating and locating hügelkultur to benefit water infiltration.

Gather the Right Tools

Building a hügelkultur system takes a bit of work and will require the right set of tools to complete the project, whether you build it by hand or with a machine. An excavator or a backhoe are perfectly suited to building these systems. Excavators grab and move logs into place, excavate the trench, backfill, and place soil on top—all the actions required to build a hügelkultur.

If you're working by hand, a pickax, shovel, and wheelbarrow will do the trick for excavating and backfilling as needed. Loppers, a pruning saw, a machete, a digging bar, and a cant hook (log-rolling tool) will be necessary for cutting and moving woody material. A chainsaw is an indispensable tool for cutting large logs that need to be sized for moving by hand.

Dig the Trench

You will bury the first layers of logs and branches in the soil below grade. This requires a trench to be excavated to the desired size.

The size of the trench will be determined by the method of installation (by hand or by machine) and the size of your largest materials. I like to build large hügelkultur systems within orchards and food forests, so mine are generally built using an excavator to create a trench that is typically 18 inches to two feet deep by eight feet wide by 40 feet or longer. I've even built systems as long as 150 feet.

The context of your project, the appropriate location when designing the hügelkultur, the materials, and the equipment on hand make up the context that helps determine what size the trench will be.

Build in Layers

Once the trench is dug, the rest of the process consists of placing the appropriate-sized material inside and on top of the trench, layering the system vertically. As you build the mound, always place the largest material at the bottom, then soil, next largest on top of that, then soil, the next largest on top, then soil, using smaller and smaller woody debris until you've placed the smallest branches in the top layers of the hügelkultur.

After every layer of woody material is placed, cover it in deep soil. The exact depth of each woody layer versus the depth of soil will be determined by your overall context and the material you have on hand.

I would suggest placing woody layers of 10 to 14 inches, followed by 6 to 8 inches of soil. Every system will be different, so use these numbers as guides, not as unbreakable rules.

As you build the hügelkultur and work up to the last top layers, consider adding manure, grass clippings, cover crop material, or other nitrogen-rich materials into the last few feet, combined with the branches and soil. These will heat up the mound—providing a beneficial microclimate in the winter—aid in decomposition, and activate biological life in the woody berm. It is best to use nitrogen-rich materials cultivated on-site but if locally sourced manure is hauled in from elsewhere, that will do.

Place the Final Layers

Once the last of the branches have been placed, cover the entire hügelkultur with a minimum of 12 inches of soil. At this point, if you're building this system by hand, your soil materials may be depleted. During the installation of your hügelkultur, make sure to continually check on how much soil is left to leave enough for the final covering.

On larger projects, excess soil may already be excavated in tandem with other projects like pond building, house foundations, rain gardens, and so forth. In that case, these excess materials will be used to their highest value inside the hügelkultur system. Always place the mineral "subsoil" materials at the bottom of the berm and any excess *biologically alive topsoil* at the top of the berm. This re-creates the natural stratification of soil and gives the biological community access to more air and plant root exchanges.

Once the final layer of soil has been placed, ideally you will cover the entire berm *again* in compost or composted manure, with a final layer of wood chips, straw, or leaf mulch. If the material is bone dry, consider wetting as you build the mound.

If you live in gopher or ground squirrel country, know that hügelkultur systems create the perfect habitat for these organisms. The woody debris creates spaces under the soil, making it nearly impossible to trap all the rodents. Ultimately, these systems become permanent refuges for burrowing animals. Even if you consider these rodents pests, don't be completely turned off by the idea of hügelkultur. There are plenty of long-lived shrubs and herbs that grow happily side by side with burrowing rodents and a settling mound.

Plant the Berm

One of the biggest issues with the mound system is that it will settle over time. As woody debris breaks down inside the berm, your soil layers settle and the entire berm will shrink. For this reason, do *not plant trees on top* of a hügelkultur. Large trees may become stressed during the settling process, leaving roots exposed to air pockets over time. It's better to plant shrubs, herbs, and ground covers that take opportunistic pleasure in the changing shape of the berm. Many rhizomatous growing species will respond favorably to these changes.

THE BENEFITS OF HÜGELKULTUR

Building hügelkultur uses up on-site biomass, as this material is incorporated into building up the raised mound instead of carting it away. The woody materials represent carbon sequestered by growing trees and stored in the trunks and branches. By incorporating these materials into the hügelkultur mound, the carbon is returned to the soil to be fed upon by microorganisms.

Microclimate Moderation

Hügelkultur moderates climate in several ways. Building these systems creates a raised mound above the natural grade of the soil, which protects areas from wind, increases drainage, and creates ecotones that provide sunnier and shadier sides to the mound. All of these produce diverse microclimates in a small area. By packing these mounds with woody material, the decomposition and breakdown generate heat, providing a slight warming to the area during the transitional fall and spring seasons and helping plant communities get a jump start on growth.

Raised Planting Bed

As a raised mound, hügelkultur generates a planting area that is easier to harvest, providing better drainage to the plant community growing on the bed, better aeration in the soil, and frost protection in some cases. Hügelkultur mounds built in rocky or hardpan soil allow for better root growth and penetration throughout the mound before roots find hardpan below.

Water Harvesting

Hügelkultur mounds are placed on or near contour, acting as water-capturing systems, slowing surface waters, and retaining significant levels of moisture in the woody, carbonaceous core that makes up the mound.

Fungal Substrate

By keeping woody material in close ground contact, hügelkultur provides a perfect substrate for opportunistic fungal growth. Fungal soil is of paramount importance for carbon sequestering, water harvesting, and generating biologically alive topsoil, which is what this mound culture turns into with time.

CONCERNS

In extremely arid environments where raised beds decrease the water-holding capacity of the soil, a system like hügelkultur is likely not appropriate. Similarly, much has been written about poorly sited hügelkultur systems in soggy environments where seasonal flooding potentially lifts biomass out of the ground. Yet every landscape decision is specific to place. Hügelkultur *has* been known to function well in both arid and wetland environments, but its applications are limited to specific contexts.

One drawback of building a hügelkultur system is an almost complete dependence on machinery for installation. Small-scale systems can be built by hand, but most hügelkultur systems require the movement of huge amounts of soil and other materials. This doesn't pose a problem on appropriate projects where equipment is already necessary for moving logs, brush, and soil. That being said, small-scale, hand-dug hügelkultur systems are ripe with potential as long as you and your team are willing to put in the hard work. If you do, you'll see it's a worthwhile endeavor.

23

The Fungal Landscape

Fungi are primordial entities that are responsible for many of the life-generating processes of the earth. They seed clouds for rain, capture and store carbon, harvest water, transform decaying biomass into living soil, protect plants, distribute nutrients in the soil food web, ferment food and drink, generate medicines of all kinds, and more. Fungi are integral to life on earth and human civilization.

Fungi are conductors of ecosystems. They make up to 50 percent of all underground biomass[1] while generating food and medicine, with many abilities we have yet to discover. The science of fungi, mycology, is still a young science indeed. New revelations are made every year as humans uncover the mysteries and origins of these organisms. They are more closely related to animals than plants and seem to operate with otherworldly intelligence.

Fungi's role in decomposition makes them one of the greatest terrestrial decomposers on planet earth. They turn excess wood, leaves, plant material, minerals, stone, chemicals, and many, many other materials into soil, usually through enzymes secreted by mycelium. Mycelium represents the underground body of the fungi, which makes up most of its mass. The fruit body (commonly called a mushroom) is the reproductive organism of the fungi, which pushes through the soil above ground to disperse spores.

The fungal phyla focused on in this book are mycorrhizal and saprophytic fungi. Mycorrhizal fungi (endomycorrhiza and ectomycorrhiza) are species with symbiotic relationships to plant roots, distributing nutrients throughout the soil community. Mycorrhizal root inoculants are commercially available in granular and powder forms, used to inoculate plant roots in the regenerative landscape prior to planting or added to compost teas for dispersal. More than 90 percent of plants form a symbiotic relationship with a mycorrhizal species.[2] A few plant families, most notably Brassicaceae, do not form mycorrhizal bonds.

Saprophytic fungi grow on dead wood and other decaying biomass—what's called *substrate*—including wood, cardboard, straw, leaves, sticks, and branches.

Edible Mushrooms

Mushrooms have been an important food source for humans for thousands of years. Many favorite edible mushrooms are capable of being grown on logs and straw directly in the landscape. Certain wild mycorrhizal species are known and wildcrafted as delectable edibles during the wet season: chanterelles (*Cantharellus*) and porcini (*Boletus edulis*), two of the most prized edible mushrooms in the world. Wildcrafting mushrooms is an art and science. Many species are poisonous and many edibles have poisonous look-alikes, which is why it's good practice to *never* pick and eat a mushroom unless you are 100 percent sure it is edible. Like all wildcrafting, harvesting mushrooms in the wild also requires a high level of sensitivity to ensure you do not decimate a mushroom patch. Best practices while wildcrafting mushrooms include: cleanly cutting mushrooms at the base without disturbing the mycelium, *never* removing all the mushrooms you find, and being sensitive to the habitat where they grow. Many mushrooms offer a full spectrum of nutrient-dense food that nourishes our bodies.

Medicinal Fungi

The science is still young but more and more medicinal benefits of mushrooms are discovered every year. Many mushrooms have highly medicinal uses, with benefits including immune system building, brain neurogenesis, detoxification, antidepressants, and much more.[3] Many of these medicinal mushrooms (the saprophytic species) are happy to grow on logs and straw.

CASE STUDY: IN THE DARK AT SOMERSET HOUSE BY DARREN SPRINGER

The Edible Utopia project is located at Somerset House, a working arts center built on a historic site in the heart of London. It is home to one of the United Kingdom's largest and most compelling creative communities.

As the mycologist in residence at Somerset House, I experiment with facilitating new ways of thinking, growing, and eating by utilizing the building's idiosyncratic architecture to create new ecological possibilities. In 2018, I started the Edible Utopia project to teach others about the unique properties of mushrooms and mycelium and their role in supporting life on earth.

The project's core mission is to provide hands-on educational sessions for people from various backgrounds to establish practical skills for creating a sustainable future in our city. We collaborate with youth groups, communities in vulnerable housing, care groups, schools, and cultural organizations.

The Edible Utopia project uses several small alcoves that were originally used for housing coal to cultivate mushrooms and other organisms that spend most of their existence in the dark, growing food in hidden and underused parts of this historic site. These old, dark coal holes have been converted into the perfect environment to create mushroom fruiting chambers. Out of the dark, we can support and create new life.

By using coffee ground waste from the on-site café that used to go straight to the landfill, we nurture and cultivate oyster mushrooms. The mushroom waste then feeds our worms, whose nutritious excrement in turn feeds the rhubarb grown on the roof. We have developed a closed-loop, organic ecosystem as a replicable example of sustainable growth in the center of the city.

Coal Hole Infrastructure for Mushroom Cultivation

Because Somerset House, including the coal holes, is grade listed—a designation for sites of exceptional national, architectural, or historical importance—we were not able to penetrate the designated coal holes in any shape or form and had to work within these limitations to design our fruiting chambers. Each coal hole has a different shape and size, which necessitated the creation of bespoke fruiting chambers for each space. Using a simple design, we built the chambers from locally sourced and treated wood. The wooden framework and flooring were then covered with PVC and installed with two ventilation grills, one near the bottom to allow fresh air in and one near the top to allow CO_2 buildup out. A mini-fan for distributing fresh air and a pond fogger to produce mist and increase the humidity were also placed in each coal hole, allowing the mushrooms to thrive.

Spawning and Incubation

First, we had to build our spawn bank, sourcing liquid culture from a local supplier. Eventually, as we expanded, we were able to make our own liquid culture using a light malt extract recipe. Once ready, we used the liquid mycelium culture to inoculate our prepared grain. Our choice for grain was wild bird seeds, which needed to be prepared by being soaked overnight, boiled for 10 minutes, sterilized for 90 minutes, and allowed to cool down before inoculation.

Mushroom filter patch bags were initially used for our grain spawn, but after a few months we started using large glass food jars for a more sustainable approach. After inoculation, it took approximately four weeks for the grain to become fully colonized and ready to use. During this incubation period, the grain spawn was placed in storage containers and located in a designated warm storage area inside the building.

In the Substrate

Once the grain spawn was ready, we had to prepare our substrate. In principle, this should have been straightforward if we didn't have to pasteurize or sterilize our substrate and could inoculate immediately. However, we faced a small challenge when, on many occasions, our buckets would be filled with not only coffee grounds but other forms of food waste and general rubbish. This was counterproductive to our goals and time-consuming to remove. Our team took this as an opportunity to do some outreach and provide more education to café staff as to why milk, yogurt, straws, tissue paper, and other anomalies were not required for this project.

Once we were able to get a consistent and clean supply of coffee waste, we thought the operation would begin easily, but it wasn't long before we found our first major hurdle—only 20 percent of the coffee bags were fully colonizing before contamination hit. It took us a few weeks to determine that the area we used to colonize our grain spawn was too warm for the coffee bags. We placed them in another slightly cooler area, which increased colonization

(continued)

rates to 50 percent. This was good progress, but it was still not suitable for our project's goals. Through further investigation, we found that regardless of how much we filled the coffee bags, the grounds were becoming too densely packed, and there wasn't enough air exchange. This slowed down and in some instances stopped colonization completely.

We decided to amend our substrate mix by introducing a new ratio of 30 percent pasteurized straw and 70 percent coffee grounds. Choosing to add an amendment was an immediate game changer for us. Our colonization success rates went up to 80–100 percent. The straw was the perfect addition, which also provided additional nutrients and broke up the density of the substrate.

At first we were using single-use plastic mushroom bags. The use of plastic (in particular single-use plastic bags) is pretty common in mushroom cultivation. Yes, plastic is a very handy product—it's cheap, adaptable, and it can also withstand high temperatures without breaking down. At the same time, we are aware of how these benefits also make plastic detrimental to the planet. We as a collective decided to use only reusable and cleanable plastic for all of our processes. We are aware that with the ever-increasing interest in mushroom cultivation and all of their sustainable qualities, we on the ground, as well as the commercial industry, need to be aware of the impact of plastic and where we are falling short.

That move also inspired us to go from pasteurizing our straw with heated water to cold-water pasteurization. This process took longer but was more sustainable and resourceful for the project and the earth moving forward.

Fruits of Our Labor

Our fully colonized bags then made their way over to the fruiting chambers. With mini-fans and pond foggers on a timer providing a fresh air supply with high humidity levels, we curated the ideal environment for our spawn bags to thrive and the mushrooms to fruit. With staggered growth cycles, depending on the variety, each coal hole produces an average of 5 to 10 kilograms of fruit per week. We sold our mushrooms, once harvested, back to the cafés and restaurants at Somerset House.

Our example of organically grown, low-tech mushrooms provides a sustainable and alternative model to food production in the heart of our city. This model is replicable in many different regions and can be adapted to various project sites with locally sourced materials.

Mushroom Cultivation Recipes

10 BASIC STEPS FOR MAKING YOUR OWN MUSHROOM SPAWN

This process will allow you to create a "spawn bank" using cardboard. A spawn bank is anything that has mycelium present, making it perfect for growing mushrooms. Because cardboard has few nutrients, you won't get mushrooms from this, but the results of this process can be added to straw, a substrate that is both nutritious and easy to break down. You can try the cardboard technique with any wood-loving mushroom, from the supermarket, forest, or previous grows—experiment! (But don't mix types of mushrooms.)

If you already have your cardboard spawn bag ready, skip to step 10.

1. Source cardboard with no ink or writing on it. Remove any tape, staples, etc. You'll need large pieces that you can cut or shred into smaller pieces.
2. Pasteurize the cardboard by pouring freshly boiled water over it. Let it cool and pour off the excess water.
3. Wait 6–10 minutes. Once the cardboard is cool enough to touch, separate the layers. Squeeze the excess water from the cardboard. This step is important to minimize the risk of contamination.
4. Next, you'll need a clean food container or bag. Make some pin-sized holes in it for air exchange.
5. Place an even layer of your pasteurized cardboard on the bottom of the container/bag.
6. Add 3 to 4 small pieces of mushroom, preferably the stem butts, to the sheet of cardboard. Less is more and will help the mycelium grow stronger.
7. Cover the mushroom stems with another layer of cardboard.
8. Repeat steps 6 and 7 until the container/bag is filled. Finish by adding a final layer of cardboard with no mushroom on the top.
9. Now seal the container/bag tightly. When sealing the bag, there's no need to squeeze out all of the air from the bag—oxygen is good.
10. Store the bag in a warm (ideally around 23°C [73°F]) dark place and leave for at least three to four weeks. The less they are disturbed, the faster they will grow. Once the cardboard has gone entirely white, it is ready to use as spawn. You can add this to straw to bulk it up and grow mushrooms with the process below.

10 BASIC STEPS FOR CULTIVATING MUSHROOMS ON STRAW

1. Take the straw and cut it into short lengths (1–2 inches) to maximize surface area.
2. Pasteurize the straw by soaking it in water at a temperature of 72°C–82°C (162°F–180°F) for 40 minutes to 1 hour. Be careful not to boil the straw as this will remove key nutrients.
3. Drain off the water and wait for the straw to cool to room temperature. This should take 5 to 10 minutes.
4. Add your prepared and cultivated spawn. A ratio of 1:10 spawn to straw is ideal. Mix them well.
5. Add the mix to a sealable plastic bag (leaving some air in the bag before sealing, as you did with your cardboard spawn prep bag).
6. Pierce the bag with 2 or 3 pin holes to allow air exchange during colonization.

(continued)

7. Store the bag in a dark and warm place (18°C–24°C [64°F–75°F]) for 10–21 days. Avoid the temptation to regularly check on them. They like to be left alone at this stage.
8. Once the bag is completely white with mycelium (sometimes this takes longer than four weeks), remove the bag and place it in a humid environment. The bag needs to be exposed to fresh oxygen, high humidity, low-level light, and cooler temperatures (between 10°C and 20°C [50°F and 68°F]). Carefully cut 2 small holes in the bag for the mushrooms to grow from.
    Tip: To maintain humidity, spray the bag with a misting bottle two or three times a day and make sure the bags have access to a light source for a few hours a day. To keep the air fresh, you can fan them once a day.
9. Over the coming days, you should start to see small pin heads (baby mushrooms) starting to grow. It takes 7 to 10 days for them to mature and be ready to harvest.
10. Once you harvest all the fully formed, matured mushrooms from the bag (called your first flush!), you can leave the bag to get a second—and possibly a third—flush every 7 to 10 days.

Erosion Control

Fungi are erosion control superstars, playing a key role in protecting soils from washing away. This is another reason why bare soil is the antithesis of a regenerative landscape. If the soil is bare, with no mulch and no living cover, it will be devoid of fungi and their erosion mitigation services. When given a chance to grow on wood chips, cardboard, straw, and forest duff, fungi create mycelium "mats" that hold soil in place. Mycorrhizal fungi also make mycelial mats in association with plant and tree roots, binding soil aggregates and providing erosion control services in this way. In the landscape, inoculate mycelial mats along road cuts, erosion gullies, and other areas in need of restoration. Add mycelium to wet cardboard, straw bales, or thick *fresh* wood chips as substrate for fungal growth in erosion zones.

Toxic Remediation with Fungi

Many species of fungi have the ability to remediate toxic substances in the landscape. They are used to clean gray and black water, oil spills, and other toxins. See the Mycoremediation case study developed by Dr. Mia Maltz in part IX of this book and learn more about this fascinating aspect of mycology.

Landscapes of Fungi

Like most ecosystems, the regenerative landscape is a network of fungi—fungi to store carbon, to distribute nutrients, as food for people, as medicine for humanity, to protect the land from toxins and erosion. These are beings that work for all of life, including your life, including mine. With a bit of intention and a lot of action, you now get to be an intentional steward: cultivating, protecting, and encouraging fungi in all its beneficial forms and functions throughout the land.

PART V
Water in the Landscape

24
Design Water Resilience

Water is the very foundation of life on earth. The planet, human beings, and every animal and plant in existence are creatures of water. How we care for, manage, and protect water is synonymous with caring for and protecting all life—this is the core responsibility of regenerative landscapers.

While the earth is abundant with water, clean freshwater is becoming more and more limited to the terrestrial biosphere. The pollution and limited access of freshwater is directly influenced by human development and civilization. As landscapers in service of a thriving earth, we are tasked with conserving water use, restoring watersheds, cleaning polluted waters, and replenishing groundwater aquifers.

All these goals are achieved in the landscape! This is one of the great joys of ecological land management. In this section of the book, we discuss ways to literally turn human-made deserts, concrete jungles, clear-cut forests, and over tilled prairies back into ecological oases; to equip every community around the planet with clean freshwater; to replenish ancient aquifers; and to regenerate freshwater springs that have been long lost due the plow and the ax. As beings of water, I believe wholeheartedly in our ability to transform our relationship to water from extractive and destructive to healing and regenerative.

We can look at water through many lenses. Your site assessment process will guide you in asking the right questions and developing appropriate design concepts for water in the landscape. Once you have thoroughly assessed the site and have a clear direction, you can begin the work of rehydrating the land and restoring the watershed.

WATER CONSERVATION

Before moving into harvesting and managing water, it's necessary to talk about conservation. For folks who live in highly developed communities, water seems like an infinite resource. Turn on the tap, open an irrigation valve, and there's always water to be had. But as long-term drought affects more and more communities around the world, the illusion of infinite water sources evaporates. Thus, the first place to engage with water is by understanding your water use.

Begin by gaining an understanding of how much the landscape currently uses and how much water newly designed landscapes will use. As you research your design plan and crunch numbers on water use, you'll quickly notice that your design strategy has a big impact on water consumption. Are you planting appropriate species to the climate? Does your design call for water-loving plants in a drought-threatened region? This process gets tricky as many food plants that humans love to consume require a fair amount of water. That being said, perennial food production (trees, shrubs, herbs) often requires more water during the first few years of growth and can then be weaned off, sometimes completely, as the landscape matures. This is a useful strategy to consider within the bigger goals of water use and water conservation over time.

To understand the water use of the current landscape and future water use projections, use tools such as the Estimated Total Water Use (ETWU) formula.[1] Many drought-stricken communities use this equation when enforcing Maximum Applied Water Allowances (MAWA).[2]

Here is the ETWU formula:

ETWU= (Eto)(0.62)[pf x HA/IE+SLA]

(Eto = evapotranspiration (inches per year); pf = plant factor from WUCOLS; HA = hydrozone area [high, medium, and low water areas in square feet]; SLA = special landscape area; 0.62 = conversion factor (to gallons per square foot); IE = irrigation efficiency [minimum .71])

Note: WUCOLS (Water Use Classification of Landscape Species) is a database that provides information about how much water plant species need to thrive. Visit https://ccuh.ucdavis.edu/wucols to access the WUCOLS database.

Regenerative Versus Degenerative Water Management

The landscape has a relationship with many sources of water, all of which require ecological management. These include water that falls as rain, melted snow, flowing creeks, and other water flowing across the land. The water pouring off the roof of your house, running down roads, or coming out of your house (laundry, bathtub, sinks) also generates landscape water management sources. How you interact with these sources makes all the difference between a regenerative or degenerative landscape. These waters literally represent life. You are now managing the living world and it starts with these waters!

Conventional landscapes throughout the western world are systems of water mismanagement. For centuries, humans have gained greater and greater skill at damming, draining, polluting, and extracting water from the land. At a minimum, the water management strategy for most conventional landscapers is to drain water away as quickly as possible using a network of drain boxes, pipes, and culverts. This drainage-based landscape culture results in extremely dehydrated landscapes completely dependent on irrigation systems, with an excessive amount of water leaving the landscape in wet seasons, compounding low-lying areas with flooding and pollution. When a large volume of water moves quickly through pipes, culverts, and across the impervious surface of roads and houses, that water becomes very dangerous. It scours the land like a high-powered drill, cutting into the soil and depositing sediment and pollution into creeks and rivers.

Regenerative landscapes work in the opposite way. Our water-management strategies focus on slowing down the movement of water, allowing it to infiltrate the soil, and moving it across nonimpervious surfaces covered with plants and their roots, where water is safely sunk and filtered before making its way slowly to underground aquifers and low-lying waterways.

Your regenerative landscape needs to manage water implementing the three S's of regenerative water management—"Slow it, Spread it, Sink it"—which were coined by my mentor and watershed regenerator extraordinaire, Brock Dolman of Occidental Arts and Ecology's WATER Institute. Brock's incredible catchphrase sums up a simple yet imperative approach to managing water in the landscape.

When water moves across the land, it not only looks for the path of least resistance but also the path of maximum absorption. When water is slowed down enough to percolate (sink) into the ground, it first feeds and gets trapped in the soil carbon sponge, then it slowly moves downward into groundwater aquifers. As the earth drinks up water, freshwater springs are recharged and low points in the topography become collection areas where water can rest on the earth. This "resting" or storage the earth provides, if maximized, ensures that water will be available during dry months. Here we make running water walk, rest, and percolate, like how one feels after a long day of work. Slowing down and resting is key to doing the important work the next day. It's the same with water—for it to do the work of providing for all life, it needs to rest *into* the land. If water is unable to penetrate the soil, then it will run across the surface instead, taking soil with it, causing erosion and downstream flooding. When the next dry spell comes around, there will be no water in the land to feed life.

Crises caused by water runoff have been so destructive that landscapes lose their ability to absorb water, resulting in significant dehydration and succession toward desert. Many landscapes around the world that once boasted impressive forests and grasslands are nothing but desolate man-made deserts and cities. The story of the land doesn't end here, however. Regenerative landscapers, farmers, and Indigenous people are working every day to help the land *slow, spread, and sink* water again.

Water Harvesting

Here are some excellent ways to harvest water in your regenerative landscaping projects.

Water Infiltration. Water infiltration is the practice of managing rainwater and surface water in such a way that it is capable of percolating through the layers of soil and into the earth. Water infiltration mitigates flooding, reduces erosion, and uses the earth as a storage system to save water for dry seasons. The ability of the landscape to hold onto infiltrated water will vary depending on the type of soil. Because water has *surface tension*, it sticks to itself and to surfaces. In the soil, water gets captured in the capillaries (the tiny spaces between soil particles), keeping it in the soil long after the last storm has passed. The smaller the particle size (clay), the more water will be held in the soil. Larger particles (sand) will still develop subsurface water storage but will facilitate better drainage with the larger pore space. This dance between drainage and hydration will come up again and again throughout the regenerative landscape design and implementation process.

As more water infiltrates into the ground and is captured by the soil, a "water plume" develops.[3] This slow-moving subsurface water can be developed over a number of years until they become reservoirs that tree roots can tap into once they have matured enough (three to five years). In addition, once-flowing, long-dead freshwater springs will eventually return and dried-up creeks and streams will flow again. In doing this work, you become a water magician with gardens and forests growing in your wake.

Roof-to-Cistern Systems. The first time I heard Australian designer Darren Doherty call a roof an "above-ground well" a lightbulb went off in my mind. Our shelters and buildings are covered in impervious materials such as tile, metal, and composite shingle. These systems drain significant amounts of water when it rains. The water lands on the roof above the ground before it runs into drains and downspouts. Gravity can be used to direct that water to strategic locations for storage.

Ponds. Ponds of all shapes and sizes are treasure troves to the water resilience of the landscape. Catching water high in the land, spreading it across the soil, and storing it in well-placed ponds is a recipe for water abundance. On smaller-scale projects, directing water from the roof of a house or the overflow of a rain tank into strategically placed habitat ponds will offer sustenance to thousands of insects, birds, and other organisms. Ponds of all sizes provide even more ecological services by moderating microclimate, providing wildlife habitat, and creating beauty in the landscape.

Water Storage. For true water resilience, you need to have water in a backup supply in case of drought, electrical shutoff, or other disruptions to your water system.

Water storage systems are some of the best ways to engineer a resilient water landscape. Storage can include above-ground tanks, underground cisterns, ponds, large bladder tanks, and even the soil itself. Synthesizing all of these potential storage systems into your regenerative landscape generates a *redundant plan* to ensure water resources are available when you need them during a crisis.

Droughts and Floods

Some of the threats we face in our communities are drought and flood. In California where I live, we've been experiencing these extremes since the early 2000s, when extended drought was followed by a big flood year followed by megafires. These extreme climatic changes from year to year are a hallmark of a warming climate, and more severe climate events are only amplifying as we move further into the twenty-first century.

How do we respond to these growing challenges and build drought- and flood-resistant landscapes? The solutions are found in the following chapters. When we create water-resilient landscapes that work with the ecosystem, within the context of topography, soil, solar orientation, water flows, and water sources, we plant water into the ground—relieving drought through the hydration of underground aquifers—and mitigate floods by spreading and capturing surface-moving water during the largest storm events. Two problems solved with the same solutions. We *can* design our way out of crisis.

Landscapes of Water, Landscape of Life

With water as our guide, the landscape design process takes further shape. Water conservation is the first step, followed by strategies to *Slow, Spread, and Sink* water in the landscape. We restore and protect watersheds, drought-proof gardens and farms, and hydrate the ecosystem, working in a *reciprocal relationship* with the land. In turn, the land comes alive with increasing levels of biodiversity. Landscapes of water are landscapes of life. We turn desolation into Eden while solving the most pressing ecological catastrophes of our era.

25

Identifying Water Sources

Every landscape requires water in some form in order to provide for plant and animal life. The specifics of climate, microclimate, topography, natural water collection, and distribution, storage, annual precipitation, and more—all dictate the availability of water resources.

Each project will have a specific set of relationships (well connected or broken) that facilitate the source of water. Assessing these connections, or lack thereof, is the first step in understanding the water context. As your grasp on the water implications of the site materialize, your design plan will need to adjust to take into account this context. It is then your responsibility to tend, protect, and care for the water resources associated with your project as part of your regenerative landscape design and management.

Let's look at common water sources from around the world.

Precipitation

As we know from part I, precipitation includes rain, snow, hail, sleet, and so on. The amount of precipitation, its *distribution throughout the year*, and the landscape's ability to store that water are major factors impacting the availability of water in the landscape.

Some folks around the world live in climates where enough rain falls throughout the year that irrigation systems are unnecessary (I'm not jealous . . . OK, maybe a little). In climates like these, planting is done with the rains, knowing that the precipitation throughout the year will keep crops and new plantings watered.

That being said, nearly every landscape in the world can be developed without irrigation by focusing on installing native plant communities during the appropriate season. The reality is that most readers and regenerative design enthusiasts are looking to grow food and medicine that people use in the modern era. This fact alone leads to a landscape approach that underutilizes native species and instead focuses on cultivars that produce desired food yields. These systems will require some irrigation to get going and persist.

You can see how the distribution of precipitation throughout the year affects the entire landscape approach. Therefore, how precipitation is captured and stored on-site makes all the difference in having a successful landscape or homestead. Measuring precipitation with rainfall and snow meters will help to understand the specifics in your climate. Most places throughout the world have open-sourced recorded rainfall data that you can research to get a sense of precipitation patterns over the years.

Rivers and Lakes

Freshwater rivers and lakes make up colossal water-harvesting and storage systems that occur naturally and through human development to store water from rain and snow. Many human-based water systems rely on these features. Unfortunately, human civilization and our overuse of water has, in many cases, drained and/or severely damaged rivers, lakes, streams, and creeks throughout the world.

These are sources of the water of life and how we manage that water is paramount for ecological health. In the case of regenerative landscape development, therefore, try to utilize lake and river water minimally or not at all in order to maintain healthy watersheds. This is always context specific, but implementing the principle of *doing the least harm* when accessing water sources must always be measured.

Wells

Most wells are holes dug deep into the earth tapping into underground water aquifers. Wells can be excellent and regenerative sources of water and they can also be highly destructive to ecology. Using groundwater for irrigation is another practice to be implemented with great consideration for overall watershed health.

Old wells were dug by hand and often only into shallow aquifers. Shallow wells, dug into high water tables, generally indicate an abundance of water and seasonal replenishment of that water.

In the twentieth and twenty-first centuries, most wells have been drilled with machines that go down hundreds of feet into the earth searching for water. Once an adequate water source is found, long perforated pipes are placed down into the hole, followed by powerful water pumps. Water can then be pumped out of the earth quickly and efficiently for use in the landscape or home. Installation of these wells gets expensive, and in arid environments drilling new wells may even be prohibited.

Wells tapping into aquifers that get replenished by rain and snow each year can be managed with a relatively low impact on the ecology if the water used is kept at a minimum. Aquifers (especially ancient ones) that don't readily replenish will one day be completely exhausted by well-pumping activities.

Wells are incredible resources for the landscape but come with a large responsibility to guarantee that misuse of precious groundwater is avoided.

Freshwater Springs

Freshwater springs are another miracle of the earth. Clean, fresh water surging from the ground is special indeed and considered sacred by cultures all over the planet. Like any water source, the volume of water emitted from springs fluctuates depending on the season. Some springs will dry up completely for a few months in the dry season only to return with rain. Springs, like every part of the landscape, have specific characteristics and patterns depending on soil, topography, orientation, and so on.

Municipal Water

Those projects located within municipal systems—urban, suburban, and annexed jurisdictions—will likely be dependent upon municipal water for the landscape. The benefit in those situations is that water is pumped directly to the project with little to no maintenance required. The downside to this water is that it's not free. Large projects dependent on municipal systems will rack up quite the water bill in the first few years of plant establishment. This is vital to consider during the design process. Alternative water resources such as gray water and rainwater catchment/storage can and should be developed. This provides *planned redundancy* for water resources and will supplement irrigation needs to alleviate the dependence upon paid municipal water. Keep in mind that it will also cost money to design, develop, and maintain alternative water systems, so savings will only be found once these new systems are built and operational.

Responsible Water Management

We all have a collective responsibility to the water of earth. Your own water systems may seem independent of your neighbors or region but that is not the case. The rainwater you catch, the groundwater taken from your well, and the river pumped into your tank are all connected to a whole watershed. The water resources that you tap and consume have far-reaching implications.

Regenerative design provides solutions to tending water resources with reverence and reciprocity. Finding the balance between using water sources to cultivate landscapes and regenerating whole watersheds is the nexus of our work as regenerative landscapers!

CASE STUDY: LAUNDRY-TO-LANDSCAPE REUSE BY CONNOR DEVANE OF DAILY ACTS ORGANIZATION

The average American family of four uses between 5,000 and 8,000 gallons of water per year through their washing machine alone. Used once to clean clothes, this "waste water" is typically sent down the pipes into the sewer. What if, instead, that water was reused to grow abundance in the landscape, saving water, energy, and money at the same time? All of this is possible through the Laundry-to-Landscape system, developed by Art Ludwig of Oasis Design.[1] At its simplest, an L2L system is just a three-way diverter valve that directs greywater from the washing machine to either a sewer or to infiltrate the soil through flat-bottomed basins or swales around the root zones of plants, which are then backfilled with mulch. They allow the greywater to enter the landscape below the soil surface and be absorbed by plants and soil without overflowing or pooling.

Laundry-to-landscape systems are safe, affordable, DIY-friendly, and, in most places, do not require a permit. By installing an L2L system, you will not only save water and money but also hydrate your landscape and boost soil health. You'll close a loop in your life and open up a new avenue to reconnect with the more-than-human world. You may even find yourself pursuing more and more resilience strategies, helping your neighbors do the same, and, before you know it, even pushing to change policy as part of a larger greywater revolution!

Before you go grabbing that washer hose and digging basins in your yard, there are a few key considerations.

Where is your washing machine located? Is it against an exterior wall? Outside the home? In the center of the home? The closer the washing machine is to your landscape, the easier it will be to direct water there.

Is the area you want to direct greywater to higher or lower in elevation than your washing machine? The pump in your washing machine will move water up and out through the pipes, but you want to work with gravity, not against it, by orienting the pipe toward a downhill slope if available. Gravity is free! Pumps are not, and they can break.

How far away from your washer is the landscape you want to direct greywater to? Your washing machine pump can move the water 50 feet on flat ground without issue. If your landscape is downhill, the water can reach further. While slightly uphill is not impossible, your pump will only take the water so far, and anything more than a 2 percent slope for a short distance will not be manageable.

What obstacles stand between your washer and your landscape? Consider the type of material your wall is made of, potential pipes and wires within the wall, and any hardscape on the ground outside your home. If your washer is inside, you will need to cut a hole through any walls that separate it from the landscape with a hole-saw drill bit. Your greywater piping will either need to run below any hardscape, or you'll need to cut through or break the hardscape. When cutting through your wall, be sure to apply silicon to the air gaps as a last step.

How many gallons of water does your washing machine use per load? Traditional washers use around 40 gallons, while newer, energy-efficient machines use about 14 gallons on average. You need to know how much water you're sending into your landscape in order to size the basins correctly to prevent them from overflowing and dispersing graywater above ground. To find the gallons per load, look on the back of the machine, in the user manual, or look up the model number on the internet. Better yet, test it yourself in a container with a known volume.

How frequently do you do laundry? Do you do a load here and there, or do you do all your laundry in one day? You want to design a system that is capable of handling the maximum amount of water you'll ever run through your washing machine, so it's important to determine both your average weekly amount and your outlier scenario maximum. Ultimately, this will impact the amount of water your plants receive and how often, along with the size of your mulch basins.

(continued)

How quickly does water infiltrate your soil? Perform a simple soil percolation test by digging a hole, inserting a ruler or yardstick, filling it with water, and observing. If you have clay soils, the water will take longer to infiltrate and you will need to develop more basin floor area and additional measures to keep the root crowns of trees from becoming oversaturated. With sandy or loam soils, infiltration will be much faster; you may want multiple mulch basins around the root zone in order to spread water out.

What kind of detergent or laundry soap do you use? Products with chlorine, boron, lye, or high amounts of sodium are not compatible with L2L greywater—your plants won't like it! Bleach and fabric softeners are likewise incompatible with L2L systems.

Do you have a sodium-based water softener? This will also be harmful to your plants and is not compatible with greywater. Consider switching to a potassium-based softener.

What kind of plants do you plan to water? Some plants are not a good fit for greywater, including turf lawns, drought-established plants (i.e., never irrigated), root crops, potted plants, and particularly sensitive plants. Trees are your best option—especially fruit trees—as they appreciate the deep and less frequent watering that comes with L2L greywater. Shrubs and large annuals are next, followed by herbaceous perennials and large annuals. You can absolutely grow food crops with greywater, as long as the water doesn't touch the edible parts. So tomatoes are a go, carrots are a no.

Can you disperse greywater without affecting the plumbing code setbacks? These setbacks are there to ensure that you do not accidently share greywater with your neighbors, send it downstream via waterways, or toward the foundation of your home. Be sure to look up the greywater code where you live to find setback requirements.

If you've determined that L2L is a good fit for you after answering the questions above, it's time to start planning. You'll need to calculate the water output potential of your system; choose your plants and determine their water needs; calculate the number and size of your mulch basins to accommodate the maximum output of your system; design the indoor components of the system; and design the outdoor components of the system.

You can find detailed information on all the above on our resources page at dailyacts.org, including Art Ludwig's book, *Create an Oasis with Greywater*. Ludwig's instructional video on the Laundry to Landscape system can be found at oasisdesign.net/laundry.

DIY-friendly doesn't mean mistakes don't happen, and it's important to remember that every system is different. You may need to recalibrate, head back to the hardware store a couple times, cut and reglue pipes, enlarge your basins . . . this is normal! You'll learn by doing, and mistakes are often the best teachers.

Once you have designed and installed your system, you'll want to test it out. Run a wash cycle and observe how water moves through the system. Are there any leaks? Mark them and fix them. It could be a glue issue, a Teflon tape issue, a hose clamp that needs tightening, or damaged irrigation tubes. Are the various outflow points letting out water at similar volume and rate? If not, try adjusting the ball valves, angling your tee couplers downward, and if need be, working to make your lines more level. Does the water drain from your basins? Does it overflow? You may need to make your basins larger.

Down the line, once your system is up and running and in regular use, be sure to keep it functioning well with a little yearly maintenance. You can flush your system with a hose by unscrewing the threaded union that connects the PVC from inside to the flexible irrigation tubing outside. Be sure to monitor inside your mulch shields (where the greywater enters the basins) to make sure the water is flowing well and unobstructed. If you have problems with gophers, moles, or voles in your garden, you can attach gopher wire to the base of your mulch

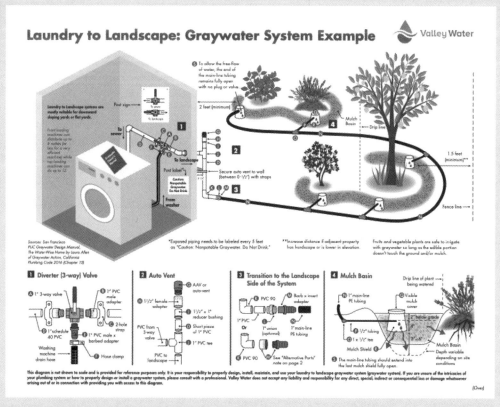

This infographic is courtesy of Valley Water, originally inspired by the graphic in Create an Oasis with Greywater."

(continued)

guards and backfill them with gravel to keep them clean. Last but not least, be sure to replace the mulch in your basins every one to two years depending on how quickly it is breaking down. You can use the old mulch as fresh compost for the garden, closing another loop.

CASE STUDY: WHY SMALL SOLUTIONS MATTER BY TRATHEN HECKMAN OF DAILY ACTS ORGANIZATION

In a world of overwhelming large problems, the power of small is bigger than you think. It's found in small daily acts of courage and conviction, small groups of unstoppable change makers—even small gardens that harvest the rain, grow food, and sequester atmospheric carbon from the air. Regenerative solutions that are low cost, low tech, nature-inspired, and people-powered like rainwater catchment, greywater, and DIY earthworks are critical for addressing the problems of our world.

Water accounts for the largest percentage of the greenhouse effect. It significantly influences our climate, yet it's not a big part of the climate conversation. You can change that. An inch of rain on my family's roof is about 600 gallons of water. On our small in-town property, it's 4,500 gallons. Covering the small city of Petaluma where we live, it's about 240 million gallons. That's a lot of water. Just percolate on the potential of small, decentralized water systems and green infrastructure solutions, such as rainwater harvesting and bioswales, at scale. We can rehydrate our soil carbon sponge, regenerate our watersheds, and transform our lives and communities from ridge to river, treating each property as a microwatershed in a reverential rehydration revolution. In an era of extreme weather, increasing drought and deluge, these strategies get all the more critical at all scales. For those of us who are passionate about regenerative solutions, it's our job to do more than just implement this stuff in our lives. We also need to be educators, advocates, organizers, implementers, and even authors of people-powered policy to reforest and rehydrate the earth.

Taking Small Solutions to Scale

Imagine what can happen when small groups apply permaculture to community organizing to amplify and spread the power of small actions and landscape strategies. One such example is Daily Acts, an educational nonprofit that unleashes the power of community to address the climate crisis. We do this through three connected strategies: training leaders and fostering networks; spreading on-the-ground solutions and models such as planting gardens and greywater education; and working with government to accelerate equitable climate programs and policies. Twenty years ago, Daily Acts was founded on the belief that to transform our communities and world, we must start with ourselves. Inspired by permaculture gardens and leaders like Erik Ohlsen—who was featured on our first Sustainability Tour and helped design our first public food forest several years later—Daily Acts has been spreading accessible eco-design solutions and influencing business, government, and even state policy ever since. We do this by partnering with engaged people and hundreds of organizations, businesses, and government agencies of all sizes.

There's Something About Greywater

I'm not sure what it is, but there's something about greywater that captivates folks. Using our water more than once is sort of a gateway drug into understanding natural systems and reconnecting to the cycles of life. In what is now a semipermanent drought, it's crazy to do laundry, shower, or wash your hands and just let the water drain away. Collectively, Californians produce about 1.3 billion gallons of greywater each day. That's a lot of water that could be rehydrating our lives and landscapes.

In the California drought in the 1970s, lots of folks reused their dish and laundry water. But then the government began overregulating anything beyond putting a bucket in the sink, based on fears of someone getting sick or potential environmental impacts. Really, laundry water? In 2009, Daily Acts removed some barriers by installing the first permitted household greywater system in Sonoma County. Soon we were installing five permitted greywater systems in a single day, then 13 over a weekend, and later running a 100 Greywater System Challenge while helping to shift California state policy with great partners like Greywater Action.

Through city and community partnerships, we went from installing one garden to dozens of landscapes at libraries, parks, schools, churches, and city halls, all while helping to innovate a city rebate program to transform over 500 lawns, saving tens of millions of gallons of water per year. Motivated by the growing urgency of the climate crisis, a big dose of inspiration, and the power of collaboration, we transformed the landscape of City Hall and mobilized the community to set a goal of planting 350 gardens in a single weekend. We ended up planting over 600 gardens and, a decade later, these efforts have catalyzed tens of thousands of resilience-building actions and projects to grow food, conserve water, save energy, and build community.

In 2008, I reconnected with a civil engineer at a permaculture workshop who had installed permitted greywater systems elsewhere and offered to collaborate with Daily Acts. When Daily Acts began partnering with the city of Petaluma on educational programs, working with a civil engineer who could design the greywater systems and had proven examples from another city made it easier to make a convincing case to the building inspector. With a more risk-averse culture, agencies often dislike being the first to do something. With

(continued)

beneficial relationships, an example in hand, and the support of friends and local businesses, we installed a constructed wetland greywater system that mimicked what a wetland does in nature to clean water. Doing this as a workshop enabled us to teach people and agency leaders from around the county. It also got us on the cover of the local newspaper and ultimately in an award-winning video seen by hundreds of thousands of people, amplifying our reach.

Underlying all this was the deeper *why* of inspiring transformative action through the power of small acts, gardens, and groups. Programmatically, our *what* evolved from inspiring people with a vision through everything from educational tours to skill-building workshops to transforming chemical, resource-intensive lawns into eco-oases. Once we transformed one landscape, given the times, we naturally pondered, how can we do *lots* more? This led to community mobilizations and fostering networks and coalitions to shift civic programs and policies for wider change.

Barriers and Challenges

While Laundry-to-Landscape (L2L) greywater systems are DIY-friendly, there are challenges and barriers that people often encounter. DIY-friendly doesn't necessarily mean easy for anyone. Not everyone has access to the required tools, and many people are intimidated by the prospect of drilling a hole through an exterior wall of their home. For those who rent their homes, an L2L system requires landlord approval. Of course, digging infiltration basins can be taxing physical work as well, even for able-bodied people, especially in clay-heavy soils. For those who aren't looking to do the work themselves, it can be difficult to hire help; landscape contractors typically aren't permitted to work inside the building envelope (i.e., they can't help with the indoor components) and they have a hard time making low-cost, low-tech systems pencil out.

Even if you overcome those barriers, one greywater system is a drop in the ocean in terms of combating drought and restoring the water cycle. You won't achieve drought and climate resiliency for your home if your community isn't working to do the same, no matter how good your design. To drive the kind of change required of us, these solutions need to be scaled, to ripple out far and wide to other communities and regions.

Call to Action

If 100 families installed a simple Laundry-to-Landscape greywater reuse system, we could collectively save 500,000 to 800,000 gallons of water each year. Scale that out to the 21,000 households in the small city of Petaluma and to countless other towns and cities. Imagine all those micro-watersheds rehydrating our soils and plants instead of sending that water to the treatment plant or the ocean, in turn boosting carbon sequestration, increasing wildlife habitat, potentially increasing local precipitation, and so much more! While watershed and water cycle restoration need to happen on massive scales, simple, decentralized solutions like greywater reuse can have a profound impact when replicated by neighbors and communities. Here are three integrated strategies to help create a rehydration revolution in your community.

Talk to Your City

Start by understanding the status of decentralized solutions like greywater in your community. Does your city or county require permits of any kind? Do they offer rebates or other incentives to install water reuse or conservation systems? Who are the people in your local agency that are interested in such solutions? Sometimes a free parts kit or a $100 rebate (which you qualify for in Petaluma, California, and Santa Rosa, California, respectively) is enough to break down the barrier to installation. If your local government doesn't offer any incentives, get a conversation started! One way to do so is to provide educational materials and examples from other cities and communities.

Inspire and Engage Your Neighbors

A next step is bringing your neighbors into this regenerative rehydration revolution by having conversations and sharing inspiring resources and the benefits of such solutions. At Daily Acts, we're big fans of the community installation party. Invite your neighbors—bring the kids!—to come get their hands dirty and gain experience installing a laundry-to-landscape system. Many hands make light work, and a day of digging basins, cutting and gluing pipes, planting fruit trees, and that special camaraderie that comes with a shared project makes for a slew of activated and educated neighbors inspired to get their own greywater out into the garden. And why not make it a potluck with tasty treats and beverages? Once the system is in place and flowing, you may already have volunteers to host the next greywater install.

Partner with Local Groups to Amplify Your Impact

Are there local nonprofits in your area who are interested in or working on these solutions? How about local landscape businesses? Consider your potential allies, whether you're looking for someone to lead your community installation or replicate the work you and your neighbors have done on a broader scale. There are countless landscapers who want to be doing things in a more regenerative way. There are caring people in every body of government just waiting for the right opportunity and leverage to drive positive change. There are people in your city and

(continued)

neighborhood who want to heal the land and water and have a good time doing it. Seek them out and explore how you can collaborate.

Find and Share Bright Spots

One of our favorite inspiring examples is water wizard Brad Lancaster, who took this approach in Tucson, Arizona, with his brother and their neighbors. It started with a few small, simple changes to the curbs in front of their house. Stormwater that used to charge down the street and cause flooding now pours into lushly planted basins that offer food, shade, habitat, beauty, and a way to store water: obstacle into opportunity. Now their techniques—curb cuts and planted basins—aren't just compliant with the law in Tucson, they're required by it! After repeating that model with rainwater, greywater, and a network of supercharged community organizations, Tucson is seeing creek and stream restoration that no one thought possible. There are more stories like Brad's every day. The rehydration revolution happens drop by drop.

You don't have to have all the skills or answers. Just find and share practical examples of what inspires you, find partners in local organizations, landscape businesses, or city agencies. Dream bigger, have fun and engage good partners, then repeat and kick it up a notch. This is how Daily Acts went from installing one greywater system and garden to hundreds, innovating and influencing civic programs and policies. Now in the face of an unending, urgent drought, we are looking at how to assemble the resources, train the workforce, and change the policies to scale these small solutions from retrofitting existing neighborhoods to ensuring all new residential construction is required to include greywater stub-outs*, making it much easier for anyone to start growing with greywater. In the end, it's all an invitation to dream bigger and find the partners to make it so.

We must be the change we wish to see. By unleashing the power of community and through a wide array of partners, Daily Acts has shown again and again the incredible power of small, passionate, committed groups of change-makers. That power is yours to wield, share, and ripple out into the world.

26
Managing and Harvesting Surface Water

Water runoff during storms is a true crisis that threatens watersheds and freshwater sources around the globe, and it stems from the use of impervious surfaces that the water does not infiltrate when it rains. Roads, buildings, roofs, and agricultural soils can all be impervious surfaces. As regenerative designers, we intercept runoff, break up compacted areas when possible, and direct surface waters into the soil for infiltration. To achieve these goals, a set of water design approaches and techniques must be implemented and developed out of the specific characteristics of each site.

TOPOGRAPHY

Comprehensively assess the topography of the landscape before developing water management strategies. In part II of this book, we discussed landforms—the valleys, ridges, saddles—that make up the shape of the landscape. Topography indicates the natural movement of water across the land, providing the foundation of understanding water on the site.

Where are the natural drainages? Where does the water *want* to move? Is it moving in those natural drainages or has it been diverted? These questions should guide you in your initial assessment. Usually, natural drainages are places where we accentuate collection in the landscape and also return overflow water once it has spread and sunk into our water-harvesting systems.

SOILS

Soils have everything to do with the land's capacity to infiltrate water. Does the soil drain easily or does water pond quickly on the surface during storm events? What's the soil's capacity to absorb water? Is the soil shallow, resting on bedrock that will create erosion when it is saturated with water? These questions about the soil help you generate the appropriate water design approach for the landscape.

SOURCES AND FLOWS

Look into all the sources and flows generating water. Explore the infrastructure of the site, looking at impervious surfaces, downspouts, roof lines, road drainage, culverts, upslope water flows, low points where water gathers, and drain pipes daylighting (releasing the water) on the project (including neighbors, seasonal drainages, and so on).

The most effective interventions in water management are small and strategic, placed in relationship to water sources, water flows, and impervious surfaces in the landscape. Intercept water as soon as possible, directing it toward infiltration systems at the first safe location.

Tracking Water Outflows

The existence of private property ownership and property boundary lines complicates our work as regenerative designers. The scope of a project is limited to the areas where authority to design and build has been given. This means that special attention must be given to adjacent properties and the effects they have on the landscape. Above the project site can be any number of water-based hazards and opportunities—an expanding erosion gully, agricultural runoff, a road culvert—and these elements may be inaccessible to you but their effects are still yours to integrate into the landscape design.

Downslope, water that leaves the landscape may do so by entering fragile ecosystems, city sewers, and other landscapes where you have no access or authority. With this reality, the only place to intervene and make any difference in the ecology are the areas we've been given to do the regenerative work. This can be frustrating, but it also pushes you as a designer to maximize the water-management design on the site to benefit both upslope and downslope neighbors. Do this by managing water in the most ecological way as it comes onto the land and ensuring that any water leaving the site does so in slow and measured flows. You can do it, for the health of your landscape and the entire watershed!

The quality of water leaving a project is an important measure of the success of your design. Striving to catch, infiltrate, clean, and slow down surface waters to protect watersheds, hydrate the landscape, and mitigate erosion are central foundations for every successful regenerative project.

LANDSCAPE GRADING

Consider that even tiny grade changes by themselves—adjustments to slope, directional changes of winter runoff, miniature landforms—provide strategic and low-cost solutions with a big impact. Simple grading is the first water management technique to implement in your design. Smoothing out a bump over here or accentuating a low point over there might be all that is needed on some sites. From your site assessment, you will be able to identify these small grading changes that will have a big impact—usually around pathways, roads, and adjusting downspouts from buildings. A simple grade change might allow water to spread into a large area, direct water to the garden or a forest for infiltration, or send water away from the foundation of a house. Start with the small and simple interventions before moving to large earthworks. Do these kinds of simple solutions excite you as much as they do me? I hope so!

Contour

Contours are magical (and scientific) levels across the land where all points are at the same elevation with each other. If we dig a ditch on contour, it will fill up in a level way, like a bathtub when water enters. Topographical maps use contours to represent the changes in elevation, the general grade of slope, and their relative steepness or flatness. That is why these maps are such great tools for regenerative designers, especially when we are designing the water layer of the landscape—the map itself tells us how water moves and collects on the land naturally, helping you attune to the water's flows.

When you find a contour, you can strategically use it to slow down and collect flowing water and nutrients in the landscape. Working with contour doesn't always mean running exactly on contour. Systems that are slightly off contour still add to the potential for absorbing and infiltrating water while also keeping areas from being oversaturated. The use of contours in regenerative design is limitless and driven by project context, values, and goals.

Here's a list of a few techniques in the landscape that leverage contour:

- Planting on or slightly off contour
- Ditches on contour, "swales"
- Farm beds on or just off contour
- Pathways and roads just off contour
- Combining contour systems with catchment systems like contour ditches directed into ponds

There are several different ways to find contour:

- Laser level—an expensive professional tool to find contour lines and lay out earthworks. Can be operated by one person.
- Transit level—this level requires two people. One person looks through a leveled scope while their partner holds a tall measuring stick at different points across the land to find a contour.
- A-frame levels—these levels are ancient technology and can be made by three sticks, a string, and a rock. The level is tied together into an A shape with the string hanging down the center and a rock on the end, crossing the horizontal stick of the A-frame. Once calibrated, the A-frame can be walked from foot to foot across the land to reveal a level contour.
- Water levels—these are low-tech, cheap levels that can be built with a single transparent plastic pipe. The pipe has to be flexible and needs to be attached to two yard sticks (one for each end of the pipe) or more simply two sticks of the same height. The tube is filled with water, usually with corks or stoppers placed in each end once full. Since water finds its own level, markings on the sticks or yards sticks can determine when each stick is standing at the same elevation.

Earthworks

Earthworks refers to any work done on the project that moves earth (soil) around. Some projects may require an extreme level of earthworks to create water-retention landscapes; fix critical drainage problems; and create roads, building pads, terraces, ponds, and water-infiltration structures like rain gardens.

Creating earthworks will have a detrimental effect on the structure and biology of the soil. Every time we dig and move soil, we release carbon dioxide to the atmosphere, damage fungal structures, and kill microorganisms in the soil. Pulling out a shovel—or jumping on an excavator, or crashing through the soil on a bulldozer—are intensive activities on the land.

Earthworks need to be approached with a high level of sensitivity. Approach this like a surgeon—very carefully, with all the safeguards in place. Try other techniques first to solve problems and achieve goals before jumping into landscape surgery through earthworks. While this kind of work may be destructive at first, if done right and in the correct context, well-designed earthworks can lead to enhanced nutrient and water distribution, erosion control, soil fertility, and many other benefits and functions.

Any time you are grading a swale, rain garden, or terrace; digging ditches; building garden beds; whatever it is—grade the slope to a stable angle. This is called the angle of repose: the natural angle the slope "wants" to settle to. If it's too steep or left ungraded, exposure to the elements will move the soil to a stable angle. When implementing earthworks, always perform a "finish" grading to make sure slopes are left at a stable angle.

Avoid Damaging the Sacred

A foundational principle to always consider is to *do the least harm*. Landscapes are special places, sacred even, and some features of the land are so precious that they must never be disturbed. Identify features such as these before any installation work commences. Sacred trees, freshwater springs, ancient stones, grave mounds, and shell mounds are some of the sacred elements you may find on a project site. Give these entities the respect and protection they deserve. Enjoy them but don't destroy them.

Equipment for Installation

Installing earthworks in the landscape is a major intervention on the land. These activities must be well thought out and taken with caution. Start with a shovel before using a machine. Understand the ramifications of both when planning your project.

Using equipment is beneficial on projects where the scale of the work is vast and you must move large quantities of heavy materials (stone, soil, gravel) or perform functions like road compaction, trench excavation, or boulder placement. If equipment is required for the project, be smart about how you use it. Have experienced operators do the work or learn under the supervision of an experienced mentor. If you're unsure about your design plan and earthworks are being called for, consult with a professional. If necessary, bring in a civil engineer to review your plans and be open to their feedback.

One of the benefits of using equipment is saving wear and tear on human bodies. When digging in hardpan soils or installing large projects, the work done in a day with a machine can be equal to a week's worth of human labor.

Time of Year

Consider the time of year when planning any earthworks or grading activities. When the soil is too wet, grading, excavating, and driving over it causes significant damage to the landscape through compaction and erosion.

When the soil is bone dry, this poses additional problems. Excavating dry soil causes dust and, on a windy day, creates a challenging environment where dust is blowing across the landscape onto neighboring properties and beyond. When the soil is too dry and particular earthmoving projects require compaction—for instance, the footings for buildings, pond dams, or roads—dry soil will need supplemental water in order to compact it to the appropriate density.

The ideal time of year to move earth is during the transitional seasons where some moisture is in the ground but not enough to exacerbate compaction. Additional factors can get in the way of implementing a project at the ideal time. If your project has such an obstacle, it is better to do the work in the dry season when supplemental water can be added rather than in the wet season where extreme compaction occurs.

Sequencing Within the Whole Project

Grading and earthwork projects are generally the first installation activities done in the landscape because major changes to the shape of the land will be required, causing a bit of chaos. Perform these activities *first* before soil conditioning, hardscapes, and planting. Having all grades (the final levels of the soil) complete before other activities begin ensures that future work will not be damaged by earthworks.

WATER INFILTRATION SYSTEMS

Rain gardens, contour swales, off-contour waterways, terraces, and soil building are all techniques for infiltrating water to hydrate the landscape. Infiltration systems slowly filter the water into the ground, hydrating the land, generating an underground water plume, and recharging aquifers. Depending on the soil, this may or may not be beneficial. Shallow bedrock, hardpan, and drainage problems can all lead to erosion or anaerobic conditions if these soils are oversaturated with infiltrated water. Place infiltration systems relative to water sources, water flows, and in places where increasing erosion is not a concern. Always be strategic and implement the *relative location* principle when placing water-catchment features.

Size Appropriately

When it comes to sizing water infiltration systems, several factors need to be considered.

Soil Type. If you have well-drained soils, extremely large infiltration systems are not necessary. If your soils are not well drained, shallow and wider systems with the capacity to handle storm surge water will be called for.

Peak Saturation and Peak Storm Surge (*Design for Catastrophe*). Once the soil inside a water-infiltration system is fully saturated, the soil's ability to infiltrate more water will be significantly limited. A large storm poised to dump rain on saturated soils is a dangerous event. All water infiltration systems need to be designed for this moment. This is when your earthworks will be tested—you need to make sure that water will be able to safely enter and exit the system without causing erosion or flooding.

Rain Gardens

Rain gardens are circular depressions (like a pond), excavated into the landscape, that catch and infiltrate water. Their circular shape makes them a good choice for many landscape projects. Smaller projects on urban and suburban sites can make excellent use of rain gardens in tight spaces to manage extreme flows of water from structures and roads. The difference between a rain garden and a pond is that a rain garden is not compacted but instead designed to catch and infiltrate water, whereas a pond is lined with a waterproof liner, catching and keeping water in the pond most or all of the year.

For small projects, a rain garden provides an excellent approach to catching and infiltrating a large volume of water. It can be built relatively small in diameter, yet deep, to adapt to the needs of the project. Rain gardens are not compacted and allow for maximum infiltration.

Surface waters, drainage pipes, and road runoff can all be directed into a rain garden. As the water enters the basin, it will slow down. Sediment carried in the water will deposit into the rain garden. This is an excellent way to clean and filter surface waters before releasing them back into the ecology.

During catastrophic events, rain gardens can relieve the pressure of overflowing pipes, tanks, swales, and ponds. Designed appropriately, rain gardens become a protective system during large storm events to keep the landscape and watershed safe.

Planting Systems. One of the greatest features of rain gardens is the ability to turn them into full-on planting beds. This is especially beneficial in areas where soil doesn't drain well and mosquitoes are a concern. A rain garden can be filled with a well-draining mix of 50 percent sand and 50 percent compost (or buy ready-made mixes on the market) and be filled up with this material (don't fill above the spillway!). Water that enters the rain garden will still percolate into the planting mix, adding to infiltration, but water will not collect on the surface, which reduces mosquito issues. Plant appropriate plant species directly into this sand–compost mix to make extra use of the concentrated water resources. Systems like these are being installed all over the world in governmental and commercial settings to handle runoff from roads and parking lots.

Habitat Creation. Anywhere water gathers is a place for wildlife to thrive. Rain gardens become a haven for birds and beneficial wildlife during the wet season. Depending on soil type and climate, some rain gardens even hold water for months at a time, providing refuge for frogs, turtles, and salamanders.

Beauty. Beauty is always woven into the regenerative design process. Accentuate your rain gardens with specimen plantings, boulders (when appropriate), and winding pathways, creating focal points in the landscape. Think of your rain gardens as aesthetic features to be discovered by people wandering the landscape.

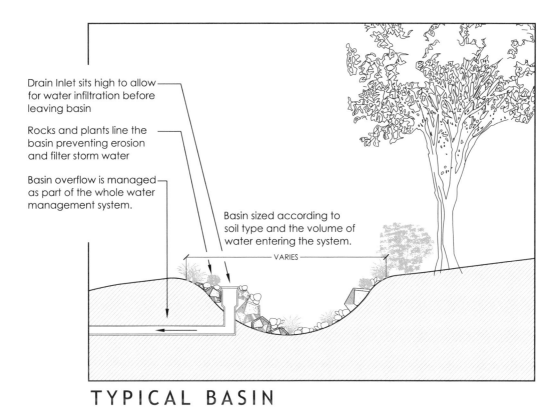

Rain garden basin detail with drain inlet overflow. Designed by Elder Creek Landscapes.

Arid Environments. In arid landscapes where precipitation and water resources are scarce, entire gardens may be designed as rain gardens—creating depressions where every drop of rain enters and is concentrated in the cultivated landscape.

Building a Contour Water-Harvesting Swale

Contour swales are large ditches excavated along contour lines with mounded soil (berms) on the downslope side, bordering the ditch. This shape of depression into a berm provides a diverse array of planting zones and the ability to catch and infiltrate significant volumes of water. Building water-harvesting swales has become a popular technique with permaculture practitioners around the world. These systems have the potential to catch and infiltrate millions of gallons of water in the landscape. They also have the potential to create significant damage, so knowing when to place a swale and when not is the first important step. If you've decided a swale is beneficial to your context and goals, here is a step-by-step process for locating and installing one.

Choosing the Starting Point. Contour swales need to be located in highly strategic places in the landscape. A randomly dug contour ditch on the side of the hillside may not provide much function, but a swale placed specifically to interrupt the flow of water, to capture runoff from a road, or receive water through a house downspout provides several beneficial functions.

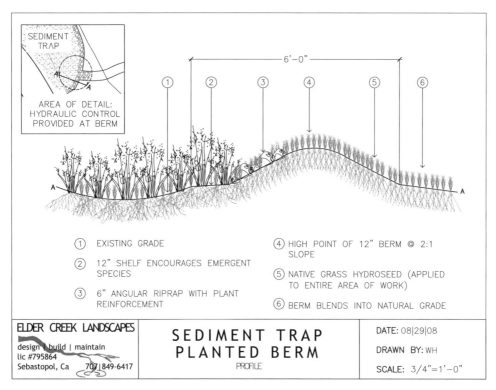

Sediment trap detail. Designed by Elder Creek Landscapes."

A contour swale also needs to have a functional relationship to the access requirements of the project. Swales are not the easiest systems to navigate (sometimes bridges or crossing culverts are used to make them more accessible) and they should be placed in such a way where efficient access throughout the landscape is still maximized.

Since swales are large excavated structures, it is also important to avoid placing them near the roots of established or old trees that might be damaged by excavation.

Placing swales on extremely steep slopes, on shallow bedrock, or directly upslope of houses are also not advised, as erosion, flooding, and structural damage might occur during large storm events.

With all those constraints in mind, place your swale inside the landscape, where it can receive surface waters and benefit trees and plants in that area.

Finding the Right Contour. Another consideration is to find the "right" contour. The very first point you use to lay out the contour (using a level of some kind) will determine where the contour moves across the land and ends up. It can be difficult, even with decades of experience, to eyeball where a contour will land.

Sometimes, a swale is being called for in a location that already has trees and other elements that are in the way. Finding a contour that moves safely between existing elements can be tricky, as the first point surveyed with your level could have a vastly different trajectory across the land than a starting point that is merely one foot below. Because of these constraints, survey a desired

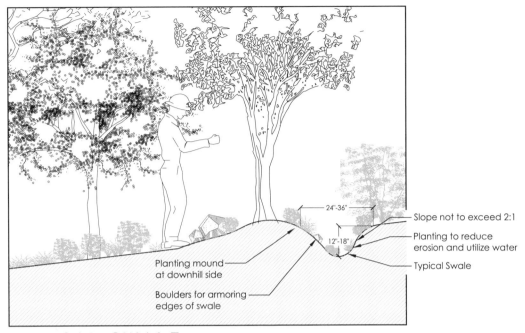

TYPICAL SWALE

Contour swale design detail. Designed by Permaculture Artisans.

contour multiple times until the contour that fits the design and context is best revealed. This looks like laying out an entire hundred-foot contour line only to lift up all the pegs and start over again once you discover the trajectory was not ideal. It's like finding the right words to write a book. Sometimes you have to delete what you wrote and try again until it's just right.

Swale Layout. Depending on the tool you use to find contour, the distance between your points may be quite different. If you place points too close to each other—for instance, a flag for every foot fall of an A-frame level it may create a very wavy contour line that is more confusing to excavate. It also adds more work. When using an A-frame, spin it at least twice (two lengths of the level, walking across the land) before pounding a wooden peg or placing a survey flag to mark the point. It's important to mark the contour in this way in order to get the level right during installation. If using a laser or transit level, I'll often place a flag or peg every 10 to 15 feet. For swales dug by hand, survey points tend to be marked closer together, and swales dug by machine points are marked farther apart.

Sizing. The length, depth, and width of the swale impacts much of the design approach. How much space is this going to take? How much work will be required for installation? What's the appropriate size in relation to the soil type and climate you're working in? How much water does the swale need to handle, especially during large storm events?

In general, shallow and wide swales are preferred as they become better integrated into the topography, are easier to navigate across, and spread water over a wider plane. Some projects will call for skinnier and deeper swales due to limited space, sandy soils, or other constraints.

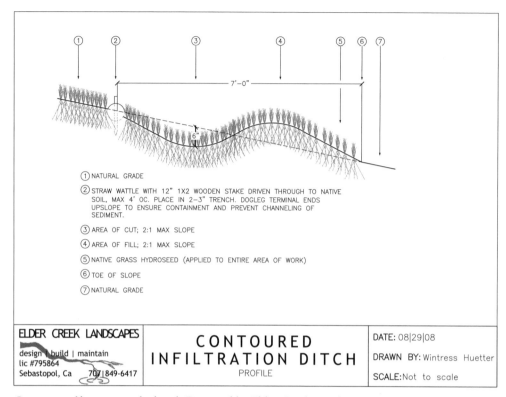

Contour infiltration swale detail. Designed by Elder Creek Landscapes.

Hand Digging a Swale. A hand-dug swale requires a slightly different approach than one excavated by machine. Digging contour swales by hand is hard yet rewarding work. It all starts with preparing the site. Once you've chosen the starting point for the swale and laid out the contour line and trajectory of the system, it is time to prep the site. The first layer of hand excavation will be to remove the vegetation (if present) over the ditch part of the swale system. Hopefully, your swale is not crossing through trees and established shrubs that require removal (though that is necessary sometimes) and the vegetation you're removing is natural growing grasses, forbs, and the like. In any case, dig out this top layer of soil plus vegetation and place it on the berm side of the ditch (downslope). If the vegetation is woody material—blackberries, poison oak, etc.—you may want to keep the material out of the berm. In case of grasses and forbs, it is fine to bury this material at the bottom of the berm.

Once you remove this first section of soil/vegetation you're ready to dig into the next layer. If the soil is highly compacted, use a pickax, digging bar, or broad fork to loosen the soil in the ditch before scraping up the next layer with shovels.

The next step is to dig out the ditch completely (to the desired depth and width) and build the berm. For every shovelful of soil you dig out, make sure it is placed where you want the soil to end up. Do not toss soil randomly at the berm, but instead place it strategically into the berm, aiming for a consistent height and width. Keep the material close to the edge of the ditch so it functions as part of a fully integrated system with the ditch.

The final grade of your swale and berm should have gentle sloping sides. Avoid building steep berms or cutting steep sides in the ditch. Take time to grade both the ditch and the berm with angled slopes (angle of repose) to mitigate future erosion and increase accessibility.

Once the swale has been dug and graded, you must cover it to protect against erosion. Heavily mulching the berm, seeding, or dense planting of the entire area are all wise options. (Note: Adding too much mulch to the ditch can cause problems. A ditch filled with mulch that floods in a storm can possibly clog outflows and lead to erosion problems. Vegetated rather than mulched swale bottoms are ideal.)

Machine Excavation. Excavating swales with machines does come with its own set of factors. The first decision to make once the swale has been surveyed and marked on the land is what type of machine to use. Excavators are by far the most versatile and sensitive machine to use when digging a swale, but they are also slow. For extremely large projects, bulldozers or road graders make more sense for installation. If you grade the slopes of a swale/berm to the angle of repose during the first pass, it will require less time later in the fine-tuning process. A bulldozer can achieve that level of efficiency.

The size of the project, the budget, the access, and end result, will all play a factor in deciding the appropriate machine for the project. For context, nine out of ten swales I dug have been with an excavator. For other practitioners it will be different.

In all cases, during the installation process, keep the risk of compaction in mind. If the soil is a little wetter than ideal, be extra sensitive to where you step or drive the machine. If the soil is bone dry, compaction may not be an issue at all.

Completing the Project

Other than those specific items mentioned above, the installation and final outcome of the swale whether built by machine or hand is exactly the same. Decisions about vegetation, grading slopes, seeding, mulching, and so on are a part of the whole process regardless of the tools used.

SPILLWAYS/OVERFLOWS

Every water-harvesting system you design *must* have a spillway. If catching and harvesting significant volumes of water—whether in rain gardens, swales, rain tanks, ponds, terraces, or ditches—*all* of these systems must have a water overflow built into the system. These *will* be tested during catastrophic storms. These overflows often act as linking elements between various water catchment and management systems; for instance, a swale overflowing into a rain garden.

Getting overflows wrong poses a huge risk of flood and erosion. When the system is full and more water is going into the system than the spillways can release, then you have a big problem. This is when the most dangerous moments in the landscape occur.

For water-harvesting structures like rain gardens, ponds, and swales, the spillway needs to be placed at an elevation above the bottom of the water-harvesting structure. This means that water needs to fill up *to* the spillway before flowing out of it. The height given to the spillway

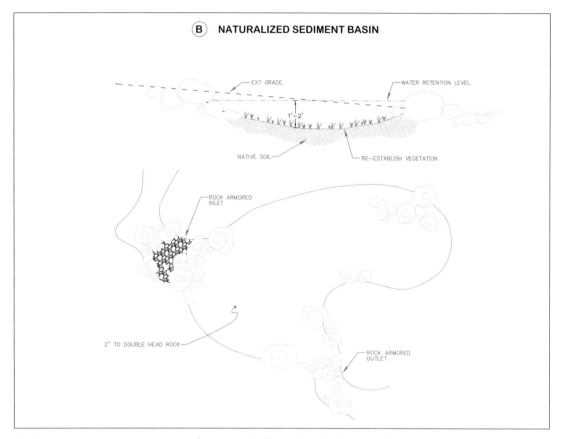

Surface water conveyance system with armored inlet and outlet. Designed by Permaculture Artisans.

dictates the volume of water that can be harvested in the infiltration structure. This fact makes the spillway a key element that facilitates the function of the water management system.

In some cases, you will have to install more than one spillway, allowing water to siphon out of the system from two locations. This way, a lower elevation spillway will function during light rain events but when large storm events occur, the second spillway, placed at a higher elevation, can provide a second outlet for the water.

Pay close attention to the differences in elevations of inflows into a water-harvesting structure, the lowest grade where the water begins to fill, and the height of the spillway. Make sure the relationship between all three of these elevations allows for both adequate water collection and a safe out for the water when the system is full.

Depending on the volume of water entering the system, the spillway might be a wide surface shelf, a large drain box with pipe, or a smaller low point where water can move out of the system. Size the spillway appropriately. During the first large storm event, make sure to visit the system and fine-tune any issues you see at the spillway to ensure that the water safely exits.

In rain gardens and swales, the spillway is where erosion is most likely to occur. This is where water leaves the system and begins to pick up velocity as it travels downstream. Spillways need to be stabilized. In many cases, armoring the spillway with rock or erosion-control blankets is advised to mitigate erosion and stabilize the spillway level.

When using stone to armor a spillway—building up along the two sides or "banks" with stone—creating an "apron" is key. The low points should *always* be in the center, the rock aprons making sure water doesn't gouge the edges of the system and create a new route for the water to leave.

Stone is often dug *into* the surface of the soil at grade to keep the rocks keyed into the ground. This way high-flow events can't wash the rocks away. Simply placing stone on top (not digging rock in) can lead to water flowing underneath the stone, eventually eroding the spillway despite the stone.

Biological armoring is also an option. Rhizomatous grasses and other rhizomatous plants can be planted in and around the spillway to stabilize the soil and mitigate erosion. Planting also attracts beneficial organisms, sequesters carbon, and adds beauty to the landscape. Avoid placing large plants in the center of the spillway, however, as this may interrupt the main function of water leaving the system.

Level sills are innovative spillways well suited to water-harvesting swales, terraces, and pond overflows. These specialized spillways are extremely wide and level along their entire edge. When water leaves a level spillway, it "sheens" over the wide area, dispersing not only water but also energy. Water can then enter a meadow, a forest, a garden, another swale, or a pond with no concern for erosion.

COMBINE WATER MANAGEMENT TECHNIQUES

There's no one technique to solve water management in any landscape, so, when designing your water-harvesting system, use a combination of techniques. A water-harvesting swale overflows into a rain garden, which spills into a pond. A terrace directs surface water to an off-contour swale leading to a pond. A road ditch enters a swale, which leads to a large rain garden. The combinations are limitless. The design always starts at the top of the landscape and slowly move downslope.

27
Landscape Drainage Systems

While a main objective of a regenerative designer is to build landscapes that catch and store water, good drainage must always be considered in tandem with water harvesting. At the most minimal level, all water-harvesting systems need to have overflows and safe means of releasing water in high-flow situations. In most landscapes, a more nuanced approach to drainage is required as you balance all the influences of water on the site. Structures such as houses, barns, and stone walls all require a form of drainage to ensure longevity. Water has the ability to rot a house foundation, push a stonewall over, or wash out a road. Water is a regenerative *and* a destructive force. In the landscape, there are elements we prefer not to be damaged by the flow of water. Pathways, patios, roads, and even certain planting systems require suitable drainage just to exist.

Harvesting water while preserving effective drainage is a tricky balance and one that is essential to get right. I have worked on many projects where poor drainage led to an inability to grow a farm, plant a fruit tree, or even walk the site. Often, landscape drainage problems aren't a consequence of natural succession but badly designed human systems. For centuries, people have been draining water off the land using culverts, drain boxes, and pipes, then releasing that water irresponsibly. Many erosion and flooding issues can be traced to these water management mistakes where old drainage systems have gone defunct and low-lying landscapes take the brunt of overly drained uplands. Striking a balance between water harvesting and appropriate drainage is the goal for regenerative landscapers.

When we design relationally, we are capable of developing effective solutions to any water problem. Like addressing human relationship problems, we can fix our water relationship problems when we seek connection. While drainage is necessary around structures, diverting the water thoughtfully can make regenerative connections throughout the landscape. Instead of releasing water along access roads, street drains, or random locations, we release these drainage systems into rain gardens, contour swales, and ponds. This turns a drainage problem into a water-harvesting solution, a sound strategy for any regenerative landscape.

Your task as a regenerative designer, then, is to develop systems that require the least amount of drainage while incorporating appropriate drainage to protect infrastructure and guard against catastrophe, while directing these flows to beneficial locations for the hydrology of the landscape.

LANDSCAPE DRAINAGE SYSTEMS

Applying a regenerative design approach to drainage means reducing the need for culverts, pipes, and drain boxes as much as possible. As soon as water enters a pipe or culvert, it increases in velocity, coming out the other end with enough force to scour the ground and create erosion.

How drainage systems are handled is directly connected to managing erosion. Like everything in this book, doing the least harm, designing for reciprocity, and designing relationships are guiding principles to strategize ecologically sound landscape drainage systems.

Drainage systems include everything from well-designed spillways, off-contour water diversion channels, french drains, and drain boxes (also called drain inlets) with solid pipe to catch and move water from one place to another to the intentional grading and buildup of infrastructure like pathways above grade, raised foundations, and slightly angled patios. There are many ways to provide drainage, some more detrimental to the landscape than others.

Grading

The most modest and primary technique for increasing drainage in the landscape is grading. Grading simply means manipulating the surface of the soil to get water to move from one place to another. Roads and pathways are always graded to sheet water in one direction or another. The outsides of structures are best graded to have rain and other surface waters sheet away from foundations. Often, when a drainage issue is present, a simple grade change in a strategic location relieves the problem.

Water Diversion Channels

One of the best techniques is to use water diversion channels. This approach, if done correctly, provides drainage while also *increasing* infiltration. Water diversion channels aren't suitable directly around structures but are best integrated with other forms of drainage to capture and move water from one place to another. From an ecological point of view, these channels are *slightly* off contour in order to move water without being so steep as to speed water movement to dangerous velocities where erosion occurs. In a regenerative landscape, these are gentle moving waterways, often planted and enhanced as highly aesthetic features of the land.

Using a water diversion channel to connect a rain garden to a water-harvesting swale, or as an intermediary between a roof water downspout and a pond, are advanced techniques for integrating a variety of water management systems.

French Drains

French drains are subsurface drainage systems used to dewater an area. These are to be used only in situations where it is absolutely necessary.

A French drain is most commonly used to protect structures from subsurface flowing water. Excessive water ponding underneath a building, rotting foundations, or the presence of mold in the house are potential indicators of too much water moving subsurface near structures. A French drain (subsurface perforated drain pipe) can be installed outside the footprint of the building to capture these underground moving rivers and divert them elsewhere.

Drain Inlets/Pipe Conveyance

There are situations in the landscape when capturing water in a drain and piping it away is necessary. Using this technique is a last resort if approaching the landscape using regenerative design principles. That being said, many projects have elements that would be damaged by water and the only way to protect these elements is to drain the water to new locations. Always, when draining water in this manner, it is best to daylight (let the water out of the pipe) at the *closest appropriate location* for infiltration or storage.

A drain inlet is a concrete or plastic box with a drain lid on top and holes cut out of the sides for installing pipes that will convey the water to new locations. In conventional buildings, drain inlets are placed at low points in the landscape, where water is directed—a patio edge, the bottom of a rain garden, the bottom of a ditch. This placement of drains maximizes drainage, moving water away from the system.

Drain inlets *do* aid in water infiltration when used as spillways for rain gardens and contour swales. I quite like this application as it enables water-harvesting systems to be implemented in places otherwise not suited for them while providing a safe and effective outlet for water.

When adding to an infiltration system (swale, rain garden, terrace), drain inlets are not placed at the lowest point. Instead, they are placed a few inches above the lowest point of the system. This allows for the infiltration structure to receive, retain, and infiltrate water. When water fills up high enough, it will enter the drain inlet and be conveyed to a new location. This type of integration between water harvesting elements and drainage techniques is especially useful in urban and suburban projects where permanent obstacles like concrete walkways, houses, or old trees need to be worked around.

Drainage and Erosion

Sometimes you will inherit a project with significant erosion caused by drainage systems that weren't built correctly, the construction of roads, culverts, poorly placed gutters, or compacted soils. And while we want to first and foremost think about catching and infiltrating water, sometimes the best, easiest, cheapest, most effective approach is actually to drain an area that's being incapacitated by fast-moving volumes of water. Capture that water and then drain it to a safer location for infiltration. Appropriate drainage is often about safely moving water from unstable or problematic areas to water-harvesting opportunities.

Drainage and Pollution

This runoff crisis is not just about erosion and dehydration, it's about pollution as well. Motor oil, hydrocarbons, heavy metals, and dioxins enter waterways, contaminating whole watersheds as a result of drainage. This is the state of human infrastructure right now, and each new generation will inherit these problems on grander and grander scales if regenerative designers don't take responsibility to design our world back into a reciprocal relationship with water. Just because we inherited a dying system doesn't mean we have to let it die. We *can* repair watersheds, heal landscapes, and remediate the poisons we have dumped in our communities. When we apply regenerative design principles to human development our infrastructure becomes a haven for life.

28
Water Distribution

How water moves around the landscape's structure—from ponds, wells, storage tanks, irrigation systems, and so on—is crucial to what you're able to accomplish in the landscape. Gravity-fed (passive) distribution and pump-based distribution provide the basis for most water conveyance techniques.

GRAVITY

Using gravity to distribute water to the landscape is the ideal regenerative approach, enabling you to forgo using electricity. Using gravity to irrigate the landscape can only happen when the source and/or storage system is sufficiently higher in elevation than the irrigated gardens. That is why one of the go-to strategies of regenerative design is locating water storage systems high in the landscape whenever possible.

Landscapes in flat terrain, with little to no topography, will not make much use of gravity unless water towers or other built structures are designed for this purpose. Approximately one pound per square inch (PSI) is generated by two feet of fall/elevation drop.[1]

Specifically, for each one foot of drop, 0.433 PSI is generated. That means if your water is stored 90 feet above your landscape, you will have approximately 40 PSI (38.97 to be exact) to pressurize water systems for the landscape.

It is important to remember that gravity-fed systems are susceptible to airlock, a condition when bubbles of air get caught inside the pipe and create a vacuum that stops all water movement in the pipe. The problem occurs when the pipe makes sharp turns or travels up and over bumps. For this reason, keep gravity-fed pipes in a constant drop with as few angles or curves as possible. When turns are made or grade changes are unavoidable, place air vents at these locations to create an outlet for air buildup. An air vent at the very top of the system is always advised to help keep airlock from occurring. Commercially available air vents are available or you can custom make one.

PUMPING WATER

The majority of water and irrigation systems around the world depend on electrical pumping. Pumping water is one of the largest demands of energy required for human civilization.[2]

While pumping water requires enormous energy, not all pumps are made the same and solar pumps, gravity pumps (Ram pumps), and other low-energy and efficient pumping mechanisms are available. The reality is, most of you will need to use water pumps to some degree on your project. Whether that be a well pump, a pressure pump, or a solar pump depends on your context and goals.

Solar High Lift

From a regenerative perspective, a solar high lift pump is one of your best options. These pumps can move water from low elevations to high elevations with incredible efficiency using energy from the sun. Incorporating these into gravity-run irrigation systems is an excellent approach. If your water sources are located at low elevations, a solar high lift pump will push that water to a storage system higher in the landscape. From the higher location, water is gravity-fed back down to the project. This uses a high-efficiency, low-energy pump to gain enough elevational "head" (a term used to describe water above your use area) to enable gravity-fed, pressurized irrigation systems.[3]

Well Pump

Most wells operate using a high-efficiency deep water pump. These pumps are placed deep down in the well casing (well pipe) and pump water directly out of underground aquifers. Well pumps, if used in agricultural or other commercial water use settings, generally burn out within 10 years and have to be replaced. For this reason, it is preferable to pump water from a well into tanks and then draw from tanks into irrigation systems. This will take *some* of the pressure off well pumps since the well only kicks on when the tanks fall to a specified water level. That said, plenty of landscape projects are irrigated directly from a well pump and pressurized by a pressure tank.

Pressure Tank (Bladder Tank)

A pressure tank is not a pump per se but a small tank with a bladder inside surrounded by pressurized air. Water enters the bladder tank via a well or booster pump and gets pressurized. When water is turned on for irrigation or domestic uses, this pressurized water is what you get.

Booster Pump

A booster pump is an external pump, generally used to pull water from water tanks, creeks, rivers, or lakes and direct this water into tanks or pressure tanks. These are powerful pumps that use a lot of energy and easily burn out through overuse. It is always safer to draw water out of a pressure tank or through gravity than to rely upon a booster pump to run an irrigation system. The booster pump is just an intermediary to get water from one system to another, not the mechanism for pressuring a system itself.

Hand Pump

Hand pumps are an ancient way of pumping water and are still relevant today in the era of rapid climate change. Hand pumps use zero electricity, relying on physical human energy to draw water out of a well, tank, or other water source. I've been recommending hand pumps more and more in recent years as power outages become more frequent due to the testing of human infrastructure by ecological and economic disasters. It may be one day that all of our pumping will have to rely on passive sources such as gravity and hand pumping as electrical grids become more and more unreliable. Sometimes the old ways endure, and that is especially true in regenerative design systems.

For large landscape projects and irrigation requirements, a hand pump system may be unrealistic, but it could still provide a reliable backup for outdoor kitchens, drinking water supply, emergency water needs, and *small-scale* irrigation.

Surface Flow

The most natural method for water to be distributed across the land is on the surface. This is *earth wisdom* in action—harnessing this power starts with identifying current surface water movement, be it creeks, streams, roads, deer trails, or ditches. When you are capable of harnessing the power of surface water, you are capable of harnessing the power of *cultivating life*.

In the regenerative approach, we direct, capture, release, and encourage maximum infiltration in the landscape. In many ecological projects, agricultural ponds are connected using contour swales and water distribution channels to reticulate water across the landscape in ecologically beneficial ways. In a process of *stacking multiple functions* into one element, landscape pathways, roads, terraces and so on can be designed as beneficial surface water distribution systems. This only works if the structures, paths, roads, and overall landscape design are in harmony with the soil and overall ecology.

Piping

The majority of landscape irrigation systems depend on plastic or metal pipes, which have a large amount of embodied energy, but when used effectively they can facilitate ecological restoration. We always have to balance the ecological benefits of a project with the embodied and destructive activities required to install that project. Laying pipe is a relatively cheap and easy solution for the majority of landscape projects despite the degenerative sources of the materials.

Natural Water Flows

Manipulating natural water courses like creeks and rivers can have catastrophic consequences in the watershed and should be avoided. The practice of watershed restoration can be benefited by interventions (woody check dams, bridge crossings, erosion control systems) in natural watercourses, but these actions should only be done after a detailed investigation process by a team of engineers, jurisdictional authorities, and you—the designer.

VEINS OF THE LAND

Water is the blood of the earth and the blood of your landscape, making water delivery systems the veins of the land. Water distribution is a structural framework for living landscapes, be it passive surface flows or high-tech pumping mechanisms. How you design and implement these systems makes all the difference in the development of landscape water resilience.

29

Roof Water Harvesting

Roof water harvesting is a tried-and-true strategy for developing water resilience in the landscape. Water from a roof is carried through watertight downspouts and directed to tanks, ponds, or water-harvesting systems in the landscape. This approach is especially useful in environments with long dry periods. When moisture is not spread evenly throughout the year, *catching and storing* water when it does rain is significant for developing water security. Utilizing rainwater for landscape irrigation reduces dependency on wells, springs, rivers, and creeks for summer irrigation needs. In this way, roof catchment systems offset some of the hydrological degeneration from groundwater and watershed extraction. And . . . catching and using the rain is incredibly satisfying and fun. Fun is an important yield, right?

CALCULATING ROOF WATER CATCHMENT

Calculating the potential volume of rain coming off a roof is the first step in designing a roof water-catchment system. You need to know the volume of water in question before making decisions about tanks, gutters, downspouts, and so on. You may discover that sufficient roof water comes from *half* the roof area, according to your needs or your budget. In many cases, the volume of water coming off a roof is significantly more than most folks can afford to store in tanks.

Every one inch of rain that falls on 1,000 square feet equals 623 gallons of water.[1] That is a significant volume of water, making roofs a major potential catchment area.

HERE IS A FORMULA IN INCHES-GALLON TO CALCULATE YOUR ROOF WATER RUNOFF.

1. Measure the footprint of the roof. For example, let's say the roof is 50 feet by 50 feet. This equals 2,500 square feet.
2. Now convert your building measurements from feet to inches. 50 feet by 50 feet equals 600 inches by 600 inches.
3. Research and calculate the average amount of rainfall in inches that falls in your project's area. For our example, let's say this project receives 10 inches of rain on average per year.

4. Multiply the roof dimensions in inches by average rainfall in inches. In this case, it would be 600 inches times 600 inches times 10 inches equals 3,600,000 cubic inches of water.

    Since there are 231 cubic inches for every gallon, divide your cubic inches of water by 231.

$$3,600,00 \div 231 = 15,584.4 \text{ gallons.}$$

For the example given above, an average precipitation of 10 inches of rain per year falling on a 50 feet by 50 feet roof, will catch approximately 15,600 gallons of water! Many readers of this book are working in landscapes that receive far more water than this example. Now you understand why we call a roof an above-ground well.

CAPTURE AND DISTRIBUTION

Before water enters conveyance systems, gutters need to be cleaned and stay clean. If gutters are filled with leaves and other debris, rainwater will potentially get caught in gutters without entering downspouts. This leads to water sheeting over gutters in locations, which can lead to erosion and water damage at the foundations of structures. In short, keep your gutters clean!

There are two kinds of water conveyance—dry line conveyance and wet line conveyance. Let's explore the differences between these two techniques and when and why you might choose one or the other.

Dry Line Conveyance

A dry line conveyance system is when water enters a tank, pond, or infiltration system via a pipe with a constant drop. This means that water passes through the pipe and once it daylights or enters a tank, the pipe is *dry*, with no water left in the pipe. A dry line conveyance system works well to fill tanks close to the building or systems downslope from the building. There are even instances where designers run a pipe with a constant drop along the side of a wall to get water into a tank using the dry line method.

Wet Line Conveyance

A wet line conveyance means that water stays in the pipe once it has come from the roof of a structure and enters into a catchment system. This happens when the *outflow* of the pipe is higher than the lowest point in the pipe. Water finds its own level such that a watertight pipe that comes off a downspout can be trenched into the ground, then rise back out of the ground and into the top of a tank or other catchment structure, filling it with water. As long as the outflow is lower than the top of the downspout, water will always move out of the pipe at the end no matter if its lowest point is underground. If it sounds like magic or some kind of miracle—in my opinion, you're right—though it is also called science.

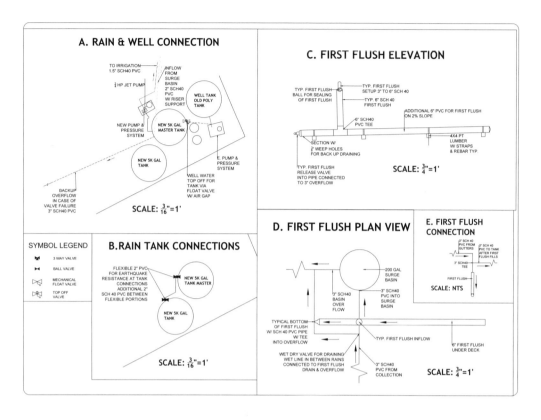
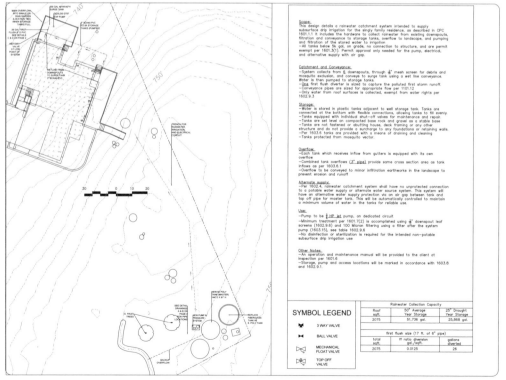

Rainwater harvesting design detail. Designed by Christopher Clarke.

We call a water line like this a wet line conveyance because there is always water sitting in the pipe. To alleviate the problem of anaerobic bacteria building up inside the pipe, a tee fitting with a ball valve is placed in the pipe at the lowest point. This point is usually underground, so a valve box is placed above the valve to facilitate access. Between storms, the valve can be opened and the extra water sitting in the pipe released.

TANK STORAGE

Storing caught water in tanks is a convenient and common approach to developing water security. Water collection sources—rain, springs, wells—all need some type of conveyance system to get water from the source to the tank. Once you get the water to the tank, then storage is secured.

Water storage tanks come in many shapes and sizes, depending on what you need. Research the various options to decide what kinds of tanks are appropriate for your project. Tanks are placed above ground on solid foundations or are buried beneath the ground as cisterns. Different tanks are designed for each application, so make sure you're not burying an above-ground tank or placing a below-ground tank above ground.

In the region where I live, tectonic fault lines spider through the hills and valleys. Earthquakes need to be taken seriously, so placing and choosing tanks requires focused attention to ensure that tanks full of water won't roll off hillsides during an earthquake.

Tanks can be purchased or built with a number of materials. High-density polyethyline (HDPE) plastic tanks are some of the most common as they are cheap, easy to install, long lasting, lightweight, and retain high water quality. The most popular underground tanks are made of reinforced fiberglass and plastic. These tanks are designed to be placed beneath the earth, where they handle the weight of soil above and hydrostatic pressure (groundwater pressure) below. These are especially useful in arid climates where above-ground tanks get too hot and also on small projects where space is limited. Underground tanks can be installed with patios, shallow gardens, and other elements placed above them.

Corrugated metal tanks are generally used for larger (20,000 gallons or more) systems, and are more difficult to install than HDPE tanks. A concrete foundation has to be poured and the tank assembled piece by piece. That being said, when you're storing upwards of 50 to 100,000 gallons of water, the costs of these tanks are worth every penny.

Concrete tanks are another option. Some concrete tanks are buried as cisterns and ferro-cement tanks built right on-site. A ferro-cement tank has the benefit of fire resistance and, if well maintained, will last many decades.

Siting Tanks

Where you place or "site" your tank is of utmost importance. There are many factors to consider.

Elevation. Placing tanks high in the landscape gives you the advantage of gravity. If the context allows, place tanks at higher elevations to gain as much gravity pressure as possible to distribute water. (Remember, approximately one pound per square inch is generated for every feet of elevation drop.)

Setbacks. Setbacks are zoning ordinances for development. Each jurisdiction and zone will have different setbacks for properties. These include setbacks to property lines, creeks, leach fields, wells, and so on. If the system you are building requires permits, tanks need to be sited outside these setbacks. Property setbacks vary from site to site, whether it's a front property line, side, or back property line. Setbacks can range from 5 to 10 feet for property line setbacks and up to 100 feet for setbacks from named waterways and leach fields.

Transfer Tanks

A transfer tank is a relatively small tank that acts as an intermediary between passively harvested water from the roof and the final storage location. Transfer tanks are located such that water from the roof of the building enters into the tank using gravity. Inside the transfer tank is a small high torque pump and an electric sensor. When the transfer tank fills to the top with water, the sensor triggers, turning on the pump. The water is then pumped from the transfer tank to higher elevation storage systems. These higher elevation systems can be more tanks, ponds, or other landscape water-harvesting elements.

Because the transfer tank pump only kicks on when the tank is full, the use of electricity is quite minimal. The pump only turns on during rain events capable of filling the tank. A 1,000-gallon transfer tank is an efficient size to use for this purpose. It's not so small that the pump has to constantly turn on to empty the tank, and not so large that it's difficult to place near structures like homes and barns. A much larger tank can be used as a transfer tank, however, if that better fits your goals.

Tank Foundations

A necessary component of a water storage tank system is a well-designed and built foundation. Tank foundations do not need to be concrete but they do need to be level. If you're placing tanks on a slope, the slope will need to be excavated to build a terrace or earthen bench to place the tanks on. In highly erosive soils or steep grades, a retaining wall may be needed to secure the terrace.

The tanks themselves are placed on well-compacted surfaces, usually covered in gravel if no concrete is used. This allows water to drain away from the tank pad but also provides a flexible and durable base.

In smaller landscape projects, water tanks are difficult to integrate because of their size and aesthetic. Keeping foundations to a minimum is generally the goal of the designer on small projects.

Gutter Retrofitting

One of the first steps in building out a roof water collection system is making small adjustments to the gutters (or installing gutters if needed). To maximize the volume of water captured by the system, you will need to combine water coming from downspouts on each side of the house into a single pipe. If the length of the roofline is relatively short, only one gutter and downspout will be needed. If the roofline is exceedingly long, two downspouts are often recommended to ensure that water doesn't sit in the gutter and rot out to the eaves of the building. Using either a dry line or wet line conveyance system, direct water from downspouts to the storage or transfer tank, infiltration basin, or pond. Multiple downspouts can be tied into each other to direct water away from the building into a single pipe that enters into your water-harvesting system.

Using Rainwater

Once you have captured roof water and collected it in tanks, cisterns, or ponds, what are its best uses? This is a tricky conundrum because the amount of water you are able to store in tanks cannot cover all the needs of a thirsty landscape. A typical rainwater harvesting system will cost somewhere between $.50 per gallon to $1.50 per gallon. This will vary from region to region and based on the accessibility of materials, labor, and equipment. Let's say a system comes out at about $1 per gallon. That would mean that, if you want a 30,000-gallon system, it would cost around $30,000 dollars! Crazy, isn't it? That's why water conservation and infiltration in the landscape are such important techniques in the water-harvesting world.

This 30,000-gallon system that costs you $30,000 to design and install will provide significant resilience in dry seasons. But if your landscape is a food-production garden with many vegetables, young fruit trees, or other water-loving plants, 30,000 gallons will not be adequate for watering in a dry climate throughout the year. This is why choosing appropriate plant communities, building topsoil, catching water in the landscape, and shading the surface of the land are all important integrated facets of your holistic approach to harvesting water.

Any amount of water you collect and store is extremely valuable. Even a 500-gallon tank filled with rainwater is precious. Once you have the water in that storage system, be strategic about how you use it. Watering the vegetable garden may not make sense, but dedicating stored water to fruit trees will provide a massive benefit; with all other design factors in place, your rain-caught water could be all the water required to keep young fruit trees thriving. Once your trees are mature, dedicate yearly caught rainwater to establish new plant communities.

Captured rainwater may also be stored for fire protection, emergency domestic uses, or used to top off water features such as ponds. Rainwater can be used for washing, toilets, and even drinking. A potable roof water system requires a well-designed filtration system to make sure the water is safe to drink. Potable water systems generally incorporate an ultraviolet light filter to kill bacteria, a charcoal filter, and a sand filter to clean particulates and increase water quality. Many jurisdictions will not permit systems such as these, so use caution when developing a rainwater-drinking system. In extreme emergency events, rainwater can be boiled and used for cooking or drinking as needed.

HARVESTING ABUNDANCE

Remember, even in drought conditions, you can catch enormous volumes of water from any kind of building or structure. One inch of rain on one acre is approximately 27,000 gallons of water! Even in a drought year, you have an immense amount of water falling out of the sky. Unless you have the budget and the space, it's unlikely you'll be able to catch and store *all* the water coming from the roof of your house and various structures.

Infiltrating water in the ground is always an option once storage tanks are full. Use terraces, rain gardens, contour ditches, ponds, and other structures and techniques to turn your landscape into a water-harvesting collection system. The more we keep water on-site, the more resilient our watersheds will be and the less your landscapes will depend on irrigation. Working with the forces of nature in this way creates a landscape system of generational longevity and wealth. With less water being pulled from aquifers, rivers, and lakes, all while increasing the ability to grow an abundance of food and medicine from the rain, the future truly is bright.

30
Landscape Ponds

Ponds in the landscape provide tremendous ecological yields along with beauty, recreation, and a tranquil atmosphere. Ponds generate *multiple stacked functions* and are linked in numerous *relationship design* connections and flows. A landscape pond serves as an exemplary system for catching surface and roof water and storing it for later use. Birds, mammals, insects, and amphibians all regularly visit year-round water features to access food, clean water, and refreshment on hot days. The microclimate benefits of ponds are numerous as they cool down a landscape through evaporative cooling, while warming the same landscape during the night through the release of radiant heat collected during the day—a function of the pond's thermal mass properties. Even the reflection of the sun off the surface of pond waters plays a role in moderating the microclimate. All these possible functions and more are designed into the landscape to integrate and harmonize with other landscape elements such as fruit trees, patios, fire pits, and native hedgerows.

The design and installation of your pond need to reflect a strong assessment of soil type, space limitation, topography, fault lines, legal constraints, budget, and more. Ponds are wonderful, but a badly designed and built pond can lead to catastrophe. They can be quite dangerous when they fail, with the potential to flood and destroy homes and property. Any pond project of a medium to large scale must be designed with the aid of engineers or people with vast experience successfully building these structures. Don't take this part lightly—it is crucial to design and build these systems correctly, with all the possible problems worked out.

That being said, small rubber-lined ponds are relatively safe and reliable, so don't get discouraged or scared by the above paragraph. Start small, learn from your mistakes, work with professionals on big projects, and take in as much knowledge as you can from these experiences.

DESIGN FUNCTIONS

Like every element in the landscape, design your pond using ecological principles. Place it in relation to other elements on the site, and design it to provide as many functions for the needs of the ecosystem as possible. Create a vision that meets the basic goals of the human and nonhuman communities integrating symbiotic relationships in as many ways as possible.

What are the services you want the pond to provide? Are you catching rainwater? Are you creating a specific microclimate for plants you can't grow elsewhere? Are you growing food in the form of an aquaculture system—growing water chestnuts, taro, and fish? Do you want to place this body of water in a specific location to enhance or create a view? Is your goal to attract wildlife and hear the chorus of frogs? All of these goals play a part in *how* you build this pond and where it is placed.

Once your goals are clear, you need to identify where the pond is to be located and how large you are going to build it. On some projects, this will be decided for you, as there will only be one location suitable for a pond, but for others you need to be diligent in your analysis about where the pond will fit in the landscape and at what scale.

Siting the Pond

Siting the pond correctly is a key decision that requires analysis of the site as well as an understanding of the overall vision and context of the project and landscape. Focus on connecting as many functions to the whole ecosystem as possible.

Here are some factors to ponder when siting a pond.

Microclimate. Ponds provide microclimatic benefits but are also affected by the existing microclimate. If the pond is placed in the full sun, there will be more evaporation and algae growth. If the pond is placed under large trees, there will be less evaporation but more leaves and debris will fall into the pond. A windy location will have more evaporation.

View. Ponds are aesthetic features on the land and thus your design will benefit from a location where the pond is visible. On the other hand, a mysterious path that leads to a tranquil

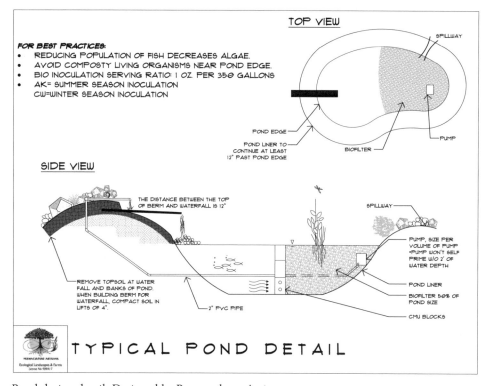

Pond design detail. Designed by Permaculture Artisans.

pond setting might be desirable. Do you want to see the pond surface from inside your house? When you're sitting by the pond, what is the surrounding view? If you want to swim in the pond, what is the view while you're swimming? Does the neighbor's second-story window look down into the pond area?

Topography. Ponds can be built on flat or sloped ground but the steeper the slope, the more challenging and dangerous it is to build a pond. The steeper the topography, the larger the pond dam. A pond dam is undisputedly the most important element of a pond and getting the dam wrong is where dangerous scenarios unfold. A failed dam usually means downstream destruction.

Ponds built on flat ground are called excavation ponds. These don't require a pond dam but do require a plan for all the soil being removed from the pond hole. A dammed pond will make use of much if not all of the soil generated during pond construction, but an excavated pond on flat ground makes use of none of the soil removed.

Landscape formations such as upper valleys and saddles make great pond locations if the topography isn't too steep and the soil type is suitable.

Soils. Soil type is a huge factor when siting and building a pond. Some soils are more erosive than others, some have clay that is great for building dams, and some soils are so sandy that water passes through like a sieve. Soils filled with large stones and boulders provide their own set of problems.

It is difficult to build earthen ponds with sandy soils and a lack of clay. In soils like these, a rubber lined pond is generally more appropriate. Bentonite clay can be added to soils lacking sufficient natural clay, but it is tricky to get the pond to seal correctly without a strong foundation of heavy soil.

Soils with large boulders and stones need to be approached with caution when building a pond. Boulders inside a dam wall are a recipe for disaster and rubber liners need to be kept protected from punctures by sharp stones.

Access. When it comes time to build the pond, are you able to get equipment and materials to the location? What effort would it take to make access possible if it isn't currently open? When excavating the pond, are other obstacles in the way like large boulders, trees, or large roots? What other elements on the site will be affected by the installation process and is the location still the best option despite these obstacles?

Engineering and Permits

Most ponds require a fair amount of excavating and moving soil. Around the world, many jurisdictions require permits and engineering plans to guarantee that the system is built safely and adheres to local ordinances.

This is especially the case for medium to large ponds built on slopes. Where I live in Northern California, we are in close proximity to many active fault lines. Placing hundreds of thousands of pounds of water on a hillside is a dangerous act. If done right, it can create abundance throughout the watershed, but if built improperly, it could cause a major secondary disaster during an earthquake.

Excavation and Shaping

Many factors influence the design and shape of your pond. Some topographies require an engineered dam, while on flatter areas the pond can be dug with no dam. The aesthetic you want, the location of the pond in relation to existing elements like trees, structures, and climate, all need to be taken into consideration during the design process and will lead you to the proper shape. The pond I built on my homestead is shaped in a general oval to fit most efficiently in the space that I have available. The central depth of my pond is nine feet because my pond is a swimming pond; and with a depth like that, the ledges around the pond needed to be shaped a certain way. I chose to build a wetland planting system, placed in a ring around the entire edge of the pond. What kind of planting areas do you foresee for your pond? These are best created through shallow ledges to place plants that are only submerged 12 to 24 inches. Ledges should be at least three feet wide, but wider is better to give ample room for stones and plants.

Another consideration for shaping are the entries and exits of the pond designed for animals and humans. In my pond, we built a beach entrance on one side and a shallow underwater patio on the other to provide two main entrances. For animals that use the pond, it is important to provide these shallow entries so they can safely get in and out of the water. If you do not provide such an element, it will lead to animals either falling into the pond and drowning or tearing the pond liner to get out.

Spillway and Leveling

Every natural pond needs to have a spillway where the pond can spill over when it is full and receiving heavy rain or inflowing waters. My pond spills into a wide, shallow ditch that leads to a large rain garden.

The spillway is not the only leveling system required for a pond. The best-looking ponds are leveled around the *entire edge* of the water with the spillway being placed at a few inches to a few feet below the leveled edge. The difference between the leveled edge of the pond and the spillway is called the freeboard. The freeboard provides a cushion for the pond when it is full and still receiving large volumes of water. The freeboard allows the surge of water to rise as water tries to leave via the spillway. You never want water to leave the pond on any embankment other than the spillway, as this will cause erosion and possible flooding.

Leveling as best as you can around the pond will give you safe places to navigate the edges but will also lend a feeling of fullness, of abundance, of a full water line. If you think I'm talking about energy and aesthetics, you are right . . . the feeling of navigating the edge of a pool or pond, where the shelf surrounding the body of water is near level—this is a real experience that is difficult to put into words.

Installing the Underlayment

If you're using a polymer plastic or rubber pond liner, you will need to use an underlayment to protect against tears and leaks. An underlayment is a soft piece of fabric placed below the liner. Geotextile underlayments are readily available throughout the world from pond or landscape supply companies. You *can* use recycled carpet scraps or rugs as an underlayment to save money. If you do, make sure to remove *all* staples left in the carpet (not doing so could result in a punctured liner).

When you install the underlayment, consider these tips:

- Your pond will likely have curvature in its shape. When you put the underlayment down, fold the material in the *middle* of curves.
- If you're using geotextile fabric, you want to stick it to the earth. This material is light and can flap around in the wind. Metal jute stakes work well to pin the fabric in place.
- Leave enough fabric outside the edge of the pond to work with later. If you underestimate the size and cut pieces of fabric that, when placed in the pond, don't reach up the sides, you may be in trouble later.

Installing the Liner

Pond liners are heavy and expensive. The only plastic pond liners you should ever use need to be made of either high-density polyethylene (HDPE) or ethylene propylene diene monomer (EPDM) plastics. These are nontoxic polymer plastics that, as long as they're thick enough, are extremely durable to water pressure and tearing.

EPDM liners are the most widely available but also the heaviest to install. A medium-sized pond approximately 30 by 20 feet across and 6 feet deep, will require a liner that weighs hundreds of pounds. A liner for a pond 10 by 8 by 4 feet deep will be light enough that it can be easily installed by one or two people.

It's important to be prepared on the day the pond liner is ready to be installed, especially for a larger pond. Extra bodies to haul in and lay out the liner will be a huge help. Larger liners require equipment in order to lift and haul them to the pond location.

Plastic liners should always be purchased a bit larger than the actual dimensions of the pond. Once the liner is installed and pressed in place against all ledges and slopes of the pond area, it should still extend out over the top edge of the pond a few feet on all sides. This will allow you to make micro-adjustments later on when installing rock and other materials in the pond and takes into account compression once the pond is filled with water.

Make sure the measurements are correct when you order a pond liner! While measuring the size of the liner, keep in mind that it is purchased in a rectangular shape (even though your pond will likely have curved edges)—you need to measure the size of the liner only by the two largest diameters plus the depth.

Once you have the pond liner at the edge of your excavated pond, now it's time to unfold or unroll the liner and place it on top of the underlayment. If the pond is large and the liner heavy, you will need a planned approach. Choose a strategic place to begin unrolling the liner and a thought-out direction to install the liner with minimum fuss.

As you stretch the liner across the pond, walk down on top of the liner and press it against the ledges and banks. The pond liner needs to sit firmly and snugly into each crevice, ledge, and slope of the pond. Once you've done that, make sure two to three feet of liner extends beyond the top edge of the pond around the entire system. If one side doesn't have an adequate extended liner past the top edge, make needed adjustments around the entire pond liner until it's right.

Rock Work

Stone, sand, and gravel can all be placed on top of the liner at this point. What kind of material and how much you use depends on the goals of your project. At a minimum for habitat ponds, stones should be placed in the bottom to create fish homes, protecting against predators like raccoons and herons. It is best to do rock work prior to filling the pond with water because it's easier to install in dry conditions.

At a minimum, shallow ledges of the pond should have some stone and gravel to protect the top section of the pond liner. This reduces damage due to the sun, wildlife entering and exiting, and falling tree branches. If placed correctly, stones help create ledges where plants are held into place in nooks within the shallow waters of the pond. You might also want a beach at the edge of the pond or stepping stones leading to a large boulder. There are so many combinations for these materials. Your context and imagination are the only limitations.

Installing Pond Infrastructure

Installing infrastructure such as skimmer boxes, submersible pumps, and other utilities are all best done when the pond is dry. This can be done at the same time as any rock, gravel, or sand work.

Sometimes biofilter wetlands are built inside ponds like these to keep the water clean. Those wetlands are often built on the ledges and can include installation of perforated pipes, air stones, and pumping systems.

The skimmer box is a common feature in medium to large ponds, often with a pump housed inside. As pond water moves into the skimmer (either through pump or wind), leaves, conifer needles, algae, and other debris enter the skimmer box where they are easily removed. The pump inside the skimmer box recirculates water to the opposite side of the pond, to a waterfall, or as an underwater jet to aerate the bottom of the pond.

Filling the Pond. Have a plan for filling the pond before you start building! Is this pond going to be filled by the rain? If so, it might be better to build the pond close to the wet season so it doesn't sit dry for too long. Are you filling the pond with well water? Is the water coming from another pond? Are you trucking in water? Using a municipal water system? Knowing the water source and how that water gets to the pond will play a major factor in your implementation plan.

Whatever the source, when you do fill the pond, watch it carefully as it fills. Notice if any of your infrastructure work is settling as the pond fills. If so, it will be easier to fix *before* the pond is full.

Burying the Liner's Edge. When the pond is full of water, now it's time to bury the liner's edge. Don't ever bury the liner of a pond before it's filled with water! A pond liner might move due to the water pressure, and that will cause problems if you've already buried the edge. Once it's full, you will see where the edges of the liner around the outside of the pond have settled.

At this point you have a couple of options: dig a trench around the edge of the pond, roll up a foot of liner, and bury it in the trench. This will effectively secure the liner from further movement and hide it from view. Another option is to bury the liner's edge by placing material on top of it such as a gravel pad, flagstone patio, beach, or topsoil to plant into. Whatever you choose, make sure that the liner completely disappears and is securely weighed down.

Hiding the Liner. When using a plastic liner for a pond, it is best to hide the liner from view during the installation. This protects it from photo degradation caused by the sun. The aesthetics of a plastic-lined pond are also greatly diminished when sections of the plastic liner are visible. Hiding it from view makes a pond look like it is meant to be where it was built, looking like it has been there forever, completely integrated into the natural surroundings like an ancient well.

These activities don't need to include the bottom depth of the pond, which is already hidden and protected by a pond filled with water. The top two to three feet and *all* edges of the pond are the most effective areas to focus on when hiding/protecting the pond liner.

Running Utilities. If the pond is designed for pumping water, then a power source must be installed at the pond. You may also want lighting, electrical outlets, and more to create an outdoor living space around the pond. All of these amenities require some form of power to operate.

CASE STUDY: WATERUP/WATER SCHOOL: JOHADS AND REVIVING RIVERS IN RAJASTHAN, INDIA, BY MINNI JAIN AND LOUISE BINGHAM (WWW.THEFLOWPARTNERSHIP.ORG)

Background

WaterUP/Water School (WU/WS) is a project started by the Flow Partnership UK in collaboration with Arup UK. The project constructs natural and traditional water-retention features to resolve local droughts and floods, revive landscapes, and enable global replication of these successful community water-harvesting methods. The current case study is of a water-retention feature called a *johad*, built in collaboration with Rajendra Singh, the "Waterman of India," in Maharajpura and Karauli in Rajasthan, India.

In addition to building water-holding features with local communities, the WU/WS project goes further by documenting the process and making language-neutral tools to enable communities living in similar regions around the globe to replicate such structures.[1]

(continued)

Johads in Rajasthan, India

Rajasthan, which is India's largest state by area, comprises 10.4 percent of India's land area, 60 percent of which is arid and 40 percent semiarid, with 90 percent of annual rainfall occurring in the monsoon months from July to September. Agriculture in Rajasthan relies heavily on groundwater, and overexploitation of this resource has led to frequent droughts and an exodus from these villages to its cities. Over the past 30 years, thousands of *johads* (small traditional earthen check dam structures) have been constructed by Rajendra Singh (widely known as the "Waterman of India") and his team, in collaboration with local communities in the arid and dry parts of this state. Johads are a rainwater collection tradition that date back thousands of years in India. They use the natural terrain to channel and store the brief monsoon downpours for year-round use. But community rainwater collection schemes fell out of favor during British rule, and after independence in 1947 their neglect, coupled with overpumping of groundwater sources, led to a severe drought in many villages throughout western India.

To date, Rajendra Singh's work has successfully restored seven rivers in Rajasthan by retaining water in these johads while providing multiple benefits for local communities. With more extreme weather events predicted as a result of climate change, the number of people affected globally is expected to increase, disproportionately affecting communities living in rural and remote areas. The WU/WS project has actively engaged with rural communities in drought and flood-stricken areas to understand their needs, unique challenges, and opportunities for change. By understanding hydrological processes and surface water management techniques of the local people, WU/WS is enabling widespread change in local water management.

Testing the Success and Benefits of Johads

Field surveys of the use of johads were conducted in the remote and semiarid Alwar region of Rajasthan in 2018. To investigate the methodologies and to ensure

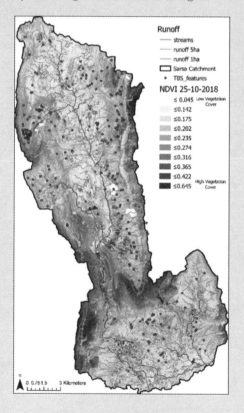

Map of the NDVI analysis of one of the catchments in Alwar, Rajasthan, indicating an increase in vegetation cover of up to 15 percent following the implementation of johads.

the principles are robust and applicable to semiarid areas around the world, they were also tested with communities in a different geographical region: La Guajira in Colombia, South America.

Annual rainfall in Karauli, Rajasthan, is concentrated within three to four months during the monsoon season (June to September), making the landscape dry and largely impermeable during the rest of the year. In unmanaged catchments, this can lead to devastating flash floods during the monsoon, followed by a prolonged drought when all the water has run off. However, the use of traditionally engineered johads, placed strategically along ephemeral flow pathways, captures and stores the rainfall on the surface and—where geological conditions allow (vertical bedrock fracturing)—recharges groundwater aquifers via infiltration. When these features are implemented on a strategic scale, the underground aquifers also revive dry rivers across the catchment.

When comparing satellite data and normalized difference vegetation index (NDVI) with catchments where the work has not been done, one can see dramatic increases in vegetation growth and health, which provides multiple benefits ranging from impacts on the microclimate to soil stabilization as well as the ability of communities to grow a second annual crop (sometimes even a third!) and/or increase grazing capabilities for pastoral farming. In addition, there is evidence of the local communities having consistently more reliable access to drinking water from their wells, even after a couple of years of drought in the area. The capture and storage of monsoon rainfall also slows the flow of surface water runoff when it is too dry to infiltrate, effectively mitigating the seasonal flash flood risk, as well as improving drought resilience.

Johads provide local communities with access to reliable, clean water for drinking via underground aquifer recharge, replenishing wells as well as surface water for washing, irrigation, and drinking water for livestock and wildlife. This positively impacts human health from a nutritional and socioeconomic perspective. Harvests are more successful, with greater, more reliable yields, enabling some communities to diversify: keeping and grazing livestock, stocking fish, and even selling surplus produce, further contributing to enhanced livelihoods. As a result, families have reported incidents of reverse migration, where local youths who previously left the area to find employment in cities have started returning or remaining local as a result of opportunities being created by improved water availability.

Case Study of Johads in Maharajpura and Karauli, Rajasthan, India

WU/WS has a three-pronged strategy. First, it enables the local community to build their own water source and hold all the water that falls in their region. This improves the condition of their land and water resources.

(continued)

Second, it creates a globally accessible film of their process and methods, which allows wide access to that knowledge, wisdom, and technique.

Finally, it ensures replicability and transferability of the methods between cultures by making it language-neutral and sharing it freely online with communities throughout the world.
Maharajpura Johads

Case Study Location: Maharajpura and Karauli, Rajasthan, India

Capacity of the water body: 10,000 m³

Number of people benefiting: 1,200

WU/WS constructed a new johad and repaired an existing one in a neighboring catchment in Maharajpura and Karauli, Rajasthan.

On-the-ground partners: Rajendra Singh, "Waterman of India," of TBS, India.

Site: Chosen in collaboration with locals who knew where the maximum run-off water could be captured.

What was built: A small check dam (johad), similar to an earthen wall, was constructed using the excavated mud and stones from the pond that would hold the water.

Time taken: Three months from start to finish (mid March 2019–mid June 2019).

On completion: Trees were planted on the earthen embankment to stop evaporation loss, some of them fruit trees to supplement local food availability.

Arup-developed digital software was used in the initial investigation of water-retention techniques in the Sarsa catchment, Rajasthan, India. Geospatially referenced data including photographs, videos, notes, and dimensions of water features were recorded in the software

Photographs of one of the new johad features before, during, and after construction. The water stored by the johad was generated by just one monsoon season and the resulting increase in vegetation cover is evident. New fields for arable production have also been built, evident in the left-hand side of the final photo.

and used to analyze the use of the traditionally engineered features. The data was later used in a hydrological model and in remote-sensing analysis to determine the value of the johads in catchment hydrology and for monitoring vegetation cover change using NDVI analysis.

Using a combination of light machinery and local equipment, members of the local community led the construction process. This enabled local people to replicate this work as needed in neighboring areas and to carry out any maintenance work as required over the years as they knew the whole process.

A language-neutral method film was created using a combination of live footage from the construction of the new and repaired water-retention feature in Rajasthan, combined with animation and graphic design to communicate the principles. Aimed at rural communities, it teaches how to deduce the best, most effective location to build a surface water management feature by appraising the natural environment, topography, vegetation, the character of the water landscape, and the underground aquifer. The film demonstrates the design principles and the physical process of building a johad, along with guidance on their use. Such a film is unprecedented in the water sector.

This method film has been tested in neighboring communities in India and in La Guajira, Colombia, to assess compatibility with contrasting cultures, geographies, and peoples. A new johad feature—which is similar to traditional structures in Colombia called *jagueys*—has now been constructed in La Guajira, which is directly benefiting approximately 800 additional people by giving them improved access to water as well as the potential to implement this on a larger, more strategic scale.

Improving global water literacy is a crucial part of tackling existing and emerging water management issues.[2]

Impact of the Maharajpura Johad

Local incomes increased by approximately £10,000 (about $12,000) per person, benefiting 900 new domestic animals and 1,200 people.

Youth are now employed selling milk in a revived cottage dairy industry (instead of joining bandits due to a lack of livelihood).

Instead of foraging wood for fuel, women were able to take up a government initiative to have natural-gas cookers in their homes, as there was more prosperity and disposable income available.

Girls have started going to school again instead of accompanying their mothers foraging wood for fuel during the day.

Crucially, during COVID-19, 120 migrants returning to these villages have been able to re-create a livelihood and live here, as opposed to those who returned to neighboring

(continued)

Enhanced crop productivity in November 2019.

water-scarce villages and had to return to the cities as soon as they could with no source of local food or income to sustain them there.

Sustainability Principles

The sustainability principles of the WU/WS project are threefold. First, the core principles and objectives focus on environmental sustainability, resilience, and reliability of water resources. Traditional engineering works on the basis that nature and the local environment, including topography and vegetation, can give an indication of the character of the water landscape and underground aquifer. For example, the height, type, and shape of trees can indicate the presence of fractures with access to the water table; the exposed bedrock can reveal the type of fractures (confined vertical fractures, unconfined horizontal fractures, or a combination of the two). This can inform the location, type, and size of surface water management features. The johad check dams themselves are primarily made of mud and stone, dug out of the area where water will eventually be stored. This solution avoids the cost implications of overusing heavy machinery and diesel while also ensuring local know-how will maintain and create more structures.

Second, the educational films are freely accessible online and can be virtually shared and rewatched innumerable times at no additional cost. The use of language-neutral tools means that each one of the method films can be used by anyone, anywhere, even via mobile phones in remote regions. In this digital age, 85 percent of the population has access to a mobile phone but almost one-third still lack access to safe drinking water.

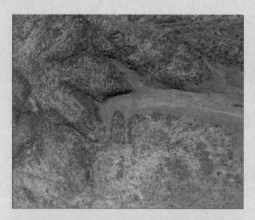
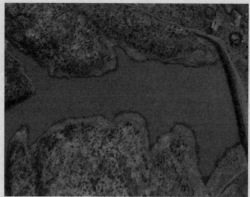

Clockwise from top left: Aerial drone footage, February 2019; Aerial drone footage, July 2019. Aerial dront footage, September 2019.

Third, the overall aim of the project is to make a meaningful contribution toward the United Nations' Sustainable Development Goals, particularly Goal 6: universal access to clean water and sanitation for all.[3] When local communities throughout the world are able to share and implement their successful methods of local landscape regeneration, the potential to meet these goals rises exponentially.

Applicability

Every day, approximately 2.4 billion people live with water shortages in the arid climates where they live. Hyper-arid, arid, and semiarid zones already cover 30 percent of the earth's surface, housing a similar proportion of the population. With more extreme weather events predicted as a result of climate change, the number of people affected globally is expected to increase, disproportionately affecting communities in rural and remote areas. It is anticipated that half of the world's population will be living in areas of high water stress by 2030. In some arid and semiarid areas, between 24 million and 700 million people could be displaced as a result, further increasing water stress in the receiving country, state, or locality. Accordingly, the size of the target audience and thus beneficiaries of this work is huge.

(continued)

> Improving global water literacy is a crucial part of tackling existing and emerging water management issues. By re-educating communities on the water cycle, catchment processes, and simple yet effective water management techniques, this project is enabling people to forge their own water-resilient future.
>
> ## Additional Links
> Water for All
> A six-minute film on the Maharajpura Johads: https://youtu.be/JKXGfyR5_SY
> Language-Neutral Method Film of Johads: https://www.youtube.com/watch?v=sx_Fre3VUU0&feature=emb_logo
> The Story of WaterUP: https://www.theflowpartnership.org/water-up
> The Flow Partnership's Water School: https://waterways.world
> Resourcing global water retention: www.onepondfund.org

Earthen Ponds

Earthen ponds are built using either clay from the site or clay brought in for the purpose. This compacted clay is used to seal the surface of the pond to hold water through the dry months. When you use resources harvested from the site, earthen ponds are the most ecological way to build a pond.

Earthen ponds potentially last longer than any type of pond system. If maintained well, they will last hundreds, even thousands of years.

For an earthen pond to be successfully built, the right type of soil must be present to seal the pond. Even in cases where sufficient soil is *not* found on-site, bentonite clay can be brought in to help seal the pond. Another alternative is to use animals such as pigs or cows to compact the pond surface when it is empty, creating a nitrogen-rich anaerobic condition that over time creates a watertight seal (called gley).

Earthen ponds are the best option for regenerative landscapers if all of the appropriate elements are in place. Urban and suburban homesteads likely will not provide adequate space for an earthen pond. Earthen ponds need slightly sloping angles (2:1 maximum) on the dam to function properly. To get to appropriate depths to reduce evaporation and provide an adequate home for aquatic life, the pond needs to be fairly large.

For larger sites, an earthen pond can provide a water-harvesting, drought-proofing solution that lasts generations. These systems require professional design and engineering to ensure safety and I highly advise getting professional support before taking on a large earthen pond project.

LOCATING A POND

When designing an earthen pond, think about the following:

Is this location accessible by equipment?

Is adequate pond-building soil present?

How will the pond fill? Is there enough surface water or other sources entering into the pond to fill it? Do roads, nearby buildings, and farmland provide impervious surfaces to collect and move water to the pond location?

How steep is the site? Is it too steep to build a pond?

Choose locations where the least amount of effort produces the greatest gain. Upper valleys, drainages (not named waterways), saddles, and lower valleys could all provide locations for an earthen pond.

What are the dangers? Is the site above homes where a blowout could cause catastrophic damage?

Can a road or trail be incorporated into the dam wall?

Is the location strategic, providing upper watershed catchment for gravity systems, habitat for wildlife, or microclimatic benefits? Optimize all of the possibilities and *stack functions* to achieve the best relationship integration throughout the landscape.

Impoundment Ponds

A simple type of earthen pond is an impoundment pond, located in wet valleys and drainages, places where water naturally gathers. It is simply an earthen dam built across a valley or upper drainage that slows surface water movement, collecting water behind the dam to form a pond. If a freshwater spring exists upslope of this pond, a simple impoundment pond may retain water all year long (depending on climate). Some impoundment ponds dry up during drier periods of the year.

The biggest difference between impoundment ponds and fully engineered earthen ponds is that the inner area of an impoundment pond is not excavated. Instead, a dam is built across an area that naturally collects water. This means a year-round watertight soil layer may not exist throughout the whole pond area. By investigating and assessing the landscape as a diligent regenerative designer, you will be looking for areas with strategic significance and water-holding features to build an impoundment pond as described here.

Test Pit. To determine whether your site has good soil for building a pond, you have to dig a test pit. This is best done with an excavator or backhoe and needs to be considered part of the site assessment and exploration process before deciding what kind of pond to build.

Dig a pit at least five feet deep in the approximate location of the proposed pond. Make sure you leave a sloping entrance that allows you to walk down into the pit and inspect the soil.

This pit will provide a snapshot of the soil profile (discussed in part II of this book). The soil profile will show the horizontal layers of the soil down to the depth of the test pit. For example, there may be 18 inches of topsoil on top of a one-foot vein of clay on top of gravel. You are digging the test pit to determine what these layers are. If you find little to no clay, then it's likely the soil will not make excellent pond-building material. If you do find a high level of clay content then you're in business.

A small vein of clay might be workable with the addition of bentonite to supplement the pond-sealing process.

Soil Segregation. Once you have determined that your project is a good fit for an earthen pond, completed the design process, and gained permits/approval as needed or desired, you are ready to begin the excavation process.

Excavating the pond needs to be done in stages with special consideration made to the type of soil being removed. Topsoil should be removed first from the entire excavation site and stockpiled nearby to be returned at the very end. The best clay in the excavation site should be stockpiled close by for use in building the dam. Other types of soil coming out of the hole (loam, sandy soils, gravel, rock) should all be segregated from each other as well as possible.

Clay—along with loam and sandy soils—may all be used in the dam-building process. Reserve the best clay for the "key way" trench (a large trench built under the center of the dam wall), plus the top few feet if clay is in short supply for sealing the pond.

Having a plan for the various soils prior to excavation will save time and money. By the time excavation begins, you should have a strong sense of what types of soil are coming out of the hole and where you will be staging them during the excavation process.

Key Way Trench. This large trench, built under the center of the dam wall, is designed to "key" the dam into the earth below. Once the trench has been excavated, use the best clay from the site to fill it. This clay should be heavily compacted as it gets added to the trench, either through "track rolling" with a bulldozer or excavator or with a sheepsfoot roller. The core of the dam is built out of the same clay material as it gets placed and compacted in layers, rising out of the trench and into the shape of the dam wall.

Layers of clay should be compacted in depths no greater than 11 inches. If the compaction tool is relatively small, then compacting in thinner layers will be necessary. Use compaction with rough surfaces so that each subsequent layer is keyed into the layer below.

When soils are saturated with moisture, they are generally difficult to compact as well. This means that semi-wet soil compacts the best and dams should ideally be built when some moisture is present; consider this fact when planning the installation schedule. Building the dam when there's still moisture in the ground but also not too wet is ideal (see the soil "squeeze test" in part II for determining ideal moisture). If this is not possible, then building and compacting in the dry season is better than building in the wettest part of the year because water can be added to dry soil to achieve the perfect compaction, while it is difficult to remove moisture from soil that is overly saturated.

Adding Bentonite. When sufficient clay is not present in the soil but you still want to build an earthen pond, bentonite clay, which can be purchased in a dry powdered form, will help.

When this material gets wet, it expands to 15 to 30 times its particle size, making it one of the best materials for sealing ponds.[4]

Sealing an earthen pond built in sandy soil with bentonite clay will still likely leak, possibly drying up each year. When some clay is present, however, adding bentonite can turn mediocre pond soil into great pond soil.

To use bentonite to seal a pond, integrate it into the top layers of the pond. Because bentonite clay particles are so small, they often cloud the pond water. To avoid this, first till the bentonite with existing soil from the pond as one of the top layers. *Then* add another layer of native soil on top of the bentonite layer to keep it from being suspended in the water when the pond is full.

Integrating bentonite into the surface of the pond is done when the pond is dry and works best when it is fully integrated into native soils. It can be rototilled, forked, disked, or some other form of integration with the native soil. Do not simply put bentonite clay powder on the surface and compact it, as this will be an ineffective way to seal the pond.

Dam Slope Angles. The inner slope of the dam wall should be no steeper than a 2:1 slope. Some soil types and locations can get away with a 1.5:1 slope, but in general, this should be avoided. Though it's possible to design for up to a 2:1 angle, a 3:1 or even gentler grade could be more beneficial for establishing planting systems, along with providing an easy entry and exit for animals (including humans).

Planting the Earthen Pond. Plantings are usually placed on the gentle slopes in shallow water. If the slopes into the pond are on the steeper side, boulders and/or heavy logs can be placed in the shallows to anchor plantings on the slope.

Avoid having medium to large trees growing on the dam wall. This can result in a catastrophic situation if a tree falls over and tears a section of dam with it. Large root systems that penetrate deep into the core of the dam can also destabilize the dam and cause leaks.[5] Shrubs and herbaceous plants, however, are usually safe to plant on the dam wall as long as the root systems are fairly shallow.

Aquaculture. The healthiest and cleanest ponds have diverse biological organisms thriving in the water. Beneficial bacteria, dragonfly nymphs, mayfly larvae, water beetles, freshwater shrimp, freshwater snails, and fish make up a complex community of organisms that keep the pond thriving. These organisms form a trophic pyramid or food web, where one organism feeds on another. A pond really comes alive when these are in balance, but it takes time to develop complex aquaculture. During its first one to two years, a new pond will go through many changes, with some organisms blooming to invasive levels only to be balanced out months later.

The microorganisms of the pond—freshwater shrimp, larvae, and bacteria—feed on the detritus generated by aquatic plants and the surrounding vegetation of the site. When leaves, flowers, and stems fall into the pond they decompose, providing food for microorganisms. Without these microorganisms, the pond can quickly become anaerobic, filling with algae and sludge. Too much food in the pond and not enough organisms to eat will cause a whole host of problems.

An aquatic plant community is a vital component of a healthy aquaculture. Plants take up excess nutrients in the pond while aerating the water through their roots and bacterial root associations. Plants provide shelter for wildlife and habitat for frog eggs, dragonflies, and more.

A newly built pond needs to be inoculated with beneficial bacteria, with diversity as the goal. The inoculation should come from multiple sources. Many biological inoculations can be purchased for this reason, but purchased bacterial inoculants can only go so far—introducing localized organisms is also necessary.

Visit the local waterways closest to the landscape (creeks, lakes, streams, or neighboring ponds). Fill a bucket halfway with water from the waterway. Then, pull a fine mesh net back and forth along the edge of the waterway for 15 to 20 seconds. Dump anything you've caught in the net into your bucket of water. Dip the net in the bucket to make sure even the tiniest microbes are deposited in the bucket. Next, get a bit of soil or gravel from the edge of the waterway and add it to the bucket. All this material constitutes an inoculation to be introduced into the new pond. Repeat this process in as many local waterways as you are able to access. This will provide a plethora of local microorganisms to inoculate your new pond.

Caution: There are invasive plant species you might want to avoid introducing into your pond. Learn what these are in your local region and be careful not to take inoculations of these from other waterways.

Aquatic Plants. The plant community you introduce to the pond will serve many beneficial functions, from edible yields to cut flowers to basketry and dye plants. Some aquatic plants root into shallow soil at the edge of the pond and other aquatic plants float on the surface.

If you desire a pond with an open surface, meaning you can look into the water, some floating plants are not advised. Tiny oxygenators like duckweed and azolla will quickly cover the entire surface of the pond. These plants are incredible carbon sequestration plants, and azolla is also a nitrogen fixer. Both can be grown in the pond and harvested for animal feed or mulch, but their aggression on the pond's surface *will* become a maintenance issue later on.

Some aquatic plants die back in the cold season and return when it's warm. If your goal is to have a vibrant, healthy plant community throughout the year, understand which plants die back and which ones are evergreen. So many factors to take into account when designing your aquatic plant community. Do your research and have fun!

AQUATIC PLANTS FOR POND SYSTEMS

Here is a short list of plant species for ponds.

Juncus Grass (*Juncus effusus*)
Water Iris (*Iris pseudacorus*)
Canna Lilies (*Canna indica*)
Seep Monkeyflower (*Erythranthe guttata*)
Taro (*Colocasia esculenta*)
Water Chestnut (*Eleocharis dulcis*)

Marsh Marigold (*Caltha palustris*)
Water Clover (*Marsilea quadrifolia*)
Sedges (*Carex*)
Water Hyacinth (*Eichornia crassipes*)

Duckweed (*Lemna minor*)
Azolla (*Azolla pinnata*)
Water Lotus (*Nelumbo lutea*)
Water Lily (*Nymphaeaceae*)

Algae Control. Algae is likely the biggest ongoing problem you'll face with your new pond. For medium to small backyard ponds, algae can be a constant nagging maintenance issue that has even led some clients of mine to fill in their ponds altogether after years of pond maintenance. That said, the larger and deeper the pond, the less algae will pose an issue.

There is no single approach to algae—only a multipronged tactic with experimentation will work. Expect algae to be an issue during the first year or two while the aquatic community is still developing. If you stay on top of the maintenance, algae will become less and less of a concern.

Reciprocity or Degradation. In the regenerative landscape, ponds provide habitat, water storage, beauty, and microclimate moderation. They are stunning examples of systems that lead to ecological yields. But this must be balanced by the energy, materials, and practices required during installation.

Be smart, be intentional, and practice due diligence when designing, locating, planning, and building a pond. A lot of embodied energy can be consumed in the process of building these elegant systems. If they are built improperly or built for the wrong reasons, then you have degraded ecosystems in the process. But when a pond is designed and built appropriately, it will be a bountiful and reciprocal element of regeneration. By building vast connections throughout the landscape with the pond through *relationship design*—connecting planting systems, wildlife communities, water resilience, and microclimates—the benefits of these systems will far outweigh the energy it takes to build them.

31

Irrigation Systems

Many regenerative landscape projects will require some kind of irrigation scheme to get landscape planting systems established. Depending on your goals for growing food, establishing forests, managing pasture, and so on, the extensiveness of the irrigation system will vary. That said, nearly every landscape (even arid landscapes) can be regenerated without the use of irrigation given enough time, focus on native species, planting at the right time of year, the acceptance of a percentage of lost plantings, and an extreme amount of patience in dry climates. For those who do need an irrigation system for your landscape project, read on.

Whether your project has an abundance of water or water is highly scarce, your water resilience design, soil-building techniques, and choice of plant communities all affect your irrigation planning decisions.

DESIGNING AN IRRIGATION SYSTEM

In this chapter, we will explore how to design and build an irrigation system. Drip irrigation will be the main focus, but within an overall look at a regenerative approach to irrigation options.

Water Demand

Before designing an irrigation system, you need to know the projected maximum water demands of the future landscape during the dry season. By crunching the numbers for what kinds of vegetation you're planting; the size of the area; and the daily, weekly, or monthly watering hours of your landscape, you'll begin to conceptualize the scale of the irrigation system required. Revisit the estimated total water use (ETWU) formula from chapter 25 to understand landscape water demand.

Water is often the biggest constraint on a site. As regenerative designers, our goal is to increase the water-holding capacity of the land. We should avoid damaging water sources through overwatering the landscape, taxing groundwater supplies, or taking excessively from natural bodies of water.

First, have a clear idea of the existing water resources on the site and a design plan to increase the water capacity; use that data as baseline information for understanding how large your irrigated planting area can be.

Sizing the System

Once you have estimated your water needs, you can begin sizing the system. Topography, pipe size, and distance all play significant roles in irrigation system design. The size of the main pipe is the first decision you'll need to make. The Manning formula will give you a sense of how increasing pipe size reduces friction loss and increases pressure for moving water across the landscape. You will also need to calculate the rise-over-run formula comparisons for the distance and slope elevation gain to see how friction loss reduces pressure across these different distances and topographical features. Do your own research on these formulas.

Work through these formulas to develop an understanding of pressure, friction loss, volume, pipe size, distance, and elevation so you can design an irrigation system that meets the needs and constraints of your project.

FLOOD IRRIGATION

For tens of thousands of years, humans have been building flood irrigation systems to water crops. A flood irrigation system uses water from ponds, cisterns, storm runoff, or natural bodies of water to move water across the surface of the land and spread *sheet flows* of water into pastures and planting systems. Water is a heavy and powerful element, and flood irrigation systems need to be designed with the utmost attention to detail, soil type, topography, erosion, healthy watershed functioning, and the social impacts of using water.

When flood irrigating, you not only hydrate the soil around your desired plants but also stimulate microbiology in the soil biome. Designed for maximum retention and infiltration, flood irrigation systems completely transform dry landscapes by building subsurface water plumes that form below flood irrigation channels.

Pulling water away from natural bodies of water like creeks, rivers, and lakes does not represent a regenerative design approach. Disrupting natural bodies of water can have disastrous impacts on watersheds, including loss of habitat, destruction of fish, turbidity, and contamination.

Ponds and water-catchment systems in the upper reaches of the watershed are important water security features that provide opportunities for developing flood irrigation systems. "Lock pipe" systems in ponds work the best for flood irrigation systems, allowing you to open valves in the landscape that will flood swales, rain gardens, and terraces with pond water. Siphons can also be developed in lieu of a lock pipe system to achieve the same results.

Freshwater springs are also a great source for a flood irrigation system if they are routed to flood channels in the landscape.

OVERHEAD SPRINKLERS

Irrigation by use of overhead sprinklers uses the most water of any irrigation system. With forty million acres of lawn in the United States alone, overhead sprinklers constitute the main approach to irrigating landscapes.

(continued)

> In some landscapes, water is abundant and overhead watering may be a reasonable choice. There *are* numerous benefits to mimicking rainfall with overhead irrigation systems. Irrigating pasture for forage, establishing native meadows, wildflower gardens, growing vegetables by seed—all benefit from overhead watering.

DRIP IRRIGATION

Drip irrigation systems have revolutionized landscape and farming industries. These efficient and water-conserving systems drip water from emitters connected to polyethylene plastic tubes or from inside the tubes themselves. Drip irrigation is the most water-conserving and highly efficient method for distributing water to plants for agriculture or landscaping, releasing water right at the root zone or drip line of trees and plants. For most temperate and dryland climates, and other environments that experience long periods without precipitation, drip irrigation systems are a great choice if designed and installed correctly.

Planning Your System

When planning your irrigation system, create zones based on the irrigation needs of each area, combining plantings with similar water requirements. Each zone will be associated with one valve line (possibly more), depending on the size of the landscape areas. An orchard with trees of similar water use needs a dedicated irrigation zone. A drought-tolerant Mediterranean herb garden with lavender, rosemary, thyme, sage, and so on would have its own irrigation zone. A vegetable garden watered every day needs its own irrigation zone.

If you mix plants that need lots of water with plants that don't, you might end up with some unhappy plants and wasted water. Remember to consider the irrigation needs of each plant community and design irrigation zones alongside your planting plans (discussed in part VI).

Water Use and Pressure. Develop a general sense of how much water is needed for each irrigation zone to decide whether sufficient pressure exists to run a zone off one valve or if additional valves are needed. Standard pressure in the water systems (pressure tank, gravity pressure, etc.), distance of pipe length, and the size of your water line pipes will dictate the pressure availability at each valve manifold and valve line.

Most irrigation systems are pressurized between 40 and 60 psi, and that pressure distributes water through drip hoses or sprinkler pipes to various planting communities. Most drip irrigation systems use pressure regulators to *reduce* (usually 15 to 25 psi) the pressure going into a drip line, ensuring that the water is spread evenly through the drip hose and that emitters don't pop off.

Gravity. A gravity-powered irrigation system is generally the most ecological as it requires little to no electricity and very few if any pumps. A gravity system can only be used when there is sufficient water storage at an elevation high enough above your irrigation zone to generate enough pressure. Since there is approximately one pound per square inch for every two feet of elevation, you would need a minimum of 50 feet of elevation to power a low-pressure drip irrigation system.[1] The biggest problem in a gravity system is when an air bubble gets caught in the line, creating vapor lock. Vapor lock creates a vacuum in the pipe where water cannot move through the pipe until the air has been released. The best way to avoid vapor lock is to install air vents at the very top of the system and at every sharp turn and grade change.

Water System Automation Timers. Keeping the landscape watered once it's installed is a tedious task to perform by hand. Timed irrigation systems make the work of watering efficient and save an immense amount of time for landscapers. Completely automated irrigation runs on timers, giving you the ability to set up an automated watering schedule for the landscape. Your watering schedule needs to take into account pressure availability in the system. Avoid the system turning on too many valves at once so the system has enough pressure to water each zone.

Furthermore, it is best to schedule watering times for nighttime when there is little evaporation and less domestic water use. For those who take vacations, a timed irrigation system provides immense relief, knowing the landscape is getting watered while you are away (usually in the hotter times of the year). Yes, you can take a vacation knowing the landscape you gave blood, sweat, and tears to will thrive while you're jumping into rivers and eating exotic food. Last, timers save *thousands* of gallons of water every year. A well-scheduled irrigation cycle can provide just the right amount of water for each plant community without *overwatering*.

Manually Operated Irrigation. Fully developed drip irrigation systems can be run manually by turning each valve on by hand. This is essentially running an automated irrigation system without the timer. This fosters a strong relationship between the landscape and the landscaper with notable benefits—you have to pay better attention to your plant communities, checking to see that they are thriving. This added observation and the need to engage with the landscape leads to a better overall relationship with more frequent harvests and other routine maintenance. You can set a timer on a watch or your phone to remind you it's time to turn the valve off.

One downside of a manual system is that valves can be left on and forgotten about, only to be remembered hours later after the irrigation zone has already been thoroughly saturated and thousands of gallons of water have been used.

Filtration. One of the big challenges with irrigation systems is when emitters and micro sprays get clogged by particles in the water. Most drip systems will need a filter to clean the water before it goes into the drip hoses. Particles that damage drip systems are sand, sediment, iron, and other minerals found in groundwater sources.

The size of the irrigation area and the quality of the water will both make a huge difference in your filter choice. Sand (found in many wells around the world) clogs filters much faster than iron and other mineral contaminants, requiring larger filters and more frequent cleaning. Keeping filters clean is a key maintenance routine for most nonmunicipal irrigation systems.

Plug-in Emitters and In-line Drip Hoses. Plug-in emitters are small fittings that plug into solid drip hose, letting water leak out when the valve is turned on. These emitters are usually placed near plant roots to water them. Each color represents a different gallon per hour the emitter releases.

An in-line drip hose contains emitters inside the hose itself, located in intervals of 6 to 12 inches. An in-line drip hose is less likely to clog over plug-in emitters and, since the emitters are inside the hose line, they never pop off and cause leaks. An in-line drip hose lets water out at every emitter interval, so the watering zone is expanded. For landscapes with planting communities placed close together (an intensive pattern), in-line drip makes sense and will water the root zones of all plants in the area. If the landscape plan places trees or other plants far apart from each other, however, using in-line drip exclusively may waste water.

In-line drip is also used to make "rings" around shrubs and trees (using pieces of in-line drip connected to solid drip pipe). The ring of in-line is placed around the dripline of the shrub or tree for an ideal watering environment. Whenever we water plants at their drip lines (the edge of their vegetated canopies) and not at their trunks, they are encouraged to grow deeper and wider root systems.

I routinely use in-line drip when growing vegetables as they water root zones fully and consistently while providing flexibility. When preparing vegetable beds, an in-line drip hose can be easily pulled off the bed to make prepping easy and then replaced with little fuss.

Drip System Installation

Water is the primary element we design for; therefore, irrigation systems are designed regeneratively when they:

- use the least amount of water
- water at the roots of plants
- are used conservatively to grow planting systems appropriate to the climate
- help perennials and trees get established with the goal of taking them off irrigation after a few years
- are designed to reduce evaporation

Irrigation systems are not one size fits all. The contexts of climate, soil, water demand, and water resources all need to be considered when designing your irrigation system.

Here is a step-by-step process for installing a professional-level drip irrigation system:

1. **Trenching.** Strike a balance between using the most direct route for moving water and doing the least harm to the existing landscape ecology. Doing the least harm takes a bit of observation and strategy. There may be features you need to be extremely careful not to dig through, over, or around (electrical lines, tree roots, sacred sites, and so on).

   If you are landscaping in the United States, use a service called US Dig. Before you dig a trench for a project, call 811 and they will send public utilities officials out for free to mark electricity, gas lines, communications wires, etc. You don't want to hit any of those underground utilities with your shovel, excavator, or trencher. (Trust me, it's an initiatory experience you can go without!)

Some sites have no public utilities but will have other (independently installed) utilities placed by land owners and contractors. Part of your landscape assessment process will be looking at any existing maps and talking to previous landowners, neighbors, and past stewards of the land to discover where underground utilities such as water lines, gas lines, and electrical lines are located before digging.

Once you've discovered underground lines, strategize your approach to trenching. Digging across existing underground utilities is acceptable as long as care is taken not to cut through or damage them in any way. Use pilot holes to gently dig down and find the actual depth of existing utilities prior to trenching. Then carefully hand dig the trench across these pipes and wires as needed. This technique is especially necessary when heavy equipment is being used to dig the trench.

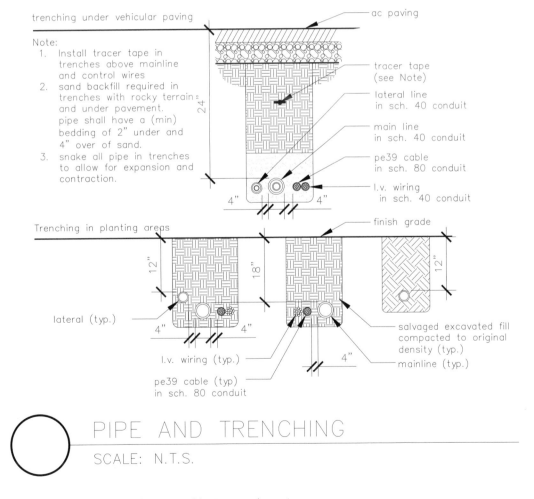

Irrigation trenching detail. Designed by Permaculture Artisans.

2. **Lay pipe.** Once your trenches are open, it's time to lay pipe into the ground. Pay close attention to this next part because there are some tricks that will make putting pipes in the ground much easier. There are three types of pipes generally installed in trenches when building an irrigation system.

The main lines, also called hard lines, are water lines that run pressurized water. These pipes, once connected and turned on, will always have pressurized water inside them and are used to activate hose bibs and valve manifolds.

The main line is the first water line to be put in the trench. Often, the main water line is larger in diameter than valve lines because this hard line needs to move water to every manifold and hose bib in the landscape. This pipe needs to be large enough to provide sufficient pressure for multiple uses of water in the landscape despite friction loss, topography, and distance. Potentially, if multiple valves are on at the same time and someone turns on a hose, the pressure will drop if the main line isn't sufficiently sized.

On small farms and homesteads I almost always run a two-inch main line to manifolds and hose bibs. The hose bibs themselves are usually only one inch or 3/4 inch in size connected to the two-inch line underground.

The main water line must be installed correctly *and tested* before the trench is backfilled. A leak in the main line could be catastrophic—emptying water tanks, overworking well systems, and difficult to find underground. By testing the line prior to backfilling the trench, any leaks developed during installation can be discovered and fixed. Ball valves or gate valves should be placed at every terminal ending of the main line to facilitate testing and pressurization in the line before backfilling.

Valve lines are water lines that come *from* the valve manifolds and run to different irrigation zones in the landscape. Depending on the overall design and the need, valve lines could run a great distance from valve to irrigation zone, or only run a short way before a drip line is connected. These valve lines are not drip hoses, but underground pipes that terminate at planting bed ends or general planting areas. Remember, each valve represents one irrigation zone. If you are running over long distances, one irrigation zone may be fed by a branching network of pipes coming from one valve. For instance, if you're running a single valve for a small orchard, you might branch the valve line and have it come up in two or more locations even though it's on the same valve. This will give you better pressure and reduce the amount of drip hose needed to be run across the surface.

In another example, if you're laying out vegetable beds, you could run two to six (or more) vegetable beds on one valve line, each bed requiring its own connection to the same valve line.

If you map how many pipes you need to run from valves to beds and main lines to valve manifolds (where multiple valves connect to main lines), you'll quickly realize that where you place valve manifolds and how many you have directly affects how many pipes need to be placed in the ground. Use this as a strategic data point while designing your irrigation system and take into account the budget and how much pipe and labor is going into the project.

If your irrigation design calls for automation, you might need to run timer cables out to valve manifolds. A timer cable is a low-voltage wire that can be buried directly in the ground, although it is always better to run the timer cable through a small piece of electrical conduit (pipe) to protect it.

If you are running timer cables to numerous valve manifolds in the landscape, you will need a dedicated timer cable for each manifold—meaning a separate line of cable and a separate run of electrical conduit for every manifold. Timer cable should be buried 18 inches or more below ground. Once all timer cables are put in the trench, it is best to cover them with a few inches of soil before putting the main water line on top of them.

PIPE-LAYING TRICKS

- If you've never run a pipe in a trench, there are a few best practices to make the process as easy as possible. Place the soil from the trench all on the same side and close to the trench when the trench is dug. On the opposite side, lay out the pipe you plan to put into the trench. Stage it piece by piece along the side of the trench, enabling you to move down the trench during installation, having the materials you need right there.
- It is always a good idea to place a piece of pipe or a piece of wood across the top of the trench. This acts like a small bridge. As you lay pipe in the trench, rest the open end up, out of the trench, on this little bridge. This will keep the end of the pipe clean and give you an easy place to connect the next section of pipe. As you connect the next segment of pipe, lay it down in the ground, lifting the new end up onto the bridge in the next location. This saves an immense amount of time, keeps the work area clean, and is easier than connecting each pipe in the bottom of the trench.
- If you use PVC (polyvinyl chloride) pipe, then you will be gluing pieces together using PVC solvent. When installing main water lines, especially if they are two inches in diameter or larger, pressure begins to build in the pipe the farther down the line you get. This means that for each new section you glue on, it is important to hold those pieces together for 30 seconds before releasing. This gives the PVC glue time to bind before the pressure building up in the pipe pops the new section out the end.
- Having a clean trench makes this entire process much easier. Make sure the trench you've dug has a fairly level bottom, not filled with chunks of soil and rock, so the pipe can lay nice and flat on the bottom of the trench.

3. **Backfilling.** After all the pipe has been placed in the bottom of the trench, it's time to backfill. Depending on whether the trench was dug with a machine or by hand and the general volume of soil to be moved, you'll need to decide whether a machine is needed or human labor is sufficient to backfill the trench.

Remember: sometimes soil gets lost in the field and compacted during the trenching process, so pay attention to that! When you backfill a trench, make sure you push *all* of the soil back in. In many cases, this will mean having a slightly raised mound on top of the trench after backfilling. That's a good sign. All that fluffed soil will compact in future rains and hopefully settle back to the normal grade. If you are unable to get all the soil back in the trench, a small ditch may develop over time, creating drainage issues.

4. **Hose Bibs.** Hose bibs are the risers that come out of the ground with a hose connector fitted on top. Most people are familiar with a hose bib, which can be found on hoses in almost every garden. Because the risers for a hose bib come out of the ground and are exposed to sunlight, it's important that *that* section of pipe not be Schedule 40 PVC or other type of plastic that degrades in the sun. Schedule 80 PVC is fine, as is metal. Metal stand pipes are more resilient in fire-prone areas and may be preferable to plastic.

    Hose bibs are connected to pressurized water main lines. Your main line is run to each hose bib and the stand pipe is connected underground, rising above for easy access. Often you will have to reduce the size of the pipe from the larger main line underground to a smaller riser for the hose bib.

    We've all done it or seen it happen. You're yanking on a hose, dragging it through the landscape, and you pull too hard, breaking the standpipe at the hose bib. It's a common issue. To avoid this problem, make sure that your hose bib is connected to a stake or post.

5. **Valve Manifold.** The valve manifold is a structure made of a set of valves linked together. When turned on (either by timer or by hand), water moves through valves into irrigation lines ("valve lines"). The valve manifold is also where the timer cables will get connected to each valve. At the top of each valve is a solenoid with two or more wires.

    Main water lines terminate at valve manifolds, so there is always pressurized water at a manifold. The best practice is to always put a ball valve between the main water line and the manifold to make repairs on the manifold easy without shutting off water to the entire landscape. You simply shut the valve off and stop feeding water to the valves so repairs can be made.

6. **Filter Installation.** Filtration is necessary for most irrigation systems as discussed above. If there is a lot of sediment in the water, you will be cleaning filters on a regular basis. In that case, a centralized filtration system might be best. This requires a fairly large filter that is placed on the main water line prior to it running out into the landscape. This means that water in the main line has to first run through the filter before going out to various valve manifolds. In some cases, filters like these need to be cleaned once a week or more.

    The big problem with a centralized filtration system is that water moving through hose bibs will also go through the filter, which is unnecessary. This only clogs the filter faster and adds to the maintenance required to keep filters clean. To avoid this, *two* main water lines can be run in the main trench—one dedicated to hose bibs and a second dedicated to valve manifolds. The filter only needs to be attached to the main line feeding valve manifolds, keeping hose bibs free from filtration.

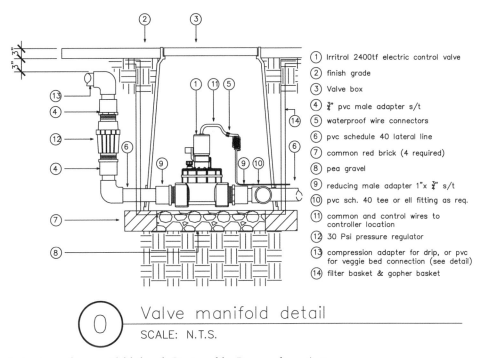

Valve manifold detail
SCALE: N.T.S.

Irrigation valve manifold detail. Designed by Permaculture Artisans.

A smaller filter placed at each valve manifold is adequate for a functioning irrigation system. The filter is generally placed between the main line and the valve manifold. This will catch sediment from the main line before entering the valve manifold.

7. **Backflow Preventer.** Backflow preventers are a special kind of check valve, which protects water systems from polluted landscape waters. A drip irrigation system can suck dirty water down through pipes and contaminate water sources. When a drip system shuts off, it creates a vacuum and can pull contaminants into the line. Water running through the backflow preventer flows in one direction, out to the landscape, but no water accidentally gets sucked back into the water source.

8. **Water Meter.** Water meters are expensive but exceedingly worth it. The water meter is placed before the main line runs out to the landscape, tracking every gallon used on that line. This gives you a sense of how much water you use each month and, just as important, helps you identify leaks.

IF YOU SUSPECT THERE IS A LEAK IN THE IRRIGATION SYSTEM, HERE'S WHAT YOU SHOULD DO.

- Make sure all valves are shut off and no hoses are running.
- Go to the water meter and see if it is still spinning. If it is spinning, then you know there is a leak along the main line between the water meter and the valve manifold and hose bibs. This is not good!

(continued)

> - If you've shut everything down, and the meter stops spinning, this means there is a leak in one of the valve lines.
> - Remember, you must place a valve between the mainline and each valve manifold to enable easy shut off. Now go to each valve manifold and turn each valve one by one, checking to see if the water meter is spinning. If it is, then you know that the manifold has a leak.

9. **Running Drip Lines.** Once all your irrigation infrastructure is installed, trenches are backfilled, manifolds are connected, and valve lines are run, it's time to connect drip lines. Drip lines are linked at the end of each valve line connected to a pressure regulator coming out of the end of the valve line. The pressure regulator makes sure the pressure in the drip hose isn't too much for emitters to handle. Too much pressure in the drip line causes emitters to pop off, which produces leaks.

Irrigation Maintenance

Drip irrigation maintenance is vital if you want the system to work leak-free for many years. Here are the most common irrigation maintenance tasks.

Cleaning Filters. Checking and cleaning filters is the most regular and important maintenance task.

Flushing Lines. If you live in a climate where your irrigation system needs to be shut off for months out of the year, then flushing your irrigation lines every year before you turn the system back on is vital. If you don't flush your lines in the spring, after it's been shut off for the winter, then all the muck that has built up inside the lines will get pushed into your emitters or in-line drip hose.

Checking for Leaks. Leaks can come from any number of sources: rats, dogs, or gophers can all chew holes in drip irrigation lines or shovels, scythes, or hoes may inadvertently clip the drip line without you noticing. Turning on manifolds one by one and walking their lines to check for leaks should be done at least once a season if not more.

Replacing Lines. Occasionally you will want to add new sections of drip line to the system when increasing the planting area or replacing an old line that has worn out or clogged. The work of maintaining and repairing drip systems is easy but can be tedious if you don't stay on top of it. The better you maintain the system and the more water you conserve, the less you'll have to replace broken parts.

32

Erosion Control

Erosion in the landscape is the wearing or washing away of soil due to the forces of wind, water, and sun. The wisdom of the earth's design is such that many ecological systems, by virtue of their behaviors, naturally mitigate erosion. Grasslands hold soil fast with their deep root systems, keeping topsoil from washing away. Forests dampen the energy of storms with their extensive canopies and cover the ground with thick mulch to keep soil in place.

Boulders, rocks, and other fixed, nonbiological elements retain the earth, keeping it from slipping down steep slopes. Trees drop their branches into creeks and rivers, slowing swift-moving water and capturing sediment. These examples of the earth's mechanisms for mitigating erosion are the patterns we emulate in the landscape.

The living systems of the earth are inherently and continuously working to cover bare soil. Bare soil is the antithesis of living ecosystems—it has difficulty absorbing water, growing vegetation, and hosting soil life. When we build landscapes, we often create bare soil during installation. It *must* be remedied before our work is complete.

Erosion needs to be taken seriously. While the water-management strategies described in this book are exemplary examples of mitigating and stopping the forces of erosion, any time we change the landscape, we are also creating new opportunities for erosion. Digging earthworks exposes soil to the elements, and if we build drainage systems incorrectly or capture hundreds of tons of pounds of water in structures that eventually wash away, then our activities significantly contribute to erosion of the land.

When erosion takes place, washing soil into watersheds, it has a dire effect on the health of aquatic communities. Sediment destroys salmon-spawning gravel beds. Unstable banks of drainage systems can cave in, taking trees and riparian forests with them. Meanwhile, uncovered soil blows away, leaving hydrophobic, inorganic, desolate, human-made deserts.

ELEMENTS OF EROSION

During landscape site assessment, read the patterns of the land with a focus not only on the symptoms but also the causes of erosion. Search out and identify erosion zones, categorize their intensity, and mark their locations on your base map.

Fixing symptoms of erosion like gullies and head cuts is not sufficient if the upslope causes are not addressed. Roads, culverts, runoff patterns, agricultural management, deforested areas—focus on these origins of erosion to develop a long-term erosion control plan.

Velocity

The volume of water moving through a landscape contributes to erosion but it is the speed—the velocity—of water that causes the most damage. When fast-moving water shoots out the end of a culvert or concrete drainage channel, it hits the ground like a big drill, displacing soil wherever it lands. That's why intercepting water in controlled settings and releasing the pressure of velocity is a key to mitigating erosion.[1]

Roads: Problem and Solution

Roads are one of the biggest contributors to erosion by becoming large water-collection systems, concentrating this water into culverts and drainage pipes. When the water is finally released, it wrecks ecosystems, causing head cuts, gullies, and mudslides.

The slope of the road is the biggest problem. The majority of roads built in the twentieth century were designed with an *in slope*, collecting water until it is released through a culvert or drainage system, which is the root of most erosion problems. An in-sloped road can provide a regenerative function if it's designed to fill a pond or other water-harvesting systems. A well-built road with an *out slope* simply sheds water safely away during storm events.

Well-designed roads are placed to provide strategic functions, increasing beneficial interactions across the landscape (e.g., catching water to fill a pond, creating a shaded fuel break for fire). Remember, when applying ecological design principles, we're *designing relationally*, placing each element in relation to another. We're *stacking functions*, so every element provides a multitude of functions for the system.

Head Cuts

Head cuts form around culverts, erosion gullies, creeks, rivers, the upslope side of roads, and so on. These are areas where the earth has literally fallen away, creating a vertically exposed soil profile. Next time you drive in the country, watch for head cuts where roads have cut through the terrain. Look for old culverts and you will likely find head cuts formed on top of them.

Head cuts can be very dangerous as they are the point where the soil continues to wash off the land. They are inherently unstable and, without treatment, will continue to slough soil, sometimes in great amounts.

Toe of the Slope

The toe of the slope is the bottom, or base, of the slope—the transition between a concave and convex topographical shape. In the landscaping process, the toe of the slope is often occurring on the downslope side of terraces, along roads, the upslope side of pathways, along the banks of drainages, the bottom edge of a large berm or mound, and so on. The toe of the slope is the weakest point as it relates to erosion. If the toe gives out, everything above it gives out. This is an exceedingly important leverage point for the regenerative landscaper. If we stabilize the toe of the slope, we stabilize the slope above. Have you ever thought about how much your toes keep you from falling over? Me either, but now it makes so much sense.

BIOLOGICAL EROSION CONTROL

Straw

Straw is a cheap and simple material with a variety of erosion control functions. Straw spread over the surface of the ground protects the soil from wind and water and adds organic matter to the soil surface. At a minimum, spreading straw like this provides a quick and easy method for covering bare soil in the short or mid-term.

Eventually, the straw will be consumed by soil biology and disappear, so it is not a long-term erosion control strategy but rather *aids* in establishing a long-term solution. The long-term approach to erosion control, of course, involves planting systems.

Straw can also be used in the form of bales. Straw bales are large rectangles of straw, compressed and tied together. A single person can usually move them around by themselves (when bales are wet, they are too heavy). Strategic use of straw bales is a powerful method for mitigating erosion. Place straw bales slightly dug into the ground on contour in rows, one after another. In this formation, they will act as a retaining wall to capture sediment carried by surface water. Even soil blown by the wind gets trapped behind straw bales as they form miniature windbreaks. Straw bales placed on contour could last up to two years in dry environments. In extremely wet environments, they decompose within a year.

Use systems like these to protect permanent plantings like hedges and orchards on a slope. Plant shrubs and trees on the *upslope* side of the straw bale wall for the best results. The straw bales also provide shade, cooling the soil and reducing evaporation if placed on the sunny side of planting systems.

Yet a third way to use straw in erosion control is to bury bunches of straw vertically in the soil in a diamond pattern across contour. Take a few handfuls of straw and spread them out into a long cylindrical bunch. Dig a hole six to eight inches into the ground where you are creating your straw erosion control system. Bury the straw in the ground with a good foot of material sticking up, almost like a cut flower arrangement coming out of the earth. Continue this pattern across contour, placing a bunch of straw every foot or so from the last, installing two or three rows of straw bunches on contour behind the first contour row. Place these new rows off-center from each other so they create a diamond pattern. When water flows across the landscape, the erect straw bundles will slow water down, capture sediment and seeds, and cast shade across the entire contour system. This simple yet effective approach can be left alone in an arid environment and achieve wonders over time. Birds and other organisms will eventually plant seeds when using the straw for protection from predators and the sun. A system such as this can grow itself into a permanent erosion-control system. Speed the process up by planting seeds or plant starts on the upslope side or among the straw bundles.

Broadcast Seeding

Another way to cover bare soil is to broadcast seeds at the right time of year to create quick vegetative cover as discussed in part IV.

Planted Overflows

Overflows from swales, rain gardens, ponds, and water channels need to have erosion control features built in to keep soil from washing away. Planting the overflows of these systems is the best long-term approach for achieving a stable, healthy, and non-erosive ecology. Plant species with strong root systems (rhizomatous or taproot) to quickly and effectively hold soil in place. Remember, overflows are often places where water speeds up as it moves out of a catchment system. These transitions are crucial locations to prevent erosion.

Contour Logs

Placing logs on contour keeps biomass on-site, slows water, catches sediment, and creates wildlife habitat. These function similar to straw wattles (described below), but last longer in the landscape. Contour logs eventually get colonized by fungi, building the soil ecosystem. Lizards, insects, and birds use these logs for habitat, and water and nutrients gather behind them, creating fertile wet zones in the landscape.

Erosion Gullies

A gully is a large scar of erosion on the land. They often look like drainages or small canyons and during storms could be mistaken for natural streams and creeks. The big difference between a gully and a naturally occurring waterway is that a gully didn't exist prior to erosion in that area. Most gullies are fairly recent (within the last 200 years); they once had *no* banks and represented only low points on the land.

Gullies are formed by the flow of water on unstable slopes or unprotected soil. Once the soil gives way, the water cuts a deeper channel. As we know, velocity turns water into a drill that scours the earth. Slowing the water down removes the power to wash soil away; instead, any sediment carried by water will be deposited wherever the water becomes still. This means that getting moving water to slow down and sink into the ground is the overall strategy to stop erosion, although additional causes of erosion include grazing animals, agricultural drainage, roads, forestry, and other human activities.

Here are some techniques for repairing erosion gullies.

Check Dams. Build check dams with brush or rock and place them across the flow of water in the bottom of the erosion gully. These slow down the velocity of the water while still allowing it to percolate into the soil. Sediment is deposited behind check dams and will begin to build the grade of the gully back to natural levels.

Packing Brush. When brush and woody debris are on hand (from fire fuel load thinning or landscape maintenance), this material can be put into erosion gullies and packed into the bottom. The woody material will slow the water down and catch sediment being carried by the water. Over time, the packed brush may fill up with sediment, repairing the overall grade of the gully. Do you love the simplicity of these restoration processes as much as I do? Basically, you could do all this with an axe and a hard day's work. Think about the impact that day will have!

Note: When packing a gully with brush, you must ensure the first layer makes contact with the ground. If the first layer does not have ground contact, water will flow underneath the brush and very little erosion control will be achieved.

Planting. Once a plan of action has been implemented to slow the flow of water in the gully, the bottom of the gully and its banks can be planted. In most cases, appropriate plants native to the region and microclimate are the best choice for planting to stabilize a gully. Choose plants that are quick-growing with strong root systems and large trees and shrubs that will take over the area over time.

In my climate, if sufficient water exists in the bottom of the gully, I might plant native roses (*Rosa californica*), willow (*Salix lasiolepis*), elderberry (*Sambucus melanocarpa*), and dogwood (*Cornus sericea*). As I move up the banks, I would be planting oak (*Quercus lobata*), bay (*Umbellularia californica*), and Douglas fir (*Pseudotsuga menziesii*).

If sufficient water is not available in dry seasons, perennial grasses, sedges, cane berries, and shrubs can all be established instead. In my microclimate, this might look like seeding creeping wild rye (*Leymus triticoides*) mixed with California poppy (*Eschscholzia californica*), lupine (*Lupine albifrons*), coyote brush (*Baccharis pilularis*), blueblossom (*Ceanothus thyrsiflorus*), and blackberry (*Rubus ursinus*).

Brush Check Dams. Brush check dams are an incredible technique for slowing fast-moving water and catching sediment in erosion gullies. Source your wood during tree management work, fire fuel load thinning, or other activities where brush is generated as part of diligent landscape maintenance. The branches are permeable, which allows water to percolate through the dam without holding it back completely. The energy is taken out of the water in this way, allowing sediment to deposit behind the check dam. As water passes through a series of check dams, it gets cleaner and moves more slowly, reducing the pattern of erosion downstream.

HOW TO BUILD A BRUSH CHECK DAM

1. Pound wooden stakes *across* the drainage or erosion gully from bank to bank where you want to build the check dam. Make sure the stakes are securely in place and no more than one foot apart. Make sure the stakes are, at minimum, two feet above grade after they have been pounded or buried in the ground.
2. Dig trenches out into each bank in line with the wooden stakes. These trenches need to go down as far as the bottom grade of the drainage but only need to be dug about two feet horizontally into each bank.
3. Take long branches and weave them between the stakes, making sure the ends of these branches are placed into the trenches in each bank. Make sure the first branch layer is in contact with the ground.

(continued)

4. Continue to weave branches above the first layer, across and through the stakes and across the drainage. Key as many as you can into the trenches on either side of the check dam. It's important that a low spillway be developed in the *center* of the check dam, about halfway up the stakes (a one-foot-high check dam in the center of the system to allow water to crest the dam during high flow events).
5. Once all branches have been woven into the stakes, backfill the trenches to key them completely into the banks.
6. Pack more brush and small logs against the bottom of the drainage or gully on the *upslope* side of the brush check dam. These materials will help slow the water and capture sediment while also creating a carbon sponge where fungi and other organisms can thrive. Make sure not to place this material above the spillway in the center of the check dam.

NONBIOLOGICAL EROSION CONTROL

Rock Armor

Rock armor is referred to throughout this book and is exactly what it sounds like. Take rock and place it against the earth in places where erosion may occur. If the erosion is severe or an extreme volume of water is flowing through that area, the rocks need to be larger. The first layer of rock is commonly buried slightly to ensure that the water can't flow underneath the first layer of rock and cause erosion anyway. In this way, rock is used to "armor" the land where the damage of erosion is a threat.

Rock Check Dams

Rock check dams are structures built of stone that are placed across a gully, creek, stream, or other waterway to slow water down and capture sediment.

Check dams are usually built from larger stones or boulders and are designed in such a way that water still percolates through the dam, though very slowly. These don't hold water back completely; instead they absorb the energy of moving water as it passes through the dam. When the water hits the stone and slows down, any sediment or nutrients in the water deposits behind the check dam. Rock check dams are usually built in succession (multiple check dams, one after another) at different intervals from each other. When these systems function during storm events, it is a sight to be seen. Once the storm passes, sediment collects behind the dam and *that* is repair taking place. Over time, the area behind a check dam can become an oasis—a wet, fertile place for life to take root.

Here's how you build a rock check dam.

Location. Check dams should be placed strategically in the landscape according to the following:

- Accessibility of tools and materials. Getting to the site is a big factor, as sometimes stone needs to be hauled to the area and placed.
- Ask yourself, "How effective will it be to stop erosion in this location?" Check dams near head cuts are highly strategic as they begin repairing the gully closer to the source of the problem. The downslope of a culvert, a rolling dip, a rain garden, or a swale are locations where water may be speeding up, and a check dam will interfere with and dissipate the energy before it causes damage.
- *Relative location* to other check dams and erosion control features is important. Check dams are often placed in succession. Take into account other erosion control features that are already functioning, and add the check dam downslope of these features where the water speeds up again.

Prep the Area. Before placing stone to build the check dam, the area needs to be prepped. This includes digging a shallow trench out of the bottom of the drainage where the first layer of rock will be partially buried. Grading back the banks around the check dam area may also be necessary to prepare for rock armor.

Place the Stone. Once the area is prepped, stone is placed across the drainage from bank to bank. Check dams are not meant to be rock walls with tight joints. It's OK to have spaces between the stones when you place them. It's necessary for water to percolate *through* the rock check dam and not be completely held back like a pond dam.

Check dams always need to feature a low spillway in the center of the dam. In high-flow storm events, you want water to flow over the center of the check dam and not to the corners or the banks.

Check dams also need to be keyed into each bank. The soil will have to be prepared to allow for stones to be partially buried in both banks. This will help knit the entire check dam together so that high-velocity water doesn't wash away the weak points, which are always against the banks.

Rock Aprons. To further shore up the banks on either side of the check dam, "rock aprons" are built. This is rock armor that extends from the two corners of the check dam slightly into the bottom of the drainage and partially up the slope. Rock armor in the corners of the upslope side of the check dam ensures that high-velocity water doesn't break through the bank and around the dam.

Clean Up. Once all of the stone has been placed and the completed check dam remains, make sure to grade any leftover piles of soil back onto the slope of the banks to the angle of repose.

If budget and time allow, the area around the check dam can be seeded with native plants, covered in straw or wood chips (only on the slopes, not in the drainage), or protected by sections of biodegradable erosion control cloth.

Rock Walls

Permanent and well-built rock walls are powerful tools to mitigate erosion. They can be installed across terraces, above roads, above structures, or in virtually any sloping area to retain the top or toe of the slope, create flat areas in the landscape, and permanently stop erosion.

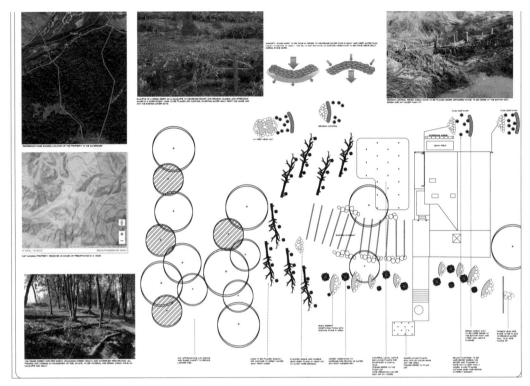

Surface water and erosion design plan. Designed by Mauricio Rivera.

Boulder Placement

Single boulders or groupings of boulders provide excellent erosion control. Boulders can be placed at head cuts, at the outflows of drainages, as natural-looking retaining walls, and so on. A large boulder is a permanent feature that usually completely mitigates erosion directly above its placement. If the erosion is significant, like a huge road cut, then many boulders in groupings will be required.

Boulders are easier to install than rock walls and create a beautiful aesthetic wherever they are placed, though installing them usually requires the use of equipment. They also change the microclimate directly around them and add interest to the landscape. Like all rock-based work, mining and hauling boulders use a lot of embodied energy if they're being brought in from off-site, a fact that always needs to be considered before introducing rock into the landscape.

Zuni Bowls

Many of the techniques implemented in regenerative landscaping have their roots in Indigenous land management practices. When it comes to erosion, native communities throughout the southwestern United States have developed numerous techniques for slowing and catching the movement of water and sediment. One such system hailing from the Indigenous Zuni tribe is called a Zuni bowl.

Zuni bowls are generally built using stone and placed at head cuts. They are designed to stabilize the head cut, develop water infiltration, capture sediment, and slow the velocity of water as it moves through the Zuni bowl.[2] Here is a simple step-by-step process for building one.

1. **Stabilize the Head Cut.** The head cut may be around a culvert or at the top of an erosion gully. The first step is to gently shape the head cut in an angle of repose, which means grading the surface so a more stable angle bends back up against the slope. Then stone (larger stone is preferable) is placed at the bottom of the head cut to form a foundation. More stones are then placed, armoring the entire graded head cut, one layer after another. Each new stone layer is placed on top of the layer below, yet pushed back slightly against the slope to create an angled wall. This stabilizes the slope above, turning the head cut into a sloped rock wall, reducing further erosion.
2. **Excavate Rain Gardens (Bowl).** On the downslope side of the head cut, a rain garden is excavated in a bowl shape. This is a wide and shallow depression where water collects and infiltrates in the soil. The bowl also removes the velocity from the water, slowing it down so it can deposit sediment at the base of the head cut.
3. **Rock Armor the System.** Once the rain garden has been excavated and the head cut is stabilized, the rest of the rain garden's surface and the sides are armored with stone as well. During strong winter storms and flash floods, significant water may enter this area, and armoring the rain garden ensures the power of water won't gouge out more soil, destroying the system.
4. **Build Check Dam.** The first rock check dam is built on the downslope side of the rain garden. Depending on the steepness of the slope and the volume of water entering the Zuni bowl, a series of check dams may be installed downslope of the first check dam. These additional systems are placed at intervals of every 10 feet to every hundred feet or more.
5. **Planting.** Zuni bowls aren't always planted, as the catchment of water and nutrients creates an environment where the ecology can repair itself with seeds that gather and sprout over time. To speed up the process of developing a biological community, cast appropriate seeds or install plants with native species that establish themselves in and around the Zuni bowl.

Water Crossings

Where roads and pathways intersect with the flow of water in the landscape, water crossings of some type are necessary. In conventional landscape development, water crossings are usually made using culverts and other piped systems not only to get across waterways but to drain water away from the site. The regenerative landscape approach is more sensitive. While crossing water is necessary, keeping water in the landscape and maximizing infiltration remain our priorities. That said, roads, trails, and pathways are structures that need regular maintenance and efficient drainage for lasting integrity.

Culverts. Culverts are metal, plastic, or concrete pipes placed under roads and pathways. A typical road uses a culvert to drain a large catchment area. Water collects down the side of a ditch and finds its way to a culvert, where this water is then released on the opposite side of the road. These are typically very damaging to the landscape, creating erosion and moving sediment and pollution into downstream waterways.

In a regenerative landscape setting, culverts can be used to allow road and pathway crossing over water to increase easy access throughout the landscape. In a regenerative setting, culverts are placed *nearly* level underneath the path. This allows water to move underneath your access way while keeping it in the landscape, where it percolates into subsurface aquifers. If the road or pathway is designed for equipment like trucks and tractors, your culverts will need to be larger and stronger in order to absorb the weight of equipment without collapsing.

Water Bars. Water bars are temporary structures that drain water off a road or pathway. It's common to see water bars sprout up through landscapes in the wet season to relieve the pressure and flow of surface water along human access ways. Water bars can be dug to be slightly more permanent (think a speed bump), and can last for a couple of years this way. Generally, a water bar is small and requires maintenance every year to every three years.

When digging a water bar, do not dig it level, but instead with a slight slope to make sure water will drain off the road or pathway. Pay close attention to where the end of your water bar leads, as this is where all the water will go. From there, divert the water into a water channel, contour swale, rain garden, or pond.

Bridges. Bridges are definitely the most aesthetic water crossing in the landscape. These can be as simple as a level bridge with planks on joists, or as elaborate as arched bridges with handrails and crafted features.

In most landscapes, simple bridges to cross waterways are fairly easy and affordable to build if they are meant only for pedestrians. If a bridge is built to support trucks and tractors, then the engineering, materials, and installation will be more expensive and elaborate. Decisions like these are dictated by the budget of the project. By using a level culvert instead of a bridge to get tractors and trucks across, you and project stakeholders will save thousands of dollars. That money can then be invested in other aspects of the landscape.

Rolling Dips. An innovative way to move water across a road or path is by using a rolling dip. These are similar to water bars in that they are a dip in the road that shunts water safely across to the other side. Trucks and tractors drive in, down, and then out of the rolling dip easily even when water is present. Rolling dips are graded similar to water bars in that the slope at the bottom of the rolling dip is moving water from one side of the path to the other. The difference is that a rolling dip is much larger and permanent. Considering what happens to the water on the other side is always required.

TEMPORARY PROJECT-BASED EROSION CONTROL

During the installation of landscape projects, temporary erosion control measures are often necessary to ensure the health of watersheds and extend the installation season. Here are a few options for temporary erosion control systems.

Straw Wattles. Straw wattles, sometimes called "straw sausages," are long tubes of straw used for temporary erosion control measures and are placed on contour and staked to the ground to slow water and catch sediment. They come in a variety of forms and materials and remain in the landscape from one to three years.

Erosion Control Cloth. One of the better inventions of the landscape and erosion control industry is the development of biodegradable erosion control cloth (think blanket). These are made out of jute, straw, and coconut fibers. They come in long rolls that are pulled out and staked across the landscape (usually on bare soil) to hold the earth in place. Many are biodegradable, but beware—some erosion control cloth contains plastic netting or has been treated with chemicals to increase longevity.

YOU ARE THE SOLUTION

Human activity has become the greatest contributor to the erosion of earth's soils. It is a catastrophe of the largest order, decimating watersheds, destroying whole ecosystems, and washing away healthy topsoil.

Humans are the problem but we are also the solution. Throughout this part of the book—looking at water in the landscape in all its forms and functions—it is easy to see that we have all the strategies and tools required to massively restore our home planet. As a regenerative landscaper, you have a responsibility to implement these methods for regenerating ecosystems. By doing this work, you also get to revel in the gratification of leaving the land in a more thriving condition than what you inherited.

PART VI
The Built Environment

33

The Built Environment

Regenerating ecosystems is as much about regenerating our own bodies, minds, and hearts as it is the external ecology. You integrate yourself fully into the landscape by developing a myriad of relationships between people and ecosystem communities.

LIVING IN THE LANDSCAPE

To facilitate this process, we create structures in the landscape that are inviting, comfortable, beautiful, and functional, weaving our living patterns with those of the land. This happens through outdoor living: outdoor kitchens, pathways, patios, wood-fired ovens, firepits, shaded hangout areas, water features, and so much more. Developing these structures in the landscape empowers you to spend more time on the land, cooking and eating, gathering with friends, telling stories, hosting parties, meditating, watching your children play, and reflecting on life. These are the structures we unpack in this part of the book: how to design, plan, and build a variety of elements that make up the built environment of the landscape.

Hardscape Versus Softscape

The terms *hardscape* and *softscape* are often thrown around in landscaping design and build communities. Hardscape refers to rock walls, stone patios, gravel pathways, fountains, fences, and other structures built with rock, stone, or wood. Softscape refers to plant communities, mulched pathways, earthen systems like rain gardens and swales, and other elements that are built solely out of the existing natural environment and vegetation.

The more hardscapes a landscape has, the more expensive it will be to build. In addition to increased costs, hardscapes have a large amount of embodied energy embedded in the materials used. Stone, gravel, concrete, metal, milled wood—these all represent natural resources that have been mined, harvested, processed, and hauled to the landscape. The greater the use of these materials, the less regenerative your landscape-building process will be. That being said, most people want outdoor living structures that will last and don't need to be rebuilt every year or reapplied every two years. Hardscapes built from stone last decades, centuries, or even millennia. These are permanent structures that, maintained even slightly, will outlive us all.

Soften the angular dimensions of stone, wood, and gravel with integrated planting systems (softscapes) throughout the landscape. These softscapes not only buffer hardscapes but also create opportunities to create beauty, grow food and herbal medicine, and provide areas where surface water draining from hardscapes is captured and infiltrated into groundwater aquifers. For instance, fencing systems can be colonized by vining plants or hidden by hedgerows, stone pathways can have planted water-catchment swales alongside them, and so on. When it comes to integrating hardscapes with softscape systems, as many combinations exist as your imagination can muster.

In your design-making process, ask yourself these questions: What aligns with your values? What aligns with your context? Be deliberate about your decisions to include hardscapes in the landscape. Find the balance that works for you, for your budget, your peace of mind, your family, and the earth.

Build to the Use

When making decisions about outdoor living structures, you must design them for the use they will be providing. You'd be surprised how often that simple approach gets looked over in fancy landscape design firms that put creative aesthetic patterns over function. Your job is to find the sweet spot between function and beauty and that all starts with identifying each structure's use. Is a pathway built for a truck or a wheelbarrow? A patio meant for a dining party of 20 people or a small family of four? Is a fence meant to keep deer out or provide privacy? In all of these cases the intended *use* defines the need of the design.

Relative Location

Relative location plays a major role in the outdoor environment design process. Placement of architectural elements and hardscapes can make them user-friendly or, on the flipside, almost unusable. You would be surprised how many times an element can become unusable due to improper placement in the landscape.

Design outdoor living elements to achieve as many functions as possible while making their access as easy as possible. An outdoor patio or deck for eating, for instance, will always be used more often if it's attached to the house or close to the kitchen. If you have to venture out into the landscape to have your outdoor meal, it's unlikely this area will get used as frequently.

There is so much possibility when built elements are designed *relationally*. Fences act as privacy screens, waterfalls filter the sound of a road, and pathways become water-harvesting features. Use your creativity and imagination to make more connections between your daily routines and the landscape. Make living in the garden as easy as possible by locating elements close to the house and outdoor living areas; bring the wonders of the landscape—wildlife, flowering trees, falling food, reflective water—into your life by virtue of the placement of elements.

Natural Building

Natural building is an ancient construction approach that uses natural materials such as clay, sand, straw, and wood. When it comes to building and house design, natural building techniques are some of the oldest in existence and still provide cutting edge, energy efficient strategies for home building today. In this book, we are focused on the landscape and will not be touching on building homes, barn, and large structures such as these.

In a landscape setting, however, natural building is an excellent approach to build benches, wood-fired ovens, walls, tool sheds, chicken coops, and so much more. In chapter 37, written by Sasha Rabin, you will find recipes for mixing cob and a complete how-to for building a cob oven. Much of what Sasha shares is also applicable to building cob benches and cob walls.

Natural building also includes naturally harvested wood, straw bale building, earthbags, natural plasters, stone structures, living structures like willow domes and willow chairs, and other arbortecture techniques.

The world of natural building is vast and infinite in its application in the landscape. As always, it is best to use on-site and local materials and build appropriate to your climate.

Use of Concrete

From patios to walkways to structural foundations, concrete is a common material used in the landscape industry. It forms into nearly any shape, is fairly easy to install, and lasts for decades. It is understandable why its use is so widespread.

The problem with concrete is in the mining and processing of this resource. It is one of the highest embodied energy products in the entire world, adding enormous volumes of carbon dioxide to the atmosphere and contributing to the destruction of watersheds.[1]

As regenerative designers we should use concrete only in the most limited capacity. I would steer you away from using concrete for patios, pathways, and gathering areas if possible. In nearly every case, stone and gravel can be substituted for concrete. In my opinion, concrete is best used in footings and foundations for structures, and for building landscapes for elderly people or people who use wheelchairs, walkers, or canes because it provides a durable and smooth surface to navigate.

Concrete may fit your needs well, but perform your due diligence, be open to alternatives, and weigh your materials choices against your core values.

Materials Sourcing

Architectural elements and hardscapes built on the land are often fabricated using stone, clay, sand, straw, concrete, gravel, wood, and metal. Sourcing materials from the site or locally is always the most regenerative option. Working with natural materials like clay, straw, locally harvested wood, and stone may provide all the resources you need to build structures.

That being said, it's likely that many materials you end up using will be purchased from local hardware stores and landscape materials vendors. Take a walk through the lumber aisle of your local hardware store or wander through the stacks of stone at the quarry. Familiarize yourself with these materials and how much they cost.

The built environment in the landscape constitutes the most expensive aspect of landscaping. When my company, Permaculture Artisans, provides hardscape installation services for clients, the choice of materials can make the difference between a $50,000 job and a $15,000 job. That's how widely the cost of different materials and the labor that follows can vary on a project. Choose and source your materials seriously. These are decisions that affect ecosystems and pocketbooks.

34

Architectural Elements

Gazebos, decks, sheds, trellises, patios, and raised beds are all architectural elements that are integrated into many landscape design projects. They play various functions like casting shade, creating spaces for outdoor recreation, and providing protection and structures for plants to grow.

When you're creating your phased developmental schedule (explained in part III), architectural elements and hardscapes are best installed after grading and earthworks but before planting takes place. Outdoor living elements sometimes need significant resources hauled over and staged on-site, foundations need to be built, equipment is used, and soil gets moved— making these high-disturbance activities in the landscape.

While many architectural elements require the use of wood and stone products, the global lumber industry is a major source of clear-cutting of old growth and second-generation forests.[1] Purchasing this lumber fuels and sponsors ecosystem destruction. If possible, use a regenerative approach and harvest material *from the site* or at least locally. Many communities have small to large mills and tens of thousands of portable mills are in use around the world. If you are able to source lumber from locally harvested and milled materials, the embodied energy and carbon footprint is drastically reduced. Hopefully the harvested wood was taken in an ecological way, during gentle thinning of crowded forests for fire protection or removal of hazardous trees.

For some of you, the forest ecosystems where you live desperately need sustainable management. Sustainable thinning is done to reduce fire fuel load and help the forest grow healthy. Portable mills used to turn material to lumber are relatively inexpensive and offer a great opportunity for a side business or new career path taking care of the forest and generating locally harvested lumber at the same time.

Electricity and water utilities are sometimes required to make architectural elements function (e.g., fountains, outdoor sinks, lighting systems). Installing these utilities is best done at the same time as other utility projects like running water for irrigation. The more developed your landscape plan is prior to installation, the more likely that the same amount of work will accomplish multiple outcomes. Running all utilities for the entire project at the same time saves a significant amount of money and labor.

Decks

A deck in the landscape is a great way to provide outdoor living infrastructure. Decks provide an easy-to-maintain, durable surface for hosting parties, eating outdoors, and relaxing in the landscape. They do have some drawbacks though. Building a deck is an expensive and laborious task with high-cost materials and complicated construction.

Because of this, a deck would not be my first choice for creating an outdoor living space in the landscape. Simple patios achieve the same functions with much less money and labor. That being said, there are scenarios where decks make sense.

In sloping environments where a staircase is required to walk from the house into the landscape, an elevated deck can offer a perfect intermediary solution if the cost of labor and materials is not an issue When building a deck, the earth does not have to be leveled like it does for a patio. Pier block foundations are used for support posts and the deck is then framed and built upon these.

Benches

A well-placed bench, paired with features like ponds, beautiful views, and cool summer shade, is perfect for making the landscape inviting and relaxing. The more places people can sit on the land, the more likely folks will listen to what the landscape has to share. To hear birds sing, to see the squirrels jump, to smell spring blossoms, to be hit on the head by an acorn. . . . We have these experiences when we are able to sit for extended periods of time, calmly, in the landscape. For me, it's an almost daily practice to sit out on a log and listen—and I always discover something new. Like the time some brown creeper birds (*Certhia americana*) built a nest *inside* the bark of a redwood tree. I never would have imagined it until I saw them tearing bits of redwood and sliding into a small crevice in the bark.

Landscape benches can be made from many materials. A cob bench built on a dry stacked rock foundation is one of my favorites, but these are more challenging to build than the common, effective, and simple wooden bench. Even a large log, or a log round turned on its end, makes an excellent bench in the landscape.

Shou Sugi Ban

Shou Sugi Ban originated in Japan as a method for treating cedar siding to make it waterproof.[2] Wood is charred with fire to create a charcoal coating that repels pests and water. This ingenious approach is now used in a variety of applications to naturally protect wood from rot. Treating wood with fire is done in one of two ways. A handheld propane torch can be used to char the outside of wood quickly. Don't let the wood catch fire, and start with short treatments until the desired effect is achieved. The goal is not to burn the wood all the way through or turn it to ash. The goal is to char the outside while maintaining the integrity of the wood.

Placing wood in a fire for treatment also works. Because the fire is stationary, the wood needs to be moved quickly around to keep it from catching fire or burning too deep into the fibers. This method requires focused attention and constant moving of the wood to achieve the desired result. Don't walk away from the fire when using this method!

Once the wood has been charred, whether by torch or by fire, it's important to brush it coarsely with a wire brush. Use the brush to scrape off loose charcoal on the outside of the wood until a smooth surface is revealed. This technique will clean up the board and produce an incredibly beautiful pattern on the wood, the natural wood hues emerging amongst a mottling of the black char patterns.

In landscape installations, this approach is used to treat posts before they go into the ground for fencing, trellises, and so on. You can also treat wooden raised beds with Shou Sugi Ban to increase longevity.

Trellises/Arbors

Trellises are structures for growing plants and they come in many forms. They can be built as pergolas, archways, fence lines, breezeways, or just shaded areas out in the landscape.

Trellises are generally built of wood or metal and used as a structure for vining plants. Plants like grapes (*Vitis*), wisteria (*Wisteria sinensis*), kiwi (*Actinidia deliciosa*), clematis (*Clematis*), passion flower (*Passiflora*), and jasmine (*Jasminum polyanthum*) are common vines used to colonize trellises. Vining plants that will grow readily on trellis systems can be found in every climate on earth.

Trellises can be bought from local fabricators, builders, and hardware stores or you can build one yourself. As an architectural element that makes use of wood and metal, trellises can get expensive, but they can also be built from locally harvested ingredients and other relatively affordable materials.

Raised Beds

Raised beds are planting areas built from a solid perimeter. These planting areas are most often used to protect plants from burrowing rodents, to provide better access for elderly gardeners, or to integrate with a contemporary, straight lined landscape design plan. Where I live, pocket gophers breed up to 300 gophers per acre. This is a lot of gopher pressure, especially for a busy family who can't spend hours every week trapping plant-eating rodents. Raised beds with wire mesh underneath are an excellent solution.

Raised beds are most often built from wood but have also been installed using metal and stone. Stone raised beds last centuries, but the wire underneath will rot well before the stone walls fall apart.

How to Build Wooden Raised Beds

Location. Locating raised beds is a good opportunity to revisit the *permaculture zone planning* method, where elements are placed in relative distance from the home due to the frequency of use. For most people, raised beds are systems for growing annual vegetables. Most annual vegetables require a high frequency of visitation and therefore are best planted in zone 1 or zone 2. Place raised beds as close to the house as you can, taking into account other contextual features like sun orientation, water, and access.

Materials. Raised beds are best built with an anti-rot wooden material like redwood, cedar, juniper, or santos rosewood. Wooden 4 by 4-inch timbers are used for corner posts, while 2 by

12s make the best choice for side panels. A raised bed is essentially a rectangular box sitting on the ground. It is best to have side panels that are one solid piece rather than have multiple panels placed together. For instance, if you use 2 by 6-inch timbers and place them one over the other to make a one-foot-high bed, the seam between them will dry the bed out faster.

Sizing. A raised bed can be nearly any shape or size you think of and can build, but that doesn't mean any shape will function well. It is best to build raised beds that allow you to easily reach into the center of the bed from either side. For folks with long arms, that means a five-foot-wide bed, but for most people a four-foot-wide bed is better (I advise the latter).

The length of a raised bed can also vary. I've seen everything from a small 2 foot by 2 foot by 1 foot raised bed all the way to a 5-foot-wide and 20-foot-long raised bed. Again, design to your context, but for the sake of this book my suggestion is not to make your raised bed any longer than 20 feet. That would make the largest bed four feet wide by 20 feet long by 1 foot deep. Four by eight feet seems to be a very common size, and many designers will build to these dimensions.

If your bed gets too long, the sideboards will eventually bow out under the weight of the soil. One way to combat this is by installing horizontal boards every 10 feet, screwing the two side boards together (usually done on the bottom of the bed to hide the boards when the bed is filled with soil). This extra structural integrity will make longer beds hold their shape.

Prepping the Area. Before you build your raised bed, the area must be prepped. Raised beds need to sit on level ground. If the landscape slopes, you will need to either cut a level terrace to place the bed on or build the bed higher on one side than the other. For the sake of this section, we are discussing beds placed on level ground.

The most important sections to level are the four corners of the bed and the distances between each corner. A bump in the earth that a side panel rests on will lift the entire edge of the bed, so each edge needs to be leveled. It's not imperative that the area *inside* the raised bed be level. This will get filled with soil eventually. (If wire mesh is to be installed, it should be at or below the grade of the *bottom* of the raised bed box.)

Building the Boxes. By now your materials will be on site, and the site will be prepped as discussed above. Now it's time to build the boxes. Ideally, you have 4 by 4s for corner posts and 2 by 12s for side panels. You've developed a design and know what size the boxes are going to be. The first step is to cut all the wood to the right dimensions. The type of bed described here is simple and therefore your 4 by 4 posts only need to be cut in one-foot lengths. In this version of a raised bed, you are *not* burying the 4 by 4 posts in the ground (though this is an option for extra durability). You are using them as added support in the corners for attaching the 2 by 12s. It's that easy.

Once the material has been cut, begin screwing side boards to the one-foot 4 by 4 corner posts. For a sturdier corner connection, bolts can be drilled and placed to connect side boards to the 4 by 4 corners.

If the raised bed is longer than 10 feet, now would be the time to attach horizontal support struts at 10-foot intervals between side boards to keep them from bowing open. Once the boxes are assembled, staple gopher wire or quarter-inch hardware cloth on the bottom of the box. You may want to attach the wire a couple inches to the inside of the sideboards to make it more difficult for ground-dwelling rodents to slip between the wire and wood.

For long beds that are difficult to flip over, sometimes placing them in their permanent home is easier. In that case, roll the metal wire out *inside* the placed bed area and staple them to the inner boards.

Filling Beds. Once the beds are built and installed level in their locations, it's time to fill the beds with soil. The soil mix used in the raised bed makes all the difference in the success of your growing endeavor. If the existing topsoil on the site is loaded with organic matter, use some of this material inside the bed, inoculating the planting area with indigenous microorganisms that will acclimate the plants to the native soil and create better water retention. However, I wouldn't fill more than 50 percent of the planting space with native soil unless it was incredibly rich. In cases of poor-quality native soil, use only 10 percent inside raised beds.

You can buy topsoil, planting mixes, compost, and other soil products at landscape supply companies. Well-aged, biologically alive compost is the best material to mix with native soil when filling the raised bed. When deciding how to fill your raised bed, take all the contextual parameters into account—the materials you have on hand, what's available to purchase, the goals of the project, and so on.

For the best results, mix more than one type of compost, composted manure, or topsoil together. The more diversity in your mix, the more diverse the microbiology being introduced to the bed will be.

Put a layer of cardboard down at the very bottom of the raised bed before filling with compost/soil mixes. This cardboard is organic matter that feeds microorganisms and will decompose. It also holds moisture, helping to keep the bed from drying out in the first year.

Make sure to fill the bed all the way to the very top. The soil will settle with time, and you may find yourself with very shallow soil after a year of natural compression if the bed has not been completely filled. Every couple years you will want to top the beds off with fresh compost.

Additional soil amendments like oyster shell, rock dust, seaweed, and compost tea can also be added to the soil while you're filling the bed. This will give the raised beds a boost of minerals, nutrients, fungi, and bacteria. And once your bed is built and filled with soil, don't forget to add drip irrigation if required in your climate. Happy growing!

BUILDING A COB OVEN BY SASHA RABIN

In its simplest form, a cob oven is a rounded, earthen vessel with space inside for a fire. The earthen material holds the heat from the fire, allowing you to cook with residual heat stored in the thermal mass of the earthen oven walls. For millennia, humanity has cooked with fire in a variety of ways. This oven is just one of many ways we use heat from fire to cook. In today's world we are disconnected from most of what sustains us. Reconnecting with the basic elements of fire and earth to cook our food and nourish our communities is one palpable way to reconnect to our sustenance. Before we dive into the oven-building process, let's look at what cob is and why it is one of the best ecological building materials on the planet.

WHAT IS COB?

Cob is a load-bearing, monolithic method of building with earth. It is a combination of enough clay to hold together the sand, enough sand to keep the clay from cracking, enough fiber (usually straw) to give it tensile strength, and enough water to make the mixture malleable. The material is worked into the wall (or oven) while still wet, creating a monolithic wall. Typically, no forms or dried bricks are used, but rather handfuls of materials are built directly onto the foundation and wall.

Adobe is a sun-dried block or brick made of mud, sometimes with the addition of straw. Adobe blocks are traditionally shaped by hand or with wood or metal molds and left in the sun to dry.

Materials

Clay is perhaps the most common building material. When we say "clay," we simply mean sediment with some clay content in it. Many naturally occurring sediments are a mixture of clay, sand, silt, and gravel. The amount of clay in the sediment ranges greatly from soil to soil. Clay works like glue in earthen building. The higher the percentage of clay in the sediment, the more other materials will be needed to produce the proper mixture. Clay soils are found in most places throughout the world. The few places where clay cannot be found are geologically young regions (volcanic terrain) or high energy depositional areas (beach shore breaks).

Clay, unlike aggregate, makes a chemical bond to water molecules, therefore expanding when wet. When it dries it then shrinks, which is why we add aggregate to the mixture. If the aggregate is already locked together and touching each other, it inhibits large cracking when the clay dries and shrinks. There are a few ways to test to see how much clay is in your soil. Since clay cracks when it dries, one way to find clay is to look for cracks on the surface of the ground. This is usually found in places where the clay was suspended in water (due to its ability to bond to water molecules) and the water evaporated.

If you don't have clay on the surface, dig down two or three feet to look for a clay layer. Clay is often confused with silt; one way to tell them apart is to do a shake test. Fill a mason jar half full of soil. Shake the jar until all the sediment is fully dissolved in the water. When you set it down, the heavy particles will settle first (pebbles and large sand), then the finer particles, and last to settle is the clay. The clay may stay suspended in water for a day or more. This is not an accurate way to determine the quantity of clay in your soil, but it can be a help in determining if you have clay in your soil. Another way to check for clay is to go wash your hands. Clay-rich soil will not wash off your hands (like sand or silt) by simply running them under water. With clay you need to rub your hands together to remove it.

Aggregate is any stone, gravel, pebble, or sand component added to an earthen mix. Sand is the primary ingredient in some earthen walls such as cob. Cob walls are more of a sand wall with just enough clay to glue it all together. Sand is most often used, but other aggregate options work as well. Aggregate does not expand when wet or shrink when dry. This is an essential part of your earthen wall, because it keeps the clay from cracking. The sand particles are already touching and locked together while the material is wet, so that when it dries it doesn't crack. It is best to use the coarsest sand available, so that it locks together and does not roll around itself. The *coarser* the sand, the stronger your material will be.

Fiber gives the wall tensile strength. This serves the same function as rebar in cement. Straw is the most common modern-day material used; however, you can use a variety of materials based on what you have. Most grasses will work, although you need them to be dry with as few seeds as possible. In some places, dung and animal hair is a common fiber added to earthen mixes.

Water is often overlooked, but if there was no water in your mix you would not be able to build.

Cob Ovens

Cooking in a cob oven takes time. Often we view this as a negative quality, but I have never regretted my time tending the fire and watching the flames as the oven heats up. It is, however, an entirely different process than turning a dial and having an oven rise to a set temperature.

Each oven is different, and the relationship you build with your oven is unique. I encourage you to not get too caught up in the details. Build an oven, then take it down and build another if you have changes you want to make. These ovens are organic and don't have to last forever.

Cob ovens are built with a combination of earthen materials and found in different forms all over the world. Our design originates from Quebec, Canada. Traditionally built using bent willow to create the void inside, our design has been adapted to use damp sand as the formwork on the inside of the oven to create a smoother interior surface as sand is a smaller aggregate than other void-filling materials. This sand gets dug out of the oven once complete.

There is a range of simple to elaborate techniques you can use in your approach to building an earthen oven. Historically, ovens were built with mostly just earth. Today we integrate fire brick for the cooking surface and other innovative details to make it more efficient. But please remember, you can also build a very basic functional oven with little more than soil found underfoot.

The first step of the oven-building process is figuring out where you want to build it. It is ideal to have your oven somewhat close to your kitchen, where I guarantee you will use it more often. My personal oven is located in such a way that I can keep an eye on the fire as it burns while inside my kitchen preparing food. The other consideration is fire safety. The flames are mostly contained inside the dome of the oven, so I recommend you treat it much like you would a barbecue grill with regard to fire and make sure nothing is flammable in the immediate vicinity.

If you intend to put a roof over it, you can place your roof approximately four feet above the door of the oven. The other siting consideration is related to how you intend to use the oven.

Do you intend to use it for pizza parties? If so, it's nice to have enough space for everyone to move around comfortably.

The next step is to decide the size of the oven you want to build. What will you be cooking in your oven? How big is the pot that needs to fit through the door? What foods will you be cooking? For example, if you plan on using it mostly for pizza, you may want a wider door to maneuver the pizza. The bigger your oven, the longer it takes to heat. The smaller the oven, the less you can fit inside. If you plan on doing bigger events, I recommend a larger oven.

Building the Foundation

There are many options for building your foundation. The main objective with the foundation is to get your oven off the ground to avoid moisture. You'll also want to set your oven at a comfortable working height. I find that elbow height is a comfortable height for cooking and glancing in to see how the fire is doing. Many details of your foundation will be determined by your climate. If you are in a wet area without good drainage, you will need to dig down farther to create more area for water to drain from under your oven. In a relatively dry climate, dig down about four inches and fill with gravel. You may dig down a foot or more if you are concerned about standing water or water freezing under your oven, leading to frost heave.

The next step is to build a stem wall using material that separates the earthen material from the ground so it won't be damaged by moisture. Stone, urbanite (chunks of concrete), earthbags, cinderblock, brick, and so on will all work. I recommend building up with at least six inches of this foundation material before applying earthen material. In rainy climates, apply earthen materials at least a foot off the ground. Your stone (or whatever material you chose) can be used to build the oven all the way up to approximately eight inches below your finished oven floor.

When you build the stem wall, you can use a cob mortar or cement to bind the stone material, whichever you are more comfortable with. A wooden structure is also acceptable to raise the oven up off the ground, which is a suitable option if you're in an extremely cold or wet climate. Make sure to build the structure strong enough to hold the massive weight of the oven. If you're building your foundation with wood, plan ahead and work your roof support posts into your foundation supports.

The next layer is to simply get the oven to a good working height. Most often I use adobe for this because it's a material we can build with easily without waiting for it to dry. You could use cob as well or continue your stem wall material all the way up. You are essentially building a strong cylinder that eventually gets filled with dirt, gravel, or whatever material is available. It is important to dampen and compact each layer as you go to avoid settling over time. If you choose to use cob or adobe in your walls, this provides an opportunity to familiarize yourself with the materials before building the oven itself.

Setting the Hearth Bricks

Insulating under the bricks that become the floor of your oven is one option for increasing efficiency. This way the heat does not get lost down into the foundation. If you are using adobe to

Cob oven fired up. Photo by Erik Ohlsen.

get your oven to height, leave a small cavity at the top to fill with insulation material. You have many options for the insulation—recycled bottles are commonly used with an infill combination of perlite and clay slip mixture around the bottles. Other options for insulating under hearth bricks are pumice or insulative kiln bricks, all depending on the materials you have access to. Make sure your insulation material is strong enough to support the weight of the oven you'll be building on top of it and won't compress over time.

On top of the insulation level, a thin layer of cob is needed to cap the insulation cavity.

Once you have covered the insulation with cob, cover the whole area with a thin layer of fine sand. If you don't have a small lip around the outside of your working surface, create one with cob to hold in the sand. There are various options for materials to use for the floor of the oven. One of the most commonly used is fire brick. If you are on a budget, you can also use red brick, but it won't last as long with frequent heat. If you have a source of used kiln shelves, that would be a great option.

If you're going for simple and traditional, smooth out a layer of cob to act as the over floor. Remember, people have been building these for thousands of years, using only what they had available. However, you won't want to cook *directly* on the cob, as it will chip away over time. Instead, cook your food in pans in the oven.

Use a two- to four-foot level to get the layer of sand as flat and level as possible. Some adjusting will still be needed as you go, but starting out as flat as possible will make the next steps easier.

I start setting my bricks from the very front so the front bricks are lined up exactly where I want them. I like to have the front bricks protruding out over the foundation just a bit so the oven is easy to clean by putting a container of some sort under the protruding bricks to sweep out the ashes when needed. If these bricks don't stay level for whatever reason, or seem to be leaning forward, build out support with a few handfuls of cob under the bricks to support them. It is worthwhile to make sure these bricks are level. A short 12-inch level is very handy for this. If you plan to cook directly on the bricks, as is common for pizza and bread, make sure your bricks are set in place as evenly as possible. Run your finger over the edges with each brick in place to make sure they are all sitting snugly with no edges sticking up or exposed gaps between them. Make sure to slide each brick down the brick next to it, not allowing any sand to get between them.

If a newly set brick is a little high, use a rubber mallet (or chunk of wood) and gently tap it down. If it sits slightly low, simply pick it back up, sprinkle a little more sand under the brick, and try again. If there are gaps, ash from burning wood will get stuck and get into your food. Make sure the bricks cover the entire bottom of what will become the cooking surface, but you don't need the bricks to extend the whole way under what will be your oven walls. In order to maximize your bricks with little waste, you will likely need to adjust some around the edges to get the shape you want.

Once you have a level, flat surface of bricks, you can draw out your oven outline onto the bricks. Find the middle of the oven floor (not counting the doorway) and draw a perfect circle with a string and pencil. The oven does not need to be a circle, but it's a good starting place. Once you have your circle, you can then adjust the shape by connecting the lines from the circle to the door opening, and make sure all the lines are how you want them. The oven floor often ends up being longer than it is wide.

Creating the Door Opening

The opening in the oven can be created with brick or cob. I tend to build a brick arch for the doorway, both for function as well as the aesthetic, but you can also do this more simply out of cob. Whatever material you use, it is a nice detail to inset the arch an inch or so from the edge of the hearth bricks so that the door has somewhere to sit.

Building a wooden form as a guide for the arch is fairly simple. In this case you would build the brick arch before creating the sand form (more on the sand form below). If you do use a wooden form to create the brick arch, it is essential that you use little shims of wood to prop the arch form up. When you are ready to remove it, you slide out the shims and the form drops down half an inch and slides out easily. If you don't do this, your form will likely get stuck.

(Trust me, it has happened!) Another option, which I've done many times, is to create the arch with the sand form itself. In that case, prop up a section of plywood in the location of what will become the door of your oven to keep the sand from falling out. If you go this route, it is helpful to trace on the plywood where your door will eventually be. Another possibility is to build your oven as an enclosed dome and cut your door opening out afterward—this is probably the simplest, easiest option.

Creating the Sand Form (the Void of the Oven)

Once the bricks are set and you have drawn out the perimeter of your oven cooking surface, you are ready to start the sand form. Once you start building the sand mold, you won't be able to stop until you have at least the first layer of cob over your sand form, so make sure you have enough time to complete these steps. At this point have your cob ready and waiting for you. I usually mix the sand in a wheelbarrow using a mixing hoe. Ideally, as one person shovels the sand into the wheelbarrow another person is misting it down, reducing the amount you need to mix it. Wet and mix the sand to a consistency that allows a ball of sand to hold its shape relatively well in your hand (exactly what you would use for building sandcastles on the beach). This will take at least two full wheelbarrows of sand and will be shaped such that the high point of the sand form is around 18 inches high. I like to give a fair bit of attention to making sure the sand form is just how I want it, nice and symmetrical, with no major lumps or bumps.

When building the sand form, keep in mind that the door needs to be between 63 percent and 75 percent of the height of the top of the oven. For example, I often make the door 12 inches and the top of the interior of the oven 18 inches. If the door is much higher than these proportions, too much heat will be lost out the door, and if it is less than that, it won't have enough oxygen for the fire to burn well.

Once you have the sand form built, cover it quickly, especially if you are in a dry or windy climate where the sand can dry and blow off the top. Having a fine mister on hand is helpful. The next step is to cover the sand form with damp newspaper. It creates a clean separation between the sand and the cob when you shovel out the sand at the end of the process.

Layers of the Oven

The only layer that is essential to building an oven in which you can cook food is the thermal mass layer. This is the layer that stores the residual heat from the fire. The insulation layer makes the oven more efficient by keeping the heat in the oven rather than letting it escape to the outdoors, but it is not essential and likely didn't exist in many ovens centuries ago. Have something to measure each newly added layer so it results in an even thickness all the way around the oven. This measuring device can be your fingers (recommended for layer one) or a stick cut to a particular length (recommended for layers two and three). As you build up each consecutive layer, keep your measurement perpendicular to the sand form, *not* parallel to the ground, to ensure an even thickness.

Although layers one and two could be applied as one layer, I tend to do them separately. For the first layer, place two fingers' thickness of cob with no straw. After this layer is on, rest and take a break or continue another day. This layer is the layer that interacts with the fire. There are many options and ways to make this layer as strong as possible. The clay in this layer of cob will eventually vitrify when fired, but you need to add either sand or fiber (or both) to keep this layer from cracking. Some people prefer adding fiber, although it will eventually burn out (which is fine within reason, as it still has plenty of thermal mass)—the resulting layer has potential to be stronger. The more sand in this layer, the more potential it has to be crumbly. There is no one right way to do this, but I generally do a fairly sandy layer to keep the clay from cracking.

While applying layer one, remember that only damp sand lies beneath. If you press too hard, you will indent the sand layer. That said, you do want to compress the cob well enough that it dries as one solid layer. Making small, sausage-shaped cob logs is a helpful way to get your layer to a somewhat even thickness. As you go up, continue to use your two fingers to check the thickness of the layer you are applying.

The next layer is also a cob layer, generally mixed with straw, adding to the thermal mass material that stores heat for cooking. The thickness of this layer depends on how long you want your oven to take to heat up and how long you want it to retain heat. The thicker the layer, the longer it takes to heat up and the longer it will stay hot. A general rule of thumb is around four inches for layer two.

Layer three functions as insulation. This layer keeps the heat that has been generated inside the oven rather than allowing it to escape. The most common insulation layer I use is a perlite-clay mixture. Using a material that won't burn is recommended, but you can also use what you have. I have used straw clay, as well as sawdust clay, when that is what's available. The goal of this layer is for it to be light, as it is the air pockets within it that create the insulation.

Mix the perlite–clay in a wheelbarrow by adding in the perlite first, followed by just enough clay slip to hold the perlite in place, but not so much that it makes the mixture too heavy and reduces its insulative properties. Wear a dust mask to avoid breathing toxic perlite dust.

Applying this layer can feel a bit strange, as the material often sticks to your hands and not the oven. Coating the cob layer with clay slip can help the perlite mixture stick to the oven. I use my hands for a bit of formwork, gently compressing the perlite mixture into shape, while continuing to measure the thickness with my measuring stick to make sure it's even. If it's really not holding together, add more clay slip. If it feels too sloppy, add more perlite.

The final step is the plaster layer, layer four. This is the layer that protects the oven, as well as the layer to use if you want to do anything sculptural on the oven. The materials we use for the base coat plaster layer are very similar to the materials used for cob, but more refined. If there are rocks or pebbles in your materials, screen them through a ½-inch or ¼-inch screen. Instead of long straw like we use for cob, use short or chopped straw. If you don't have a method for chopping it, you can always screen regular straw and use the short pieces that fall through the screen.

> ## EARTHEN PLASTER RECIPE
>
> 1 part clay slip—screen through a ¼-inch screen
>
> 1 part sand—probably don't need to screen, only if rocks are present
>
> 1 part chopped straw
>
> Your mix may vary depending on your clay soil. I can't stress enough the importance of making samples!

The way the plaster is applied is just as important as the plaster mix itself. The more the plaster is compressed, the stronger it will be. The plaster can be applied with your hands or using a wooden float. If applying with your hands, it won't be quite as strong as using a float. This takes some practice before you get the hang of it. Since it is just clay and sand, just keep working it, adding water with a mister if needed, until you get the shape and smoothness desired. This layer won't result in a super smooth surface but rather a durable outer layer.

If you add sculptural elements into this layer, make sure that none of them have potential to catch rain. Water needs to run off the oven surface as easily as possible. The goal for this layer is to sculpt the shape you want without leaving an overly smooth surface. The final layer of plaster wants some sort of rough surface to grab onto. If it's too smooth, the final plaster layer will have a harder time adhering to the layer under it.

Oven Roof

Roofs keep your oven from needing additional maintenance. Even more, they can be designed to provide a protected place when using the oven in rainy weather. Roofs can be built from wood, as the fire does not lick out of the oven far enough to pose a threat. If your roof is at least three to four feet above your oven, it will be fine. At that height it will get black with soot but won't catch on fire.

Oven Door

Contrary to what you might think, an oven door can be built out of wood. The door is not on the oven when fire is present, so it doesn't burn. Once you have burned the fire for as long as needed, scoop out the coals and ash (as you would for baking bread) and put the door on. At this point the oven might be 500 or 600 degrees but shouldn't catch the door on fire.

COOKING IN YOUR COB OVEN

This is when you get to develop a relationship with your oven, learning how long you need to fire it and with what kind of wood to cook what you want to cook. You can cook anything from cookies to bread, from pizza to slow-roasted meats. I cook a lot of things in the door of the oven while the oven is heating up. If I am firing the oven to bake bread, I often cook a whole dinner in the door with the flames licking out the door above a variety of cast iron pans with veggies, sausages, and flatbreads. You can also use the residual heat left over from cooking. Put a pot of beans in the oven to cook overnight or, if it's a bit cooler, you can make granola or even use it to dry fruit. Experiment and come up with your own recipes and methods of cooking.

The volume of sand and clay you will need to build an oven varies greatly depending on the clay content of your clay soil and the size of the oven you chose to build, but here are some rough quantities to start with.

MATERIALS AND TOOLS FOR A COB OVEN (26-INCH DIAMETER COOKING SURFACE)

52 gallons sand (plus 2 wheelbarrows full for sand dome form)

37 gallons clay soil

5 cubic feet perlite (can be increased for a more insulated oven)

1 bale of straw for cob layers

12½ gallons chopped straw (¼ bale)

16 wine bottles

41 fire bricks

Newspaper

Rock for foundation (if using)

Foundation Materials (foundation can be built from different materials)

    45 premade adobe bricks (7½ by 9 by 4 inches)

    24 gallons sand

    14 gallons clay soil

    20 stones (roughly soccer ball size)

    8 gallons gravel

    4–5 wheelbarrows of fill dirt

Tools

Buckets	Dust masks (for perlite)
Shovels	String
Hoes (ideally mixing hoes)	Pencil
Plaster floats/trowels	Level
Hose	Rubber mallet
Hose nozzle/mister	Mixing tarps
Wheelbarrows	Tape measure

Additional (optional) tools you may find useful

- Drill with mortar mixing paddle to make clay slip
- Wood chipper or weed eater to chop straw
- Tile saw to cut custom brick sizes

RECIPES

I list all recipes with some hesitation, because any of the recipes will be different from what I have listed here depending on the composition of your soil. Please use these as a starting place, but not as your *actual* recipe. In order to find your recipe, you will need to make samples. Start with these recipes and make samples, some with more clay and some with more sand. Make sure to label all your samples! I know in the moment it *really* feels like you will remember what you did, but after 10 different mixes, you *will* forget. These cob recipes can also be used for other architectural and landscape elements like benches, walls, chicken coops, and even houses.

Clay Slip

To make clay slip you just need to soak clay in water. Different clays need to soak for different amounts of time. Some clay only needs to soak for 10 or 15 minutes before becoming a nice milkshake consistency, while some will soak for weeks and still remain in huge clumps. If the latter is the case, either break it up with your hands or feet (by getting into the barrel) or use a mixing attachment on a drill, which speeds up the process. The end result needs to roughly be the consistency of a smoothie.

Chopped Straw

Some recipes require long straw, some chopped straw. If you don't have an easy way to chop straw, just take your regular bale of straw and screen it through a ½-inch screen, screening out all the longer pieces (be sure to save them for your cob). Chopping straw with a chipper shredder is the easiest. Another option (with a more common tool) is to chop it with a weed eater in a garbage can. This is a very messy process, so make sure to wear good eye protection and a mask.

Cob

Even throughout the oven build, the cob recipe often changes due to the different needs of our cob mixture. Note: I use the same recipe for cob as I do for adobes. Here is the recipe.

BASIC COB RECIPE

2 parts sand
1 part clay soil (not soaked, unless your clay is in hard-to-manage clumps)
Long straw to feel
Water to feel

Variations

Cob with no straw (first layer of oven)
3 parts sand
1 part clay soil
Water (less water than the other mixture, because we are not adding straw, which dries out the cob)

How to Mix Cob

There are many ways to mix a batch of cob, and no doubt you will find what works best for you. My preferred way is to put my dry clay soil and sand on a tarp and roll it back and forth to mix the dry ingredients. Once it's mostly mixed, make a well (think volcano crater) in the center and add water. The amount of water you add varies depending on existing moisture in your materials and how much straw you are adding. Once you have added water, it is time to mix the materials with your bare feet. Once the water is mixed in, start adding straw.

Continue to use the tarp to turn the materials, piling them back into the middle of the tarp, and then stomping them out again. When you do add water, use the tarp to get the water to the bottom of the pile; it will make mixing a lot easier to have the wet *under* the dry, rather than having your dry materials under your wet materials. Add the straw in thin layers, stomp the straw in with your feet, turn the materials with the tarp, and add more straw. Do this until the mixture has stiffened up and you no longer sink through the material when you stand on it. It should start to resemble a burrito when rolled with the tarp.

Ratios for Cob Mixes

Always start with samples. Depending on how clumpy your clay is, you may need to soak it overnight to break up the big dried masses. If you just screen it, you might be screening out the clay chunks you actually want. If you do soak it for your samples, try your best to be relatively consistent with your mix, so that you're not making samples with runny slip, and then your finished material with significantly thicker slip.

Make These Samples

1 part clay : 3 parts sand
1 part clay : 2 parts sand
1 part clay : 1 part sand
2 parts clay : 1 part sand
3 parts clay : 1 part sand

I recommend samples roughly the size of a shoebox. If the sample feels erodible (falls apart easily), then it needs more clay; if it cracks, then it needs more sand (or straw). Generally, you will add more sand to keep it from cracking, although there are times (like with our plasters) where we add fiber to mitigate cracks.

There will likely be more than one sample that is in the acceptable range. If that is the case, then choose the sample that uses more of the materials that you have on-site, which are more accessible, cheaper, or have less destructive ecological impact.

THERMAL MASS VERSUS INSULATION

- Most building materials are rated for their insulation value. In the United States that's an R value (R for resistance). This is a material's ability to resist temperature transferring through it.

- Insulation is created by the thousands of tiny air pockets in a material, meaning that the lighter a material is, the better insulation it has.

- Thermal mass is the opposite of that. The heavier a material is, the more thermal mass it has. The denser a material is, the more it can hold onto and store temperature. Rocks have a high amount of thermal mass, as does water.

35
Landscape Patios

If you build it, *you* will come. Having places in the landscape that make it easy to have a party, relax in the sun, eat your daily meals, and do outdoor craft projects is the best way to live daily in the landscape. Landscape patios provide these functions.

For some, the idea of a patio might feel overwhelming as you envision sprawling stone or concrete. But a patio doesn't need to be an expensive and complex feature; it can be as simple as a graveled area or as complex as a mosaic of flagstone shapes and sizes. The materials and design of your patio need to meet the context of your project including your budget and labor resources.

SIZING

The size of a patio matters. If it is too small it will be limited in its function; if too big, the costs will be higher and some parts of it may get little use. Don't build a patio with a diameter smaller than roughly 12 feet, as it's hard to fit people in a space smaller than that.

Make sure you size the patio relative to:

- The space that you have available, but also work within the natural spaces you have in the landscape.
- What the function is going to be. Size the patio appropriately to your context and your planned use. Outdoor dining? Outdoor classroom?
- Drainage and direction of water flow. This will help you decide on the exact shape, size, and location of the patio. For example, a perfectly flat patio will not drain. You need at least a 1 percent slope (that's 1/8 inch per foot slope to get the patio to drain correctly). A 2 percent slope (¼ inch per foot) will work as well, but don't make the slope steeper than that or you will feel a slant when sitting or walking on the patio.

SURFACE MATERIALS

Know what patio surface materials you're going to use before you prep the area and build the foundation. Patio surface materials come in different thicknesses, which is helpful to know before building the foundation so you can make adjustments to foundation thickness and materials. As you will see below, surface materials can include flagstone, pavers, brick, decomposed granite, and gravel. As these materials constitute hardscapes, they are expensive and consume energy. Build the foundation to the right height to ensure that the surface material you install meets the desired final grade.

PATIO FOUNDATIONS

If you're building a patio from stone or gravel it will need a *solid* foundation. Here is how to build one.

1. Lay the shape of the patio out with either landscape paint, survey flags, or stakes and string to arrange the area to be prepped.
2. To prep the site, soil and organic matter must be removed. Excavating the patio area to the appropriate depth is a key step in the process. The final grade of your patio will be four to six inches *above* the base of your foundation. That means you need to excavate the area four or six inches *below* your desired final grade. If the patio is meant to connect with a house entrance, a deck, or a staircase, getting the final grade correct is crucial. Grading out this excavated area needs to be done with drainage in mind. It is easier to install a patio with perfect drainage when the starting foundation already has a 1 pecent slope built in.
3. Once the area has been excavated, the earth needs to be compacted in the patio area. This is the first of many compaction processes that take place during the foundation installation. If you're building only with hand tools, a hand tamper will do to achieve compaction. In the ideal setting, a vibratory compactor plate is used to achieve the most stable compacted base.
4. Once the area has been excavated and compacted, next you can install the edging. Edging comes in many forms: metal edging, plastic edging, stone, brick, wood. Metal and plastic edging can be purchased from landscape materials vendors in a bendable and ready-to-install sections of 10 to 20 feet by four or six inches wide. The most important part of edging installation is ensuring that it follows the 1 percent drop angle. Once the edging is installed, it becomes the guide for the rest of the patio-building process. Get the edging wrong and your final patio may not drain. To help with placing the edging material to the correct angle, use a laser level or water level. When you have the edging installed, screw it into wooden or metal stakes pounded into the ground to keep it secure. If using stone or brick, use mortar or just backfill and compact with native soil and/or gravel around the stone edging to lock it in place.
5. If the patio is being built in an environment riddled with burrowing rodents, I advise you to roll out gopher wire or hardware cloth across the entire patio area and attach it to the edging. This will keep rodents from slowly excavating underneath your final patio, creating slumps and divots over time.
6. Once the edging and metal wire is in place, dump the first layer of gravel within the edging across the patio area. A minimum of two inches of gravel is necessary to create a strong

foundation. Depending on your final surfacing (flagstone, pavers, gravel, decomposed granite), your compacted gravel may need to be three or four inches deep. If your edging material is six inches in depth, use four inches of gravel to build the foundation. If the edging is four inches in depth, use two to three inches of gravel.

7. Now it's time for the second compaction. Once you've spread the gravel throughout the entire patio area, use a vibratory compactor plate or tamper to create a solid gravel foundation.
8. Now the foundation is ready for the final surfacing. If you're using decorative gravel or decomposed granite, they can be spread directly on top of the compacted gravel base and compacted into place. If you're using flagstone or pavers, you can use some sand in between the gravel base and the final material to help level each stone or paver.

FLAGSTONE PATIO

A patio made of flagstone is beautiful and durable, offering a certain flair to the landscape with its angular shapes, patterns, and colors.

If you have been following the recipe for a patio foundation given above, flagstone can be laid right on top of compacted gravel. Flagstone at 1½ to 2½ inches *in thickness* is recommended for building a patio. Smaller pieces are too brittle (unless they're mortared), and anything thicker will require extensive labor when hauling, cutting, and placing the stone. The benefits of flagstone:

- Flagstone is beautiful, interesting, and anchors the entire landscape design aesthetic.
- Stone is durable and long lasting, making a flagstone patio an investment into the future.
- A dry laid flagstone patio (no use of mortar in the joints) allows water to percolate between the gaps between the stones, creating significantly less water runoff than a concrete or paver patio.

Here are some tips for installing your flagstone patio:

If the patio is going to be used for outdoor dining, install the flagstones with the smallest joint space between them (joints are the gaps between the stones) so that chair legs do not get stuck and become a hazard.

If you want to soften the stone look, wider joints can be left open, filled with compost, and planted with groundcover plants like mosses and thyme, bestowing veins of green plants upon the flagstone.

You will need rock chisels and cutting saws if you hope to install flagstone in tight interlocking patterns. The stone needs to be cut and/or broken along the edges to achieve tight joints and follow any curvature of sinuously edged patio designs.

Thicknesses are approximations when it comes to flagstone. If you buy two-inch-thick pieces, some may be thicker, some thinner. With the slightly varying thicknesses of each stone, you will need to add loose gravel or sand underneath to help get each stone set to the ideal level.

PAVERS/BRICK

Many varieties of pavers exist, some large and some small, with different colors, patterns, and thicknesses. Pavers require *less* labor to install than a tightly fitted patio of flagstone because the pavers are already all the same size and shape and can be fit into the desired pattern with little effort. They are durable, long-lasting, and fit together like a glove, making their joints nearly nonexistent. This means pavers are a better option for elderly people and those who use wheelchairs and walkers. Pavers are a good middle ground choice between flagstone and concrete for this reason.

Here are some tips for installing pavers:

Pavers need to be set tightly together to make sure one doesn't pop out and destabilize the whole patio. Pounding each one into a thin layer of sand during leveling adds to their durability. In order to follow curving edges, pavers need to be cut to fit against the edging. A stone-cutting wet saw is the best tool to use for this. (Use a wet saw to mitigate dust, and always wear safety gear.)

Sand is often brushed into the tiny joints between pavers/bricks to lock them in place.

DECOMPOSED GRANITE

One of the easiest ways to build a patio is with decomposed granite. This is crushed granite, which comes in a golden or gray color. Follow the patio foundation specifications given above, leaving one inch from the surface of the edging unoccupied with gravel. This final inch is where decomposed granite is spread and compacted on top of the gravel foundation.

Some of the benefits of using decomposed granite include:

- While decomposed granite is more expensive than gravel, it is much cheaper than flagstone, pavers, or concrete and much easier to install.
- The simple aesthetic of decomposed granite makes it a flexible element in almost any design.
- A patio made with decomposed granite retains effective percolation of rainwater, mitigating runoff.

Here are some tips for installing decomposed granite:

Using the edging as your guide, a long 2 by 4 wood timber or similar surface can be used to scrape the surface of the decomposed granite to the exact level of the edging.

Once the first layers have been spread, it needs to be compacted. Add more decomposed granite in any low points you discover and compact again. Continue scraping the surface using the edging as your guide until you have a perfectly compacted decomposed granite patio.

36
Landscape Pathways

Pathways are the connecting flows between landscape stewards and the land, connecting people to the garden. With well-placed and well-built pathways, you can mitigate problems in the landscape. If you can't navigate the site, how do you notice when a tree branch breaks from an old tree and needs to be cleaned up? How will you observe when disease hits a tree or when a pest issue appears in a garden bed? Part of developing easy access to the landscape is cultivating a relationship for observation, assessment, ongoing monitoring, evaluation, and tweaking. With that in mind, place the pathways in *relative location* to tools, materials, and other elements needed to care for the landscape.

Before designing a pathway, take the context in consideration. First and foremost, observe the *natural flows* and work with them. The more you work with existing walking patterns, connection points, and destination areas, the more intuitive and seamless the design will feel. Look for destinations where a beautiful view exists or a special place under a large tree can be discovered along (or at the end of) a pathway.

Pathways and trails are the networks that distribute people, resources, and yields between the landscape and the home. They provide landscape stewards access to pruning, watering, harvesting, and managing a landscape.

Pathways are built and sized for their intended use; a pathway meant to convey a tractor will look different than one meant for a wheelchair. A pathway for a wheelbarrow looks different from a path meant for a truck. For this reason, a landscape will have more than one kind of pathway. Some larger paths might be designed for daily use while others are used infrequently and only meant for seasonal harvesting.

Pathways, when built through a regenerative lens, provide ecological yields, reciprocal relationships, protection from catastrophe, and much more. A pathway can be a water-harvesting structure, catching and directing water to rain gardens and ponds. Large trails act as fuel breaks when managed in such a way with the surrounding environment. Pathways made of stone moderate microclimates, and pathways growing with nitrogen-fixing plants become soil-building superstars.

Pathways are made from many different materials. The materials you choose are driven by context. A pathway meant to be walked during a wet winter may require a stone surface material, whereas wood chips are adequate for one only used in summer months.

Similar to the veins in our bodies or the structure of irrigation systems, pathways function like arteries and capillaries. Larger pathways (arteries) provide access to equipment, fire breaks, and open areas in the landscape for recreational activities like horseshoes, throwing a frisbee, or children playing. Pathways that function like capillaries tend to be smaller, accessible with the wheelbarrow or simply sized for your two feet. These smaller paths split off from larger pathways into various planting areas and farming zones.

Pathways become a major part of the aesthetic structure of the landscape. Turn to part III of this book, where Emily Mallard talks about the difference between lines and curves in design. If a contemporary and linear design aesthetic is desired, then pathways will be designed in straighter lines and grids, whereas meandering pathway patterns can create pleasing curvatures.

WATER RUNOFF/DRAINAGE

Because pathways are major hydrological features in the landscape, do not place them randomly. Depending on the location, flow, and materials, pathways can be either beneficial or detrimental to water movement and management. Consider how they affect grading and drainage, the proximity to terraces, water-harvesting swales, rain gardens, and other drainage systems. Pathways raised up, built above grade, or placed higher in the landscape can be used to convey surface water into the contour swales and rain gardens. Your materials choices can help or hinder this process since some materials, like concrete, are completely impervious. The shape of the pathway itself will also affect drainage. Is it flat or does it have a slope? Is it crowned in the middle, curving, following contour, climbing up or down the slope? Account for all of these design factors to achieve hydrologically regenerative pathway systems.

SHAPE AND FLOW

When laying out your path, consider whether it will cross contours. When you enter the pathway or when you move from an elevated position down to a lower position, steps, landings, or junctions may be required. How you deal with these changes in elevation will affect and accentuate function, flow, and connection.

MATERIALS FOR PATHWAYS

Explore the merits of different materials for pathway design.

Gravel

Gravel pathways are some of the easiest paths to build. Also, gravel comes in so many varieties—it can be anything from gold-colored ⅜-inch chip to ½-inch salt and pepper cobbles to small round pea gravel and everything in between.

Benefits of Gravel Pathways

- During large storm events, gravel pathways percolate easily, providing a mud-free surface during wet weather.
- A gravel pathway with landscape fabric underneath is relatively low maintenance with little if any weeding required. That said, putting landscape fabric underneath gravel is an additional use of a plastic material with high embodied energy.
- Built with decorative rock, gravel paths provide a high-quality aesthetic.

Installation Tips

- Gopher wire netting underneath the gravel will mitigate damage from gophers, ground squirrels, or other burrowing rodents.
- If you're using decorative, expensive gravel for the final surface, only buy enough to cover the top inch of the pathway. Below this material, compact common blue shale gravel to act as the foundation for the more expensive decorative rock. This will save you money!
- Make sure the gravel is being put down in a graded pathway area free of organic matter. If you throw gravel down on top of wood chips or healthy topsoil, it will disappear within a year or two as it gets integrated into the biology below.

Flagstone

Some of the most beautiful landscape paths are made from flagstone. They are often built with the beautiful colors and patterns of large stones, which are both durable and flat.

Benefits of Flagstone Pathways

- The aesthetic beauty is nearly unmatched if built correctly with well-chosen stone.
- The thermal mass properties of stone aid in moderating the microclimate.
- Flagstone is a great choice for winter pathways when the land is wet or muddy.
- A flagstone pathway built with tight joints (the seams between stones)—either mortared or compacted with fine materials—makes a great surface for wheelchairs and walkers.

Installation Tips

- Choosing the right flagstone is crucial. The thickness of the stone has consequences for its durability and the labor required to move it. In general, I would never use flagstone that is less than 1½ inches thick. The thinner material is better used in concrete and mortar settings, but for a normal, dry laid flagstone pathway it would be too brittle. The best way to choose flagstone is in person, at your local materials supplier, so you can assess its color, thickness, and cost (which can vary wildly).
- Build a strong foundation. The foundation is the most important part of the pathway. If you're using flagstone with tight joints (not as stepping stones), then your foundation needs

to be well compacted and prepped to the appropriate grade. As each piece of flagstone is installed, use the edging of the foundation as a guide for leveling.

- Have stone-cutting tools on hand such as a small handheld sledgehammer, rock-cutting wedges, and possibly a stone-cutting saw. If your goal is to have clean and tight joints between stones, then you'll need to cut the stone to match edges with each other.
- If tight joints are not necessary, do your best to place stone with joints that are aesthetically pleasing and fit together as best as possible. You can plant ground cover in the spaces between the stones—for example, Corsican mint (*Mentha requienii*), elfin thyme (*Thymus serpyllum*), blue star creeper (*Isotoma fluviatilis*), and so on.
- When leveling flagstone, use some loose gravel or sand on top of the compacted area to provide some flexibility beneath the stone to get it leveled. In some cases, digging out some of the compacted material might be necessary. Take your time with leveling each stone! Make sure it is sturdy and close to perfect. This will avoid the slumping of stones down the line, which will turn your pathway into a hazard.

Stepping Stones

Stepping stone pathways are a cheaper technique than flagstone while still enabling a durable, all-season, highly aesthetic path with many benefits.

Stepping stone paths are built from large stones or pavers. These are placed as single stepping pads a few inches from one another. Vegetated areas (grasses, groundcover, or simple mulch) are usually placed between the stones.

Benefits of Stepping Stone Pathways

- Stepping stone pathways allow for excellent drainage as water can infiltrate into the soil around each stepping stone, as opposed to solid stone pathways where water has a difficult time infiltrating and runs off the surface.
- Stepping stone pathways are beautiful and whimsical, invoking a sense of mystery as they venture out into the landscape.
- A path system such as this retains the durability of a stone path while reducing the resources (using minimal stone).
- Stepping stones are much easier to install than full hardscaped pathways, saving labor, time, and money.
- These pathways function in all weather, allowing you to walk through wet and muddy conditions with relative ease.

Installation Tips

Choose stone that is two to four inches thick. A four-inch stepping stone will be much sturdier but a two-inch stone will suffice. Families may be better served by stones large enough for an adult and a child to stand on one stone together.

- Place the stones a natural walking distance from each other. The average step for most people is 18 inches, so make sure to center the stones and place them between 18 and 24 inches apart to ensure an easy walking experience for most people.
- When placing each stone, make sure they are raised slightly above the surrounding grade. Over time, if you are planting ground covers, mulching, or adding compost, stepping stones can end up buried in the landscape. It is better to raise them half an inch to an inch above grade to accommodate future changes in the landscape.
- Stepping stones need to be placed level with each other to avoid hazardous tripping conditions.

Wood Chips

Wood chip pathways can be as simple as dumping four to six inches of wood chips where you want a pathway with little to no prep underneath. Or you can place the wood chips on top of cardboard in a sheet mulching system to suppress weeds and aid in soil building. And that, folks, is all you need to do! Probably one of my favorite acts is just to dump a wheelbarrow of chips in a path and walk away. So many functions and ecological yields in that one simple act.

Benefits of a Wood Chip Path

- When you add up materials and maintenance, wood chip pathways are one of the cheapest types of pathways. Sheet-mulched paths like these will last one to two years depending on climate. You can source wood chips either for free from local arborists in your community, or they can be bought cheaply from landscape materials vendors. If you are living in an ecosystem with limited wood chip material, thick layers of straw can achieve the same result with a different aesthetic.
- A wood chip path builds soil. Cardboard and wood chips feed fungi and microorganisms in the soil, adding organic matter and carbon. This leads to better water-holding capacity of the soil and nutrient availability to plants.
- Wood chips create a "sponge" over the soil, absorbing water, reducing runoff, mitigating erosion, and aiding in overall water catchment.
- Wood chips are light and easy to move, making them one of the least labor-intensive materials for a pathway.
- Wood chips are sometimes considered a "waste" product (I think that's completely ridiculous) and making use of them can save them from being put into a landfill. (Can you see me putting my head in my hands?)

Installation Tips

- When you spread wood chips on your pathways, don't spread anything less than three inches of chips or they will be quickly consumed by soil biology and disappear. Four to eight inches is the best.

- Never use wood chips that have been dyed black or some other color. The dye impregnates the wood chips with chemicals, which are inherently degenerative instead of regenerative. A wood chip pathway is an opportunity to *reciprocate*, providing benefits to the ecology rather than adding more toxins.
- Avoid using bark mulches. These barks interact differently with water and biology. Often they are hydrophobic (repel water) and therefore reduce one of the greatest benefits of a wood chip pathway.
- Other than avoiding the bark mulch, don't be concerned with the type of wood the chips come from. Even trees that have allelopathic tendencies (meaning that plants don't like to grow under them) are fine to use as mulch because once they are ground and dried up, the volatile oils gas off and the material is ready to be consumed by fungi.
- For an added yield, you can inoculate your wood chip pathways to grow *Stropharia rugosoannulata*, a giant edible mushroom.

Vegetated Pathways

Pathways can also be growing areas for clovers, grasses, and other ground covers. This approach leverages the power of photosynthesis to generate ecological yields, turning the entire pathway into a conduit for liquid carbon to feed the biology in the soil.

Benefits of Vegetated Pathways

- Vegetated pathways add to the vibrant green of the landscape, providing a verdant, natural aesthetic.
- Vegetated pathways are better at absorbing and infiltrating water than any hardscape.
- Pathways grown from clovers and grasses aid in building soil's organic matter and feeding microorganisms.
- As long as thistles, nettles, and other spiky plants are dealt with, a vegetative pathway is the best sort of trail for walking on barefoot.
- If it is a wide path (artery) that's big enough to play games on, the grassy trail can be used for many recreational purposes.
- If clovers and other flowering ground covers are allowed to bloom, the vegetated pathway becomes a source of forage and habitat for beneficial insects. (Some might sting your bare feet so be careful.)

Installation Tips

- It is best to use seed to establish a vegetative pathway. Rolls of sod and grass are acceptable but lead to a lawn system with less biological diversity.
- Whether seeding or sodding a vegetative pathway, the path needs to be prepped. A path that has already been disturbed by tractors or other means can be graded, fertilized with compost (optional), and seeded with little prep.

- A path covered in sod will first have to be *completely* denuded of existing vegetation and prepped with compost prior to rolling sod onto the area.
- Native bunch grasses mixed with clovers make an excellent soil-building combination of seed for vegetative pathways.
- Work with the appropriate season when establishing your pathway. Seeding a vegetated pathway in the middle of a hot summer will have less success than one seeded during a wet fall, warm winter, or early spring.

Decomposed Granite

Granite crushed into nearly sand-sized aggregates is called decomposed granite. This usually comes in golden and gray colors. Decomposed granite is an excellent material for using on the surface of pathways.

Benefits of Decomposed Granite

- Easy to install once the foundation of the pathway has been built.
- Decomposed granite allows for decent water percolation into the path itself.
- Granite pathways provide some thermal mass properties, aiding in microclimate moderation.
- Many people love the aesthetic of decomposed granite pathways.

Installation Tips

- Decomposed granite is placed on top of a compacted gravel foundation.
- Use no less than one inch of decomposed granite over your gravel foundation. Up to two inches is fine if a deeper granite surface is desired.
- Use a 2 by 4 board to scrape the top of the pathway and line it up with the top edge of the pathway's foundation edging.
- The granite itself is compacted using a vibratory compactor plate (best option) or a hand tamper, providing a smooth and even surface to the pathway.

Pathway Chases

Before building the foundation for a pathway by laying stone or gravel (or any other surface for that matter), make sure to install chases underneath the pathway. This is not necessary for wood chip or vegetative pathways, but installing chases underneath every other type of pathway will save tremendous amounts of time and labor in the future.

A chase is a large pipe (usually three to four inches in diameter) placed under the path before pathway construction. These pipes provide a place to push other pipes under the pathway as needed. If you ever need to run an irrigation line, a lighting cable, or electricity, rather than having to dig up the pathway to do it, you can install your new utilities through the chases.

Water-Harvesting Pathway

Pathways can be water-harvesting systems. Making your path a water-harvesting and filtration system as described below is best done when working in small areas like urban or suburban landscapes. These pathways, while they function well, have some limiting factors when it comes to accessibility for elders, people with disabilities, and the movement of wheelbarrows and garden carts. But if you have a small space and want to gain multiple purposes out of your pathway, manage water, and provide good access to manage the garden, then this system is for you.

Design Components of a Water-Harvesting Pathway

- Place this structure far enough away from buildings that infiltrating water can't damage building foundations. Do not place your water-harvesting pathway within 10 feet of a house or any other structures.
- To achieve water catchment and infiltration, the pathway is built and dug *on contour*. That means that water will fill the path like a bathtub (or a contour swale).
- Grading of the pathway needs special consideration to get right. An overflow must be designed to ensure the pathway never washes out and that high rain events are able to move through the system without causing erosion. This means the water must have somewhere to go—a drain inlet, a rain garden, a ditch, a swale—to provide an outlet for water once it moves through the pathway.
- Once the pathway has been graded appropriately to catch, infiltrate, and release water, the next step is to fill the path with gravel. This makes walking on this water-catchment area possible. Gravel, half an inch or larger, is heavy enough that it won't float away when water enters the pathway. Make sure the gravel is *higher* than the level of the spillway. This way, during high rain events, you can still walk the path without sloshing through water.
- Large stone steps can be placed in the gravel pathway to offer a sturdier walking platform when navigating this area. Just make sure the top of the stone steps are higher than the spillway and the surrounding gravel.

Landscape Steps

In steep areas, a pathway system with landscape steps is essential. Planning a staircase in the landscape first requires an understanding of rise over run. Fortunately, we have a formula to help determine the rises and run of your steps. You'll have to make some decisions. How many steps can you fit in the area in question and what sizes can you use to determine how many to build? The steeper the area, the more steps are likely needed. But the size of the treads (where you place your feet) makes a huge difference. They should be at least one foot in depth. Also, the steeper the slope, the more material needs to be dug out and retained for deeper, wider treads.

A standard staircase design calls for a minimum of a 7¾-inch rise and a 10-inch tread for house-building purposes. This offers a natural and comfortable stepping condition for the majority of people, but conditions don't always provide for these exact dimensions, especially in topographical landscapes.

When you add rise and run (tread), it should equal approximately 18 inches (anything between 17 and 19 inches will work). Call this r(rise) + R(run) or r + R = 18 inches. Getting the steps within an inch of this formula is ideal.

The second formula is 2r + R = 25 inches. That is two rises plus one run equals 25 inches. Getting the steps within an inch of this formula is ideal.

Use these basic formulas to design landscape stairs and steps. The landscape is always confined by topography, and building steps with 7 inches risers and 11-inch treads (18-inch r + R) is not always possible.

You can make adjustments as needed. For example:

5½-inch rise + 13-inch tread = 17½-inch r + R and 24-inch 2r +R
6½-inch rise + 12-inch tread = 18½-inch r + R and 25-inch 2r +R
8-inch rise + 10-inch tread = 18-inch r+ R and 26-inch 2r + R

There are many ways to build a staircase. It can take a turn halfway up, providing a landing area. It's possible that a small number of steps with deep treads between them make it easier to walk the path than taller rises and shorter treads. If the slope is steep and the treads of the steps are on the smaller side, a railing will be necessary. For *any* sort of steep staircase, a railing is a kind gesture to elders or people with disabilities navigating those steps. Don't forget about grandma and grandpa! Once you've developed a plan and know the height of your risers and the depth of your treads, you can build the staircase.

Stone Steps. If using stone fits your budget, values, and design plan, the final result will be breathtaking. Stone makes a great staircase material because it provides an all-weather, durable tread for heavy use. In addition, stone steps anchor the landscape with stunning beauty.

Single Stone Steps. If the budget allows, single large stones prefabricated with 6-inch to 8-inch thickness (risers) make an excellent stair system. Each stone is large and heavy duty and, when the staircase is built from the bottom up, each stone placed in the system weighs down the stone *beneath* it. Make sure always to overlap them, which further stabilizes the entire staircase.

Wooden Landscape Staircase. The simplest landscape steps to build are made with wood. The same procedure is followed as above—planning out the rise over run, number of stairs, depth of treads, excavation, and prepping of the area.

These steps use wood as their risers, with eight by eight inch (or sometimes six by six) lengths acting as mini retaining walls for the earth behind each section. Wood will rot over time, so it is best to use anti-rot wood like cedar, juniper, redwood, or pressure-treated wood. (I avoid using pressure-treated wood as much as possible, but many folks use it in this application because it lasts so long.)

The wood sections can be placed on a bit of gravel to increase their longevity, but the most important part of installing a wooden step is to pin it into the earth to stabilize it completely. The best way to do this is to drill holes from the top down toward the soil. Then pound metal rebar or another metal conduit through the wood and into the earth below. This will stake each wooden step to the ground and keep it from shifting or rolling under the weight of use.

The treads behind the wooden steps can be made of compacted earth or surfaced with gravel, mulch, or any surface tread that you want. If you add gravel or mulch to the treads, make sure your riser has a *small lip* to keep these materials from slipping or washing away.

37

Terrace and Rock Wall Systems

Terraces have been used for thousands of years to provide agroecological functions in nearly every region of the planet. These systems provide generational food and shelter to agrarian communities, but even more than that—they manage water, erosion, soil health, and carbon sequestrations over vast areas. If built and maintained correctly, terraces can last for hundreds of years.

One of the best regenerative agriculture systems I've ever seen was when visiting Cinque Terre, Italy. The steep, coastal bluffs of this region are managed by a network of miles of thousand-year-old rock wall terrace systems. Among these ancient farming communities, olive forests mixed with figs, capers, grapes, and stone fruit are flourishing. This is a kind of multigenerational food system that all humans on earth deserve to live within. And, with the climate crisis on our doorstep, humanity *needs* localized food production to survive.

When terraces are integrated into the landscape, they harvest water, create accessible spaces in sloping terrain, catch and store nutrients, make for incredible planting areas, change the microclimate, and make sweeping aesthetic statements across the land.

While terraces have their place as an epic ecological design solution, I have to caution you on integrating them into your landscape plan. Terraces are *massive* interventions, which usually require large-scale earth moving and sometimes large quantities of stone or wood to retain each terrace.

Be realistic. Before designing big terraces in the landscape, make sure it's within the budget to build them. That being said, a terrace can also be built smaller; something as simple as placing a log on contour and slightly grading behind it can develop into a larger terrace over time. Work within natural patterns. Any time you slow the flow of water and sediment, it will turn into a terrace if given enough time. Be strategic and utilize terraces to increase access on slopes, increase water infiltration, and retain nutrients.

WALLS OR NO WALLS

Large terrace systems are expensive projects, sometimes the most expensive installations within a regenerative landscape, especially if rock walls are part of the system. If you are going to terrace, you need to assess whether the slope and terrace system requires retaining walls or not. Deciding on walls depends on the soil, the slope, the size of the area, the design context, your budget, and the overarching goals of the project.

With no walls, a terrace project will be much cheaper and easier to build. Without walls, terraces need to be spaced farther apart from each other. Terrace slopes need to be graded to gentle angles of repose to ensure their stability over time. Strategic planting is commonly used to secure the sloping areas between terraces with masses of roots.

Terraces on steep slopes or terraces placed close to each other do need walls. Walls are often used when the landscape is small and/or steep with few flat areas. Terrace wall systems maximize usable space by providing flat zones in an otherwise sloped landscape.

When building terraces, equipment is commonly used to excavate the large amounts of soil needed to install the project.

TO CONSIDER WHEN EXCAVATING TERRACES

- If the terraces are over eight feet wide, it's best to segregate the topsoil from subsoil during excavation to make sure the topsoil ends up on top when the project is complete. If you start the terraces from the bottom of the slope, then topsoil can be removed from the above terraces and dumped on the terraces below, but this method leaves the top terrace without topsoil. In that case, topsoil from the first terraces can be hauled to the top terrace or topsoil excavated from the site (from a road, patio, or pathway, for instance) can be hauled to cover the top terrace.

- In addition, segregating the materials results in the most stable system. Build the base of each terrace out of the subsoil first—keying into the subsurface—then return topsoil for the final layer. Your entire approach will depend on the situation, the size of the terraces, the size of the area, and the equipment you have on hand.

- If you're building smaller, shallower terraces, then segregating the soil is probably not necessary and would add complexity and extra labor/machine costs to the project. In this case, terraces are barely cutting into the subsoil at all and each earthen bench is cut straight from the ground with all material left in place in the new shape of a terrace.

- Be highly strategic when excavating your terraces to ensure soil and wall-building materials are moved the least number of times. It happens too often on these projects that material is staged in such a way that it has to be moved two or three more times than needed to get the job done. Getting this part right could save weeks of labor and thousands of dollars.

Staging Terrace Projects

The correct staging of material is crucial when you're building retaining wall terraces. For large projects it is best to stage and build walls section by section to keep the work area clean and the movability of machines, people, and materials as flexible as possible.

Avoid overly compacting areas that are going to be planting zones. Staging and moving soil and how machines move across the land as the walls are built all have compaction consequences. By spending time planning the staging, phasing, and installation of materials, you could save tens of thousands of dollars on a large project.

Combining Terraces, Swales, and Rain Gardens

A terrace system can be integrated with contour swales and rain gardens to optimize their water-harvesting functions. Sometimes terraces have contour ditches on the upslope side with pathway systems into them, following along running surface water.

Terraces are commonly built on or near contour to grant the best flat areas and to harvest water. Water flowing from terraces may still need management once it leaves the terrace. Place rain gardens and contour swales at these junction points to keep the water moving slowly and infiltrating into the aquifer. Combine all the water-harvesting and erosion control tools described in part V that work harmoniously with your terrace systems.

ROCK WALLS AND ALTERNATIVES

If the goals, contexts, and values of the project lead you to design rock walls, you won't be disappointed in the end result. But before you make that decision, make sure to look into less expensive wall-building materials such as wood and cinder block. Neither of these two options will last as long or provide as many functions as a rock wall, but the savings on materials and labor might be the difference between being able to build a terrace retaining wall or not.

Benefits of Rock Walls

Longevity/Stability

Not many systems that humans build are as durable and long lasting as rock wall structures. If built correctly, with the right stone, these are systems that will outlast everything else in the built environment.

Habitat

Rock walls are remarkable habitats for lizards (and many other beneficial beings). The small, cool cavities between stone joints provide a perfect home for lizards, who are voracious insect eaters and will beneficially impact pest problems in the landscapes.

Microclimate Moderation

By installing a rock wall, you create a microclimate around the walls that warms the area at night, potentially combating frost in temperate climates. In hot climates, rock walls absorb heat during a hot day, which cools the surrounding area and provides opportunities to grow sensitive plants behind and around walls that may not thrive elsewhere in the landscape.

Disadvantages of Rock Walls

Costs

Rock walls are incredibly expensive to build. If stone materials need to be purchased, they could amount to tens of thousands of dollars just for the materials.

Labor

Stone is heavy and awkward to move and stack, making a rock wall one of the most labor-intensive systems to build in the landscape—not an endeavor that can be rushed. It takes not only heavy work but also a focused and calm mental strategy to complete the project. Large walls could take months to build.

Embodied Energy

If rock resources are present in the landscape, then a rock wall has little embodied energy. Unfortunately, the majority of rock walls are sourced from stone material that has been mined and potentially hauled from far away. It is always best to use stone mined from your local community to reduce the embodied energy of the product. Do your research and try to source materials as locally as possible.

URBANITE WALLS

Urbanite is broken pieces of concrete that are destined for the landfill, created during construction processes where old concrete walls and foundations are dismembered and the materials thrown away. This material offers a highly functional solution to the regenerative landscape.

Generated in urban communities in great quantities, urbanite can usually be sourced easily and for free. This material is perfect for building hardscaped walls as an alternative to using stone.

An urbanite wall has all of the same benefits of a stone wall without many of the high energy and high-cost disadvantages. It is easier to build with since it comes preformed in thicknesses of four to six inches. The top and bottom of each piece is flat, making them easy to stack. Simply build the wall like you would a dry stacked rock wall, but it will be easier and faster.

BOULDER WALLS

Boulder walls are the most natural-looking type of rock wall. I love building boulder walls because they are less labor intensive than a dry stacked wall and are built to look as though they have been there for thousands of years.

Boulders are heavy, but placing a single boulder will fill a large space. This means that boulder walls can be installed fairly quickly and without the enormous labor required of a dry stacked rock wall. It's important to note that boulders are installed using machines these days, so an experienced operator is required. Boulder walls will last hundreds to thousands of years.

Placing Boulders

Avoid placing boulders in a straight line. Sometimes you have to work with straight lines at the edge of a road or other structure, but in general, the best approach is to place some boulders farther back, some higher up, some clumped in groups of two or three. Aim to make the boulder wall look like something you would find in a mountain range or on a hike through rocky terrain. Leave gaps—some small, some large—between the boulders to enhance the natural and organic look and allow for water to percolate between them.

Use a mix of different sized boulders when building the wall so it feels like it belongs in a natural setting. Create interest and plan for a diversity of functions when creating these systems—use flat-topped stones for benches and tabletops, create small caves and grottos—get as creative as possible when placing boulders to make your landscape a paradise.

PART VII
Planting Earth

38
Revegetate the Planet

We all know the world is in crisis—extreme climate events, food shortages, failing energy systems, income inequality, culture wars, health crises. Reading the news or scrolling through social media, one can witness catastrophe happening all around. Regenerative concepts, when put into action, form one antidote to global catastrophe. My hope is that you find some sense of empowerment here. Revegetating planet earth starts in your own backyard. It starts with every inch of land where you can plant seeds, cuttings, and roots. Your actions make a difference. And *planting earth* offers many beneficial implications that ripple across generations.

In part I of this book we explored the processes that the earth implements to create the conditions for life. The core of these processes—sequestering carbon, building healthy soil, regulating the climate and the atmosphere, and transforming sunlight into food—is photosynthesis. When we focus our lives on revegetating the planet—turning man-made deserts back to forests, diversifying our landscapes with multilayered systems of plant communities, turning schools into gardens, cities into forests, and managing ecologies with biodiversity in mind—we repair broken water cycles and draw down carbon from the atmosphere.

Through the act of planting, we can grow enough food to feed everyone in our communities and create habitats for threatened species to bounce back from the edge of extinction. We cool our cities down, reducing the use of electricity to power air-conditioners. We grow local materials for building our homes and businesses. Famine disappears, freshwater returns, and we live in paradise gardens once again. This is why planting the earth is one solution that solves many problems. This is the power of a seed in your hand and the power of a community that thinks like a watershed. I know it sounds idealistic but this is the future we all deserve. It's a future worth planting for.

REPAIRING THE WORLD WITH PLANTS

The plant world literally turns sunlight into life through the process of photosynthesis. But plants do so much more. Revegetating the land also means repairing erosion, filtering water, providing food for all life, generating building materials, saving endangered species, developing healthy soil, and sequestering carbon. In your landscape you can generate these functions simply through the plants you choose for your garden.

An Ecological Planting Strategy

Much of what makes up the material fabric of basic human civilization can be cultivated, harvested, and processed in our regenerative landscapes. Plants are powerful allies for restoring the biosphere and our place in the webs of life. The plant world is highly diverse, complex, and generous with its offerings to people and ecosystems. We have only to accept their gifts, listen to their ways, and propagate them at will. If we focus on revegetating the earth, every corner of our world will once again be its own version of a paradise garden.

Plant Medicine

Many modern and ancient medicines are derived from plants. This time-tested herbal healing is accessible to you through the landscape. Remedies to reduce anxiety, aid sleep, support digestion, heal skin issues, relieve pain, and so much more can all be grown and made in the landscape. Herbal salves and poultices are easy to make as needed for you and your family. Many of these plants serve multiple functions—they attract beneficial insects, build soil, create beauty, and provide food.

Making herbal medicine in the garden has become one of my favorite activities. We experience the abundance of plant relationships by using our garden salves and drinking herbal teas every day. My kids know the exact plants to harvest in emergencies. They start by using yarrow (*Achillea millefolium*) to mitigate infection and follow that up with poultices made with the amazing tissue-healing properties of plantain (*Plantago*).

Plants for Controlling Erosion

The loss of topsoil and sediment into watersheds is a global catastrophe of epic proportions.[1] Unchecked erosion leads to the complete destruction of waterways and the loss of arable lands. Managing water is the first step, but it's the plant community that provides the long-term solution to not only mitigating erosion but stopping it completely. Land covered in appropriate plants will not blow or wash away. It's as simple as that.

Soil Building

Plants build soil through many methods—fixing nitrogen, feeding the soil biomass, releasing plant exudates to feed soil biology, cooling the surface of the ground, creating living mulch, and so much more. In your planting plan, incorporate these functions and species throughout the entire landscape to continuously support a thriving soil ecology.

Water Filtration

Plants serve as primary or secondary filtration systems for virtually every type of pollution of the world's waters. Through the process of phytoremediation, plant communities filter toxins from water and soil.[2] By taking advantage of this process in the landscape, we can filter ponds, clean graywater and blackwater, and—in conjunction with bacteria, fungi, and other organisms—use plants to filter water polluted with chemicals and heavy metals.

Food Production

One of the greatest benefits of developing ecological landscapes is becoming a producer rather than a consumer of an agricultural system that devastates the biosphere. In the regenerative landscape, the act of growing your own food not only saves you money and increases your health, but you also become a vehicle for managing water and soil with regenerative practices.

Not all regenerative landscapes have to grow food. The planting system must adhere to all the complex layers of context that make up the project and its goals. That being said, growing food doesn't have to look like raised vegetable beds and fruit trees. Stacking functions by restoring a native savannah with oaks (*Quercus*) and native grasses is a different kind of food production system—one that has lasted millennia and will remain to feed our descendants long after our own bodies have returned to the soil. Native people have survived eating these wild foods for hundreds of generations while ecosystems thrived. Ecological yields and human yields are not mutually exclusive.

Nutrient-Dense Food

Food is more than its color, its taste, and its shape. A tomato (*Solanum lycopersicum*) grown on a conventional farm is vastly different from one grown on an organic farm. And the tomato grown on your own regenerative homestead, in soil tended with the highest principles of soil health, will be different from an organic monocultural tomato.

Obviously the conventionally grown tomato is sprayed with pesticides and fungicides, but what makes all these tomatoes most different from each other is the volume of nutrients available from each one. Nutrient-dense food is food filled with minerals, vitamins, proteins, and other nutrients that are easily taken up by your body when eating.[3] A fruit or vegetable grown in ecologically managed soil, grown in a biodiverse setting, where the above and below ground biology is diverse and thriving, will yield food with more readily available nutrients for your body.

When we grow food in the regenerative landscape, we are growing the most nutrient-rich food on the planet in our own front and backyards with our own hands. It may seem simple, and for some it may even seem ridiculous. But the truth is, this is how humans lived for thousands of years before the advent of conventional agriculture. Whether as hunters and gatherers harvesting nutrient-dense food from the ecology or as farmers tending the land, selecting and breeding their foods, most of our ancestors had a personal connection with the plants and animals they consumed. And because these plants and animals thrived in complete ecosystems, the food itself was more nutritious.[4]

Edible Landscaping

Growing food in the landscape doesn't just mean raised beds planted with vegetables. Many species of plants are edible and medicinal while also providing numerous landscape functions. In fact, many plants listed as "ornamental" and used in conventional and large-scale landscapes are also edible. Edible plants come in every form and shape you can imagine, from low-maintenance ground covers to towering hundred-foot-tall trees.

Edible species can be evergreen, deciduous, biannual, or annual. Choose species that are not only edible but that also provide privacy screens, cut flowers, crafting wood, and so much more. Don't be afraid to plant edible species throughout the landscape. The future of the globalized food system is unknown and will be affected by many factors including climate change, access to arable land, cost of transportation, and health hazards. You'll be happy about your edible landscape when your favorite foods become too expensive or nonexistent. Even more, having a relationship with the land and feeling the satisfaction of harvesting, prepping, and eating the nutrient-dense food you've grown in a garden that cares for all life is one of the greatest feelings of all. It's a service to your own health and the health of the entire world.

PLANT HARDINESS ZONES

Plant hardiness zones describe a variety of different climates and microclimates around the world. When you know the zone your landscape is within, you can better choose species that will thrive there. Plant hardiness zones are categorized by their average extreme *minimum* temperature.

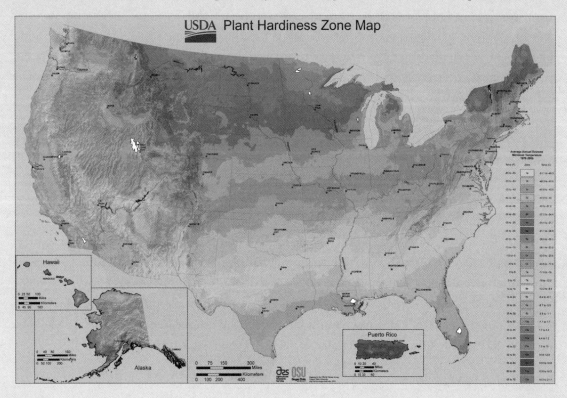

There are 13 plant hardiness zones averaged over data collected 1976–2005. While the climate is changing and the zones are moving around, the hardiness zones categories are still helpful:[5]

Zone 1	Zone 3	Zone 5	Zone 7	Zone 9	Zone 11	Zone 13
-60 to -50F	-40 to -30F	-20 to -10 F	0 to 10F	20 to 30F	40 to 50F	60 to 70F
-51.1 to -45.6 C	-40 to -34.4C	-28.9 to -23.3C	-17.8 to -12.2C	-6.7 to -1.1C	4.4 to 10C	15.6 to 21.1C

Zone 2	Zone 4	Zone 6	Zone 8	Zone 10	Zone 12	
-50 to -40F	-30 to -20F	-10 to 0F	10 to 20F	30 to 40F	50 to 60F	
-45.6 to -40 C	-34.4 to -28.9C	-23.3 to -17.8C	-12.2 to -6.7C	-1.1 to 4.4C	10 to 15.6C	

39
Landscape Planting Plans

The term *landscape planting plan* comes right out of professional landscape design jargon. These plans are specific layers in a landscape map that represents every plant proposed for the landscape. Each species of plant has its own graphic symbol, which is sized to correspond with the scale of the design. Existing plants that will be kept in the landscape also get their own graphic symbol. The whole planting plan is developed in great detail with each symbol representing the size of the plant at maturity. For instance, an avocado (*Persea americana*) tree placed on the plan will show a canopy size that reflects how large the avocado tree will grow.

Hatching marks are used for ground covers, grasses, and wildflowers and decoded by a legend on the plan. Planting plans will look quite busy, especially for larger projects. Because every plant is represented on the plan, this can mean hundreds of symbols.

A spreadsheet of the species and number of plants is often placed on the plan or added along with the planting plan. These plant details will often include the common name, Latin name, and sometimes the functions or uses of each plant.

If you are a professional providing a planting plan to a client, this level of detail and information represents an incredible service to your client. For folks who are designing landscapes for themselves, a detailed planting plan as described above is probably not necessary. A simpler form of planting plan will help you design plant communities, functions, and locations before you plan out the materials and installation budget for the project. Let's take a deeper look at the many facets of creating a planting plan for your regenerative landscape.

Assess Existing Vegetation

What, if any, existing vegetation do you need to remove to achieve your regenerative landscape goals? Ask yourself, why do they need to be removed? Don't make this decision lightly. What ecological functions does the existing vegetation provide the landscape? Are human yields being provided by existing vegetation? Identify the benefits of all existing vegetation and keep as much of it as you can to avoid unnecessarily disturbing the ecology.

Plant Lists

Make lots of plant lists! Use plant community categories. Make a list of edible plants that grow in the shade. Make a list of edible plants that grow in full sun. Make a list of privacy hedge plants that build soil. Make a list of plants that work under an oak. Make a list of perennial

LANDSCAPE PLANTING PLANS

Code	Botanical Name	Common Name	#	Size
AFCG	Achillea filipendulina 'Coronation Gold'	Fernleaf Yarrow	10	4"
API	Achillea millefolium 'Pink Island Form'	Common Yarrow	15	4"
AR	Agastache rupestris	Sunset Hyssop	24	4"
ASFA	Asclepias fasicularis	Narrow-Leaf Milkweed	8	4"
BOF	Borago officinalis	Borage	37	4"
CEVE	Ceanothus velutinus	Snowbrush	5	5G
CILI	Citrus × limon	Lemon	1	5G
CRMU	Citrus reticulata 'Murcott'	Murcott Mandarin	1	5G
CIRE	Citrus reticulata	Mandarin	1	5G
DKFU	Diospyros kaki 'Fuyu'	Fuyu Persimmon	1	5G
ES	Echinacea Sombrero Adobe Orange	Coneflower	32	4"
ELMU	Elaeagnus multiflora	Goumi	4	1G
ERG	Erigeron glaucus	Beach Aster	31	4"
FESE	Feijoa sellowiana	Pineapple Guava	1	1G
FCOS	Ficus carica 'Osborne'	Osborne Fig	1	5G
FA	Fragaria vesca 'Alexandria'	Alpine Strawberry	15	4"
HAVI	Hardenbergia violacea	Lilac Vine	4	1G
LIPE	Limonium perezii	Statice	12	4"
LM	Lobularia maritima	Sweet Alyssum	31	4"
LUAB	Lupinus albifrons	Silver Lupine	4	1G
PEFR	Passiflora edulis 'Frederick'	Frederick Passion Fruit	1	1G
PABA	Persea americana 'Bacon'	Avocado 'Bacon'	1	5G
PAME	Persea americana 'Mexicola'	Avocado 'Mexicola'	1	5G
PABL	Prunus armeniaca 'Blenheim' on Citation	Blenheim Apricot	1	5G
PCSE	Pyrus communis 'Seckel' on OHxF333	Seckel Pear	1	5G
RHRH	Rheum rhabarbarum	Rhubarb	2	1G
RUCP	Ribes uva-crispa 'Pixwell'	'Pixwell' Gooseberry	8	1G
RICA	Rubus idaeus 'Caroline'	raspberry	2	1G
RIHE	Rubus idaeus 'Heritage'	raspberry	2	1G
SLSB	Salvia leucantha 'Santa Barbara'	Santa Barbara Sage	9	1G
SIM	Sidalcea malviflora	Checkerbloom	32	4"
SYOF	Symphytum officinale	Common Comfrey	26	4"
TLCO	Tagetes lemmonii 'compacta'	Copper Canyon Daisy	41	1G
VCSO	Vaccinium ' Southmoon'	Southmoon Blueberry	6	1G

Plant list for ordering. Designed by Damien McAnany.

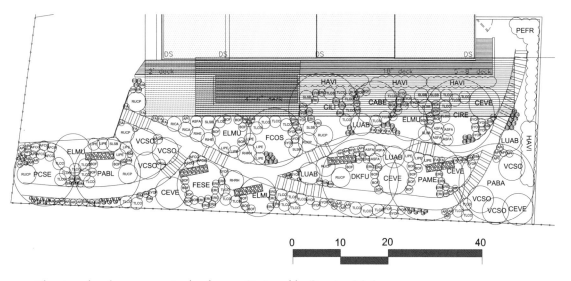

Planting plan for regenerative landscape. Designed by Damien McAnany.

cut flowers that bloom most of the year. Whatever context you have inherited in the landscape, develop as many different plant community lists as possible. Let your imagination, creativity, and excitement run wild for a time. This helps get you into researcher mode where you discover new exciting species that meet the context and goals of the landscape.

Once you've developed and refined your plant lists and plant communities, put them onto the planting plan. What you will quickly realize is that the landscape itself can only fit so many plants. Your plant list gets further refined as you start to map the planting plan onto the design.

Mapping Your Planting Plan

Your planting plan is a stand-alone design layer that doesn't include the other design concepts like grading and utility systems. The planting plan itself is so detailed and busy that there won't be no room for many other features. You have to figure out how to fit every plant on the design, scaling the symbols to represent smaller and larger plants. This way, you quickly discover how many plants and what kinds fit in each planting area.

Play around with different plant communities and planting formations until you form a design that meets all design needs and integrates ecologically and aesthetically. Once you have a workable version, clean it up and scan it to present to the project stakeholders.

Useful Plants

In a regenerative landscape, the goal is to advance the life-generating process of the earth, generating yields for all beings. To better achieve this goal, choose planting systems that provide a multitude of yields and benefits. Many plant species provide not only food but also habitat for beneficial insects, beauty, and more. Avoid developing a planting plan populated only with plants with little use (often called ornamentals).

Choosing plants with multiple uses exemplifies regenerative design principles. Some plants provide five or more reciprocal functions in the landscape. A well thought out combination of plants and their uses creates resiliency and redundancy throughout the system, ensuring a level of relationship diversity usually found only in pristine ecosystems.

The Right Plants for the Space

For years I have wanted to grow avocados, so much so that I researched the best varieties for my area and planted many avocado trees in different microclimates hoping to someday obtain a harvest. Well, none of those trees have worked out so far. The Northern California coast doesn't always make for a good avocado harvest. Only very special microclimates in my bioregion sustain avocados from seed to fruit.

You may have plants and trees that you love, crave, and want to grow that your landscape and your climate do not support. Accept this and move on. There is no point in spending money and time trying to grow plants that do not want to grow in your landscape. Sure, you can get them to sprout and maybe even to grow into a sickly tree or plant. These plants will most likely always need more attention than better-suited species, and they might eventually succumb to pests or disease.

Choose plants that thrive in your landscape setting and that literally fit the space. Specifically, don't plant trees and shrubs that will grow too large for the intended space. If you do, you will spend time every year cutting them back and retraining them. If your landscape is a tiny urban lot, it's probably ill advised to grow a 200-foot redwood tree (*Sequoia sempervirens*). It seems obvious, but this concept is clearly not practiced throughout landscaping and gardening industries.

Extending Flowering Times

In temperate and subtropical climates, flowering plants grow all year round. With a little extra planning, your landscape can also provide nectar and forage for birds and insects throughout most of the year. An extremely cold climate will need a greenhouse but it can be done.

I try to incorporate flowering and insect/bird forage plants in every zone of the landscape in every season possible.

In the winter, food sources are generally scarce for the pollinator community as many trees and shrubs die back in the cold.[1] That is why, in many environments, some native plants and trees flower at this time of year, providing sustenance to pollinators. For instance, where I live, one of the first trees to flower—California bay (*Umbellularia californica*)—does so in late winter. This evergreen species provides important food for pollinators when nearly all other trees are dormant. My guess is that there are similar species that provide the same function in your environment as well.

In the landscapes you design, you must mimic this pattern if possible, providing year-round resources to feed ecosystem communities. Some plant choices provide for both the wild community and the human community simultaneously, adding even more function to the landscape. Choose wisely.

Evergreen Versus Deciduous

While creating your planting plan, pay close attention to how many evergreen or deciduous species you place in the plan, referring to your aesthetic goals for the project. Plant not only trees but also herbaceous perennials—plants that either remain covered in leaves throughout the year or die to the ground only to come back in the springtime.

If you accidentally design a section of the landscape that will be dominated by deciduous trees and dormant perennials, the winter aesthetic of that area will be sparse. If that is acceptable then there's no problem, but if you hope to develop a landscape that invokes a vibrant green aesthetic for as much of the year as possible, integrating evergreen trees and perennial plants among the deciduous species is the best option.

In a backyard food forest, for instance, you might plant many deciduous cultivars like apple (*Malus domestica*), pear (*Pyrus*), plum (*Prunus domestica*), and peach (*Prunus persica*). In the winter, all these trees drop their leaves and only the branches remain. Beneath these species, consider

PLANTING LEGEND

CODE	Botanical	Common	#	Size
AO	Acer pal. 'Orangeola'	Orangeola Japanese Maple	1	5G
AC	Achillea filipendulina 'Coronation Gold'	Coronation Gold Hybrid Yarrow	9	4"
AP	Achillea millefolium 'Pink Island Form'	Island Pink Yarrow	19	4"
AD	Actinidia deliciosa	Kiwi 2- female, 1 male	3	BR-S
AR	Agastache rupestris	Licorice Mint	24	4"
AQ	Akebia quinata	Five-Leaf Akebia	1	1G
AF	Asclepias fasicularis	Narrow-Leaf Milkweed	7	4"
BO	Borago officinalis	Borage	16	4"
CA	Citrus aurantifolia 'Dwarf Bearss Seedless'	Dwarf Bearss Seedless Lime	1	5G
CR	Citrus reticulata	Mandarin Orange	1	5G
CI	Citrus X 'Improved Meyer'	Improved Meyer Lemon	1	15G
DI	Diospyros kaki 'Izu'	'Izu' Oriental Persimmon	1	BR-T
EG	Elaeagnus ebbingei gilt edge	Elaeagnus	10	1G
EM	Elaeagnus multiflora	Goumi	3	1G
EE	Elaeagnus x ebbingii	Elaeagnus	3	1G
EW	Erigeron glaucus 'Wayne Roderick'	Seaside Daisy, Beach Fleabane	20	4"
EJ	Eriobotrya japonica	Loquat	1	5G
FS	Feijoa sellowiana	Pineapple Guava	2	1G
FE	Fragaria × ananassa 'Earliglow'	Earliglow June Bearing Strawberry	7	4"
FA	Fragaria vesca 'Alexandria'	Alexandria Alpine Strawberry	8	4"
FW	Fragaria x 'Wonderful Pine'	Wonderful Pine Strawberry	8	4"
HV	Hardenbergia violacea	Purple Lilac Vine	2	1G
HF	Heuchera 'Firefly'	Firefly Coral Bells	12	4"
JN	Juniperus procumbens 'Nana'	Dwarf Japanese Garden Juniper	4	1G
LP	Limonium perezii	Sea Lavender	27	4"
LH	Lonicera japonica 'Halliana'	Hall's Japanese Honeysuckle	2	1G
LA	Lupinus albifrons	Silver Bush Lupine	7	1G
MM	Malus Multi-Graft	Multi-Graft Apple	1	BR-T
MD	Muhlenbergia dumosa	Bamboo Muhly, Giant Muhly	5	1G
ON	Ophiopogon planiscapus 'Nigrescens'	Black Mondo Grass	16	4"
PF	Passiflora edulis 'Frederick'	Frederick Passion Fruit	1	1G
PT	Pinus thunbergii 'Thunderhead'	Thunderhead Japanese Black Pine	1	BR-T
PC	Prunus avium 'Craig's Crimson' on Newroot-1	Craig's Crimson Cherry	1	BR-T
PP	Prunus persica 4 in 1 (curl resistant)	4 Curl Resistant Varieties of Peach	1	BR-T
PB	Prunus salacina 'Beauty'	Beauty Asian Plum	1	BR-T
PM	Pyrus pyrifolia Multi-graft	Multi-graft Asian Pear	1	BR-T
RD	Rhododendron 'Dora Amateis'	Dora Amateis Rhododendron	4	1G
RC	Ribes nigrum 'Consort'	Consort Black Currant	3	BR-S
RB	Ribes rubrum 'Blanka'	Blanka White Currant	3	BR-S
RW	Ribes sativum 'Wilder'	Wilder Red Currant	3	BR-S
RA	Rubus idaeus 'Addison'	Addison Raspberry	2	BR-S
RF	Rubus idaeus 'Fall Gold'	Fall Gold Everbearing Raspberry	2	BR-S
RJ	Rubus idaeus 'Jewel Black'	Jewel Black Raspberry	2	BR-S
SM	Sidalcea malviflora	Checkerbloom, Prairie Mallow	20	4"
TL	Tagetes lemmonii	Mexican bush marigold	7	1G
TJ	Trachelospermum jasminoides	Star Jasmine	2	1G
UM	Ugni molinae	Chilean Guava	2	1G
VC	Vaccinium corymbosum 'Chandler'	Chandler Blueberry	3	BR-S
VL	Vaccinium corymbosum 'Legacy'	Legacy Blueberry	2	BR-S
VO	Vaccinium corymbosum 'O'Neal'	O'Neal Southern Highbush Blueberry	2	BR-S
WS	Wisteria sinensis	Chinese wisteria	1	1G

Planting plan legend. Designed by Damien McAnany.

planting evergreen shrubs like rosemary (*Salvia rosmarinus*), sages (*Salvia* spp), or any evergreen, shrub, or herb that fits your climate and context. These understory species will maintain a vibrant green or silver hue throughout the winter (unless covered in snow). Plan the aesthetic of each landscape zone using the lens of evergreen versus deciduous to grow fuller, more verdant gardens.

Permaculture Zoning in Planting Plans

In part III of this book, we explored the use of the zoning method in permaculture design. This is the placement of plants and elements in the landscape by their relationship/management needs. Items that need daily attention are in zone 1, weekly attention in zone 2, monthly attention in zone 3, and so forth.

This concept is also highly useful when developing your planting plan. If you don't plant according to zones, it could cause problems down the line. For instance, if you place a lemon tree (*Citrus limon*) in the back corner of the garden where nobody visits, there's a good chance that when the lemons are ready to be harvested, they will be forgotten. A walnut tree (*Juglans* spp) planted right outside the back door won't require much tending for most of the year until it drops its leaves or nuts. In this way, placing a large walnut tree in zone 1 doesn't make a lot of sense if other aspects of the plan require a daily relationship.

Plan for Maturity

Don't plan based on what your plants look like immediately after they're planted. Imagine what they are going to look like 5 or 10 years from now. That is what you're designing—not next year or the year after, but the mature phase once everything has grown in.

Choosing Plant Sizes

You've developed the palette of plants you're going to use for the landscape. You know the species, cultivars, and structure of your planting plan. Now it's time to make decisions about how to source your plants (propagating them yourself is always the best) and what size plants are best to put in the ground. If you are purchasing plants from the nursery, the size of the plants is a huge decision. The larger the plant you buy, the more expensive it's going to be. If you want a five-foot oak tree, purchasing a tree that size may cost over a hundred dollars, whereas a one-gallon-sized tree costs only around $6 or $7.

Smaller plants also have the advantage of root systems that have been less disturbed. Larger plants have often been transplanted into larger and larger pots during their lifecycle, with bound-up root systems that grow more slowly once put in the ground. Smaller plants will sometimes grow more vigorously and become larger over time than larger plants installed at the same time. Sometimes it pays off to start small as the yields are greater if you're willing to wait for them.

Buying larger plants makes sense when a need for an immediately established landscape is driving the project. It's great to plant smaller plants for the reasons mentioned above, but it can take them three to five years to establish themselves. If your landscape is located at a business or school, it's likely that a more established landscape early on is necessary.

Factor in the context of the project, the budget, and the time available for establishing the plant community when choosing the size of your plants. My personal approach is generally a strategic mix of smaller and larger plants. I'll often order 75 percent of the planting plan in smaller plants and the remaining 25 percent in 15- to-24-gallon size. The more mature plants can be spread out across the landscape to create an immediate sense of establishment.

40
Plant Communities

The term *plant community* is a loose phrase used in this book to describe different groupings of plants. In essence, a plant community is a collection of plants that, when grown together, either support each other in some way or combine to meet a specific aesthetic or function. A plant community can be as simple as a native landscape, a vegetable bed, or an erosion-control planting—each represents a specific community of plants.

In regenerative landscapes, choose plant communities that perform as many functions as possible while generating as many ecological yields as possible. Make sure to choose plants that are compatible and the landscape will flourish. Characteristics like growth structure, sun, and water needs all need to work together. Avoid incompatible combinations; for instance, if you design a plant community that combines drought-tolerant plant species with wetland plants, you'll either be giving too much water or not enough for the whole community to be happy.

Structural Plant Combinations

The structural growth pattern of plants is of vital importance in your planning process. How tall and wide will each plant grow? Does it have low-growing branches or will it grow tall and lanky, reaching for the stars? Is it a plant that sprawls across the ground yet needs partial sun, or a short-growing herb that lounges in full shade? The size and shape of plants at maturity makes a huge difference in their success when combined with others to form a plant community.

Below we discuss the vertical layering of plants within a food forest. This is helpful when thinking about plant shapes and structure in a forest setting. Design using plant structures for each specific planting area; each zone gets its own structure while also considering the interaction with other landscape areas. Blend shapes and sizes into a visual feast of natural beauty and function.

STRUCTURAL GROWTH PATTERNS OF TREES AND PLANTS

Upper Canopy

The upper canopy of an ecosystem (landscape) consists of the tallest trees in the system. These tower above the landscape, providing shade, habitat, and other yields. Upper canopy trees need to be placed carefully to make sure they support, rather than hinder, the growth of the rest of the landscape. **Approximate growth height 25 to 250 feet.**

(continued)

Lower Canopy

Below the soaring upper canopy are lower canopy trees, which still produce a medium to large canopy but are kept below 25 feet in height. Many fruit and nut trees fall into this category; in many food forest and orchard systems, lower canopy trees make up the largest vertical layer of growth in the landscape. **Approximate growth height 10 to 25 feet.**

Shrubs

Shrubs are perfect for hedges, creating privacy and obtaining a variety of yields without growing too large. Shrubs often exist in the edges of a forest ecosystem or as a unique ecology unto themselves (chaparral), making way for larger tree systems to succeed them. Many glorious species like citrus trees, berries, guavas, nitrogen fixers, and more grow in shrub form. **Approximate growth height 4 to 10 feet.**

Vines

In the tropics, vines grow up trees, using them as scaffolding. In temperate climates, vines sprawl across the ground or use live, dying, or dead trees to grow on. In the regenerative landscape, vines are used to colonize arbors, trellises, fences, and other architectural systems to provide shade, privacy, beauty, and other yields. **Approximate growth length 4 to 100 feet long.**

Herbaceous Plants

Herbaceous plants include thousands of different species and potential fits for your landscape. These are plants that provide flowers, food, medicine, habitat, and so much more. These species fit into many niches, whether they need full sun or full shade and everything in between. **Approximate growth height 6 inches to 6 feet.**

Ground Cover

Ground covers are living mulches that spread across the ground, protecting it from sun, wind, and rain. These species also come in many forms, providing food like berries, mints, and flowers. **Approximate growth height 1 inch to 3 feet.**

Bulb/Rhizomes

Underground bulbs and rhizomes are another great addition to the landscape. These species usually grow for one season and then die back until the next year depending on the climate. Some bulbs and rhizomes offer the best foods, medicines, and flowers, such as ginger (*Zingiber officinale*), tulips (*Tulipa* spp), saffron (*Crocus sativus*), and turmeric (*Curcuma longa*). **Approximate growth height 1 to 4 feet.**

Zone by Zone

When developing your landscape plan, notice that each landscape area has a specific microclimate that also overlaps with your specific permaculture zones. For each of these areas, develop a community of plants that fits all design goals, structurally fits the area, and complements the existing ecology. That's a lot of factors! But don't get overwhelmed—be patient with the process and trust your site assessment process and your intuition. When the correct plant community comes together, you'll know, and it will be simpler than you think. Remember the regenerative design principle of *relationship design*? This principle is fundamental to the process of creating plant communities.

PLANTS BY FUNCTION

In a regenerative landscape, as in all pristine natural settings, plant communities develop through the functional niches that plants provide the ecosystem. Function is anything from food production to building soil, casting shade, providing for wildlife, and filtering graywater. The best landscapes combine and synthesize various functions in order to achieve as many diverse relationships as possible.

Soil-Building Plants

As discussed in part IV, plants that feed microorganisms, produce heavy loads of biomass, and fix nitrogen are all considered soil-building plants. Really, every plant is a soil builder but some are better than others.

Throughout your entire landscape, the function of soil-building plants is best incorporated into all plant communities. This is reciprocal design at its finest—organize plant communities in such a way where the soil is constantly being renewed with nutrients and fed with biomass, providing surrounding plants with the benefit of available nutrients and water-holding capabilities.

Native Gardens

If we want to follow the original operating systems of the land, then we must look to native plants first. These are the plants best suited to your environment, having evolved over thousands if not millions of years with the soils, geology, climates, and seasons of the land.

Many regenerative landscapers believe that native species do not meet the goals of growing food, providing beauty, and designing ideal spaces for recreation. That kind of thinking is a result of the shallow relationship landscapers have with native plant communities. In the most regenerative model of repairing living systems, native species are nearly always at the forefront. When you protect and grow native plant communities, you protect and grow native insects and native wildlife communities. These are organisms that have coevolved together. The more we regenerate native ecosystems, the better chance we have of protecting threatened plants and animals.

Unless you carry the indigenous stories of these plants, your relationship with them is likely not as rich as it could be. Though countless have been lost, many of these stories are still carried today by Indigenous wisdom keepers. If you're diligent in your research and build relationships with the keepers of knowledge, you will greatly deepen your understanding of native plant communities and their ecological niches, functions, and yields. Exploring the world of the native plants generates a stronger two-way connection between you and the ecosystem where you live.

Where I live, oak trees grow in abundance from mountain to valley. But most ecological designers and food producers I know don't grow or harvest acorns for food. We grow different food plants that we are used to enjoying instead. We've gone for the modern food palate, leaving the ancient foods to fall and wither all around us. This is one of many examples of the broken relationship landscape designers (and modern humans) have with native plant communities.

Drought-Tolerant Gardens

In arid and drought-stricken climates, drought-tolerant plant species fit the landscape best. These miraculous communities of plants are some of the toughest plants in the world, surviving the hottest and driest places on earth while still providing many services to the ecosystem. Hardy plants such as these aren't limited to growing in dry places; many yield benefits to other ecosystems and human communities. Contrary to conventional thinking, drought-tolerant plants can be aesthetically pleasing, edible, and much more.

Cut Flowers

Splendor rides the wind on the smell of fresh flowers. Your landscape is not only a place for food and ecological function but also to cultivate beauty in all forms—a feast for all the senses. Flowers grown throughout the year not only attract beneficial insects and birds but also provide beautiful flowers to be cut and taken inside. Within every functional category found in this chapter, there are species that will produce a perfect cut flower to brighten your home.

Medicinal and Culinary Herbs

Since time immemorial, humans have been harvesting, cultivating, and using medicinal and culinary herbs. For much of human history these herbs (along with folk magic) were the basis for treating all sorts of ailments and diseases. Even in our modern world, useful herbs have an important place in the home apothecary to treat everything from skin rashes to joint pain. Many are both edible and medicinal and often splendidly beautiful, covered in blooms for much of the year while providing food and habitat for innumerable beneficial insects and birds. In short, every regenerative landscape needs to integrate medicinal and culinary herb communities into the planting plan for the benefit of all life, human and nonhuman alike.

Grains

For larger landscapes and farms, growing your own grain by sowing into farm beds and agricultural meadows is absolutely possible. The most ecological approach is to grow grain in the correct seasons (usually sowing in the fall or spring) when limited to no irrigation is required. Adding grain to a pastoral community of plants is ideal for generating a host of ecological benefits like fixing nitrogen, forage for wildlife, and diversifying the soil ecology through diversified root systems. If you are maintaining a native meadow system, use native grain alternatives rather than common varieties. Keep in mind that growing grain is generally easy but harvesting and cleaning the grain can be quite time-consuming and may require special tools. Make sure you have the determination and patience to see the endeavor through all the steps and you will be rewarded with the final harvest.

Plant Fibers

Where I live in Northern California, the native people (Pomo, Miwok) use many kinds of plants—including nettles (*Urtica dioica*), dogbane (*Apocynum cannabinum*), sedges (*Carex* spp), and blackberries (*Rubus* spp)—to make baskets and other useful materials. Similar plants grow in every biome around the world. The roots and stalks of these types of plants have countless uses for crafting, clothing, rope making, and so much more. Many fiber-producing species provide other benefits as well—food, flowers, medicine, soil building—and will share their gifts with you when incorporated into the ecology.

Crafting Wood

Your landscape is a source of wood materials for making tool handles, benches, tables, trellises, bowls, sculptures, and more. Certain species of shrubs and trees work better for these uses than others. When you plan your landscape plant community, include species such as hazelnut (*Corylus* spp), black walnut (*Juglans nigra*), bamboo (*Bambusoideae*), or ironwood (*Ostrya*) to grow materials for any wood project you can imagine.

Wetlands

A whole host of plants grow in wetland environments. If your landscape includes bogs, riparian edges, graywater, blackwater, ponds, rain gardens, or other highly saturated areas, a wetland plant community will be the best choice for these areas.

Insectary Plants

Insectary plants attract, feed, and repel insects in a number of ways. When thinking about insectary plants, always consider that form follows function. Not every flower is formed the same way, and for good reason. The shape of certain flowers is better for butterflies, while other flowers have a better shape for bees, and still other flower shapes benefit hummingbirds, bats, or moths. When we're laying out our planting strategy, ponder a diversity of flower shapes and colors to attract a greater diversity of insects and birds to the landscape.

Merge these three different kinds of insectaries with the landscape:

Attractor Plants. These plants attract butterflies, bees, parasitoid wasps, lacewings, tachinid flies, and other beneficial insects that not only pollinate the landscape but also manage pests in the system. They are like all-you-can-eat buffets for the winged folk, who then gorge themselves on pollen, nectar, and smaller bugs. The more you attract these beneficial insects, the more they will feed on aphids, cucumber beetles, and caterpillars.

Repellent Plants. Repellant plants exude strong-smelling oils through their leaves. Many plants in the mint family—rosemary, salvias, mints (*Mentha* spp), oregano (*Oregano vulgare*), lavender (*Lavandula* spp)—produce these stinky oils, repelling pests from the garden.

Larval Food. Larval food plants feed the larvae of insects such as butterflies. In some cases, these insects are completely dependent on specific larval food plants for the survival of their entire species. For instance, milkweed (*Asclepias* spp) is the larval food for the endangered monarch butterfly. That means that monarchs lay their eggs on the milkweed and when the caterpillars hatch, they eat only the milkweed until they can transform into butterflies. No milkweed, no monarchs—it's as simple as that. Many butterfly species have the same co-evolved relationship with another specific plant species. When developing your landscape planting plan, add larval food plants that will provide for the native insects in your region and be part of the solution for saving the biodiversity of planet earth.

Animal Forage

When you have integrated chickens, goats, sheep, or other animals into your regenerative landscape, incorporating animal forage plants into the design is an important part of developing a holistic ecology. Many trees, shrubs, herbs, and grasses provide complex nutrients for animals while cutting down on feed costs and building health and immunity in your animal community. Tree species such as apples, mulberries (*Morus alba*), and mesquite (*Prosopis* spp), are excellent animal forage for humans and nonhumans.

NATIVE PLANTS VERSUS EXOTIC PLANTS

The debate about native plants versus exotic plants is a long-running, opinionated, and sometimes nasty discussion among native plant enthusiasts, landscapers, permaculturists, agroecologists, and others. I won't spend too much time on this topic here because there are volumes of books and articles written on the subject. Both sides of the debate have valid points and I personally fall somewhere in the middle. One reason *purely* native landscapes are less popular among conventional landscapers and gardeners of all stripes is that, in some environments, they are seen as less beautiful, less functional, and less desirable. From the edible landscaping point of view, most people want to grow food they are used to eating (though learning to eat a native food diet would solve so many problems). Most of these edible species do not pose a risk to native ecosystems. They are plants we grow close to our homes with loving care, and it's unlikely the majority of those species will propagate themselves into the surrounding ecosystem.

The worry that exotic plants we grow in our landscapes will become invasive and spread into native ecosystems is one of the chief concerns of native plant enthusiasts. While most of our chosen edibles and medicinal plants won't spread, it is a valid concern that can't be overlooked.

Invasive species that are released into the environment can have damaging effects to native plant communities and in some cases outcompete them altogether.

Proponents of using exotic plants in certain cases argue that we should encompass a larger timescale, one where we see that all ecosystems on earth have evolved through the constant mobility of plants and animals taking over new areas and creating new ecosystems where they establish themselves until the next cycle of change. The question is often posed: "Native to *when?*" I do not share this notion here to debunk the concerns of native plant lovers, as these folks are working to protect the ecosystems we live in today, which have evolved and been established over the last few thousand years.

On the other hand, the climate is changing faster now than it has in thousands of years. Recent climate projections predict drastic changes to climate and vegetative composition by 2080.[1] This means that, as regenerative designers, we need to look into the future and the changing patterns that are coming to prepare landscapes and ecosystems for survival as permanent changes in the climate settle in.

Every microclimate is different; your landscape has its own specific needs and will experience its own specific changes in the coming decades—another reason why having a deep understanding of your local environment is paramount for designing and managing regenerative landscapes.

My personal solution to the natives-versus-exotics issue is this: I plant non-native species in landscapes and homesteads only close to where people live, focused mostly on food and medicine production along with carbon sequestering. Large orchards and agricultural projects may also include proven non-native, noninvasive species in order to obtain specific yields. In my approach, any work done in surrounding ecologies outside food production is focused solely on native plant management and restoration.

In addition, every landscape or farm design I develop incorporates hundreds if not thousands of native plantings throughout the system. Even though I grow apples, pears, and mulberries, I still plant them in relationship with natives—grasses, salvias, wildflowers, and shrubs. Many of my landscapes are incorporated within redwoods, oaks, firs, and other woodland species native to my bioregion. As you can see, my approach is not an either/or, it's a both/and. No matter what, it complements the context of the project's unique landscape.

I do my best to not cultivate plants that are known to be wildly invasive—specifically plant species that easily spread into surrounding native ecologies and cause damage. It's one thing not to plant these species, but the debate about whether to eradicate existing invasives is another can of worms entirely. In my region there are many "invasive" species that are providing vital functions in the ecosystem at present. To remove these from the land would cause significant damage in the short term. From the regenerative design point of view, we need to take the entire context into account; leaving these species for now might be the better choice in some cases. Weigh all your plant choices based on what they offer the ecology and the community, and always seek to do the least harm for the greatest benefit to all life.

CASE STUDY: EARTHSEED FARM

What does it mean to design a truly holistic society? A regenerative place in which every human and more than human kin are honored. A place where every person is accepted, nourished, and given space to heal. What does it mean to create a place that cares for people and the earth with love and dignity? EarthSeed Farm has asked these questions and generated a solution-based model to make this vision a reality.

EarthSeed Farm is a place where the needs of our more than human kin and humans are at the center of an Afroindigenous, agroecological farming model, one that drives its roots deeper into the cultural soil than the modern conceptions of organic farming, permaculture, or regenerative design ever could. EarthSeed Founder Pandora Thomas and her team have created a center that symbiotically develops the health of the land with the health of Black and Indigenous communities.

At the farm, "environmental education meets ecological design rooted in the wisdom of AfroIndigenous traditions." Afroindigenous traditions are rooted to the cultural synchronism of African earth-based spirituality and Native American practices. When Africans were forcibly removed from their native landscapes and brought as enslaved people to what is now called the Americas, they were forced to work the land. During the same time, Indigenous communities of the Americas were experiencing genocide and the settlement of hostile colonialists in their territories. African descendants and Indigenous people fostered important relationships with each other in order to survive. This is where the AfroIndigenous tradition emerged.

The ethos of Earthseed is not only to learn about current land stewardship practices but more important, the ancient wisdom traditions of African and Native American heritages, whose people have been stewarding ecosystems regeneratively for thousands of years. In this way, EarthSeed is a place of *reclaiming*. Reclaiming the wisdom, the practices, and the legacies that were stolen from Black and Indigenous people during the European colonization of the Americas. All of this ancestral healing, ancient stewardship practices, and learning is taking place on a 14-acre organic orchard in transition from a conventional organic farm to a holistic, regenerative landscape.

As many regenerative designers and farmers know, an organic farm is not necessarily regenerative or ecological. The process required to transition from conventional organic practices into a whole systems, ecological approach is immense. Pandora and EarthSeed farm represent a living model of what it means to make this transition—not only the transition away from a capitalistic agriculture model but also the societal transformation of what it looks like to center the needs of people and our more than human kin in the effort to restore the land. For EarthSeed Farm, neither is separate from the other. As sure as the morning sun rises,

Pandora Thomas and friend in the EarthSeed fruit stand. Photo credit: Devin Ariel of Mahogany Visions.

EarthSeed embraces the notion that in order to heal the land, we must heal the people and vice versa.

The farm itself is composed of 4,000 fruit trees planted in rows, sprawled across a dozen acres of sandy loam soil. The Farm produces marketable crops of Asian pear (14 varieties), apple (10 varieties), pluots (four varieties) blackberries (three varieties), and pineapple guavas. EarthSeed inherited not only the land and trees, but also the entire farm operation. This includes the clients, equipment, and labor force, which has kept this farm humming year to year. Pandora quickly realized what many farmers, the previous owners included, understand about our current agricultural system–it's based on capitalist frameworks that aren't set up to pay all workers a salary beyond a fair wage. This is especially true for what we call "seasonal" workers. This is at odds with the values and vision of EarthSeed. Many of her employees had worked this farm for years and for some even decades without receiving enough compensation to cover basic needs. One of Pandora's first changes was to raise everyone's salaries (however, she stresses the need to raise them even more) as a way to honor the men and women who have been stewarding the land for years.

(continued)

During her observation, listening, and site assessment of the land it became clear to Pandora that the farming model she inherited was extractive and the land needed a rest. As a result, she left some areas fallow to give the land time to replenish habitat and soil. For EarthSeed, money is not the only indicator of wealth. Other measures of success include health of the soil, water catchment and conservation, biodiversity, enhanced wildlife habitat, and the creation of a sacred place for the community to gather, rest, and be nourished by the natural world. The transition happening on the farm reflects these goals and values and is bolstered by a mission-driven structure where grants, creative funding, and a future goal of collective buy-in can generate the resources to make EarthSeed thrive for generations.

While transition steps are taking place, EarthSeed Farm still needed to maintain a farm income. The previous farm owners established a prosperous U-pick and wholesale market, which EarthSeed retained at reduced capacity. To hold true to the EarthSeed values, Pandora made adjustments to the farm model to provide access to farm products for Black and Indigenous communities. To facilitate this vision, they opened access to the farm to urban and rural black and brown community members. In this way, EarthSeed provides a safe and nurturing home for folks in the urban core to get out of the city to a place where the values of justice, acceptance, connection, and healing are celebrated.

Transitioning away from an extractive form of organic farming and toward a regenerative system included building high-quality compost on site, diversifying crops into multistory polycultural ecosystems (alley cropping between tree rows with ancient grain varieties and herbs), incorporating animals to ecologically manage the farm, and enhancement of beneficial insect and wildlife habitat. In addition, they are shifting away from a tillage-based model toward no-till practices. Piles of seasonally pruned branches that were previously burned will be made into biochar. These are just *some* of the transformational practices taking place at EarthSeed; most if not all have been practiced by people of African ancestry for decades.

EarthSeed is a microcosm, a model of what it takes to transform our communities into centers for landscape regeneration and cultural healing. The logistics of shifting conventional agricultural practices are immense and yet increasingly necessary around the world. Changing agricultural models pose a huge financial burden in the first few years until the new systems are up and running. But once a regenerative system is developed, it generates incalculable wealth in the form of soil, water, climate, and—for EarthSeed—cultural healing, personal empowerment, community building, and ancestral connection. Earthseed's mission is to help people reconnect with these ancient practices in the modern era. To help the community recognize that *all* our ancestors—no matter the color of their skin or heritage—come from earth-based stewardship traditions. Reclaiming these traditions is the path to a thriving future. At EarthSeed, the human right of connection to earth is celebrated, ancestral legacies and stories are told, and a new generation of earth stewards are emerging.

41
Regenerative Agroforestry

Regenerative agroforestry is the practice of planting tree crops using the principles of regeneration. Tree crops include everything from fruit and nuts to timber, fuel, and fiber. Agroforestry systems often generate multiple benefits, utilizing the behaviors of grazing animals beneath tree systems to develop multiple yields and also to create a closed loop ecosystem.

The Dehesa system in Spain and Portugal is one of the world's greatest examples of regenerative agroforestry. Cork oak (*Quercus suber*) woodlands provide cork materials, used for flooring and bottling, without killing the tree. Beneath the oaks, pigs, cows, and sheep graze the understory in low densities, eating fallen acorns and oak leaves while providing fertilizer. Some of the highest quality animal products in the world are generated from this system, which has been operating continuously for approximately 2,000 years.[1] This is also called a silvopasture system—the combination of woodlands with large pastoral areas in between, creating a diverse setting for plants and animals alike.

Regenerative agroforestry systems also include food forests, multilayered orchards, woodlots, productive hedgerows, and tropical forest restoration. Throughout the world's biomes, innovative cultures have developed agroforestry systems that provide yields for humans and the surrounding ecologies and can be managed productively for hundreds to thousands of years.

Regenerative agroforestry offers one of the best solutions for restoring degraded environments while also producing food. This approach is the future of agriculture in a world dominated by climate crisis and food shortages. In many ways, this entire book is a love letter to regenerative agroforestry models meant to meet your needs (or that of your clients, family, community) and the needs of the ecosystem through mutually beneficial relationships.

FOOD FOREST AGROFORESTRY

Many reading this book have heard the term *food forest* before. This term is a fun way of describing a highly intensive, vertically layered, diverse perennial landscape. Specifically, what makes a forest a food forest is that it is designed to produce food. These systems have been cultivated around the world for thousands of years. In some cultures, they are called kitchen gardens, but the principles remain the same—a multistacked landscape populated by perennial (mixed with annuals) and edible species composed of a highly diverse and intensive planting system.

The inspiration for food forests comes from observing natural forest ecosystems. How many vertical layers do you find in the forest ecosystems of your region (if you have them)? Designing a food forest entirely mimics a natural forest ecosystem, where many relationships between plant species, animals, soil biology, and climate take place. A food forest is designed to achieve the same functions and relationships—to manage water, build soil, provide forage and habitat for wildlife, and to produce food for all life.

Food forests take into account sun and shade, maximizing both for the benefits of plants that need one or the other. In many permaculture circles, the concept of the seven-layer food forest (a concept developed by Robert Hart in his groundbreaking book *A Forest Garden*) is very popular. These seven layers include bulbs, groundcover, herbs, vine, shrubs, low canopy, and upper-canopy species. A seven-layer food forest system takes inspiration from subtropical and tropical forests where this level of diversity and vertical stacking takes place. In many arid and temperate climates, however, forest ecosystems are unlikely to achieve seven vertical layers of growth. I've found that mimicking the composition of healthy forest in your own bioregion tends to have great results when developing a food forest. The forests in my bioregion don't usually have more than four or five vertical layers, though I have found more in special microclimatic areas.

Orchards

An orchard is a food-producing perennial system like a food forest but with less diversity and a minimum of vertical layers. The greatest difference between an orchard and a food forest is that an orchard tends to have only two layers: the tree layer—usually a lower canopy or upper canopy tree species—and a groundcover layer composed of grasses and clovers.

For smaller, intensive landscapes, a food forest maximizes space and grows an abundance of food while creating incredible beauty. However, when scaling to larger agriculture systems, an intensive, many layered food forest often doesn't make sense (with the exception of subtropical and tropical settings). Too many layers over extremely large areas of the landscape will become difficult to maintain and harvest. Orchards, on the other hand, are an excellent design solution for larger scale agricultural production as they are designed for easy access when harvesting and maintaining trees. Ecologically managed orchards boast impressive diversity and ecological functions without the chemical and inversion plowing techniques that constitute the backbone of conventional orchards with pure monoculture systems.

Orchards can be developed with alley cropping systems to create even more diversity. Alley cropping is the production of food and medicine in between tree rows. These alley crops usually consist of annual herbs, berries, animal forage, and so on. Each year they are cut back or grazed and then replanted. Cover crops are incorporated into alley cropping systems to continually build and feed the soil underneath orchard trees.

Managing Biomass

The core maintenance task in an agroforestry system, once it has been set up, is managing vegetative growth. If planned regeneratively, these systems generate large volumes of biomass that can be used as mulch, for composting, and for animal forage. Here are a few methods for managing biomass.

Chop and Drop. The practice of chop and drop was discussed briefly in part IV. In a food forest or larger scale agroforestry system, cutting back trees/plants and leaving their biomass on-site as mulch is effective and powerful in maintaining plant health and building soil fertility. In syntropic agriculture, an agroforestry system developed in Brazil,[2] entire tree crops are grown solely for biomass production. These pioneer species are cultivated for their fast growth and the volumes of biomass they create. This is a brilliant way to jumpstart a degraded ecosystem—by quickly infusing it with huge amounts of biomass. Remember, biomass doesn't mean only the leaves and branches for mulch but also the roots that are left in the ground to either decompose or sprout back.

To manage biomass, a chop-and-drop system is as simple as walking into the food forest with a large knife or a small sickle and chopping down plants that are shading other plants, getting in the way of the pathway, or are ready to be cycled into soil to make way for more desirable crops. This method is one of my favorites for maintaining a food forest system, but managing biomass by hand will become infeasible when moving to large-scale agroforestry. At the large scale, tractor implements, chainsaws, and use of animals makes the most sense.

Managing Vertical Layers. When managing biomass in an agroforestry system, consider how vertical layers interact with each other. Correctly time the pruning cycles with the seasons and growth of adjacent plants to make sure that trees get the sun or shade they need at the right time of year. Remove plants here and there, with intention, to make way for additional sunlight in areas that are too shaded.

Pruning multistacked agroforestry systems manages lower and upper canopies in such a way that a maximum amount of sun filters through the system. Carefully planning what you cut and when will stimulate growth throughout the entire agroforestry system while generating mulch and soil-building materials. Remember, you're always managing successions—at some point, species whose time has come will take over the system while others need to be chopped and removed. These management cycles also play out in the timing of when species are flowering and fruiting. Pay close attention to what cycle trees are currently in, cutting, harvesting, and pruning in the appropriate seasons.

Animal Integration. Animals can be integrated into an agroforestry system on nearly every scale to help you manage weeds, increase fertility, manage pests, and browse back undesirable plants like blackberries and poison oak (*Toxicodendron diversilobum*). Silvopasture and other large-scale agroforestry projects benefit from the behaviors of grazing and browsing animals, who graze down the grasses, eat the lower limbs of tree species, clean up fallen fruit and nuts, and provide yields of meat, fiber, and dairy products for farmers.

Evolving Systems. It can't be stressed enough that perennial agroforestry systems are landscapes that evolve over many years. The first few years will look very different from year three, year five, year ten, or year twenty. If you plant slow-growing, long-living species that produce for hundreds of years (olives, figs, apples), you need to plan for their maturity. Short-living crops can be grown in the early years, then turned to mulch when larger trees come into maturity.

Soil Seed Bank

We have arrived at one of my favorite topics: managing the soil seed bank. The soil in your landscape is filled with millions of dormant seeds. When sufficient moisture and light is available, some of the seeds will sprout and push their leaves above the ground. These are what people normally call weeds. Some of these weeds are edible, medicinal, soil building, and habitat producing. Other seeds that sprout end up taking on invasive forms and make it difficult to manage those areas.

The first step in managing the soil seed bank is to identify existing weeds that you don't mind having growing naturally in the landscape. Clovers (*Trifolium* spp), native grasses, and wildflowers are ecological superstars and make great additions to a regenerative landscape. Common weeds such as yellow dock (*Rumex crispus*), dandelion (*Taraxcum* spp), chicory (*Chicorium intybus*), and plantain are all incredible superfood plants. Allow these species to go to seed. Meanwhile, make sure undesirable weeds are cut or removed *before* they go to seed.

This is the beginning of a soil seed bank management strategy, but we can go much further. Establish useful reseeding and biennial plants in your agroforestry system. On my homestead I've established calendula (*Calendula* spp), dill (*Anethum graveolens*), fennel (*Foeniculum vulgare*), evening primrose (*Oenothera biennis*), mullein (*Verbascum thapsus*), borage (*Borago officinalis*), California poppy (*Eschscholzia californica*), clary sage (*Salvia sclarea*), miner's lettuce (*Claytonia perfoliata*), chickweed (*Stellaria media*), and clover. All of these species provide beneficial functions to human and nonhuman communities alike.

Allow beneficial reseeding plants to naturalize in areas where they don't smother other prized plants. Let these species grow through their entire life cycle until their seeds are ripe. Then disperse the seeds around the landscape and cut back the seed stalks.

In the first five years on our homestead, I would send my children to venture on the land and knock ripe seeds from dried stalks. Sometimes I would give them sticks to "swordplay" with the seed stalks, thereby dispersing the seed. Other times, we rolled our bodies down across areas where clover seed was ready to be planted. I would encourage them to just whack seed heads when they walked by, a game I myself still play today.

Little by little, each year, the soil seed bank gains new deposits of seed you want to grow. After a number of years, the dominant "weeds" in the landscape become useful plants you harvest and enjoy.

Pollination

When it comes to growing tree crops, good pollination—the mixing of pollen between flowers—is a must. Pollen is dispersed by insects and wind, or self-pollinated by the tree itself. Once a flower has been pollinated, it has what it needs to produce a fruit. But not just any pollen will do. Depending on the tree species, specific types of pollen must be sourced from specific cultivars in order to pollinate the tree.

For instance, avocado trees grow two types of flowers called type A and type B. The best yields come from avocados trees that have a mix of both A and B flowers. Within each of these two categories, a number of cultivars exist. This means special planning is required when choosing your trees to ensure that flowers type A and type B are present.

Universal Pollinators. Apple trees also have specific pollination requirements but with the benefit of having a universal pollinator in the form of the crabapple (*Malus sylvestris*), which will readily pollinate any apple tree. Many apple pollens will mix with each other, too. That being said, planting a few crabapples within a large agroforestry system will help the overall pollination of the system. Universal pollinators exist within many cultivar species included in regenerative agroforestry systems.

Self-Pollination. Many tree species self-pollinate. They have the right combination of pollen and flower parts to produce food no matter the surrounding pollen. These are convenient species to plant because you can be sure that a harvest is coming. Pollination is foundational for growing, selecting, and harvesting the characteristics and varieties of seed that you want.

Prepping Planting Areas

Before rushing out to place plants in the ground, make sure the area has been thoroughly prepared to enable your baby plants to thrive. Prepping planting areas begins with a focus on soil. Is the soil compacted or devoid of organic matter? Located on a steep slope? These areas need to be prepped before planted.

Planting is one of the final activities in a landscape-building process. By the time you put plants in the ground, planting zones have already been graded, fertilized with compost as needed, and sheet mulched with irrigation infrastructure close by. When it's time to plant, your new baby plants will be placed in excellent soil conditions and undisturbed by landscape development activities.

Growth Pattern and Longevity

Always plan for the longevity and mature size of each species. A peach tree may live 10 to 15 years, an apple tree 50 to 100 years, an olive (*Olea europaea*) 200 to 1,000 years. The peach will produce fruit in year one, whereas a seeded apple might take seven years or more to fruit. An olive tree could take 5 to 10 years before providing consistent harvests.

As you plan your edible landscape, work with succession by understanding the patterns and growth rate of tree species you are planting. Some species take time to grow into their mature shapes. During these growth periods, understory harvests can be generated with faster-growing species. Eventually, the slower-growing trees reach maturity and the fast-growing species are phased out.

The growth patterns of the species you plant will have a significant impact on how the landscape grows and matures. Consider sunlight, wind flows, access, and views as you develop your planting plan.

Extending Harvests

If your goal is to grow as much food as possible to feed you, your family, and your community, then your planting plan should extend the harvest season for as long as possible.

Extending the harvest throughout the year is dependent on both climate and microclimate, with some climates providing year-round growing conditions. If the climate is too cold, consider using greenhouses, preserving and storing food, and hunting and foraging as a means to produce food during the winter.

Beyond that, extend your harvest season by choosing a diversity of edible cultivars. Being strategic about the varieties of edibles you put into the landscape extends your harvest, limits waste, and builds resilience across the system. If you want apples, for instance, consider planting three apple cultivars instead of one, choosing cultivars that harvest at different times of the year. There are literally thousands of apple cultivars throughout the world. In some climates, you can plant a variety of apples and enjoy fruit from July through January—that's half the year harvesting fresh apples! Wherever you are in the world, whatever fruits and nuts and edibles you love to eat, it is very likely that more than one cultivar or variety exists for each edible you love. It's even more likely that these varieties don't harvest at the same exact time of the year. Not only are you harvesting a larger variety of food over a longer period of the year, but you also mitigate having a glut all at one time.

Diversity builds resilience not only during harvest but throughout the year. As an example, some cultivars may get damaged in spring storms where later varieties don't even start blooming until those storms have passed. Implement this strategy not only with fruit trees but with perennials, nuts, herbs, berries, and vegetables. This is working smarter, not harder.

For many perennial vegetables and medicinal herbs, multiple harvests per year is possible. In fact, harvesting actually stimulates plants to produce more. If you harvest calendula flowers for tea and dry them for making salve, for example, the plant will respond by sending a plethora of new blossoms. If you harvest them continuously, they will continue to bloom throughout much of the year. If you don't harvest the blooms, it sends a signal to the plant that it is time to set seed instead. The relationship between you and these organisms is one of shared abundance—a reciprocal experience between you and the plant.

Strategically choose plant species, considering harvesting cycles and seasonal activities, to achieve the highest level of successional harvests. Do this and you will generate vast abundance for yourself and the ecosystem.

PLANTING TREES

There is no one correct way to plant a tree, but there are a few best practices to implement for most situations. Are you planting by seed, a tiny tree sprout, bare root, or a tree grown in a large pot? These each require a different approach. Before planting, you need an overall understanding of the landscape so you can adjust your approach to meet the patterns and constraints of the land.

Soil Structure

Compacted clay soil or soil with a shallow, hard pan is difficult for many tree species to root into. On the other hand, soil that is extremely sandy may be erosive, and trees you plant might sink into the ground a few weeks after planting.

In heavily compacted soils, I highly advise you to excavate the hole in the shape of a square rather than a circle and to dig the hole twice the size of the root ball. Digging a circular hole in heavy clay soil may cause the roots of your newly planted baby tree to spin around in circles, fulfilling the prophecy of clay pot syndrome. Your tree will suffer and potentially die if this occurs. In a square hole, the roots spread out into the loosened soil while the surface area of the corners allows them to penetrate laterally into the adjacent soil, avoiding the spinning roots of death.

In sandy soils, be sure your hole is not too deep. Digging deep into sandy soil sometimes results in the tree sinking into the soil (settling). To avoid damage due to settling (such as trunk rot), water the hole to speed up settling *prior* to tree installation. While you're planting, pack the soil around the roots and push out air pockets to settle the soil further.

In arid environments, planting in pits or depressions ensures catchment of what little rain will visit the landscape. Even though you're planting in depressions, do your best to avoid settling after planting by keeping the root ball at grade.

Orientation

The orientation to sun and wind can mean life or death for the tree you are planting. Plant in shade, sun, or a mixture of both according to its preferences. Many tree species prefer to grow in the shade in their early years to get established and then stretch toward the sun for the remainder of their life. Get to know the species you're planting and the environments they need to thrive.

In hot, arid, and highly exposed areas, it is best to provide newly planted tree species with shade by placing them in the shade of existing vegetation (a shrub or tree) or next to a fast-growing shrub that provides shade in the early years. Another option is to place a protective tree guard or shade structure around each tree.

Strong winds can be as damaging as strong sun. If the area you're planting is windy, do what you can to protect your young trees from wind by staking them until they're established. Many conventional landscapers will stake all the trees they plant; however, if the area is devoid of damaging winds, then the stakes are not necessary.

Tree trunks might get inadvertently damaged by the stake or tying method, and sometimes trees become dependent on their stakes, growing weaker and more susceptible to wind damage later in life. If possible, training trees to grow into and withstand winds is the best way to nurture a strong species. In every case, stakes should only be used in the first year or two of the tree's life until it has become established. Remove the stakes once the trees are large enough to withstand the wind on their own.

Water Table

Planting trees in an ecology with a high water table is tricky if the species you hope to plant is not a riparian or bog plant. Most tree species do not like their feet in water all the time unless they have evolved to have their roots wet for long periods of time. If the wrong tree is planted in these conditions, it can lead to root and trunk rot.

There are some ecologies, however, where the soil is saturated with water for only a few months of the year; the rest of the year, the soil dries out. Here it is possible to plant a wide variety of tree species. To help these trees during the saturated months, plant them on mounds or berms. This keeps the crown of the tree out of the high water table while still allowing the tree to penetrate into the same water resources from a safe distance. This is the best of both worlds.

Planting on mounds and berms is also a strategy for soils with shallow bedrock and extreme compaction. The mound provides the trees with a loose area to establish roots before the hard work of penetrating into a nearly impervious earth.

Tree Guards

In areas where wild or domestic animals are present, tree guards are necessary to protect each tree from the threat of animal browsing. Hundreds of different tree guard products exist and can be purchased for this use. Usually, these are small plastic tubes attached to one or two stakes and placed around the tree. Tree guards come in different sizes ranging from one to four feet, giving trees adequate protection until they've grown above animal browse lines.

Tree guards need to be translucent, allowing sunlight to penetrate through the guard and reach the tree. Many innovative tree guards act as mini greenhouses to provide heat that helps the tree grow. Larger tree guards can be built from fencing wire and stakes that are three to four feet long. This is useful in environments where tall browsing animals are present and the tree needs to be protected until it's six to eight feet tall.

Another alternative is to build simple circular or square fences individually around each tree, two to three feet from the trunk of the tree itself. Once the trees are sufficiently established— tall enough with thick bark—these fences can be removed so that browsing animals can have access to fallen fruit and the lower branches and leaves of the tree.

In old silvopasture systems, shepherds would build wooden split rail fences around each tree to keep sheep and other livestock from peeling off the bark and damaging the tree. It is a way of incorporating animals with tree systems that goes back thousands of years.

PLANTING TREES BY SEED

One of the most satisfying processes in a regenerative landscape is sprouting a tree from seed. I sometimes hold the seeds in my hand in awe at the miracle of these tiny seeds that will grow into massive entities that provide food, shade, and shelter to the community. I feel like a participant in generational abundance, as though I'm holding hands with both my ancestors and my descendants—engaging in one of the simplest yet effective solutions to many of the crises on the planet today.

The problem with planting trees from seed is that it can be quite difficult to get some species to germinate (sprout). Before planting tree seeds, understand the species you're planting and what they need to germinate.

Seeds into the Ground

Many tree species' seeds will sprout when put directly into the ground during the wet season. The seeds need to be collected the year before and stored in a cool, dry, dark place until the time of planting. When harvesting tree seeds, always look for the largest, healthiest seeds, which usually result in stronger and happier trees.

It is advisable to plant more seeds in the ground than trees you want to grow. Seeds can be eaten by birds and soil organisms or can be rotten from the inside. It is always good to overplant; later, if too many trees grow, you can transplant them to other locations or thin them out as needed. Keep in mind that some tree species actually take two whole years of being in the ground before they sprout. Research this ahead of time to avoid disappointment if the seeds don't sprout in the first year.

One of the biggest benefits of planting by seed is that trees grown in this way generally develop into the largest and healthiest specimens. This is because the root systems are never disturbed, and the tree is able to grow deep into the soil without interruption.

Seeding into Pots

Most tree species will germinate in a pot. While planting in a pot seems simple and easy, it does require a lot of care and attention and most species need to be kept moist until the tree sprouts.

The huge benefit of growing trees in pots, of course, is that you can grow them in a well-tended environment until they have an established root system. Growing trees in pots has a huge downside, however. Trees grow large root systems fairly quickly. A tree planted in a pot will need to be transplanted into a larger pot sooner rather than later. If the tree grows too long in a small pot, the roots will get bound up and the tree will be stressed.

It is even better to skip transplanting into a larger pot and plant them into the land as soon as they have grown into a small sapling. This is a highly efficient way to grow trees by seed as thousands can be sprouted in a relatively small area. The trick here is that the trees need to be planted into the landscape within the first year or two.

Stratification

Cold-hardy tree species have evolved within frigid conditions. To mimic these conditions, many species require a period of cold stratification before the seeds become viable for planting. This can be accomplished by leaving seeds in the freezer for two to three months in a medium of sand or peat moss.[3] Once the seeds have experienced their desired length of cold, they are ready to be sprouted and planted out.

Wet Versus Dry Seed

Tree seeds have all kinds of needs and preferences for germination. Some species germinate better when the seed is planted directly after the fruit was consumed, meaning while the seed is still wet. Other types are better germinated after the seed has been stored and dried, then planted at the right time of year. In short— do your research!

PLANTING A BARE ROOT TREE

Bare root trees are usually sold as deciduous fruit and nut trees. They are grown in the ground for two years before they are dug up during dormancy and sold to gardeners and farmers with the roots bare of soil.

Purchasing bare root trees is one of the best ways to establish a food forest or orchard. The trees come strong and healthy most of the time, and because the root systems are two years old, they establish and grow very quickly after planting.

Bare root fruit trees are always purchased when they are dormant. This is usually in the winter time but some nurseries will place trees in cold storage to keep them dormant for longer.

The majority of bare root trees are trees that have been grafted. This is the process of taking scion wood (stratified branches of the cultivar you want to grow) and splicing it onto a carefully selected root stock.

Since bare roots are grafted trees, you must pay attention to the graft union—the place where the scion is attached to the root stock. These graft unions need to be placed opposite the sun or wind side during planting. These are usually the weakest points in the tree, where disease and infection can take hold.

PLANTING A BARE ROOT TREE

1. Dig the hole to twice the size of the root ball in width. The depth should be a few inches deeper than the length of the roots. If the soil is compacted or has excessive clay, shape the hole into a square.
2. While prepping the hole, soak the bare root tree in a large tub or wheelbarrow filled with compost tea on the day of planting. Make sure to keep it in the cool shade. The bare root tree will soak up the compost tea and the beneficial biology will attach itself to the roots. This way, the tree will be preinoculated with beneficial soil microorganisms prior to planting. In my experience, trees presoaked in compost tea before planting establish and grow much faster in the first few months.
3. Plant the tree with a mix of approximately 50 percent native soil and 50 percent aged compost, adding biological amendments (mycorrhizal fungi powders, rock dust, oyster shell) and additional compost tea to the hole at the time of planting. This will provide accessible nutrients and an active soil biology to help the tree grow strong.
4. Place the tree in the hole with the graft wound pointed *away* from prevailing sun and wind. This will help protect the graph wound until it heals over completely. In the Northern Hemisphere, the graph wound would be pointed to the north or northeast.
5. When you place the tree in the hole, bury the root crown four to six inches deeper than the top grade of soil (only at first). Pay attention to the often chaotic root systems of bare root trees during planting. Planting these trees at grade initially will often leave roots

bound up or splayed in an upward direction, which may stunt the growth of the tree. I've seen it many times, including roots that were sticking *above* ground after a novice planted the tree. To mitigate this issue, plant the tree deep and then gently pull (from the trunk) and lift the tree's root crown to the top of the soil. This will ensure that the roots of the tree point in a downward direction.

6. Push air pockets out from around the roots with your hands and add more soil until you've gently packed soil over all the roots and up to the root crown of the tree.
7. Water the tree deeply after planting. You will notice additional settling of the soil in some areas. Add a top dressing of compost or more soil to get the grade correct.
8. You now need to mulch around your newly planted bare root tree. Mulching with additional compost, composted manure, wood chips, straw, or cardboard sheets are all appropriate. Use what you have. Consider whether you need to smother weeds out or not. A two-inch layer of compost will benefit both the tree and any grasses growing near the trunk. I like to put two inches of compost, then a layer of cardboard, then three inches of wood chips around each bare root tree.
9. This next part is optional but a common practice for most professional orchardists. Prune back the top of the tree heavily. Make cuts for shape and structure. Many growers don't perform a heavy prune but I usually do. When bare root trees are pulled out of the ground and sold to you, some of the roots get torn off and left in the ground. To balance out this stress I like to prune heavily upon planting so the tree focuses its energy in the first year on establishing the root system rather than nourishing a large canopy. If you don't feel comfortable doing this, don't worry; use whatever pruning best practices you know and do what feels comfortable to you.

CHOOSING FRUIT AND NUT CULTIVARS

Choosing cultivars is not a decision to make lightly. Climate, personal preference, and harvest time are all factors to consider. Below, you will find details to help your decision-making process. Choose wisely!

Chill Hour Requirements

Before fruit trees form fruit buds, they require a minimum number of hours below the temperature of 45°F and above 32°F. We call these *chill hour* requirements.[4] They vary from tree species to tree species and from cultivar to cultivar.

Apples and pears tend to have high chill hours—1,000 hours or more—while many peaches need from 200 to 600 chill hours. Some apples have been selected for lower chill hour requirements (200 to 800) and some peaches for higher chill hours (600 to 1,200). The same pattern takes place throughout the entire world of fruit trees.

Imagine how disappointing it would be if you planted an orchard with trees that need 1,000 hours or more below 45°F and above 32°F per year but your climate doesn't provide that. You end up with an orchard that doesn't bear fruit. For this reason, take chill hour requirements seriously in your planning process. Have an understanding of the minimum temperature averages of your climate and choose cultivars that receive the chill hours they need to produce fruit in your landscape.

Occasionally there are landscapes in sloping environments that have extreme differences in microclimate. I once designed a 10-acre landscape where we grew apples at the base of the property and oranges (*Citrus sinensis*) at the top. There were enough chill hours at the bottom for 1,000 chill hour apples but no frost on the higher slope to damage the orange trees.

Varieties You Like to Eat

Temper that desire you have to grow every exotic fruit that's available for your region. I would never discourage you from experimentation, but first and foremost grow species and cultivars that you know you're going to eat. Check that off the list first before planting strange fruits you've never tried before. If you feel drawn to plant unfamiliar fruits, try and taste the fruits before planting the tree.

Even among species that you know you want to grow, look for cultivars that you specifically like. On my homestead, I have at least 12 different types of apples that ripen at different times of year. I don't regret planting a single one of them, but there are three or four of these cultivars that no one in my family especially likes to eat. They are better used for sauces and ciders, but, if we don't get to them one year, those apples get composted.

Storing and Longevity

Ensure that the cultivars you choose for the landscape are not only for fresh eating. It's better to incorporate a few varieties that are meant for long-term storage.

Long-term storage isn't the only way to achieve longevity. Varieties that *stagger* their fruit-setting times are pure gold in my opinion. On our homestead we have Santa Rosa plums (*Prunus salicina*), which are delicious. The only problem is that they drop all of their fruit over a two-week period. Usually that's at the beginning of summer, and sometimes (or hopefully) we've gone away on a camping trip. Just a few days away and we come home to half the harvest on the ground. These fruits do not stagger their harvest; they dump it all at once.

The pluots (*Prunus brigantine*) however, are another story. Their fruit slowly ripens on the tree over a six- to eight-week period! This means we are harvesting fresh pluots from the tree for nearly two months of the year.

Cultivars for Fermentation

If you are interested in making cider, wine, and mead, then consider choosing fruit cultivars bred specifically for fermentation. These often have existing tannins, are loaded with juice, grow large, and ripen late in the season. Cultivars bred for fresh eating can also be added to ciders and wine of course. Having a diversity of options will make a variety of delicious beverages.

HEDGEROWS

A hedgerow is an ancient regenerative agriculture system that comes from old Europe. Some hedgerows still in existence today date back thousands of years. These are long, forested strips that generate food, fiber, fuel, and habitat for wildlife. In the old days, hedgerows were built to section pastures for grazing animals and to protect villages, castles, and sacred sites from invasion.

Centuries later, these hedgerows still provide a bastion for diverse life and ecological functions. In a regenerative agroforestry system, hedgerows are best used anywhere where space needs to be divided—a property line, a private area, animal pastures, along the road, along a waterway, or to break up farm and grazing land with wildlife corridors.

In farming systems, hedgerows become an important part of integrated pest management. Populated with native trees, shrubs, and herbs, the hedgerow provides forage, pollen, and nesting sites for the insect and wildlife animal community. The same organisms living in the hedge venture onto the farm, eating pests and pollinating crops.

The difference between the ancient hedgerows of Europe and what people commonly think when they hear the word *hedge* is the amount of plant diversity that forms the system. In modern day landscape architecture, most hedgerows are designed as a wall made of a single species of plants. Designing a hedgerow that resembles the ancient ones requires highly diverse planting with multiple vertical planting dimensions. These are the types of hedgerows referred to in this book.

Tips for Growing Regenerative Hedgerows

Biodiversity is key to ecological function. A hedgerow provides the most environmental benefits when it is composed of five or more species. If possible, add even more diversity to the hedgerow to generate additional ecological yields. Rather than focusing on a single tall species, incorporate smaller shrubs and herbaceous plants throughout the system to create a multilayered hedgerow. Different vertical layers filter prevailing winds and provide nesting and forage for a wider range of bird and insect life.

Make your hedgerows wide, increasing the opportunities for biodiversity and vertical stacking in the system. The more species in the hedgerow grown to their full size and spreading their canopies, the better. A productive hedgerow is a source of food, medicine, fuel, and fiber. Incorporate systems such as coppicing and pollarding into the hedgerow to design it for many functions. You'll be able to harvest firewood, furniture wood, basketry materials, crafting supplies, herbs, fruits, and nuts once it's established.

Hedges are generally tall— a minimum of eight feet— and some grow as tall as a forest. When designing your hedgerow, consider the size of the area you're planting and the functions you hope to facilitate. That will narrow down your plant options. Choose native species first—they are havens for native insects, native plants, and native wildlife. A diversity of species will enable the hedgerow to have a plant blooming at all times of the year (the best outcome possible in cold climates). The hedgerow will constantly be attracting beneficial organisms by providing yearly forage to the landscape.

Hedgerows can also provide a level of climate moderation for the system itself, serving as wind filters, buffers for cold air, evapotranspiration, cooling the soil surface, and reflective surfaces for increased light. Filtering the wind means moving it around, taking the energy out of it, and providing protection for crops and structures.

Orient your planting to manage sun and shade. We can plant to create solar bowls—trapping as much sunlight as possible with our planting systems—by putting our taller trees on the north side in the Northern Hemisphere and south side in the Southern Hemisphere to make sure we're not shading out the other plants. This orients the solar bowl toward the sun side to harvest as much sunlight as possible.

In arid environments or in places where there is too much sun and evaporation, we plant strategically to create more shade, keeping more water in the ground and creating opportunities to plant more diversity within that shade.

You can mitigate frost by strategically planting bigger trees to provide some insulation, creating microclimates in different protected pockets of the landscape.

42
Managing Tree Systems with Pruning

Caring for trees in an orchard or food forest requires careful planning and seasonal action. In many settings, pruning trees for structure, shape, size, health, and harvest is necessary. Most pruning books will tell you to start with the three D's: dead, diseased, and directional. Removing diseased material is always the highest priority. Dead material comes next unless you're pruning for size and shape. Beyond this, pruning is used to manage fruiting wood and accessibility in the landscape.

(The term *directional*, referring to the direction branches are growing on the tree, can be misleading and is not always necessary. You may not have the time to tackle every tree and prune every branch to the best direction by removing branches growing *into* the center for instance. Times like these require prioritization, and directional branches are low priority.)

You have to ask yourself how much time you have to get the job done and what you hope to achieve. Before you start a pruning project, generate a few goals for each tree. Are you pruning for size, shape, food, or something else?

Some trees only require two or three large cuts before moving on to the next tree, while other trees require half a day of your attention to prune. When it comes to pruning neglected mature fruit trees, an extensive pruning session could last all day. For most people this becomes daunting and many trees are left unpruned as all the energy was consumed by one or two trees.

Managing your personal energy is always the first and most important planning approach. If you start there when planning a pruning session, the project tasks become more efficient and the decisions less paralyzing.

Dead

When trees are evergreen or deciduous trees are leafed out, it is easy to identify dead branches—the leaves will be dead, brown, or nonexistent. You can also test the tips of branches like these by gently breaking the first couple inches. If it snaps right off and no green is present inside the branch, it is dead. In an ecology where the danger of fire is present, most dead branches and often all branches need to be removed up to approximately 10 feet off the ground. This helps keep ground fires from traveling up the lower branches and surging into the tree canopy. Removing dead branches opens airflow, reduces the risk of disease, and help the tree focus on new growth.

When branches are dormant, the best way to identify a dead branch without damaging it is to *gently* scrape the outside bark. One fingernail scrape of the young bark will show either green or brown. If you scrape and find no green, the branch is dead. If you find green, you're looking at a living cambium layer, which means that the branch is alive and sending sugars and nutrients up and down the tree.

Diseased

It is always a priority to remove diseased branches when pruning trees. Any casual observer can notice signs of disease once it gets really bad. Bark peeling away in an unusual fashion, orange or translucent material draining from branches, blisters, fungi, and discoloration are all indicators of disease.

Pruning diseased branches must be done carefully and at the right time of the year because the pruners or loppers you use can become infected with the disease when you make a cut. Without thorough disinfecting, you may infect other trees when pruning them with the same tools. Remove diseased branches during the dry season when spread of disease is limited.

Prepare a spray bottle with a 50/50 mix of water and hydrogen peroxide. Bring the spray bottle out to the field during pruning projects and prevent tree-to-tree spread of disease by disinfecting your tools after you have finished pruning each tree.

Once you've removed the diseased wood, now you must deal with the pruned material. Avoid chop and drop (leaving pruned material on the ground) with diseased wood. This can lead to reinfection of the tree and leave adjacent species susceptible to the disease.

Burning diseased branches is highly effective yet must be done outside of fire season. Hauling the material to a thermophilic industrial composting facility works, as well as creating your own hot composting system that reaches temperatures hot enough to rid the disease from the site.

Directional

The growth habits of trees sometimes make for chaotic branching systems. Branches growing into the center of the tree block out light, branches extending into pathways block access, and branches growing against buildings creates fire danger.

Pay attention to the direction branches are growing and prune accordingly. Prune for light, prune for better harvest, and prune to remove branches over buildings and pathways as needed.

Pruning for Size

In medium and small landscapes, pay special attention to managing the size trees are allowed to grow. When you are growing a food forest in a small area, for instance, you will likely overplant the landscape to generate maximum food production, wildlife habitat, and ecological yields. Eventually, your trees may start to crowd each other, blocking light and growth. One strategy for managing this is to prune each tree specifically to manage its size. It's best to choose the right-sized tree for the space but that is not always possible.

Pruning fruit trees to their buds (heading) generates vertical growth, whereas pruning to the next branch (thinning) stimulates lateral growth. Pruning in the summer will stunt trees, keeping them smaller. In addition, trees that can be coppiced, or pollarded, are cut on specific cycles, which opens up the surrounding landscape to light. All these techniques are employed to manage how large trees will grow.

Pruning for Shape

Any time you're pruning a shrub or tree, you are dictating its current and future shape. Many conventional landscapers prune for a "lollipop" shape or rectangular and square forms. These are artificial shapes that nearly always have detrimental effects on the health of the plant or tree.

A more beneficial approach is to accentuate the natural shape of the plant or tree. In the process of accentuating its natural shape, you can also prune it for size and for its structure in relation to surrounding plants and trees. You might shape it to open up light for herbaceous plants underneath or work with its natural growth pattern by thinning small branches and leaves a little bit here or there to bring out its natural shape and pattern. Every plant becomes a landscape showpiece—a specimen plant—when given this level of care during pruning.

Many landscapes are too large and wild to do this to every plant, but, when and where it matters, shape plants to their natural pattern or other functions, whether aesthetic or ecological. And for the love of all that is sacred, please don't default to cutting plants into lollipops and rectangle shapes. This dominance of the landscape is not the regenerative way. Remember to compose with—not impose upon—the land.

Pruning Times of the Year

Generally, the best time to prune fruit and nut trees is when they are dormant because it induces the least amount of stress in the tree as most of the tree's attention is down in the roots. This is nearly always in the wintertime.

Trees can be kept small through strategic pruning in early summer. This is usually the time when trees have shifted away from pushing springtime energy into vegetation and instead focus on flower and fruit.

Springtime is when the trees' life forces surge, pushing their leaves and branches to the sky. This is also when residual winter moisture is still present in many climates. It is a perfect time for fungus and disease to proliferate when the land warms and mingles with spring rains and winter moisture. Pruning at this time risks opening wounds on the tree where disease can enter.

Pruning evergreen edibles like citrus and olives is best done in mid- to late spring or early summer. These trees are more susceptible to cold damage if trimmed in the winter. Many evergreen edibles are also subtropical or tropical plants and thrive in warmer weather. This is why pruning when it's warm tends to cause less damage to these species. If your project is in a subtropical/tropical environment, cold weather is less of a concern and you'll need to consider other factors like time of flowering, time of fruiting, and the storm season when pruning your trees.

Pruning Fruit Wood

Not every tree fruits on the same kind of wood. Apple trees fruit on fruiting spurs,[1] whereas peaches and nectarines (*Prunus persica*) fruit on one-year-old wood.[2] You need to know the fruiting wood you are dealing with every time you prune a tree. Without this knowledge, you run the risk of cutting all the fruiting wood from a tree and destroying that year's harvest.

A conscious attempt at pruning fruit wood gives you the power to help trees avoid the self-destructive pattern of growing too many fruits on a weak branch, which results in branches breaking off the tree during peak harvest season, sometimes permanently damaging the tree. Identify weak branches and carefully thin fruiting spurs or cut back fruiting wood to keep the tree from overproducing on those branches.

For peaches and nectarines, prune hard each year to stimulate new growth. This new growth becomes next year's fruiting wood. If a peach tree is not pruned, it grows only a small amount each year and produces little fruit.

As you can see, it's important to know what sort of fruiting wood a tree produces to avoid mistakes and help the tree grow strong.

Pruning Angles

When pruning food-bearing trees, select and train the angles of branches attached to the trunk to between a 45- and a 60-degree angle.[3] These are the strongest connection points for these branches, which we call scaffold branches. The scaffold branches (usually four to six on a fruit tree) will bear the weight of all of the fruit or nuts that grow on the subsequent branches of each scaffold. The scaffold branches need to be trained at correct angles starting in year one. Training branches happens early in the life of the tree when branches are still pliable and springy. After two to three years, the branches will harden into place.

THREE WAYS TO TRAIN SCAFFOLD BRANCHES

Strategic Cutting

When you initially prune the tree the first three years, strategically prune off branches growing from the trunk that have poor angles and keep branches that have the correct angle or can confidently be trained at the correct angle.

Branch Spacers

Spacers are used between the trunk of the tree and the scaffold branch you are training. For branches whose angle is less than 45 degrees, a spacer is pushed between branch and trunk until a workable angle is discovered. Leave spacers in place until the branch has stiffened into the correct angle.

Be extremely careful when installing spacers. Make sure you don't pull the branch down so hard that it breaks and tears down the trunk of the tree. Tree spacers can be bought, but my preference is to make them from previously cut branches. Cut a branch at the needed length to make a spacer and then, using pruners or a knife, cut a notch into each end of the spacer. Gently slide it down between the trunk and the branch until the correct angle is found.

Tying Branches

A third method for training scaffold branches is to put stakes in the ground beneath the tree and tie a flexible ribbon between the stake and the branch you're training. Pull the branch to the desired angle and attach it to the stake. Again, do this only on young branches that don't run the risk of breaking when you pull down on them. Once the branch has grown and accepted its new position, remove the ribbons from the tree.

THE POWER OF YOUR CUTS

How you cut the tree has major implications for the future. This is a hugely overlooked aspect of pruning trees. You're not pruning just for today's benefit—you're pruning the tree with next year or, even better, five or ten years in mind. Cuts you make now, along with how you train and manage new growth, will help develop the overall structure of the tree.

When you prune a tree, you are managing where energy goes. Cutting to a bud or to a branch, which branches you cut, and which branches you leave all tell the tree where to push energy through the tree and in which directions new growth will go. In the long-term growth of a tree, cuts you made two or three years ago are still influencing the way the tree is growing now. You will understand these concepts better over time with practice. Hopefully, when you prune a tree, you'll be able to maintain a relationship with that tree for years to come. If so, observe and track how the tree grows in response to cuts you make. The tree itself is a better teacher than anything found in a book.

Central Leader

The central leader of a tree is the tallest leading branch of the tree. A cultivar that hasn't been topped (leader branches cut) will follow the central leader and grow as tall as possible. This is great for large trees where yields such as shade, fog harvesting, and wind filtration are prioritized. If it is a fruit- or nut-bearing tree, you may want to train the tree to grow shorter, so harvesting is easier, which would steer you away from a central leader form.

Modified Central Leader

If you want the tree to grow more slowly, you can top the leader branch down to a leaf bud. A new leader will form at the leaf bud. This becomes your *modified* leader. Cutting and training a northern branch to act as modified leader will slow the vertical growth of the tree over time while maintaining a leader branch structure.

Open Vase

Another technique for keeping trees smaller and generating more productivity involves cutting out central leader branches entirely, leading to an open vase tree structure. Prune your tree into a "vase" shape by focusing on four to six scaffold branches to create an open center where sunlight penetrates.

Sunscald

When the bark of a tree is exposed to intense sun day after day, the bark blisters and breaks. This is sunscald, a damaging disorder that is most threatening to young trees. After a few years, sunscald will kill a tree. Many products exist to protect against sunscald in orchard settings; often trunks are painted with a lime wash or white paint. These techniques work, but so does shading tree trunks with leaves from their own branches. If you're concerned about sunscald, keep the lower branches on the trunk the first time you prune your tree. When the lower branches leaf out, they will shade the base of the tree. Planting herbaceous species around the tree also provides protection from the sun.

Branch Flexibility

Test the "spring" or flexibility of a branch to determine how much fruit wood to leave on the branch. The young branches of trees are generally flexible and weak. When you bend them down, do they spring back into place? If the branch is too flexible, it's best to remove fruiting wood from the branch so it doesn't get overburdened and break off during harvest season.

As you manage each tree, year after year, you'll notice branches that were once too weak now have no "spring" to them and are strong enough to carry a full harvest of fruit.

THINNING FRUIT

For some reason, many species like apples and pears frequently produce more fruit on a branch than it can handle. This results in branches breaking off in the summertime if no help has been given. In addition, when too many fruits grow on a branch, competing for resources, all of the fruits end up small.

To avoid these calamities, you simply need to thin the fruit. This is the process of pinching off baby fruits in the springtime. Wait until the flowers have been pollinated and fruit has been set. Once the fruits are the size of a marble, begin the process of thinning. Depending on the size of the mature fruit, you might thin to every three inches or every six inches. Many factors are taken into account, such as the age and strength of the branch, the variety of fruit, and what the fruit will be used for once harvested. Thinned fruit can be dropped to the ground unless it is infected with a fungal or bacterial disease. In that case, thinned fruit should be removed from the site or burned up in a hot composting system.

COPPICING

Coppicing is a tree management technique in use for thousands of years.[4] Trees are managed in such a way that they grow long and straight shoots that can be used for tool handles, basketry, house construction, trellising, fuel, and waddle building. The best part of this technique is that the tree is never killed. This means the successional harvesting of materials can take place for decades and in some cases centuries.

The act of coppicing begins with cutting a tree a few inches from the ground. This is only done to trees and shrubs that are known to *sprout again* from the stump (hazelnut and willow are two favorites). After the tree has been cut, the new sprouts need to be managed accordingly to train for size and shape. If you're growing them for fuel or fiber of some kind, choose the new sprouts with the straightest form. Grow them out until they are the desired length and diameter (for your desired use—e.g., tool handle or house post), which usually takes one to four years.

The season of harvest makes a big difference in the health of the tree and the quality of the wood. Even the cycle of the moon makes a difference. Are you harvesting when the sap is flowing, when the wood holds more water, or when curing will lead to cracking? How long do you need to cure the wood before use? Keep these questions in mind as you plan out your coppice groves. In addition, if coppice groves are being used in hedgerows or as privacy screens, the time of year will also be a factor in how the system meets these functions at the time of harvest.

The best way to harvest coppiced wood is to cut stalks in a successional pattern. Don't cut every stalk at the same time on the same tree. Strategically thin the coppice grove in order to maintain a variety of aged stalks. In this way, a full aesthetic remains after every harvest. Remember to select and thin new sprouts after each harvest. Once you successfully guide the grove into a successional system, you'll be able to harvest every year without clear-cutting the grove. These systems eventually become permanent sources of regeneratively grown and harvested materials.

The act of coppicing stimulates trees to grow new young wood every year. This keeps the tree from getting old and weak, which helps them grow for centuries. Some coppice groves around the world have been managed for a thousand years! Imagine providing a rich legacy of abundance like this for future generations.

POLLARDING

If you drive around a city, eventually, you'll notice strange looking trees. They usually have four or more large branches all cut off at the same exact height. These trees are pollarded. The tops of each main branch are thick and often covered in burled wood. In the growing season, long branches sprout from the tops of the knobby tree branches, only to be cut again the next winter.

In the urban environment, this technique is used to keep trees from growing too big, a classic case of planting the wrong species in the wrong space. Pollarding was traditionally developed for a much better reason than combating poor urban planning. Another ancient technique, pollarding is used in agroforestry systems to produce fodder for animals.[5] The trees are cut low enough to make harvesting fodder easy by hand.

With trees kept small, larger species can be interplanted with little competition for vertical space and light. By growing trees as dry season fodder, food for animals can be harvested when the grasses have died back. Trees are grown tall enough to allow pasture systems to thrive underneath while remaining harvestable. Pollarding provides a whole set of dynamic interaction within the agroforestry system.

Oak is the traditional pollard tree because leaves and acorns provide nutritious forage for pigs, goats, and cows. New shoots on a tree are harvested as a perennial feed as needed throughout the year and dropped to the ground for animals to eat.

Just like coppicing, pollarding keeps trees producing young wood, which keeps them alive for decades longer. Pollarding can help some trees live for hundreds of years.

In small intensive landscapes, pollarding doesn't make sense most of the time, but in large-scale, multi-yield agroforestry systems, this technique provides a wide array of benefits with a minimum of management effort.

43

Growing Vegetables

The majority of people on earth consume some form of vegetables every day. Vegetables come in two main forms—annual and perennial. An annual plant grows for a single season, dying after one annual cycle. A perennial grows and comes back year after year.

Why grow your own vegetables? For some it may seem like too much work. Maybe you're too busy. If it's not feasible to grow your own vegetables, then please, please support your local farmers, through farmers markets, CSA programs, or farmstands. Growing vegetables and supporting local farmers is so important because the agricultural industry producing most crops is a devastating force to ecosystems. Hundreds of thousands of acres of soil are plowed every year and millions of tons of pesticides and herbicides are sprayed on farmlands.[1] The average vegetable travels 1,500 miles before getting to your plate.[2] If you want to protect ecosystems, mitigate the effects of a changing climate, and develop true resilience in your community, growing your own food achieves it all.

Nutrient Density

Another reason to grow your own vegetables is because they are healthier for you than the vegetables you buy at the store. Many regeneratively grown vegetables provide a full spectrum of nutrients to nourish your body and your health.

Saving Money

Healthful food is getting more and more expensive to purchase. This trend is unlikely to go away. If you want access to the healthiest food in the world and don't want to pay half your paycheck for it, then grow your own. But wait! I hear you. "But Erik, setting up my garden is expensive. Saving money by growing my own food is a myth." Valid point, friends.

Setting up your landscape to grow vegetables does take an enormous amount of labor and materials. The initial startup costs for even a single raised bed could be a few hundred dollars. It is true. But you must think longer term. If you build one 4 by 8-foot vegetable bed, it could cost you $300 to $400 to construct. But how much food can you grow in there the first year? How about after three years? How about after five years? The initial investment in developing vegetable gardens is substantial, but the rewards more than make up for it.

Conduct an experiment on yourself and track how much money you spend on vegetables. Track what you spend every month and include a few meals out. You will be utterly surprised by how expensive it is to purchase your own vegetables. Consider that a head of lettuce in an organic supermarket today costs approximately $3. Now consider that in a four by eight-foot vegetable bed, you can grow more than 25 heads of lettuce (*Lactuca sativa*) every three months. If the climate allows, you could do this year-round, growing 100 lettuce heads or more in a year. One hundred heads of lettuce at $3 a piece is $300 worth of lettuce per year. That alone more than pays for the cost of building the garden bed. But you get to grow lettuce again next year and the year after that. If you implement vegetable growing cycles like those discussed in the Singing Frogs Farm case study in part IV, you might be growing two to three other crops in the bed at the same time. If you add it all up, you could grow over $1,000 worth of vegetables in that one four by eight-foot bed every single year. Now compound that by two of these vegetable beds, or six of them. This equates to thousands of dollars of food that can be grown every year. And not just any food—the healthiest, most nutrient-rich food with the least embodied energy. Food that is best for the climate, best for the soil, best for your body—all from your own backyard.

Food Sovereignty

Growing your own food is the act of creating food sovereignty. Now expand this notion beyond your backyard landscape into the neighborhood, into the community. Organizing regenerative food-growing systems in your community develops resilience and food abundance. Endeavors like these can alleviate hunger for the houseless, provide healing, medicinal food for the sick, nourish children through school lunch programs, and create an ecotourist destination where local, regenerative food is celebrated.

I have been part of, or witness to, examples of every one of these food sovereignty strategies. In my own community, the production and celebration of local food has worked its way through all levels of the economy. People come from all over the world to tour these landscapes, including my own farms and gardens. Growing your own food doesn't have to be done in isolation. Developing food sovereignty in your community is an act of joy, a cause for celebration, and a multigenerational process.

Given time, communities can establish cooperatives for growing and distributing food, for processing high value products like olive oil and grain flour, and for cooking and preserving food for the community. A community that functions like this is not beholden to large agricultural businesses and a government subsidized food system. A community that develops food sovereignty is resilient in disaster and economic meltdown.

The best part is, all of this starts in your own vegetable bed. It starts when the first seed is placed into the ground.

Healthy Soil Equals Healthy Food

When I think about growing vegetables one quote always comes to mind. This one is from biointensive garden pioneer John Jeavons. He says, "People don't grow plants, soil grows plants." This is an excellent way to think about growing vegetables. As we discovered in part IV of this book, the soil is where the magic begins. Another old phrase comes to mind: "You are what you eat." Take that one step further and you see that "a plant is what it eats."

If the soil is dead, filled with chemicals, dry, and stressed, it's likely vegetables won't grow well there. On the other hand, when you focus on healthy soil, you get healthy plants. If your soil is rich with biological activity, minerals, and amino acids, then the vegetables you grow there will be rich with minerals, vitamins, and proteins. The plants we consume are as healthy as the soil they grow in and we are as healthy as the plants we eat.

FOUR SEASONS OF HARVEST

If you live in a climate where year-round vegetable production is possible, then you are fortunate. If you don't, continue below to find tips on how to extend your growing season for as long as possible. Growing four seasons a year is optimal if you intend to produce a large percentage of your own food.

Growing in the Right Season

If you haven't already, now is the time to learn about different species of vegetables and the optimum seasons they grow in. This is the simplest step for planting a year-round harvest. Grow vegetables that grow well in each season. Tomatoes (*Solanum lycopersicum*) and peppers (*Capsicum* spp), for instance, are very sensitive to the cold weather. In many places around the world, people have given up growing tomatoes at all because they just don't ripen in cold weather.

The optimal time to grow tomatoes is after the last frost has passed and before the next frost comes. As you research each vegetable, you may be surprised by the climatic and seasonal associations of some vegetables. Lettuce, for instance, grows better in cool weather. It's frost resistant to a degree and in many temperate climates can be grown all year. At the peak of summer, however, lettuce has a hard time growing because of excessive heat. This makes the lettuce go to flower (otherwise known as bolting), which gives the leaves a bitter taste.

By simply planting crops in their favorite time of year, you will automatically expand your growing season.

Frost Protection

Frost is a force that changes the vegetable growing season when it strikes. In many climates, vegetable production ends when the first frost hits and begins after the last frost has passed. It doesn't have to be this way, though. Many organic farmers today use frost blankets, fine-meshed white cloth that can be bought in long rolls, that are literally just placed over the top of your vegetable beds to protect them. This material insulates the ground from frost and cold weather, giving your plants a chance to grow longer into the fall/winter season or get a jump start on the spring season. The frost blankets keep heat stored in the earth and trap it around your vegetable plants, while the cold, frosty air has a hard time penetrating them to get to your tender plants. (Planting under the drip line of trees provides a similar effect as tree branches insulate the earth below them.)

Choosing the right microclimate in the landscape also helps protect against frost. A south-facing zone against a building has much better frost protection than an exposed area.

When you combine all these strategies together, it's possible to extend the harvest by weeks. In the end, however, an extremely hard frost or bitterly cold weather system will be too powerful for these strategies to work long term. Every little bit counts; you can win a few extra weeks here or there that produce a harvest you wouldn't get otherwise, but the only permanent frost protection comes in the form of greenhouses and hoop houses.

Greenhouse/Hoop House

To significantly extend the growing season, a greenhouse or a hoop house is the way to go. These are structures built from frames of wood, metal, or plastic, which are covered by a variety of greenhouse plastics or glass. A simple hoop house consists of plastic or wooden arches stretched over a planting area and staked to the ground, then covered by a large sheet of pliable greenhouse plastic. Doors are often framed into the side of a hoop house, or the plastic can be folded over and held with a simple clip system to open each end for access and ventilation.

A greenhouse is a more permanent structure framed from metal and wood, then covered with thick double-walled plastic panels or glass. In both cases, a large area is being isolated from the surrounding cold air and winds. Sun penetrates through the glass or plastic, heating up the growing area. These significantly increase the growing season of most vegetable crops. In cold climates, a greenhouse means year-round production that wouldn't be possible any other way.

Greenhouses can be heated, ventilated, and insulated to create year-round growing conditions in the coldest places on earth. If you're in a climate that gets really cold, setting up a greenhouse may be one of the greatest investments toward growing food year-round.

CHOOSING VEGETABLE VARIETIES

Most vegetable gardeners have had this experience: The excitement bubbles up when it's time to plan the vegetable garden. With a little bit of research, one quickly discovers there are *hundreds* of different kinds of tomatoes, dozens of types of lettuce, strange-colored beets (*Beta vulgaris*), insanely hot peppers, and colorful watermelons (*Citrullus lanatus*) you can choose to grow. It is a miracle—the colors, shapes, textures of the vegetables on earth. When you're growing your garden, it's hard not to feel the pull to experiment wildly with many new varieties. It's a feeling you come to know well if you don't know it already; the results can be great but sometimes disappointing. Experimenting with new varieties poses a risk of growing plants that don't work with your landscape or cultivating varieties you don't like to eat.

It's a risk, but in the first few years it's a worthy risk. I say go for it! Most vegetables are grown annually, so you get to start over every year. If a variety doesn't grow well, or you don't like the flavor, you don't ever have to grow it again. I wholeheartedly encourage you to take the first one to two years of vegetable growing to experiment with new varieties. But the operative word here is *experiment*, because you'll want to plan for long-term food security after a couple years. Use the experiment to develop a list of vegetables that not only grow best in your landscape but ones you actually eat. That is the ultimate goal—finding that community of vegetables that meets these needs.

Grow What You Eat

One of the biggest wastes of a vegetable garden is when you grow varieties that you don't eat or use in other ways. I don't mean varieties you don't like, but specifically species you don't eat. It's easy to say you want to grow 100 percent of your food in the garden, but the reality is that some types of vegetables will be hard for you to incorporate into your daily eating patterns.

For instance, you might be interested in growing kabocha winter squash (*Cucurbita maxima*) for their unique look, huge size, and great flavor. Let's say you plant five of these squash plants and end up with 15 huge kabocha at the end of the year. Much investment in the form of water, space, nutrients, and labor went into growing those 15 squash, but the reality is that you don't typically cook winter squash and the amount of work to peel and open it is more than you bargained for. Maybe you work full time and processing winter squash is not realistic for you very often. In instances like these, the squash may sit around the kitchen for a while, reminding you of your failure to cook it. Months go by until one day you roll it over and it's rotten. Ask me if this has ever happened to me . . . yes, yes, it has. This is why I encourage you to grow what you eat!

We used to grow 8 to 10 different varieties of tomatoes on our homestead—Purple Cherokee, Green Zebra Stripe, Brandywines, Early Girl, Sungold, Marvel Stripe, cherry tomato, and many more. For years I was fascinated with all the different tomatoes that can be grown and so I wanted to grow them all. It was great fun! The problem we kept running into, however, was the limited use for many of the varieties. Some were extremely large and juicy and only made sense in an heirloom tomato salad or sliced on a sandwich. I love those meals, but when I've got a hundred pounds of these tomatoes, there's only so much heirloom tomato salad I can eat. Of course, we gave them away as fast as possible but we couldn't give them away fast enough.

Over the years, we discovered two or three varieties of tomatoes that we would eat regularly. We make them into pasta sauces and salsas and add them to salads and soups, along with other staple meals we regularly eat in our house. The first time we decided to plant only varieties we knew we would eat, it was such a relief. I felt so guilty all those years, wasting tomatoes by the pound. Now hardly any tomatoes go to waste. The same goes for all varieties of vegetables. Experiment, yes, but eventually find the vegetable varieties you actually eat and focus on growing them.

Growing in Season

When choosing varieties of vegetables, grow the right variety at the right time of year. Look even deeper into the growing time required for each variety. How many days does it take for a vegetable to ripen and become ready for harvest? A cabbage (*Brassica oleracea var. capitata*) that takes 90 days from seed to harvest is very different from cabbage that takes 120 or 150 days to harvest. In some climates, 150 days of good growing conditions just doesn't exist.

Perennial Vegetables

Perennial vegetables are species that grow year after year. Some of them may die back in the winter but return again in spring. The advantage of growing perennial vegetables is that they don't need to be replanted every year. Over the years, these perennials grow and expand, providing tons of food and propagation materials to grow new plants.

Perennial vegetables can also be used in a landscape setting. Artichoke (*Cynara cardunculus var. scolymus*), for instance, is a beautiful plant with a gorgeous flower. Artichokes are grown as food crops but, if left unharvested, produce large purple blossoms, dotting the landscape with beauty.

There are hundreds of perennial vegetables around the world that can be incorporated into your landscape. Similar to many native foods, many perennial vegetables are too exotic for the modern-day palate. You might find yourself growing a number of perennial vegetables that you only eat once—unless you retrain your tastes!

NOTABLE PERENNIAL VEGETABLES

- **Tree Kale (*Brassica oleracea var. viridis*).** A perennial purple kale with year-round edible leaves. The leaves are best in the cold season when they get sweet and tender. These species readily propagate by a rooted cutting, making them easy to spread around quickly
- **Rhubarb (*Rheum rhabarbarum*).** Strikingly beautiful with large leaves and reddish stalks. These often die back in the winter but come back larger and larger each year if happy. Harvest the stalks for jams, jellies, and pies.
- **Artichoke (*Cynara cardunculus var. scolymus*).** Artichokes are an exotic-looking edible shrub. These stunning short-lived perennials produce bunches of edible flowers harvested before the blossom opens. Artichokes respond well to harvesting by producing more flowers in succession. Left alone, artichokes turn into beautiful purple flowers that attract bees and butterflies.
- **French Sorrel (*Rumex scutatus*).** These tangy perennial greens produce large, spearlike leaves and can be added to soups and salads. They love to grow in full to partial shade.
- **Asparagus (*Asparagus officinalis*).** Asparagus plants are sold as bare root bunches and planted in late winter. In the spring they produce tall, edible stalks that can be steamed or sautéed. In the winter, the feathery stalks produce gorgeous red berries and die back until the next spring.
- **Garlic Chives (*Allium tuberosum*).** These are one of the easiest perennial vegetables to grow. They are easy to propagate (by seed or root divide) and grow abundantly. The stalks are used fresh or cooked and the spicy flowers make great additions to salads.

- **Horseradish (*Armoracia rusticana*).** Horseradish is a rhizomatous root crop that sprouts from the ground every year. The long white roots are dug up throughout the year as needed and can be grated to make a horseradish spread or added to recipes that need an extra spicy kick.
- **Walking Onion (*Allium proliferum*).** This truly special variety of perennial bunching onions have one of the best onion flavors. New bunches spread from the base, but the best part is their seed stalks. Walking onions form seed bunches *on top* of their stalks, and these stalks fall over, planting the next bunch. This behavior is where they get their "walking" moniker.

PLANTING IN CYCLES

To increase your harvest and extend the growing season, always plant your garden in cycles.

Interplanting Successions. If you follow the advice of Paul and Elizabeth Kaiser of Singing Frogs Farm, you will quickly understand what successional planting is all about. It's the practice of having more than one crop in a bed at a time. These crops grown together are in different phases of their life cycle. One crop can be vegetating while the other crop is ready to harvest, which allows you to successfully grow two to three crops in the same bed in the same season.

Timing Harvests. Another form of succession is planting varieties you want to eat all year on a staggered planting schedule. This gives you better control over the timing and consistency of harvests. If you plant all your crops in the same weekend and never plant again that season, eventually you'll harvest those wonderful and tasty plants. But once harvested, that's all for the season, which will result in having too much come in at the same time and it will be hard to make use of it all.

Let's say you want to eat broccoli (*Brassica oleracea var. italica*) nine months out of the year. To achieve this, plant a few broccoli plants every two weeks for a few months and your harvest will arrive spaced out over as many months. My wife, Lauren, and I learned long ago that if we want fresh salads year-round, we have to plant lettuce every two weeks like clockwork. I can't say we've ever achieved that for an *entire* year but we did succeed over large portions of the year, saving us from the high cost of our salad-eating habits.

Renewing Soil Health

If you took anything from reading part IV of this book (you did read part IV, right?), it is that soil health is paramount for growing food successfully. In the vegetable garden, this is as true as in any landscape system—maybe more so. Many vegetables are considered "heavy feeders" as they take up large amounts of nutrients from the soil to produce food.

If you're not careful, you will exhaust the soil in your vegetable garden by continuously growing food, season after season, harvesting and extracting from the land without renewing the soil. Adding compost, composted manure, spraying compost tea, and spreading soil amendments are important techniques for revitalizing soil in your vegetable garden. Occasionally, you also need to take a break from vegetables and plant cover crops to build soil health. When you grow cover crops, you are renewing the soil with organic matter, biological activity, nitrogen, and carbon.

COMPANION PLANTING

Companion planting is the practice of interplanting diverse communities of plants that aid each other. Plants help each other in many ways.

Maize (corn), beans (*Phaseolus vulgaris*), and squash are an old North American indigenous plant community affectionately called the "three sisters." The maize provides a stalk for the beans to climb and the beans fix nitrogen, feeding the soil. Squash sprawls along the ground, keeping weeds from encroaching and acting as a living mulch.

Dill (*Anethum graveolens*) interplanted with cabbage will help repel cabbage loopers. The cabbage plants provide structural support for the dill to keep it from falling over when it gets tall.

Sweet alyssum (*Lobularia maritima*) planted beneath kale (*Brassica oleracea var. sabellica*) attracts beneficial insects, which feed on the aphids that attack your kale.

Many associations like these exist throughout plant communities. Learning what associations work best in your vegetable garden helps you determine what kinds of interplanting and cyclical harvests you can grow while gaining the benefit of helpful interactions between well-matched companions.

HARVESTING

You've done the hard work of building and prepping the planting areas, sprouting your vegetable starts, and planting them in the earth. You've put in irrigation systems or watered the garden by hand and now, after all this time, it's time to harvest. But how do you know when veggies are ready to be harvested? Do you already know when each vegetable is in its prime harvesting phase? If you do, that's great—enjoy dinner. If you experiment with many varieties of vegetables, have a clear idea of the optimal harvest times and characteristics of ripe fruit.

For example, if you want to eat sweet corn, harvest it when the tassels turn brown but the husks are still green. Then you will enjoy the fresh summer flavor of sweet corn. But if you're growing corn to grind into flour for tortillas, leave the corn on the stalk until the entire stalk has gone brown. The seeds will have begun to shrivel and dry. If you harvest sweet corn late, or the grain corn (dent) early, the harvest will be lost.

Know what varieties you're planting, what they are used for, and what characteristics of the plant show that they're ready to be harvested. Before you harvest, have a plan for what you're going to do with the food.

Preserving the Harvest

Growing and harvesting food is one thing, but preserving it as a long-term food source is an art in itself. Ideally, many of your vegetables are being eaten fresh the day they were harvested or close to it. If you implement planting cycle strategies mentioned above, you'll be harvesting throughout the year and hopefully won't be left with much food that goes unused in the process. Even then, there will always be a need to preserve the harvest for later consumption.

Below are the best methods for preserving food.

Fermentation

Fermentation occurs when naturally occurring yeasts and bacteria feed on the sugars in food. These beneficial organisms also live in our bellies and help digest our foods. Fermentation is used in everything from winemaking and cheesemaking to breads, pickles, and sauerkraut. Many highly valued foods and beverages are made through the process of fermentation.

Good food and drink are one thing, but the fermentation process also helps cure food so it lasts longer. Some fermented food and drinks last years on the shelf. The more I've experimented with fermentation, the more I recognize how easy it is to turn garden cucumbers (*Cucumis sativus*) into pickles, cabbages into kimchi, and fruits into mead. Try out fermentation—you won't be disappointed.

Drying

Many fruits and vegetables can be dried and stored for later use. Fancy dehydrator units have become popular for drying all kinds of vegetables, fruits, and herbs. One popular choice is kale, which can be cut into medium-sized pieces; dressed with oil, salt, and other flavors; and lightly baked in the oven. This creates wildly popular kale chips, which can be found in many supermarkets these days.

One of my favorite dried, homegrown foods are sun-dried tomatoes. We call them "sun-dried" but most of the dried tomatoes you see were dried in a dehydrator. Either way, I love adding them to pasta dishes and my secret sun-dried tomato and olive pesto recipe. Drying food is fun and delivers complex flavors, but the best part is that once your fruits and vegetables are dry, you can store them for years.

Canning

Canning is another method to preserve and store the harvest. Canning is a process of filling heatproof jars (quart-size mason jars work well) with sauces, soups, jams, jelly, or simply chopped fruit and vegetables in water.

After the jars have been sterilized, they are filled with your processed food product, the lid is placed, and then they are heated inside a hot water or steam bath. The heat seals the jars and protects them against rot. Canned food like this can last on the shelf for months if not years.

Canning is quite a lot of work and can be a complex process. My suggestion is that, if you're going to can food, do a large amount all at once. I like to devote an entire day to canning as much food as possible to get the most out of the preparation and labor process. The truth is, I don't can as much food as I used to because, in my home, we usually take the easy route instead—freezing food.

Freezing

Freezing food is by far the easiest method for storing and preserving your precious garden harvests (though it uses the most electricity). Simply chop up the fruit or vegetable you want to store, put it in an airtight bag or jar, and stick it in the freezer. When you want to use it, simply take it out of the freezer, thaw, and cook your favorite dishes.

HARVEST/PRESERVATION TIPS BY VEGETABLE (A SHORT LIST)

Leafy Greens

Lettuce (*Lactuca sativa*). Harvest the outer leaves of loose heads as needed for fresh eating; the plant will continue to grow. Head lettuce is best left to form tight heads and harvested all at once. Store harvested lettuce in the refrigerator or cold storage and consume within a few days.

Kale (*Brassica oleracea var. sabellica*). Harvest the lower leaves of kale by popping them off at the stalk. Work your way up to the top each time you harvest. Our favorite way to eat kale is to pull the leaves off leaf stalks, chop it up, and massage it with salt and olive oil (lemon juice and nutritional yeast are optional additions). Salt wilts the kale and makes it extra tender. Even the kids eat kale this way. To store, add kale to your favorite soups and can or freeze.

Spinach (*Spinacia oleracea*). Spinach is best grown in partial shade, the outer leaves harvested when still young and tender. Baby spinach can be added to salad mixes while larger leaves can be cooked into soups, wilted over eggs, or used in specialty dishes like spanakopita. Spinach is one of the few greens that handle freezing well. Pack washed greens into a bag and freeze until ready for use.

Collards (*Brassica oleracea var. viridis*). These nutritious greens are highly versatile and take well to being frozen for long-term storage. Harvest the outer leaves when still tender. Steamed collards mixed with your favorite seasoning are a great addition to a meal or add them to soups and other specialty dishes like beans and greens. One of my favorite ways to eat collards is to take a large leaf in the garden and wrap it around other fresh greens and flowers like a burrito wrapping. Try it out! It's a fun way to consume fresh garden goodies. You can use the large leaves as nutritious wraps for all kinds of foods.

Root Crops

Carrots (*Daucus carota var. sativus*). Carrots come in many shapes, colors, and sizes. Know what you're planting before you sow those seeds. After you harvest carrots and wash them thoroughly, you can cut them into long strips and put them in a glass container with a little bit of water in it. The water keeps the carrots fresh and crisp instead of wilting as they often do. Keep them in a cool, dark place (refrigerator is best). Make a carrot soup or turn them into crunchy carrot pickles for long-term storage.

Potato (*Solanum tuberosum*). Potatoes originate from South America and there are literally thousands of traditional varieties. Some are better for baking while others are better for mashing and still others are better for frying. Mmmm, so many options. Harvest potatoes when the top vines (leaves) have completely died back. This crop takes patience but it's worth it. They often grow 15:1 meaning that one potato planted will produce 15 new potatoes. Store them in a cool, dry, dark place. Burying them in sawdust is a great way to keep them from sprouting. Whip them up into any of your favorite potato dishes and can or freeze them for long-term storage.

Beets (*Beta vulgaris*). Beets are another root crop that has many variations, coming in many colors and patterns and flavors. Beets are delicious steamed and thrown into a salad or turned into borscht—a favorite in my house. Make a large pot of borscht, eat for a few meals, and then can or freeze the rest.

Onion (*Allium cepa*). Onions are a staple food in my house as we use them in most of our cooked dishes. Harvest onions when their necks have flopped over. Onions have some of the best storing qualities but they need to be cured to achieve longevity. To cure them, spread them out in a single layer, making sure they don't touch. This is best done in warm temperatures (75°F–80°F) and a dry breeze is helpful. Leave for a few weeks until the stalks and papery skins are dry. A properly cured globe onion can last up to a year.

Garlic (*Allium sativum*). Garlic is best planted in October and harvested in June. Harvest garlic when the stalks turn brown. Remove the roots but leave the stalks. One of the most enjoyable ways to store garlic is to braid the stalks into long bunches of garlic, which are then hung in a dry location. Hang this in your kitchen and harvest garlic directly off the braid as needed.

Tomatoes (*Solanum lycopersicum*)

Sauce Tomatoes. There are hundreds of tomato varieties but only a few that are best for making sauces. San Marzano, Early Girl, and other red tomato varieties make for great sauces.

(continued)

Harvest tomatoes ripe off the vine and cook them down into sauce. Use it for your favorite pasta and pizza dishes and can or freeze the rest.

Slicing Tomatoes. Slicing tomatoes are of the large variety and can be added to sandwiches or used to make caprese salad. Tomatoes do not store well and need to be eaten fresh within a couple days of harvest. The best storage option for large tomatoes is to chop them up as a base for sauce or salsa, which can then be frozen or canned for later use.

Cherry Tomatoes. Cherry tomatoes are small, bite-sized tomatoes often picked and eaten right in the garden. Use cherry tomatoes in salads, sauces, soups, or roasted tomato dishes. Add to salsa or sauces and freeze or can for preservation.

Cucumbers (Cucumis sativus)

Pickling Cucumbers. Most fresh eating cucumbers make great pickles. That being said, there are few varieties that are specifically grown for pickling. Pickling cucumbers is easily done by fermenting them in a simple salt brine. After a few days of fermentation, they are ready to eat. Preserve pickled cucumbers by canning them for long-term storage or keep in the refrigerator and they will remain good for weeks.

Squashes (Cucurbita)

Winter Squash. Winter squash are varieties that are harvested in the winter once the vine has begun to die back. This means they need to be planted in the late spring and early summer. Most winter squash has thick skin and, once harvested, will stay fresh for many months if kept in a dry location. Squash can be turned into soups or chopped up and preserved by canning or freezing for even longer storage.

Summer Squash. These varieties need to be harvested when they are small and tender. If left on the plant for too long, they will lose flavor and become pithy. Use these for stir-fry, frittata, soup, and roasting. Summer squash can be chopped up and stored in the freezer or made into soups and other favorite dishes for canning and preservation.

Corn (Zea mays)

Sweet Corn. Sweet corn varieties are meant for eating fresh. Sweet corn needs to be harvested when the tassels start to turn brown but before the husks brown at all. If left on the stalk too long, sweet corn will become starchy and lose its flavor. Eat fresh, grill, steam, boil, roast— sweet corn is versatile in its use. Cut the corn from the cob and make into cream of corn soup that can be canned or freeze cut corn as is for later use.

Dent (Flour) Corn. Dent corn (maize) varieties are important food sources for many Indigenous communities of the Americas including Cherokee, Seminole, Hopi, Pueblo, Omaha, Ponca, and others. Maize is considered sacred and has provided the nutritional foundation for many ancient societies. Harvest maize once the entire plant has died back and the corncobs are brown and dry. If rains are a threat, corn can be harvested early and dried to completion in the home. Dried dent corn can last years if kept dry. To use this corn, it is best to first follow a traditional nixtamalization (alkaline lime wash) process to soak the corn before grinding. This process dehulls the corn, increases its nutritional value, and makes it easier to grind. Once ready, maize is ground into a fine flour for tortillas and tamales.

Beans (Phaseolus)

Green Beans. Green beans are harvested when the pods are still green and tender. Green beans can be eaten fresh or roasted. One of the best ways to preserve them is to pickle them like you would traditional pickled cucumbers. This is an excellent way to store and eat them.

Dry Beans. Beans are harvested dry and cooked for tacos, soups, and other traditional bean dishes. Wait until the pods are completely brown before harvesting. Remove the dry beans from the pods and they are easily stored as-is for years in a cool, dry, dark place.

PESTS AND DISEASE

Pests and disease *will* find their way to your vegetable garden. It can be very disappointing if your garden is small and has been heavily attacked by an invasion of pests. It's beyond the scope of this book to get into the details about every pest and disease that can occur in your garden. I maintain that focusing on soil health, planting the right plants for the right area, and prioritizing biodiversity deals with many pest and disease issues in the landscape.

Aphids are one of the most common pests. They will attack anything from roses to kale and even some fruit trees. Many folks try to rid the plants of aphids to protect the crop. I almost always do the opposite and leave aphids because many insects and birds feed on them. By leaving aphids I'm implementing a "trap crop," a plant that is sacrificed to pests in order to attract beneficial organisms and keep the pests from other crops.

Diseases are more difficult to deal with in the vegetable garden than pests. Once disease is present, it is likely that the crops will be lost. Once blossom end rot, powdery mildew, or rust fungi arrives, there's not much you can do in the moment other than remove infected plants. What you can do, however, is focus on a healthy soil ecosystem. The healthier your soil, the less likely diseases will crop up in the landscape. In addition, keep a high level of biodiversity throughout the vegetable garden. Diseases often infect and spread among the same species. If you have 50 of them growing together then all 50 will quickly become infected. If you've implemented interplanting techniques discussed above, you can break the spread of disease and still obtain a harvest.

Keep in mind that pests and diseases are almost always seasonal. In the late spring, a pest infestation may occur, while powdery mildew may form on your precious plants in early autumn. In both cases, these are seasonal changes that bring about conditions for pests and disease to thrive. Do what you can to save your plants, but don't despair—these phases will pass and the next season is always around the corner. Look to part VIII for a larger discussion of integrated pest management and the various techniques used in the regenerative landscape to balance pest issues.

44
Plant Propagation

The plant world never ceases to share its wonders and miracles. Plants provide food, medicine, and shelter, sequester carbon, feed the soil biology, and regulate the gases in our atmosphere. But there is yet one miracle we have barely touched upon in this book—the way plants propagate—the magic of using a seed, a stem, or a root of a plant to cultivate another plant.

PROPAGATE BY SEED

The seed cycles of plants are awe-inspiring. A plant that grew from a single tiny seed then produces hundreds of thousands of new seeds. One seed holds the potential for thousands of new plants—the definition of abundance.

Sowing Seeds

Starting your own vegetable and herbs by seed is a satisfying, affordable, and effective means of developing your garden. When buying, saving, and starting seeds, the size and species of seed is the key to sprouting successfully. Like fruits and nuts, starting veggie and herb seeds requires a varying approach depending on the context. Let's look at the different options for sprouting your own plant starts from seed.

Soaking. Above all other species, legumes germinate better when their seeds have been soaked in water. Corn, pumpkin, and beets are other species that enjoy being soaked prior to planting.

It is most common to soak your legumes and other species in a bowl, jar, or bucket of water for 10 to 24 hours prior to planting. This helps the seed expand and thins the outer walls, enabling roots and shoots to emerge. Once the seeds have been soaked, plant them based on their preferred method, either in the ground or a pot.

For many species of tree and perennial legumes, hot water is preferred for soaking. For this method, use hot water from the tap and soak seeds for 10 to 24 hours. Do not use water hotter than hot tap water as you will cook the seeds instead.

Scarification. Scarification is a process of scarring the outside shell of the seed to aid in germination. Many seeds evolved by being scarified by animals that eat them, or by passing through the gizzard of a bird.

For seeds such as gourds (*Cucurbitaceae*), a light sanding down of the dog-eared corner is sufficient. For peppers, it's best to put them in a blender. Check the seed for its optimal germination method to give it the best chance of sprouting and growing.

Inoculation. Legumes have a symbiotic relationship with rhizobia bacteria. These bacteria are the force that fixes atmospheric nitrogen into a plant/soil-based nitrogen capable of being absorbed by plant roots. For many legumes, pre-inoculating seed before planting greatly increases rhizobia bacteria populations on roots, thereby increasing the nitrogen-fixing functions.

Rhizobia bacteria inoculant is readily purchased throughout the world. Place seeds in a bucket and fill with water to the level of the seeds. Add rhizobia bacterial powder and mix. Let soak for an hour before planting.

Depth of Seed Planted

For the sake of planting seeds, size really does matter. When you place a seed into the soil, it is best to bury the seed twice its size in depth. This is a basic rule applied across the spectrum of trees, herbs, and vegetables. This means a one-inch-long pumpkin seed is placed two inches into the soil, whereas a 1/8-inch lettuce seed is placed ¼ inch beneath the soil.

Tiny seeds such as yarrow (*Achillea millefolium*), poppy (*Papaver somniferum*), and clover (*Trifolium*) are so small it is best not to put them beneath the soil. Many herbaceous perennials like these have tiny seeds, some hardly visible to the naked eye. Seeds such as these can be sprinkled lightly on top of the soil instead of pushing them below the soil's surface. Simply sprinkle the seeds lightly on top of the soil surface and gently press down. Water them in immediately. This is the best method for germinating seeds of this sort. If you plant too deep into the soil, they're unlikely to sprout.

Covering Seeds

Cast small and medium seeds on the surface of the soil and sprinkle a thin layer of compost or soil over the top to avoid inconsistencies and soil settling.

Seeding in Ground Versus Pots

Planting seeds in the ground (called direct seeding) and planting seeds in pots require different approaches. Direct seeding is best done during the wet season or in irrigated areas that get watered every day. One disadvantage of sowing seeds in the ground is the possibility of slugs, birds, and other members of the ecology feeding on your sprouting seeds. This is disappointing but can be alleviated with the addition of frost cloth or some other material placed over the seeds, protecting them until they sprout and grow.

Germinating seeds in pots often means placing them in a hothouse, a greenhouse, or outside in a location you visit every day. In this way, seeds are better protected from hungry wildlife with a better chance of growing into a young plant. Daily watering is required until seeds have sprouted and established a root system. On hot days, watering twice a day is necessary to give seeds a chance to sprout.

GROW YOUR OWN PLANTS

Anyone who's built a garden or landscape knows that purchasing plants gets expensive really fast. When I visit a plant nursery, I hope I can buy just a handful of plants I really need and get out before I go broke. But once I'm there, I can't imagine leaving without filling my car or truck to the brim with new plants. The problem is, they add up quickly and next thing you know, you're spending hundreds or even thousands of dollars on a truckload of plants.

Purchasing plants is fine, but it's the easy and expensive way to go. If you want to save money, engage in the miracle of propagating your own plants. In this chapter, we explore the primary techniques for propagating plants by cutting, by root, and by grafting. My hope is that at the end of reading this chapter, you feel empowered to go out right now, today, and propagate one of your favorite plants.

Cuttings

A plant propagated by cutting is clone grown from clipping off the stem or young branch of a mother plant you want to grow. Thousands of plant species around the world are grown by cutting. Everything from small ground covers to enormous trees can be propagated in such a simple fashion. There are many species that don't take by cutting, though, especially woodier tree species. Know ahead of time if the species will grow from cuttings or just have fun experimenting and expect both success and failure.

Here are two ways to take cuttings.

Cuttings in the Ground. Propagation by cuttings in the ground is one of my favorite activities in the landscape. It's ridiculously easy, costs nothing, and if conditions are right, a new plant will grow healthy and strong. Taking and rooting a cutting in the ground is best done during the wet season, when you are confident of wet soil for long periods. If sufficient moisture is not available in the soil, the cutting will never grow roots.

Select the plant you're taking cuttings from and snip off a few long branches (two feet is plenty). Make sure the bark isn't too woody on these branches and that they are between one and three years in age. Some species root better on one-year wood and others better on two- or three-year-old wood.

Choose a location where you want to place your cutting. Make sure it's a suitable location for the species you're planting there. If the soil is soft enough to push the cutting into the ground, that is a great sign. If the soil is compacted and hard, take a piece of metal rebar or a wooden stake and prepound a hole before placing your cutting into the earth.

Before placing it into soil, you must prep the cutting. One big benefit of putting a cutting in the ground is the ability to push a longer section of branch into the earth than is possible in a pot. Having more branch in the ground provides a longer shaft for growing roots and wicking moisture. Destem the section of the branch that will go beneath the soil—six inches to one foot will be pushed into the ground. The cutting must have little vegetation above ground to ensure energy is focused on roots and not leaves but it's important to have a minimum of two to four leaves on top for photosynthesis to take place. Trim the top of the cutting as needed; light scraping along the outer wall of the branch is OK and often stimulates growth.

Once the cutting is ready and the hole has been prepounded (if needed), push the cutting all the way into the ground, deep enough that the bottom two leaves nearly touch the soil. Don't stick a cutting part way into the soil with a lanky stem sticking above the ground. That will dehydrate the cutting and make it difficult for roots to grow. Place as much of the branch underground as possible.

And that's it! You've taken your cutting. If taken at the right time of year with a species that readily forms roots, in a few months you'll know it has rooted when new leaves start to grow. My preference is to leave these in the ground so they can grow into mature plants. Transplanting them from ground is acceptable as well. Dozens of cuttings can be grown in a small area in this way.

Potted Cuttings. Growing cuttings in pots follows many of the same principles as propagating in the ground. The difference with potted cuttings is the need to manually water them every day. The benefit is that you can take cuttings at any time of the year this way.

To get the most out of the process, put cuttings in pots at least two inches from each other. You have to transplant them into bigger pots later, so take advantage by sprouting as many cuttings in one pot as possible.

Take your cuttings the same way described above for in-ground propagation—for potted cuttings, the difference is the length of the cutting you're rooting. Trim branches to a length that is shorter than the pot is tall. If using a one-gallon pot that is eight inches tall, make your cutting six to seven inches long to ensure the bottom tip of the cutting doesn't touch the plastic pot. If you're using taller pots, it's still advised to keep the cutting length rather short as it will make it easier to transplant to a new pot later.

Cuttings take best if they're not initially grown in fertile soil. For best results, use a well-drained, sterile soil medium until roots have formed. Coconut coir, sand, or seed-starting soil mixes all work great for cuttings.

Once the cutting forms roots and grows a new set of leaves, it is time to transplant to a larger pot. When transplanting, you may place the rooted cutting in fertile soil for vigorous growth. Once established in the second pot, the cutting can be planted out into the earth.

When prepping the cutting, remember not to leave more than four leaves above the soil line. Push your cutting all the way into the soil until the bottom leaves are nearly touching.

Cuttings need to be watered every day. This bears repeating. *Cuttings need to be watered every day.* If the soil dries out around the cutting, then it will die.

This process can also be done by putting a single cutting, rather than multiple cuttings, in a pot and letting it grow into a fully established plant ready for transplanting into the earth.

Another method is to place cuttings in a wet sandy medium in a deep bucket, and place the whole bucket inside a plastic bag. This keeps the system moist and may buy you a few days between watering the cuttings.

Dig and Divide Roots

Propagating by roots—simply breaking off a rooted section of a plant from a mother plant—is called dig and divide. It's most common to dig and divide herbaceous perennials, cane berries, and shrubs that sprout multiple stems from the root ball. Anytime a plant has a matted root ball with multiple stems, rather than a single trunk, it is possible to propagate through digging and dividing.

Digging a rooted section from an established plant is the least disruptive method of propagating from the root. This is done with the use of a shovel (and axe if necessary for cutting strong roots). Stomp into the plant with the shovel and separate a piece of plant root from the mother. This new plant should be put in a pot or ground immediately so the roots don't dry out.

A more drastic yet effective way to dig and divide is to dig the *entire* plant out of the ground. Once the mother plant is dug up, take a shovel or an axe and chop the entire plant into a number of smaller plants. For varieties like thyme (*thymus*), garden sage (*Salvia officinalis*), and other mat-forming plants, you can literally divide dozens of new plants from the single mother plant. Once you've divided all these plants, put them in pots or plant them into a new landscape area. Make sure to place one divided plant back where the original plant was dug.

Grafting

Many of the fruits and nuts people enjoy around the world come from grafted trees. These are cultivars that don't grow true from seed and are difficult to take from cutting. Cultivars that don't grow true from seed originally developed through open pollination and/or selective plant breeding. The only way to propagate these varieties and have them produce the same fruits and nuts each time is through grafting.

Grafting is taking the scion wood (branch tip) of the cultivar you want to propagate and then attaching it to a root stock. When the attachment—or graft wound—heals, the branch tip (scion) will grow the fruit and the root stock remains as the root system and lower trunk of the tree. Scion wood is usually trimmed from desired cultivars in the fall just after leaves have fallen from the tree. They are then placed in bags of sand and put in the freezer for two to three months. Make sure you label your scion wood! Once cold stratified, the scion wood is ready to be attached to a root stock. Grafting must be done when the tree is dormant. The window for grafting lasts from leaf fall until spring bud break.

There are many commercial rootstocks developed that are resistant to disease, grow in a wide variety of soil conditions, and dictate whether the plant will be a dwarf, semidwarf, or standard size tree. The root stock facilitates many characteristics of the tree but not the fruit. If you want to learn more about the art of grafting, do your own research and access the huge volume of books written on the subject.

45
Landscape Maintenance

Landscape maintenance is a critical set of cycles that govern how a landscape grows and functions. In conventional landscape maintenance programs, the greatest two priorities are aesthetics and affordability. These are not mutually exclusive, but the aesthetic of a landscape is up for debate. In much of the Western world, a clean and kept landscape, resembling English rose gardens (but with less function), is the primary landscape aesthetic. Often these landscapes are centered around large lawns, surrounded by many ornamental (less functional) low-maintenance plantings. In general, this aesthetic is counter to the regenerative principles and goals of an ecological garden.

CHANGING CULTURAL AESTHETICS

Since landscape maintenance is heavily influenced by the dominant cultural aesthetic, we as regenerative designers must endeavor to change what people in the Western world view as an acceptable image of a landscape. Let's collectively shift the cultural aesthetic of landscapes toward a "normal" that is wild, biodiverse, and ecological. This shift in aesthetic demand will have a massive impact on ecosystem and community health around the world.

When the landscape grows wilder, freer, more like a jungle, less maintenance is required to maintain a clean aesthetic. But if you're growing food, then a different set of management tasks related to pruning, harvesting, and preserving will be required. This change of maintenance priorities focuses on ecological yields rather than following invented cultural norms about aesthetics.

VEGETATION MANAGEMENT

Vegetation must be managed to ensure the diversity, health, and desired composition of plant communities—at least once every year and at times daily or weekly.

Vegetation management depends on the behaviors of animals, natural disasters, the cycles of seasons, and human-based management. Humans have spent so many generations managing the environment that we have now created hundreds of different tools and methods for trimming, mowing, chopping, grinding, splitting, and killing plant life. Managing the vegetation is the landscape management task that will take the most amount of time so it's important to be thoughtful in your approach. One human with a weedwacker can do a lot of damage if the work is done carelessly.

Each tool and approach first has to take into consideration the context of the site:

- What type of vegetation is being managed? What time of year is the work being done? What ecological processes are being performed by the existing plants in question?
- What are your goals (fire fuel load management, aesthetics, managing seed dispersal)?
- What resources do you have at your disposal to make this happen? A handsaw, a chainsaw, a scythe, a tractor?

Once you have a good sense of the context, refine your goals. Each tool will have a different effect on the landscape. A more aggressive approach may be called for in a high fire danger area, while a more reserved approach might be called for in an arid or desert ecosystem.

Unfortunately, most people in the developed world are more motivated by aesthetics than ecological function in landscaping. Aesthetics are important, but a clean look often comes through sacrificing biodiversity, habitat, carbon farming, water storage, and soil health. As we all know from this book—right?—ecological landscapes are the lifeblood of human civilization. They are our resilience to natural disasters and the safety net for future generations. They also bring joy and connection into our lives when we let them.

When seeing through this lens, aesthetics can't be at the forefront of our approach to management. If you are managing ecological goals, you need to understand the how, the when, and the what to use in achieving your regenerative management goals.

Mowing

One process that mimics good grazing behavior is strategic mowing. Mowing, in this book, can mean weedwacking, scything, using a tractor, or walk-behind mowing. At the right time of year and/or the right time in the vegetative cycle of the plant, mowing can have incredible benefits for building soil, sequestering carbon, managing opportunistic species, increasing aesthetics, and reducing fire danger.

It's important to know why you are mowing. For instance, if the goal is to reduce the spread of opportunistic plants, like some invasive grasses, then you need to time your mowing regime to cut the undesired plants back before they go to seed. This may be required two, three, or four times in a season. This process will likely need to be repeated over a period of years to enable a transition from undesirable species to your replacement species. If your goal is to build soil, you may allow plants to go to flower prior to cutting them as nitrogen fixation is maximized when plants are cut during flowering.

Some constraints may crop up that affect when you can mow or cut back. The soil might be too moist, species like birds and insects might be nesting in the area, or you might want to save seed. In all of these cases, delay mowing until appropriate conditions present themselves. Mowing is an art that requires careful decision making and planning to achieve varying regenerative goals.

String Trimmers. String trimmers (commonly known by the copyrighted name Weedwackers) are easy to use on any topography and offer the ability to surgically mow around existing plants and trees. Nearly every other kind of mowing tool has difficulty in these conditions.

String trimmers are a better choice for mowing in fire-prone ecologies during fire season. Because plants are being cut by a plastic string rather than a metal blade, there's no danger of accidentally sparking a fire when hitting a rock.

These tools have many benefits but they can also be very damaging. The person doing the trimming needs enough plant literacy to avoid cutting beneficial plants that will resprout. This is the big problem with most string trimming endeavors—it's too easy to just mow everything in sight to the ground, which is a kind of devastation. In agroforestry systems and ecological landscapes, we are managing many cycles of plant growth, and we want to keep 90 percent of the vegetation intact. A full-scale string trimmer attack often results in cutting emerging wildflowers, breaking the successions of clovers and other herbs we want to go to seed, and damaging other cyclical processes in the ecosystem. On the other hand, in the right hands, a weed trimmer is one of the best tools for managing mowing. Because they don't roll across the ground, the operator has incredible control over the tool. A smart operator mows the tall grasses of a meadow without damaging the clover and poppies coming up beneath. With the weed trimmer you can carefully mow around trees without destroying the perennial herbs of the understory. It's more difficult and time-consuming to mow this way, but the ability to manage plant cycles with such accuracy is empowering.

Scythe. A scythe is an old-world mowing tool and happens to be one of my all-time favorite tools in the landscape. Scythes have been used for thousands of years to manage and clear land and also to harvest grain. A scythe is not operated by an engine and is therefore better for the environment and the climate. Scything is a full body and core workout—if you do it every day, you'll stay strong.

Scythes are composed of long, curved blades on handles called snaths. They are operated with two hands, a swinging of the arms, and a twist of the hips. The blade runs across the ground, slicing plants and dropping cut stalks into a pile. These tools are excellent for a regenerative landscaper to hand-trim vegetative pathways, pastures, and fields and to harvest grain. I love using my scythe to cut down cover crops and reseed wildflowers.

In highly intensive food forests, it is more difficult to use a scythe. They are hard to use around trees, irrigation lines, and herbaceous vegetation. One wrong slice with the scythe and you will damage a tree trunk, cut an irrigation line, or destroy adjacent plants. In such cases, it's better to use a hand sickle—a miniature version of a scythe.

An experienced scythe operator can cut over an acre per day! If this is an alley crop of winter wheat in the middle of an orchard, the scythe is modified with a grain cradle for harvesting the wheat. Imagine one person harvesting an acre of grain per day with no power tools. That is the power of a scythe.

Tractor Mowing. For large landscapes with open fields, vegetated roads, and pastures, mowing with a tractor might be necessary. Of all the methods for managing vegetation, tractor mowing is my least favorite—but it also gets the job done fastest. The times when I have been overwhelmed by dozens of acres of tall grasses and fire season around the corner, I felt blessed to access a tractor with a mowing attachment to take the grasses down in a day. It's a love/hate relationship.

The obvious downside to tractor mowing is the use of fossil fuels and the embodied energy they carry. Mowing with a tractor is also damaging to much of the life living in the pasture. If you walk into a field on the day it was mowed by tractor, it's easy to notice a few patterns. The first will be the presence of crows and ravens hopping around the field. They know that when a tractor mows a field, it leaves death in its wake. If you look closely, you will eventually discover snakes, lizards, and even ground-nesting bird eggs that could not escape the mower.

If you need to mow with a tractor implement, go for it. Most mowing implements can cut anywhere from one inch to six inches above the ground. I suggest sticking with four to six inches unless you are mowing to reduce fire danger. Keeping grass taller simulates a healthy grazing pattern; if the grasses are not demolished, they are stimulated to grow again, and the cycle of sequestering carbon in the soil continues. This is how mowing with a tractor can have some strategic, beneficial impacts in the regenerative landscape.

Nontoxic Herbicides

There are plenty of nontoxic herbicides that can be made or purchased. Clove oil, black walnut husk decoction, vinegar, and boiling water all make for effective nontoxic herbicides.

Occultation

Occultation was discussed in part IV as a no-till method of preparing planting areas. The reason it works so well is because the plant life under the occultation tarp dies. It is used to eradicate invasives, but I warn you, some invasives are happy to go dormant in the ground. With species like these, occultation will have the opposite effect. Instead, all vegetation dies back and the roots of the invasives are now free to completely take over once the tarp has been removed. Know the behavior of the invasives you're working with so you can determine whether occultation is a risk or not.

The Art of Weeding

Throughout my decades of teaching permaculture courses and landscape programs and working with volunteers, students, and apprentices, the chief complaint and least desirable task is always—weeding.

Weeding seems to turn landscape maintenance into a hellscape demanding the most menial of jobs. But I have a different take on it. Be prepared to shift your perspective! Are you ready? Apply the permaculture principle of turning problems into solutions, and approach this task from a different mindset. A changed mindset unlocks wonders.

I wouldn't say weeding is my favorite task, but it is definitely one of the most meditative. Slowing down, getting your body close to the surface of the earth—these are some of the benefits you gain from weeding. Often when I am weeding a garden bed, I am assessing the soil, looking at the biology, and listening to the language of birds. I relish the feeling of the air and the sun on my skin. When weeding, I am able to drop into an awareness with the land, yielding incalculable knowledge and observations about the site. It's rare that I leave a weeding session without a new idea, a revelation, or a new action plan. What I am speaking of is the art of weeding. It is a practice that turns an unpopular menial task into a grounding moment for yourself and a moment to check on the processes and interactions happening in the landscape.

46
Saving Seed

The act of saving seeds in the garden—whether they are vegetables, fruit, herbs, flowers, or medicinals—develops untold ecological resilience for ourselves and future generations. Many of us wouldn't be here today if our ancestors hadn't cultivated food and saved and planted the seeds. If your goal is to give our descendants a livable earth, we need to know how to grow, collect, and save our own seeds.

Saving seeds from the landscape is joyous. If you think about reciprocity, there's almost nothing as abundant and life-giving as a single plant providing hundreds to thousands of seeds. It's akin to a perpetual motion of energy as each single plant holds the potential for thousands more.

If you step in and engage with this process, you will quickly understand what I mean. Someday you'll be cleaning your seed and the realization will hit you—all of the potential life that is in your hands. When you experience that moment, all you can do is bask with a deep sense of gratitude, a reverence for the wisdom of the earth and the role you get to play in its bounty.

POLLINATION

If you hope to grow and save varieties of fruits and vegetables, you first need to know how they are pollinated. Some species grow true to seed (the seed will grow the same plant as its mother), while other species will produce a new, open-pollinated variety as a result of cross-pollination. For instance, if you save squash seeds, make sure not to end up with a "spucchini" (spaghetti squash/zucchini hybrid) as spaghetti squash and zucchini readily cross with each other. If you plant those seeds you're not going to get a spaghetti squash or zucchini; you'll get an unpalatable hybrid we like to call spucchini. (Note: Not all squash types cross-pollinate. Know your varieties before planting.)

Many cultivars of fruit like pear, apple, and plum are open-pollinated and will not grow true to seed. Every now and then an incredible new cultivar will emerge from these seeds, but you'll never grow a copy of the mother tree this way.

Self-Pollinated

Self-pollinated species do not require pollen from another plant in order to produce a fruit. Tomatoes, peppers, and peas are self-pollinating. Generally, self-pollinated plants will grow true to seed as their flowers have already been fertilized before they open. Sometimes cross-pollination does occur, but it is rare.

Insect-Pollinated

These species depend on insects like bees, flies, lacewings, and moths to move pollen from one flower to another, which fertilizes flowers to produce a fruit. Depending on the species, insect-pollinated varieties will not grow true to seed, though in some cases they do.

Wind-Pollinated

Many of the pollens that blow on the wind and give people allergies are wind-pollinated species. Grasses, corn, chard, conifers—all these depend on wind to carry their pollen across the landscape, spreading onto everything in their path. This is why corn generally needs a minimum of 50 plants to ensure a good crop. Enough pollen needs to drop to thoroughly fertilize those precious ears of corn. Most wind-pollinated plants will cross-pollinate with their own species. This is why, if growing corn, you only want to grow one variety at a time and hope your neighbors aren't growing a different one close to your patch.

Hand-Pollination

Many diligent seed savers hand-pollinate crops to ensure they get the same variety back that they sowed. Hand-pollination means that you first collect the pollen of a plant you wish to save as seed. Next, brush the pollen onto the female part of the plant (the flowers that will produce fruit) and quickly bag those flowers. You have placed the correct pollen on the correct flower and, by bagging it, have excluded any further pollen from fertilizing that flower. This guarantees the seeds you save from those flowers will grow true to the mother plant.

WHEN TO HARVEST SEED

For most grasses, herbs, and flowers, harvest the seed when the flower heads turn brown and die. You must wait until the plant is naturally ready to drop its seed before harvesting. This ensures viability when planting out those sweet little seeds. Harvesting too soon will result in immature seed, which may struggle to sprout and grow vigorously. Saving seed in this way may require a shift in aesthetics as you manage the landscape. You cannot keep a perfectly clean-looking aesthetic when you're letting plants literally die to save their seed. But by letting them die you are harvesting the potential of a thriving future.

Harvesting Wet Seeds

When harvesting seeds from fruits and vegetables you'll usually be harvesting the seeds wet, meaning the fruit or vegetable is in a living state when you harvest the seed.

There are countless variations on how to harvest and process seeds from fruits, vegetables, and trees. Some need scarification, some need cold stratification, others need heat, while others need to be planted immediately—yet others need fermentation, and still others need to simply be dried and saved for later. I don't have space to get into the nuances of every different species of tree and vegetable out there. Make sure to research each one before saving seeds. Overall, most fruit and vegetable seeds are harvested from the fruit, cleaned under water, then placed on a screen of some sort to drain and dry. Once seeds are dried, they can be stored for many years.

SEED PROCESSING

There are three steps to processing dry seed from grasses, herbs, flowers, greens, and grains. The three steps are threshing, screening, and winnowing.

Threshing

The first stage of processing seed is to separate it from the seed chaff. You need a seed that is as clean of chaff as possible, which starts with breaking the chaff from the seed. Most seeds are encased by the flower heads and need to be removed from this material. This is where threshing comes in. Threshing involves crushing, stomping, and/or beating the seed heads to separate them from the rest of the plant. Depending on the seeds you are saving, this can be a fairly quick and easy process—as is the case for beans and brassicas—while grains like wheat and barley require a fierce amount of threshing to be cleaned. Many cultures over millennia have developed innovative threshing techniques for this purpose.

In the regenerative landscape, threshing will most often look like cutting and placing seed heads into a bag or bucket and stomping and/or crushing it with your hands or feet. It is best not to use metal tools for crushing the seed as this will likely break and damage the seed itself. Crushing it with wooden implements, however, is fine. Once you have separated the seed from the chaff, you will have a big mix of seed plus all the broken plant parts. At this point, it's time to screen the seeds.

Screening

The quickest way to separate seed from broken chaff is to pour the seed and chaff mix through different-sized screens. The screens will either filter out small pieces of chaff, leaving larger seed behind, or allow seed and small chaff to drop through, leaving larger pieces of chaff behind. Usually, you end up using a variety of screen sizes to remove either seed or chaff to get the cleanest seed possible. At this point, you will have semi-clean seed with remaining bits of small chaff.

Winnowing

The final step in cleaning your seed is the process of winnowing. In this step, you use either the wind, a fan, or your own breath to blow the small pieces of chaff off the remaining seed.

If using wind or fan as a method, it is common to lay down a tarp and drop the seed into the wind or in front of the fan. The seed will blow and collect in one location on the tarp and the chaff will blow and collect in another location (or blow away altogether). Be warned that some seeds are so light they will literally blow away in the wind. For seeds like this, it is best to use only your breath!

Most of the time, your breath will be your go-to for winnowing. Place the seed and chaff mix into a wide, shallow bowl. Gently shake the material back and forth until the seed falls to the bottom and the little bit of chaff rises to the top. Gently blow this chaff across the seeds, up and out of the bowl. Continue this process of gently shaking the bowl and blowing the chaff that rises to the surface off the seeds. If your seeds are light, sometimes they will blow out of the bowl with the chaff. Don't worry! You have ultimate control of your breath, so look for the sweet spot where only the chaff blows away. Continue this process until your seeds are clean.

SEED STORAGE

Dry seeds that are stored correctly can stay viable for a number of years.[1] In cold and sterile environments, seeds could theoretically stay viable for hundreds to thousands of years. For most of you reading this book, with a few simple items, you can store your seed and retain viability for five or more years.

Seeds want to be stored in a cool, dark, dry location. Store dry seeds in envelopes or glass jars with labels, or in a refrigerator or freezer, which are excellent places to store seeds but use a lot of electricity. A cupboard, cellar, or simply a water-sealed container are all great options as well. We keep our seeds in water and rodent-proof containers in a dark corner of our garage. A small closet devoted to seed saving is ideal. Filing your seeds in a file cabinet or drawers is an excellent way to keep your seeds well organized and accessible.

Labeling

Always label your seeds with the name, specific variety, date harvested, and location. This level of tracking gives you all the information you need to manage your seed stock. It's a wise practice to plant out varieties of seed approximately every five years. This way, if you are holding onto special varieties of vegetables or grains, you have a chance of growing and saving the seed again, keeping it viable for another storage cycle.

Share the Abundance

Have fun and share the abundance! Seed saving is one of the most satisfying activities in the landscape. I suggest sharing the abundance with your friends, family, and community. Participate in or organize seed exchanges, give them away as special gifts, and/or help plant other people's gardens with the seeds you have saved. This not only leads to a blossoming of new regenerative gardens but also continually renews the potential of the seeds you saved. Every garden where they grow is an opportunity to save more seeds and exponentially spread abundance in your community. It is a powerful act indeed, one of deep reciprocity with our ancestors, our descendants, the land, and each other. Saving seeds is an act of resilience that maintains the potential to grow your own food and medicine.

THE HIDDEN SEEDS

When I was nineteen, saving seed was my first initiation into ecological and regenerative design. The nonprofit I cofounded, Planting Earth Activation (PEA), gave free gardens away to the community with the purpose of saving 25 percent of those gardens for seed. Developing this type of community resource and safety net is as relevant today as it was then. Led by these tiny gems of living potential, I spent many years growing, cultivating, and saving seeds, giving tens of thousands of seeds away to the community.

One day I heard something that has always stuck with me: Viable seeds have been discovered in various gravesites around the world that have been sitting there for thousands of years. This blew my mind. Seeds sitting in the ground for 2,000 years are still able to sprout today! What does that mean about our world? We are living through an ecological catastrophe where biodiversity is being lost every day—plant species going extinct, animal species dying out—sometimes it feels insurmountable. But . . .

What about the hidden seeds? The seeds we hid from ourselves underneath our asphalt, our concrete, and our factories? What happens when we let the earth breathe again? When water and sun fall in these places where seeds are hiding? I believe the future is hidden underneath the asphalt of our cities. Ancient seeds lie in wait until the time is right to revegetate earth once again.

THE CULTURAL CONSERVANCY AND HERON SHADOW BY MAYA HARJO

Based in San Francisco, California, Ramaytush Ohlone Territory, Turtle Island, The Cultural Conservancy (TCC) is a Native-led organization that serves Indigenous cultures and collaborates with intercultural communities, organizations, and individuals. Since our founding in 1985, TCC has been dedicated to our mission of protecting and restoring Indigenous cultures, empowering them in the direct application of traditional knowledge and practices on their ancestral lands. We work with tribes, communities, organizations, movements, and individuals throughout Turtle Island, Abya Yala (the Americas), and Moananuiākea (the Pacific) who are dedicated to Indigenous rights. Our programs protect the sanctity of Native foods, illuminate our world with new and ancestral media, support Native-led organizations by funding Indigenous communities, create alliances for Indigenous solidarity, and offer Indigenous learning and educational programs through intergenerational workshops, internships, and leadership programs.

At the root of all our programs is the sacred relationship of Indigenous peoples to their land and waters and the importance of that relationship to the physical, mental, and spiritual health of Indigenous communities. Our focus on *eco-cultural* revitalization, deeply rooted in *biocultural diversity*, aims to renew and restore the health of traditional knowledge, foodways, landscapes, and practices of Indigenous cultures that have been directly targeted by the last 500 years of colonialism. By supporting Indigenous ways of knowing and being, TCC cultivates a vision of Indigenous wellness that extends from seed to plate, soil to sky, song to recipe, and ancestors to future generations.

Foundational to this vision is a practice of land stewardship that promotes a reciprocal restoration of ecological health and cultural lifeways. In addition to our support of other communities, The Cultural Conservancy stewards 7.6 acres of land in Sonoma County, on the ancestral lands of the Coast Miwok and Southern Pomo Peoples of the Federated Indians of Graton Rancheria. This land is known as Heron Shadow: An Indigenous Biocultural Heritage Oasis—a home for the dreaming, building, growing, and transmission of The Cultural Conservancy's mission and vision. From a neglected, fallow property to a holistic Native place of refuge and relearning, Heron Shadow will focus on the protection and regeneration of Indigenous agriculture, Traditional ecological knowledge, Native sciences, and ancestral lifeways.

We understand that the wellness of Indigenous peoples and the health of the land are inextricably connected. The destruction of homelands and habitat has been disastrous for the health of Indigenous communities, while the forced removal of Native people and violent separation of them from their lifeways has been equally genocidal to the ecosystems and beings with whom they are kin. We aim to cultivate Heron Shadow as a space for ecocultural healing, where community members are safe to step back into their inherited role as stewards and root themselves in reciprocal relationship with the land.

Core to this vision is our *responsibility to the seeds*. As the bearers of life, they are also the carriers of the ancestral memory and Elder wisdom that lead us in this work. While many of the most sacred seeds have been stolen from or lost to Native communities, a flourishing seed sovereignty movement is recentering our ancestral seeds as the heart of our collective cultural revitalization.

Heron Shadow is now the home to TCC's Native Seed Library, started in 2007, through which we keep safe Native heirloom seeds that have come into our care through traditional intertribal trading routes and relationships. Locally, community members gift us with their ancestral seeds or request that we seek out certain crops and varieties that they have lost access to or been disconnected from. Nationally and internationally, TCC is in deep relationship with farmers, tribes, and seedkeeper networks with whom we exchange important seeds and traditional seed-saving practices. We grow dozens of Native seed varieties each year on our farm and distribute them into the hands of Indigenous growers through our community distribution program.

At Heron Shadow, we practice holistic seed stewardship that honors the generational commitment we have made to each seed in our care. It is through the Native Seed Library that we uplift the core values and visions that guide our seed stewardship—revitalization, resilience, resistance, and rematriation.

Seed Stewardship
"Those agreements that our ancestors made with their plant relatives, they run like wild rivers in our blood and bones. And so there is an invitation for all of us, no matter what your

(continued)

ancestry is, we all have a responsibility to engage with this work of rematriation. Even just picking up a seed and beginning to grow that seed, it will rehydrate those agreements inside of you and bring this beautiful remembrance up from your very core.

This is powerful healing work of cross-cultural reconciliation, this work is cultural, spiritual, and political—this is seed justice."

—Rowen White, *Seed Mother: Coming Home* (2021)

PART VIII
Creatures of the Landscape

47
Of Wing, Hoof, Claw, and Scale

Landscapes are not things, or a collection of separate parts—they are communities. They are filled with the complex webs of relationships that exist between all aspects of life and are rooted in the processes of carbon, water, photosynthesis, and predator-prey relationships.

In the environment, animals are no less important than plants, water, soil, care, and love. They play an immeasurable role in managing the life processes of earth and keeping a thriving world possible. The animal community itself, as managers of the landscape, generate abundance in the landscape by providing a host of services, from what and how they eat to how, where, and when they move around. From a tiny ant to a 10-ton elephant, mammals, reptiles, insects, birds, and aquatic life are foundational aspects of the ecosystem that you want to support as a landscape designer and builder. Approach every project from this point of view. Step onto every landscape as a beneficial member of the current and future animal community. The decisions you make and actions you take should both utilize the beneficial behaviors of the animal world, ensuring not only their survival but their ability to thrive.

In part I of this book, I discussed the importance of keystone species. These are species (plant or animal) that an ecosystem fundamentally depends on for survival. Removal of these species results in ecosystem collapse. Developing your landscape plan will require an understanding of the current keystone species in your bioregion and past keystone species that may have gone extinct. The latter leads you to question which functions in the ecosystem may have been broken and need to be repaired for optimal health. You are one of many who can make decisions to restore optimal health in the landscape.

PREDATOR-PREY RELATIONSHIPS

The food webs of animal communities contain complex relationships between predator and prey. Witness a robin eating a worm. Contemplate the vital role a mountain lion plays when killing a deer. These relationships dictate not only the movements of animals throughout the landscape but also the bioavailability of nutrients, minerals, proteins, and plant communities. For instance, a community overrun by deer with no predators to keep them in check may experience a decline in important plant species as deer overgraze the landscape. An infestation of aphids in the landscape with no predators (parasitoid wasps, ladybugs, or tachinid fly larvae) will result in the loss of a crop. When the predator-prey ratio is kept in balance, those plant species can thrive again.

The predator–prey dynamic is foundational in the evolution of many landscapes of earth; this relationship is one of the key, consistent management processes of most ecosystems on the planet.[1] Humans have been regeneratively herding livestock for thousands of years. Indigenous communities like the Sami reindeer herders have an inseparable relationship between their own survival, the movement of herding animals, and ecosystem health.[2] Many cultures such as the Sami sustain a reciprocal relationship with their landscapes for generations.

Through the growth of industry, population, and a growing disconnection from earth's processes, people began breeding and keeping more and more livestock. Rather than moving them through the landscape regeneratively, they instead feed them grains and keep them on contained pastures or feedlots where degeneration takes place through overgrazing and overcompaction.

The movement of animals in the landscape is like the movement of water through the land. It is a fundamental part of managing a healthy ecosystem distributing nutrients and resources. Human industrialization has broken these flows. Private property laws, fencing, roads, overhunting, loss of apex predators—these human-induced disturbances have been instrumental in destroying many of the fragile and verdant ecosystems that once sprawled across nearly every part of the globe. We *can* return to a version of that lost world. We *can* repair the man-made deserts and the clear-cut forests. But we can *only* do it in community, and that means collaboration with all the creatures of the landscape.

NATURE AWARENESS

Much of the language of nature and its processes can be understood through observing animal communities and their behaviors. Birds, insects, mammals, reptiles—they all relay messages to each other and interact in specific ways within ecological webs that have wide-ranging benefits and meanings. In part II of this book, I discussed methods for bringing your awareness to the land—sit spots, observation walks, and spending time in various parts of the landscape to listen and observe are powerful techniques for connecting with and perceiving the forces of nature around you.

These nature awareness practices are fundamental for comprehending animal behaviors, migrations, communications, and working in harmony with landscape communities to manage the land ecologically. The practice of nature awareness in and of itself encompasses many facets of landscape interaction—bird language, tracking, ancient skills, wild land tending, basket making—all constitute the roots of many animistic societies. The deeper you listen to birds, follow animal paths, and watch the wind through the trees, the more you tune yourself to the same frequency, patterns, and cycles as the creatures of the land.

As you become an aware participant in the ecological webs, you access new layers of data about how the environment is functioning. Then, when mundane issues such as a proliferation of pests, a drainage problem, or a newly built fence come into play, the decisions you make in response will take into account the lives of the whole landscape community. This is essentially the most regenerative mindset you can develop as a designer, practitioner, or just plain earthling.

It takes practice and commitment to attune yourself to the patterns of plants and animals and their ecosystems. This goes beyond merely observing landscape features and practicing site assessment prior to design. This is much deeper. Here we are building intimate relationships within the ecosystem. Here we pay attention to fox, raccoon, and finch. We observe their patterns without passing judgment. We listen to the calls, follow their paths, and read their scat. In doing so, we gain not only understanding of the behaviors and life of these creatures, but we also adapt our landscapes to fit the needs of all beings. We don't dig up and disturb the fox den. We leave the seed heads that the finch is consuming even though they look dead and "ugly." We notice the pile of raccoon poop at the base of that tree and understand that there's a raccoon family living up there. This is what it means to be in relationship. Nature awareness practices are part of the methodology for building these relationships, leading us to make decisions that serve not only your needs but the needs of all members of the ecological community.

Bird Language

Understanding the language and communication network of birds—the main orators of the landscape—helps you track animal movements and seasonal changes while deepening your relationship with the earth. Birds announce the movement of predators, claim territory, check in on each other, and more. Birds tell of the weather, the ripeness of fruit, the change of the seasons—they sing the songs of the land. These messages are sent from bird to bird, even between bird species, literally moving miles across the land.[3]

"A mountain lion is here!" "A human is running this trail!" "Weasel just caught a gopher!" Bluejay shouts into the forest. The warning is picked up and recast by sparrow, then crow. The news ripples across the landscape, and every animal within range, big or small, is listening. You should be listening too.

Before fully grasping the voices of birds you need to know what their baseline is. When any animal is resting, feeding, or playing, they are in a baseline state—a state of feed and breathe. When you're taking observational walks or spending time in a sit spot, you will eventually notice this behavior throughout the landscape. The more you become present (at baseline) within the landscape, the more at ease the wildlife community will be around you. Once you know the baseline, you will be able to distinguish better the messages birds are sharing.

Animal Ancestral Compulsion

Birds, deer, elephants, rattlesnakes, salmon, butterflies—these species have been following their seasonal migratory pathways for thousands of years. These creatures have an electromagnetic sense and a generational responsibility to forage, nest, and reproduce in the same locations at roughly the same time of year as past familial generations.[4]

This ancestral compulsion fascinates me endlessly. In another grave warning that the earth is experiencing ecological catastrophes, many animals are unable to follow their ancestral impulse. They change and adjust their ancient patterns, trying to evolve, but in many cases they cannot evolve fast enough. As a result, species like the monarch butterfly are on the brink of extinction, suffering from climate change, loss of habitat, and unprecedented drought. This is part of earth's insect apocalypse—an unprecedented, unfolding catastrophe. At the time of this writing, approximately 40 percent of the world's insects are in a declining state and nearly one-third are already endangered.[5] When the insects are gone, many of the plants we and other species of wildlife depend on will disappear with them. Once that happens, mammals and other large animals will follow suit.

This story doesn't have to play out in the extinction of more species on earth. Regenerative designers, *you* are a key part of the solution. The practice isn't solely to protect what's left of the animal species on earth, but to literally regenerate ecosystems in collaboration with these organisms, to generate enough biological resources for the animal world to thrive again. Many of the decisions we make in the landscape intersect with the migration and movement of animals. By understanding the patterns and movements of the species in your region, your landscape design practices can be integrated to aid and support the animal world and its primordial ways of moving across land and water.

In my region, deer are known to travel the same trails, generation after generation, passed down for thousands of years. As a result of private property and fencing, many of these old trails no longer exist, or if they do, they are shredded by roads, homes, and agricultural areas. Pay attention to visiting bird life throughout the year, making sure your landscape provides adequate forage and nesting sites during their temporary stay between long migratory journeys.

On my homestead we have a 10-foot tall perennial Chilean tree tobacco (*Nicotiana*) that is covered with pink, tubular flowers much of the year. One spring, I heard a ruckus in the tobacco tree. Hummingbirds were locked in a fierce battle. This is behavior I'm used to, but not at the scale I experienced that day. That day, there were at least 15 hummingbirds screeching and crying, diving and buzzing, all around the nicotiana. I'd never seen so many at one time before. Over the course of the next week, I sat under this tree every day at sundown, enthralled by their territorial battle. Each day, I would count the various hummingbirds and note what they looked like. I was surprised to notice 12 of these hummingbirds were a full-body, bright orange. These were a type of bird I hadn't seen very often. When I looked them up, I discovered they were a *Rufous* hummingbird species, which migrates thousands of miles every year. That year, they turned my tree tobacco into their personal metropolis for a period of two weeks. After that, they disappeared on their long trek to the Gulf of Mexico. Since that wonderful experience, the same hummingbirds come back to visit each year in the spring. Never have I seen as many as I did that first year, but when I recognize them now I feel grateful that my homestead provides a wide diversity of hummingbird forage for them during their brief visits.

OBSERVING ANIMAL HABITAT

In this part of the book, we explore many ways to create habitat for beneficial wildlife in the landscape. But the idea of creating habitat almost assumes that functional habitat doesn't exist already. Ecological designers take stock of the existing environment, observing existing habitat and its functioning before rushing in to make changes. It's quite possible you'll feel an urge to remove existing habitat in the process of building your dream regenerative homestead. Push against that urge until you have a clear sense of what habitat already exists in the landscape.

Existing habitat structures come in many forms. A dead old tree makes a perfect woodpecker metropolis. A couple of large stones make a perfect lizard village and a large blackberry patch the site of a fox den. Until you take the time to watch the animal community interact with the landscape, you won't know to leave these areas alone.

I can't emphasize this enough.

Before you take action in the landscape, learn about the ecological processes and community dynamics already taking place. If you are truly about regenerating ecosystems, you won't remove these habitat systems without a plan to re-create them in the landscape.

ANIMAL BEHAVIORS

The general behavior of animals is integral to ecosystem management—what and how they eat, the effect of their poop on the soil, how they move seeds around, the messages they send to each other, and their nesting and breeding behaviors. For instance, bees, wasps, flies, and other creatures move pollen from plant to plant, fertilizing vegetables, fruits, and nuts. The movement of pollen also helps plant and tree species evolve to better withstand their changing environments.

Having a bird-friendly landscape, where many varieties of forage plants provide food and habitat, also yields an increase in the amount of phosphorus in the soil, delivered in the form of guano dropped by birds.[6] This further enhances soil health, which further builds the immune systems of the plants and trees that are visited by the birds. It's a holistic, reciprocal cycle we get to take part in. Seed dispersal by birds, squirrels, and other creatures sow edible and medicinal landscapes everywhere. Many tree and berry species coevolved and are even dependent upon animals for processing and dispersing seed to ensure the tree reproduces itself for generations.

We are caught in webs of relationships between the behavior of animals, the abundance of plants, and our own animal behaviors, instincts, and needs. When we all work together in exchange and reciprocity, we literally create paradise.

Leave Landscape Habitat Intact

Leave their homes alone! Let it be messy a little bit longer! These are the thoughts I want to yell out when I see people cutting back their gardens heavily in the fall. Those dry stalks, the seed heads, the blanket of leaves covering the ground, these are literally the homes and habitats for beneficial organisms hoping to overwinter in the landscape. The westernized cultural aesthetic of a clean and pruned landscape, where nothing is left to stand or rot, is the antithesis of the ecological requirements of the wildlife community.

I understand, there must be a middle ground. If you're a business or a school hosting special events, you want the landscape to look amazing at all times. Situations like these require you to clean up the landscape and make it feel welcoming. You must find the balance between aesthetics and ecological function. But take heed: removing the habitat for beneficial birds, insects, reptiles and so on means that the next spring will come with significantly fewer beneficial organisms in your landscape. As a result, a proliferation of pests will ensue.

People sometimes remove old trees and other beneficial habitat systems because of their unsightly aesthetic or reduced production. This is not holistic thinking. Many old apple orchards where I live have been transformed into vineyards over the last few decades. As the apples grew old and produced less, and the demand for these apples changed (mostly because the Gravenstein apples of this region have a short shelf life), people considered these trees more of a nuisance than a benefit. But if you ever walk through an old apple orchard, you will notice that birds and rabbits make extensive use of these hollowed-out old beings. These trees offer homes to bluebirds, oak titmouse, tree swallows, and more. What do these birds eat? Bugs. They eat lots of bugs. Their behaviors benefit a balanced and healthy ecosystem and an old hollowed-out tree provides the perfect natural home. Many of these trees continue to provide harvest for humans and other animals as well.

Before rushing to clear your overgrown landscape, think about the organisms that nest, forage, and depend upon the leaves, stalks, seeds, and branches of this decomposing ecosystem. Allow some landscape plants to age and wither. They might become unsightly, but they provide habitat for many beneficial organisms.

Insectary Superstars

Insectary plants are one of the easiest ways to attract these beneficial birds and insects into the landscape. But you must remember that form follows function. Not every flower is made the same way, and some flowers attract a higher diversity of insects than others. Take yarrow flower (*Achillea millefolium*) for instance. This white flowering, herbaceous perennial is a food source for hundreds of different insect species. Its pollen attracts everything: bees, butterflies, hummingbirds, tachinid flies, and lacewings.[7] As you develop a planting plan suited to your climate and soils, choose plant species that attract a large diversity of insects.

Integrated Pest Management (An Ecological Approach)

When we design ecological landscapes, we are designing ecosystems. A healthy ecosystem is capable of keeping a healthy balance between pests and predators. When we create new landscapes, however, it takes time for the pest–prey balance to find its equilibrium. As a result, we will have seasons where pests become a big issue on our crops. This is where Integrated Pest Management (IPM) comes into play, an approach that has gained in popularity in the twenty-first century. IPM looks at many options for pest control including the use of beneficial insects, birds, pesticides, and more. In the following chapter, we will explore IPM from an ecological point of view. This means making use of all the regenerative techniques without the use of synthetic chemicals.[8]

48
Integrated Pest Management

Integrated Pest Management (IPM) is a tailored, ecological approach to managing pests in the landscape that incorporates several strategies at the same time. This thinking is based on the notion that there is no one way to handle a pest in the landscape. The more diversity in your approach to managing pests, the better your success. IPM has been embraced throughout organic farming, gardening, and landscape communities.

Dealing with an aphid infestation through the lens of ecological IPM could look like this:

- Help beneficial insects like ladybugs and parasitoid wasps overwinter in the landscape. These insects will consume aphids and proliferate from the aphid population.
- Provide bird boxes and sufficient bird habitat to feed a large diversity of birds in the landscape year-round. Many birds such as goldfinch and chickadee will eat aphids directly from the stalks of brassicas and other plants.
- Organic, nontoxic insecticides such as neem oil or nontoxic mint soap can be sprayed onto heavily infested areas to kill off and deter the aphids.
- Spray compost tea, add healthy compost, and water sufficiently to build soil and provide enough nutrients for plants to grow healthy and strong. The healthier and stronger the plant, the better they fend off any pest attacks on their own.

In the above example, we've integrated four different approaches to deal with aphids, all of which can be implemented simultaneously. With this many solutions in play, it's unlikely aphids will pose a huge problem in the landscape. (Note: Building healthy soil and inviting in a diversity of beneficial organisms takes time and you may not see the yields from these efforts for one to two years.)

The same integrated approach can be applied for any pest concern in the landscape. Use as many biological solutions as possible to develop a landscape that empowers biodiversity in all its forms and major pest problems can be avoided.

SEASONALITY

Seasonality plays a huge role in the activity of pests and predators. In most cases, a pest outbreak only lasts for a few weeks, possibly a month, until the season and climate factors have shifted and are no longer ideal for the pest to proliferate. As you learn about the potential pests in your region, plan for an IPM approach that is activated in the right season to ensure the best possible management throughout the year. For instance, you can boost the immunity of the garden by applying compost in the early springtime or let the fall garden overwinter so beneficial species are present when springtime pests come to forage.

STRESSED PLANTS

Any time a major pest issue exists, the overall vigor of the plants must first be assessed. Pests are a key indicator of unhealthy soil, lack of water, too much water, wrong climate pairing, and so on. Building soil by providing organic matter and feeding soil biology ensures that plants have what they need to fight pests off themselves. Plants that are stressed out because they're not in their right climate or microclimatic zone are also going to be weak and thus attract pests. Pests indicate a whole set of possible systemic issues and lead us to better manage the ecological interactions of the entire ecosystem.

BENEFICIAL PREDATORY INSECTS

Predatory insects come in all shapes, sizes, colors, and attitudes. They can be as intimidating as a bald-faced hornet or as fairy-like as a blue dragonfly. The one thing they all have in common is that they eat other insects, often the kind that consumes plant tissue. Attracting these organisms into the landscape is one pillar of the ecological pest management approach.

Dragonfly (Anisoptera)

Dragonflies are one of the most ancient winged insect species on earth. These beings evolved around three hundred million years ago and are still with us today. Dragonflies only hunt while flying and have a voracious appetite for mosquitos. A single dragonfly eats up to 30 mosquitos on average per day.[1] If the landscape is making use of the water-harvesting and pond-building systems featured in this book, there's a good chance dragonflies will inhabit the landscape year-round. When that happens, you have serious insect-devouring predators on your side.

Parasitoid Wasps (Ichneumonidae and others)

There are thousands of different kinds of wasps—some as small as a midge and others as large as a paper wasp. Most of them are harmless to humans but pose a serious threat to smaller insects. All wasps are beneficial to the regenerative landscape but a few families of wasps we call parasitoids have a very specific diet—mainly aphids and caterpillars.

The reproduction process of parasitoid wasps is an example of the viciousness found in the natural world. Using their stingers, they pierce the skin of their prey and inject eggs into its body. When the eggs hatch, the larvae eat their prey from the inside out, piercing a hole through its body to fly away when mature. Spend time looking at any plant covered in aphids. With enough searching, you would likely find paralyzed aphids with a tiny hole in them. These were the host body for a parasitoid wasp.

I know it sounds gruesome, but these organisms are highly beneficial in the landscape. Take note, however, that in order for these wasps to reproduce in any great number, they need plenty of host bodies in order to lay their eggs. This means if you remove all aphids and caterpillars from the garden, you're unlikely to have a large population of these beneficial wasps.

Ladybugs (Coccinellidae)

Yay, lady beetles—everyone's favorite sweet and cute little insect, right? Well, these pretty bugs are actually vicious killers (just forget that fact when you put that cute ladybug printed onesie on your baby). They have piercing jaws to help them chomp on aphids and other small insects. This behavior, of course, makes them great companions to the landscape. Ladybugs migrate in large masses over long areas but many will also reside in the landscape. Many generations of ladybugs will hatch in the garden throughout the year if they have a food source, shelter, and access to water, all available in a regenerative landscape. Once ladybugs settle onto a food source, they lay their eggs on infested plants, and soon lady beetle larvae will be all over the garden. When you see this phenomenon take place, don't cut those plants back! Leave them alone to allow the ladybugs to go through their full life cycle.

Lacewings (Neurotera)

The garden is full of delightful creatures, no less the green lacewing. When I spot these in the garden, I know we are doing something right. These flying insects are incredible pollinators, attracted especially to plants in the *Asteraceae* family such as sunflower, dill, and dandelion. They feed on nectar, yeasts, and honeydew. Lacewing larvae are voracious eaters of scales, aphids, and other pests, each one capable of eating up to 200 aphids per week.[2]

Tachinid Flies (Tachinidae)

When most people think of flies, they conjure in their minds black flies that feed on dung and death. But not all flies are the same. There are thousands of species with many functions in the ecosystem. The tachinid fly in particular, with its 1,300 species in North America alone, is a great ally to the landscape. They have a variety of methods for killing pests, especially beetles and caterpillars. Some lay their eggs inside the host bodies or lay eggs for hosts to consume. In both cases, the larvae eat the host from the inside. Tachinid flies visit many plants in the garden, providing an abundance of pollination services.

Hoverfly (Syrphidae)

Hoverflies are a seldom sought-after beneficial pollinator that is vital to our changing climate and food-production systems. They are true flies that mimic bees and yellowjackets with their striped markings. Hoverflies are known to visit approximately 72 percent of food crops globally[3] while also protecting said crops from pests. There are nearly 6,000 species of hoverflies throughout the entire world. Adult hoverflies feed on nectar and pollen while the larvae feed on aphids and other pests.

MAMMALS

Mammals sometimes get a bad rap in the garden. Deer, rats, gophers, skunks—these creatures often are thought of as pests in the landscape. While many of these species *are* pests, that mindset is inherently disconnected from seeing the landscape as a whole ecosystem functioning on reciprocal relationships. All creatures have a place in this whole, whether in or outside your landscape project. Mammals move to and from the landscape and are therefore part of a wider world than the artificial confines of your project. If you put out rat poison to kill rats, they will eventually get eaten by hawks, foxes, or other predators. Now those predators are poisoned. The landscape is always connected to the wider biome.

As the ecosystem becomes more diverse, you'll notice an increase in mammalian visitors to the landscape. Fallen fruit and seed will attract browsing animals and rodents. Then the rodents will attract predators like fox, skunk, opossum, or whatever the equivalent is in your bioregion. This is how the food web of the landscape works. Maintain biodiversity and all beings benefit.

For some, the idea of a skunk or an opossum is horrifying. That is because modern culture has demonized these animals. We have skunks on our homestead and they have never been a problem. Actually, they have been a huge benefit to the landscape. Did you know that skunks dig up and eat yellowjacket hives? Every time I see one, they mind their own business without ever looking at me. Opossums (*Didelphis virginiana*) are another creature that doesn't live up to its bad rap. Did you know one opossum will eat up to 5,000 ticks a season?[4] They eat rats as well. Opossums are one of the great antidotes to disease in the environment. (Note: If you are keeping chickens, many beneficial mammals become a threat to the flock. Keep your chickens in predator-proof coops and they can all coexist together. That is the best way!)

Mammals have their own specific patterns and relationships to discover and manage in the landscape. Sometimes you will need to keep mammals out of the garden and sometimes you invite them in. If the aim is regeneration, then the aim is biodiversity. Trust in the wisdom of the earth, its complex food webs, and interspecies relationships.

ATTRACTING BIRDS TO THE LANDSCAPE

The bird community is a vital part of every landscape—they sing, they peck and scratch, they eat, and they flit from tree to tree. As the diversity of birds in the garden increases, the benefits (and possible downsides) grow exponentially. Birds are attracted to the landscape if they find food (insects, fruit, seeds, worms, rodents), water, shelter, and nesting sites. By developing these resources in the regenerative landscape, you are creating habitat for a thriving bird population.

In some ecosystems, rodents (rats, mice, gophers, etc.) wreak havoc on the homestead. Nature has solved this problem through the hunting behavior of owls, raptors, and predatory mammals. Building owl boxes is a great way to invite this beneficial predator onto your project. These nighttime stalkers cruise silently through the woods, farmland, and urban environments devouring every rodent they can find. A male barn owl may catch up to 10 rodents a night to feed a family of owlets.

My neighbor has barn owls (*Tyto alba*) living in his 1916 water tower, and he tracks their behavior with an infrared camera. He records the owls through the seasons to watch their habits and behaviors. One year, between May 1 and May 18, papa owl caught 91 gophers to feed the owlets and the mama.

Attracting birds of all kinds is foundational to a functional regenerative landscape. The following sections will help you design systems to attract these winged landscape superheroes.

Nesting

You would be amazed at the incredible places birds build their nests. I've seen them build nests on top of a broom left outside, inside a small box, in a cavity of redwood bark, attached to the side of a bamboo pole, and even in the gravel of a landscape patio. Every species of bird has an ideal (though sometimes quirky) nesting habit. Generally, nesting behavior breaks down into the following categories.

Ground Nesting. Killdeer, quail, bowerbirds, peacock, and turkey build their nests on the ground, usually beneath established plants, in mounds, in pits, or in other protected areas. This is not always the case, however. The killdeer (*Charadrius vociferus*) builds its nest in open pastures, on gravel, or on sand, hoping its camouflaged eggs and feather patterns keep it from being noticed.

Cavity Dwellers. Cavity-dwelling birds build their nests inside the holes of trees, bird boxes, the sides of buildings, and nearly any type of cavity that is off the ground where the bird feels safe.

Tree Canopies. When most people think of a bird's nest, they imagine birds that build their homes in the branches and leaves of trees. These types of nests are usually built in hidden parts of the tree to protect them from predators.

Regenerative landscapes are inviting to birds, both for visiting and for permanent residence. You can take their nesting requirements into consideration throughout the landscape by providing sufficient habitat through vertical layering—ideal for bird species that prefer to nest in tall trees and those that build their nests a few feet off the ground—and nurturing sufficient perennial and woody plant communities to protect ground nesting birds. Additionally, waiting to clean up landscapes and mowing later in the springtime will help ground nesting birds rear their young from incubation through hatching.

Cover/Shelter

As you identify the volume and diversity of bird species in your community, you may notice a few patterns. Notably, birds are constantly vigilant about being attacked. Most birds will not venture out into the open for fear of being picked off by a hawk or other predator. If your landscape boasts lots of open areas—trees separated by huge expanses of manicured grass— your environment is not optimal for a wide diversity of birds. Birds need protective cover in order to hide and feed.

Developing cover in the landscape is as easy as letting a patch of brambles stay where it is, planting thick hedgerows, or developing perennial shrub layers throughout your gardens. These plant structures provide plenty of spaces for birds to dive into cover when a predator is nearby. Cover that connects various parts of the landscape allows the bird community to move through the entire landscape at a baseline state and provide ecological services like eating seeds, insects, and bird guano fertilization.

Forage

No bird will care to visit your landscape if there is no food. Since different bird species eat different foods, it is in your best interest to provide as many different kinds of forage as possible. Many birds love eating nuts, berries, and seeds. You provide this forage in two different ways. First of all, establish a diverse plant community that provides berries, nuts, and seeds. Make sure this forage arrives at different times of the year to keep a more diverse bird community around for longer periods through the year. Many forage plants provide human food as well, and you may end up fighting the birds for some of your favorite crops like raspberries, cherries, and peaches. Many fruit farmers actually hate birds for the damage they do to their crops and go to great lengths to deter birds from the crops.

Try not to hate birds for eating fruit. If you grow enough diversity, when the system is mature, there will be enough for all. That being said, sometimes different birds visit from year to year or their behaviors change and you may lose a crop to them. In the spring season of 2022, birds ate all the cherries off our three trees. This was the first time that had happened and led me to reflect on what had changed. After a couple months of observing the situation, my conclusion is that when the neighbors cut down 15 large pine trees, they evicted a large murder of crows. Those crows moved onto our homestead and became very territorial. They also ate all the cherries.

The second method for providing forage for birds is to let weeds and cultivated landscape plants (including vegetables) go to seed. Instead of cutting everything back as soon as it bolts or flowers, allow a percentage of your landscape to go to seed first. Use this both for harvesting seed as a safety net for future propagation and to provide seed-loving birds with important forage.

Bird Boxes

Many cavity-dwelling bird species will happily make their home inside homemade bird boxes. When building a bird box, first consider the types of birds you are hoping to attract. The size of the hole in the bird box will determine which birds can and want to make a nest there and which will not.

See the chart to the right for a range of holes to attract different sorts of birds.

Whenever possible, it is best to focus on attracting native bird species to your bird boxes—those that provide beneficial services to the landscape, such as eating insects and weed seeds.

Once you have built or bought a bird box, be thoughtful about the location and placement of your box. One of the most dangerous predators to songbirds are domesticated cats, so place your box out of reach of feline friends. Generally, boxes are placed on a single round pole around the garden and farm, away from trees and fences where predators can stalk the nest.

(Note: Be careful with outdoor cats in the landscape—they are responsible for over 2.4 billion bird deaths a year in the United States alone.[5] If you're hoping to have a large and diverse bird population on the site, then you may want to make sure outdoor cats don't decimate these populations.)

Bird Species (North American)	Bird Box Hole Size (Inches)
Barn Owl (*Tyto alba*)	6
Bluebirds (*Sialia spp.*)	1.5
Brown Creeper (*Certhia americana*)	1.375
Brown Headed Nuthatch (*Sitta pusilla*)	1.125
Chickadee (*Poecile spp.*)	1.125
Crested Flycatcher (*Myiarchus crinitus*)	1.25
Downy Woodpecker (*Picoides pubescens*)	1.5
Hairy Woodpecker (*Picoides villosus*)	1.5
House Finch (*Carpodacus mexicanus*)	2
Kestrel (*Falco tinnunculus*)	3

MASON BEE HABITAT

Mason bees (*Osmia*) are widespread throughout much of the world. These cavity-dwelling bees make their homes inside hollowed-out branches and cracks in stone. These incredible pollinators readily make their home in nesting sites you build for that purpose in the landscape.

Constructing mason bee habitat is quite simple, yet also beautiful and almost always effective. Mason bees make homes in hollowed out tubes, which can easily be made using bamboo, elderberry, or by drilling holes in a block of wood.

MAKING MASON BEE HOTELS

1. **Design Approach.** Gather hollowed twigs of bamboo, remove the inner pith of elderberry, find adequate dried reeds, or use other hollow branches from species local to your region. Alternatively, drill appropriately sized holes into blocks of wood to create the tubular shapes mason bees and other solitary pollinators like to use as homes. Avoid using treated wood or insect-repelling species like cedar for your nesting material.

2. **Drill Holes.** Mason and leaf cutter bees are solitary creatures that don't build large communal nests. The females use a single tube to gather pollen and lay their eggs. Providing ample nesting sites will grow larger populations in the landscape and harness the pollination powers of these creatures. More holes equal more potential homes. Drill

5/16-inch-wide holes for mason bees and 3/8-inch-wide holes for leafcutter bees, all six inches deep.

3. **Rain Protection.** To keep your pollinator hotel from getting damaged by sun, rain, and predators, keep it up off the ground and protected with a small roof (with eaves) to keep dry. This will increase the chances of attracting a thriving bee population.

Once you have built your pollinator home and set it up, check the tubes every now and then to see if they are being inhabited by bees. You'll know a tube has been claimed when a mother bee covers the entrance to protect her egg. Replace nesting materials annually to keep these habitats functioning year after year and avoid buildup of kleptoparasitic mites and Houdini flies, which prey on solitary bees.

INSECTARY PLANTS

In part VII, I discussed the various insectary types of plants: attracting, repelling, and larval food plants. These plant species should be integrated into every regenerative landscape to maximize biodiversity and beneficial insect populations. To the right is a list of insectary plants and the species they attract/feed.

Flower Shapes

Choose plants with flower structures formed for different types of pollinators. If you desire a hummingbird garden, choose flowers with a tubular shape made for a hummingbird's beak. For butterflies, choose flowers with wider "landing pads."

Plants coevolved with their pollinators for millions of years. Their shape, color, and aromas

Insectary Plant Species (Short List)	**Beneficial Insects**
Sweet Alyssum (*Lobularia maritima*)	Minute Pirate Bugs, Parasitoid Wasps, Hover Fly
Sunflower (*Helianthus spp.*)	Braconid Wasp, Butterflies, Bees, Minute Pirate Bug, Chalcid Wasps, Green Lynx Spider, Big eyed Bugs, Lady beetles, assassin Bugs, Predatory Stink Bugs, Lacewings
Thyme (*Thymus spp.*)	Hover Flies, Parasitoid Wasps, Tachinid Fly
Lavender (*Lavandula spp.*)	Hover Flies, Parasitoid Wasps, Bees, Lady Beetles, Butterflies
Bee Balm (*Monarda spp.*)	Bees, Butterflies, Hummingbirds
Elderberry (*Sambucus*)	Minute Pirate Bug, Lace wings, Bees, Butterflies
Mountain Mint (*Pycnanthemum*)	Bees, Butterflies, Solitary Wasps, Beetles
Mexican Sunflower (*Tithonia spp.*)	Butterflies, Bees, Spined Soldier Bug, Minute Pirate Bugs, Hover Flies
Yarrow (*Achillea millefolium*)	Braconid Wasp, Damsel Bug, Lady Beetle, Minute Pirate Bug, Spined Soldier bug, Chalcid Wasps
Dill (*Anethum graveolens*)	Lacewings, Hover Flies, Lady Beetles, Parasitoid Wasps, Minute Pirate Bug
Sage (*Salvia spp.*)	Bees, Lady Beetles, Butterflies

all attract their animal counterparts in order to be pollinated and spread seeds. The more intention you devote to planting different shapes and colors of flowers in the landscape, the more biodiversity will be generated.

Trap Crops

Trap crops are used as sacrificial plants to trap pests that would normally have a negative effect on the rest of your landscape. Rather than planting crops specifically for this purpose, you can simply leave pest-infested plants undisturbed as martyrs. This has two purposes.

First, allowing pests to focus on a few plants can keep them busy and reduce their spread to other plant species. Second, and more important, letting a pest population coexist in the landscape provides an ample food source for beneficial insects like parasitoid wasps, ladybugs, hoverflies, and tachinid flies to expand their populations and beneficial impacts on the land.

BURROWING MAMMALS

Burrowing mammals are often considered pests in landscapes around the world. Moles, voles, groundhogs, ground squirrels, gophers, and wombats are all burrowing animals that tend to damage the roots of agricultural crops. Managing these beings in the landscape is tricky business and needs to be approached with a combination of techniques such as placing plants in rodent-proof metal baskets, trapping, and attracting predators.

REPTILES

Snakes, lizards, turtles, and skinks all readily make regeneratively managed landscapes their home. These beings provide incredible pest management services and should be regarded as beneficial in the landscape (aside from poisonous snakes and the issues they pose). Creating habitat for lizards is especially helpful because they have a voracious appetite for insects. If you create dark, protected, cool environments, lizards are virtually guaranteed to post up in the garden.

AMPHIBIANS

When you harness the powers of both water and land, you are also harnessing the power of amphibians. These organisms, which live part-time in the water and part-time on land, are incredibly beneficial to the ecosystem as a whole. Many frogs, salamanders, and snakes spend their days eating insects and smaller life across the landscape, both in and out of the water. In this way, amphibians are managing the food webs of the entire landscape ecosystem. Develop year-round water sources in your design if possible to create habitat for these world-hopping beings.

Apply the principle of *relative location* when you're placing water features to integrate landscape-regulating functions with the patterns of thirsty wildlife. Place water features in a central location where the organisms they are attracting can play beneficial roles in the landscape.

LIZARD HABITAT

Lizards all over the world provide many beneficial processes to their ecosystems, consuming bugs, dropping scat as fertilizer, and making their homes in the cool, dark crevices of stones and wood. Your regenerative landscape must be filled with habitat for the beneficial lizards in your region. Depending on the context, your project may already have an ample amount of existing habitat sufficient to host large lizard populations. If that is the case, make sure to consider any changes or demolitions you propose in regard to lizards as those activities may remove this vital habitat and you will need to develop new environments for them.

Making lizard habitat is as simple as placing a rotting log on the ground, or it could be as complex as building rock cairns with deep cavities in the middle. When the system gets overgrown by plants, they'll make an even better habitat for the lizard community. Lizard habitats built near water sources like hoses, ponds, natural waterways, and cool shady areas are all the more enticing for many lizard species. They want it moist but not wet, and having easy access to water is a plus.

EDGE EFFECT

Organisms of all kinds thrive in the gaps and edges between water and land, forest and meadow, garden and orchard, near building foundations and in rock piles. Creatures like snakes, lizards, and turtles take cover and hide, nest, burrow, hunt, cool down, and hibernate at these edges. With that in mind, accentuate habitats in these transitional spaces.

AVOID INSECTICIDES (CONVENTIONAL AND ORGANIC)

Before spraying insecticides (organic or conventional), assess the whole situation and make sure you are not killing beneficials and destroying the health of topsoil or water systems. Remember the reciprocity principle, which already governs the role of pests. If you kill all the pests manually, you've taken food sources away from beneficials. It's a tricky balance to manage. The goal is that someday there will be so many beneficials that pests cease to be a major issue (except during stress times).

Insecticides are responsible for innumerable damages to ecosystems, including poisoned waterways, biologically dead soils, and loss of beneficial insects. The most concerning and dramatic example of this is the widespread use of neonicotinoids on farms and in urban centers. These toxic chemicals get absorbed by pollen and become toxic to bee populations. Over time, they poison bee colonies, even affecting the health of queen bees, which reduces a bee colony's ability to reproduce.[6]

In short, a regenerative landscape is a safe haven for insects where insecticides of all kinds are *not* employed in pest management.

HABITAT PONDS

Year-round water sources are vital to wildlife habitat and survival. Many wildlife partners who manage the landscape require water, not only to stay hydrated but also for reproduction. Frogs, dragonflies, damselflies, and salamanders all require sources of water for laying and hatching new generations. Birds, mammals, snakes, and lizards all visit year-round water sources for food and drink. No matter what climate you're in (yes, even freezing cold climates), year-round water features can be designed and implemented in the landscape. These features range from cheap or free to highly expensive systems. Ponds are discussed at length in part VI of this book if you want to explore water systems in more depth. Below, I focus on their benefits as habitat systems.

In most projects, I design a year-round water source of some kind for the bees, the birds, and everyone else. These havens of life become not only attractions for wildlife but also destinations for the human community. I still get surprised and delighted by the diversity of organisms I observe visiting these waterholes throughout the year. The edge of a habitat pond is a great place to witness the patterns of landscape and the ecological community we share.

Years ago, when stewarding a new homestead, I planned the installation of a well-sized habitat pond for my garden. One scorching summer day of 106°F, I walked out to visit my pond project, now halfway built. That week my crew and I had completed the shaping and installation of the pond liner and filled the pond with water. Only the final planting, finishing touches of the waterfall, and edging the liner with rock remained. Though, on a sweltering day such as this, who would want to work outside? I approached the pond, sun glaring in my eyes. The water looked cool and calm as I sat at the edge. A loud buzzing filled the air around me and, looking around, I saw hundreds of honeybees lining the edge of the shallow ledge around the pond. This ledge had much of the rock and gravel installed, and the shallow gravel area gave the bees a perfect pad to land and drink from the pond water. As I sat, dropping into an observational state, I noticed the steady stream of bees coming and going from the northwest. Then it hit me. This is the closest water they have to drink on this hot day! They must be desperate for water; the honey bee scouts must have sent a map to the hive communicating where the closest water source was—our new pond. My body tingled with excitement, gratitude for the bees, and the privilege of providing them such important nourishment on a blazing hot summer day.

49

Fencing

They say good fences make good neighbors but this is not always the case. Sometimes tearing the fence down enables relationships to flourish. Neighbor relations aside, we often need to consider fences for other practical and important reasons, like keeping deer from eating 90 percent of the plants we are trying to grow for sustenance or protecting animals like chickens, goats, and sheep from wild creatures of the night. With that in mind, you may find yourself in need of building a fence.

For deer, you will need a wire mesh standing fence, built seven to eight feet tall. These are the typical fences that protect gardens, farms, and vineyards in deer country. The same fences are often built strong enough to keep other critters like wild hogs and rabbits from entering and damaging the landscape.

I want to stop here for a moment. Take this moment to consider whether a fence is necessary and what kind it would be. You can build fences that keep deer out but let rabbits in. It doesn't have to break all connections with four-legged creatures outside the landscape. Keep in mind that a deeply regenerative system is woven into the ecosystem, the whole environment, and the landscape's inhabitants.

SINGLE TALL FENCE

A single, seven- to eight-foot tall fence is a major investment that allows your landscape to thrive without the pressure of browsing animals.

Siting the Fence

The first step is deciding where to put the fence. Most often people place fences on property lines. This makes sense for marking territory and provides protection for your landscape but should not be considered the only or best possible location.

When considering whether to exclude animals from an area, keep the whole ecosystem in mind. Are you cutting off and fencing all pathways that deer and other animals have been traversing for generations? Consider relationships and reciprocity here. Take the time needed to understand the wildlife patterns in the landscape before throwing fences up around the property.

If you're set on having a property line fence, it could be shorter, which still allows animals to pass through but marks the property's edge. A taller deer fence could then enclose only the landscape areas where desirable, deer-sensitive plants are cultivated. Placing fences on contour can stack the added functions of slowing water and sediment flow across the landscape; then, if the fence is planted, these species will gain the benefit of contour-influenced topography.

Choosing Fencing Materials

As with every decision about landscape materials, the two major factors are whether to source your materials locally and budget. If time, energy, and budget allow, regenerative harvesting of fence posts from the landscape is ideal. To be done ecologically, these resources would come from congested forests where thinning to protect against fire is needed or from coppiced woodlots where wood is grown to be harvested again and again in subsequent regenerative cycles. Additionally, you can reuse suitable materials from the site, be it metal posts from an old fence or vineyard or reclaimed materials from an old building.

The fencing material itself can also be used to weave branches in a wattle formation, build split rail or log pole fences, and everything in between. Humans have been building fences like these, harvesting needed material from the environment, for thousands of years. These techniques are still as relevant today as they ever were. The biggest challenges in building fences like these is finding natural resources in suburban and urban communities and the labor it takes to build. Most of us walking a regenerative path had to learn the hard way, over time, that most regenerative activities are more expensive and definitely more time-consuming than simply purchasing manufactured materials from the hardware store to build a landscape structure. It is a sad state of affairs, one that is brought to us by the industrial economic system we are currently living in. It is for this reason that your specific situation in life and that of your project may be more realistically suited to fences built from purchased rather than harvested materials.

If you are purchasing fencing materials, there are many options.

Wooden Posts. Any wood pole, post, or right-sized lumber can be used as a fence post, but not all will have the sort of longevity and strength most designers want in their fencing. Most conventional practitioners use some form of pressure treated 4 by 4, 6 by 6, or larger posts to secure their fencing. The benefit of chemically treated materials is their rot resistance (longevity). These posts are buried in the ground with soil compacted at the base and will last for decades without rotting. Corner and gate posts are frequently buried with concrete to provide extra stability.

Nontreated wooden posts will rot more quickly than treated ones, but they are placed in the landscape without the addition of potentially harmful chemicals. Nontreated wooden posts can be treated by using the Shou Sugi Ban wood-burning method discussed in part VI. Interestingly enough, this method of wood burning is also used in Northern Europe, where fence posts have been charred before installation into the ground for hundreds of years.

Using rot-resistant materials like redwood (*Sequoia sempervirens*), cedar (*Cedrus*), locust (*Robinia*), teak (*Tectona grandis*), yew (*Taxus baccata*), juniper (*Juniperus*), or Osage orange (*Maclura pomifera*) decreases the chances of rot. To add even more longevity, posts can be buried in a foot of compacted gravel and/or concrete. If you use concrete, make sure the top of the concrete comes out of the ground and is angled to slant water away from the post.

Very old reclaimed materials such as old-growth redwood and cedar from demolished old structures will last a very, very long time on their own. Redwood itself takes as long to decompose as it did to grow, which means a thousand-year-old redwood will take a thousand years to decompose. That being said, I don't support the cutting of *any* old-growth forest! Our old-growth forests are in danger of disappearing forever, and the only old-growth wood you should use in any aspect of your landscape is reclaimed material from old barns, homes, ports, and other infrastructure being demolished to make way for new structures.

Metal Posts. Metal lasts almost forever, and thick, galvanized metal lasts the longest. That's why this material is an excellent choice for building fences. Metal stakes and posts come in a wide variety. T-posts are the most common metal fencing material on the market. These thin metal posts are pounded into the ground using a heavy post driver. T-posts come in a variety of thicknesses and lengths. They are mass produced and easily accessible worldwide for relatively low cost.

Thick metal conduit is a step above T-posts. These are hollow metal tubes that range in diameter from three inches to more than eight inches. Metal conduit is expensive but once installed will last for generations with little to no maintenance. If pounded deep into the ground, these posts require no concrete, and with tractor-assisted pounding implements, large permanent fences can be erected quickly.

Fencing Mesh. The actual mesh that is stretched from post to post creating the animal barrier comes in many forms, material choices, and styles. Many high-end architectural firms design fancy fences, incorporating stained wood with corrugated metal panels and adding special lighting features, while most agricultural fencing uses rolls of simple "nonclimb" metal mesh.

For most regenerative designers, fences will be kept simple as the goal is to generate as much plant life as possible. This means that we may choose to plant or train vines across our fences rather than use expensive, aesthetically driven fencing systems. That being said, if you have the time, desire, and budget to build a beautiful fence that features artistic expression, then go for it!

In the twenty-first century, wire fences are the most popular and inexpensive style of fence. Rolls of wire mesh (usually 100- to 150-foot rolls) can be purchased in a variety of thicknesses, mesh patterns, and heights. For instance, if you are building a fence to keep out deer or other browsing animals, you might choose a seven-foot wire mesh, nonclimb fence, with a two by four-inch mesh grid.

The best part about using rolls of wire mesh fencing is how easy it is to quickly roll them across the landscape and attach to preinstalled fence posts. Plan the correct distance between fence posts—commonly seven to eight feet "on center" (meaning that you measure from the center of each post)—and methods to pull tension along the fence (using a winch, for example). Wire mesh fencing is a breeze to install.

Plastic mesh fencing is also available and is the cheapest and quickest option for stringing up a fence, but this material is not advised for any long-term application. The plastic mesh often degrades in the sun, falls down in sections, and sometimes traps small animals. It's best to avoid this unless you need a quick, temporary solution.

Wooden Fencing. As mentioned above, humans have been building wooden fences for thousands of years, using wattle, split rail, and other techniques. These fences make beautiful and long-lasting features in the landscape, derived from locally harvested materials. Connecting fence posts with wooden panels or lumber is more common in these modern times. If you install the majority of the wood paneling a few inches above the ground, the fence can last for decades. These fences are installed in many patterns but normally consist of lateral boards that are secured horizontally from post to post at the top and bottom, creating a frame where you can attach vertical panels. These create visual privacy and guard against animals like deer and rabbits.

The downside of fences like these is the expense of the lumber. Also, much of this material is sourced from an ecologically destructive timber industry. You always need to know where your wood is coming from to understand its embodied energy cost.

DOUBLE LOW FENCES

An ingenious way to keep deer and other undesirable animals out of the garden is by using a double low fence. These are two five-foot fences, placed five feet apart. Deer will not jump into the small space between the two fences, nor will they jump across two five-foot fences. These can also be used as chicken runs and protected areas to plant trees and hedgerows. What is nice about a double low fence is that it keeps the profile of the fence short so as not to block views or areas you might rather accentuate.

ELECTRIC FENCING

These days, electric fence technology has completely changed how humans interact with domesticated animals such as cows, sheep, goats, and chickens. Solar-powered electric fencing in the form of electrified netting, electrified tape, and electrified rope are incredible options for creating temporary, movable, lightweight, and easy-to-install fencing solutions for small to broadacre landscapes.

For large landscapes in particular, building permanent fencing from wood and metal is often cost prohibitive and can be akin to scars across the landscape. Instead, set up quickly installable electrified fencing to create paddocks. This type of fencing can be removed and reinstalled in just a few hours. Electrified fencing is an empowering tool for shepherding animals across the landscape in a beneficial way, mimicking the shepherds of old in a modern setting.

On a small scale, electrified netting can be used to section off parts of the landscape or garden for moving chickens and other animals around as a type of chicken tractor system. This enables you to put chickens in a small area of the landscape, where they eat weeds and bugs and fertilize. They can then be quickly moved into new areas to avoid overgrazing and compaction. Fencing can be moved seasonally or more frequently to achieve the desired effect, using the behavior of the animals to serve specific management needs in the landscape.

To combat the raging wildfires here in California over the last decade, some innovative people have been using quickly erected electric fencing systems to deploy the grazing/browsing habits of sheep and goats among the tall, dry grasses and overgrown forests. Using electrified fencing and mobile water tanks, these animals graze fire fuel load (dead, tall, congested vegetation), fertilize these ecosystems, and aid in water retention. They can quickly be moved off the landscape at the ideal time to avoid overgrazing. I have seen this used effectively throughout our parklands and have been impressed at the tender care these shepherds bring to our landscapes. It is truly a win for the animals, the land, and the safety of our communities.

50

Choosing the Right Animals

Integrating domesticated animals into a regenerative landscape comes with a lot of bonuses, a lot of work, and—depending on the project—can generate either an ecological benefit or ecological disaster. Your dream of going out your back door to harvest eggs, milk your cow, make cheese, and so on is totally attainable *if* the context of the project allows.

Chickens, ducks, and rabbits can be kept in smaller landscapes and still provide ecological benefits. Keeping cows, horses, and even goats and sheep in small areas is often a recipe for chaos. This is where your "*compose with* the land" contextual design lens must be activated.

With that in mind, this chapter is devoted to exploring whether specific animals are a good fit for your landscape project. This topic could be discussed at length and fill a whole book on its own. *This* book can't do the topic justice in the space available, so I will give as much guidance as I can; I direct you to look for the many exhaustive resources on the subject that are readily available. The following chapter focuses on chickens as they are probably the easiest and most beneficial animal for a landscape. For now, let's explore some of the habits of bees, cows, sheep, and goats and when they might belong in your regenerative landscape.

BENEFICIAL RELATIONSHIPS

The first approach to integrating animals in the design process is to understand the mutually beneficial relationships the landscape community will have with these domesticated animals. For instance, if your project is large enough, filled with grassland meadows or grassy paddocks, then you might consider a flock of sheep. The trick is to make sure that the behaviors of the sheep are beneficial to the landscape throughout the *entire* year. To figure that out, you can use a standby analysis tool that we've used in permaculture circles for decades. It's called the *input/output analysis*, described below.

Are the behaviors of sheep—eating, pooping, walking around, and eating grass—beneficial to the entire landscape in the way they build soil, collect water, and manage healthy vegetation? Are the sheep managing invasive plants, providing or building habitat, or providing any other services that aid biodiversity and a healthy, functioning ecosystem? If the benefits outweigh the negative impacts, then they can be included in the project.

Introducing new animals to a landscape must be done carefully, with reciprocity in mind. The new members of the community need to benefit the landscape while also receiving what they need to thrive from the same landscape. The goal here is to create closed loop systems, where the activities of the animals in question generate surplus for the ecosystem and the ecosystem generates food and shelter for the animals. This reciprocal relationship is what makes these systems regenerative.

For these types of mutually symbiotic relationships to blossom, evaluate the factors below.

Stocking

Stocking refers to the population of a flock of chickens, a drove of cattle, a herd of goats, and any other animal collectives. Are you bringing 2, 100, or 1,000 animals onto the land? Getting the stocking correct is one of the first design factors to consider. As you ponder stocking, you will need the answer the following questions:

How much land are you working with?

What are the dominant vegetation types in that landscape?

How much precipitation do you get throughout the year?

What are your water resources?

If you're trying to manage summertime dry grass fuels on 50 acres and hoping to do that with five goats, you're missing something. Three hundred goats maybe, but if you bring 300 on, can you keep that many goats on the land 365 days of the year without doing more harm? The correct stocking ratio will depend on the availability of vegetation, moisture, and terrain.

So maybe 300 goats on 50 acres makes sense in the spring and summer, but what happens during fall and winter when there is less forage? What happens if 300 goats start overbrowsing the landscape, causing damage to trees and compacting the soil? How much supplemental feed do you need to bring in when forage is little to none? How much will that cost you?

You can see that choosing the stocking ratio (the number of animals relative to the amount of land) and assessing the resources you have available is a key, first-level decision. Let's explore other design factors that will help you make realistic regenerative design decisions.

Vegetation

The kind of vegetation, existing and/or added by you, will help you rule out certain animals real fast. If your landscape is primarily forest, then sheep (beloved grass eaters) are not likely to be a great choice. Goats and pigs, however—two animals that have evolved in forest ecosystems around the world—would be. These species eat thicker, woodier plants and are a much better fit for a forested landscape.

Most of you reading this will have either a mix of open areas and forest or no forest at all. In that case, sheep or cows could work if there is sufficient grass and herbs to forage throughout the year. Or maybe the landscape is a large patch of brambles and poison oak, or covered in an invasive shrub land. What then? Goats? Cows? Horses?

Get to know the behaviors of the types of animals you're interested in building community with and make sure they will complement the land. If so, they will bring the landscape to a higher level of thriving complexity. Get the math wrong and you will destroy the ecosystem or create an inhospitable environment for the animals you've introduced, and they will become stressed and sick.

Deciding what kinds of animals you might be incorporating also depends on what kinds of vegetation you want to add to the landscape. If you are planning to plant an orchard and also hope to have goats, for example, then your system will require significant management to keep the goats from damaging the orchard—goats love to strip the bark off trees.

If you're growing a large vegetable garden and also want to have chickens, the behaviors of chickens and growing many vegetables are not so compatible. Either the chickens will be stuck in a coop for most of their life (if they have no other place to go), or they will destroy every baby plant you carefully place into the soil.

Terrain

The terrain plays another significant role in choosing animals for the landscape. Some animals are better equipped for handling steep, rocky terrain than others. That being said, the breed of each animal makes a difference too. There are some varieties of cows that do great on plains or mostly flat terrain, but put them on steep ground and they will struggle. In places like Switzerland and Scotland, however, cows have evolved on the flanks of steep mountain communities for thousands of years. These are the landscapes they know and love, and these breeds are a perfect match for steep landscapes.[1]

Frequency

In this context, frequency refers to the amount of time a group of animals has access to a part of the landscape (rotational grazing). How long do you keep your chickens in that chicken run without giving it a break? How long do you keep your goats tethered in the edge of that forest without giving the edge of the forest time to regrow?

The best frequency simulates a predator-prey dynamic, where animals are stocked in denser groupings but move from location to location with increased frequency—every day to twice a day or more. With denser stocking ratios, this level of frequency tends to create one big impact over a short period of time followed by a long period of rest. These regenerative disturbances stimulate vegetative growth. The short frequency also avoids compaction of the soil ecosystem (unless the soil is waterlogged) and aerates the soil with a day's worth of activity from sheep, cows, chickens, etc.

As you will see in the next chapter on chickens, your landscape can be designed so that animals move across it, from section to section with short frequency, harnessing their behaviors as regenerative benefits for managing each area for pests, weeds, aeration, and fertility.

Human Resources

As you design this paradise landscape, have you been keeping tabs on what it will take to manage? How are your time management skills? Do you have a plan to care for all the lives (plants and animals) that you bring to the landscape? Make sure to understand this before introducing domesticated animals to the site. They are depending on you.

Having a plan for how to use your own personal resource—your time—to manage water systems, harvest, mitigate fire danger, and so on is an integral part of your landscape design process. The moment you bring domesticated animals into the mix, the management needs of the landscape go way up. A fruit tree can sit in the landscape with no management for months, but you can't go a single day without taking care of your chickens. You can't go a single day without making sure your animals have everything they need to survive through the night.

In no way do I want to discourage you from incorporating animals responsibly into the landscape. All the benefits that come from it—both potential benefits to the ecology and food produced for the human community—all of it is possible, and can evolve into a truly resilient system in the face of global disaster. But these are not decisions to take lightly, especially if you are career oriented and don't have time for the responsibilities that come with raising animals.

Input/Output Analysis

To help identify whether an animal is compatible with your project context, use input/output analysis. This process is as simple as it sounds. Let's use ducks as an example. First, generate a list of all of the inputs required to keep ducks, followed by a list of the outputs they produce.

Inputs

Protection: Protection from predators (either a closed coop or a floating nesting box in the middle of a pond). Possibly fenced runs.

Forage: Ducks need to forage, either on water plants or on herbs and grasses throughout the landscape. They have an insatiable appetite for bugs, snails, and other small creatures and need these for optimal health.

Supplemental Feed: If you're keeping ducks and sufficient forage can't be found, then supplemental feed will need to be grown or bought, stored, and provided to the ducks.

Water Source: Ducks are water birds; to grow happy and healthy, they need access to water, be it a large pond or a small children's pool.

Egg Harvesting: If you are keeping ducks to harvest their protein-rich eggs, then you'll need to set up a system for easy harvest.

Companionship: Ducks are social creatures and need other ducks around to be content.

These are the basic inputs to keep ducks, but other inputs may be required in your particular context. If you are unable to provide them, then ducks are probably not the best match for your landscape. (Note: Wild ducks know how to survive without human intervention. If they visit your landscape or take up residence in your pond, feel free to let them be or drive them off if they are causing problems.)

Output

Foraging: Ducks love to eat plants and insects. This can be either a positive contribution to the landscape or a negative impact. Letting ducks run wild in your vegetable garden may not yield the best results, but letting them forage in pastures, forests, orchards, and perennial zones focuses their foraging activities in ways that are beneficial to managing pests and weeds.

Manure: Ducks provide an incredible manure source of phosphorus and nitrogen. Integrated into a rotational scheme throughout the landscape or added to compost piles, their manure will build soil and help grow healthy plants.

On the other hand, ducks defecate in their water sources. If you give ducks access to your habitat pond, they will add a significant nitrogen load to the water. If sufficient biofiltration is not present, the pond will turn into stagnant, algae-ridden muck.

Eggs: Duck eggs are larger with a more complex set of nutrients than chicken eggs. They make a great chicken egg replacement for many recipes, and can be eaten the same way, with adjustments for the higher fat content.

Aggression: Male ducks have quite the reputation for being aggressive. I would even consider calling some male ducks I've met mean. If children are around, watch out for interactions with male ducks. An angry duck will attack a child, or an adult for that matter, but most of the time it is not an issue.

These are the basic outputs that ducks provide. As you can see, there are many benefits, but if your ability to meet the required inputs feels insurmountable, then don't have ducks.

The following lists provide a synopsis of inputs and outputs for a variety of domesticated animals to help you decide what makes the most sense in your landscape. (Note: This input/output analysis for each species is not exhaustive, but hopefully it's enough information for you to ponder whether these species are a match for your landscape project. As always, do extensive research beyond this book before committing to keeping any of these animals.)

KEEPING BEES

Over 10,000 years ago, people began gathering honey from wild hives, the start of a blossoming relationship. Over the next thousand years, beekeeping practices emerged among the people of North Africa, who began keeping bees in earthenware hives,[2] and the continuously refined beekeeping practices of Egypt began to spread across the globe. Cave drawings in Spain show images of beekeeping going back around 7,000 years.[3] By 300 BCE, the Mayans were keeping melipona bees (stingless bees) in log hives, harvesting beeswax and royal jelly, and cultivating some of the best honey in the world.[4] (Melipona bees don't produce as much honey as the European honeybee, but the honey is sweeter and gathered from inside sacks of wax rather than combs.)

Keeping bees not only benefits the pollination of crops and produces honey and wax for consumption; it also protects humanity. As mentioned in part I, bees are a keystone species on which the human race is dependent for survival. One of every three bites you eat is thanks to the bees.

Is keeping bees the right fit for your landscape and life context? Let's find out!

Beehives

There are many types of beehives you can purchase, the most common being the Langstroth, the Warre, and the Top Bar. Each has its benefits and drawbacks. If you're new to beekeeping, research the options to find one that best fits your landscape. All of these choices are designed to protect bees, give them a home where they can build their combs, and for easy honey harvesting.

Log Hives

Log hives mimic the natural habitats of bees. Wild beehives are often observed inside old oaks, maples, eucalyptus, and other trees. Building log hives is an incredible way to develop habitat for both wild and domesticated bee communities. These log hives are not usually designed for easy honey harvesting, instead prioritizing the best possible conditions for a bee colony to thrive. That said, there are some creative log hive builders out there who have developed log systems where honey *can* be harvested. The logs' thick walls insulate bees and protect them in cold winter months. Log hives are placed up to 20 feet above the ground and attached to trees to emulate wild hive conditions.

Furthermore, log hives and their wild hive prototype provide an excellent environment for the natural growth of mushroom mycelium. Recent discoveries in the field of mycology through renowned mycologist Paul Stamets have revealed that mycelium from polypore mushrooms plays a beneficial role in beehive immunity, helping bees fight off viruses.[5] Paul and his team have developed a mycelium mushroom extract that can be offered to bees via a special bee feeder, giving wild and domesticated bee colonies instant access to these important mycelium medicines.

Inputs

Equipment: If you're keeping bees for honey and wax production, then you'll need to purchase a variety of equipment including hives, bees, a smoker, and protective gear.

Supplemental Feed: In the first year of keeping bees and in times of stress, you may need to offer them sugar water to help them get through hard times. This is a concoction of one part granulated sugar and one part water mixed into quart jars and sealed with a bee-feeding lid. It's important to closely monitor how much sugar water the bees are consuming and remove it as soon as the bee activity has stabilized. Sugar water is only to be used when absolutely needed; it's not something bees should have access to otherwise. It dilutes the honey and can lead to other problems like attracting ants.

Water: Bees need a source of water to drink—a nearby pond, a birdbath, or simply a dish of water.

Weekly Monitoring/Maintenance: In this era of widespread bee colony collapse, bees need constant monitoring to make sure mites, parasites, ants, and small hive beetles are not destroying the hive and eating the brood. If problems do arise, immediate action and constant monitoring must be undertaken until the problem is solved.

Location: Beehives are best located facing east where they can get the earliest sunlight and at least 50 feet away from zones with high foot traffic.

Outputs

Honey: It usually takes a year for a healthy brood to grow, so usually little to no honey is available for human harvest during the first year. The bees are working hard and need the honey they produce to build a robust and healthy hive. By the second year, the honey should start flowing and will be as sweet as you imagine.

Wax: Bees create wax to build their combs. When it comes time to harvest the honey, you will also be harvesting the wax. A slow but simple process of straining the honey out from the wax, followed by placing the leftover wax into a pot of hot water, will separate the remaining wax when it melts and floats to the top. Once that is done, you can make your own candles, add it to herbal salves, and so on.

Pollination: In the regenerative landscape, pollination makes the difference between a minimal harvest and robust food crops. By increasing your pollination through keeping bees, you're guaranteeing excellent pollination throughout the landscape. In general, two bee hives per acre is sufficient.

SHEEP

Humans have nurtured symbiotic relationships with sheep going back near 10,000 years.[6] Sheep were one of the first animals to be domesticated and contributed to the rise of many civilizations around the world. Shepherding is the backbone of many rural grassland communities. Sheep provided clothing, food, companionship, and ecological management. Many shepherding communities were seminomadic, and their seasonal movements through the landscape provided regenerative disturbances, maintaining plant biodiversity and mitigating catastrophic wildfire, all while developing life-giving resources for the community.

In the modern era, much of what was once public and common land is now held as private property. Our private property laws and the fences that followed have disrupted shepherding culture in many parts of the world. In the regenerative landscape, sheep are still great companions to your homestead ecosystem. As long as there is plenty of grass forage and room to move sheep seasonally, the relationship between the ecological functions of the land and the behaviors/needs of the sheep can be well balanced, closing many waste loops, building soil, increasing water capacity, and providing beneficial resources to the human community.

On very small landscapes, however, it is unlikely that a flock of sheep will be beneficial ecosystem managers. Sheep can certainly be kept in smaller spaces, but the cost of supplemental feed, concentration of manure and soil compaction, and the mobility needs of sheep can all have degenerative impacts.

Inputs

Freshwater: Like all animals, sheep need access to fresh water at all times.

Mineral Lick: Sheep need minerals such as sodium, chloride, and selenium. Some of these minerals they get from forage, but if their forage doesn't provide sufficient minerals, they will need a supplemental mineral lick.

Green Pasture: Sheep are grass eaters and are best suited for grassland environments as opposed to forest or chaparral ecosystems.

Supplemental Feed as Needed: Depending on climate and space, there may be times where adequate forage isn't available to your flock and supplemental feed must be provided.

Protection from Predators: Sheep are a favorite prey of predators like wolves and lions. Make sure your sheep are protected at all times either by electrified fencing or appropriate guard animals.

Wool Shearing: Sheep have been bred for thousands of years for their wool. As a result, most varieties of sheep produce a large coat of wool every year. This material must be sheared off every year to keep the sheep healthy and happy.

Trim Hooves: Sheep's hooves need to be trimmed at least once a year. This will prevent them from developing diseases, getting sick, and dying. Foot rot is one of the most common diseases that plague sheep and can be mitigated through regular hoof trimming.

Cleaning Enclosures: Monthly maintenance of animal enclosures (cleaning out manure) is always necessary to prevent parasites and disease and to provide general welfare for your animals.

Outputs

Wool: Wool is a regenerative fiber produced by sheep that can be made into nearly every type of clothing as well as blankets, hats, and belts, and used in crafts projects such as felting and jewelry making.

Meat: Some varieties of sheep (such as Suffolk, Hampshire, and Dorset) were specifically bred for meat and can be raised for this purpose.

Milk: Many varieties of sheep bred for meat were also bred for milk production. Cheese made from sheep's milk is world renowned, such as the Spanish manchego. If you hope to milk, make sure to select the right breed, such as East Friesan, Awassi, or Assaf.

Grasslands Management: Sheep are living lawnmowers. If managed rotationally and regeneratively, sheep drastically improve the health of grasslands through periodic grazing. This manages invasive species and activates the nutrient pump of photosynthetic exudates, sequestering carbon and increasing water absorbability.[7]

Manure: Sheep manure is a great soil-building resource for fertilizing homesteads, pastures, and orchards.

GOATS

Goats are among the first animal species to be domesticated by humans, over 10,000 years ago in what is now called Iran.[8] Today, they are one of the most widely distributed domesticated animals and are vitally important to human settlement and ecological management throughout the globe. They are capable of thriving in nearly every environment, from hot deserts and alpine altitudes to urban settings and rainforests.

On a regenerative homestead or agroforestry system, goats play a number of important roles including managing vegetation, browsing fire fuel loads, spreading fertility, and generating resources such as milk and meat. Keeping goats in the landscape is also a challenge because they will eat almost anything. They will forage on any trees in the landscape, slowly killing them off by peeling their bark. Goats would be a challenge to integrate into a highly intensive food forest but are well suited as ecosystem managers in forested and chaparral environments. Many varieties readily eat blackberries, poison oak, and other undesirable shrubs.

Tethering smaller herds of goats in smaller, intensive landscapes has proven quite effective not only in providing great forage for each goat but also keeping them from running freely into gardens and farms, destroying everything in sight. The downside to tethering is the daily management required to pull the goats out, tether them to a stake pounded in the ground, and then move them to a new location once they've browsed that area down. They need to be moved multiple times a day.

There are hundreds of varieties of goats, all with different behaviors, input and output needs, and characteristics. Do your research on the different types of goats, what their needs are, and how best to integrate them into the landscape. They are not all the same! I can't stress this enough—the variety of goat greatly affects how well they will meet the context of your project.

Inputs

Protection from Predators: Like most domesticated animals, goats will fall prey to large predators. They must be protected through nighttime enclosures, fencing, use of guard animals, or electrified wire.

Forage: Goats love to eat . . . and then . . . they love to eat some more! They will eat nearly every kind of vegetation, from grasses to shrubs to whole trees. They are best suited for environments where their foraging capabilities provide a benefit to the ecosystem.

Loose Mineral Licks: Goats need supplemental minerals to thrive, including copper. Because of the mechanics of their jaws, they need *loose* mineral supplements rather than blocks.

Strong Fences: Goats love to climb to reach areas for foraging. If you are using perimeter or permanent fencing, make sure it is strong enough to withstand a goat climbing onto it to reach low-hanging tree branches or vines.

Hoof Trimming: Just like sheep, goats need their hooves trimmed to avoid foot rot and other diseases.

Climbing Structures: Since goats love to climb, give them structures to climb on. Large stones, logs, and wooden built structures all make great climbing structures. One of the funniest examples of this I have seen is a place a few miles from my home. Someone mounted a surfboard up in a tree. They must have built a set of platforms to reach the surfboard because every time you drive by there's a goat standing on the surfboard riding an imaginary wave. Surf's up!

Companionship: Goats are social animals. Even if you are integrating goats with other livestock, make sure there is at least a pair of goats to ensure their happiness.

Outputs

Vegetation Management: By now you've gathered that goats have one of the largest appetites of any animal. They will eat nearly any type of plant or tree. For this reason, they are a perfect fit for landscapes that have been neglected or where fire has been suppressed for decades.

Milk: Goat's milk is very similar to human milk; for many people, drinking goat's milk is easier to digest than cow's milk.[9] Goat's milk can be turned into cheese, ice cream, yogurt, and so on.

Meat: There are some cultures whose whole diet is based on goat meat, making it an important food source around the world. If this is an output you wish to harvest, make sure that you raise varieties best suited for meat production.

Manure: Goat manure is excellent for the garden, farm, or added to compost piles.

COWS

From the sacred cow of India, the cosmic cow Auðumbla of Norse mythology, and the Buffalo people of Turtle Island, bovine ruminants are revered and even worshiped throughout cultures and ecosystems.

Over 10,000 years ago, humans began breeding the modern cow from wild aurochs.[10] Meanwhile, on Turtle Island (North America), the relationship between Indigenous people and bison has lasted over 10,000 years and still exists today.[11]

In the modern world, the breeding of cattle for meat and dairy consumption has been disastrous. These industrial factory farms are not only terrible and unethical places for animals but also destroy the soil, pollute the water, warm the atmosphere, and poison our communities. People have lost the reverence that permeated older cultures and still exists in some places today.

In the regenerative landscape, cows can be used to mimic the beneficial behaviors of ruminants that once managed our landscapes. In the region where I live, there were once herds of elk, antelope, and bear, all functioning as ecosystem managers. They grazed grasslands and browsed forests, cleaning out fallen nuts and fruits and reducing the congestion of woodland environments susceptible to catastrophic wildfire. Most of these species were overhunted and no longer exist in great numbers in our landscapes.

Cows in the regenerative system clearly have a potential to heal the land if stocking ratios, correct frequency of disturbance, and loving care are all accounted for. Cows will provide the missing management that native ruminants once provided the ecosystem. (Note: I would always advocate for regenerating native species first, but in many cases this is just no longer possible.)

Cows are large animals and need enough space for adequate forage. They are generally not a good fit for small landscapes or even small homesteads. Their impacts are just too great to keep them on small sites. That said, there are regenerative farmers who keep a single milking cow (usually a smaller jersey cow) as part of their herd of animals. This *can* work and your cow will provide incredible fertility and food sources.

Depending on the breed you choose, there are many ways cows can regeneratively fit the context of your project. Look into all the different types out there, their size and their needs, because not all cows are the same.

Inputs

Fresh Water: Cows need to have access to fresh water at all times.

Salt Lick: Cows need access to a mineral salt lick to ensure they have all the micronutrients they need to thrive.

Ample Forage and Movement: The ecological method of raising cows requires ample forage and movement. Cows spend a short period of time in each area and then are moved in quick succession to find new forage and mitigate overgrazing.

Supplemental Feed: Managing cows will always include supplemental feed in the form of hay. Even if they are grass fed throughout their entire life, providing them hay in small amounts is a great trick to get them to move from one place to another.

Outputs

Soil-Building Superstars: When cows are used as beneficial members of the ecological community, they become soil-building superstars. Their manure composts easily and even attracts beneficial organisms that help build the soil. Dung beetles (*Scarabaeinae*) are one of the foremost soil-building insects. They collect manure from ruminants, roll it into a ball, and bury it into the ground.[12] This of course feeds the soil nutrients but also provides food for soil biology. Frequently moving dense herds across the land will stimulate prairie growth, pumping nutrients into the soil while also increasing plant growth.

Milk: Dairy cows will produce ample milk for a family or community. If milking cows are integrated into your regenerative system, keep in mind that this requires daily management as well as caring for your cows through pregnancies, births, and aftercare.

Meat: Cows are of course a favorite food source around the world and can be raised and harvested in the regenerative landscape for this purpose. The logistics of killing and butchering a cow are complicated, however, and you will need to find local professionals to help you.

Fuel Load Management: In this age of catastrophic megafires, rotational grazing manages dry vegetation (fire fuel load) and helps to mitigate the catastrophic impacts of fire.

SAFETY CONSIDERATIONS FOR DOMESTICATED ANIMALS

Many domesticated animals are favorite food sources for the apex predators of our environments. Wild cats, coyotes, wolves, eagles—these creatures see your sheep or goat, and even your cow calf, as a potentially easy meal. You must have a plan for protecting animals from predators, which will likely include a combination of efforts—incorporating temporary and/or permanent fencing, protective nighttime enclosures, and guard animals that deter predators from attacking. (It's noteworthy that, with the exception of daytime predators like eagles and dogs, it's rare for your animal companions to be attacked during the day.)

There are many types of guard animals—llamas, donkeys, and dogs are common. Many dog species have been bred not only to herd sheep and cows across prairies but also to live in the pastures with them, scaring off predators in their midst. Llamas and donkeys also live with herds and flocks as permanent members of those communities.

51
Chicken Systems

Chickens and humans have coevolved for thousands of years. There is evidence that chickens were originally domesticated by South Asian rice farmers 7,000–10,000 years ago before migrating westward into Europe and Africa.[1] These days, chickens represent the homesteading movement in many ways and have become important companions in the regenerative landscape.

This relationship is based on reciprocity. We give them a home, protection, and care, and they provide us with food and landscape management services. It's an amazing trade if done ethically by implementing the principle: *do the least harm*. In this context, doing the least harm to the chickens means creating the best scenario for them to thrive, and doing the least harm to the landscape by integrating the chickens in such a way that their activities are beneficial and not detrimental to the landscape as a whole.

Where chicken coops are placed and built, how chickens are managed, and the choice between movable chicken coops and permanent chicken runs—all of these decisions determine whether the relationships between humans, chickens, and the land are beneficial or detrimental.

First, have an intimate understanding of the context of your project. Diligently research these questions before bringing chickens to the landscape: How big is the landscape? Where can the chickens venture? How many people live on the site, if any? What predators are in the area?

A well-integrated system will have chickens in a stocking ratio most beneficial to the area they will roam *and* the ability to move chickens to different areas, providing them with healthier forage. The best designs direct their behaviors into beneficial management processes throughout the landscape. If you're keeping chickens in the coop all of the time with no chicken run, never letting them out into the open, then you have not created an integrated design plan. This type of chicken system, all too common on homesteads, does not provide the chickens with their ideal environment, but it also means that you have to provide them with more feed sources generated off-site then you would in a fully integrated system. An integrated system means that chickens move to different areas of the landscape at different times of the year, thereby accessing a wide variety of forage plants and insects, while also spreading manure and weed seed-eating services to the landscape.

Varieties

Chickens are as diverse as people; each variety has different characteristics related to their size, how often they lay eggs, how good they are at raising babies, if they're good to eat for meat, and behaviors such as scratching, flying, noise making, and so on. Plus, chickens have their own personalities just like every animal.

With so many possibilities at play, doing diligent research into the different types of chickens, their behaviors, yields, and attitudes will help you decide which type is the right fit. Once you have your first flock of chickens, you will learn more about their behaviors and you may develop a favorite type of chicken for your landscape community over time.

Araucana chickens are great mothers and produce plenty of colored eggs. Buff Orpingtons are incredible layers, very calm, and due to their large size are good for eating. They also are less likely to escape because they're unable to jump or fly very far. California White chickens produce incredibly throughout the year in varying environments, but they like to roost high, and they know how to escape and survive the wild—a tenacious chicken indeed but also quite annoying if you don't want them to get out of carefully built coops and runs.

INTEGRATING CHICKENS INTO THE REGENERATIVE LANDSCAPE

Incorporating chickens into a regenerative design is a great way to produce a protein-rich food source *and* have these landscape maintenance allies woven into the tapestry of the landscape. Chickens can be extremely beneficial and they can also be extremely damaging. A well-designed system will enable all of the benefits and hopefully none of the drawbacks of raising chickens.

Here are a number of ways to design a beneficial chicken system into the landscape.

Determine If Chickens Are Appropriate for Your Project

Not every landscape will be appropriate for keeping chickens. What does your understanding of the context tell you? Is there sufficient energy at home or among project stakeholders for someone to care for the chickens daily? Are you in a city where keeping chickens is illegal? What other factors come up when making this decision?

Locating the Chicken Coop

Chickens can be loud and they can be smelly. Locate your chicken coop far enough away from living quarters that sound and smell are not an issue. Some folks are more sensitive to this than others, so the needs of the people involved are important.

Chickens are highly susceptible to predators. It turns out just about everything likes to eat them. Raccoon, fox, hawk, weasel—chickens make a snack for them all. You will find tips below for protecting them, but when it comes to locating the chicken coop, safety factors need to be taken into account. Are you placing the chicken coop next to the neighbor's dog house? Are you placing it so far away that you couldn't hear a commotion in the night if there was one?

You will have to visit the coop every single day. Most people who keep chickens visit their chicken coop at least twice a day—first thing in the morning to collect eggs and to let the chickens out of the coop, and at sundown when the chickens need to be locked back up. There are automatic door openers that can be installed and programmed to open and close the coop.

These are convenient but they don't preclude the need to visit the coop daily. At a minimum, eggs must be harvested each day. If eggs are left in the coop for too long, the chickens will peck and eat the eggs, and a chicken who gains a liking for the taste of eggs will begin eating them every day. That means no eggs for the humans in this relationship.

PROTECTING YOUR CHICKENS

As mentioned above, many predators love the taste of chicken. And one of your main jobs as a steward of a flock of chickens is to ensure their safety. That is why they have a coop to begin with. Most predators come out at night, and if your chickens aren't safely tucked away behind a sturdy door, walls, and roof they will be eaten.

Permanent Runs

When integrating chickens to the landscape, the principle of *relationship design* begs creativity from the designer. What does it mean to integrate chickens in the landscape? How do you go about doing that?

Permanent runs (dedicated, permanent areas for chickens to forage) are one technique that can lead to the positive integration of chickens throughout the landscape, harmonizing many types of biological relationships. Like any technique, the where and the how make all the difference.

Permanent runs are best in medium to small landscapes where large pastures and forested areas are not accessible. Permanent perimeter runs (around the perimeter of the landscape)—by far one of my favorite techniques for integrating chickens—are excellent for this. First, a perimeter run is made around the landscape using small mesh fencing materials. Many landscapes have fencing already, and putting a second fence up to create a protected run area for chickens can complement an existing fence. This perimeter run connects directly to the chicken coop, which is where the chickens sleep and lay their eggs.

The perimeter run itself serves a multitude of functions.

- Chickens in the perimeter run are protected from wild animals and kept out of places in the landscape or garden where they could cause damage. It protects the garden and the chickens at the same time.
- The behavior of chickens (scratching, eating weeds, eating bugs, and dropping manure) is focused around the perimeter of the landscape, which reduces the movement of pests and weeds from neighboring landscapes. This area can also be planted with trees and shrubs (protect them with tree guards) that provide forage for chickens, humans, and other organisms, and in this way the behaviors of the chickens are adding fertilizer and other services to these trees.
- Additional fence lines can intersect with the perimeter run, separating parts of the landscape. This will enable you to let the chickens into areas of the landscape at the appropriate time of year to benefit from their behaviors without risking damaging other parts of the landscape. This is akin to creating a permanent rotational grazing system.

Movable Systems

Chicken Tractors. A few minutes into researching movable chicken systems and you will inevitably find the term *chicken tractor*. The original chicken tractor design is a mobile chicken coop with an open or fenced bottom that lays on the ground. The coop itself is built small enough to be rolled from one area to another by hand or by machine, while keeping the chickens inside at all times. The chicken tractor is moved to fresh pasture or untouched garden areas and placed down to give chickens access to new grass, weeds, bugs, and plants to forage. When the new area has been well grazed but not overgrazed, the chicken tractor is moved to a new area. This way, the chickens always have great forage and do not damage the land. A well-built chicken tractor protects chickens from predators but leaves them stuck in the small, moveable coop.

Rotational Chicken Grazing. While chicken tractors provide some benefits to the land, I personally don't like keeping chickens in small, cooped areas for most of their life. They have to be moved daily and this adds to daily maintenance chores. Many alternative chicken tractor systems have been innovated by chicken farmers around the world. My favorite movable chicken system is a combination of a movable coop and movable fencing. A system like this allows you to direct the impact of your flock—where they're scratching, foraging, pecking, and defecating— while also providing the flock an open area where they can roam freely inside a temporarily fenced zone.

A movable coop is often built on a small trailer and can be dragged by a tractor or truck from area to area. For much smaller flocks, hand-trucked coops can also be built, then lifted up and rolled by hand into a new fenced area. To make moving fences easy, electrified netting is usually the fencing material of choice, especially when the variety of chickens are not prone to jump and fly as often. Electrified netting can be taken down and put back up to fence off a new area in less than an hour.

The most regenerative egg farmers in the world are using large movable coops built on trailers and dragged by tractors onto new fenced and fresh pasture. Once each area has been beneficially grazed (not overeaten or compacted), they are then moved to a new area. This is "mob" chicken grazing at its finest. No area gets overimpacted by the chickens, but they all get a decent mowing and fertilization during the chickens' stay. These same systems can be designed for small landscapes or used for massive regenerative agriculture systems.

The biggest downside to having a movable chicken system is the added maintenance and labor required. In order to keep the system as regenerative as possible, chickens need to be moved out of an area before they begin to damage the soil or eat too much of the vegetation. That means you need to monitor each area and move the chickens at the right time. If the context is a small homestead—one where chicken eggs are grown solely for your family's consumption—then I would steer you away from a movable system and toward some of the more permanent and user-friendly rotational chicken system designs discussed in this chapter.

HARVESTING

One of the biggest joys of living with chickens is making use of the eggs they provide. These protein-rich food staples are small colorful treasures you and your family discover every day.

Eggs grown in the regenerative landscape are not your typical store-bought eggs. Your chickens will be healthier, foraging from more diverse and nutrient-dense sources of food than the typical egg farm would produce. Eggs grown regeneratively have a more colorful yolk, a longer shelf life, and are packed with readily available nutrients.

To make harvesting the eggs easier, the best coops are built with direct access to nesting boxes, enabling access to eggs from outside the coop. This makes harvesting convenient and quick. One of the most important practices is to harvest eggs every day, which is why easy access is so important. Get them fresh before they accidentally break. As I mentioned, once a chicken has had a taste of egg, it's likely to peck and eat eggs daily from then on. To mitigate this possibility, harvest the eggs every day.

As any veteran chicken keeper will tell you, once your flock is established, the eggs come every day for much of the year. You quickly end up with more eggs than you could possibly consume, even with a small flock. Eggs make a great gift to friends and neighbors and can even be turned into a small roadside business. Share the surplus in whatever way you can, and make sure your labeling and storage system is adequate so you don't spread bad eggs around.

BASIC CHICKEN COOP DESIGN

Building a home for your chickens doesn't have to be fancy or expensive, but it does need a few basic elements to keep the chickens safe and happy. If the chickens have ample room to roam inside runs, open pasture, or forest, then the coop can be quite small for a tiny flock (up to 12 chickens). Chickens will only go in there to sleep at night and lay their eggs. On smaller landscape projects, coops tend to be larger, as the chickens will inevitably spend more time in their coop without as much room to roam.

Every coop needs nesting boxes. A nesting box is where the hens lay their eggs. If they are broody, then this is also where they will sit on their eggs, waiting for their chicks to hatch. In general, chickens do not sleep in their nesting boxes; they sleep on roosts. For this reason, you don't need to build a separate nesting box for each chicken. Three chickens or more will often use the same nesting box. A fitting rule is to have at least four nesting boxes per 10 chickens. As you design your landscape and decide on the size of your chicken flock (stocking ratio) that meets the resources of the landscape, you can expand or reduce the number of nesting boxes as needed. A flock of 30 chickens would need 12 boxes, while six chickens would be OK with two or three boxes. Ten inches square is a sufficient size for most nesting boxes. Remember, the hens will not spend a lot of time in these boxes as most of them only go there to lay eggs.

Like many in the bird world, chickens like to roost. When they want to rest or sleep, their reflex is to climb onto their roosts to feel protected from predators. These instincts carry over from their ancient ancestors who flew up into the tops of trees to avoid getting eaten in the night. Every coop needs to have a roost. The roost can be as simple as a long branch placed off the ground and attached horizontally with room enough for chickens to jump onto it.

It's best to have one single roost that your entire flock can use. If you install multiple roosts at differing heights, you will inadvertently trigger a social hierarchy instinct within the flock and the chickens will fight each other (sometimes to great bodily injury) to use the uppermost roost and confirm their role as alpha. Chickens, just like humans, have a unique psychology all to their own. The better you understand how they work and how their social system functions, the better you create a peaceful chicken community and healthy flock.

PROTECTION FROM PREDATORS

Let's be clear, the main reason to have a chicken coop is to protect them from being eaten by predators. Your coop needs to be fully enclosed—top, sides, and bottom. A solid rainproof roof needs to be mounted to protect the chickens in the wet season.

In moderate to warm climates, chicken-wire walls mounted on solid wooden posts are acceptable, especially when the wire mesh extends 12 inches into the ground. The buried wire protects the chickens from burrowing predators like dogs and weasels sleuthing their way into your coop for a midnight feast.

In colder climates, small greenhouses make better chicken coops, or any structure with fully enclosed walls to provide better insulation and protect against the cold. Whatever your walls are made of, there can be no holes larger than ¾ inch in diameter around the outside. That is why chicken wire comes as a tightly woven mesh as opposed to other fencing wires that have larger gaps. Doors need to be installed in the coop to allow the chickens to get out in the morning. These doors are often connected to a pulley system and literally slide up to let the chickens out and slide back down to close them in at night.

Somewhere in the coop, a large door should be installed or an easy way to take one wall off. This enables you to muck out the chicken coop every month, utilizing that nitrogen-rich material to build compost for the landscape. After the coop is cleaned out, deep bedding material must be spread throughout the coop.

Smaller coops can be even better situated if they are built off the ground, on piers or stilts, which makes burrowing animals a nonissue, as well as getting the chickens out of the rat zone to deter these egg-devouring creatures. Having your coop off the ground also makes harvesting the manure-filled bedding easier each month as you're able to scrape it right out of the coop and into a wheelbarrow for easy transport. Work smarter, not harder.

WATER SOURCE

You need to make sure an adequate water source is available to chickens at all times. Many chicken-watering systems are available for purchase, and if you do a little research, you can find all kinds of tricks and hacks for creating innovative chicken-watering systems. The most important aspect is that their water is kept clean, which is why it's best off the ground.

FOOD

The ideal ecological set-up for chickens in the landscape would have chickens eating nearly 100 percent of their diet from foraged seeds, leaves, and insects, with possible additions of kitchen scraps and vegetable surplus from the garden. This is ideal, and we should strive for this level of harmony in the ecosystem, but it's unrealistic to think you will do that in the first year. Unfortunately, for most of us, purchased feed is still an important staple of the chicken's diet. This is because there is generally not sufficient forage and fodder to keep chickens well fed; they will need access to more food. Supplementing their forage with organic feed is the best option if possible, though it can get expensive. Typically, having at least some feed always available to the chickens if they need to eat it is a best practice. The more forage and alternative fodder you provide them from the landscape, the less feed they will need to consume.

DEEP BEDDING

I personally believe that the healthiest chickens are the ones that live in deep bedding. Whenever I see chicken coops or chicken runs that are scratched to bare earth, I cringe for those birds. Deep bedding means that, at a minimum, the chicken coop is filled with a thick layer of fresh mulch. This can be leaves, straw, or wood chips. Six to 10 inches deep is best.

In permanent runs where chickens may overgraze, deep bedding protects the soil from runoff and helps incorporate chicken manure in a self-composting system. The deep bedding system also generates forage for chickens. Worms, grubs, beetles, and more are attracted to the bedding for their own reproductive and foraging processes. As chickens scratch the bedding, they dig up these insects to eat, and also mix their manure into the bedding. This reduces flies, which can be a major nuisance with any domesticated animals.

When the coop is cleaned out each month, the material you dig out is deep bedding mixed with chicken manure. This is perfect for adding to composting systems, placing around trees, or even spreading directly on the surface as a mulch. (Note: Chicken manure is quite hot, so it is usually better not to put raw chicken manure straight into the garden. But if it's part of a deep bedding system, then much of it will already be in a decomposing state and well balanced with the bedding material, suitable for placing around trees. This material should be composted for five to six weeks before applying it around vegetables.[2]

PART IX
Restore the Wild

52

Stewards of the Earth

BIODIVERSITY

Biodiversity is the foremost indicator of ecosystem resilience.[1] The more plant and animal biodiversity, the better an environment weathers changes in climate, pest pressure, disease, and other natural disasters. Enhancing plant biodiversity (and therefore wildlife diversity) is a fundamental goal in all work we do as ecological designers. The existing state of biodiversity must be assessed before restoration plans are developed. Based on your assessment, a phased management approach is created with regenerative stewardship tools including forest management, rotational grazing, prescribed fire, seed drilling, and reforestation.

Assessing biodiversity is ideally performed throughout the seasons to render a full understanding of the succession, vegetative cycles, and animal migrations that impact the region. Avoid making ecosystem conclusions after only a few visits to the landscape. A field covered in invasive grasses in March will look very different in June. A herd of bison or elk may have migrated through the area, shearing the grass and leaving dung behind. Newly exposed plant species may then emerge. On the other hand, when you return to the grassland and a single grass species is dominating season to season, biodiversity is in decline.

Next time you go for a walk or a drive or spend time in a park, pay close attention to the vegetative arrangement of these spaces. Whether wild land, green zone, or park, see if you can identify how much biodiversity is present. At first glance, the health of an ecosystem is hard to decipher. What looks like a beautiful forest or verdant grassland may still be experiencing a state of ecological catastrophe. Part of the problem is that not enough people have adequate assessment skills to determine true ecological health. My hope is that this book has given you that edge. Use the tools in this book to your best abilities and find mentors to help you deepen this path.

In assessing biodiversity, first look at the state of succession. If, while walking through a grassy meadow, you observe hundreds of knee-high oak trees, what do you think that meadow will be like in five years? How about in 10 years? In 50 years, it will be a mature oak woodland. In a case like this, how much intervention is necessary? What can you do to protect the oaks until they mature?

Invasive Grasses

Once large areas are consumed by a single plant species, these landscapes are moving toward barrenness. When only a few species are present, they are susceptible to pests, disease, and climatic events. What happens when a single species that is anchoring a place dies off? It is a precursor to desertification and a process we have the responsibility to repair. As stewards of the environment, we use our actions and resources to enhance biodiversity on a broad scale. It's easier than it sounds as long as we are willing to do the work.

The ecosystem restoration techniques (regenerative disturbances) described in this section of the book—fire, reforestation, forest management—represent tools in the toolkit that, if used with intelligence and in the spirit of partnership, will grow biodiversity in great magnitude.

The work of enhancing biodiversity is the work of generating a thriving future for our descendants. It's the act of being a good ancestor. Each of us has the capacity to create biodiversity wealth right now, today. Put this book down and go outside, day or night. Plant a seed. Cut back invasive grasses. Root the cutting of a favorite plant. Plant an heirloom seed garden or organize your community to restore the parks in your neighborhood. Support these types of efforts in ways that fit your skills and resources. Biodiversity is our measure of success; with a few strategic actions, we can all be heroes to the land.

Site Specific

Stewarding the land with regenerative disturbances can be the right strategy, but we also need to know when leaving it alone is what's called for. There's no one-size-fits-all approach to landscape repair work. Every site is specific, every season is specific, and restoration of the land has to take generational succession into account. What is the current state of the project? What management or disturbances are needed and/or what needs to be left alone for the season?

Unfortunately, centuries of deforestation, overgrazing, human development, fire suppression, and agriculture have led to a fairly disastrous state of much of what we call wild areas. This is why active stewardship is often necessary. As ecosystem managers, it is our responsibility to look out into the wild and see the work that must be done. To introduce fire in a good way. To become the bear, the elk, the antelope, and manage the forest similar to how it was done for tens of thousands of years.

Emergency Resilience

This entire book is a manual preparing you for social, economic, and ecological emergencies. Once you understand that you can be a producer of life's basic needs, then you fully grasp the power of a regenerative landscape. Every year from 2017 to 2020 my family and I experienced multiple catastrophes—multiple wildfires threatened our community, we were evacuated twice, had power outages, dry lightning events, flooded roads, damaging wind events, and the COVID-19 global pandemic.

In all these cases, our regenerative homestead provided resources that gave us resilience to weather these events. We had nutritious food ready to harvest at all times. Our 11-thousand-gallon rain storage meant we had water abundance when the power went out *and* surplus water to fight the fires if they got too close. In an emergency, our homestead readily provides wood for heat and cook fires, medicinal herbs for nearly any ailment, and enough abundance to share and trade with neighbors. Even a well-designed urban lot can provide residents with backup basic resources during a crisis. Your home can too.

Reforestation

Struggling forests, clear-cut timberlands, overgrazed woodlands, fire-scarred landscapes, and suburban developments are all candidates for reforestation projects. Reforestation includes nurturing existing trees, planting saplings, and sowing tree seeds. Sourcing the correct saplings at scale can be difficult and is often done by contract growing with a local nursery. That said, growing your own trees is feasible—thousands of trees can be propagated by seed or cutting in a fairly small space. Species like oaks are best sown from the seed (acorn) directly into the land in the fall. Find the approach that best fits your situation.

Bring Back the Prairie

Grassland prairie ecosystems are some of the most diverse, carbon-sequestering, life-giving ecosystems on earth. Throughout this book I have touched on grasslands, their ecology, and regenerative management practices appropriate to these systems. An ecologically managed grassland is a major carbon sink and supports a wide diversity of wildlife and domesticated animals.

Grassland biodiversity is as important as woodland biodiversity. Walk into a meadow or grassy field and kneel close to the ground. How many species of plants and herbs are growing there? Is it a single invasive grass species, or a mix of nitrogen fixers, broadleaf herbs, and a variety of grasses? The level of biodiversity indicates much about the landscape's health.

In part II of this book, we discussed water infiltration assessment. In part IV we took a deep dive into soil health and assessment. When it comes to grasslands, these two analysis techniques are used to understand whether grassland restoration efforts are successful. Tending grasslands in such a way that increases carbon also increases water availability. As we know, a 1 percent increase of soil carbon over one acre equals approximately 25,000 gallons of increased water-holding capacity per acre. With more water held in the soil throughout the year, grass and herbs that make up the biome grow stronger and longer into dry seasons. If these grasslands are managed responsibly by animals such as cows, sheep, or goats, the added forage is a boon to these animal endeavors.

When colonizing settlers landed in the Americas and spread across the continent, they described an ecological paradise unparalleled in their known world. They spoke of park-like ecosystems filled with animals, plant diversity, with millions of birds overhead. Little did they know that these fecund ecosystems emerged from the cultural tending of Indigenous people. The verdant grasslands didn't just happen, they were tended—cocreated—by people.

Native folks introduced fire to the land, clearing underbrush and opening wide grassland ecologies to benefit herding ruminants of bison, elk, and antelope; these animals provided crucial food and spiritual resources for the people. Humans, fire, animals, plants, and trees all worked in symbiotic harmony within the grassland ecosystem. Today that symbiotic harmony has been fractured. But we are here to reknit those broken links.

The grasslands and meadows of our environments can be tended in the old way again. With the smart introduction of fire, rotational management of wildlife or cattle, and a focus on building healthy soil, we can regenerate these abundant grasslands throughout our communities.

Perennial Grasses and Herbs

One hallmark of settler practices around the world is the introduction of non-native grass species and their degenerative impacts. Grassland ecologies coevolved with specific grass and herb species to work in those microclimates and soils. Much of the time, perennial grasses make up the ancient grassland ecology. In fact, purple needlegrass (*Nassella pulchra*), a perennial bunching grass, is the official grass of California. There were once twenty million acres of purple needlegrass throughout California. That number has been greatly reduced to approximately 100,000 acres today.[2]

Much of the grasslands in California have been taken over by introducing rye, oats, and highly invasive species such as medusa head and harding grass. The dominating growth of these grasses (some of which are annual) and the decrease in perennial bunchgrass prairies has greatly increased fire danger, reduced water availability, and resulted in a series of other ecosystem problems.

Purple needlegrass specifically evolved in landscapes as part of a complex web of relationships that includes frequent fire and elk migration. With its deep roots, purple needlegrass not only rebounds after fire but also taps into deep water tables, keeping its leaves green further into the summer. If you look around much of modern California in July, the grasslands are almost entirely brown. But Indigenous and settler lore tells that this was not always the case. There was a time where areas of California's grassland ecology remained green all through the year.

This is partly due to native perennial grasses and their deep rooting abilities. What is astonishing is that some purple needlegrass lands are hundreds years old. Let that sink in. There are not only old-growth forests but old-growth prairies. And they need to be protected just as much as any old-growth biome.

CASE STUDY: MYCOREMEDIATION WITH DR. MIA MALTZ

Even small things can make a big impact. Microscopic bacteria and fungi that live in soil can provide a spate of services to support ecosystems and human livelihoods. Once we are proficient in deciphering their language, we can then engage with these microbes and measure their activity. Given the detrimental impact of humans on the planet, we can collaborate with

(continued)

these unlikely allies to get our collective needs met and restore degraded environments. Moreover, as we grow to understand microbial resilience and sensitivity, we can determine how to enhance mutual benefits in relating with fungi or bacteria as well as discern how our activities can affect microbial processes.

Conservation Mycology

Historically, fungi have not been prominently featured within global conservation agendas. Yet, as they emerge on the conservation and restoration scenes, fungi are attracting considerable attention. In 2012, Chile was the first nation to include mushrooms in their legislation. With Giuliana Furci and Fundacion Fungi[3] at the helm of this movement, mushrooms are now afforded legal protection as the impacts of land management and development on fungi have been included within environmental impact assessments for Chilean ecosystems. In Ecuador, the rights of nature are memorialized in their nation's constitution;[4] Ecuador's Constitutional Court has to approve requests from extractive industries after assessing the effect on the land. When a team of mycologists conducted fungal biodiversity surveys[5] in the Reserva Los Cedros[6]—11,861 acres encompassing premontane wet tropical forest and cloud forest in northwestern Ecuador—this evidence was used to uphold sanctions against mining in this protected forest. Yet, regulatory decrees that sanction the impact of extractive industries on nature may not be sufficiently executed. Without advocates or spokescouncils of affected community members, such as Unión de Afectados por Texaco (UDAPT)[7] in Ecuador, reckless or oppressive acts that pollute air, water, and soil resources in remote locations may remain shrouded by dense vegetation, coupled with poorly enforced legislation.

Some Latin American and South American nations have launched mycological conferences, including Ecuador's first mycological congress in 2022. That same year, Dr. Nahuel Policelli, an Argentinian researcher of mycorrhizal ecology, gave a keynote address[8] emphasizing fungi in restoration at an event hosted by the Society for Ecological Restoration. After a well-attended international workshop on mycorrhizal symbiosis at Universidad Austral de Chile, the South American Mycorrhizal Research Network was launched to promote research in local communities and highlight work from a diversity of researchers, including BIPOC mycologists, through events such as the second Coloquio Colombiano de Micología in Colombia in 2021. Meanwhile, the Mycological Society of America hosted a "LatinX Mycelium" event in 2022 to highlight the innovative research of many LatinX mycologists across disciplines, including fungal ecology, identification, and conservation.

While the impacts on plants and animals have been historically integrated into modern US conservation efforts, fungal conservation has not been routinely considered within either US legislation or the global conservation movement. Although fungi are the engines of nutrient cycling and serve as essential drivers of ecosystem processes, they are rarely included in conservation planning and site assessments. As a response, the Society for the Protection of Underground Networks (SPUN) has launched their Underground Explorers grant program for supporting mycologists in mapping mycorrhizal fungal communities and advocating for their protection in understudied systems. My Ecuadorian colleague, mycologist Paulette Goyes, and I were recently invited to become scientific advisors for SPUN and support their mission of mapping mycorrhizal fungal communities worldwide. Organizing more Mycoblitz events[9] to engage community scientists in forays to collect, identify, and produce vouchered records of surveyed macrofungi (e.g., mushrooms) within particular geographic areas would be helpful in gathering baseline data to combat the exclusion of fungi in conservation efforts.

The geographic distribution of fungal species is related to climate and nutrient availability. Therefore, different types of mushrooms fruit in temperate, boreal, and tropical rainforests; likewise, cold-tolerant fungi from the frozen tundra may have different traits than those found in arid deserts. These environments select for microbes with a particular combination of traits that promote their survival. In some of my work, I examine how fungi (and other microbes) can be indicators of harsh environmental conditions and how adding in microbes (i.e., microbial inoculation) supports restoration outcomes.

As our climates change, novel habitats emerge; the geographic ranges of species shift to keep pace with these emergent environmental conditions (i.e., climate adaptation).[10] Now, in the Anthropocene Era,[11] we have cutting edge tools to peer below ground into the zone of fungal interactions and influence (the hyphosphere) and probe fungal responses to our activities. Since environmental conditions select for certain species, manipulating environmental features—like soil moisture or nitrogen content—may empower us to deliberately select for microbes that are meaningful in our lives or gardens by encouraging their growth in these novel environments. Techniques such as adding fungal spores, tissue, or microbial slurries into the environment can be employed to augment microbial abundance or promote microbial ecosystem services, increasing biodiversity, cycling nutrients, and enhancing plant performance. Through these methods, we become more capable of practicing land management along with these ancient microbial allies. It is likely that, without an explicit consideration of fungi, we may be undermining our conservation, management, and restoration efforts.

As a fungal ecologist, I incorporate fungal processes into land management. Using a variety of tools, I interpret fungal responses to stimuli and evaluate how to leverage fungal processes to accentuate soil remediation and restore habitat across both natural and managed ecosystems. In this spirit, I have launched projects and founded organizations[12] in the nonprofit sector like CoRenewal,[13] which works with fungi to preserve biodiversity and ameliorate the impacts of natural disasters and ecological disturbances on community and ecosystem health. At CoRenewal, we emphasize the role of fungi in restoring contaminated or

(continued)

fire-affected ecosystems by facilitating research and collaborative community-led solutions for supporting ecological resilience.

Through CoRenewal and as a PhD scientist, I find it rewarding to work on a range of sites impacted by industrial pollution and natural disasters. In these degraded sites, fungi promote nutrient cycling below and above ground, and resources can be exchanged among microbes that live together in symbiosis with plants (i.e., plant–microbial symbioses). Symbiotic root-associated fungi—the mycorrhizal fungi[14]—provide nutrients to plants, which usually leads to increased photosynthetic rates and improved plant productivity.[15] To enhance revegetation outcomes and plant root–fungal interactions that promote resource exchange within the hyphosphere, some land managers incorporate mycorrhizal spores or fungal strands (hyphae) into restoration projects.

Overall, I explore how microbial inoculation and community-inclusive approaches to restoration may address the damage caused by multiple drivers of global change. Below I will share several projects that align with, or emerged from, CoRenewal in examining how microbes respond to severe contamination within inhospitable habitats as well as how inoculating microbes may help rehabilitate these severely degraded, toxic, or fire-affected systems.

Ecotoxicology and Bioremediation

In 1567, Paracelsus stated: "All things are poison, . . . nothing is without poison: the *Dosis* alone makes a thing not poison." If every substance taken beyond its dose is poison,[16] then the appropriate dose differentiates poison from remedy.[17] Environmental toxicologist S. V. Rana[18] drew a parallel conclusion about substances that produce undesirable effects on humans and the environment (i.e., pollution).

One of Bill Mollison's permaculture principles[19] posits that pollution is an unused resource—the output of any system component that is not being used productively by another component. Therefore, any excessively abundant material can not only be considered pollution but also a resource for use in another system. Often, it is a matter of perspective. For instance, the macronutrient phosphorus (P) is essential for many biological processes, including membrane and DNA synthesis, as well as food production and modern agriculture.[20] However, when phosphorus runoff is discharged from farms or wastewater, aquatic systems suffer via eutrophication, resulting in toxic conditions. Riparian buffers around farms,[21] including those planted with native plant polycultures and inoculated with mycorrhizal fungi,[22] may reduce total phosphorus loading. On unceded Abenaki territory, Jessica Rubin researches phosphorus movement out of soil via mycorrhizal fungi. When cyclically coppiced, these plant–microbial symbionts remove phosphorus from the landscape, leaving behind remnant habitat for pollinators and providing food, medicine, and useful resources.

Human activities across environments yield biodegradable debris, and microbial infallibility suggests that all of this debris—every naturally occurring substance—can be taken up or broken down by at least one microbe. For instance, composting takes food waste and outputs soil microbial amendments. If we apply that perspective to coffee or bicycle repair shops, residual coffee grounds or greasy rags take on new life: as substrate for growing fungi and reducing toxicity of industrial compounds or debris.

Danielle Stevenson, a board member of CoRenewal, founder of DIY Fungi (https://diy-fungi.blog), and PhD candidate in Environmental Toxicology at UC Riverside, has worked with small businesses to attenuate biodegradable debris fields, such as grease rags drenched with teflon-based bicycle lubricant. In addition to decomposing urban debris, Danielle explores the connection between root-associated mycorrhizal fungi and metal contaminated "brownfields" (previously developed land that is no longer in use) specifically in arid systems. Danielle grew up in Ontario, Canada, in an area considered to be a "Cancer Alley,"[23] because this corridor contains large numbers of petrochemical and automotive industry plants[24] and other forms of industrial pollution.[25] As a small child, she identified this link between human health and environmental pollution, but she was inspired to see plants like sumac and poplars, along with fungi—such as the charismatic shaggy mane mushroom—growing through asphalt alongside a nearby oil refinery. At five, she created an outdoor mud kitchen to play with soil and concoct solutions; by 13, she was spending time in a lab inside her closet, created for "solving world problems." Today, Danielle conducts research in a high-tech environmental science lab where she tests soil and looks to nature for these remedies. Her bioremediation work investigates how plants and microbes can biodegrade contaminants or extract toxic metals from contaminated soil by viewing these pollutants as food sources.

Danielle leverages the power of plant–microbial symbioses to determine whether mycorrhizal fungi serve as gatekeepers that inhibit or enhance the uptake of toxic metals. Danielle explains that context is incredibly important. When contaminated land is lying fallow, like a superfund[26] or brownfield site, then we may want to add in microbes, such as mycorrhizal fungi, that "reverse-mine" contaminants and toxic metals from fallow land. Elements, including metals, are nonbiodegradable; therefore, they move into soil food webs and are translocated through hyphal networks of fungal tissues (mycelium) to the root zone (rhizosphere), where they may be incorporated into their plant host's roots, leaves, or fruits. This extractive process is known as phytoextraction or myco-phytoextraction. However, it may not always be beneficial to promote phytoextraction, such as when contaminated land is slated for development and green space planning includes recreation or food production in urban farms or community gardens. Fungi that live in plant roots have the capacity to absorb or retain metals in their tissue. If fungi transport these metals into the edible portion of food crops, this would

(continued)

have toxic implications for human consumption. In these contexts, we may ally with microbes to *inhibit* the uptake of toxic metals into plant or fungal tissues, as opposed to enhancing this process. In specific cases with food crops, plant-supporting mycorrhizal fungi may be coaxed to retain metals within their mycelium, rather than transfer these elements to their host plant for storage in either edible or nonedible plant tissues. Danielle's work provides evidence about how fungi affect where metals ultimately travel in a plant and how to leverage fungal processes for reducing these impacts and supporting food security.

Within a municipal scale project with the City of Los Angeles, the Department of Toxic Substances Control, neighborhood council groups, community groups, other collaborators, and regulators of brownfields in California, Danielle scales up approaches that have previously shown promise at smaller scales. Taking a biological approach to remediation (bioremediation), she translates the findings from her experiment into practice. She communicates with policy makers and governmental representatives to set precedents and explore applications for her work with fungi and environmental toxicology. Danielle identifies which microbes are volunteering on contaminated sites—these pioneer species brave inhospitable terrain and pave the way for ecological succession by enhancing the viability of severely contaminated landscapes. After identifying pioneers, she next assesses their capacity to tolerate contaminants present on the site. Finally, she investigates mechanisms, processes, and interactions to consider how to accelerate, support, or enhance what microbial volunteers could be doing to restore degraded sites and conducts comparisons between enhancing volunteer species or introducing known remediators.

In this work, Danielle experiments with microbial inoculation and phytoextraction at contaminated sites that have been sitting for decades. Conventional *ex situ* (off-site) cleanup may include excavating and shipping soils far distances or bringing in clean soils to cap the remnant brownfield. Therefore, it may be more energy efficient to clean up these contaminated sites *in situ* with ecologically sound approaches—by either adding microbes or manipulating soil properties—than it would be to haul soil from impacted locations for subsequent *ex situ* microbial processing.

In contrast to phytoextraction, organic pollutants may be treated biologically by leveraging microbial catabolic pathways,[27] which use enzymes to digest and biodegrade compounds. Humans generate unprecedented quantities of artificial compounds that are foreign to biological systems (i.e., xenobiotics).[28] Because xenobiotics are difficult to remove from wastewater, exposure to these emerging contaminants can cause health effects downstream. Selection experiments introduce difficult to degrade or xenobiotic compounds to fungal mycelia, which may unlock catabolic pathways in fungi capable of biodegradation[29] or biologically induced mineralization.[30]

Bioaugmentation—adding microbes directly into contaminated media—can occur either *in situ* or within an *ex situ* mesocosm,[31] a greenhouse, or in microcosm experiments.[32] Microbial inoculum can originate from varying sources, representing single species isolated from an environment or a complex microbial mixture or community. Native microbes can be sourced from local ecosystems or microbial inocula can be purchased from commercial sources. Native microbes can be collected from neighboring reference ecosystems[33] or isolated and selected based on their capacity to support a desired function. Some bioremediation practitioners use spent mushroom spawn (SMS), a by-product of mushroom cultivation, which is often discarded by mushroom farms in large quantities and can be applied to help with soil remediation.

In lieu of bioaugmentation, microbial communities in native soil can be encouraged to proliferate by adding biostimulants, such as kelp and seaweed or molasses-based amendments. In biostimulation, food sources are added to promote microbial growth, reproduction, and metabolism within the target environment. A variety of these types of biostimulation experiments may trigger microbial acclimation.[34] Given that microbes have fast generation times, in some cases, exposure to a substance or condition may elicit microbial adaptation, with subsequent generations of these microbes retaining the capacity to tolerate, degrade, or use these substances via microbial processing and metabolism. Adding in these microbes—bioaugmentation with known remediators—or stimulating with nutrients, substrates, or substrate analogs *in situ* on degraded sites might enhance endemic microbial volunteer species and stimulate the capacity of the microbial community to promote biodegradation, remediation, or cometabolism.

Many practitioners of fungal bioremediation (mycoremediation) are interested in jump-starting fungal enzymatic processes because enzymes produced by particular groups of decomposer fungi can catabolically or hydrolytically break down compounds with digestive enzymes in a similar fashion to how we digest our food. Fungi have elegant metabolic pathways for decomposing the structural components of woody plants, lignin, and cellulose.[35] Their enzymes break apart strong chemical bonds in compounds found in woody debris and fungally derived substances from mycelium (exudates) depolymerize and then repolymerize these compounds into substances that are easier to break down,[36] which are then used as food sources by other bacteria and fungi.

The complete breakdown of these substances, as well as the sloughed cells of fungi and other microbes, contribute to soil organic matter (SOM). SOM can persist over long periods of time below ground in soil organic carbon (SOC) pools, building fertile topsoil and helping to support revegetation and ecological succession. SMS is rich in enzymatic compounds, fungal biomass, and necromass (dead fungal tissue), which further contribute to SOC pools.

(continued)

Fungi and Fire

Bioaugmentation, biostimulation, and SMS amendments can also be applied in the wake of natural disasters, such as post-fire systems throughout the western United States. This post-fire restoration has been initiated through both community-led and collaborative experiments, as well as through federal, state, and local agencies. With CoRenewal, I explore biological questions related to fungal dynamics, biodiversity, and the ecological consequences of fire—both prescribed and natural—on surrounding ecosystems. Moreover, we aim to optimize these approaches for different environmental contexts across bioregions.

In recent years, I have observed an increase in the frequency and severity of wildfires, megafires, and gigafires[37] (depending on the acreage of burned land). Concurrently, I have witnessed and participated in community efforts to deploy conventional and emerging approaches, including soil bioremediation and microbial inoculation to aid in post-fire ecosystem recovery. I gather data to better understand the intended—and unintended—consequences of microbial inoculation as a post-fire management strategy to inform decision-making, as catastrophic megafires become more commonplace across our landscapes.

Along with university researchers and graduate students, I have set up multifactorial experiments comparing bioaugmentation treatments in post–prescribed fire settings. Some measured variables include soil microbial diversity and composition, soil nutrients, and native plant communities. Thanks to Annika Rose-Person (UC Riverside PhD candidate), we have monitored greater pollinator visitation in our treated plots, linked to higher floral diversity, the use of furrows, and the addition of soil from unburned reference sites into these regenerating systems. Above- and below-ground ecosystems are inextricably linked—the services performed by soils enhance pollination and biodiversity, with implications for food security.

CoRenewal members Maya Elson and Taylor Bright[38] coordinated a long-term fungal inoculation study following the catastrophic megafires of 2020. They launched this post-fire biofiltration initiative (PFBI) to mitigate toxic effluent and reduce erosion in these post-wildfire systems using community-led *in situ* methodologies in 27 replicated experimental blocks across five burn scars in California. PFBI compared methods of using conventional erosion-control wattles[39] for physically filtering effluent versus similar myco-wattles inoculated with the oyster mushroom, *Pleurotus*. These treatments were aimed at reducing sediment erosion, mineralizing heavy metals, and reducing polluting effluent or toxic ash from entering high-risk waterways. Fungal inoculation of these wattles may support these desired outcomes by biologically filtering sediment and polluting compounds via biofiltration. Through this scientific research, we will assess if these approaches yield any desired outcomes and, if so, determine the efficacy of these treatments.

In addition to biophysical filtration, chemical and metabolic processing of difficult-to-degrade residual contaminants may be important on sites where structures burned in the blaze. Since wattles were deployed near structure burns, this team is monitoring changes to biological, chemical, and physical soil properties by analyzing metals and other elements, quantifying petroleum hydrocarbons, characterizing water stable aggregates, and analyzing soil microbial communities. Fieldwork, sampling campaigns, and soil processing for PFBI were performed by in-kind and volunteer efforts, facilitated by community members and generous financial support from Metabolic Studio, an environmental arts studio in Los Angeles.

Among fire survivors that incorporate fungal remediation post-fire, I would like to highlight one complementary researcher, Cheetah Tchudi from Turkey Tail Farms. Cheetah's home, farm infrastructure, outbuildings, and water systems burned to the ground in the 2018 Camp Fire in Butte County. Shortly thereafter, Cheetah launched Butte Remediation, a nonprofit that aims to create open-source methods of remediation through researching fire-based contamination and providing baseline information and no-cost fungal bioremediation services to underserved Camp Fire survivors. These types of community-led projects emerged from a collective sense of urgency, as we and our loved ones were evacuated from our homes and witnessed the magnitude of western wildfires. As fire survivors document their experiences,[40] I remain in awe of the destructive and transformative force of fire. However small, microbes also harness powers of decomposition and facilitation to aid in regenerating these fire-adapted systems.

In 2021, the Wildlife Conservation Society's Climate Adaptation Fund selected CoRenewal and our partners to evaluate the benefits of inoculating custom erosion control wattles with different sources of microbial inocula. In collaboration with farmers and ranchers across California and Oregon, CoRenewal is setting up replicated field experiments in five different fire boundaries across a western US climate gradient. Spanning across bioregions, the findings from this work will allow us to monitor the benefits of post-fire microbial inoculation across sites with different climates and vegetation communities and then tailor these post-fire microbial approaches to locations with unique on-site resources. Ultimately, we aim to synthesize these findings to create recommendations for community members and land managers in those locations, highlighting techniques for working with fungi and other microbes to restore post-fire habitat in an ecologically and management-relevant timeframe.

Microbial Translocation

Much of this work relies on augmenting degraded land with microbes from intact ecosystems. Salvaging soil has been used as a restoration technique[41] and is particularly effective when the recipient ecosystem is severely degraded, with a depleted plant seed bank and a diminished fungal (e.g., mycorrhizal fungal) spore bank. Introducing beneficial microbes to

(continued)

foster mutualistic interactions with plants may promote seed germination. Adding soil from an intact reference ecosystem—typically, a local ecosystem that emulates characteristics found in the recipient system, prior to any disturbance—can increase species interaction, such as between mycorrhizal fungi and plant roots. In addition to these mutualistic microbes, diverse suites of reference soil microorganisms are also introduced to recipient soils.

Any time soils are translocated far distances, there may be an associated risk because translocating opportunistic, invasive, or pathogenic microbes into the recipient sites may influence biodiversity[42] and ecosystem functioning. Although microbial invasive species are not necessarily designated as noxious threats,[43] careful consideration is recommended when choosing donor sites in salvaged soil translocation projects. Ecologically sound, ethical, and appropriate microbial translocation could be enhanced by an expanded perspective on baseline data collection and ecological contexts. Ideally soils or microbes would be translocated short distances, and not include exotic plant or microbial propagules. Of the few data-driven studies that have investigated invasive fungi,[44] some have discovered invasive fungi in tree plantations[45] or growing throughout midwestern forests.[46] More work evaluating the unintended consequences of introducing opportunistic microbes with salvaged soil or commercial or exotic species would be germane, even for promoting putatively beneficial outcomes within a restoration context.

Reflections from the Ground Up

Fungi are sensitive to factors that degrade landscape and therefore can serve as "canaries in the coal mine," speaking volumes about the impacts of extractive industries or landscape degradation on soil organisms and microbial processes. Once we refine the tools to listen to them, assessing these fungal impacts may help us elucidate how global change drivers affect soil organisms like fungi. Commonly used landscaping or restoration methods could also alter the environment and change the structure of soil-based or plant-associated fungal groups. In addition, as climates change and humans modify natural environments, this may create novel habitats for non-native microbes or fungal pathogens to proliferate, with potential implications for fungal nutrient cycling or plant establishment in these novel environments.

Even though fungi are sensitive to these stressors, many fungi are also resilient. This ecological resilience can be exhibited at all levels of organization, from an individual to an ecosystem. For instance, a mushroom, fungus, or fungal population may first shrink in abundance when initially exposed to an environmental pollutant. Eventually (at either fast or slow time scales), following exposure, these fungi may learn to grow again, proliferate, and ultimately harness an arsenal of tools to use the pollutant as a food source. We have a lot to learn from fungal resilience as we too adapt to our changing planet.

Mycoregeneration. Illustration by Taylor Bright. Species featured: Turkey tail (Trametes versicolor), Shiitake (Lentinula edodes), Phoenix Oyster (Pleurotus pulmonarius), King Stropharia (Stropharia rugosoannulata), and Shaggy Mane (Coprinus comatus).

The tools we use to document these processes are cutting edge. However, these practices are not novel. In fact, we are building on more than a hundred centuries of traditional land-management techniques that maintain environments, promote polyculture plant palettes, and translocate organic materials to new sites. Whether tending the oak trees with oyster shells[47] or conducting controlled burns to reduce fuel loads[48] in forest understories, human management

(continued)

of ecosystems has promoted the adaptive success of human populations by changing environmental conditions to promote microbial proliferation and essential nutrient cycling.

Working in collaboration with diverse communities, we are relearning how to restore the balance by exploring tools that address the social and environmental injustices that are rampant in contemporary society, determining the efficacy of these approaches at small scales. There is mounting evidence for applying the use of fungal ecology to improve the structure and functioning of biological communities and support ecosystem regeneration after ecological disturbances, technological shifts, and exposure to industrial pollution. We are now faced with a paramount challenge to extend this work beyond the scientific realm, into the sociopolitical and technological dimensions of environmental problems that pose unprecedented challenges for humanity and the environment. Truly addressing these environmental issues means scaling these applications for home, community, industrial, and municipal settings.

To learn more, check out these books and resources:

Arevalo, Willoughby. *DIY Mushroom Cultivation: Growing Mushrooms at Home for Food, Medicine, and Soil*. Vol. 6. New Society Publishers, 2019.

Benyus, Janine M. *Biomimicry: Innovation Inspired by Nature*. Morrow, 1997.

Cotter, T. *Organic Mushroom Farming and Mycoremediation: Simple to Advanced and Experimental Techniques for Indoor and Outdoor Cultivation*. Chelsea Green Publishing, 2014.

Darwish, Leila. *Earth Repair: A Grassroots Guide to Healing Toxic and Damaged Landscapes*. New Society Publishers, 2013.

Dorr, Alex. *Mycoremediation Handbook: A Grassroots Guide to Growing Mushrooms and Cleaning Up Toxic Waste with Fungi*. Simon & Schuster, 2021.

Kellogg, Scott T., and Stacy Pettigrew. *Toolbox for Sustainable City Living (A Do-It-Ourselves Guide)*, 2008.

Kellogg, Scott. *Urban Ecosystem Justice: Strategies for Equitable Sustainability and Ecological Literacy in the City*. Routledge, 2021.

McCoy, Peter. *Radical Mycology: A Treatise on Seeing and Working with Fungi*. Portland, OR: Chthaeus Press, 2016.

Satori, D., and M. Wainhouse. "Unseen Connections: The Role of Fungi in Rewilding." In *Routledge Handbook of Rewilding*. Cardiff University: Natural England, in press.

Stamets, Paul. *Mycelium Running: How Mushrooms Can Help Save the World*. Random House Digital, Inc., 2005.

SEED DRILLING

In large, no-till agriculture and grassland restoration ventures, a seed drill quickly establishes new plantings with minimal soil disturbance. A seed drill rolls over the ground, pushing seeds into the surface without inverting topsoil. The seed drill will push seeds through many different mediums—a crimped cover crop, mulch, bare soil, or grazed pasture.

BUILD RELATIONSHIPS WITH WILD PLANTS

Building gardens and farms are noble tasks if done ecologically. But prior to the advent of agriculture, all our ancestors practiced a different form of living on earth. "Hunters and gatherers" is what we call them, and these people of our past (and present) sustained their way of life directly from the wild itself. Here we will focus on "gathering."

These days, the term *wild crafting* invokes images of damaging harvests of endangered native plant species. Sorting out whether wild crafting has any benefit at all to the environment other than a personal yield is confusing. Harvesting wild plants does have beneficial effects when performed with the right practices. Work with regenerative principles, primarily reciprocity and succession, when approaching wild plants for harvest. A symbiotic exchange between you and the plant community is a must. If a plant is severely threatened or endangered, however, then *don't harvest them!*

Don't wild harvest threatened or endangered plants. These are plants on the brink of survival. Unless you are a trained biologist working to expand populations through propagation, it's best to keep your hands and shears off these wild species. To make matters worse, culturally significant plants like white sage (*Salvia apiana*) have been overharvested, threatening their survival in the wild. This plant has significant cultural importance in many Indigenous tribes, especially in the Southwest. Burning white sage has become a popular phenomenon for all kinds of spiritual people. Sadly, the demand for white sage has resulted in the loss of many patches of wild white sage.[49] This type of harvesting should be avoided at all costs unless you are a member of the communities that have tended this plant for generations. Growing plants such as white sage in your own landscape or farm is great! I myself have large patches of white sage, and I harvest and send it as gifts to friends and communities around the United States. It's a fabulous offering and always received with great appreciation.

It's not true that harvesting wild plants is always damaging to the environment. That thought has hopefully been weeded out of your mind during the reading of this book. You must see yourself as an ecosystem manager, as one of the creatures of the forest and the meadow, and from there your actions become symbiotic and beneficial. Wild crafting is an ancient practice not only meant for harvesting food and medicine but also to expand plant communities through propagation and cultivation. It's not about taking resources as much as it is about nurturing wild plant species into prolific feral gardens. Harvesting wild plants ecologically turns you into a wild gardener, spreading native seeds, cuttings, and bulbs to swell wild crops for present and future generations.

Ethical Wild Harvesting Techniques

A core tenet of wild crafting is to never harvest all of a single plant. When harvesting, only take a small volume from each plant and spread the impact of your harvest throughout an entire patch or multiple patches. You know you've done it right when you look at a harvested patch or plant and it looks the same as it did preharvest. Use this as your guide for appropriate wild crafting. Remember, you're not only leaving behind herbs, flowers, fruits, roots for other humans but for the entire landscape ecology. Don't break the links of biological resilience by harvesting all of a plant. Other species depend on those plants too.

Tending Wild Plants

When harvesting wild plants there is an opportunity to provide wild tending. If an invasive exotic is taking over a native plant community you're wild crafting from, then in exchange, weed the invasive and create room for native plants to thrive. If you observe disease or other issues threatening the wild plants you harvest, help them by cutting out the diseased or sick material.

The deeper your understanding of ecology, the more you can determine what kinds of problems might persist that affect wild plants you hope to harvest. Are they able to propagate themselves? Or have keystone species or other ecological processes disappeared that would generally help this plant reproduce? For instance, in heavily fire-suppressed plant communities, many species may find it difficult to reproduce because they require fire to make seeds viable. Help solve this by harvesting the seeds and heating them gently on a warm skillet. This fire simulation will activate seed viability. Next time you return to the mother plants, sow their seeds for them. This is true reciprocity and the type of regenerative thinking and action required when building relationships with wild plant communities.

Stimulate Growth and Propagate

How you harvest plant material makes a huge difference—not only the amount taken from each plant or patch but also the parts you cut. Use your knowledge of plants and make cuts in such a way that stimulates vigorous growth. This is as simple as cutting to a bud or, when harvesting roots, digging up a plant and breaking it into many new plants (only if the plant is propagated by root). For the latter, take one plant, harvest 25 percent of the root, then break up the remaining 75 percent of roots into three new plants to replant them in their natural area.

Seasonality

For wild crafting activities to be beneficial, they must be done in the appropriate season. It's easy enough to know when a species is ready to be harvested like a fruit or a flower, but when is the best time for those plants to propagate themselves? What other living organisms are depending on these plants and at what times of the year? If you happen upon a native plant community you hope to harvest from but it is currently being visited by dozens of bird species and insects, does that change how you harvest? If you're paying attention to the life around you, you will be sensitive to removing this food and habitat from the landscape community when they need it most. Time your activities appropriately, take feedback from biological communities, and make every action one of symbiotic exchange with the plants you are harvesting from in the right season.

53

Lands of Fire

More than fifty thousand years of fire develops a dependency in the landscape.[1] Many landscapes literally need fire to stay free of pests and disease, to access nutrients, and to grow in a thriving manner. Fire-evolved tree and plant species require fire to scarify their seed for viability. The seeds literally need fire!

A good fire scours the land, seeds are released from plant life, and a new generation of robust vegetative growth occurs. Biodiversity skyrockets and these systems continue to grow until the need for fire returns and the cycle starts anew. These are fire-dependent landscapes, and they exist on nearly every continent on the planet. Are you in such a landscape right now?

CATASTROPHIC (HIGH INTENSITY) VERSUS GOOD FIRE (LOW INTENSITY)

Fire in the landscape has occurred for millions of years. Some ecosystems evolved more closely with fire than others and eventually became fire ecologies. But after witnessing the devastation and destruction of catastrophic fire in the modern era, most see wildfires as a terrible and frightening phenomenon.

In truth, fire is both catastrophic and beneficial. The measure of the regenerative or destructive impacts of fire is the intensity—the actual heat the fire produces. High-intensity, very hot fires are generally burning on heavy fuels—the crowns of trees, tall dry grasses, homes, and other human infrastructure. With enough fuel, a high-intensity fire can create its own weather systems. Pyrocumulus clouds, fire-made winds, and fire tornadoes are all possible once the fire grows large enough.[2] A fire of this magnitude does not regenerate; instead it incinerates much in its path. That said, it's impossible to call every part of a high-intensity fire negative. Such fires create many microclimates and various sister fires. The fire burns at different intensities in different areas—large areas around the perimeters of high-intensity fires are of lower intensity and act as beneficial disturbances.

A low-intensity fire, what we call "good" fire, provides ecological benefits to ecosystems. These fires burn on lighter fuels and are generally set intentionally by the people of those landscapes. These fires burn cooler and therefore don't destroy all the biology in their path, instead burning out the understory, removing disease, alkalinizing soil, and scarifying seeds of native plants that require fire to become viable. In the wake of a low-intensity fire, immense vegetative growth by pioneering plants occurs, providing food for wildlife. These fires also create conditions for larger and more mature forest ecosystems to flourish as disease is removed and a balanced soil pH is generated.

Low-intensity fires occur through Indigenous cultural ignition (fire lit by Native people), by modern-day prescribed burns, at the edges of large wildland fires, or in lightning-struck areas where ecological management practices have removed large fuel loads. Managing forests and grasslands ecologically is managing them in preparation to receive low-intensity, healing fire.

Walking among the charred ruins of the woodlands where I live, I can see where low-intensity fires occurred around the edges of the bigger fire. Grasses are resprouting, trees are pushing leaves, and fungi cover the surface of the ground. Hiking to the ridgetops where the fire was hottest was walking into a literal wasteland. Not even the remains of burning trees were left behind. Instead, holes in the ground mark where fire burned out the root systems. This hotter fire burned down and into the soil, killing all life there. Where low-intensity fire landed, life surges forward in response to the regenerative disturbance. On the ridge where fire burned hot, only dust and ash remained.

FIRE FREQUENCY

Ecologies that coevolve with periodic fire do so with specific frequency. The frequency of fire is specific to each environment's microclimate, topography, soil, and vegetation. In many fire ecologies the world over, governments suppressed fire in the landscape throughout the twentieth century; removing fire from the landscape pushed fire-dependent biomes toward disaster.

The Indigenous people of Turtle Island have been savvy ecosystem managers for hundreds of generations. They use fire as a cultural tool, revering its power not only as a sacred life-giving element but also as a beneficial management tool in the environment. Whether induced by humans or from a lightning strike, the frequency of fire in the environment remained similar over the course of more than 10,000 years until just before the age of fire suppression.[3]

On the land you are called to manage, when was the last time fire burned? What about the time before that? How far back can you find the patterns of fire in that landscape? What is the natural frequency of fire in the area? Most likely, the best data you can find is held within the Indigenous communities of the region. What you discover may be remarkable. Some landscapes need fire every five years, others every seven, while some burn every 50 years. As you analyze fire frequency in the landscape, keep in mind that these patterns are changing now. With the warming earth and a shifting climate, the frequency of megafires has greatly increased. This is also due to what is essentially a fire debt in the landscape. Decades of fire suppression have left the landscape ripe for more frequent megafires.

Once fire comes to the land, it is imperative that we reintroduce it frequently from then on. Fire becomes less catastrophic when it burns at the right frequency. Small, controlled burns and Indigenous cultural fires introduced to fire-dependent landscapes regenerate ecology while keeping communities safe from harm.

LESSONS FROM THE FIRE

From 2017 to 2020, my community experienced a succession of traumatic wildfires. Thousands of homes and businesses burned to the ground, along with many thousands of acres of forests. Fires like these change a community, and our community is forever changed. The fire patterns were sporadic at times, skipping over some houses and trees while burning their neighbors. For many it was just a stroke of luck, a quick change in the wind or a feature of topography. For others, the landscaping itself played a role in deciding whose home burned and whose didn't.

Analyzing why some homes got burned and others didn't, fire experts distinguished a number of patterns and made conclusions. Many homes that burned were ignited by the ember cast ahead of the main fire. These embers would land on the roofs of buildings and, if sufficient fuel from leaves, branches, wooden shingles, and/or composite roof were present, the house went up in flames. Embers also blew against homes and got into debris-filled gutters and even vents. Landscapes with dead and dying trees trapped embers and burst into flame. Interestingly, it has been noted that healthy trees that burned adjacent to houses were largely burned due to the house fire and not the other way around. Healthy neighborhood trees remained slightly scarred or unscathed when not in proximity to buildings. Finally, some homes were protected by green hedges and irrigated landscapes—embers were caught and went out and/or heat was buffered, keeping those houses from harm.

The psychological trauma experienced around huge fires is all too real. Many homeowners and rebuilding developers became so concerned about flammable materials and fuel load in the landscape that they essentially "moonscaped" their projects. They cut down healthy trees, removed every old shrub, poured concrete, scraped soil, and left landscapes devoid of life. I don't blame folks for responding to the fear and trauma they experienced by hardening their homes in such an emphatic way. But this level of fire hardening has negative ecological consequences that might make fires worse in the long run.

Removing wildlife habitat, photosynthesis, and carbon sequestration in the landscape is not a recipe for human survival. Combine this with landscape dehydration caused by impervious concrete and the removal of natural shade and these environments move closer to deserts than fire-resilient landscapes. It's imperative to find the balance between tending ecosystem processes and living with the forces of fire. Obviously, homes and livelihoods need to be protected, but at the same time, how much ecological destruction is required to protect our stuff?

Balancing these goals is possible. Regenerative landscapes surrounding our homes can mitigate fire danger, integrating the needs of ecosystems with the needs of humans to find the sweet spot in this work. Incorporate water-harvesting structures as tools to mitigate fire. Shade the soil with useful plantings to cool the soil surface and keep moisture present—these techniques reduce fire danger. Be smart and remove combustible fuels like dead and diseased trees close to your home. Focus on building soil and turning it into a year-round carbon sponge. Combine all these techniques and you will fireproof your landscape while implementing ecological practices at the same time.

ANIMALS AND FIRE MANAGEMENT

Large animals have played an important management role in our ecosystems for millions of years, but extensive hunting and industrialization have wiped out many of these important species in our ecosystem. Grazing ungulates like elk and antelope stomp accumulated dead organic matter (fuel load) into the ground where it comes in contact with soil-level moisture and microorganisms that cause it to further decompose. Other animals like bears have been important forest managers as they break down the low branches and small trees in the forest while scavenging for food. As a result, material that would otherwise volatilize and release greenhouse gases into the atmosphere—namely, CO^2—instead builds organic matter and stores carbon in the soil.

Elk and antelope never overgrazed areas because they were followed by wolves, coyotes, and mountain lions that kept these hooved animal herds bunched up and on the move. This predator–prey relationship results in a beautiful and dynamic ecosystem management pattern that has been lost in contemporary ecosystems.

All debates around humans eating animals aside for now, if we specifically look at the activities of well-managed animals in the right environment and the impact that has on an ecosystem, we can easily see that from an ecological point of view, integrating animals (even domestic) into land management has huge benefits if managed appropriately. Pigs, goats, cows, and sheep could all play important roles in managing fuel load and getting carbon into the ground on public and private lands. The realities of such endeavors will have to be specific to each site and carefully monitored by the community for optimum ecological health. There are plenty of cases where the use of domestic animals in managing ecosystems is not appropriate, from either social or economic issues or cultural and ecological ones. In all cases, success depends on understanding the specific needs of an ecosystem and community to decide on the best practices for that place.[4]

Fuel Ladders

One technique for mitigating wildfire catastrophe and rebuilding forest health is to keep fire from moving from the ground into the crowns (tops) of trees. A healthy fire, a good fire, stays low to the ground and burns at a lower intensity. If fire has a chance to climb vertically into the canopy, the intensity of the fire and the rate of spread (ROS) significantly increases.

Vegetative material (dead or living) that connects the crowns of trees to the understory are called ladder fuels. It generally consists of low branches, small trees, and shrubs. Depending on the composition between understory species and forest canopy species, the optimum height of ladder fuels will vary. Generally speaking, approximately 8 to 12 feet from the ground is recommended. If understory shrubs are present, then a 10-foot distance between the tops of shrubs and lower tree branches is desired. Around buildings and in the wildland/urban interface, fuel ladders may be cut to 18 feet from the forest floor. Every local context requires a specific approach and depends on climate, forest species, and forest structure.

Prune back the understory plants. Make sure to prune dead and diseased material completely, and then move to living vegetation, cutting it back to levels appropriate to your situation.

Use the material generated from these activities in any number of woody debris management systems discussed in this book.

Prescribed Burning

Many First Nations communities around the world sustain intergenerational cycles of ecological health for themselves and the ecosystems they maintain. Let's heed the wisdom of Indigenous communities who have been managing earth's landscapes using prescribed burning and other methods. North America has no chance of achieving this with our current land management practices as we have destroyed much of the ecology in just 150 years and counting. We must make an immediate shift toward ecological, place-based, and appropriate land management practices with a timescale of managing health for future generations.

Prescribed burning is the practice of intentionally setting low-intensity fires in the forest to consume and reduce the accumulated fuel load of dead limbs, thatch, and outcompeted smaller trees. The timing, technique, and location are thoroughly assessed for optimal effect and mitigation of catastrophic consequences. These burns are often carried out in spring when plants are still green and humidity is present in the ecosystem to ensure that the fire cannot spread into the canopy of established trees and the people managing the prescribed burn can keep it controlled.

Shaded Fuel Break

In fire-prone ecologies, shaded fuel breaks are developed to slow the movement of fire and provide defensible space to battle fire when it comes. For most people, when they hear the term *fuel break* they imagine a large clear-cut swath through a forest, or an industrial agriculture system like a vineyard. These certainly provide adequate fuel breaks but with little ecological function. A shaded fuel break retains some ecological functions while also acting as a fire break.

Strategically, shaded fuel breaks make the most sense along existing or newly developed roads and trails. These access ways already assist in getting tools, equipment, and water to a fire. But they also constitute an area with a break in vegetation. To turn a road or trail into a shaded fuel break, you must intentionally manage the forest 100 feet on either side of the trail. Within this 100-foot area, a more aggressive thinning regime is required to create the shaded fuel break.

Within this area, trees are thinned to create up to 10-foot spaces between the canopies of the trees. In this way, the canopy is not fully enclosed—no tree canopies are touching each other. The next treatment is to leave minimal to no understory in the shaded fuel break area. Personally, I find it difficult to remove all understory in areas as large as these, but, the less understory there is, the more functional the shaded fuel break will be.

Finally, make sure there are no contour brush piles or other woody debris on the forest floor inside your designated zone. All these techniques combined work well to slow a fire from spreading. If a fire burns to a shaded fuel break, it will slow its rate of spread with little fuel to keep it burning. If the shaded fuel break is along a road or trail, access for firefighters might be sufficient to fight fire from there.

THE FIRES WILL RETURN

October 8, 2017, was a life-changing experience for me and the community where I have lived my whole life. Due to a perfect combination of extreme drought followed by a historic wet season—encouraging vegetative growth—and a strong, hot inland wind, a massive firestorm erupted overnight. It consumed hundreds of thousands of acres of land and thousands of homes and businesses. This is what it means to live in a fire ecology in the age of fire suppression.

It was a deeply emotional experience living through such an event, and the long-term recovery and collective trauma will be felt for years to come. After witnessing the level of destruction to lives, homes, and property, it's easy to want to do everything in our power to stop fires from ever returning. But is that even possible? What if I told you that the idea that "We can prevent the fire" is the most dangerous and ineffective approach to protecting people and property?

What if I told you, in order to reduce the risk of catastrophic fires in our lives, we have to embrace wildfire? Fire is not the enemy. Wildfire is a raw and powerful expression of nature, and learning to design our communities and steward our environment with fire in mind is our best chance to decrease the threat of catastrophe. But how do we learn to live with firestorms? Who can teach our land stewards and community developers how to embrace the power of fire?

Indigenous people have known how to live in harmony with wildfire for tens of thousands of years. The wisdom and stories still carried by native communities provide some of the best

Redbird Willie (the illustrator of this book) surveys the dogbane patch after fire.
Photo Credit: Erik Ohlsen.

kept records of the world's natural history. To truly listen to this generational wisdom is to wake up to a deeper dimension of relationship to the land.

Three Lessons from Native American Ecologist Edward "Redbird" Willie

During the recovery from the 2017 California firestorm, I had the privilege to learn from a Native American ecologist named Edward "Redbird" Willie (Pomo, Wintu, Wailaki), who is also the illustrator for this book. He graciously attended many fire recovery events to share his knowledge about the historical role fire plays in ecology.

As an ecological designer, I feel pretty confident in my understanding of ecosystems, fire ecology, and everything encompassed therein. What Redbird taught me and our community was much deeper than I had expected. It expanded my relationship to the land in fundamental ways, along with my view of development, and has given me a sense of hope. Here are three lessons from Redbird about fire.

Lesson 1: Forest Fires Cannot be Prevented

Let me be clear that while the fires themselves cannot be prevented, the level of catastrophic impacts can. Why can't wildfires be prevented? Nothing sends that message home more than learning how long these fires have been returning to the same exact places in the landscape. According to Redbird, the Pomo have been observing the fire zone most recently known as the Tubbs Fire (October 8, 2017, Santa Rosa, California) for at least the last 10,000 years. This fire has been returning to the same place *for 10,000 years*.

The Napa, California, Atlas Fire that burned in October 2017 has been observed by the Indigenous people of those lands, the Onasatis (Wappo), for over 10,000 years. Redbird shares that the Onasatis even have a word in their language for the hot east winds that return each October. Imagine that—to be so in tune with the cycles of fire that you give the exact fire winds in an exact location a name to pass through the generations. Redbird describes these fires as "geysers," natural phenomena that reoccur in regular intervals like any other type of geyser.

Cultivating Relationship with Recurring Fire Events

Over millennia, knowing the firestorm was destined to return, Redbird's Pomo ancestors cultivated an approximately five-square-mile patch of dogbane (*Apocynum*) plants directly in its path—exactly where the Tubbs Fire hit in 2017. Dogbane is an important native plant to the Pomo people. They make fishing and hunting nets out of the thick fibers of the plant's stalk. It takes approximately 60,000 stalks of dogbane to make one net for a whole family.

Fire plays an important role in managing dogbane, which I learned when Redbird and I visited a small, protected area of what is left of the ancient Pomo dogbane patch. Fire clears

(continued)

out competing plants and causes the dogbane to grow tall lanky stalks the following year. This creates longer fibers to harvest for nets and cordage—forming a deep relationship between people and fire.

Lesson 2: Learn the Story of Place

One of the more important lessons Redbird shares is the understanding that every place is different. Topography, microclimate, and vegetation type all contribute to the environmental processes and functions of a place. He encourages us to learn the stories of each place; each valley, each ridgetop, each tree, each generation of animal has its own story to tell us about the land. With this listening approach, we deepen our sense of time and the succession of a landscape. To understand the ecological pattern of place is to better understand the role fire may play there. The more we listen and learn, the more we change our stewardship practices and planning endeavors from a fight against nature to a collaboration with it, just like native communities have done for generations.

Learning the story of a place means that the solution for one location may be different from that of another location. Geographically close areas are still differentiated due to microclimate, water, and other site-specific conditions—the expression of natural hazards like fire and drought are varied.

Without understanding the story of each place, we are intentionally cultivating ignorance of the forces of nature. As twenty-first-century firestorms have regrettably demonstrated, we are in a fight for our lives, but only because we made it so. Nature will always have the last word. That is why we need to remember that we are nature too. Remember that we can live in right relationship with ecosystems. We will never go back to the exact ways of our ancestors, but we can strive for a new kind of harmony—a new balance of ancient wisdom with the modern world.

The more I learn from Redbird and other Indigenous wisdom keepers, the more I realize that our environment has a story that has been told, retold, edited, and revised for millennia, changed by generation after generation. The oral records of the past are a prediction of the future and can point us toward solutions. Our modern-day culture puts too much trust in the promise of technological solutions. Maybe the solutions to many of our problems have already been figured out by our ancestors who lived through catastrophes that we have never witnessed.

Lesson 3: Steward the Land with Prescribed Fire

Redbird shares how native people intentionally use fire as a tool to steward the land. They introduce fire at regular intervals to manage the growth of vegetation, reduce fuel load, and activate fire-dependent plant communities. With fire occurring more often, fuel load is generally less of an issue and these fires burn at a lower intensity and therefore lead to less destruction.

Today we call the practice of using fire for management "prescribed burning" and it has widespread use in many places across the globe. It's important to note that introducing fire to a landscape for the purpose of management must be done at the correct time of year with many important best practices in place. The danger is low if done right. In fact, 99 percent of prescribed burns are completely controllable by fire tenders.[5]

Using prescribed fire in fire ecology landscapes is good way to avoid large-scale disasters like we saw during the 2017 California firestorms. Introducing more fire will also support a healthier relationship with native plants and animals as they have coevolved with fire, possibly even longer than humans.

FIREPROOFING THE LANDSCAPE

Hardening your home landscape to fire is the best personal strategy to avoid catastrophic damage during wildfire season. A fire-resilient landscape is heavily managed up to 100 feet from the home in all directions, commonly called *defensible space*.

A landscape layout that breaks the movement (continuity) of fire through the area is an important strategy. When fire does come, will it climb vegetation and gain purchase onto your house or burn into the canopies of tall trees? Here are a few techniques to fire-harden your landscape and home.

Gutters. Keep gutters and roofs clear of leaves and debris.

Flammable Materials. Remove all flammable material like propane tanks, wood piles, and tool sheds to at least 30 feet from the home.

Gravel Mulch. It is best to use gravel as a mulching material rather than straw, wood chips, or leaves directly around your house. A 5- to 10-foot area around buildings and decks should be free of flammable mulch materials.

Green Landscapes. Keep the plant communities around your house well irrigated (especially within the 30-foot range). Green plants provide protection to the home by buffering the wave of heat that precedes an oncoming fire. Green plants can burn but require higher fire intensity in order to combust. Some plants are even resilient to fire, including succulents, cacti, and water-loving trees such as fig.

Plant Spacing/Layering. In high-risk fire zones, plant and tree species should be placed farther from each other (than normally found in an intensive food forest system) to break up fire movement. In part VII, vertical layering within food forests was discussed in detail. In fire zones, the vertical layering strategy is a bit different. To keep fire from spreading, trees are spaced far enough from each other to keep mature canopies from touching. Understory plants are placed far enough away from tree trunks (five or more feet) to keep fire from using the understory as fuel ladders.

Waterscapes. The regenerative landscape is managed to catch and infiltrate as much water as possible using ponds, terraces, rain gardens, and contour swales. All of these systems build fire resilience in a number of ways. Each water-catching structure can act as a fire break when managed for such. The building of localized water aquifers keeps vegetation greener for longer, reducing the length of fire season.

Healthy Topsoil. A focus on building healthy soil creates landscapes that act as sponges. As carbon and organic matter are fed to soil biology, the water-holding capacity of the soil increases, keeping plants greener longer and reducing highly combustible fire fuels from forming.

Fuel Breaks. Throughout the landscape, pathways, ponds, roads, patios, irrigated grassy areas, and so on all act as fire breaks if managed accordingly. If it fits your context, intentionally design these spaces to act as fire breaks at well-spaced intervals away from the house. A managed trail around the edge of a forest, for instance, provides a fire break for the landscape if the forest catches fire.

54

Regenerative Forest Management

The forests of the world provide life-giving resources to the whole planet. They produce oxygen, sequester carbon, and provide fuel, food, and fiber for untold thousands of species including humans. Deforestation, clear-cutting, catastrophic fires, bark beetle infestations, disease, and a changing climate have put many forest ecosystems in great peril. Forests depend on complex webs of interactions in order to grow and thrive, retaining biodiversity and resilience to pests, disease, and fire. These webs have been broken for centuries due to mismanagement. As ecological stewards, we must reintroduce ecological management and Indigenous techniques back into our forests to protect us all.

ECOLOGICAL FOREST MANAGEMENT

Ecologically minded folks, you're being called to the forefront of the restoration efforts of this era. We need people willing and capable to read the language of the land and reintegrate into the reciprocal relationships necessary for forests and humans to thrive together again. That means you! Ecological management techniques provide a variety of ways to understand forest ecosystems and to use targeted regenerative disturbances such as selective thinning, prescribed fire, lop and scatter, chipping, mycoremediation, replanting, and so on to restore woodlands.

Silviculture is an umbrella term used to describe large-scale forest management techniques geared toward timber harvesting. Under the banner of silviculture, we find forest clear-cutting, forest plantations, and dozens of techniques with a general mindset of seeing the forest as a commodity rather than an ecology. Silviculture practices aren't all bad, though; when they are incorporated with an ecological lens, they can lead to responsible forest management at the largest scale possible. An ecological approach looks at all biological functions, from the underground mycelial networks up to the canopy-dwelling microcommunities and everything in between. Look into water quality and availability, soil health, animal diversity, and understory species composition—all this analysis must be complete before developing a forest management plan.

Managing a forest ecologically is managing the land in the way Indigenous people have since ancient times. Tending a forest is more than selective thinning and introducing fire; it is the threshold of relational reciprocity. The forest gave life to many human civilizations, those embedded in its web of relationships. The give-and-take between forest and people is a mutually beneficial dance of relationships that yields a flourishing forest, and flourishing people. It's as simple as that. This is the perspective I hope you adopt before you take a saw into the woods.

See yourself as one of the missing animals of the woodland forest, here to manage regeneratively. You are there not only to take but to exchange. Dedicate every step, every saw stroke, every axe swing, every sapling planted or herb harvested to the forest. Dedicate these actions to the thriving future you are cocreating.

Selective Thinning

Due to the suppression of fire and the loss of large animals like bear, antelope, and elk, many forest ecosystems are highly overcrowded. That means there are too many trees per acre trying to grow in a crowded environment. A congested forest is plagued by many problems including limited sunlight, which filters through to the forest floor and reduces understory biodiversity. Many goals can be met by thinning selected trees and opening the canopy—reduced fire danger, enhanced understory growth, disease resistance, and small-scale timber harvests.

Selective thinning through an ecological lens is not the same as the thinning practices performed by many corporations and governments that make the case for removal of old-growth trees. Thinning techniques have been greenwashed in the media, held up as methods to tend forests responsibly, but in truth these act as a guise for timber extraction.

Death and Decay

In an overcrowded forest, many trees are competing for light and end up shading each other out. Eventually, the too-small or slower growers get stressed and die. These trees all together constitute a colossal fire hazard, turning the forests into tinder boxes of dead trees full of ladder fuels. If fire strikes a forest like this, it will quickly reach the crown of the forest and unnecessarily result in catastrophic damage. (Note: When selectively thinning in a forest, *do not* cut every dead tree. Leave well-established snags to continue as havens for wildlife. Some dead trees in the forest are beneficial. But when the forest is mostly dead, action needs to be taken.)

Disease Vectors

The more stressed and congested the forest, the more it becomes a vector for pests and disease. Lack of light and ventilation causes the perfect conditions for these vectors. Once disease and pests move through a forest, they leave behind an even greater fire risk. Only a blade or a flame will bring a situation like this back to balance. In response to these degenerative scenarios, selective thinning within the forest can be a regenerative act. Implementing this technique is the moment you become the good fire. Your use of a saw blade to thin dead and dying material, remove ladder fuels, and thin stressed trees mimics the clearing power of fire without catastrophe. The wood you cut is then chipped, lopped, scattered, and/or used for erosion control. This builds soil, catches water, enhances wildlife habitat, and more. As an overcrowded forest opens, understory biodiversity increases, fire danger decreases, and pest and disease conditions are minimized.

Selecting Trees to Cut

Once dead and dying trees have been removed (with the exception of habitat trees), you must decide which living trees to cut. Trees that should be left are trees that are strong and healthy and don't show signs of pests and disease. Identifying the healthiest trees first will help you make decisions about what to cut around each healthy tree. There's no need to cut every small tree from the forest, leaving only the large beautiful trees. You need to consider ecological succession and leave trees of all ages in the forest—this means the oldest trees, semi-old trees, medium-size trees, and also saplings. A mix of ages ensures that the forest will last many generations.

So, what is a healthy forest? A healthy forest is one that has fewer stems per acre and therefore more space between the trees. The question of how many stems per acre depends on the species of trees, the climate, and many other factors. An ecologically thinned forest (fewer stems per acre, a balance of different ages of trees) also increases light and air on the forest floor. Airflow helps reduce disease and prevents parasites from establishing themselves in the forest. Just as houses with poor ventilation can be subject to mold, the same goes for forests. In helping the forest gain light and reduce congestion, we reduce potential disease and pathogens.

Light on the forest floor is key because the floor is home to a staggering diversity of native vegetative life. This native vegetation is often edible and/or medicinal and provides incredible food sources for wildlife.

Ecologically based forest products as a result of thinning may provide a small-scale economic solution to some of the financial obstacles to making this work happen. Entrepreneurial thinkers may start small-scale businesses selling furniture, tools, soil-building products, mushrooms, sustainably harvested building materials, and other potential value-added products that come from the ecological management of the forest.

Lop and Scatter

Significant volumes of woody material are generated through forest management techniques such as removing ladder fuels, understory pruning, and selective thinning. One method to handle this carbon-filled fuel is called *lop and scatter*. This is the process of cutting trunks and branches into medium to small pieces, then spreading them across the forest floor. This returns biomass to the ground where fungi and bacteria decompose it into living soil. This material also provides habitat for lizards, snakes, birds, and rodents, supporting a robust wildlife community.

Placing large volumes of woody debris on the forest floor does pose a fire danger. It's important your piles are no taller than three feet from the ground, placed an appropriate distance from tree trunks, and no larger than approximately 10 by 30 feet in length and width. It's best to leave approximately 50 feet of distance between lop and scatter piles to diminish the spread of fire. In the first year after material has been lopped and scattered, an increase of fire danger is present in the forest. By year two, once sufficient moisture wicks into the piles and decomposition begins, fire danger is reduced to pre-pruning levels.[1]

Lop and scatter piles can be managed and modified in a number of ways. They can be set out and then burned, returning minerals and ash to the land without endangering the forest. They can be inoculated with mycelium, speeding up decomposition and providing fungal growth and the benefits that come with mushrooms. Covering a lop and scatter pile in wood chips also speeds up decomposition and soil-building processes.

The lop and scatter technique makes the most sense on very large-scale projects where integrating brush into check dams and gully repair is not possible or the volume of wood being harvested far surpasses the need for erosion-control measures. Whatever method you employ, whether it be solely lop and scatter or a hybrid of carbon sponge techniques, the actions you take need to match the specific project context. The size of the area being worked, time of year, budget, access to the landscape, available tools and equipment, labor force, and local permitting laws all impact the approach you take in forest management.

Protect Existing Saplings

If you hope to protect the next generation of forest or woodland, then you have to pay attention. Environments where tree-based ecologies endeavor to grow are frequently mismanaged in the modern era. The extinction of keystone animal species, the effects of private property ownership, the predator–prey imbalance, and overgrazing prevent our forests from regenerating themselves. Where I live, many oak woodlands strive to reestablish themselves in agricultural fields, parklands, on overgrazed ranches, and other agricultural areas. But due to wild and domesticated animal grazing, herbicides, tall unmanaged grasses, and our mowers, plows, and tractors, young saplings are unable to grow and mature.

When walking through the landscape, I regularly see the knee-high seedlings of oaks, bay, and other species that will get mowed or grazed down each year. These young trees trying to grow represent the future, and with a little care, they can become a woodland. An easy way to remedy the situation, to help the forest grow again, is simply to protect these saplings.

Put a simple tree guard around any sapling or seedling you find to protect against grazing and mowers. This reforestation technique, called Farmer Managed Natural Regeneration (FMNR), is one of the easiest and most effective ways to nurture the next generation of forest. Many of these saplings have fully developed root systems, sometimes many years old. If given a chance, these trees grow extremely fast. The greatest inspiration for the efficacy of FMNR is found in Nigeria and is now being introduced throughout Africa and Asia.[2] As a response to increased desertification, malnutrition, and limited access to freshwater, communities in Nigeria had to manage their landscape differently. These subsistence communities have been dependent on goat herding for many decades. Unfortunately, the goats were eating down all vegetation, pushing the environment toward desert and collapse.

Inspired by Australian agronomist Tony Rinaudo, villages in Nigeria and beyond began to seek out and protect any small saplings they found on the land.[3] They cut the lower limbs, then make use of those bottom limbs to fuel cook fires. The result of protecting these small trees is nothing short of a miracle. Over two decades, this technique spearheaded by Rinaudo has regenerated approximately 240 million trees, providing food, fuel, fiber, and water, not only for millions of people but entire wildlife communities. Never underestimate the wisdom of earth. Sometimes all that's needed is a tiny bit of help; earth's self-healing mechanisms are exponentially powerful.

I love this strategy for its simplicity and low-budget approach. Any of us can go onto the land and find a young tree to protect. Whether it's using a tree guard (a purchased plastic guard) or building a small twig fence around the tree to keep animals from browsing, this action leads to forest regeneration faster than any new planting efforts.

Contour Brush Piles

Managing woody debris in fire-prone landscapes requires a careful approach to keep biomass on-site without adding to fire danger. When placing logs and brush on contour, the first layer of materials must be slightly dug into the ground for ground contact. This helps moisture wick into the wood, attracting fungi and speeding up decomposition. If material is suspended off the ground, it dries out faster, decomposes at a slower pace, and becomes a more flammable fuel load.

The best brush contour systems are built with smaller cut material and packed tight to close air gaps and encourage soil development. This kind of pile makes a great fungi habitat, holding water like a sponge and breaking down into carbon-rich soil in a short time. Built on contour, these carbon sponges slow water runoff and capture nutrients behind them. This simulates a tree falling in a forest. Head into a forested ecosystem and see for yourself. An old fallen tree becomes a habitat for wildlife, plants grow behind where the nutrients gather, and these fallen trees create ecotones of their own on the forest floor. Our contour brush piles do the same.

Biochar

In some parts of the world, biochar has been used to sequester carbon and build topsoil for agriculture productivity for millennia. Biochar and prescribed burning are a powerful combination.

In simple terms, a burn pile (often used in prescribed burning) can be created by tightly stacking logs and then lighting the top rather than the bottom of the pile with fire. A low oxygen pile like this burns off the least amount of carbon while still burning the rest of that material in a process called pyrolysis.[4] What's left is a kind of charcoal with strongly bonded carbon that takes hundreds of years to release back into the atmosphere. It becomes a carbon battery. Once this material comes in contact with microbiology, it becomes a highly sought-after host for beneficial microorganisms. Use biochar to amend soil, boost fertility, support living biology in the soil, and improve water retention. This technique creates biochar and manages fuel load at the same time.

FOLLOW INDIGENOUS WISDOM

If we want a way out of this mess, then it's time to put the colonialist mindset aside and embrace the deep and generational wisdom of Indigenous communities. More than 50,000 years of relationship to this land is more astute, more aware, and more able to assess solutions to ecological issues than the colonial mindset of the last few hundred years ever will be.

Maybe, if we have real intention to heal landscapes, we also get an opportunity to heal cultural wounds. Maybe these "natural" disasters are a wake-up call, not only to understand the need for ecological management but also in cultural healing. Humans have been integral to the ecological management of landscapes for hundreds of generations. You can continue this path, roaming it yourself. Integrate yourself into the landscape as one of the many members of the biological community. In this way, you will leave a legacy of healing our earth. Become an ecosystem manager—be the solution—and take meaningful action for the benefit of all life.

We are at a threshold to the future. Do we continue down the path of destruction and degeneration of the waters, the soils, the forests, and the oceans? Do we build landscapes that extract and pollute or do we become the solution to a dying world? Hopefully it is clear by now that humans did not always meet Mother Earth with destruction. Once, our ancestors revered all life and cared for it with love. We could even equate this caring of the land with caring for a family member, for these landscapes care for us in return. They embrace us when we are sick, feed us when we are hungry, nourish the waters of our bodies, shelter us from the cold, and give us tools and materials to thrive.

This reciprocity of mutual benefit, of symbiosis, was understood by our ancient ancestors, and these are relationships that have not been lost. This book is but one small collection of the wisdom of the earth and the ancient ways of living in balance. Walk the path with reverence, with hope and confidence for a thriving future—with seeds in one hand and someone you love holding the other. If you are reading this, you are on this path of remembering, reintegrating, and bringing the nature that is you in harmony with the nature that is . . . everything.

ACKNOWLEDGMENTS

A book of this scale literally takes years to write and produce. Along the way, many people showed up to support the vision, the process, and remind me time and time again that this project was worth it.

Where would I be without my community? Where would I be without my allies of plants, animals, watersheds, and soils? When pulling together the strands of gratitude, these are the questions I ask myself. And in short, this book, like myself, would not exist if it were not for the collective of beings, human and nonhuman alike, that helped me get here.

To my family, my wife Lauren, my kids Phoenix and Iyla: I thank you for the enduring years of support, believing in me even when I didn't believe in myself, and giving me the space and time to leave on monthly writing retreats to get sections of this book complete.

To all the staff at Permaculture Artisans and the Permaculture Skills Center who keep the lights on, the shovels digging, the designs flowing, and the projects growing: without you, the roots that makes up this book would not exist.

I want to thank my publishers, especially Doug, for believing in this project from the start and for guiding me into the process of developing this book and having my back all the way through. My editorial team, especially Noelle, for being a gentle yet on point editor helping me find the right topics, the right words, and the voice that sprawls across these pages. It has been an absolute pleasure. And thanks to all of the folks who made this book happen over at Synergetic Press: Deborah, Amanda, Allison, Chloe, Sandy, Jasmine—what a team to have to breathe life into this project and get it out to the world!

To all of my contributors, Maya Harjo, Minni Jain, Sasha Rabin, Darren Springer, Pandora Thomas, Kendall Dunnigan, Emily Mallard, Elizabeth and Paul Kaiser, Trathen Heckman, Connor Devane, Mia Maltz, Rick Taylor: you have made this book a community voice, a collective effort, and to each and every one of you I say thank you for your support and the deep wisdom and inspiration you give us all with the work you do in the world. I want to give an extra special heartfelt thanks to our illustrator Edward "Redbird" Willie. You have brought this book to life with your artwork.

Last but not least, I want to thank the ancestors. The ancestors of the lands that I live, eat, and drink upon. The ancestors of my heritage and traditions, that gave me life, breath, and hundreds of generations of connection to this earth.

REFERENCES

Chapter 1: Earth's Design Intelligence

1. Ann Gibbons, "Are We in the Middle of a Sixth Mass Extinction?" *Science*, March 1, 2011, https://www.science.org/content/article/are-we-middle-sixth-mass-extinction.
2. "Freshwater (Lakes and Rivers) and the Water Cycle," U.S. Geological Survey, Overview, accessed January 24, 2023, https://www.usgs.gov/special-topics/water-science-school/science/freshwater-lakes-and-rivers-and-water-cycle#overview
3. Obbe A. Tuinenburg et al, "High-resolution global atmospheric moisture connections from evaporation to precipitation," *Earth Syst. Sci. Data*, 12, 3177–3188, 2020, https://doi.org/10.5194/essd-12-3177-2020.
4. Kevin E. Trenberth, "Atmospheric Moisture Recycling: Role of Advection and Local Evaporation," *Journal of Climate* 12, 5 (1999): 1368-1381, accessed Jan 24, 2023, https://doi.org/10.1175/1520-0442(1999)012%3C1368:AMRROA%3E2.0.CO;2.
5. T. Deshler, "Observations for Chemistry (In Situ) | Particles," in *Encyclopedia of Atmospheric Sciences*, edited by James R. Holton, Academic Press, 2003, pages 1476–1484, https://doi.org/10.1016/B0-12-227090-8/00264-5. Accessed January 24, 2023, https://www.sciencedirect.com/topics/earth-and-planetary-sciences/cloud-condensation-nucleus.
6. Susette Horspool, "How Rain Forms Naturally: Pseudomonas Syringae," *Owlcation*, July 28, 2022, https://owlcation.com/stem/The-Rainmaker-Pseudomonas-syringae.
7. MO Hassett et al, "Mushrooms as Rainmakers: How Spores Act as Nuclei for Raindrops." Figure 1 in *PLOS ONE* 10(10): e0140407. October 28, 2015, https://doi.org/10.1371/journal.pone.0140407
8. Tara Lohan, "'Megadrought' and 'Aridification'—Understanding the New Language of a Warming World," *The Revelator*, June 8, 2020, https://therevelator.org/megadrought-aridification-climate/.
9. Carol Konyn, "What Are Carbon Sinks?" Earth.Org, August 24, 2021, https://earth.org/carbon-sinks/.
10. Alberto Canarini et al, "Root Exudation of Primary Metabolites: Mechanisms and Their Roles in Plant Responses to Environmental Stimuli," *Frontiers in Plant Science* 10 (2019), https://www.frontiersin.org/articles/10.3389/fpls.2019.00157/full.
11. Zhiying Ning et al, "Comparison of Leaf and Fine Root Traits Between Annuals and Perennials, Implicating the Mechanism of Species Changes in Desertified Grasslands," *Frontiers in Plant Science* 12 (2022), https://www.frontiersin.org/articles/10.3389/fpls.2021.778547/full.
12. "Introduction to the Cyanobacteria: Architects of Earth's Atmosphere," UC Museum of Paleontology, accessed January 25, 2022, https://ucmp.berkeley.edu/bacteria/cyanointro.html.
13. Calvin Norman and Melissa Kreye, "How Forests Store Carbon," College of Agricultural Sciences, Pennsylvania State University, September 24, 2020, https://extension.psu.edu/how-forests-store-carbon.
14. David Ellison et al, "Trees, Forests and Water: Cool Insights for a Hot World," *Global Environmental Change* 43 (2017), 51–61, https://doi.org/10.1016/j.gloenvcha.2017.01.002.

15. Joanna Mounce Stancil, "The Power of One Tree—The Very Air We Breathe," U.S. Department of Agriculture, June 3, 2019, https://www.usda.gov/media/blog/2015/03/17/power-one-tree-very-air-we-breathe.
16. Ken W. Krauss et al, "Managing Wetlands to Improve Carbon Sequestration," *Eos*, November 16, 2021, https://eos.org/editors-vox/managing-wetlands-to-improve-carbon-sequestration.
17. "Mississippi River Flood History 1543–Present," National Weather Service, National Oceanic and Atmospheric Administration, updated August 10, 2019, https://www.weather.gov/lix/ms_flood_history.
18. "Wetlands," Think Global Green, accessed January 25, 2022, https://thinkglobalgreen.org/wetlands/.
19. Chris Marlowe, "How the Salmon Spawn Works," HowStuffWorks.com, November 20, 2008, https://adventure.howstuffworks.com/outdoor-activities/fishing/freshwater-tips/salmon/salmon-spawn.htm.
20. "FAO's Global Action on Pollination Services for Sustainable Agriculture," Food and Agriculture Organization of the United Nations, accessed January 25, 2023, https://www.fao.org/pollination/background/bees-and-other-pollinators/en/.

Chapter 3: Land-Use Directive
1. Rebecca Harrington, "Grass takes up 2% of the land in the continental US," *Business Insider*, February 19, 2016, https://www.businessinsider.com/americas-biggest-crop-is-grass-2016-2?amp
2. "The Impact of Watering Lawns—235,224,000,000,000 Gallons Per Year," Synthetic Grass Warehouse, February 29, 2012, https://syntheticgrasswarehouse.com/how-much-water-can-turf-conserve-try-235224000000000-gallons-a-year/.
3. "Bird, Pollinator, & Wildlife Habitat Not Just for National Parks Anymore," National Park Service, March 14, 2022, https://www.nps.gov/articles/bird-pollinator-wildlife-habitat-not-just-for-national-parks-anymore.htm

Chapter 4: Contextual Design
1. "History of Bald Eagles and DDT," James River Association, accessed January 25, 2023, https://thejamesriver.org/wp-content/uploads/2020/04/Bald-Eagles-and-DDT-Lesson.pdf.

Chapter 6: Reading the Land
1. Françoise Watteau and Geneviève Villemin, "Soil Microstructures Examined Through Transmission Electron Microscopy Reveal Soil-Microorganisms Interactions," *Frontiers in Environmental Science* 6 (2018), https://www.frontiersin.org/articles/10.3389/fenvs.2018.00106/full.
2. "How Landforms Affect Global Temperature and Weather," World Landforms, accessed January 25, 2023, http://worldlandforms.com/landforms/how-landforms-affect-global-temperature-and-weather/.
3. "Diablo Winds," Fire Safe Marin, accessed January 25, 2023, https://firesafemarin.org/prepare-yourself/red-flag-warnings/diablo-winds/.
4. "What Is Thermal Mass," Heat Geek, November 16, 2018, https://www.heatgeek.com/what-is-thermal-mass/.

Chapter 7: Create a Base Map
1. Owen Hablutzel, "Planning for Permanence with Yeomans' Keyline Scale," Permaculture News, Permaculture Resesarch Institute, June 30, 2012, https://www.permaculturenews.org/2012/06/30/planning-for-permanence-with-yeomans-keyline-scale/.

2. "Frame Finder," UC Santa Barbara Library, accessed January 25, 2023, https://mil.library.ucsb.edu/ap_indexes/FrameFinder/.
3. "What will climate feel like in 60 years?" University of Maryland Center for Environmental Science, accessed January 25, 2023, https://fitzlab.shinyapps.io/cityapp/.

Chapter 10: Conceptual Design Process
1. Julian Brave NoiseCat, "The western idea of private property is flawed. Indigenous peoples have it right," *The Guardian*, March 27, 2017, https://amp.theguardian.com/commentisfree/2017/mar/27/western-idea-private-property-flawed-indigenous-peoples-have-it-right.
2. Gleb Raygorodetsky, "Indigenous peoples defend Earth's biodiversity—but they're in danger," *National Geographic*, Novermber 16, 2018, https://www.nationalgeographic.com/environment/article/can-indigenous-land-stewardship-protect-biodiversity-.
3. Jacob Faber, "Impact of Government Programs Adopted During the New Deal on Residential Segregation Today," Fast Focus Research/Policy Brief No. 51-2021, Institute for Research on Poverty, University of Madison–Wisconsin, February 2021, https://www.irp.wisc.edu/resource/impact-of-government-programs-adopted-during-the-new-deal-on-residential-segregation-today/.
4. Scott Hoffman Black, "Leave the Leaves to Benefit Wildlife," Xerces blog, Xerces Society for Invertebrate Conservation, November 12, 2020, https://xerces.org/blog/leave-leaves-to-benefit-wildlife.

Chapter 16: Living Soil: The Foundation of Regenerative Landscapes
1. "24 billion tons of fertile land lost every year, warns UN chief on World Day to Combat Desertification," United Nations, June 16, 2019, https://news.un.org/en/story/2019/06/1040561.
2. Hannah Ritchie and Max Roser, "Land Use," *Our World in Data*, September 2019, https://ourworldindata.org/land-use.
3. Jay Fuhrer, "Soil Health: Principle 1 of 5-Soil Armor," Natural Resources Conservation Service, U.S. Department of Agriculture, accessed January 25, 2023, https://www.nrcs.usda.gov/wps/portal/nrcs/detailfull/nd/soils/health/?cid=nrcseprd1300631.
4. Kris Nichols, "Does Glomalin You're your Farm Together?" USDA-ARS-Northern Great Plains Research Lab, United States Department of Agriculture, accessed January 25, 2023, https://www.ars.usda.gov/ARSUserFiles/30640500/Glomalin/Glomalinbrochure.pdf.
5. David H. McNear Jr., "The Rhizosphere—Roots, Soil, and Everything in Between," *Nature Education Knowledge* 4(3):1 (2013), https://www.nature.com/scitable/knowledge/library/the-rhizosphere-roots-soil-and-67500617/.
6. Alberto Canarini et al, "Root Exudation of Primary Metabolites: Mechanisms and Their Roles in Plant Responses to Environmental Stimuli," *Frontiers in Plant Science* 10 (2019), https://www.frontiersin.org/articles/10.3389/fpls.2019.00157/full.
7. James J. Hoorman, "Role of Soil Bacteria," College of Food, Agricultural, and Environmental Sciences, Ohio State University, June 6, 2016, https://ohioline.osu.edu/factsheet/anr-36
8. Elaine R. Ingham, "The Living Soil: Fungi," Natural Resources Conservation Service Soils, United States Department of Agriculture, accessed August 14, 2022, https://www.nrcs.usda.gov/wps/portal/nrcs/detailfull/soils/health/biology/?cid=nrcs142p2_053864
9. "Biointensive No-Till," Community Alliance with Family Farmers, accessed January 25, 2023, https://caff.org/ecologicalfarming/biointensive-no-till/.

10. Don Comis, "Glomalin: The Real Soil Builder," Agricultural Research Service, February 5, 2003. https://www.ars.usda.gov/news-events/news/research-news/2003/glomalin-the-real-soil-builder/

Chapter 17: No-Till Landscaping

1. "Global Greenhouse Gas Emissions Data," Global Emissions and Removals, United States Environmental Protection Agency, last updated February 25, 2022, https://www.epa.gov/ghgemissions/global-greenhouse-gas-emissions-data.
2. Mahdi Al-Kaisi et al, "Frequent tillage and its impact on soil quality," Integrated Crop Management, Iowa State University, June 28, 2004, https://crops.extension.iastate.edu/encyclopedia/frequent-tillage-and-its-impact-soil-quality.
3. Aleš Kučera et al, "Forest Soil Water in Landscape Context," in *Soil Moisture Importance*, ed. Ram Swaroop Meena (IntechOpen 2021), https://www.intechopen.com/chapters/72698.
4. "Forest Carbon Stocks," Indicators of Biodiversity and Ecological Services, World Resources Institute: Global Forest Review, accessed January 25, 2023, https://research.wri.org/gfr/biodiversity-ecological-services-indicators/forest-carbon-stocks.
5. Asis Mukherjee et al, "Role of irrigation and mulch on yield, evapotranspiration rate and water use pattern of tomato (Lycopersicon esculentum L.)," *Agricultural Water Management* 98(1):182-189, December 2010, https://www.researchgate.net/publication/227411269_Role_of_irrigation_and_mulch_on_yield_evapotranspiration_rate_and_water_use_pattern_of_tomato_Lycopersicon_esculentum_L.
6. "Ecological effects of using worming agents," Project, Wageningen University and Research, accessed January 26, 2023, https://www.wur.nl/en/show/Ecological-effects-of-using-worming-agents.htm.

Chapter 18: Vermiculture

1. Food Waste FAQs, U.S. Department of Agriculture, accessed January 26, 2023, https://www.usda.gov/foodwaste/faqs.
2. Jayakumar Pathma and Natarajan Sakthivel, "Microbial diversity of vermicompost bacteria that exhibit useful agricultural traits and waste management potential." *Springerplus* 1:26 (October 4, 2012), https://www.ncbi.nlm.nih.gov/pmc/articles/PMC3725894/
3. Meghan Knowles et al, "Earthworms in Forests," University of Vermont / Vermont Department of Forests, Parks, and Recreation / Northeastern States Research Cooperative, https://fpr.vermont.gov/sites/fpr/files/Forest_and_Forestry/Forest_Health/Library/EarthwormsInForests_final.pdf.

Chapter 19: Composting

1. Jack Kittredge, "Making Fungal Compost," The Natural Farmer, July 22, 2011, https://thenaturalfarmer.org/article/making-fungal-compost/.

Chapter 21: Cover Cropping

1. Huan Gao et al, "Cover Crop Species Composition Alters the Soil Bacterial Community in a Continuous Pepper Cropping System," *Frontiers in Microbiology* 12 (2021), https://doi.org/10.3389/fmicb.2021.789034.
2. Stephen C. Wagner, "Biological Nitrogen Fixation," *Nature Education Knowledge* **3(10)**:15 (2011), https://www.nature.com/scitable/knowledge/library/biological-nitrogen-fixation-23570419/.

Chapter 23: The Fungal Landscape

1. "Fungal Biomass," ScienceDirect, accessed January 26, 2023, https://www.sciencedirect.com/topics/biochemistry-genetics-and-molecular-biology/fungal-biomass.
2. Colin Averill et al, "Global Imprint of Mycorrhizal Fungi on Whole-Plant Nutrient Economics," *PNAS* 116 (46) 23163–23168, October 28, 2019, https://doi.org/10.1073/pnas.1906655116.
3. Giuseppe Venturella et al, "Medicinal Mushrooms: Bioactive Compounds, Use, and Clinical Trials," *Int J Mol Sci*, 22(2):634, January 10, 2021, https://www.ncbi.nlm.nih.gov/pmc/articles/PMC7826851/.

Chapter 24: Design Water Resilience

1. "How Your Estimated Total Water Use is Calculated," County of Santa Cruz Planning Department, accessed January 26, 2023, https://www.sccoplanning.com/Portals/2/County/Planning/bldg/How_your_Estimated_Total_Water_Us_%20is_Calculated.pdf.
2. "How Your Maximum Applied Water Allowance Is Calculated," County of Santa Cruz Planning Department, accessed January 26, 2023, https://www.sccoplanning.com/Portals/2/County/Planning/bldg/How_Your_MAWA_is_Calculated.pdf
3. "Interaction of Ground Water and Surface Water in Different Landscapes," United States Geological Survey, USGS Publications Warehouse, accessed January 26, 2023, https://pubs.usgs.gov/circ/circ1139/pdf/part1bb.pdf.

Chapter 25: Identifying Water Sources

1. Art Ludwig developed the first laundry detergent that biodegrades into plant food and wrote popular books on greywater, as well as the laundry greywater exemption of the California Plumbing Code. Oasis maintains a hub for greywater information at oasisdesign.net/greywater.

Chapter 28: Water Distribution

1. Lee Johnson, "How to Calculate Pounds Per Square Inch in Elevated Water Storage Tanks," *Sciencing*, December 5, 2020, https://sciencing.com/calculate-elevated-water-storage-tanks-5858171.html.
2. Sara Dadar et al, "Impact of the Pumping Regime on Electricity Cost Savings in Urban Water Supply System." *Water* 13, no. 9: 1141 (2021), https://doi.org/10.3390/w13091141.
3. Sergio Gualteros and Daniel R. Rousse, "Solar water pumping systems: A tool to assist in sizing and optimization," *Solar Energy*, Volume 225, 2021, pages 382–398, https://doi.org/10.1016/j.solener.2021.06.053.

Chapter 29: Roof Water Harvesting

1. "Harvest Rain," University of Arizona Cooperative Extension, accessed January 26, 2023, https://waterwise.arizona.edu/harvest-rain.

Chapter 30: Landscape Ponds

1. These are available on the free, online water school https://waterways.world.
2. The film is freely accessible via the Flow Partnership's flagship water school at https://www.theflowpartnership.org/the-water-school.
3. Sustainable Development Goal 6 is one of 17 Sustainable Development Goals established by the United Nations General Assembly in 2015.

4. Muhammad Ashraf et al, "Effectiveness of Sodium Bentonite Clay for Reducing Seepages from Earthen Rainwater Harvesting Ponds," Sugarcane Biorefinery, the Eco-Friendly Appealing Option. *Int J Environ Sci Nat Res* 2021, 28(3): 556240, https://juniperpublishers.com/ijesnr/IJESNR.MS.ID.556240.php.
5. "Common Problems at Dams—Trees," Dam Safety, Nebraska Department of Natural Resources, accessed January 27, 2023, https://dnr.nebraska.gov/dam-safety/trees.
6. "Gravity Feed System Basics: Elevation, Pressure, Water Quality, and Timers," Articles, Irrigation Solutions, Dripdepot, April 20, 2022, https://help.dripdepot.com/support/solutions/articles/11000044367-gravity-feed-system-basics-elevation-pressure-water-quality-and-timers.

Chapter 32: Erosion Control

1. "Reduce Peak Flow, Runoff Velocity, and Soil Erosion," Climate Change Resource Center, U.S. Forest Service, accessed January 27, 2023, https://www.fs.usda.gov/ccrc/approach/reduce-peak-flow-runoff-velocity-and-soil-erosion.
2. Jeremy Maestas et al, "Hand-Built Structures for Restoring Degraded Meadows in Sagebrush Rangelands: Examples and Lessons Learned from the Upper Gunnison River Basin, Colorado," Natural Resources Conversation Service, State of Colorado, U.S. Department of Agriculture, May 1, 2018, https://www.researchgate.net/figure/It-is-critical-to-ensure-the-top-rocks-of-the-Zuni-bowl-wall-match-the-existing-elevation_fig4_325651474.

Chapter 33: The Built Environment

1. "Embodied Carbon," MIT Concrete Sustainability Hub, accessed October 1, 2022, https://cshub.mit.edu/embodied-carbon.

Chapter 34: Architectural Elements

1. "Timber," Responsible Forestry, World Wildlife Fund, accessed January 27, 2023, https://www.worldwildlife.org/industries/timber.
2. "Shou Sugi Ban: The Traditional Art of Charred Cedar," accessed January 27, 2023, https://shousugiban.com.

Chapter 38: Revegetate the Planet

1. Wiktor Halecki et al, "Loss of topsoil and soil erosion by water in agricultural areas: A multi-criteria approach for various land use scenarios in the Western Carpathians using a SWAT model," *Land Use Policy*, Volume 73, 2018, Pages 363–372, https://doi.org/10.1016/j.landusepol.2018.01.041.
2. Sigurdur Greipsson, "Phytoremediation," Nature Education Knowledge 3(10):7, 2011, https://www.nature.com/scitable/knowledge/library/phytoremediation-17359669/.
3. David R. Montgomery et al, "Soil health and nutrient density: preliminary comparison of regenerative and conventional farming," *PeerJ*, January 27, 2022, https://peerj.com/articles/12848/.
4. "Ancient Indigenous Diets Are More 'Nutrient Dense,' Say Global Experts," Women News Network, January 25, 2014, https://womennewsnetwork.net/2014/01/25/ancient-indigenous-diets/.
5. "USDA Plant Hardiness Zone Map," U.S. Department of Agriculture, accessed January 27, 2023, https://planthardiness.ars.usda.gov.

Chapter 39: Landscape Planting Plans

1. Dean Fosdick, "Winter-Blooming Plants Help Bees Overwinter in Your Yard," *AP News*, October 17, 2017, https://apnews.com/article/11a89d12a0174df79a237949cf25d1c3.

Chapter 40: Plant Communities

1. Hugo Ahlenius, "Projected Agriculture in 2080 Due to Climate Change," UNEP/GRID-Arendal, 2008, https://www.grida.no/resources/7299.

Chapter 41: Regenerative Agroforestry

1. Martin Crawford, "Dehesa Agroforestry Systems," Association for Temperate Agroforestry, April 5, 2014, https://www.aftaweb.org/latest-newsletter/temporate-agroforester/92-2005-vol-13/october-no-4/97-dehesa-agroforestry-systems.html.
2. Simon West et al, "Just What Is Syntropic Agroforestry?" Word Forest, April 22, 2022, https://www.wordforest.org/2022/04/22/just-what-is-syntropic-agroforestry/.
3. Sarah Rodriguez, "3 Ways to Cold Stratify Seeds and Why," New Life on a Homestead, January 16, 2023, https://www.newlifeonahomestead.com/cold-stratification-of-seeds/.
4. Eric T. Stafne, "Chilling-Hour Requirements of Fruit Crops," Agricultural Communications, Mississippi State University, 2020, http://extension.msstate.edu/publications/chilling-hour-requirements-fruit-crops.

Chapter 42: Managing Tree Systems with Pruning

1. Angelo Eliades, "What Age Do Fruit Trees Flower and Fruit On?" *Deep Green Permaculture*, September 28, 2020, https://deepgreenpermaculture.com/2020/09/28/what-age-wood-do-fruit-trees-flower-and-fruit-on/.
2. Marie Iannotti, "How to Prune Peach Trees," Gardening, *The Spruce*, June 9, 2022, https://www.thespruce.com/how-to-prune-peach-trees-4125536
3. "Pruning 101," Not Far from the Tree, accessed January 27, 2023, https://notfarfromthetree.org/tree-health/pruning/.
4. William Bryant Logan, "From One Tree, Many: On the Ancient Art of Coppicing," *Literary Hub*, June 9, 2020, https://lithub.com/from-one-tree-many-on-the-ancient-art-of-coppicing/.
5. Sandrine Petit and Charles Watkins, "Pollarding Trees: Changing Attitudes to a Traditional Land Management Practice in Britain 1600–1900," *Rural History* 14 (October 2003): 157–176, https://www.researchgate.net/publication/216340331_Pollarding_Trees_Changing_Attitudes_to_a_Traditional_Land_Management_Practice_in_Britain_1600-1900.

Chapter 43: Growing Vegetables

1. Michael C.R. Alavanja, "Pesticides Use and Exposure Extensive Worldwide," *Rev Environ Health* 24(4), Oct–Dec 2009: 303–9, https://www.ncbi.nlm.nih.gov/pmc/articles/PMC2946087/.
2. "How Far Does Your Food Travel to Get to Your Plate?" Foodwise, accessed January 27, 2023, https://foodwise.org/learn/how-far-does-your-food-travel-to-get-to-your-plate/.

Chapter 46: Saving Seed

1. Rachel Kaufman, "32,000-Year-Old Plant Brought Back to Life—Oldest Yet," *National Geographic*, February 23, 2012, https://www.nationalgeographic.com/science/article/120221-oldest-seeds-regenerated-plants-science.

Chapter 47: Of Wing, Hoof, Claw, and Scale

1. Mark S. Boyce and Robert L. Byrne, "Managing Predator-Prey Systems: Summary Discussion," *Transactions of the 72nd North American Wildlife and Natural Resources Conference* (September 2016): 19–33, https://wildlifemanagement.institute/sites/default/files/2016-09/19-Summary_Discussion.pdf.
2. Ole Henrik Magga et al, eds, "Reindeer Herding, Traditional Knowledge, and Adaptation to Climate Change and Loss of Grazing Land," Ealát Project, Norway / Association of World Reindeer Herders / Arctic Council, Sustainable Development Working Group, 2009, http://hdl.handle.net/11374/43.
3. Jon Young et al, "Expand Your Senses with Bird Language," Bird Language, accessed January 27, 2023, https://birdlanguage.com/bird-language/.
4. Davide Castelvecchi, "Magnetic Sense Shows Many Animals the Way to Go," *Scientific American*, January 1, 2012, https://www.scientificamerican.com/article/the-compass-within/.
5. Dave Goulson, "The Insect Apocalypse: 'Our World Will Grind to a Halt Without Them,'" *Guardian*, July 25, 2021, https://www.theguardian.com/environment/2021/jul/25/the-insect-apocalypse-our-world-will-grind-to-a-halt-without-them.
6. "How Do Birds Help the Environment? (4 Key Reasons)" Birdfact, last updated August 2, 2022, https://birdfact.com/articles/how-do-birds-help-the-environment.
7. "Know What You Grow! Yarrow," UC Master Gardener Program, University of California Agriculture and Natural Resources, accessed January 27, 2023, https://ucanr.edu/sites/RiversideMG/newsletters/Fact_Sheets_for_Flowers89644.pdf.
8. "What Is Integrated Pest Management (IPM)?" University of California Agriculture and Natural Resources Statewide Integrated Pest Management Program, accessed January 27, 2023, https://www2.ipm.ucanr.edu/What-is-IPM/.

Chapter 48: Integrated Pest Management

1. Sarah Zielinski, "14 Fun Facts About Dragonflies," *Smithsonian Magazine*, October 5, 2011, https://www.smithsonianmag.com/science-nature/14-fun-facts-about-dragonflies-96882693/.
2. Marissa Schuh, "Lacewing," Beneficial Insects, University of Minnesota Extension, last reviewed 2022, https://extension.umn.edu/beneficial-insects/lacewing.
3. Toby Doyle et al, "Pollination by hoverflies in the Anthropocene," *Proc. R. Soc. B.* 287: 20200508 (May 20, 2020), http://doi.org/10.1098/rspb.2020.0508.
4. Jane Kirchner, "Opossums: Unsung Heroes in the Fight Against Ticks and Lyme Disease," National Wildlife Federation blog, last updated December 16, 2021, https://blog.nwf.org/2017/06/opossums-unsung-heroes-in-the-fight-against-ticks-and-lyme-disease/.
5. Grant Sizemore, "Cats and Birds," American Bird Conservancy, accessed January 27, 2023, https://abcbirds.org/program/cats-indoors/cats-and-birds.
6. "How Neonicotinoids Can Kill Bees," Summary of Report, Xerces Society for Invertebrate Conservation, accessed January 27, 2023, https://www.ipswichma.gov/DocumentCenter/View/11328/How-Neonics-Can-Kill-Bees.

Chapter 50: Choosing the Right Animals

1. "Highland," The Cattle Site, September 29, 2022, https://www.thecattlesite.com/breeds/beef/40/highland/.
2. Maris Fessenden, "Our Ancient Ancestors Probably Loved Honey Too," *Smithsonian Magazine*, November 11, 2015, https://www.smithsonianmag.com/smart-news/relationship-between-humans-and-honeybees-goes-back-9000-years-180957245/.
3. "History of Beekeeping," Buzz About Bees, last updated February 7, 2021, https://www.buzzaboutbees.net/history-of-beekeeping.html.
4. K. Kris Hirst, "Ancient Maya Beekeeping," ThoughtCo, May 11, 2018, https://www.thoughtco.com/ancient-maya-beekeeping-169364.
5. Paul E. Stamets et al, "Extracts of Polypore Mushroom Mycelia Reduce Viruses in Honey Bees," *Scientific Reports* 8, 13936 (2018), https://doi.org/10.1038/s41598-018-32194-8.
6. William T. T. Taylor et al, "New Discovery Reveals Early Dispersal of Neolithic Domesticated Sheep into the Heart of Central Asia," *Nature: Human Behavior*, Max Planck Institute of Geoanthropology, April 8, 2021, https://www.shh.mpg.de/1977786/taylor-sheep.
7. Jason Johnson, "Focusing on Grazing Management and Soil Health," OSU Sheep Team, Ohio State University College of Food, Agricultural, and Environmental Sciences, April 16, 2019, https://u.osu.edu/sheep/2019/04/16/focusing-on-grazing-management-and-soil-health/.
8. Michael Marshall, "Goats Were First Domesticated in Western Iran 10,000 Years Ago," *New Scientist*, June 7, 2021, https://www.newscientist.com/article/2280046-goats-were-first-domesticated-in-western-iran-10000-years-ago/.
9. Hui-Fang Kao et al, "Goat Milk Consumption Enhances Innate and Adaptive Immunities and Alleviates Allergen-Induced Airway Inflammation in Offspring Mice," *Frontiers in Immunology*, 11:184 (February 18, 2020), https://doi.org/10.3389/fimmu.2020.00184.
10. Ludovic Orlando, "The first aurochs genome reveals the breeding history of British and European cattle," *Genome Biology* 16, 225 (2015). https://doi.org/10.1186/s13059-015-0793-z.
11. Cynthia O'Brien and Jamie Kiffel-Alcheh, "Native People of the American Great Plains," National Geographic Kids, accessed January 30, 2023, https://kids.nationalgeographic.com/history/article/native-people-of-the-american-great-plains.
12. Paul Manning et al, "Dung Beetles Kep Keep Ecosystems Healthy," Frontiers for Young Minds, 9:583675, April 22, 2021, https://kids.frontiersin.org/articles/10.3389/frym.2021.583675.

Chapter 51: Chicken Systems

1. David R. Laatsch, "Origin and History of the Chicken," Livestock Division of Extension, University of Wisconsin–Madison, accessed January 30, 2023, https://livestock.extension.wisc.edu/articles/origin-and-history-of-the-chicken/.
2. R. Saliga III and J. Skelly, "Using Chicken Manure Safely in Home Gardens and Landscapes," Extension | University of Nevada, Reno, FS-13-23 (2013), https://extension.unr.edu/publication.aspx?PubID=3028.

Chapter 52: Stewards of the Earth

1. Elsa E. Cleland, "Biodiversity and Ecosystem Stability," *Nature Education Knowledge* **3(10)**:14 (2011), https://www.nature.com/scitable/knowledge/library/biodiversity-and-ecosystem-stability-17059965/.

2. "Purple Needle Grass," More Mesa Preservation Coalition, accessed January 30, 2023, https://moremesa.org/purple-needle-grass/.
3. "Giuliana Furci," FFungi, accessed January 30, 2023, https://www.ffungi.org/en/meet-giuliana.
4. "Ecuador First to Grant Nature Constitutional Rights," *Capitalism Nature Socialism* 19:4 (2008), 131–33, DOI: 10.1080/10455750802575828.
5. Dylan Stirewalt and Solange Yépez, dirs., *Marrow of the Mountain*, Handlens Productions, LLC, 2023, https://marrowofthemountain.com.
6. Patrick Greenfield, "Plans to Mine Ecuador Forest Violate Rights of Nature, Court Rules," *Guardian*, December 2, 2021, https://www.theguardian.com/environment/2021/dec/02/plan-to-mine-in-ecuador-forest-violate-rights-of-nature-court-rules-aoe.
7. Texaco Toxico.Net / Oil Pollution in the Ecuadorian Amazon, UDAPT, accessed January 30, 2023, http://texacotoxico.net/en/.
8. Nahuel Policelli, "Back to Roots—Fungi and Forest Restoration," Society for Ecological Restoration, August 10, 2022, https://www.ser.org/events/EventDetails.aspx?id=1656555.
9. Tom Bruns and Michael Wood, "Pt. Reyes MycoBlitz," MycoWeb, accessed January 30, 2023, https://mykoweb.com/PtReyes.
10. Climate adapation is the process of adjustment to actual or expected climate change and its effects (IPCC 2014). Adaptation interventions may seek to moderate or avoid harms, facilitate adjustments to climate and its effects, or even benefit from changing conditions.
11. Anthropocene Era: a time when humans, and human activities, have made a substantial, detrimental impact on the planet.
12. Return Intention Towards Ecological Sustainability; R.I.T.E.S: The RITES Project, Sebastopol, California, and the Amazon Mycorenewal Project https://www.amazonmycorenewal.org (Nueva Loja, Ecuador).
13. CoRenewal, U.S. federally approved nonprofit organization, Irvine, California, http://corenewal.weebly.com.
14. Michael F. Allen, *The Ecology of Mycorrhizae* (Cambridge: Cambridge University Press), 1991; Michael F. Allen, *Mycorrhizal Functioning: An Integrative Plant-Fungal Process* (New York: Chapman & Hall, 1992).
15. Kathleen K. Treseder, "The extent of mycorrhizal colonization of roots and its influence on plant growth and phosphorus content," *Plant and Soil* 371, no. 1 (2013): 1–13, https://doi.org/10.1007/s11104-013-1681-5.
16. Hugh Crone, *Paracelsus: The Man Who Defied Medicine: His Real Contribution to Medicine and Science* (Melbourne: Albarello Press, 2004).
17. M. Alice Ottoboni, *Dose Makes the Poison: A Plain-Language Guide to Toxicology* (New York: Van Nostrand Reinhold, 1991).
18. S. V. Rana, *Environmental Pollution: Health and Toxicology* (Oxford, UK: Alpha Science Press 2006).
19. Bill Mollison, *Permaculture: A Designers' Manual* (Tasmania, Australia: Tagari Publications, 2002).
20. Dana Cordell and Stuart White, "Peak phosphorus: clarifying the key issues of a vigorous debate about long-term phosphorus security," *Sustainability* 3, no. 10 (2011): 2027–49.
21. Samson O. Ojoawo et al, "Phytoremediation of phosphorus and nitrogen with Canna x generalis reeds in domestic wastewater through NMAMIT constructed wetland," *Aquatic Procedia* 4 (2015): 349–56; Jessica A. Rubin and Josef H. Görres, "The effects of mycorrhizae on phosphorus mitigation and pollinator habitat restoration within riparian buffers on unceded land," *Restoration Ecology* (2022): e13671.

22. Jessica A. Rubin and Josef H. Görres, "Potential for mycorrhizae-assisted phytoremediation of phosphorus for improved water quality," *International Journal of Environmental Research and Public Health* 18, no. 1 (2021): 7.
23. The abnormally high cancer risk and concentration of petrochemical operations inspired the "Cancer Alley" moniker; Brian Cross, "Windsor and Essex County Region Has Higher Rates for 3 of 4 Most Prominent Cancers," *Windsor Star*, May 18, 2016, https://windsorstar.com/news/local-news/windsor-and-essex-county-region-has-higher-rates-for-3-of-4-most-prominent-cancers.
24. Harriet A. Washington, *A Terrible Thing to Waste: Environmental Racism and Its Assault on the American Mind* (New York: Little, Brown Spark / Hachette, 2019).
25. M. Gilbertson and J. Brophy, "Community health profile of Windsor, Ontario, Canada: Anatomy of a Great Lakes area of concern," *Environ Health Perspect* 2001 Dec;109 Suppl 6(Suppl 6):827-43. https://www.ncbi.nlm.nih.gov/pmc/articles/PMC1240618/.
26. Polluted locations in the United States requiring a long-term response to clean up hazardous material contaminations. They were designated under the Comprehensive Environmental Response, Compensation, and Liability Act (CERCLA) of 1980.
27. "Catabolism" is the breakdown of complex molecules to form simpler ones, together with the release of energy; "metabolism" occurs when the contaminant serves as a substrate for microbial growth and energy; whereas "cometabolism" occurs when the contaminant is modified by a microbe but does not serve as a nutrient for microbial growth or energy.
28. "Xenobiotics" may include, or are found in polymers, gases, chlorinated or fluorinated compounds, pesticides, detergents, solvents, and some personal-care or pharmaceutical products. They contain structures and bonds not found in nature.
29. "Biodegradation" is the breakdown of organic chemicals by the biological action of living organisms.
30. "Mineralization" converts organic substances into minerals through decomposition of substances into inorganic ions and CO_2.; Stephen Mann, "Biomineralization and Biomimetic Materials Chemistry," *Journal of Materials Chemistry* 5, no. 7 (1995): 935–46. https://doi.org/10.1039/JM9950500935; Dennis A. Bazylinski and Bruce M. Moskowitz, "Microbial Biomineralization of Bagnetic Iron Minerals: Microbiology, Magnetism and Environmental Significance," in *Geomicrobiology: Interactions Between Microbes and Minerals*, ed. Jillian F. Banfield and Kenneth H. Nealson (Boston: De Gruyter, 1997), 181–224, https://doi.org/10.1515/9781501509247.
31. A mesocosm is a bounded and partially enclosed outdoor experiment to bridge the gap between the laboratory and the real world in environmental science; Eugene P. Odum, "The mesocosm," *BioScience* 34, no. 9 (1984): 558–562, https://doi.org/10.2307/1309598.
32. Microcosm experiments are artificial, simplified ecosystems that are used to simulate and predict the behavior of natural ecosystems under controlled conditions.
33. Reference ecosystems are intact neighboring ecosystems that exhibit characteristics intended of the restored ecosystem, as per Mia R. Maltz and Kathleen K. Treseder, "Sources of inocula influence mycorrhizal colonization of plants in restoration projects: a meta-analysis," *Restoration Ecology* 23, no. 5 (2015): 625–34.
34. "Acclimation" is when individual microbial species or populations may tolerate a substance or condition but will return to their ambient state when the substance is removed or the condition is alleviated. This process is known as *acclimatization* when referring to complex microbial communities becoming accustomed to a new climate, condition, or historic exposure to a polluting substance.

35. There are many different types of cellulose and, likewise, numerous types of enzymes to biodegrade these different forms of cellulose (i.e., cellulases). Lignin is a difficult to degrade compound (i.e., recalcitrant), which is similar in its chemistry and structure to many types of industrial contaminants (e.g., petroleum hydrocarbons, PCBs, etc.). While brown-rot fungi use fenton chemistry, the genomes of white-rotters are architected with genes that encode for enzymes that biodegrade lignin (e.g., lignin peroxidases, manganese peroxidases, laccases, versatile peroxidases, etc.).

36. Labile substances are easy to break down, as compared to recalcitrant substances.

37. Gigafires expand to at least 1,000,000 acres across the burn scar; Bill Gabbert, "Where did the term 'gigafire' originate," *Wildfire Today*, October 7, 2020, https://wildfiretoday.com/tag/gigafire/.

38. Maya Elson can be reached at https://www.mycopsychology.org for embodied remediation. Taylor Bright can be found on her site https://www.symbiiotica.com and through her outdoor log mushroom farm https://www.moonfruitmushroomfarm.com.

39. Wattles are cylindrical tubes, wrapped with jute, cotton, or wood fiber netting and filled with straw or woody debris.

40. Brian Fies, *A Fire Story* (New York: Abrams, 2019).

41. Salvaged soil is a soil translocation technique that includes the bulk transfer of soil, plant seeds, and soil microbes from an intact reference ecosystem (i.e., the donor site) to a different, often degraded, location (i.e., translocation to a recipient ecosystem).; Katharina T. Schmidt, et al, "Identifying mechanisms for successful ecological restoration with salvaged topsoil in coastal sage scrub communities," *Diversity* 12:150 (2020), https://doi.org/10.3390/d12040150; Mia R. Maltz and Kathleen K. Treseder, "Sources of inocula influence mycorrhizal colonization of plants in restoration projects: A meta-analysis," *Restoration Ecology* 23 (2015): 625–34, https://doi.org/10.1111/rec.12231; Michala L. Phillips et al, "Native and Invasive Inoculation Sources Modify Fungal Community Assembly and Biomass Production of a Chaparral Shrub," *Applied Soil Ecology* 147 (2020), https://doi.org/10.1016/j.apsoil.2019.103370; M. R. Gerrits et al, "Synthesis on the effectiveness of soil translocation for plant community restoration," *Journal of Applied Ecology* (in review).

42. Katrina M. Dlugosch and Ingrid M. Parker, "Founding events in species invasions: genetic variation, adaptive evolution, and the role of multiple introductions." *Molecular Ecology* 17, no. 1 (2008): 431–49.

43. Anne Pringle and Else C. Vellinga, "Last chance to know? Using literature to explore the biogeography and invasion biology of the death cap mushroom Amanita phalloides (Vaill. ex Fr.: Fr.) Link," *Biological Invasions* 8, no. 5 (2006): 1131–44, https://pringlelab.botany.wisc.edu/documents/PringleVellinga_000.pdf.

44. Anne Pringle et al, "The ectomycorrhizal fungus Amanita phalloides was introduced and is expanding its range on the west coast of North America," *Molecular Ecology* 18, no. 5 (2009): 817–833.; Benjamin E. Wolfe et al, "Amanita thiersii is a saprotrophic fungus expanding its range in the United States," *Mycologia* 104, no. 1 (2012): 22–33.

45. Marc-André Selosse et al, "Structure and dynamics of experimentally introduced and naturally occurring Laccaria sp. discrete genotypes in a Douglas fir plantation," *Applied and Environmental Microbiology* 65, no. 5 (1999): 2006–14.

46. Andrea L. Bruce, "Population genomic insights into the establishment of non-native golden oyster mushrooms (*Pleurotus citrinopileatus*) in the United States." M.S. diss., 2018.

47. M. Kat Anderson and Michael J. Moratto, "Native American land-use practices and ecological impacts," in *Sierra Nevada Ecosystem Project: Final Report to Congress*, vol. 2, pp. 187–206 (Davis: University of

California, Centers for Water and Wildland Resources Davis, 1996), https://pubs.usgs.gov/dds/dds-43/VOL_II/VII_C09.PDF.
48. Arielle A. Halpern et al, "Prescribed fire reduces insect infestation in Karuk and Yurok acorn resource systems," *Forest Ecology and Management* 505 (2022): 119768.
49. Jan Timbrook, "White Sage in Danger," *Santa Barbara Independent*, January 21, 2022, https://www.independent.com/2022/01/21/white-sage-in-danger/.

Chapter 53: Lands of Fire

1. Katarina Zimmer, "People May Have Used Fire to Clear Forests More than 80,000 Years Ago," Scientific American, May 5, 2021, https://www.scientificamerican.com/article/people-may-have-used-fire-to-clear-forests-more-than-80-000-years-ago/.
2. Doyle Rice, "From Fire Clouds to Fire Tornadoes, Here's How Wildfires Can Create Their Own Weather," *USA Today*, July 20, 2021, https://www.usatoday.com/story/news/nation/2021/07/20/wildfires-can-create-their-own-weather-including-fire-tornadoes/8030811002/.
3. William T. Sommers et al, "Fire History and Climate Change: The View from Ecosystems," in *Synthesis of Knowledge: Fire History and Climate Change*, Joint Fire Science Program, Project 09-2-01-09 (2011), https://www.firescience.gov/projects/09-2-01-9/supdocs/09-2-01-9_Chapter_6_Fire_History_The_View_from_Ecosystems.pdf
4. "Grazing for Fire Prevention," Livestock and Natural Resources Information Center—Plumas, Sierra, and Butte Counties, University of California Agriculture and Natural Resources, accessed January 30, 2023, https://ucanr.edu/sites/Rangelands/Grazing_for_Fire_Prevention_/.
5. Rob Jordan, "Setting Fires to Avoid Fires," *Stanford Earth Matters Magazine*, January 20, 2020, https://earth.stanford.edu/news/setting-fires-avoid-fires.

Chapter 54: Regenerative Forest Management

1. "Forestry: Before the Fire," Natural Resources Conservation Service–Washington, United States Department of Agriculture, accessed September 24, 2021, https://www.nrcs.usda.gov/wps/portal/nrcs/detail/wa/technical/landuse/forestry/?cid=nrcseprd367217.
2. Nicola Heath, "Australian Agronomist Tony Rinaudo Is Turning African Deserts into Forests," *ABC News* (Australia), July 23, 2022, https://www.abc.net.au/news/2022-07-24/tony-rinaudo-forest-maker-fmnr-land-regeneration-africa/101189330.
3. "Tony Rinaudo," Laureates, Right Livelihood, accessed January 30, 2023, https://rightlivelihood.org/the-change-makers/find-a-laureate/tony-rinaudo/.
4. "Biochar Production," US Biochar Initiative, accessed January 30, 2023, https://biochar-us.org/biochar-production.

INDEX

aesthetics, 80, 96, 222, 225, 364
agroforestry, 91, 41, 143, 323
afforestation, 7
Afroindigenous, 320
agroecological, 128, 296, 320
airlock, 209
aphids, 36, 318, 357, 376, 382-384
alley cropping, 322, 324
animal habitat, 379
animal integration, 325
animism, 15, 16
angle of repose, 196, 203, 255, 257
apple, 309, 318, 319, 321, 325, 327, 333, 339, 342, 368, 381
architectural elements, 23, 86, 96, 263, 265
aridification, 5, 6
arthropod, 121, 123
aquaculture, 219, 235, 236
asteraceae, 384
awareness practice, 34, 377, 378

bald eagle, 32
bare root, 159, 329, 332,333, 350
base map, 37, 50-56, 60, 93, 98, 249
bee balm, 389
bees, 2, 11, 164, 317, 350, 369, 380, 384, 388, 389, 391
beekeeping, 402-404
bentonite, 221, 232, 234, 235
bioavailability, 121, 123, 376
biochar, 322, 449,
biodiversity, 2, 20, 21, 40, 76, 181, 302, 318, 322, 335, 357, 365, 372, 385, 389, 390, 404, 418-420, 422, 435, 445, 446
biomass, 14, 42, 122, 132, 137, 138, 143, 156, 160, 163, 166, 169, 171, 252, 315, 324, 325, 447, 449
biome, 10, 239, 317, 323, 420, 436

bird boxes, 382, 386, 387,
bird habitat, 382
bird language, 377, 378
bloom time, 29
boulder wall, 299, 300
bridges, 200, 258
broadcast seeding, 162, 164, 251
broad fork, 125, 126, 130, 202
brush check dam, 253, 254
budget, 23, 38, 39, 50, 51, 64, 80, 96, 102, 105, 106, 108, 109, 135, 159, 203, 212, 218, 244, 255, 258, 263, 273, 283, 294, 296, 306, 312, 394, 448
building with cob, 264, 266, 269-276
burrowing animals, 169, 390, 415
butterflies, 2, 164, 317, 318, 350, 378, 381, 389

canning, 353, 356
carbon, 2, 3, 6-10, 14, 18, 28, 39, 41, 48, 66, 75, 78, 120-123, 131-133, 137, 138, 141, 153, 154, 162, 166, 169, 170, 171, 190, 196, 205, 236, 264, 265, 290, 291, 296, 302, 319, 352, 359, 365, 367, 376, 405, 420, 437, 438, 444, 447-449
carbon cycle, 3, 6, 7, 9
carbon sequestration, 9, 18, 121, 236, 296, 437
carbon sink, 6-8, 166, 420
carbon sponge, 120, 121, 180, 437, 448, 449
cardboard, 22, 24, 25, 83, 138, 139, 141-143, 149, 150, 163, 171, 174-176, 269, 290
case study, 55, 81, 113, 127, 172, 184, 188, 225, 320, 421
check dam, 211, 226, 228, 230, 252-255, 257, 448
chickens, 12, 84, 106, 159, 161, 385, 393, 396, 398, 399-401, 410-416
chicken tractors, 413
chicken coop, 31, 84, 264, 279, 410-416

chicken run, 84, 396, 400, 410, 416
chill hours, 333, 334
chop and drop, 143, 325, 338
clients, 36, 55, 63, 71, 96-100, 104, 109-112, 145, 237, 264, 321, 323
climate analogue, 58
cob oven, 83, 264, 269, 271, 277, 278
corn, 352, 356-359, 369
comfrey fertilizer, 160
compaction, 20, 44, 124, 137, 196, 197, 203, 324, 283, 298, 330, 377, 396, 400, 405
companion planting, 352
composted manure, 141, 150, 169, 269, 333, 352
composting, 126, 140, 153-157, 160, 324, 338, 342, 416, 425
compost tea, 125, 135, 136, 155, 158, 159, 164, 269, 352, 382
community gardens, 14, 77, 78, 425
computer drafting, 99
conceptual design process, 50, 70, 85
conservation mycology, 422-424
construction drawings, 96
contextual design, 18, 29, 162, 398
contour, 51, 57, 82, 94, 95, 167, 170, 194, 195, 197, 199-201, 205-208, 211, 251, 252, 258, 287, 293, 296, 298, 394, 439
coppicing, 335, 342- 344
core values, 65, 67, 109, 112, 373
cow, 12, 13, 141, 154, 161, 232, 323, 344, 396, 398-400, 407-409, 420, 438,
cover crops, 106, 130, 136, 155, 162, 324, 352, 366
clay slip, 273, 276, 277, 279
climate, 3, 6-8, 10, 14, 28, 29, 35, 36, 38, 39, 41, 44-48, 51, 120, 136, 149, 150, 156, 162, 167-169, 178, 181, 182, 188, 198, 201, 210, 215, 217, 219, 220, 233, 238, 240, 242, 248, 253, 256, 264, 267, 272, 275, 290, 296, 302, 309, 311, 316, 319, 323, 324, 328, 333, 334, 336, 339, 345-349, 366, 379, 381-384, 405, 415, 418, 436, 438, 445, 447
cloud condensation nuclei, 5
cultural aesthetics, 364
cultural history, 113,

culverts, 179, 193, 200, 206, 208, 249, 250, 257, 258
cuttings, 78, 302, 361, 362, 433
cycles, 3, 5, 6, 9, 12, 17, 18, 29-31, 45, 49, 85, 105, 108, 123, 302, 325, 328, 339, 346, 351, 359, 364, 366, 377, 394, 418, 439, 441

damsel bug, 389
decks, 47, 66, 103, 265, 266, 443
decomposed granite, 282, 283, 285, 292
demolition, 81-83, 103, 391
design plan, 9, 16, 70-73, 89, 90-95, 97-100, 101, 110, 113, 157, 178, 182, 196, 238, 256, 262, 267, 294, 306, 410
design process, 14, 18, 22, 31, 34, 40, 41, 47, 48, 50, 51, 58, 61, 67, 70, 72-74, 79, 85, 96, 108, 109, 112, 113, 181, 184, 198, 222, 234, 263, 398, 401
design contract, 109, 110
dew, 4
dig and divide roots, 363
disease, 11-13, 15, 49, 122, 142, 153, 156, 157, 286, 309, 316, 332, 337, 339, 342, 357, 358, 363, 385
double low fence, 396
drainage, 41, 44-46, 89, 103, 104, 130, 146-148, 150, 169, 179, 180, 193, 195, 197, 198, 206-208, 233, 246, 249, 250, 252-257, 272, 282, 283, 287, 289, 377
drafting, 2, 53, 54, 70, 89, 92-94, 97-99
dragonfly, 235, 383
drip irrigation, 38, 238, 240-242, 247, 248, 269
dry line conveyance, 213
ducks, 12, 141, 153, 161, 398, 401, 402
dung beetle, 40, 142, 408

earthen pond, 221, 232-235
earthworks, 22, 44, 82, 101, 104-106, 120, 137, 194-198, 249, 265
earthworms, 123, 129, 152
ecological garden, 77, 116, 364
ecological planting strategy, 302
ecological yield, 17-19, 77, 78, 80, 106, 127, 137, 143, 166, 219, 286, 290, 291, 304, 313, 335, 338, 364

edible forest, 83
edging, 22, 283-285, 289, 292, 392
electric fencing, 396, 397
elevation, 34, 45, 46, 51, 57, 92, 94, 95, 194, 195, 203, 204, 209, 210, 215, 216, 239-241, 287
embodied energy, 17, 41, 75, 87, 211, 256, 262, 264, 265, 288, 299, 346, 366, 396
erosion control, 87, 88, 120, 140, 141, 176, 196, 205, 249, 251-256, 258, 259, 298, 313, 446, 448
estimated total water use formula, 179, 238
evergreen vs deciduous, 309
extending the harvest, 328
extending flower times, 309

farmer managed natural regeneration, 448
fencing, 102, 263, 267, 330, 337, 379, 393-397
fermentation, 334, 353, 369
filtration, 5, 217, 241, 246, 257, 293, 303, 341, 429
fire, 9, 13, 22, 29, 41, 46, 47, 63, 87, 88, 140, 215, 217, 219, 246, 250, 252, 253, 265, 266, 269, 271, 275-277, 337, 338, 365-367, 394, 397, 401, 406, 407, 418-421, 428, 434, 435-447
fire ecology, 440, 441, 443
fire frequency, 436
fire hardening, 437
fog, 6, 8, 40, 45, 49, 173, 174, 341
food forest, 17, 38, 81, 102, 116, 141, 168, 189, 309, 313, 314, 323-325, 332, 337, 338, 366, 406, 443
food production, 11, 28, 66, 77, 84, 120, 174, 217, 296, 303, 304, 315, 319, 338, 384
food sovereignty, 346
forest, 4, 7-9, 13-15-19, 21, 22, 29, 30, 32, 38, 40-42, 44, 48, 87, 88, 102, 120, 124, 137, 138, 140, 141, 152, 163, 168, 178, 180, 194, 205, 238, 249, 265, 296, 302, 309, 313, 323-325, 332, 335, 377, 378, 391, 394, 395, 397, 399, 400, 402, 405, 408, 414, 418, 420, 421, 433, 436, 437, 439, 443-450
forestry, 13, 252

forage, 84, 164, 240, 291, 309, 317, 318, 324-336, 344, 378-381, 383, 387, 399, 401, 402
flagstone, 75, 83, 103, 225, 282, 283-285, 288, 289
flood irrigation, 239
flood plain connectivity
flowering times, 309
freezing, 272, 354, 356, 392
french drains, 104, 207
frequency, 35, 110, 267, 377, 400, 408, 436
frost protection, 347, 348
fruit trees, 77, 83, 88, 186, 191, 217, 219, 228, 304, 321, 328, 332, 333, 337, 338, 357
fruit wood, 339, 340, 342
fruit and nut cultivars, 333
fuel ladders, 438, 444
fungi, 5, 6, 9, 24, 35, 42, 45, 76, 80, 121-123, 129, 132, 135, 137-139, 140, 142, 154, 156, 158, 159, 166, 171, 172, 176, 252, 254, 269, 290, 291, 303, 304, 332, 338, 357, 421, 422-430, 436, 447, 449

Gantt chart, 106-108
geology, 40-41, 55, 315
goals, 14-17, 20, 29, 33, 40-41, 65-67, 71, 73, 75, 77-78, 92, 109-112, 127-128, 135, 153, 163, 173, 193, 195-196, 199, 210, 216, 219-220, 224, 238, 269
goat, 12, 153, 154, 318, 344, 393, 396-400, 406-407, 420, 438, 448
good fire, 13, 22, 435, 438, 446
grading, 23, 103-105, 194, 196-197, 203, 207, 255, 257, 265, 287, 293, 296, 308
grain, 88, 162, 164, 173, 316-317, 322, 352, 366, 370-371
graphic scale, 90-91
grassland, 3, 5-7, 10, 19, 21, 40, 120, 124, 180, 249, 348, 404
gravel, 10, 30, 44, 81, 92, 143, 188, 196, 216, 224-225, 234, 236, 249, 262, 264, 270-272, 278, 287-288, 443
gravity, 46, 102, 181, 185, 209-211, 215-216, 240-241
greenhouses, 48, 51, 328, 330, 348, 415
greenwashing, 74
greywater, 38 185-192
gully, 31, 44, 47, 194, 252-255, 257, 448

habitat ponds, 181, 224, 392
habitat enhancement, 23
Haney test, 131, 133-134
hardscaping, 22, 81, 101, 103
hardscape plan, 103
harvesting, 8-9, 17, 120, 132, 145, 151-153, 163, 172, 178, 180, 183, 188, 193, 199, 203-208, 212-213, 217, 352, 369, 401, 413, 433
head cut, 44, 249-250, 255-257
hedgerows, 129, 219, 269, 323, 335-336, 387, 396
homesteads, 76, 115, 120 232, 244, 319, 406, 408, 410
hover fly, 389
hügelkultur, 166-170
hydrophobic soils, 124

impoundment pond, 233
Indigenous, 10, 13, 16, 29, 31, 34, 56-57, 59, 61-62, 76, 85, 113, 120, 150, 180, 256, 269, 315-316, 320, 322, 357, 372-373, 377, 420-421
industrial agriculture, 11, 120, 439
infiltration, 4, 23, 49, 82, 123, 125, 167, 180, 186, 190, 193-195, 197-198, 202, 207-208, 213, 217, 239, 257, 293, 296, 420
inoculation, 158, 173, 236, 360, 423-424, 426, 428-429
input output analysis, 398, 401-402
insectary plants, 317, 381, 389
invasive grasses, 365, 418-419
irrigation, 17, 22-25, 38, 93, 95, 102, 107, 129, 138, 162, 164, 178-179, 182-184, 187, 209-210, 214, 238-243, 247-248
integrated pest management, 335, 358, 381-382

keystone species, 10-12, 22, 32, 376, 403, 434
keyline design, 55-56, 125, 136

ladybugs, 36, 164, 376, 382, 384, 390
lacewings, 36, 164, 317, 369, 381, 384, 389
land access, 75, 78
landscape implementation, 120
landscaping, 2, 14-17, 20-21, 23, 31, 75-76, 78-80, 85, 106, 124, 137, 180, 240, 242, 250, 256, 262, 264, 304, 309, 318, 365, 437

Land Back, 40, 76
landform, 31, 41, 45-46, 55, 193-194
landscape steps, 293-294
lawns, 10, 20-21, 23, 186, 189-190
lawn transformation, 22, 25
leaf fall, 142, 153, 363
leafy greens, 354
level sill, 205
LIDAR, 51, 56
living soil, 23, 120-121, 123, 129, 167, 171, 447
lizard home, 391-392
lop and scatter, 445, 447-448

managing biomass, 324-325
managing stormwater, 82
mason bee, 388-389
master plan, 70, 73, 100-102
materials calculation equation, 143
maximum applied water allowances, 179
microbiology, 121, 129, 135, 143, 160, 162, 239, 269, 449
microclimate, 14-15, 38, 45-49, 55, 113-114, 132, 167-169, 181-182, 219-220, 227, 237, 253, 256, 286, 288, 292, 296, 298, 305, 308, 315, 319
migration, 12, 227, 377, 379, 418, 421
milkweed, 310, 318
mulching, 22-24, 108, 125-126, 137-142, 203, 290, 333, 443
mushrooms, 5, 23, 35, 42, 171-176, 403, 422-423, 432, 447
mycelium, 122, 171-176, 403, 422, 425-427, 432, 447
mycoremediation, 176, 421, 427, 432, 445
mycorrhizal fungi, 24, 121-122, 135, 159, 171, 176, 332, 424-426, 430
mowing, 13, 21, 364-367, 386, 413

native landscape, 113, 313, 318, 320
native vs exotic plants, 318
natural building, 140, 263-264
nature awareness, 36, 377-378
nematode, 121-123, 132
nesting, 335, 365, 367, 379-380, 386, 388-389, 401, 414
nesting boxes, 414
nitrogen fixer, 163, 216, 314, 420

noninversion, 125
no-till, 129, 137, 139
nutrient dense, 3, 61, 172, 304–305, 414
nutrient pumps, 38, 183, 185, 209–210, 224, 240

observation, 22, 31–32, 37–38, 88, 97, 120, 124–125, 241–242, 286, 322
observation walks, 377
occultation, 129–130, 138, 367
orchards, 42, 82, 98, 141, 159, 168, 251, 319, 323–324, 381, 402, 406
orientation, 29, 35, 41, 45, 48, 60, 87, 96, 181, 183, 267, 329
organic farming, 127, 320, 322, 382

parasitoid wasp, 36, 164, 317, 376, 382–383, 389–390
pathways, 22–23, 60, 66, 72, 82, 88, 92, 95, 97–98, 101, 104, 143, 149, 163, 194–195, 206, 250, 257, 262–264, 283, 286–295, 338, 366, 393
patio, 22, 24, 48, 66, 75, 82–83, 89, 106, 143, 207–208, 219, 222, 262–266, 282–286, 297, 386, 444
patio foundations, 282
pattern recognition, 30, 86, 120
pavers, 282–285, 289
perennial vegetables, 328, 350
permaculture, 16, 24, 29, 55, 62, 74, 81, 85–86, 94, 97, 138, 143, 149, 188–189, 199, 201, 204, 220, 243, 247, 264, 267, 311, 315, 320, 324, 367, 398, 424, 451
permaculture zoning, 88, 149, 311
permanent runs, 412, 416
pests, 122–123, 129, 150–151, 154–157, 164, 169, 266, 309, 317–318, 325, 335, 357–358, 381–385, 390–391, 400, 446–447
phasing plan, 105
phospholipid fatty acid, 131–133
photosynthesis, 6–8, 18, 48, 122–123, 128, 291, 302, 362, 376, 437
plan sets, 101–103, 110
plant communities, 45, 102, 116, 122, 124, 129, 131, 169, 182, 217, 238, 241, 262, 302–303, 306, 308, 313–317, 319, 321, 352, 364, 376, 386, 428, 433–434, 443

plant exudates, 6, 121–122, 129, 303
plant hardiness zones, 305
planting plan
pollination, 23–24, 92–93, 101–102, 108, 240, 303, 306–312, 316, 318, 327, 329, 332, 381
pond, 9, 14, 23, 30–31, 44–46, 48, 51, 59, 64, 106, 181, 220–221, 233
pond liner, 222–225, 392
pollarding, 335, 343–344
pound per square inch, 209, 216, 241
precipitation, 3–4, 6, 8–9, 59, 182, 190, 199, 213, 240, 399
predator prey, 12, 376–377, 400, 438, 446
prescribed burn, 436, 439, 443, 449
principles, 14, 16, 20–21, 65, 67, 70, 73, 86, 88, 93, 113, 120, 128–129, 207–208, 219, 227, 229–230, 250, 304, 323, 362, 364, 424, 433
project parameters, 111–112
project stakeholders, 36, 41, 48, 51, 62–65, 70–72, 74, 80, 89, 93–97, 99, 100, 105, 108–109, 113, 308, 411
protozoa, 45, 121–123, 132, 158
propagation, 350, 359, 361–362, 387, 433
pruning, 13, 143, 153, 155, 167, 186, 325, 333, 337–343, 364, 447
pumping, 183, 209–211, 224–226, 408

rain, 3–6, 49, 82, 162, 197–198, 208, 214, 255
rain garden, 23, 82, 107, 167–168, 195–199, 203–208, 214, 218, 239, 252, 255, 257–258, 262, 286–287, 293, 298, 317, 444
rainwater harvesting, 9, 17, 107, 120, 163, 170, 180, 183, 188, 193, 199, 203–208, 212–218, 225, 232, 250, 263, 286–287, 293, 298
raised bed, 166–167, 170, 265, 267–269, 304, 345
reading the land, 34, 38–41, 97
reciprocity, 6, 17, 31, 37, 77, 121–124, 142, 184, 207, 237, 368, 380, 391, 393, 434–435, 445, 450
redlining, 76
red mangroves, 9, 11
redwoods, 8, 45, 319

reforestation, 418–420, 448
regenerative agriculture, 73, 78, 120, 128, 296, 335, 413
regenerative disturbances, 12, 400, 404, 419, 445
restoration, 77, 81, 106, 124, 176, 181, 192, 211, 252, 319, 323, 373, 418–420, 422–424, 428–430, 432, 445
reverse engineering, 66–67
revisions, 73, 93, 98–99, 214
rhizobia, 122, 132, 164, 360
rhizosphere, 121–123, 425
ridge, 28–29, 44–48, 131, 188, 193, 436
road base, 81
roads, 5, 38, 46, 51, 53, 55, 81, 113, 137, 143, 179, 193, 195, 197–198, 206–208, 211, 233, 250, 252, 255, 257
rock wall, 98, 103, 255, 257, 262, 296–299
rock armor, 254–255, 257
rolling dip, 255, 258
roof water, 207, 212–213, 215–217, 219
roosts, 414–415
root crops, 186, 355
rotational grazing, 400, 409, 412, 418
ridges, 29, 45–46, 193
runoff, 208, 212, 227–228, 239, 249, 277, 284–285, 287, 290, 416, 424, 449

sacred, 10, 17, 61, 65, 132, 183, 196, 242, 322, 335, 339, 357, 372, 373, 407, 436
saprophytic fungi, 132, 171
satellite image, 35, 37, 50, 51, 56, 57
sector map, 59, 60
sediment, 6, 11, 81, 124, 179, 198, 200, 204, 241, 246, 247, 249, 251–254, 256–259, 270, 296, 303, 394, 428
seed bank, 326, 429
seeding, 5, 126, 137, 162–165, 203, 251, 253, 292, 326, 331, 360
seed saving, 78, 371, 373
selective thinning, 445–447
sequencing, 105–107, 197
scale bar, 50, 52, 91, 98
scythe, 248, 365, 366
screening, 279, 281, 370
seeps, 39, 46
shaded fuel break, 250, 439

sheep, 12, 141, 153, 234, 318, 323, 330, 393, 396–400, 404–407, 409, 420, 438, 460
sheet mulching, 22–24, 138, 139, 141, 142, 290
shelter, 46, 48, 181, 236, 296, 330, 359, 384–386, 399, 450
Shou Sugi Ban, 266, 297, 394, 457
silviculture, 445
silvopasture, 323, 325, 330
site analysis, 37, 38, 97, 111
site assessment, 37, 41, 46, 48, 49, 55, 58, 60, 73, 102, 178, 194, 233, 249, 315, 322, 378, 423,
sit spot, 36, 37, 377, 378
slake test, 135
spillway, 198, 203–205, 208, 222, 254, 255, 293
springs, 38, 39, 178, 180, 183, 196, 212, 215, 239
softscape, 262, 263
soil building, 23, 66, 120, 132, 135, 136, 142, 143, 162, 163, 197, 238, 286, 290, 292, 303, 315, 317, 325, 326, 406, 408, 447,
soil fertility, 83, 120, 122, 166, 196, 325
soil profile, 41, 43, 44, 234, 250
soil moisture, 44, 423, 455
soil regeneration plan, 135, 136
soil structure, 41, 42, 44, 121, 123, 137, 154, 328
soil tests, 42, 59, 124, 130–132
soil type, 35, 39, 44, 59, 82, 197, 198, 201, 219, 221, 235, 239
solar bowl, 336
spent mushroom spawn, 427
staircase, 266, 283, 293, 294
staging materials, 49, 103, 106, 143, 234, 270, 278, 297, 298
staging equipment, 17, 63, 81, 102, 103, 106, 113, 126, 168, 196, 229, 233, 258, 265, 287, 297, 321, 403, 439, 448
stepping stones, 81, 224, 288–290
stocking, 227, 399, 400, 408, 410, 414
storage, 4, 7, 14, 39, 82, 86, 87, 122, 123, 137, 173, 180, 181–184, 208–210, 215–218, 227, 237, 240, 332, 334, 354–356, 365, 371, 414, 420, 426
story of place, 29, 442
stratification, 169, 331, 369

straw, 24, 83, 88, 116, 140, 141, 150, 151, 153, 155, 157, 165, 169, 171–176, 251–252, 255, 258, 259, 263, 264, 270, 271, 276, 277–281, 290, 333, 416, 443
straw flake, 141
storm surge, 9, 197
sub soiling, 59, 125, 126, 135, 137, 163, 169, 297
suburban, 11, 81, 98, 140, 143, 184, 198, 208, 232, 293, 394, 420
succession, 19, 29, 31, 40, 63, 75, 100, 124, 128, 132, 162, 180, 206, 254, 255, 325, 327, 328, 343, 350, 351, 366, 408, 418, 419, 426, 427, 433, 437, 442, 447
surface tension, 5, 180
surveyed map, 50
swale, 82, 95, 107, 137, 163, 184, 188, 195–208, 239, 298
sweet alyssum, 352, 389
symbiotic relationships, 15, 163, 171, 219, 399, 404

tachinid fly, 376, 384, 389
taking feedback, 100
tanks, 82, 102, 181, 198, 203, 209, 210, 212, 213, 215–218, 244, 443
terraces, 44, 82, 95, 104, 137, 163, 195, 197, 203, 250, 211, 218, 239, 250, 255, 287, 296–298, 444
thermal mass, 49, 219, 269, 275, 276, 281, 288, 292
thermophilic, 141, 142, 156, 157, 158, 338
threshing, 370
throughfall, 9
thinning, 88, 252, 253, 265, 338, 342, 446
tilling, 6, 44, 126, 129, 137, 138, 163
timers, 25, 241
title block, 52, 91, 92, 94, 98
toe of the slope, 250, 255
topography, 23, 29, 35, 38, 41, 46, 48, 51, 55–57, 67, 182, 193, 221, 229, 230, 238, 442
tracing, 53, 54, 93, 94, 98, 99
traditional ecological knowledge, 16, 59, 373
trap crop, 357, 390
transpiration, 3, 4, 5, 8, 179, 336, 455
tree guard, 24, 329, 330, 412, 448

tree planting, 342
trees, 3, 7, 15, 24, 53, 54, 66, 83, 84, 115, 116, 145, 166, 179, 186, 191, 228, 230, 249, 313, 314, 321, 328, 330, 332, 337, 339, 343, 386, 431, 446
trellis, 86, 103, 267, 314, 317, 343
trenching, 102, 242, 243, 246
triangulation, 50, 52–54

urban, 8, 11, 12, 29, 36, 52, 61, 81, 83, 98, 102, 115, 116, 120, 137, 140, 143, 154, 163, 184, 198, 208, 232, 265, 272, 293, 299, 309, 322, 343, 377, 385, 391, 394, 400, 404, 408, 420, 423, 425, 430, 432, 436,
urbanite, 272, 299
utilities, 52, 101, 102, 224, 225, 242, 243, 265, 292
utility plan, 102

vegetables, 11, 23, 66, 115, 132, 136, 145, 153, 164, 217, 240, 242, 267, 304, 328, 345, 348, 349, 350, 352, 360, 368, 371, 380, 400, 416
velocity, 46, 204, 206, 250, 252, 255, 257
valleys, 21, 32, 45, 46, 193, 215, 221, 233
vegetation management, 20, 364, 407
vegetated pathways, 291
vermiculture, 140, 145–147, 149, 150
vertical layer, 313, 314, 323–325, 335, 386, 443
vision statement, 65, 67

water bars, 258
water conservation, 39, 178, 179, 181, 217
water crossings, 257
water runoff, 5, 29, 47, 81, 82, 180, 193, 212, 227, 284, 287, 449
water plume, 180, 197, 239
water use classification of landscape species, 179
wetlands, 3, 9, 39, 224, 317
wet line conveyance, 213, 215, 217
wildfire, 12, 15, 29, 31, 140, 163, 397, 404, 408, 419, 428, 429, 435, 437, 438, 440, 441, 443
woodchips, 22, 24, 82, 83, 140–144, 153, 157, 165, 166, 169, 176, 255, 286, 288, 290, 333, 416, 443, 447

worms, 45, 123, 129, 138, 143, 145–152, 156, 172, 319, 385, 416
worm bins, 88, 146, 147, 149
worm castings, 145–148, 150–152, 158
weeding, 13, 288, 367
weed whacking, 364, 365

wildcrafting, 88, 171, 172
wind filter, 336
winnowing, 370

Zuni bowl, 256, 257